OCR
A LEVEL

FURTHER MATHEMATICS A

Mechanics

Jean-Paul Muscat

Series editors
Roger Porkess
Catherine Berry
Consultant editor
Owen Toller

Boost
integral
HODDER EDUCATION
LEARN MORE

This resource is endorsed by OCR for use with specification H235 OCR AS Level Further Mathematics A and with specification H245 OCR A Level Further Mathematics A. In order to gain OCR endorsement, this resource has undergone an independent quality check. Any references to assessment and/or assessment preparation are the publisher's interpretation of the specification requirements and are not endorsed by OCR. OCR recommends that a range of teaching and learning resources are used in preparing learners for assessment. OCR has not paid for the production of this resource, nor does OCR receive any royalties from its sale. For more information about the endorsement process, please visit the OCR website, www.ocr.org.uk.

Hachette UK's policy is to use papers that are natural, renewable and recyclable products and made from wood grown in well-managed forests and other controlled sources. The logging and manufacturing processes are expected to conform to the environmental regulations of the country of origin.

Orders: please contact Hachette UK Distribution, Hely Hutchinson Centre, Milton Road, Didcot, Oxfordshire, OX11 7HH. Telephone: +44 (0)1235 827827. Email education@hachette.co.uk Lines are open from 9 a.m. to 5 p.m., Monday to Friday. You can also order through our website: www.hoddereducation.co.uk

ISBN: 978 1 5104 1451 8

First published in 2017 by

Hodder Education
An Hachette UK Company
Carmelite House
50 Victoria Embankment
London EC4Y 0DZ

www.hoddereducation.co.uk

Impression number 10 9 8 7 6 5 4

Year 2022

Typeset in Bembo Std Regular 11/13 by Integra Software Services Pvt. Ltd., Pondicherry, India

Printed in CPI Group (UK) Ltd, Croydon, CR0 4YY

A catalogue record for this title is available from the British Library.

Contents

Getting the most from this book

Mathematics is not only a beautiful and exciting subject in its own right but also one that underpins many other branches of learning. It is consequently fundamental to our national wellbeing.

This book covers the Mechanics elements in the Mechanics elements in the OCR AS and A Level Further Mathematics specifications. Students start these courses at a variety of stages. Some embark on AS Further Mathematics in Year 12, straight after GCSE, taking it alongside AS Mathematics, and so have no prior experience of Mechanics. In contrast, others only begin Further Mathematics when they have completed the full A Level Mathematics and so have already met the Mechanics covered in OCR A Level Mathematics (Year 2). Between these two extremes are the many who have covered the Mechanics in AS Mathematics but no more.

This book has been written with all these users in mind. So, it provides a complete course in Mechanics up to the required level. Those who already know some Mechanics will find some revision material in the early chapters.

Chapters 1 to 8 of this textbook cover the content of Further Mathematics AS Y533 Mechanics. Chapters 1 to 14 (the whole book) cover the content of Further Mathematics A level Y543 Mechanics.

Between 2014 and 2016 A Level Mathematics and Further Mathematics were very substantially revised, for first teaching in 2017. Changes that particularly affect Mechanics include increased emphasis on

- Problem solving
- Mathematical rigour
- Use of ICT
- Modelling.

This book embraces these ideas. A large number of exercise questions involve elements of problem solving and require rigorous logical argument. Mechanics often provides descriptions of real world situations that make them tractable to calculations, and so modelling is key to this branch of mathematics. It pervades the whole of this book.

Throughout the book the emphasis is on understanding and interpretation rather than mere routine calculations, but the various exercises do nonetheless provide plenty of scope for practising basic techniques. The exercise questions are split into three bands. Band 1 questions (indicated by a green bar) are designed to reinforce basic understanding; Band 2 questions (yellow bar) are broadly typical of what might be expected in an examination; Band 3 questions (red bar) explore around the topic and some of them are rather more demanding. In addition, extensive online support, including further questions, is available by signing up to MEI's Integral platform (http://integralmaths.org).

In addition to the exercise questions, there are three sets of Practice questions. The first of these covers Chapters 1 to 5, the second covers Chapters 6 to 8, and the third covers Chapters 9 to 14. These include identified questions requiring problem solving PS, mathematical proof MP, use of ICT T and modelling M.

There are places where the work depends on knowledge from earlier in the book or elsewhere and this is flagged up in the Prior knowledge boxes. This should be seen as an invitation to those who have problems with the particular topic to revisit it. At the end of each chapter there is a list of key points covered as well as a summary of the new knowledge (learning outcomes) that readers should have gained.

Those using this book will need a working knowledge of pure mathematics including calculus and trigonometry. So, for example, differentiation and integration are used in kinematics, radians in circular motion and the scalar product in the work–energy principle in vector form.

Two common features of the book are Activities and Discussion points. These serve rather different purposes. The Activities are designed to help readers get into the thought processes of the new work that they are about to meet; having done an Activity, what follows will seem much easier. The Discussion points invite readers to talk about particular points with their fellow students and their teacher and so enhance their understanding. Another feature is a Caution icon ❗, highlighting points where it is easy to go wrong.

Answers to all exercise questions and practice questions are provided at the back of the book, and also online at www.hoddereducation.co.uk/MEIOCRFurtherMathsMechanics.

Much of the material is shared with a fourth edition MEI textbook and so is tried and tested. However, as a consequence of the changes to A Level requirements in Further Mathematics, large parts of the book are either new material or have been very substantially rewritten.

Catherine Berry
Roger Porkess

Prior knowledge

No prior knowledge of mechanics is needed for this book. It does however assume that the reader is reasonably fluent in basic algebra and graphs: working with formulae and expressions; solving linear and quadratic equations and inequalities; changing the subject of a formula; working with parametric equations; using logarithms and exponentials.

Basic trigonometry is used throughout, including the identity $\sin^2\theta + \cos^2\theta = 1$. Pythagoras's theorem is used to find the resultant of two vectors. A working knowledge of calculus is also required. In the first half of the book polynomial functions are integrated and differentiated with respect to time; calculus is used to find turning points and second derivatives are sometimes used. From Chapter 10 onwards, more advanced calculus is required, including the chain rule and differential equations with separable variables or those that require an integrating factor.

Some Pure Mathematics content is required from *OCR A Level Mathematics Year 2* and *OCR A Level Further Pure Mathematics Year 2*.

- **Chapter 1: Kinematics** introduces the basic ideas and vocabulary associated with motion. It requires basic algebra and calculus.
- **Chapter 2: Forces and motion** introduces Newton's laws of motion. This involves forces and equilibrium. Vectors are introduced and they require the use of elementary trigonometry.
- **Chapter 3: A Model for friction** builds on Chapters 1 and 2. The algebra includes inequalities.
- **Chapter 4: Moments of forces** builds on the work on forces in Chapter 2. There is further use of trigonometry.
- **Chapter 5: Work, energy and power** introduces new concepts based on ideas in Chapters 1 and 2. Algebra is used throughout and there is some use of elementary trigonometry.
- **Chapter 6: Impulse and momentum** broadens the work in Chapter 5. It requires the algebra of indices.
- **Chapter 7: Dimensional analysis** reviews the dimensions and units used in mechanics.
- **Chapter 8: Circular motion 1** extends the ideas of forces and vectors from Chapters 1 and 2. Fluency in basic trigonometry is expected, and there is some calculus.

The material in the remaining chapters of this book is all in the OCR specification for A level Further Mathematics. It is assumed that anyone taking this qualification has either already taken A level Mathematics or is taking it at the same time. So the Prior Knowledge for chapters 9 to 13 includes the content of A level Mathematics, both the Pure Mathematics and the Mechanics.

- **Chapter 9: Centre of mass 1** extends the use of moments in Chapter 4, and of vectors in Chapter 2. No calculus is used in this chapter; cases that require its use are covered in Chapter 13.
- **Chapter 10: Motion under a variable** force extends the work on variable acceleration from Chapter 1 and on vectors from Chapter 2. The use of calculus to find velocity and acceleration in Chapter 1 is extended to more than one dimension. The following topics from pure mathematics are required: The scalar product from Chapter 7 of OCR AS Mathematics (Year 1) or from chapter 1 of OCR A Level Mathematics Year 2, solving differential equations using separation of variables from Chapter 13 of OCR A Level Mathematics Year 2, and using integrating factor from Chapter 9 of OCR A Level Further Pure Mathematics Year 2.
- **Chapter 11: Circular motion 2** extends the work from Chapter 9. It uses conservation of energy from Chapter 5 and builds on formulae from Chapter 1. It also uses projectile motion from Chapter 21 of OCR A Level Mathematics Year 2.

- **Chapter 12: Hooke's law** builds on the concepts of force from Chapter 2, work and energy from Chapter 5 and variable acceleration from Chapter 10.
- **Chapter 13: Centre of mass 2** extends the work in Chapter 9 to cover shapes requiring the use of calculus to find volumes and their centres of mass. It also requires elementary trigonometry.
- **Chapter 14: Oblique impact** extends the ideas introduced in Chapter 6 to cases where the impact is not necessarily along the line of motion. It requires the use of vectors from Chapter 2 and of elementary trigonometry.

Acknowledgements

The publisher would like to thank the following for permission to reproduce copyright material.

Practice questions have been provided by David Holland (MEI), Roger Porkess and Owen Toller (pp.122-123, pp.181-184 and pp.333-335).

Photo credits

p.1 © goce risteski – Fotolia; **p.25** © bolina - 123RF; **p.58** © andreigilbert - 123RF; **p.70** © Matjoe – Shutterstock; **p.73 (top)** © Evan-Amos - Wikipedia Commons (Public Domain), **(bottom)** © ConstantinosZ - Shutterstock; **p.79** © MarVil – Shutterstock;; **p.95 (top)** © kasiastock - Fotolia. com; **p.95 (bottom)** © All Canada Photos / Alamy Stock Photo; **p.114** © Steve Mann – Fotolia; **p.124** © Blend Images / Alamy Stock PhotoJGI/Tom Grill; **p.185** © huaxiadragon – Fotolia; **p.146** © Image Source / Alamy Stock Photo; **p.161 (left)** © styleuneed – Fotolia; **p.161 (middle)** © Nicholas Piccillo – Fotolia; **p.161 (right)** © NickR – Fotolia; **p.171** © Rick Rudnicki - Getty Images; **p.204** © StockTrek/Photodisc/Getty Images/ Science, Technology & Medicine 2 54; **p.228** © Avind Balaraman/ Fotolia; **p.239** © Colin Anderson - Getty Images; **p.251 (left)** © elina – Shutterstock; **p.251 (centre)** © ChameleonsEye – Shutterstock; **p.251** (right) © ArtemZ – Shutterstock; **p.263** © Nick Kennedy / Alamy Stock Photo; **p.266 (top)** © Aggie 11 – Shutterstock; **p.266 (bottom)** © Matthew Ashmore / Alamy Stock Photo; **p.279 (left)** © Brandon Bourdages – Shutterstock; **p.279 (right)** © BasPhoto – Shutterstock; **p.279 (centre)** © Zoonar GmbH / Alamy Stock Photo; **p.280** © André Karwath aka Aka (https://creativecommons.org/licenses/by-sa/2.5/deed.en); **p.285** © Robert Gendler/Visuals Unlimited, Inc. via Getty Images; **p.286** © spacekirs – Fotolia; **p.287** © Alex Yeung – Fotolia; **p.288** © domnitsky – Shutterstock; **p.308** © Photo courtesy of Millbrook Proving Ground Ltd**; p.316** © barfisch via Wikipedia Commons https://creativecommons.org/licenses/by-sa/3.0/ (https://en.wikipedia.org/wiki/Rules_of_snooker#/media/File:Snooker_Freeball.png).

1 Kinematics

The journey of a thousand miles begins with a single step.

Lao Tzu

Discussion point

Describe the motion of the person in this photograph.

1 The language of motion in one dimension

Think of throwing a marble straight up in the air so that it reaches a height of 1.25 m above your hand, before it falls back to the ground 1 m below your hand. The marble moves as it does because of the gravitational pull of the Earth. It is moving vertically up then down. The vertical direction is along the line towards, or away from, the centre of the Earth.

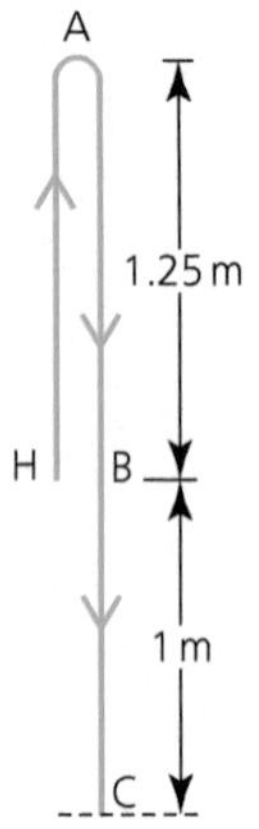

Figure 1.1

A quantity which has only size, or magnitude, is called a **scalar**. One which has both magnitude and direction is called a **vector**.

- The total **distance travelled** by the marble at any time does not depend on its direction; it is a scalar quantity. The distance it travels before hitting the ground is 1.25 + 1.25 + 1 = 3.5 m.
- The **position** of the marble is its distance above a fixed origin, for example, the place where it first left your hand. At the top, the position is +1.25 m. When it hits the ground the position is –1 m. Position is a vector quantity.
- A position always refers to a fixed origin but a **displacement** can be measured from any position. When the marble reaches the ground, its displacement is –1 m relative to your hand but –2.25 m relative to the top. Displacement is also a vector.

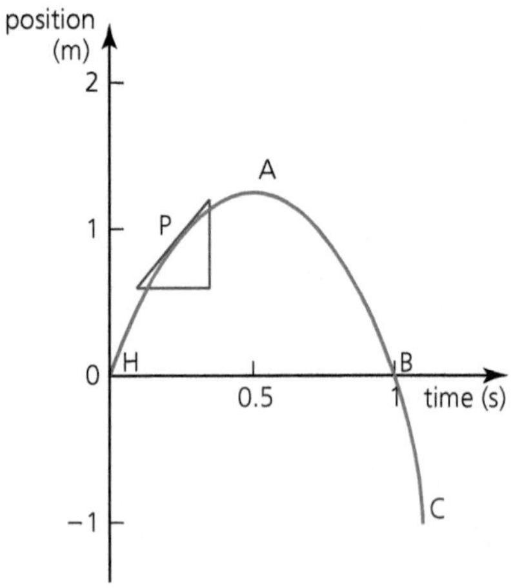

Figure 1.2

Figure 1.1 shows the direction of motion of the marble and relevant distances. The direction of motion is indicated by an arrow. Figure 1.2 is a graph showing the position above the level of your hand against the time.

- **Speed** is a scalar quantity and does not involve direction.
- **Velocity** is the vector related to speed; its magnitude is the speed but it also has a direction. The velocity of an object is the rate at which the position changes.

When a position–time graph is curved, as in Figure 1.2, the velocity changes with time. At any instant the velocity is given by the gradient of the tangent to the curve at that point.

This means that the velocity, v, can be written as

$$v = \frac{ds}{dt}$$

where s is the position.

Figure 1.3 shows the velocity–time graph for the marble.

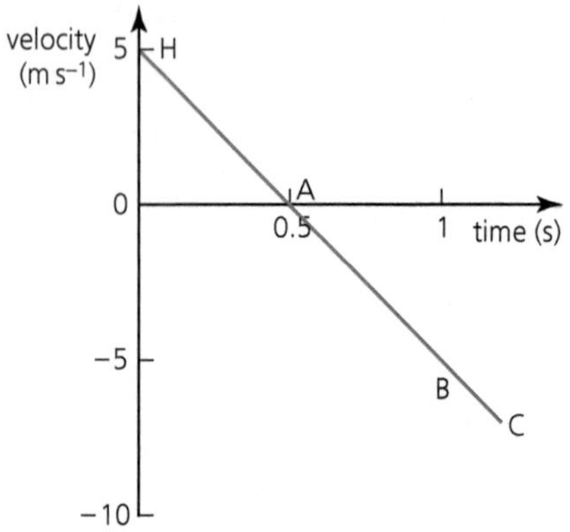

Figure 1.3

- At the point A, the velocity and gradient of the position–time graph are zero. The marble is instantaneously at rest.
- The velocity at H is positive because the marble is moving upwards.
- The velocities at B and C are negative because the marble is moving downwards.
- **Acceleration** is the rate at which the velocity changes. It is a vector quantity and can take different signs in a similar way to velocity.
- The equivalent scalar quantity is **magnitude of acceleration**.

This means that acceleration, a, can be written as $a = \dfrac{dv}{dt}$.

Acceleration is given by the gradient of a velocity–time graph.

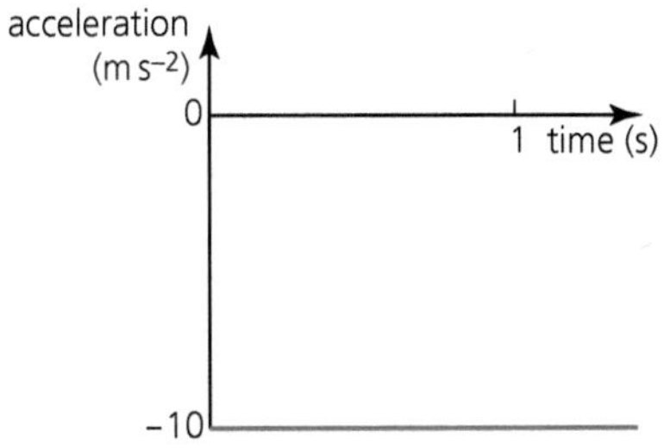

Figure 1.4

Note

You will recognise −10 as an approximation to *g*, the acceleration due to gravity.

When an object is slowing down it is often said to be decelerating. Retardation is another word for deceleration.

The gradient of the line in Figure 1.3 is constant because the line is straight and it is negative because the line is sloping downwards. Using the first 0.5 seconds, its value is found to be

$$\frac{0-5}{0.5-0}=-10$$

So the acceleration–time graph is as shown in Figure 1.4.

Notation and units

As with most mathematics, you will see in this book that certain letters are commonly used to denote certain quantities. This makes things easier to follow. These are the letters commonly used for motion in one direction:

- s, h, r, x, y and z for position
- t for time measured from a starting instant
- u and v for velocity
- a for acceleration.

Vector quantities are usually printed in bold, for example, **r**, **u**, **v** and **a**, particularly when this work is extended to 2 and 3 dimensions.

The S.I. (Système International d'Unités) unit for **distance** is the metre (m), for **time** it is the second (s) and for **mass** the kilogram (kg). Other units follow from these, so speed is measured in metres per second, written $m\,s^{-1}$.

Next steps

The next example uses and extends the ideas developed so far.

Example 1.1

Tara has a letter to post on her way to college. The post box is 800 m east of her house and the college is 3.2 km to the west. The road is at a slight incline from west to east. Tara cycles at a steady speed of $5\,m\,s^{-1}$ while travelling east to the post box. She takes 40 s at the post box to find her letter and post it. She then cycles at a steady $12.5\,m\,s^{-1}$ while travelling west to college.

(i) Draw a diagram to illustrate Tara's journey to college.

(ii) Find the total distance Tara travels and the time she takes.

(iii) Draw (a) position–time (b) velocity–time (c) distance–time (d) speed–time graphs to illustrate her journey.

(iv) Explain why an acceleration–time graph would not be very interesting.

Solution

(i)

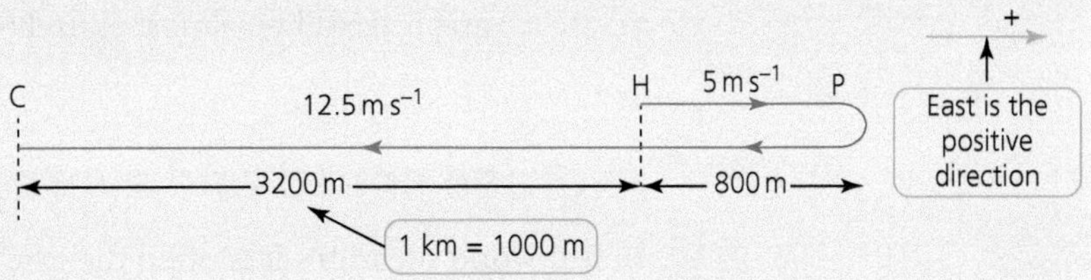

Figure 1.5

(ii) The distances and times for the three parts of Tara's journey are:

	Distance	Time
Home to post box	800 m	$\frac{800}{5} = 160$ s
At post box	0 m	40 s
Post box to college	4000 m	$\frac{4000}{12.5} = 320$ s
Total	4800 m	520 s

(iii)

(a) position–time

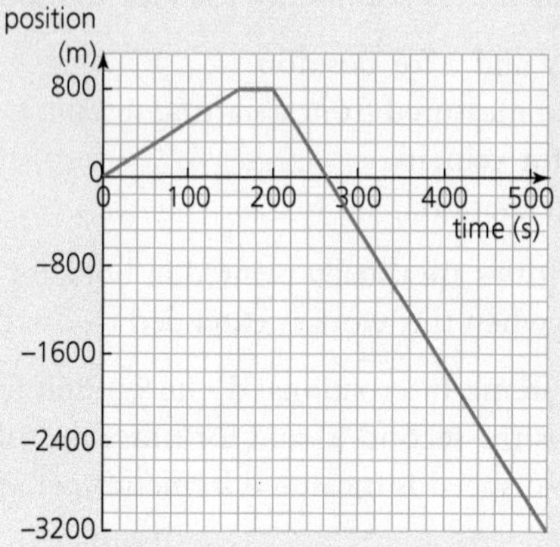

Figure 1.6

(b) velocity–time

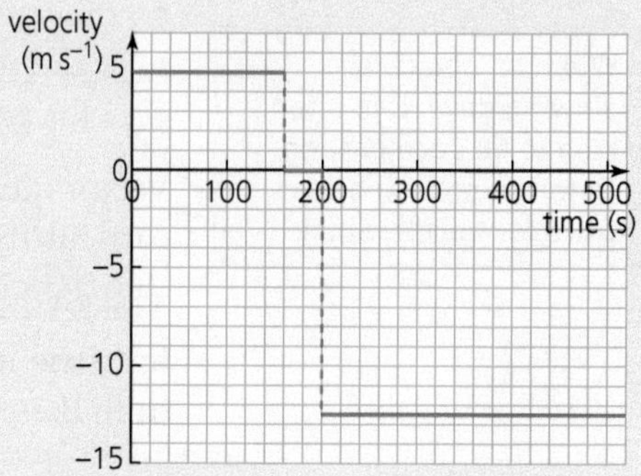

Figure 1.7

(c) distance–time

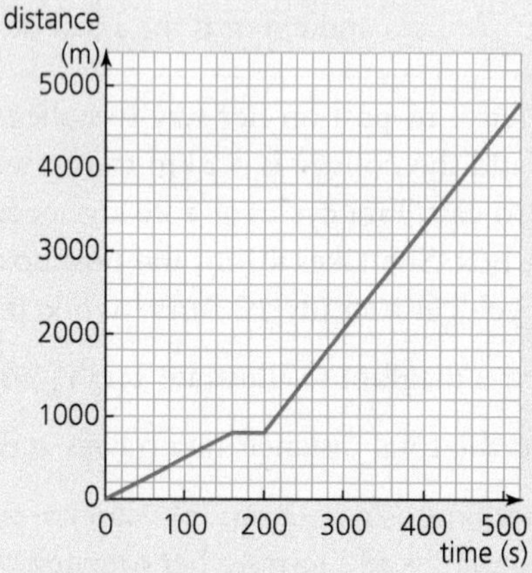

Figure 1.8

(d) speed–time

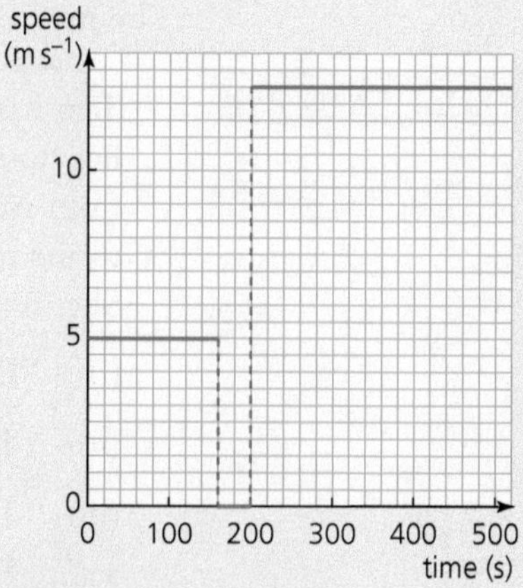

Figure 1.9

Note

The distance–time graph of Tara's journey differs from the position–time graph as it shows how far she travels irrespective of her direction. There are no negative values. The gradient of the distance–time graph represents Tara's speed rather than her velocity so it too has no negative values.

(iv) Tara travels at a steady speed for both parts of her journey so, apart from the short time when she gets up speed, her acceleration is zero. It is also zero when she is posting the letter. So the acceleration–time graph would be almost entirely along the horizontal axis.

Average speed and average velocity

In real world situations it is often the case that you are interested in average values. For example, even on a 'good run' you do not maintain a steady speed

Note

Notice that the average used here is not the same as that commonly used when finding the mean of a set of numbers. This is not a situation where you add all the numbers together and divide by how many they are.

when driving on the motorway. Instead you are often slowing down and speeding up because of the other traffic.

The definitions of average speed and average velocity are

$$\text{average speed} = \frac{\text{total distance travelled}}{\text{total time taken}}$$

$$\text{average velocity} = \frac{\text{displacement}}{\text{time taken}}$$

In the previous example,

- Tara's average speed is $\frac{\text{total distance travelled}}{\text{time taken}} = \frac{4800\text{ m}}{520\text{ s}} = 9.23\text{ m s}^{-1}$
- Her average velocity is $\frac{\text{displacement}}{\text{time taken}} = \frac{3200\text{ m west}}{520\text{ s}} = 6.15\text{ m s}^{-1}$ west (or -6.15 m s^{-1})

In the calculations the units and direction are included at an early stage for clarity. It is quite usual to leave them out until the final answer.

Changing units of speed

Quite often speeds are expressed in terms of km h^{-1} (kilometres per hour). To convert to m s^{-1} you need to multiply by 1000 (1 km = 1000 m) and divide by 3600 (1 hour = 60×60 = 3600 s). Or, in other words, you need to divide by 3.6. Conversely, to convert from m s^{-1} to km h^{-1}, you need to multiply by 3.6.

Tara's average speed is thus $9.23 \times 3.6 = 33.23\text{ km h}^{-1}$. This may also be found from the calculation

Distance in km

Time in hours

$$\frac{4.8}{\frac{520}{3600}} = \frac{4.8 \times 3600}{520} = \frac{432}{13} = 33.23\text{ km h}^{-1}$$

Tara's average velocity is $-6.15 \times 3.6 = -22.15\text{ km h}^{-1}$ which may also be found from the calculation

Displacement in km

Time in hours

$$\frac{-3.2}{\frac{520}{3600}} = \frac{-3.2 \times 90}{13} = \frac{-288}{13} = -22.15\text{ km h}^{-1}$$

Using areas to find distances and displacements

More strictly, the area under the graph is the area of the region bounded by the lines, or curves, and the horizontal time axis.

Speed–time and velocity–time graphs give you a lot of information. You have already seen that, as well as the actual values on the graph, the gradient gives you the acceleration. But it doesn't end there. In addition, the area under the graph represents the distance travelled (in the case of a speed–time graph) or the displacement (for a velocity–time graph).

Note

Since the area under a curve can be found by integration, it follows that $s = \int v\,dt$ and $v = \int a\,dt$.

Similarly, the area under an acceleration–time graph represents the change in speed or velocity.

The next two examples illustrate these points.

Example 1.2

Tom is cycling home. He turns onto the main road, which is straight, at 5 m s^{-1} and accelerates uniformly to 8 m s^{-1} over the next 6 s. He maintains this speed for 20 seconds and then slows down uniformly for 4 seconds to stop outside his home.

Note

Many speed–time and velocity–time graphs consist of straight-line sections. The area can easily be found by splitting them up into triangles, rectangles or trapezia.

(i) Draw a velocity–time graph for Tom's journey and use it to find how far Tom cycles.

(ii) Draw an acceleration–time graph. Explain the significance of the area between this and the time axis.

Solution

(i)

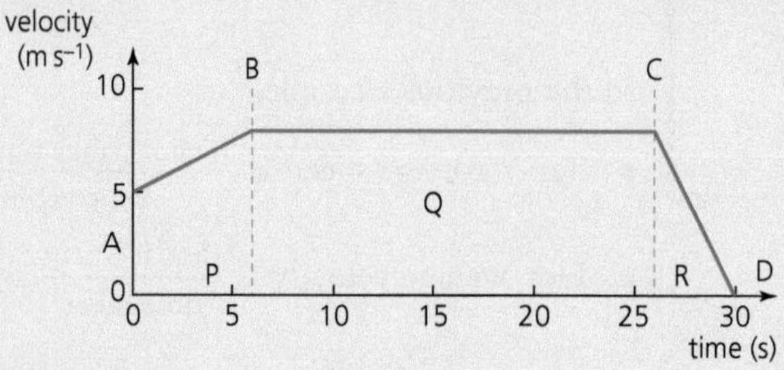

Figure 1.10

The area is split into three regions.

P trapezium: area $= \frac{1}{2}(5+8)\times 6 =$ 39 m

Q rectangle: area $= 8 \times 20$ = 160 m

R triangle: area $= \frac{1}{2}\times 8\times 4$ = 16 m

total area = 215 m

So Tom cycles 215 m.

(ii) The acceleration–time graph is shown in Figure 1.11.

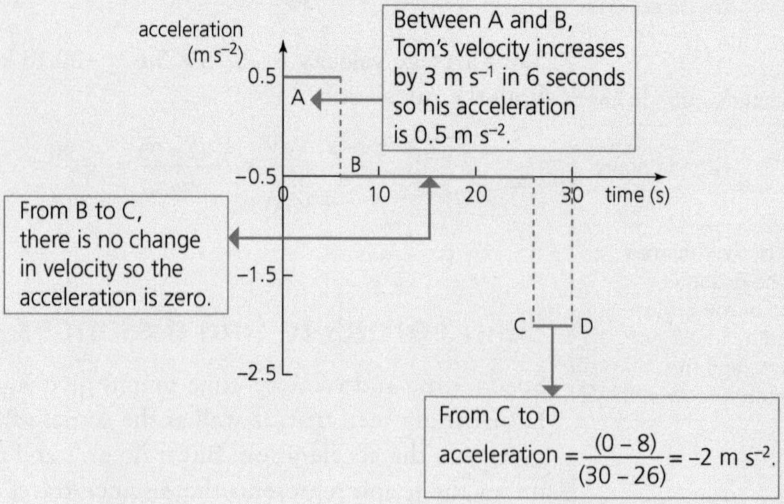

Figure 1.11

From C to D Tom is slowing down while still moving in the positive direction towards home.

The area between the graph and the time axis is
$0.5 \times 6 + 0 \times 20 + (-2) \times 4 = -5$.

So Tom's velocity decreases by $5\,\text{m}\,\text{s}^{-1}$, from an initial speed of $5\,\text{m}\,\text{s}^{-1}$ to being stationary.

Example 1.3

A car is moving between two sets of traffic lights 1500 m apart on a straight road. Starting from rest at the first traffic light, it accelerates uniformly to a maximum speed, which it maintains for 2 minutes before decelerating uniformly until it stops at the second traffic light. The whole journey takes 2.5 minutes. Find the maximum speed.

Solution

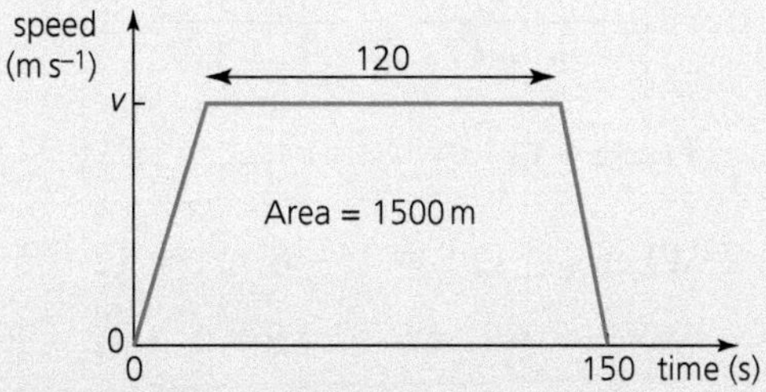

Figure 1.12

The sketch of the speed–time graph of the journey shows the given information, with suitable units. The maximum speed is $v\,\mathrm{m\,s^{-1}}$.

The area is $\frac{1}{2}(120+150)\times v = 1500$

$$v = \frac{1500}{135} = 11.\dot{1}$$

The maximum speed is $11\,\mathrm{m\,s^{-1}}$ (to 2 s.f.).

Information given algebraically

So far the information about the motion of an object has been given either in words or in a diagram. However, sometimes you will be given it in algebraic form, as in the next example.

Example 1.4

The position of a particle moving along a straight line is given by $x = t^2 - 8t + 12$ for $0 \le t \le 9$ where x is the displacement from a fixed point O in metres and t is the time in seconds.

(i) At what times is the particle at O?

(ii) Draw the position–time graph of the particle for $0 \le t \le 9$.

(iii) Give the displacement and the distance travelled between $t = 1$ and $t = 9$.

(iv) Give the average velocity and the average speed between $t = 1$ and $t = 9$.

Solution

(i) When the particle is at O, $x = 0$

$\Rightarrow t^2 - 8t + 12 = 0$

$(t - 2)(t - 6) = 0$

$t = 2$ or $t = 6$

The particle is at the origin at 2 seconds and 6 seconds.

(ii)

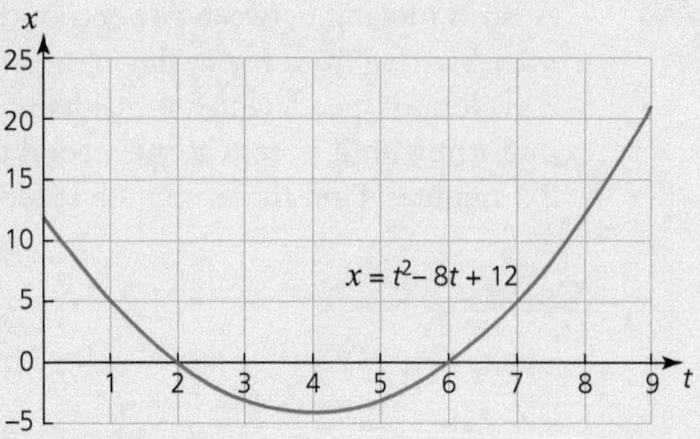

Figure 1.13

(iii) When $t = 1$, $x = 1^2 - 8 \times 1 + 12 = 5$

When $t = 9$, $x = 9^2 - 8 \times 9 + 12 = 21$

The displacement from $t = 1$ to $t = 9$ is $21 - 5 = 16$ m.

When $t = 4$, $x = 4^2 - 8 \times 4 + 12 = -4$

As you can see from the graph, the particle is at its most negative at time 4 seconds.

From $t = 1$ to $t = 4$ the displacement is $-4 - 5 = -9$; distance travelled = +9

From $t = 4$ to $t = 9$ the displacement is $21 - (-4) = 25$; distance travelled = +25

Total distance travelled is $9 + 25 = 34$ m

(iv) Average velocity $= \dfrac{\text{displacement}}{\text{time taken}} = \dfrac{16\text{ m}}{8\text{ s}} = 2\text{ m s}^{-1}$

The time taken is $9 - 1 = 8$ seconds.

Average speed $= \dfrac{\text{distance travelled}}{\text{time taken}} = \dfrac{34\text{ m}}{8\text{ s}} = 4.25\text{ m s}^{-1}$

Exercise 1.1

① For the following position–time graphs, calculate the total overall displacement and the total distance travelled.

(i)

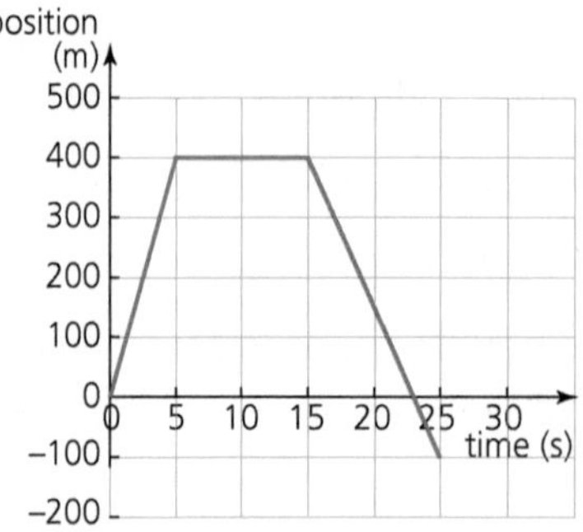

Figure 1.14

(ii)

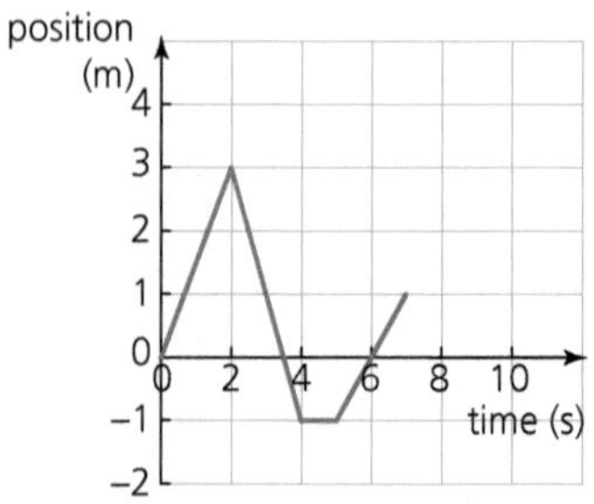

Figure 1.15

② For the following position–time graphs, find

(i) the initial and final positions

(ii) the total displacement

(iii) the total distance travelled

(iv) the velocity and speed for each part of the journey

(v) the average velocity for the whole journey

(vi) the average speed for the whole journey.

(a)

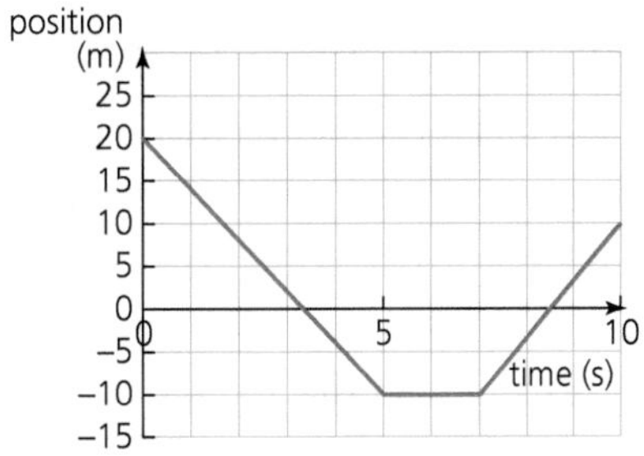

Figure 1.16

(b)

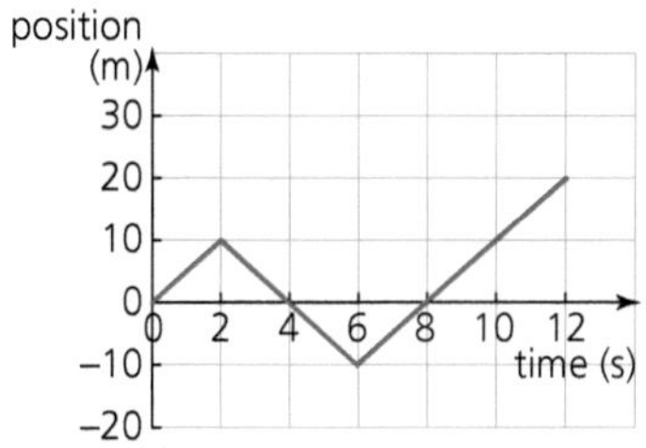

Figure 1.17

③ The position of a particle moving along a straight line is $x = 3t^2 - 14t + 11$ where x is in metres and t is in seconds with $0 < t < 5$.

(i) At what time is the particle at O?

(ii) When is the particle furthest from its starting point?

(iii) How far has the particle travelled in the first 5 seconds?

④ A ball is thrown straight up in the air so that its position x m at time t s is given by $x = 2 + 12t - 5t^2$.

(i) Sketch a position–time graph for $0 \le t \le 2.5$.

(ii) From what height is the ball thrown?

(iii) Find the ball's displacement relative to its starting position after 2.5 s.

(iv) At what time is the highest point reached and how high does the ball go?

(v) What is the total distance travelled in the 2.5 s?

⑤ A car travels 50 km from A to B at an average speed of 80 km h^{-1}. It stops at B for 30 minutes and then returns to A travelling at an average speed of 60 km h^{-1}.

(i) Find the total time taken for the whole journey.

(ii) Find the average speed for the whole journey.

(iii) Find the car's average velocity.

⑥ The speed of light is 3×10^8 m s^{-1}. The average distance from the Sun to the Earth is 1.5×10^8 km. How long does it take light from the Sun to reach the Earth?

⑦ A cyclist rides uphill a distance of 2.5 km at an average speed of 4.5 m s^{-1} and returns downhill on the same course with an average speed of 14 m s^{-1}. Find the average speed for the whole trip.

⑧ The velocity–time graph shows the motion of a particle along a straight line.

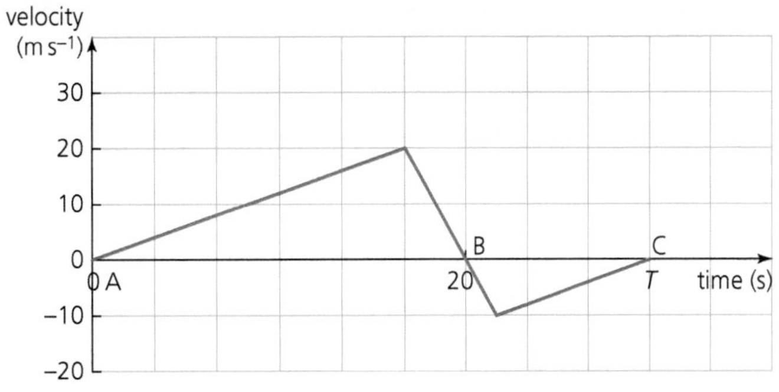

Figure 1.18

(i) The particle starts at A at $t = 0$ and moves to B in the next 20 s. Find the distance AB.

(ii) At a time, T seconds, after leaving A the particle is at C, a distance 50 m from B. Find T.

(iii) Find the displacement of C from A.

⑨ The distance between Victoria and Paddington stations on the London Underground is 3.5 miles. The average speed of the moving tube train is 15 mph and it stops for 2 minutes at each of seven intermediate stations.

(i) Find the average speed for the journey.

(ii) What would the average speed be if the stop at each station was reduced to 45 s?

⑩ A particle starts from rest at time $t = 0$ and moves in a straight line, accelerating as follows:

$a = 2;\quad 0 \le t \le 20$

$a = -1;\quad 20 < t \le 60$

where a is the acceleration in m s^{-2} and t is the time in seconds.

(i) Find the speed of the particle when $t = 10$ and 60.

(ii) Sketch a speed–time graph for the particle in the interval $0 \le t \le 60$.

(iii) Find the total distance travelled by the particle in the interval $0 \le t \le 60$.

⑪ A particle moves along a straight line. It starts from rest, accelerates at 3 m s^{-2} for 2 seconds and then decelerates uniformly before coming to rest in a further 6 seconds.

(i) Sketch a velocity–time graph.

(ii) Find the total distance travelled.

(iii) Find the deceleration of the particle.

(iv) Find the average speed for the whole journey.

⑫ A train starts from rest and accelerates uniformly for 2 minutes, by which time it has reached a speed of 1.2 kilometres per minute. It runs at this speed for 9 minutes and then decelerates uniformly, coming to rest in 1 minute.

(i) Draw the velocity–time graph.

(ii) Find the total distance travelled.

⑬ The figure shows a velocity–time graph for the motion of a particle in a straight line.

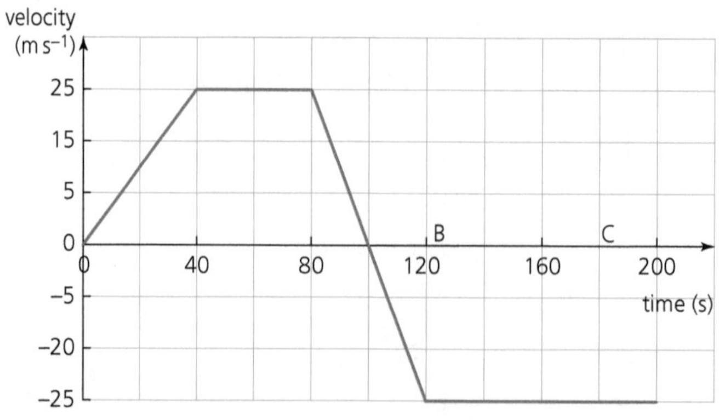

Figure 1.19

(i) Find the displacement of the particle at times $t = 40$, $t = 80$, $t = 120$ and $t = 200$.

(ii) Find the total distance travelled.

(iii) At what time does the particle pass its starting point?

⑭ A tram travels from rest at one station to rest at another station 5 km distant in a time of 10 minutes. The tram gets up to full speed uniformly in the first 250 m and slows down uniformly to rest in the last 125 m. Find the maximum speed of the tram.

⑮ The driver of a train travelling at $90\,\text{km h}^{-1}$ on a straight level track sees a signal to stop at a distance of 500 m and, putting the brakes on, comes to rest at the signal. The train stops for 1 minute and then resumes its journey, attaining the original speed of $90\,\text{km h}^{-1}$ in a distance of 750 m. Assuming that the train accelerates and decelerates at a uniform rate, find the time lost due to the stoppage.

⑯ Two stations A and B are 2 km apart on a straight track. A train starts from rest at A and comes to rest at B. The train accelerates uniformly for $\frac{3}{4}$ of the distance and decelerates uniformly for the remainder. The journey takes 4 minutes. Find

(i) the acceleration

(ii) the deceleration

(iii) the maximum speed of the train.

2 The constant acceleration formulae

In the velocity–time graph shown in Figure 1.20 the initial velocity is $u\,\text{m s}^{-1}$ and the velocity t s later is $v\,\text{m s}^{-1}$. The increase in velocity is $(v - u)\,\text{m s}^{-1}$.

The line is straight and so the acceleration $a\,\text{m s}^{-2}$ is constant; it is given by

$$\frac{v-u}{t} = a$$

So

$$v - u = at$$

$$v = u + at \qquad ①$$

The area under the graph represents the displacement, s metres, and is given by the area of the trapezium

$$s = \frac{1}{2}(u+v)\times t \qquad ②$$

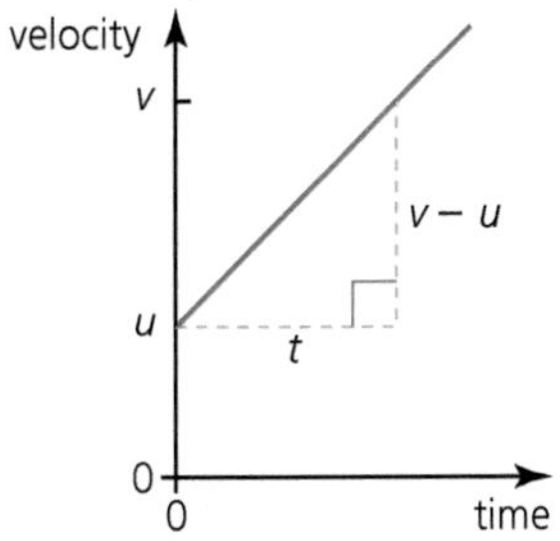

Figure 1.20

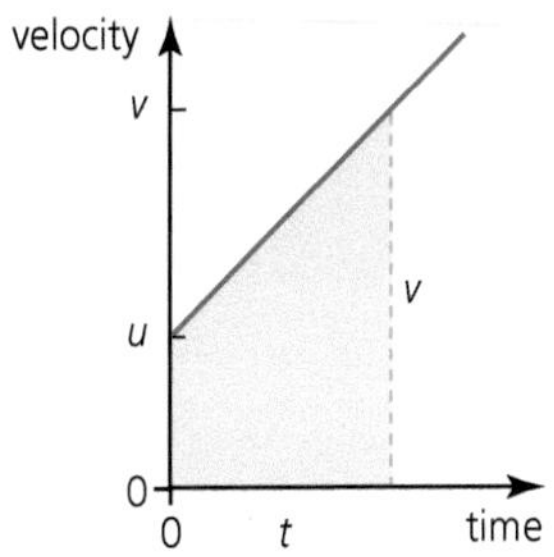

Figure 1.21

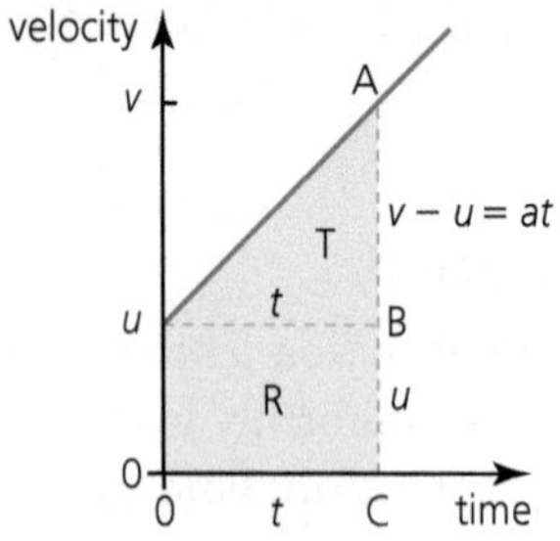

Figure 1.22

The area under the graph may be viewed in a different way, using the rectangle R and the triangle T, as shown in Figure 1.22.

$$AC = v \text{ and } BC = u$$

so that $AB = v - u$

$= at$ from equation ①

total area = area of R + area of T

so $$s = ut + \frac{1}{2} \times t \times at$$

giving $$s = ut + \frac{1}{2}at^2 \qquad ③$$

Alternatively, you could write the area as the difference between the larger rectangle of area $v \times t$ and the triangle, giving rise to

$$s = vt - \frac{1}{2}at^2 \qquad ④$$

To find a formula which does not involve t, you need to eliminate t.

One way to do this is first to rewrite equations ① and ② as

$$v - u = at \text{ and } v + u = \frac{2s}{t}$$

and then multiply these to give

$$(v-u)(v+u) = at \times \frac{2s}{t}$$

$$v^2 - u^2 = 2as$$

$$v^2 = u^2 + 2as \qquad ⑤$$

Equations ①–⑤ can be used for any motion in a straight line with **constant acceleration**. There are five equations involving five variables (s, u, v, a and t). Each equation involves four variables with the fifth one missing.

Equations ①–⑤ are sometimes called the **suvat** equations. Equations ③, ④ and ⑤ can all be derived from ① and ②. Do it for yourself.

① $v = u + at$ has s missing

② $s = \frac{1}{2}(u+v) \times t$ has a missing

③ $s = ut + \frac{1}{2}at^2$ has v missing

④ $s = vt - \frac{1}{2}at^2$ has u missing

⑤ $v^2 = u^2 + 2as$ has t missing.

So, in any problem involving linear motion with constant acceleration, if you know three of the variables, then you can obtain the other two.

Example 1.5

A car is travelling at $10\,\text{m s}^{-1}$ and accelerates at $\frac{1}{4}\,\text{m s}^{-2}$ for 30 s.

(i) How fast is it travelling at the end of the 30 seconds?

(ii) How far will it have travelled in that time?

Solution

(i) Use the formula $v = u + at$ with $u = 10$, $a = \frac{1}{4}$ and $t = 30$.

$$v = 10 + 0.25 \times 30 = 17.5$$

The speed of the car is $17.5\,\text{m s}^{-1}$ after 30 s.

(ii) Use the formula $s = ut + \frac{1}{2}at^2$ with $u = 10$, $a = \frac{1}{4}$ and $t = 30$.

$$s = 10 \times 30 + \frac{1}{2} \times \frac{1}{4} \times 30^2 = 412.5$$

The car has travelled 412.5 m in 30 s.

Example 1.6

A train starts from rest at station A and accelerates uniformly at $0.2\,\text{m s}^{-2}$ for 2 minutes. It then travels at constant speed for 10 minutes, after which it is brought to rest at station B with constant deceleration $1.5\,\text{m s}^{-2}$. Find the distance AB.

Solution

The distance travelled by the train while it is accelerating is found by use of the formula $s = ut + \frac{1}{2}at^2$ with $u = 0$, $a = 0.2$ and $t = 120$.

$$s = \frac{1}{2} \times 0.2 \times 120^2 = 1440\text{m}$$

The constant speed of the train is found by using the formula $v = u + at$ with $u = 0$, $a = 0.2$ and $t = 120$.

$$v = 0.2 \times 120 = 24\,\text{m s}^{-1}$$

The distance travelled in 10 minutes at this speed is given by $24 \times 600 = 14\,400$ m.

The distance travelled by the train while it is decelerating from $24\,\text{m s}^{-1}$ to 0 is found using the formula $v^2 = u^2 + 2as$ with $u = 24$, $v = 0$ and $a = -1.5$.

$$0 = 24^2 + 2 \times -1.5\,s$$

$$s = \frac{24^2}{3} = 192\text{ m}$$

The distance between the stations is AB = 1440 + 14400 + 192 = 16 032 m.

The acceleration due to gravity

When a model ignoring air resistance is used, all objects falling freely under gravity fall with the same acceleration, $g\,\text{m s}^{-2}$. This varies over the surface of the Earth, but it is assumed that all situations encountered here occur in a place where $g = 9.8\,\text{m s}^{-2}$.

Example 1.7

A coin is dropped from rest at the top of a building of height 12.25 m and travels in a straight line.

Find the time it takes to reach the ground and the speed of impact.

Solution

Suppose the time taken to reach the ground is t seconds. Use the formula $s = ut + \frac{1}{2}at^2$ with $u = 0$, $a = 9.8$ and $s = 12.25$

$$12.25 = 0 + \frac{1}{2} \times 9.8 \times t^2$$

$$t^2 = \frac{12.25}{4.9} = 2.5$$

$$t = 1.58 \text{ (to 3 s.f.)}$$

To find the velocity, v, a formula involving s, u, a and v is required.

$$v^2 = u^2 + 2as$$

$$v^2 = 0 + 2 \times 9.8 \times 12.25$$

$$v^2 = 240.1$$

$$v = 15.5 \text{ (to 3 s.f.)}$$

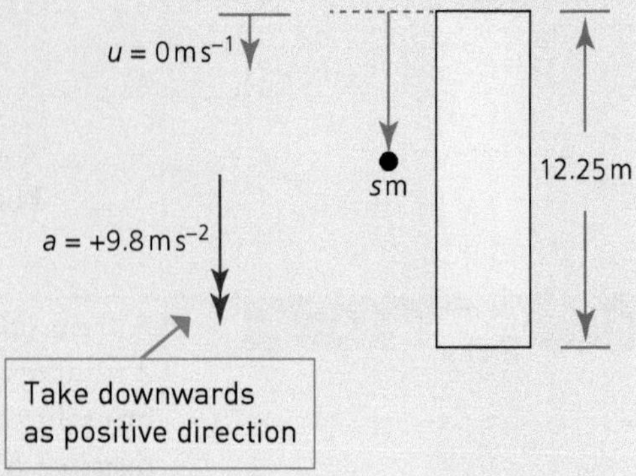

Figure 1.23

The coin takes 1.58 s to hit the ground and has a speed 15.5 m s^{-1} on impact.

The next example illustrates ways of dealing with more complex problems. None of the possible formulae has only one unknown and there are also two situations, so simultaneous equations are used.

Example 1.8

A train decelerating uniformly passes three posts A, B and C spaced at intervals of 100 m. It takes 10 seconds to cover the distance between posts A and B and 15 seconds to cover the distance between posts B and C. Find the deceleration of the train and the distance beyond the third post where the train comes to rest.

Solution

Figure 1.24 shows all the information, taking the acceleration to be a m s^{-2} and the speed at A to be u m s^{-1}.

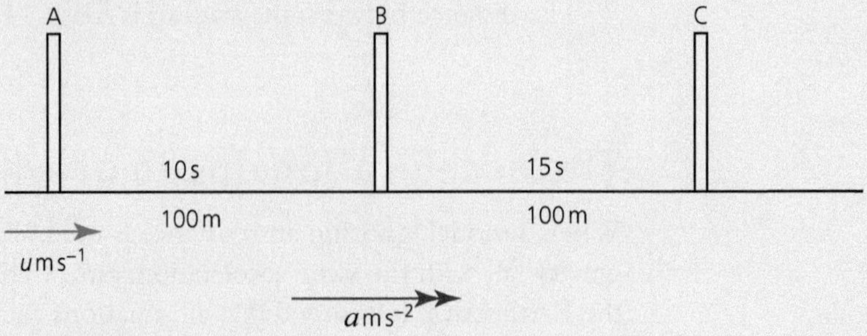

Figure 1.24

Travelling from A to B: You know that s = 100 m, t = 10 s, the speed at A is u and the acceleration is a, so you use $s = ut + \frac{1}{2}at^2$

$$100 = u \times 10 + \frac{1}{2} \times a \times 10^2$$

$$100 = 10u + 50a \qquad ①$$

To use the same equation for the part from B to C, you would need the velocity at B which brings in another unknown. It is better to consider the whole of the journey from A to C, in which case $s = ut + \frac{1}{2}at^2$ with s = 200 m, t = 25 s and u and a as before.

$$200 = u \times 25 + \tfrac{1}{2} a \times 25^2$$

$$200 = 25u + 312.5a \quad ②$$

The two simultaneous equations in u and a can be solved more easily if they are simplified.

① ÷ 5	$20 = 2u + 10a$	③
② × 0.08	$16 = 2u + 25a$	④
④ − ③	$-4 = 15a$	
	$a = -\frac{4}{15}$	
	$u = 10 - 5 \times \left(-\frac{4}{15}\right) = 11\frac{1}{3}$	

The train stops at D. To find the distance AD, use the constant acceleration formula $v^2 = u^2 + 2as$ with $v = 0$, $u = 11\frac{1}{3}$, and $a = -\frac{4}{15}$

$$0 = \left(11\frac{1}{3}\right)^2 + 2 \times \left(-\frac{4}{15}\right)s$$

$$s = 128\frac{4}{9} \times \frac{15}{8} = 240\frac{5}{6}\text{ m}$$

The distance beyond the third post where the train comes to rest is $240\frac{5}{6}$ m.

Exercise 1.2

① The following questions involve motion under constant acceleration.

(i) Find v when $u = 5$, $a = 2.5$ and $t = 2$.

(ii) Find s when $u = 2$, $a = -1.5$ and $t = 4$.

(iii) Find u when $a = -2$, $s = 4$ and $v = 4$.

(iv) Find s when $a = 2$, $v = 5$ and $t = 8$.

(v) Find v when $a = -2$, $s = 100$ and $t = 5$.

② A car travelling at $30\,\text{m s}^{-1}$ decelerates uniformly to rest in 15 s. Find the deceleration and the distance travelled in this time.

③ A stone is dropped down a well. It takes 5 seconds to reach the bottom. How deep is the well?

④ A ball is thrown vertically upwards with a speed of $20\,\text{m s}^{-1}$. One second later another ball is thrown vertically upwards from the same starting height with a speed of $15\,\text{m s}^{-1}$. Find when the two balls are at the same height and find the velocity of each ball at this moment.

⑤ A sprinter accelerates uniformly from rest for the first 10 metres of a 100 metre race. He takes 2 seconds to run the first 10 metres.

(i) Find the acceleration in the first 2 seconds of the race.

(ii) Find the speed of the sprinter after 2 s.

(iii) The sprinter completes the 100 m travelling at that speed. Find the total time taken to run the 100 metres.

(iv) Calculate the average speed of the sprinter.

⑥ Use the equations:

(i) $v = u + at$ and $s = \frac{1}{2}(u + v)t$ to derive the equation $s = ut + \frac{1}{2}at^2$

(ii) $v = u + at$ and $s = ut + \frac{1}{2}at^2$ to derive the equation $s = vt - \frac{1}{2}at^2$.

⑦ A particle, X, is projected vertically upwards at $28\,\mathrm{m\,s^{-1}}$ from a point O on the ground.

(i) Find the maximum height reached by X.

When X is at its highest point, a second particle, Y, is projected upwards from O at $20\,\mathrm{m\,s^{-1}}$.

(ii) Show that X and Y collide 2 seconds later and determine the height above the ground that this takes place.

⑧ Two runners are nearing the end of a fun run. Janet is 100 m from the finish line and is running at a constant speed of $5.25\,\mathrm{m\,s^{-1}}$. Steven, who is 150 m from the finish line and running at $4\,\mathrm{m\,s^{-1}}$, decides to accelerate to try and beat Janet. He accelerates uniformly to his maximum speed of $8\,\mathrm{m\,s^{-1}}$ in 4 s and then maintains that speed to the finish line.

(i) Which of the two crosses the finish line first?

(ii) How far ahead is the winner?

(iii) What is the time margin between them?

⑨ Two trains are running on parallel tracks. When they are initially level with each other, one is moving with a uniform speed of $25\,\mathrm{m\,s^{-1}}$ and the second has a speed of $10\,\mathrm{m\,s^{-1}}$ but is accelerating at a uniform rate of $0.5\,\mathrm{m\,s^{-2}}$. How long will it be before they are level again and how far will they have travelled?

⑩ A stone dropped into a well reaches the water with a velocity of $30\,\mathrm{m\,s^{-1}}$ and the sound of the splash is heard 3.19 s after it was dropped. From these data, calculate the velocity of sound in air.

⑪ A train, moving with constant acceleration, is seen to travel 1500 m in one minute and 2500 m in the next.

(i) Find the speed of the train at the start of the first minute.

(ii) Find the acceleration.

(iii) Find the speed of the train at the end of the second minute.

⑫ A ball is thrown vertically upwards and returns to its point of projection after 4 seconds. Calculate its speed of projection and the maximum height reached.

⑬ A stone drops from the roof of a building and takes $\frac{1}{8}$ s to pass from the top to the bottom of a window, 1.20 m high. How high is the roof above the top of the window?

⑭ Which would win a 100 metre race, a sprinter who can cover the distance in 10 s or a motor car which can accelerate to 60 miles per hour from rest in 16 s?

⑮ Two cars are travelling along a straight road. Car A is moving at $30\,\mathrm{km\,h^{-1}}$ when it is overtaken by car B travelling at $40\,\mathrm{km\,h^{-1}}$. A immediately accelerates uniformly and after travelling 500 m overtakes B which has kept its speed constant. Calculate

(i) the time taken

(ii) the acceleration of car A

(iii) the greatest distance between the cars during that time.

⑯ Two trains start together from rest at a station. They travel for 3 minutes and come to rest together at the next station. One train, A, accelerates uniformly at the rate of $1\,\mathrm{m\,s^{-2}}$ for 30 s, continues at that speed for the next 2 minutes and decelerates uniformly for the last 30 seconds. The other train, B, has a uniform acceleration for 90 seconds and uniform deceleration for the remaining time.

(i) Draw on the same diagram, velocity–time graphs for the two train journeys.

Find

(ii) the distance between the two stations

(iii) the acceleration of train B in the first part of its journey

(iv) the largest distance between the trains.

⑰ Two particles P and Q are moving in the same direction along neighbouring parallel straight lines with constant accelerations of $3\,\mathrm{m\,s^{-2}}$ and $2\,\mathrm{m\,s^{-2}}$, respectively. At a certain instant, P has velocity $3\,\mathrm{m\,s^{-1}}$ and Q is 30 m behind P and moving at $11.5\,\mathrm{m\,s^{-1}}$.

(i) Show that P and Q will be level twice.

(ii) Find the velocity of P when the particles are level for the first time.

(iii) Find the maximum distance Q gets ahead of P.

3 Variable acceleration

The equations you have used for constant acceleration do not apply when the acceleration varies. In such cases, you need to go back to first principles.

The velocity of a moving point is the rate at which its position changes with time. When the velocity is not constant, the position–time graph is a curve.

The rate of change of position is the gradient of the tangent to the curve, which can be found by differentiation,

$$v = \frac{\mathrm{d}s}{\mathrm{d}t} \qquad ①$$

Similarly, the acceleration is the rate at which the velocity changes, so that

$$a = \frac{\mathrm{d}v}{\mathrm{d}t} = \frac{\mathrm{d}^2 s}{\mathrm{d}t^2} \qquad ②$$

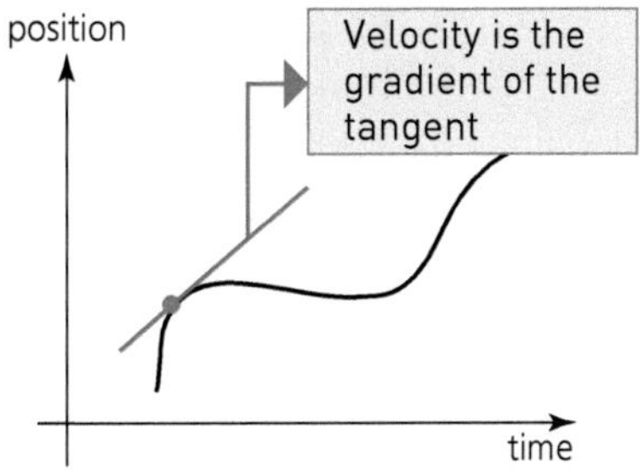

Figure 1.25

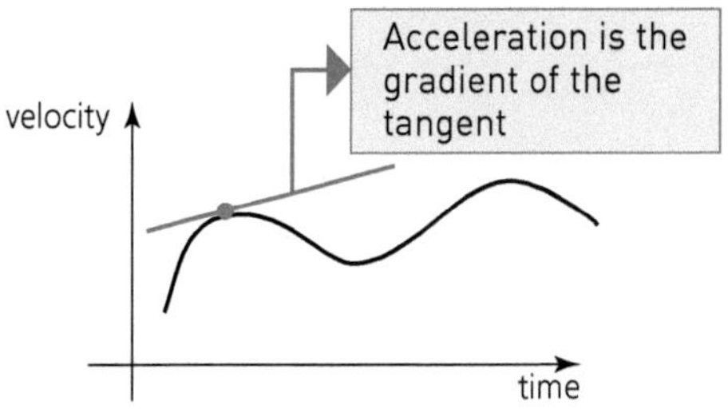

Figure 1.26

When you are given the position of a moving point at time t you can use equations ① and ② to solve problems even when the acceleration is not constant.

Example 1.9

A particle is moving in a straight line and its displacement s from a fixed point O is given by the equation

$$s = 18t - 21t^2 + 4t^3$$

(i) Find expressions for the velocity and acceleration of the particle at time t.

(ii) Sketch the graphs of s, v and a against time in the interval $0 \leq t \leq 4$.

(iii) Find the distance travelled between the two times when the velocity is 0.

(iv) Find the distance travelled in the interval $0 \leq t \leq 4$.

Solution

(i) Position $s = 18t - 21t^2 + 4t^3$

Velocity $v = \frac{ds}{dt} = 18 - 42t + 12t^2$

Acceleration $a = \frac{dv}{dt} = -42 + 24t$

(ii) The three graphs of s, v and a are shown one above the other.

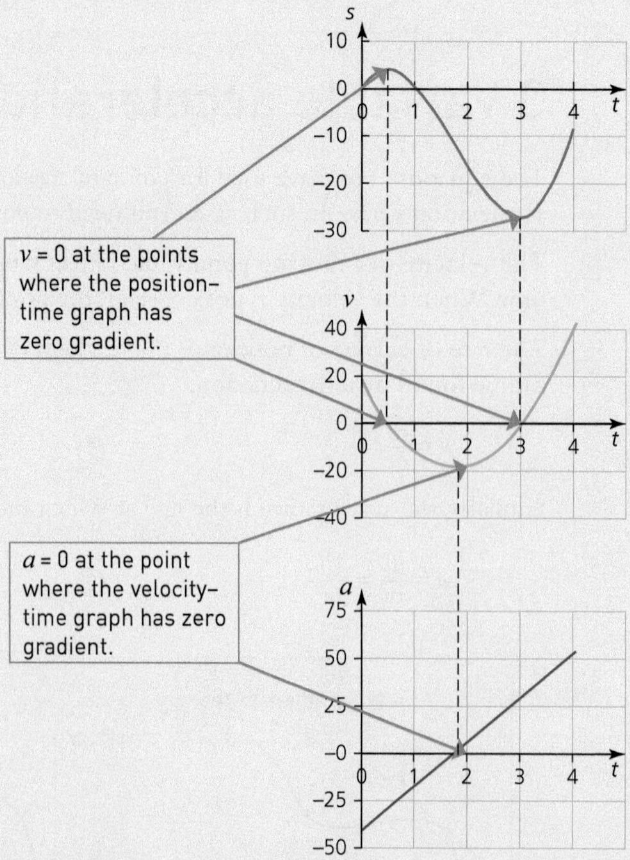

Figure 1.27

(iii) The velocity is zero when

$18 - 42t + 12t^2 = 0$

$6(2t - 1)(t - 3) = 0$

$t = \frac{1}{2}$ or $t = 3$

When $t = \frac{1}{2}, s = 18 \times \frac{1}{2} - 21 \times \frac{1}{4} + 4 \times \frac{1}{8} = 4\frac{1}{4}$

When $t = 3, s = 18 \times 3 - 21 \times 9 + 4 \times 27 = -27$

The total distance travelled between $t = \frac{1}{2}$ and $t = 3$ is

$27 + 4\frac{1}{4} = 31\frac{1}{4}$.

(iv) When $t = 4, s = 18 \times 4 - 21 \times 16 + 4 \times 64 = -8$

The total distance travelled between $t = 0$ and $t = 4$ is equal to

$4\frac{1}{4} + 31\frac{1}{4} + 27 - 8 = 54\frac{1}{2}$.

Distance between $t = 0$ and $t = \frac{1}{2}$.

Distance between $t = \frac{1}{2}$ and $t = 3$.

Distance between $t = 3$ and $t = 4$.

Finding displacement from velocity

Note

The dt indicates that you must write v in terms of t before integrating.

To find an expression for the position of a particle when the velocity is known you need to integrate with respect to time.

$$v = \frac{ds}{dt} \text{ implies that } s = \int v\,dt$$

Example 1.10

Find the position s of a particle at time t, given that $s = 3$ when $t = 0$ and its velocity is given by $v = 5t - 2$.

Solution

The position at time t is given by

$s = \int (5t - 2)\,dt$

$s = \frac{5}{2}t^2 - 2t + c$

Using the initial condition that $s = 3$ when $t = 0$, gives $3 = c$, resulting in

$$s = \frac{5}{2}t^2 - 2t + 3$$

Finding velocity from acceleration

You can find the velocity from the acceleration by using integration.

$$a = \frac{dv}{dt} \text{ implies that } v = \int a\,dt$$

Example 1.11

The acceleration of a particle (in m s^{-2}) at time t seconds after starting from rest at the origin is given by

$$a = 3t - 2$$

(i) Find expressions for the velocity v and position s at time t.

(ii) Sketch the graphs of a, v and s.

(iii) Show that the particle returns to its starting point after 2 s and find the distance of the particle from the starting point after a further 2 s.

(iv) Find at what time the particle's velocity is 0.

(v) Find the total distance travelled by the particle in the first 4 seconds.

Solution

$c = 0$ as the particle starts from rest.

(i) Acceleration $a = 3t - 2$

Velocity $v = \int(3t-2)\,dt$

$$v = \frac{3}{2}t^2 - 2t + c$$

$$v = \frac{3}{2}t^2 - 2t$$

$k = 0$ as the particle starts from 0.

Position $s = \int\left(\frac{3}{2}t^2 - 2t\right)dt$

$$s = \frac{1}{2}t^3 - t^2 + k$$

$$s = \frac{1}{2}t^3 - t^2$$

The particle starts at 0, goes back at first, stops instantaneously at $t = \frac{4}{3}$, changes direction, returning to 0 at $t = 2$. It then continues moving forwards with increasing speed.

(ii) The graphs are drawn under each other to show how they relate to one another.

(iii) To show that the particle returns to its starting point after 2 seconds, you need to show that $s = 0$ when $t = 2$:

$$\frac{1}{2}(2)^3 - 2^2 = 4 - 4 = 0$$

The displacement of the particle when $t = 4$, is equal to

$$s(4) = \frac{1}{2}(4)^3 - 4^2 = 32 - 16 = 16\text{ m}$$

(iv) The velocity is zero when

$$v(t) = \frac{3}{2}t^2 - 2t = 0$$

$$t\left(\frac{3}{2}t - 2\right) = 0$$

$$t = 0 \text{ or } t = \frac{4}{3}$$

The velocity is 0 when $t = 0$ or $t = \frac{4}{3}$ s.

(v) The particle goes backwards in the interval $0 < t < \frac{4}{3}$, turns round at $t = \frac{4}{3}$ and then moves forwards in the interval $\frac{4}{3} < t < 4$.

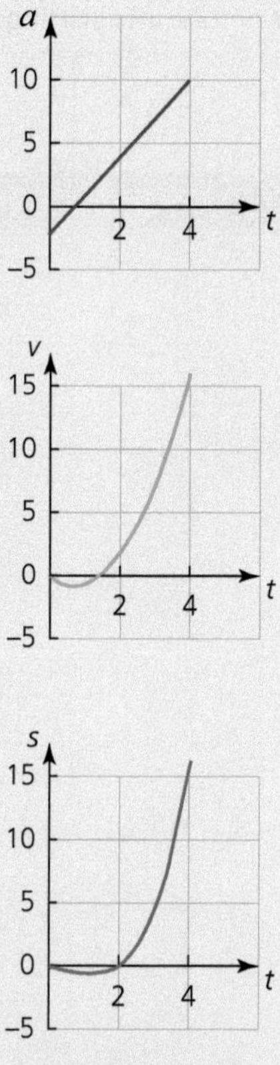

Figure 1.28

The displacement from $t = 0$ to $t = \frac{4}{3}$ is $\left[\frac{1}{2}\left(\frac{4}{3}\right)^3 - \left(\frac{4}{3}\right)^2\right] - [0] = -\frac{16}{27}$.

So the distance travelled from $t = 0$ to $t = \frac{4}{3}$ is $+\frac{16}{27}$.

The distance travelled in $\frac{4}{3} < t \leq 4$ is equal to $16 - \left(-\frac{16}{27}\right) = 16\frac{16}{27}$.

The total distance travelled in the interval $0 \leq t \leq 4$ is $\frac{16}{27} + 16\frac{16}{27} = 17\frac{5}{27}$.

The particle travels $17\frac{5}{27}$ m in the first 4 seconds.

Exercise 1.3

① In each of the following cases:

(a) $s = 2 + 4t - t^2$

(b) $s = 5t^2 - t^3$

(c) $s = t^4 - t^2 + 2$

(i) find expressions for the velocity

(ii) use your equations to write down the initial position and velocity

(iii) find the time and position when the velocity is zero.

② The position s of a moving point A at time t seconds is given by

$$s = 2t^3 - 3t^2 + 4t - 10$$

Find the velocity and acceleration of A at the instant $t = 4$.

③ Find the position s m of a particle at time t s if its velocity v m s^{-1} is given by

(i) $v = 5t - 2$, and $s = 3$ when $t = 0$

(ii) $v = 3t^2 + 4t$, and $s = 2$ when $t = 1$.

④ Find the velocity v m s^{-1} and displacement s m of a particle at time t s, if its acceleration is given by

(i) $a = 12t - 8$ and when $t = 0$, $s = 5$ and $v = 3$

(ii) $a = 0.5t^2 - 0.2t + 1$ and when $t = 1$, $s = 0.5$ and $v = 1$.

⑤

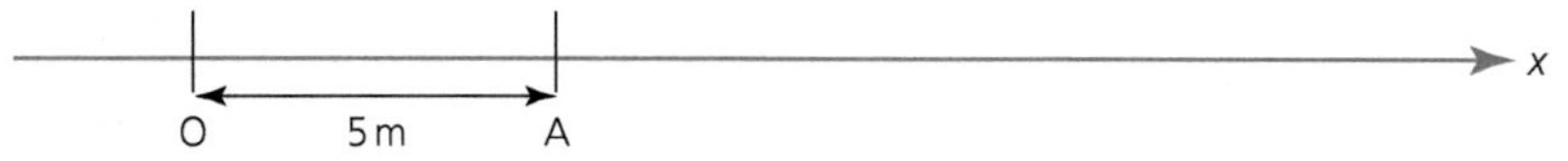

Figure 1.29

A toy car is moving along the straight line Ox, where O is the origin. The time t is in seconds. At time $t = 0$ the car is at A, 5 m from O, as shown in Figure 1.29.

The velocity of the car, v m s^{-1}, is given by

$$v = 2 + 9t - 1.5t^2$$

Calculate the distance of the car from O when the acceleration is 0.

⑥ A particle moves along a straight line so that after t seconds, $t \geq 0$, its distance s from the origin O on the line is given by

$$s = (t - 1)^2(t - 2)$$

(i) Find the velocity and acceleration of the particle on each occasion that it passes the origin.

(ii) Find the distances of the particle from O each time the velocity is 0.

(iii) Find the acceleration when the velocity is 8 m s^{-1}.

⑦ During braking, the speed of a car is given by $v = 12 - 3t^2$ until it stops moving. Find the distance travelled from the time that the braking starts.

⑧ The velocity of a sprinter at the start of a 100 metre race is given as

$$v = 10t - 2.5t^2, \quad 0 \leq t \leq 2$$
$$v = 10, \quad t > 2$$

(i) Find the acceleration of the sprinter at $t = 2$. Hence write down the maximum speed of the sprinter.

(ii) How far does the sprinter run in the first 2 seconds?

(iii) How long does the sprinter take to run 100 metres?

⑨ A particle moves along the x-axis. Its displacement from the origin, O, is given by

$$x = 10 + 36t + 3t^2 - 2t^3$$

where t is the time in seconds and $-4 \leq t \leq 6$.

(i) Write down the displacement of the particle when $t = 0$.

(ii) Find an expression in terms of t for the velocity $v\,\text{m s}^{-1}$ of the particle.

(iii) Find the values of t for which $v = 0$ and find the values of x at those times.

(iv) Calculate the distance travelled by the particle from $t = 0$ to $t = 4$.

(v) How many times does the particle go through O in the interval $-4 \leq t \leq 6$?

⑩ A particle P is moving in a straight line. At time t seconds, for small values of t, after starting from the origin, O, its velocity is given by

$$v = t^2(3 - t)$$

(i) Find the values of t when the acceleration is zero.

(ii) After what time does the particle come to instantaneous rest?

At that time, the particle has reached its furthest point A from O and then reverses back towards O.

(iii) Find the distance OA.

(iv) Find the time taken for the particle to return to O.

⑪ A car moves between two sets of traffic lights, stopping at both. Its speed $v\,\text{m s}^{-1}$ at time $t\,\text{s}$ is modelled by

$$v = 6t^2 - t^3$$

(i) Find the times at which the car is stationary.

(ii) Find the maximum speed of the car.

(iii) Find the distance between the two sets of traffic lights.

⑫ A particle is moving in a straight line. The position s of the particle at time t is given by

$$s = 3t^2 - t^3, 0 \leq t \leq 4.$$

(i) Find the velocity v at time t and the values of t for which $v = 0$.

(ii) Find the values of t for which the particle has zero displacement.

(iii) Find the total distance travelled by the particle in the interval $0 \leq t \leq 4$.

⑬ The distance of a particle from a point O at time t is given by

$$s = 6 \sin 3t + 8 \cos 3t$$

(i) Find expressions for the velocity and acceleration in terms of t.

(ii) Show that the acceleration a and the displacement from O, s, satisfy the equation $a = -9s$.

(iii) Show that the velocity v and s satisfy the equation $v^2 = 9(100 - s^2)$.

⑭ Two sprinters are having a race over 100 m. They both start from rest. Their accelerations in m s^{-2} are as follows:

Sprinter A	Sprinter B
$a = 10 - 5t, \quad 0 \le t \le 2$	$a = 15t - 7.5t^2, \quad 0 \le t \le 2$
$a = 0, \quad t > 2$	$a = 0, \quad t > 2$

(i) Find the greatest speed of each sprinter.

(ii) Find the distance run by each sprinter while reaching greatest speed.

(iii) How long does each sprinter take to finish the race?

(iv) Who wins the race, by what time margin and by what distance?

⑮ Two walkers, John and Euan, are on a long hike. John walks at a uniform rate of 5.15 km h^{-1} throughout. Euan's speed v_E km h^{-1} is $\frac{30}{4.5+t}$, t hours after he started. How long does it take for John and Euan to finish the 15 km hike? Who gets to the finish line first? How far ahead is the leader at the end of the walk?

KEY POINTS

1

Vectors (with magnitude and direction)	Scalars (magnitude only)
Displacement	Distance (travelled)
Position: displacement from a fixed origin	
Velocity: rate of change of position	Speed: magnitude of velocity
Acceleration: rate of change of velocity	Magnitude of acceleration
	Time

2 Graphs

The gradient of a position–time graph is the velocity.
The gradient of a velocity–time graph is the acceleration.
The area under a velocity–time graph is the displacement.
The gradient of a distance–time graph is the speed.
The gradient of a speed–time graph is the magnitude of the acceleration.
The area under a speed–time graph is the distance.

3 Averages

$$\text{Average speed} = \frac{\text{total distance travelled}}{\text{total time taken}}$$

$$\text{Average velocity} = \frac{\text{displacement}}{\text{time taken}}$$

$$\text{Average acceleration} = \frac{\text{change in velocity}}{\text{time taken}}$$

4 Constant acceleration formulae

$$v = u + at$$
$$s = \frac{1}{2}(u+v)\times t$$
$$s = ut + \frac{1}{2}at^2$$
$$s = vt - \frac{1}{2}at^2$$
$$v^2 = u^2 + 2as.$$

5 Relationships between variables describing motion

Position	Velocity	Acceleration
⟶	differentiate	⟶
s	$v = \frac{ds}{dt}$	$a = \frac{dv}{dt} = \frac{d^2s}{dt^2}$

Acceleration	Velocity	Position
⟶	integrate	⟶
a	$v = \int a\,dt$	$s = \int v\,dt$

LEARNING OUTCOMES

When you have completed this chapter, you should know

- the difference between position, displacement and distance travelled
- the difference between speed and velocity and between acceleration and the magnitude of acceleration
- how to draw and interpret position–time, distance–time, velocity–time, speed–time and acceleration–time graphs and how to use these to solve problems connected with motion in a straight line
- how to find average speed and average velocity
- how and when to use the constant acceleration formulae to solve problems involving linear motion
- how to use two constant acceleration formulae to derive a third formula
- how to deal with problems involving motion under gravity
- how to use calculus to derive expressions for position, velocity and acceleration as functions of time, given suitable information
- how to solve problems involving linear motion with variable acceleration.

2 Forces and motion

In the beginning (if there was such a thing) God created Newton's laws of motion together with the necessary masses and forces. This is all; everything beyond this follows from the development of appropriate mathematical methods by means of deduction.

Albert Einstein

→ This tightrope walker is stationary. There are a number of forces acting on the walker which cancel each other out, resulting in no motion. In order for that to be possible, the cable must make small angles to the horizontal so that the vertical components of the tension can cancel out the weight of the walker. In that case, the tensions in the cable will be greater than the walker's weight.

1 Forces and Newton's laws of motion

Modelling vocabulary

Mechanics is about modelling the real world. In order to do this, suitable simplifying assumptions are often made so that mathematics can be applied to situations and problems. This process involves identifying factors that can be neglected without losing too much accuracy. Here are some commonly used modelling terms which are used to describe such assumptions:

- negligible: small enough to ignore
- inextensible: for a string with negligible stretch
- light: for an object with negligible mass
- particle: an object with negligible dimensions
- smooth: for a surface with negligible friction
- uniform: the same throughout.

Forces

A force is defined as the physical quantity that causes a change in motion. As it depends on magnitude and direction, it is a vector quantity.

Forces can start motion, stop motion, speed up or slow down objects, or change the direction of their motion. In real situations, several forces usually act on an object. The sum of these forces, known as the resultant force, determines whether or not there is a change of motion.

There are several types of force that you often use.

The force of gravity

Every object on or near the Earth's surface is pulled vertically downwards by the force of gravity. The size of the force on an object of mass M kg is Mg newtons where g is a constant whose value is about $9.8\,\text{m s}^{-2}$. The force of gravity is also known as the **weight** of the object.

Note

g varies around the world, with $9.8\,\text{m s}^{-2}$ being a typical value. Singapore, at 9.766, has one of the lowest values, and Helsinki, with 9.825, has one of the highest.

Tension and thrust

When a string is pulled, as in Figure 2.1, it exerts a **tension** force opposite to the pull. The tension acts along the string and is the same throughout the string. A rigid rod can exert a tension force in a similar way to a string when it is used to support or pull an object. It can also exert a **thrust** force when it is in compression, as in Figure 2.2. The thrust acts along the rod and is the same throughout the rod.

The tension on either side of a smooth pulley is the same, as shown in Figure 2.3.

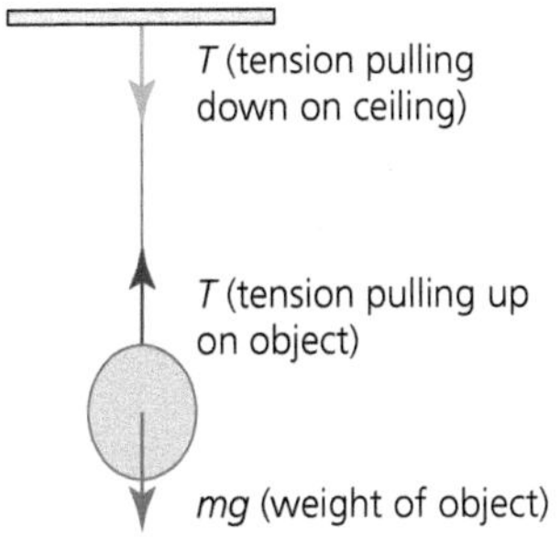

Figure 2.1

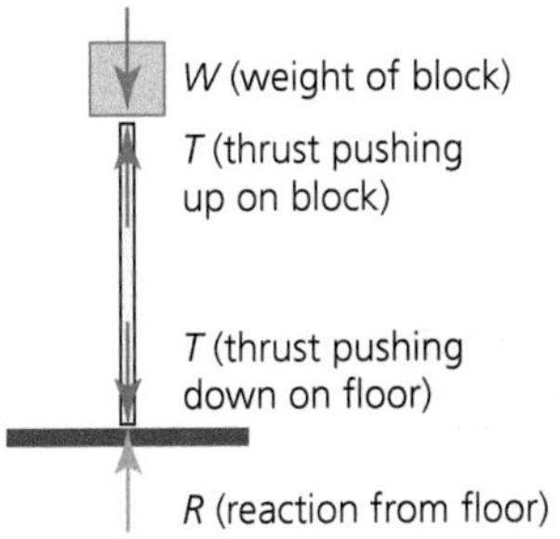

Figure 2.2

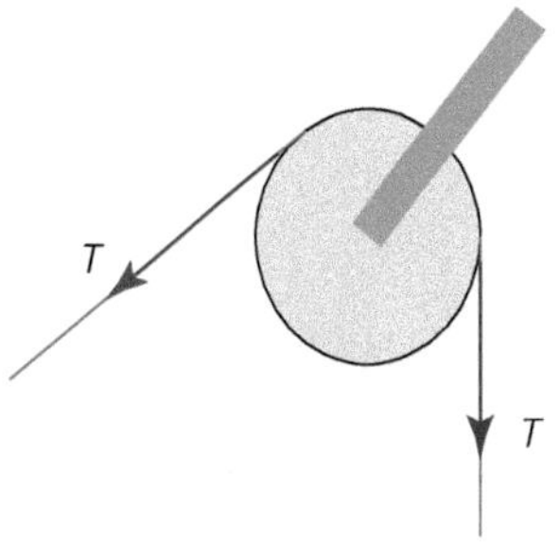

Figure 2.3

Normal contact force

A book resting on a table is subjected to two forces, its weight and the **normal contact force** of the table. It is called 'normal' because its line of action is normal (at right angles) to the surface of the table. Since the book is in equilibrium, the normal contact force is equal and opposite to the weight of the book.

> **Note**
>
> In Figure 2.4, the normal contact force is vertical but this is not always the case. For example, the normal contact force on an object on a slope is perpendicular to the slope.

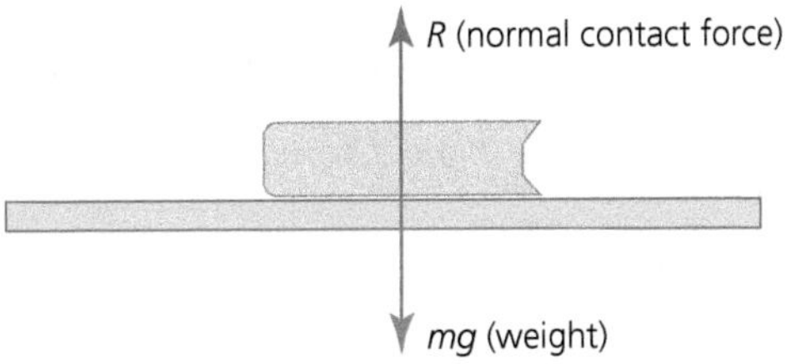

Figure 2.4

If the book is about to lose contact with the table (which might happen, for instance, if the table is accelerating rapidly downwards), the normal force becomes zero.

Frictional force

In Figure 2.5, the book on the table is being pushed by a force P parallel to the surface. The book remains at rest because P is balanced by a **frictional force**, F, in the opposite direction to P. The magnitude of the frictional force is equal to the pushing force, $P = F$.

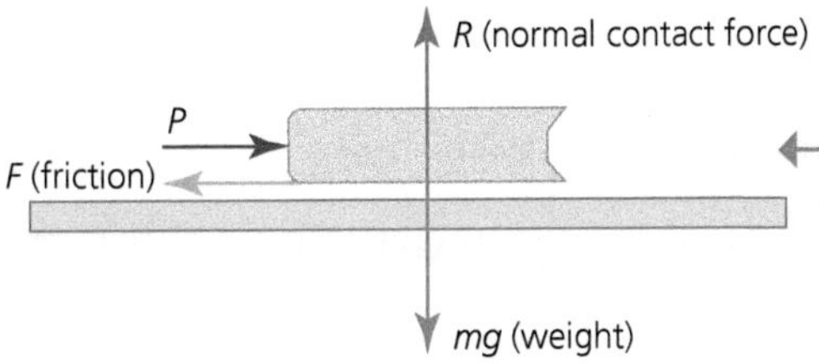

The frictional force is also sometimes called the frictional contact force.

Figure 2.5

If P is increased and the book starts to move, F is still present but now $P > F$. Friction always acts in the opposite direction to the motion. Friction may prevent the motion of an object or slow it down if it is moving.

Driving force

In problems about moving objects such as cars, all the forces acting along the line of motion can usually be reduced to two or three: the **driving force**, the **resistance** to motion and, possibly, a **braking force**.

Figure 2.6

Example 2.1

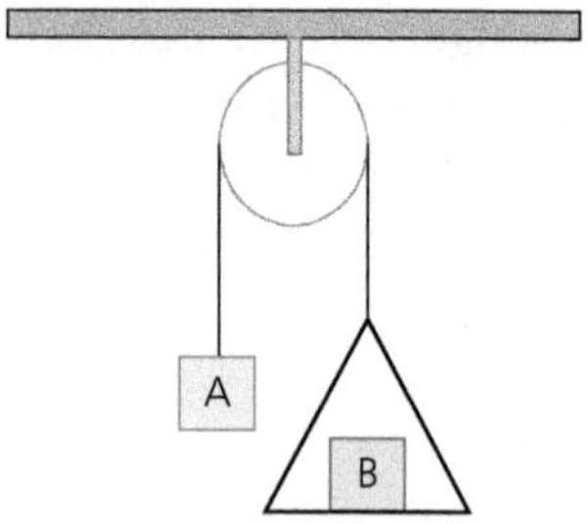

Figure 2.7

Figure 2.7 shows a block A of mass 10 kg connected to a light scale pan by a light inextensible string that passes over a light smooth pulley. The scale pan holds block B, also of mass 10 kg. The system is in equilibrium.

(i) On separate diagrams, show all the forces acting on each of the masses, the scale pan and the pulley.

(ii) Find the value of the tension in the string.

(iii) Find the tension in the rod holding the pulley.

(iv) Find the normal contact force of B on the scale pan.

Solution

(i)

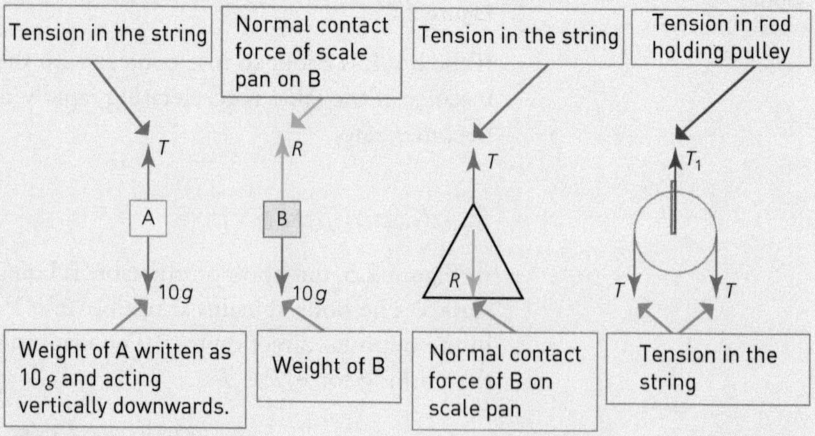

Figure 2.8

(ii) Block A is in equilibrium $\Rightarrow$ $T = 10g = 98$ N.

(iii) The pulley is in equilibrium $\Rightarrow$ $T_1 = 2T = 196$ N.

(iv) Block B is in equilibrium $\Rightarrow$ $R = 10g = 98$ N.

Newton's laws of motion

1 Every object continues in a state of rest or uniform motion in a straight line unless it is acted on by a resultant external force.

2 The acceleration of an object is proportional to, and in the same direction as, the resultant of the forces acting on the object.

F is the resultant force.
m is the mass of the object.
a is the acceleration.

$\mathbf{F} = ma$

Historical note

Isaac Newton was born in Lincolnshire in 1642. He was not an outstanding scholar either as a schoolboy or as a university student, yet later in life he made remarkable contributions in dynamics, optics, astronomy, chemistry, music theory and theology. He became Member of Parliament for Cambridge University and later Warden of the Royal Mint. His tomb in Westminster Abbey reads 'Let mortals rejoice that there existed such and so great an ornament to the Human Race'.

Notice that this is a vector equation, since both the magnitudes and directions of the resultant force and the acceleration are involved. If the motion is along a straight line it is often written in scalar form as $F = ma$.

3 When one object exerts a force on another there is always a reaction from the second object on the first, which is equal and opposite in direction to the acting force.

Equation of motion

The equation resulting from Newton's second law is often described as an **equation of motion**, as in the following examples.

Example 2.2

An empty bottle of mass 0.5 kg is released from a submarine and rises with an acceleration of $0.75\,\mathrm{m\,s^{-2}}$. The water causes a resistance of 1.1 N.

(i) Draw a diagram showing the forces acting on the bottle and the direction of its acceleration.

(ii) Write down the equation of motion of the bottle.

(iii) Find the size of the buoyancy force.

Solution

(i) The forces acting on the bottle and the acceleration are shown in Figure 2.9.

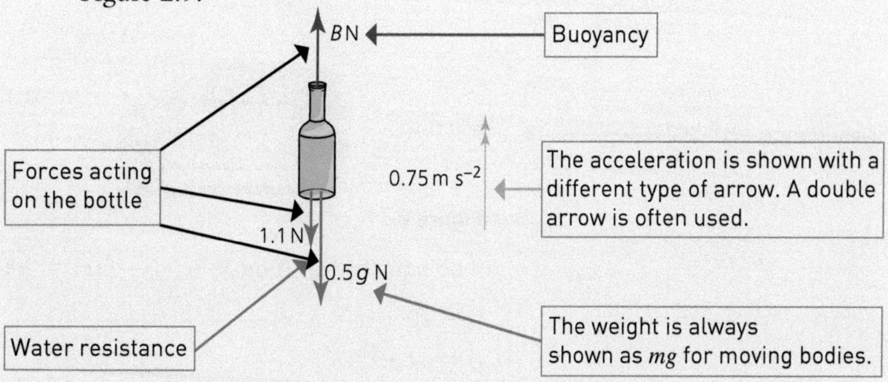

Figure 2.9

(ii) The resultant force acting on the bottle is $(B - 0.5g - 1.1)$ upwards.

The resulting equation

$$B - 0.5g - 1.1 = 0.5a$$

is called the **equation of motion**.

(iii) $B - 4.9 - 1.1 = 0.375$ ← 0.5 × 0.75

$$B = 6.375$$

The buoyancy force on the bottle is 6.375 N.

Example 2.3

A car of mass 900 kg travels at a constant speed of $20\,\text{m}\,\text{s}^{-1}$ along a straight horizontal road. Its engine is producing a driving force of 500 N.

(i) What is the resistance to its motion?

Later the driving force is removed and the car is brought to rest in a time of 5 s with the same resistance to motion.

(ii) Find the force created by the brakes, assuming it to be constant.

Solution

(i) The car is travelling at constant speed, so that the resultant force acting on the car is zero.

Resultant = $500 - R$

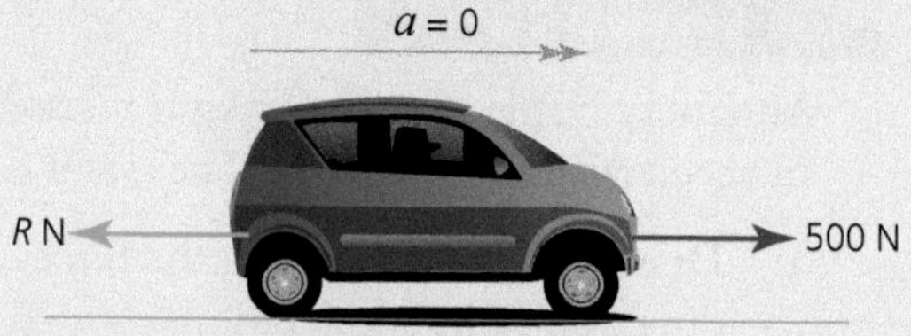

Figure 2.10

Let the resistive force be R N.

$$500 - R = 0$$

$$R = 500$$

The resistive force is 500 N.

(ii) The car is slowing down.

So you expect a to be negative.

Resultant = $-B - 500$

Figure 2.11

B is constant, so that a is also constant and you can use the constant acceleration formulae.

The equation of motion is $-B - 500 = 900a$ ①

$0 = 20 + a \times 5$

Use $v = u + at$ with $u = 20$, $v = 0$ and $t = 5$.

$a = -4\,\text{m}\,\text{s}^{-2}$

Substituting in ①: $-B - 500 = 900 \times -4$

$\Rightarrow B = 3100\,\text{N}$

The braking force is 3100 N.

Example 2.4

Two boxes A and B are descending vertically supported by a parachute. Box A has mass 100 kg. Box B has mass 75 kg and is suspended from box A by a light vertical wire. Both boxes are descending with downwards acceleration $2\,\mathrm{m\,s^{-2}}$.

(i) Draw a labelled diagram showing all the forces acting on box A and another diagram showing all the forces acting on box B.

(ii) Write down separate equations of motion for box A and for box B.

(iii) Find the tensions in both wires.

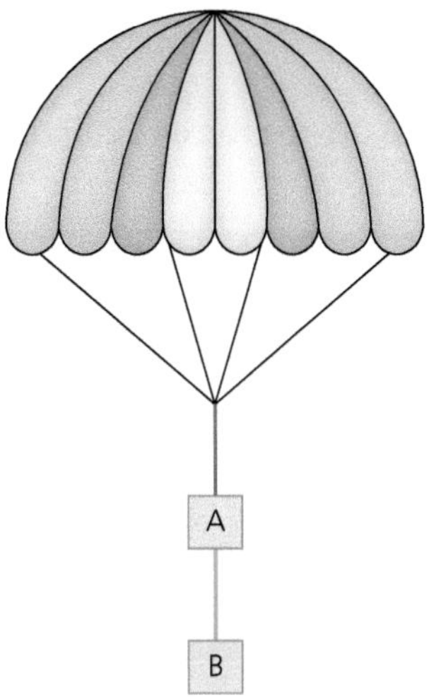

Figure 2.12

Note

T_1 is the tension in the blue wire linking A to the parachute. T_2 is the tension in the green wire linking A to B.
$T_1 \neq T_2$

Solution

(i)

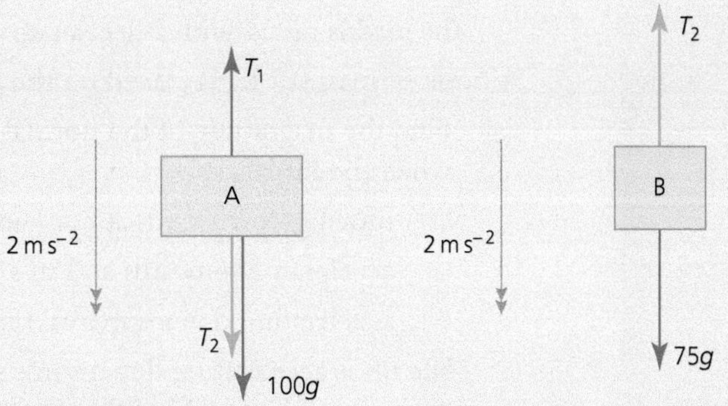

Figure 2.13

(ii) Box A: The resultant downwards force is $T_2 + 100g - T_1$ so the equation of motion is

$$T_2 + 100g - T_1 = 200 \quad ①$$

Since $100a = 100 \times 2 = 200$

Box B: The resultant downwards force is $75g - T_2$ so the equation of motion is

$$75g - T_2 = 150 \quad ②$$

Since $75a = 75 \times 2 = 150$

(iii) From ②: $T_2 = 75 \times 9.8 - 150$

$= 585\,\mathrm{N}$

Substituting in ①: $T_1 = 585 + 100 \times 9.8 - 200$

$= 1365\,\mathrm{N}$

The tension in the blue wire linking A to the parachute is 1365 N.
The tension in the green wire linking A to B is 585 N.

Exercise 2.1

① Find the accelerations produced when a force of 100 N acts on an object

(i) of mass 15 kg

(ii) of mass 10 g

(ii) of mass 1 tonne.

② A bullet of mass 20 g is fired into a wall with a velocity of $400\,\mathrm{m\,s^{-1}}$. The bullet penetrates the wall to a depth of 10 cm. Find the resistance of the wall, assuming it to be uniform.

③ A car of mass 1200 kg is travelling along a straight level road.

(i) Calculate the acceleration of the car when a resultant force of 2400 N acts on it in the direction of its motion. How long does it take the car to increase its speed from $4\,\text{m s}^{-1}$ to $12\,\text{m s}^{-1}$?

The car has an acceleration of $1.2\,\text{m s}^{-2}$ when there is a driving force of 2400 N.

(ii) Find the resistance to motion of the car.

④ A load of mass 5 kg is held on the end of a string. Calculate the tension in the string when

(i) the load is raised with an acceleration of $2.5\,\text{m s}^{-2}$

(ii) the load is lowered with an acceleration of $2.5\,\text{m s}^{-2}$

(iii) the load is raised with a constant speed of $2\,\text{m s}^{-1}$

(iv) the load is raised with a deceleration of $2.5\,\text{m s}^{-2}$.

⑤ A book of mass 0.7 kg is placed on the floor of a lift.

(a) Find the magnitude of the normal force from the lift on the book when the lift is

(i) moving downwards at constant speed 3 m s^{-1}

(ii) accelerating upwards at 3 m s^{-2}

(iii) accelerating downwards at 3 m s^{-2}.

(b) The lift is accelerating downwards so that the normal force from the lift on the book is zero. Find the magnitude of the minimum acceleration of the lift.

(c) What happens to the book if the lift accelerates downwards at 12 m s^{-2}?

⑥ A block A of mass 10 kg is connected to a block B of mass 5 kg by a light inextensible string passing over a smooth fixed pulley. The blocks are released from rest with A 0.3 m above ground level, as shown in Figure 2.14.

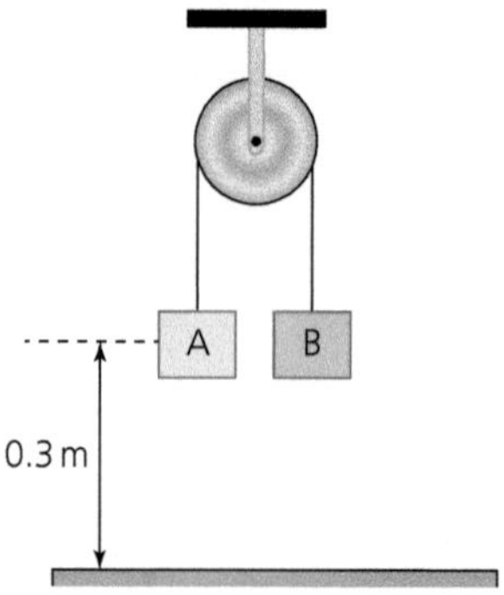

Figure 2.14

(i) Find the acceleration of the system and the tension in the string.

(ii) Find the speed of the masses when A hits the ground.

(iii) How far does B rise after A hits the floor and the string becomes slack?

⑦ A block A of mass 10 kg is lying on a smooth horizontal table. Light inextensible strings connect A to particle B of mass 6 kg and particle C of mass 4 kg, which hang freely over smooth pulleys at the edge of the table.

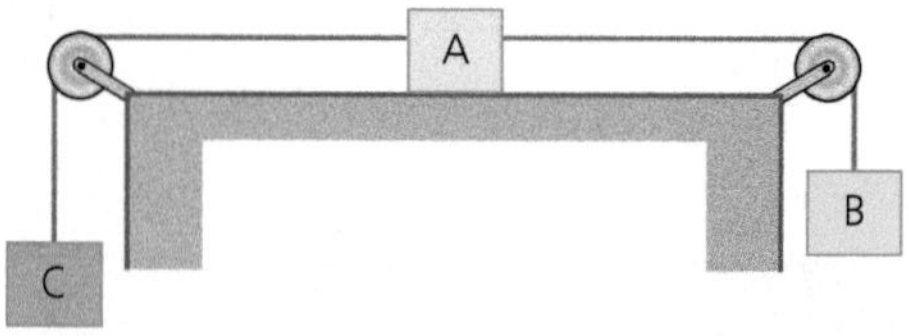

Figure 2.15

(i) Draw force diagrams to show the forces acting on each mass.

(ii) Write down separate equations of motion for A, B and C.

(iii) Find the acceleration of the system and the tensions in the strings.

⑧ A truck of mass 1250 kg is towing a trailer of mass 350 kg along a horizontal straight road. The engine of the truck produces a driving force of 2500 N. The truck is subjected to a resistance of 250 N and the trailer to a resistance of 300 N.

Figure 2.16

(i) Show, in separate diagrams, the horizontal forces acting on the truck and the trailer.

(ii) Find the acceleration of the truck and trailer.

(iii) Find the tension in the coupling between the truck and the trailer.

⑨ A train consists of a locomotive and five trucks with masses and resistances to motion as shown in Figure 2.17. The engine provides a driving force of 29 000 N. All the couplings are light, rigid and horizontal.

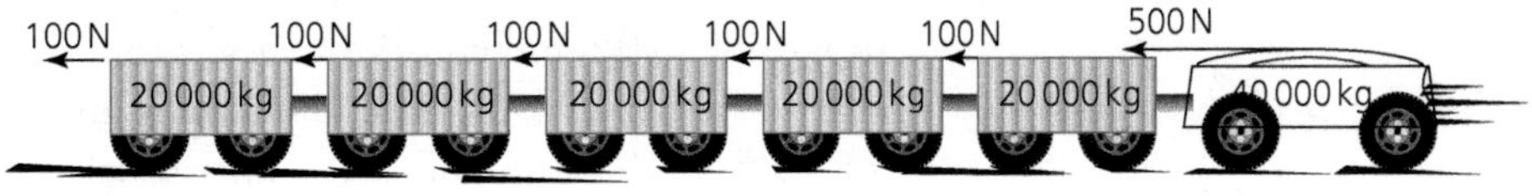

Figure 2.17

(i) Show that the acceleration of the train is $0.2\,\mathrm{m\,s^{-2}}$.

(ii) Find the force in the coupling between the last two trucks.

With the driving force removed, brakes are applied, so adding additional resistances of 3000 N to the locomotive and 2000 N to each truck.

(iii) Find the new acceleration of the train.

(iv) Find the force in the coupling between the last two trucks.

⑩ Block A of mass 2 kg is connected to a light scale pan by a light inextensible string which passes over a smooth fixed pulley.

The scale pan holds two blocks, B and C, of masses 0.5 kg and 1 kg, as shown in Figure 2.18.

(i) Draw diagrams showing all the forces acting on each of the three blocks.

(ii) Write down equations of motion for each of A, B and C.

(iii) Find the acceleration of the system, the tension in the string, the normal force between B and C and the normal force between C and the scale pan.

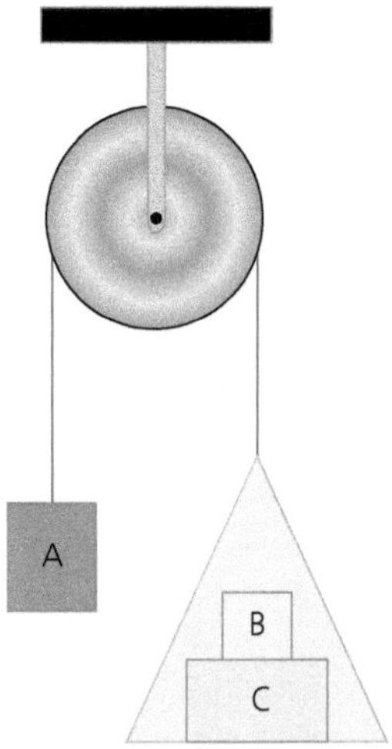

Figure 2.18

⑪ A block A of mass 5 kg is lying on a smooth horizontal table. A light inextensible string connects A to a particle B of mass 1 kg which hangs freely over a smooth pulley at the edge of the table. B is connected to a third particle C of mass 2 kg by another string, as shown in Figure 2.19.

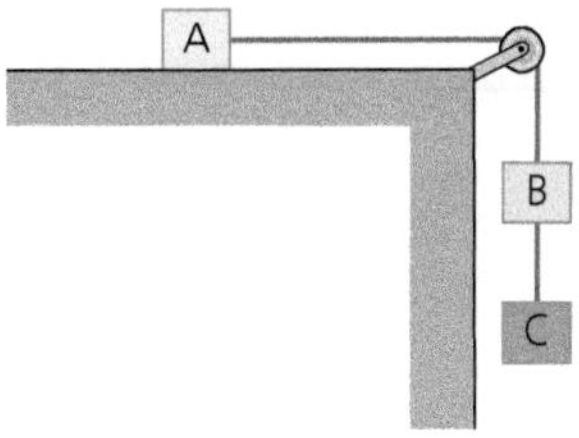

Figure 2.19

(i) Draw diagrams showing all the forces acting on each of A, B and C.

(ii) Write equations of motion for each of A, B and C.

(iii) Find the acceleration of the system and the tension in each string.

2 Working in vectors

A force is a physical quantity that causes a change of motion. A force can start the motion of an object, stop its motion, make it move faster or slower, or change the direction of its motion. By its very nature, a force is a vector quantity just like displacement, velocity or acceleration. It has magnitude and direction, unlike scalar quantities such as distance, speed, mass or time, which have magnitude only.

Notation and representation

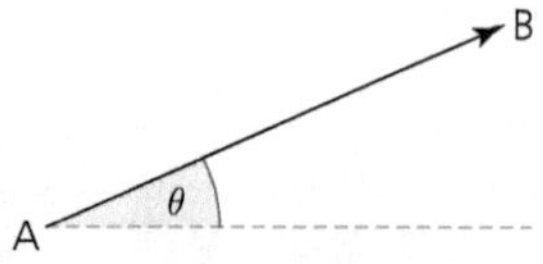

Figure 2.20

A vector can be represented by a directed line segment in a diagram.

In writing, $\overrightarrow{AB}$ represents the vector with magnitude AB. The magnitude can also be written as $|\overrightarrow{AB}|$. The direction is given by the angle θ which AB makes with a fixed direction, often the horizontal.

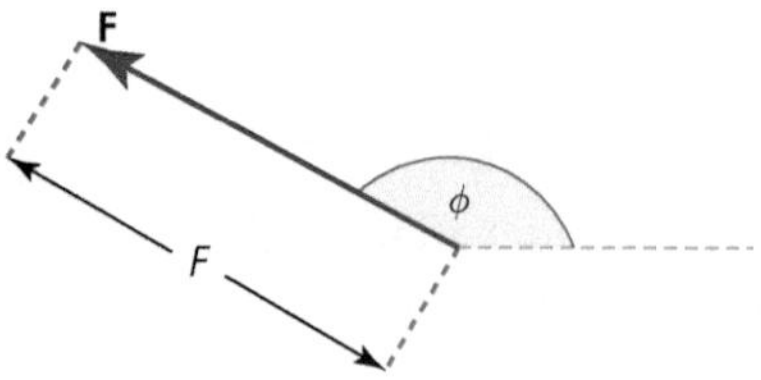

Figure 2.21

In Figure 2.21, **F** is a vector with magnitude $F = |\mathbf{F}|$ and direction ϕ.

Vectors are often written using lowercase letters, like **a**, **b** and **c**. It is common to use **a** for the vector $\overrightarrow{OA}$ where O is the origin.

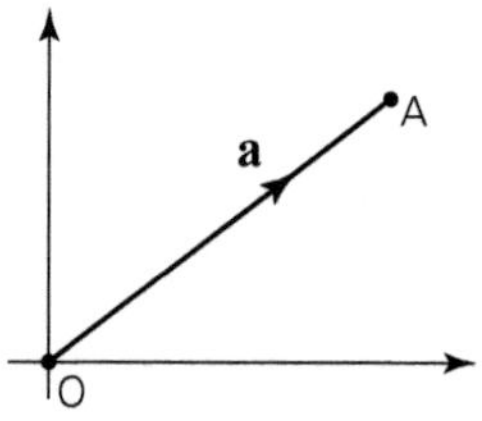

Figure 2.22

To determine the direction of a vector in the *xy* plane, a mathematical convention is used. Starting from the *x*-axis, angles measured anticlockwise are positive and angles in a clockwise direction are negative.

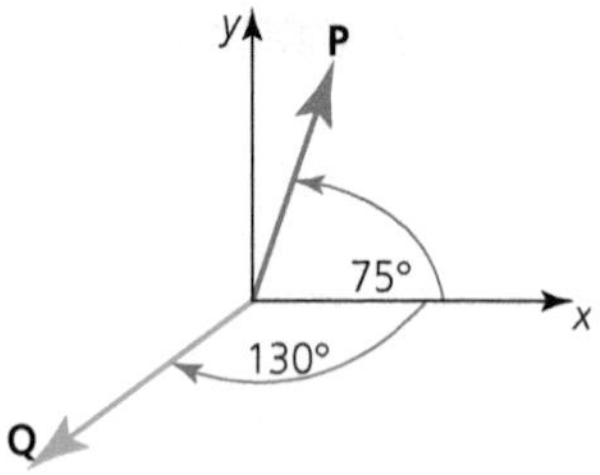

Figure 2.23

In the example shown in Figure 2.23, **P** has direction +75° and **Q** has direction −130°.

Adding vectors

One way to add vectors is to draw them one after another, i.e. where one finishes the next one starts.

$$\overrightarrow{AB} + \overrightarrow{BC} = \overrightarrow{AC}$$

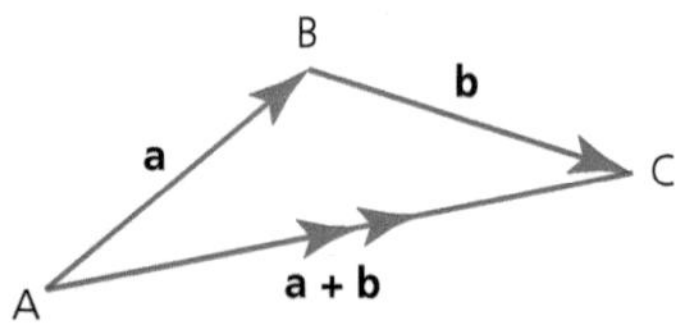

Figure 2.24

Alternatively, you can make **a** and **b** start at the same place and take the diagonal of the ensuing parallelogram.

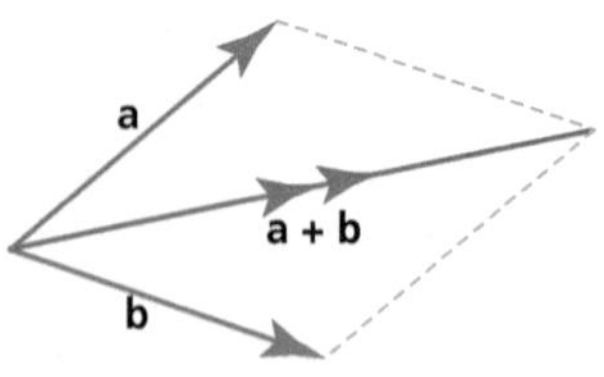

Figure 2.25

This gives the same result, because opposite sides of a parallelogram are equal and in the same direction, so that **b** is repeated at the top right of the parallelogram in Figure 2.25.

Resultant forces

The resultant of a number of forces is equal to the sum of these forces. As each force is a vector, the resultant is a vector starting at the start point of the first force and ending at the end point of the last force (Figure 2.26).

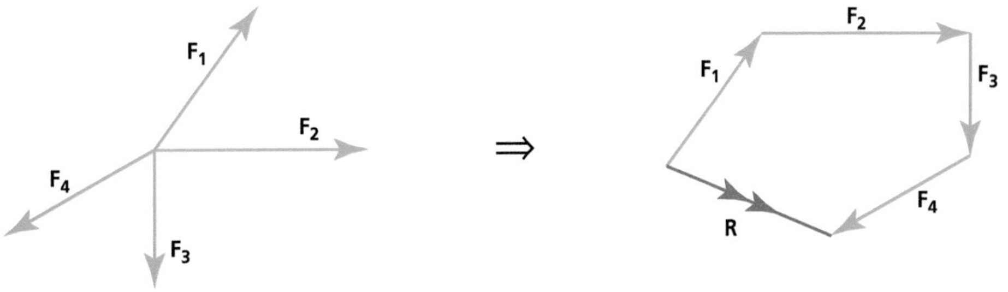

Figure 2.26

$$\mathbf{R} = \mathbf{F}_1 + \mathbf{F}_2 + \mathbf{F}_3 + \mathbf{F}_4$$

The resultant **R** of the four forces ($\mathbf{F}_1$, $\mathbf{F}_2$, $\mathbf{F}_3$ and $\mathbf{F}_4$) can be found by drawing consecutive lines representing the vectors. The line which completes the polygon is the resultant.

You have met the contact forces of normal reaction force **R** and frictional force **F**. The resultant of them is the **total contact force** (Figure 2.27). This has magnitude $\sqrt{F^2+R^2}$.

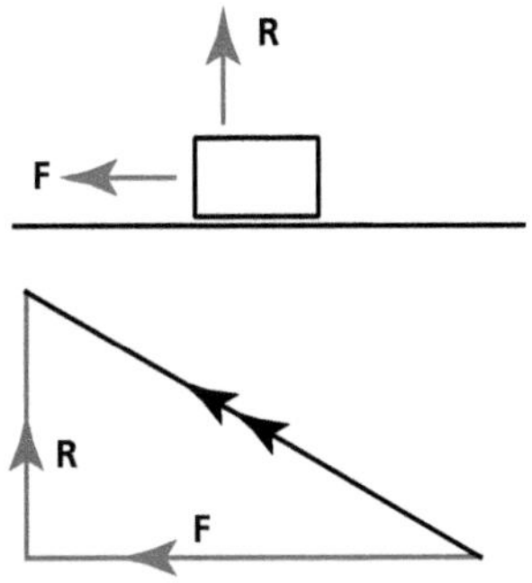

Figure 2.27

Components of a vector

Finding components is the reverse process of adding two vectors. It involves splitting a vector into two perpendicular components.

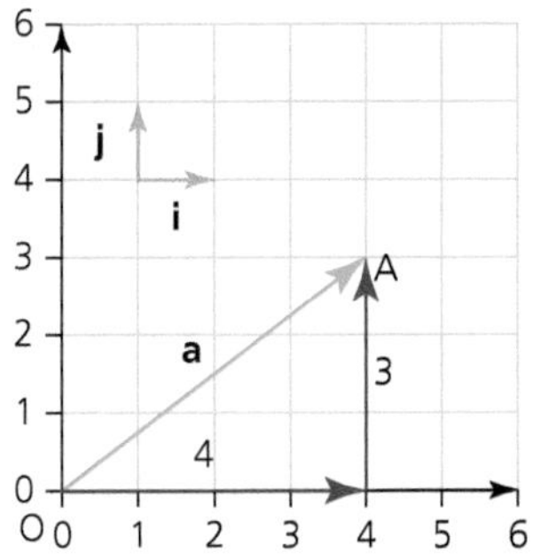

Figure 2.28

The result is often described using unit vectors **i** and **j** along the x and y axes respectively. The vector **a** in Figure 2.28 may be written as $\mathbf{a} = 4\mathbf{i} + 3\mathbf{j}$.

Alternatively, **a** can be written as the **column vector** $\begin{pmatrix} 4 \\ 3 \end{pmatrix}$.

In general, if **i** and **j** are unit vectors along the x and y directions respectively then **a** can be written in terms of components as $\mathbf{a} = a_x\mathbf{i} + a_y\mathbf{j}$ or in column vector form

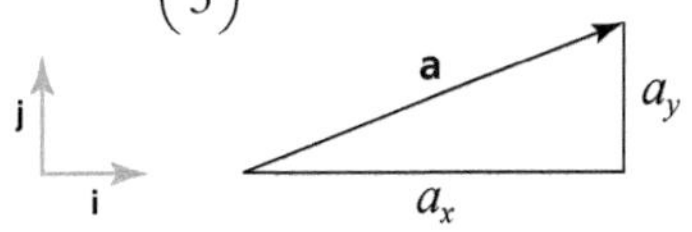

Figure 2.29

$$\mathbf{a} = \begin{pmatrix} a_x \\ a_y \end{pmatrix}$$

$$\mathbf{a} = a_x\mathbf{i} + a_y\mathbf{j} = \begin{pmatrix} a_x \\ a_y \end{pmatrix}$$

Example 2.5

The four vectors **a**, **b**, **c** and **d** are shown in Figure 2.30.

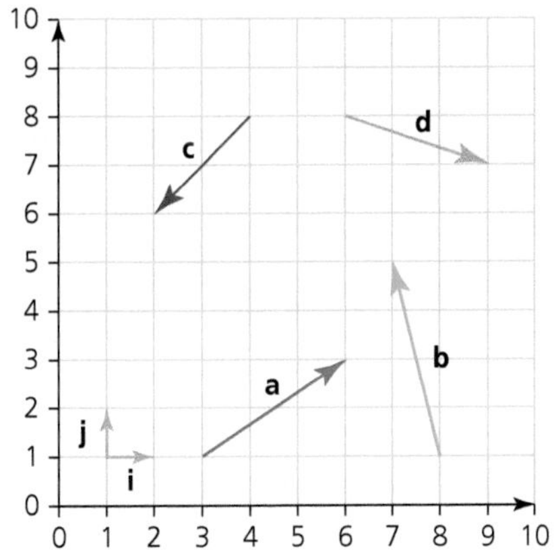

Figure 2.30

(i) Write them in component form and as column vectors.

(ii) Draw a diagram to show the vectors 2**a**, –**b** and 2**a** – **b** and write these in both forms.

Solution

(i) $\mathbf{a} = 3\mathbf{i} + 2\mathbf{j} = \begin{pmatrix} 3 \\ 2 \end{pmatrix}$, $\mathbf{b} = -\mathbf{i} + 4\mathbf{j} = \begin{pmatrix} -1 \\ 4 \end{pmatrix}$, $\mathbf{c} = -2\mathbf{i} - 2\mathbf{j} = \begin{pmatrix} -2 \\ -2 \end{pmatrix}$,

$\mathbf{d} = 3\mathbf{i} - \mathbf{j} = \begin{pmatrix} 3 \\ -1 \end{pmatrix}$

(ii)

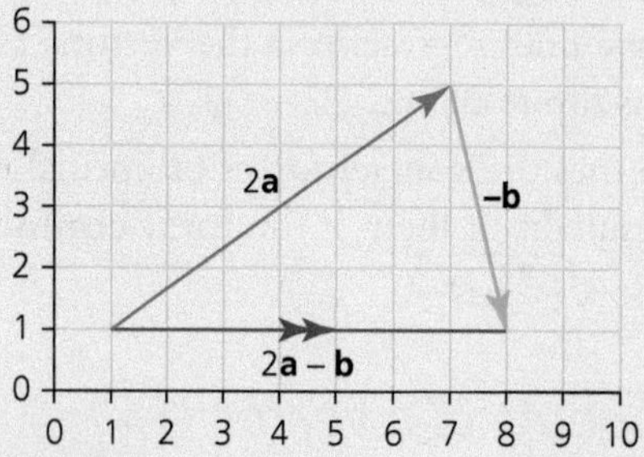

Figure 2.31

$2\mathbf{a} = 2(3\mathbf{i} + 2\mathbf{j}) = 6\mathbf{i} + 4\mathbf{j} = \begin{pmatrix} 6 \\ 4 \end{pmatrix}$

$-\mathbf{b} = -(-\mathbf{i} + 4\mathbf{j}) = \mathbf{i} - 4\mathbf{j} = \begin{pmatrix} 1 \\ -4 \end{pmatrix}$

$2\mathbf{a} - \mathbf{b} = 2\mathbf{a} + (-\mathbf{b}) = 6\mathbf{i} + 4\mathbf{j} + \mathbf{i} - 4\mathbf{j} = 7\mathbf{i} = \begin{pmatrix} 7 \\ 0 \end{pmatrix}$

Position vectors

To specify the position of an object, you define its displacement relative to a fixed origin. **a** and **b** are usually used to define the position vectors of A and B.

The vector between two points

$\mathbf{a} = \overrightarrow{OA}$, $\mathbf{b} = \overrightarrow{OB}$
$\overrightarrow{AB} = \overrightarrow{AO} + \overrightarrow{OB}$
$\overrightarrow{AB} = -\mathbf{a} + \mathbf{b}$
$= \mathbf{b} - \mathbf{a}$

The displacement AB can be replaced by the displacement from A to O followed by that from O to B.

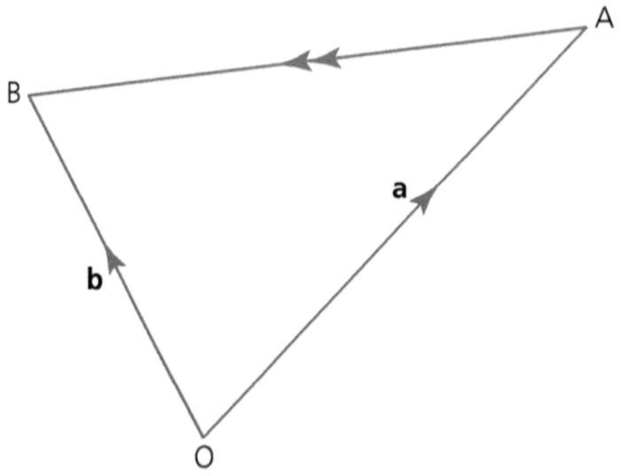

Figure 2.32

Any displacement vector AB can be written in terms of the position vectors of its two end points.

The magnitude and direction of vectors written in component form

The magnitude of a vector is just its length and can be found by using Pythagoras' theorem.

$$a = \sqrt{a_x{}^2 + a_y{}^2}$$

The direction is related to the angle the vector makes with the positive x-axis.

$$\theta = \arctan\left(\frac{a_y}{a_x}\right)$$

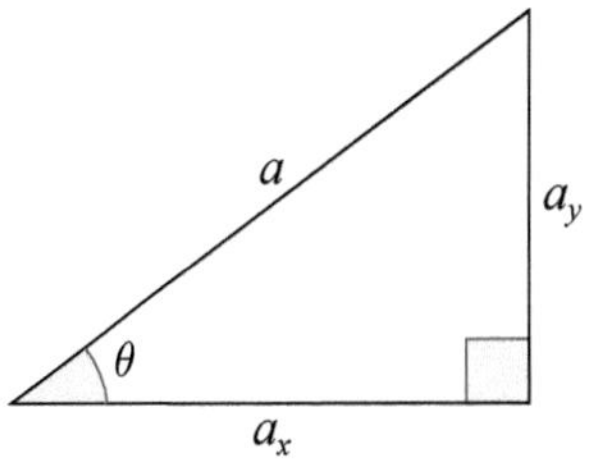

Figure 2.33

or $\theta = \arctan\left(\frac{a_y}{a_x}\right) + 180°$, depending on which quadrant θ is in.

Example 2.6

Find the magnitude and direction of each of the four vectors

$\mathbf{a} = \begin{pmatrix} 3 \\ 2 \end{pmatrix}$, $\mathbf{b} = \begin{pmatrix} -1 \\ 4 \end{pmatrix}$, $\mathbf{c} = -2\mathbf{i} - 2\mathbf{j}$ and $\mathbf{d} = 3\mathbf{i} - \mathbf{j}$.

Solution

$\mathbf{a} = \begin{pmatrix} 3 \\ 2 \end{pmatrix}$

Magnitude $|\mathbf{a}| = \sqrt{3^2 + 2^2} = \sqrt{13} = 3.61$

Direction $\theta = \arctan\left(\frac{2}{3}\right) = 33.7°$

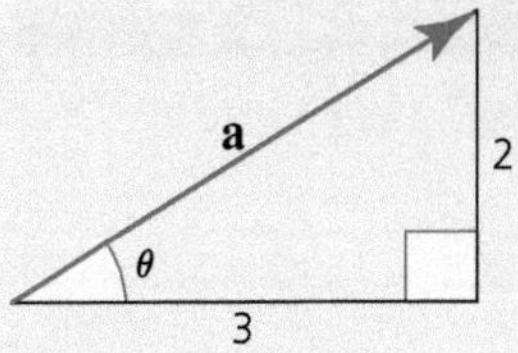

Figure 2.34

$\mathbf{b} = \begin{pmatrix} -1 \\ 4 \end{pmatrix}$

Magnitude $|\mathbf{b}| = \sqrt{(-1)^2 + 4^2} = \sqrt{17} = 4.12$

$\tan\phi = \frac{4}{1} \Rightarrow \phi = \arctan 4 = 76.0°$

Direction $\theta = 180 - \phi = 104°$

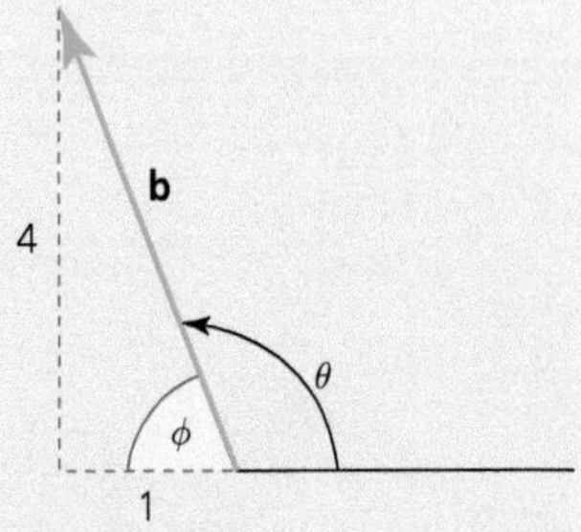

Figure 2.35

$\mathbf{c} = -2\mathbf{i} - 2\mathbf{j}$

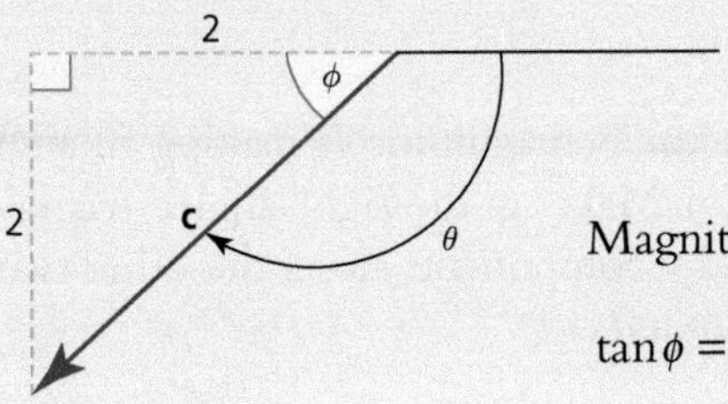

Figure 2.36

Magnitude $|\mathbf{c}| = \sqrt{(-2)^2 + (-2)^2} = \sqrt{8} = 2.83$

$\tan\phi = \frac{2}{2} = 1 \Rightarrow \phi = \arctan 1 = 45°$

Direction $\theta = -(180° - 45°) = -135°$

$\mathbf{d} = 3\mathbf{i} - \mathbf{j}$

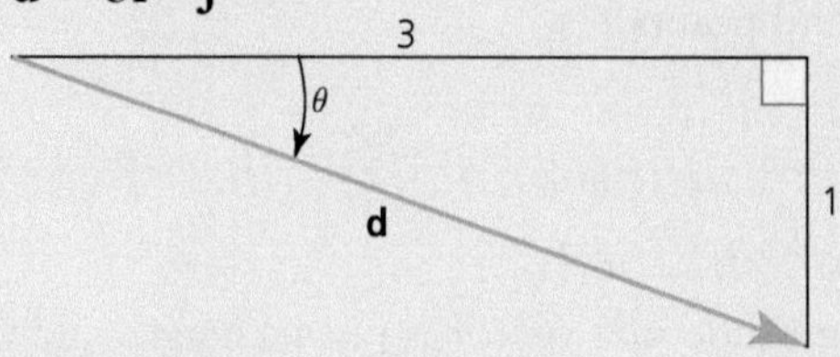

Figure 2.37

Magnitude $|\mathbf{d}| = \sqrt{3^2 + (-1)^2} = \sqrt{10} = 3.16$

Direction $\theta = -\arctan\left(\frac{1}{3}\right) = -18.4°$

Finding unit vectors along given directions

If $\mathbf{a} = a_x\mathbf{i} + a_y\mathbf{j}$, the magnitude of $\mathbf{a}$ is $|\mathbf{a}| = \sqrt{a_x^{\,2} + a_y^{\,2}}$. A unit vector along $\mathbf{a}$ (denoted by $\hat{\mathbf{a}}$) has magnitude 1. $\hat{\mathbf{a}}$ is parallel to $\mathbf{a}$ but has a magnitude which is scaled by the factor $\frac{1}{|\mathbf{a}|}$.

$$\hat{\mathbf{a}} = \frac{\mathbf{a}}{|\mathbf{a}|} = \frac{a_x}{\sqrt{a_x^{\,2} + a_y^{\,2}}}\mathbf{i} + \frac{a_y}{\sqrt{a_x^{\,2} + a_y^{\,2}}}\mathbf{j}$$

Example 2.7

(i) Find a unit vector along $\mathbf{a} = 3.5\mathbf{i} - 12\mathbf{j}$.

(ii) Find a vector along $\mathbf{a}$ which is 25 units long.

Solution

(i) The magnitude of $\mathbf{a}$ is $|\mathbf{a}| = \sqrt{3.5^2 + (-12)^2} = \sqrt{12.25 + 144}$

$= \sqrt{156.25} = 12.5$

A unit vector along $\mathbf{a}$ is $\hat{\mathbf{a}} = \frac{3.5}{12.5}\mathbf{i} - \frac{12}{12.5}\mathbf{j} = 0.28\mathbf{i} - 0.96\mathbf{j}$

(ii) $\hat{\mathbf{a}}$ has magnitude 1, so you are looking for a vector along $\mathbf{a}$ which is 25 units long, i.e. $25\hat{\mathbf{a}} = 25(0.28\mathbf{i} - 0.96\mathbf{j}) = 7\mathbf{i} - 24\mathbf{j}$

Resolving a force into components in two perpendicular directions

Draw the vector $\mathbf{F}$, magnitude F, making an angle θ with the x-axis, taken as the $\mathbf{i}$ direction. Make up the right-angled triangle with $\mathbf{F}$ along the hypotenuse and the x and y components along the other two sides. These are then evaluated using trigonometry.

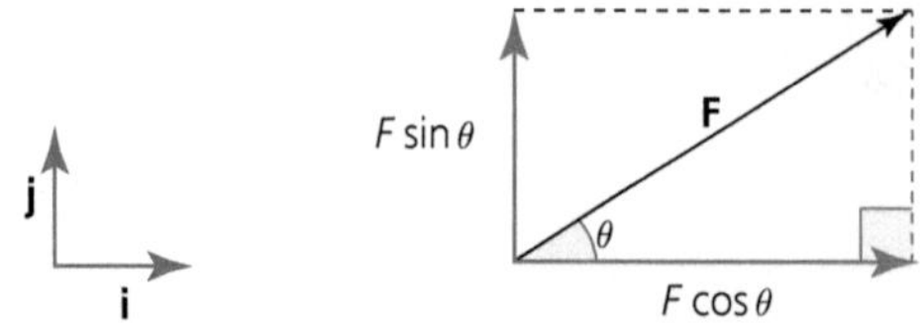

$$\mathbf{F} = F\cos\theta\mathbf{i} + F\sin\theta\mathbf{j} = \begin{pmatrix} F\cos\theta \\ F\sin\theta \end{pmatrix}$$

Figure 2.38

Example 2.8

Resolve a weight W N in two directions which are along and at right angles to a slope making an angle θ with the horizontal.

Solution

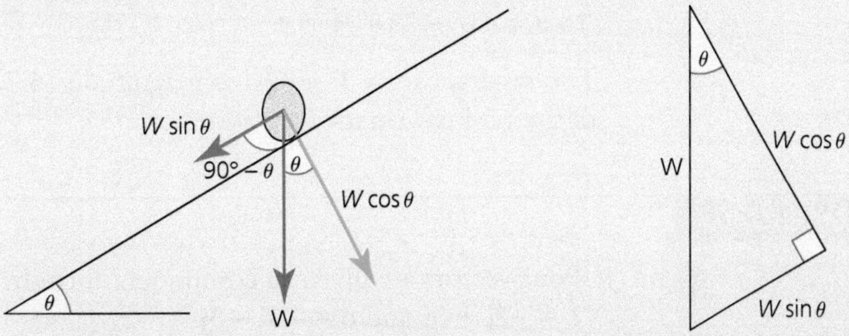

Figure 2.39

W is the hypotenuse of the right-angled triangle. The components are along the other two sides. The component parallel to the slope is $W\cos(90° - \theta) = W\sin\theta$.

The component perpendicular to the slope is $W\cos\theta$.

Example 2.9

Two forces **P** and **Q** have magnitudes 10 N and 15 N in the directions shown in Figure 2.40.

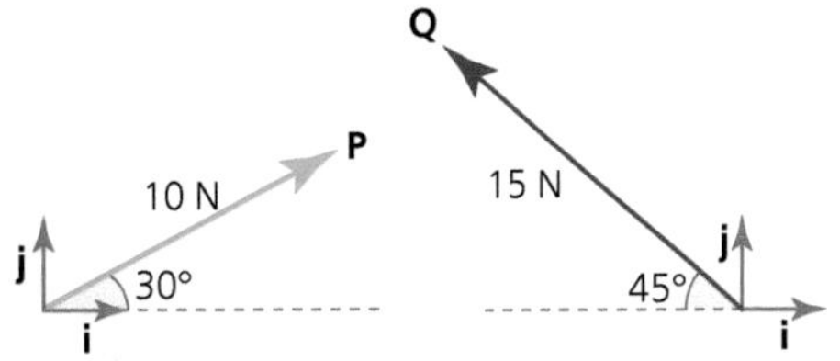

Figure 2.40

Find the magnitude and direction of the resultant force **P** + **Q**.

Solution

Note
$\mathbf{P} = 10\cos 30°\,\mathbf{i} + 10\sin 30°\,\mathbf{j}$
$= 8.66\,\mathbf{i} + 5\,\mathbf{j}$

Note
$\mathbf{Q} = -15\cos 45°\,\mathbf{i} + 15\sin 45°\,\mathbf{j}$
$= -10.61\,\mathbf{i} + 10.61\,\mathbf{j}$

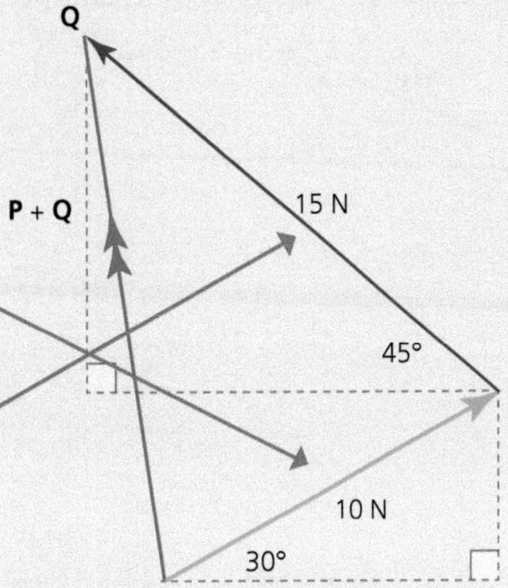

Figure 2.41

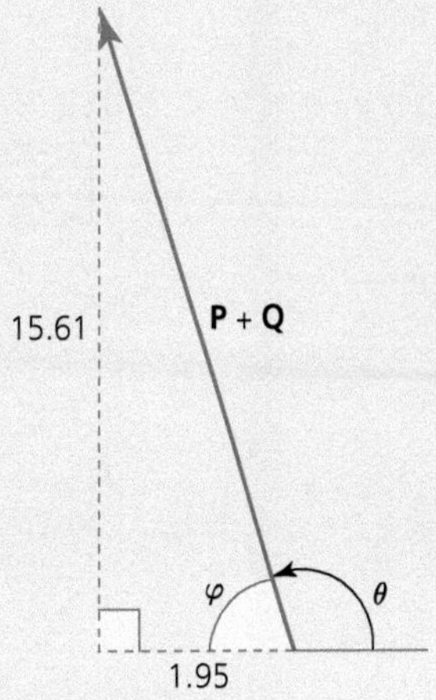

Figure 2.42

The resultant is $\mathbf{P} + \mathbf{Q} = (8.66\mathbf{i} + 5\mathbf{j}) + (-10.61\mathbf{i} + 10.61\mathbf{j})$

$= -1.95\mathbf{i} + 15.61\mathbf{j}$

It is shown in Figure 2.42.

The magnitude of the resultant is $|\mathbf{P}+\mathbf{Q}| = \sqrt{(-1.95)^2 + 15.61^2} = 15.73$

The direction of the resultant:

$$\tan\varphi = \frac{15.61}{1.95} \quad\Rightarrow\quad \varphi = \arctan(8.01) = 82.9°$$
$$\theta = 180° - 82.9° = 97.1°$$

The resultant force $\mathbf{P} + \mathbf{Q}$ has magnitude 15.73 and direction 97.1° relative to the positive x-axis.

Exercise 2.2

① Four vectors are given in component form by $\mathbf{a} = 3\mathbf{i} + 4\mathbf{j}$, $\mathbf{b} = 6\mathbf{i} - 7\mathbf{j}$, $\mathbf{c} = -2\mathbf{i} + 5\mathbf{j}$ and $\mathbf{d} = -5\mathbf{i} - 3\mathbf{j}$.

Find the vectors

(i) $\mathbf{a} + \mathbf{b}$ (ii) $\mathbf{b} + \mathbf{c}$ (iii) $\mathbf{c} + \mathbf{d}$

(iv) $\mathbf{a} + \mathbf{b} + \mathbf{d}$ (v) $\mathbf{a} - \mathbf{b}$ (vi) $\mathbf{d} - \mathbf{b} + \mathbf{c}$

② A, B, C are the points (1, 2), (5, 1) and (7, 8).

(i) Write down in terms of $\mathbf{i}$ and $\mathbf{j}$ the position vectors of these three points.

(ii) Find the component form of the displacements $\overrightarrow{AB}$, $\overrightarrow{BC}$ and $\overrightarrow{CA}$.

(iii) Draw a diagram to show the position vectors of A, B and C and your answers to part (ii).

③ Three vectors $\mathbf{a}$, $\mathbf{b}$ and $\mathbf{c}$ are given by $\mathbf{a} = \begin{pmatrix} 1 \\ 1 \end{pmatrix}$, $\mathbf{b} = \begin{pmatrix} -1 \\ 2 \end{pmatrix}$ and $\mathbf{c} = \begin{pmatrix} 3 \\ -4 \end{pmatrix}$.

R is the endpoint of the displacement $2\mathbf{a} - 3\mathbf{b} + \mathbf{c}$ and (1, −2) is the starting point. What is the position vector of R?

④ Find the magnitude and direction of the following vectors.

(i) $12\mathbf{i} - 5\mathbf{j}$ (ii) $7\mathbf{i} + 24\mathbf{j}$ (iii) $-\mathbf{i} + \mathbf{j}$

(iv) $3\mathbf{i} + 4\mathbf{j}$ (v) $2\mathbf{i} - 3\mathbf{j}$ (vi) $-\mathbf{i} - 2\mathbf{j}$

⑤ Write down the following vectors in component form in terms of $\mathbf{i}$ and $\mathbf{j}$.

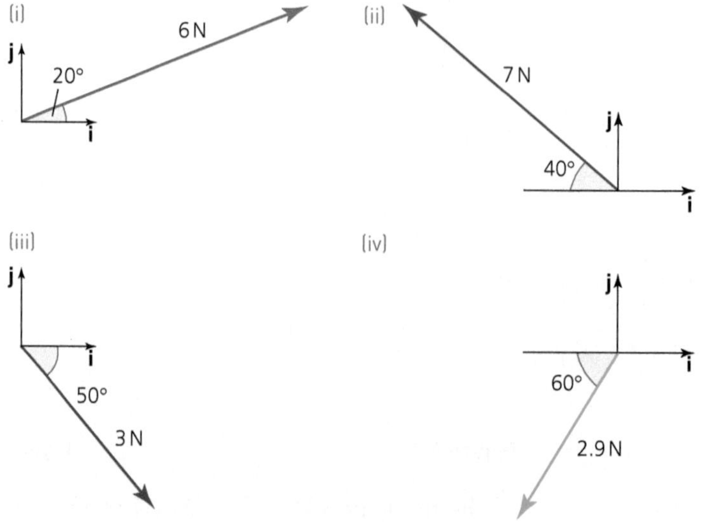

Figure 2.43

⑥ (i) Find a unit vector in the direction of $\begin{pmatrix} 10 \\ 24 \end{pmatrix}$.

A force $\mathbf{F}$ acts in the direction of $\begin{pmatrix} 10 \\ 24 \end{pmatrix}$ and has magnitude 39 N.

(ii) Use your answer to part (i) to write $\mathbf{F}$ in component form.

⑦ Find the vector with magnitude 8.2 that is parallel to the vector $40\mathbf{i} - 9\mathbf{j}$.

⑧ Write down each of the following vectors in terms of $\mathbf{i}$ and $\mathbf{j}$. Find the resultant of each set of vectors in terms of $\mathbf{i}$ and $\mathbf{j}$.

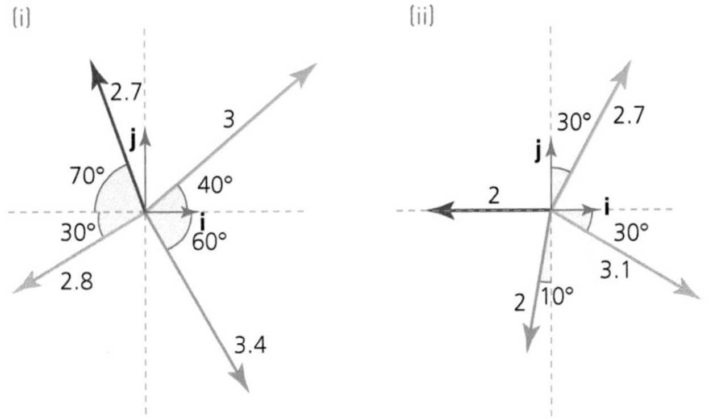

Figure 2.44

⑨ The displacement of B from A is $\begin{pmatrix} 4 \\ 1 \end{pmatrix}$. The displacement of C from A is $\begin{pmatrix} -2 \\ 3 \end{pmatrix}$. The displacement of D from A is $\begin{pmatrix} 0 \\ -4 \end{pmatrix}$.

Draw a diagram showing the relative position of A, B, C and D. Find

(i) $\overrightarrow{DB}$ (ii) $\overrightarrow{DC}$ (iii) $\overrightarrow{CB}$ (iv) $\overrightarrow{BC}$

⑩ Three vectors $\mathbf{a}$, $\mathbf{b}$ and $\mathbf{c}$ are represented by the sides of a triangle ABC, as shown in Figure 2.45.

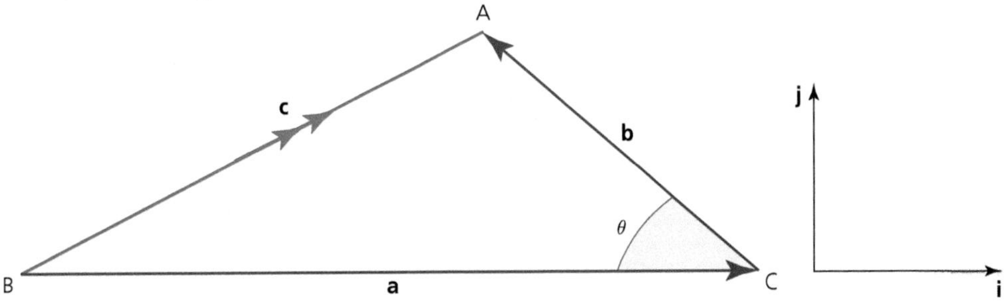

Figure 2.45

The angle C is θ and $|\mathbf{a}|$, $|\mathbf{b}|$ and $|\mathbf{c}|$ are a, b and c. Answer each part in terms of θ, a, b and c.

(i) Write $\mathbf{a}$ and $\mathbf{b}$ in terms of $\mathbf{i}$ and $\mathbf{j}$.

(ii) Find $\mathbf{a} + \mathbf{b}$ and hence $|\mathbf{a} + \mathbf{b}|^2$.

(iii) Use your answer to part (ii) to express c^2 in terms of a, b and θ.

3 Forces in equilibrium

When forces are in equilibrium their vector sum is zero and the sum of the resolved parts in **any** direction is zero.

Example 2.10

A brick of mass 5 kg is at rest on a rough plane inclined at an angle of 35° to the horizontal. Find the frictional force F N, and the normal contact force R N of the plane on the brick.

Solution

Figure 2.46 shows the forces acting on the brick.

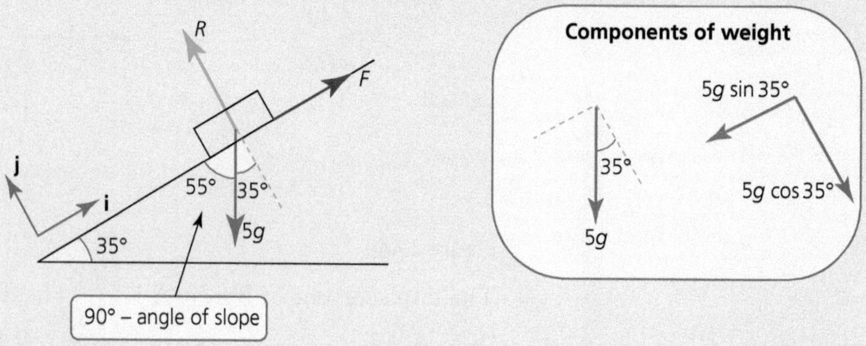

Figure 2.46

Take unit vectors **i** and **j** parallel and perpendicular to the plane, as shown.

Since the brick is in equilibrium, the resultant of the three forces acting on it is zero.

$5g = 49$

Resolving in the **i** direction: $F - 49 \sin 35° = 0$ ①

$$F = 28.10 \ldots$$

Resolving in the **j** direction: $R - 49 \cos 35° = 0$ ②

$$R = 40.13 \ldots$$

Written in vector form this is equivalent to

$$F\mathbf{i} + R\mathbf{j} - 49 \sin 35°\mathbf{i} - 49 \cos 35°\mathbf{j} = 0$$

or, alternatively,

$$\begin{pmatrix} F \\ 0 \end{pmatrix} + \begin{pmatrix} 0 \\ R \end{pmatrix} + \begin{pmatrix} -49 \sin 35° \\ -49 \cos 35° \end{pmatrix} = \begin{pmatrix} 0 \\ 0 \end{pmatrix}$$

Notice that both of these vector equations lead to the equations ① and ② above.

The triangle of forces

When there are only three (non-parallel) forces acting and they are in equilibrium (Figure 2.47), the polygon of forces becomes a closed triangle, as shown for the brick on the plane.

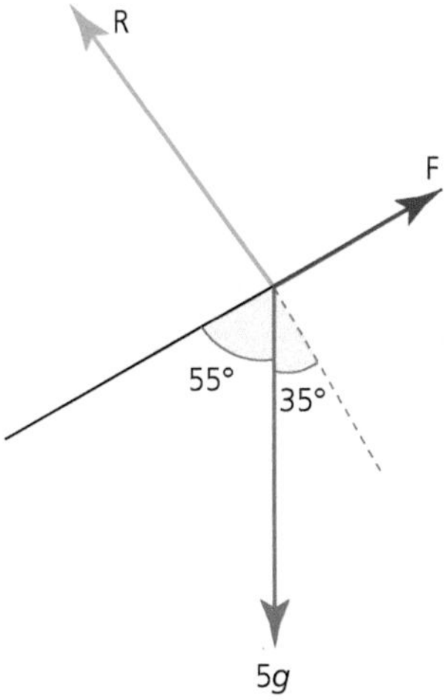

Figure 2.47

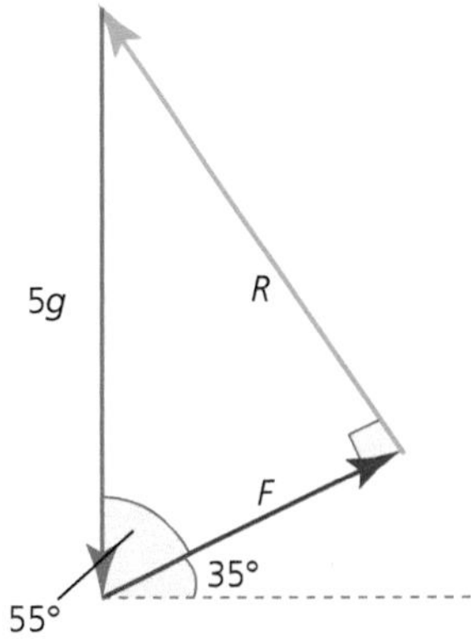

Figure 2.48

Note

The triangle is closed because the resultant is zero.

When a body is in equilibrium under the action of three non-parallel forces, then

(i) the forces can be represented in magnitude and direction by the sides of a triangle

(ii) the lines of action of the forces pass through the same point. They are concurrent.

Then $\frac{F}{5g} = \cos 55°$

$F = 49\cos 55° = 28.1\text{N}$

And similarly $R = 49\sin 55° = 40.1\text{N}$

This is an example of the theorem known as the **triangle of forces**.

When more than three forces are in equilibrium, the first statement still holds but the triangle is then a polygon. The second statement is not necessarily true.

The next example illustrates two methods for solving problems involving forces in equilibrium. With experience, you will find it easier to judge which method is more suitable for a particular problem.

Example 2.11

A sign of mass 10 kg is to be suspended by two strings arranged as shown in Figure 2.49 below. Find the tension in each string.

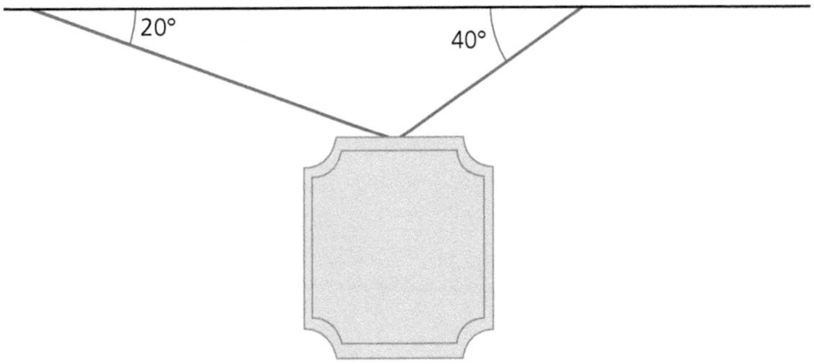

Figure 2.49

Solution

The force diagram for this situation is given in Figure 2.50.

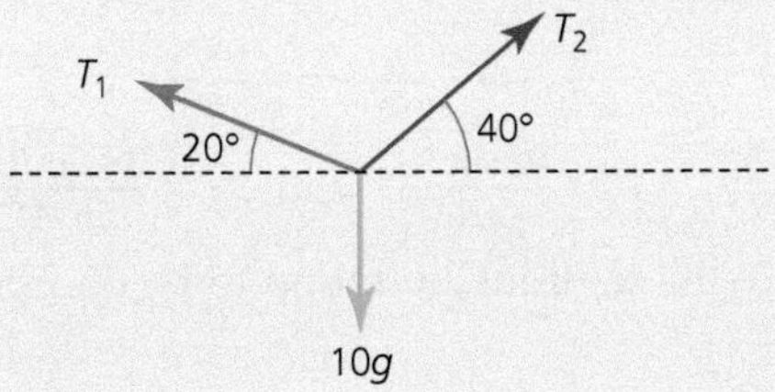

Figure 2.50

Method 1: Resolving forces

Vertically (↑): $T_1 \sin 20° + T_2 \sin 40° - 10g = 0$ ①

$0.342\ldots T_1 + 0.642\ldots T_2 = 98$

Horizontally (→): $-T_1 \cos 20° + T_2 \cos 40° = 0$ ②

$-0.939\ldots T_1 + 0.766\ldots T_2 = 0$

The set of simultaneous equations is solved in the usual way. Whether you are using the equation solver on your calculator or working it out on paper, it is important that you keep as much accuracy as possible by substituting for the different sines and cosines only at the very end of the calculation.

Multiply ① by cos 20° and then add ② × sin 20° to give

$$T_2(\sin 40° \cos 20° + \cos 40° \sin 20°) = 98 \cos 20°$$

You may recognise that this is the compound angle form for sin(40° + 20°) and so is the same as sin 60°.

$$T_2 = \frac{98 \cos 20°}{\sin 40° \cos 20° + \cos 40° \sin 20°}$$

$$T_2 = 106.33\ldots$$

Substituting back in ② now gives

$$T_1 = \frac{T_2 \cos 40°}{\cos 20°} = 86.68\ldots$$

The tensions in the strings are 86.7 N and 106.3 N.

Method 2: Triangle of forces

Since the three forces are in equilibrium they can be represented by the sides of a triangle taken in order.

Discussion point

In what order would you draw the three lines in this triangle of forces in Figure 2.51?

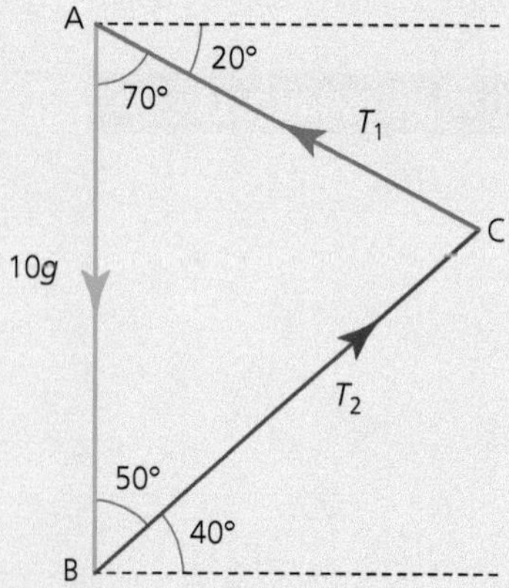

Figure 2.51

You can estimate the tensions by measurements. This will tell you that $T_1 \approx 87$ and $T_2 \approx 106$ in newtons.

Alternatively, you can use the sine rule to calculate T_1 and T_2 accurately.

In triangle ABC, $\widehat{CAB} = 70°$ and $\widehat{ABC} = 50°$, so $\widehat{BCA} = 60°$.

180° − 70° − 50° = 60°

So $$\frac{T_1}{\sin 50°} = \frac{T_2}{\sin 70°} = \frac{98}{\sin 60°}$$

giving $$T_1 = \frac{98 \sin 50°}{\sin 60°} \text{ and } T_2 = \frac{98 \sin 70°}{\sin 60°}$$

As before the tensions are found to be 86.7 N and 106.3 N.

Discussion point

Lami's theorem states that when three forces acting at a point as shown in Figure 2.52 are in equilibrium then

$$\frac{F_1}{\sin\alpha} = \frac{F_2}{\sin\beta} = \frac{F_3}{\sin\gamma}.$$

Sketch a triangle of forces and say how the angles in the triangle are related to α, β and γ. Hence explain why Lami's theorem is true.

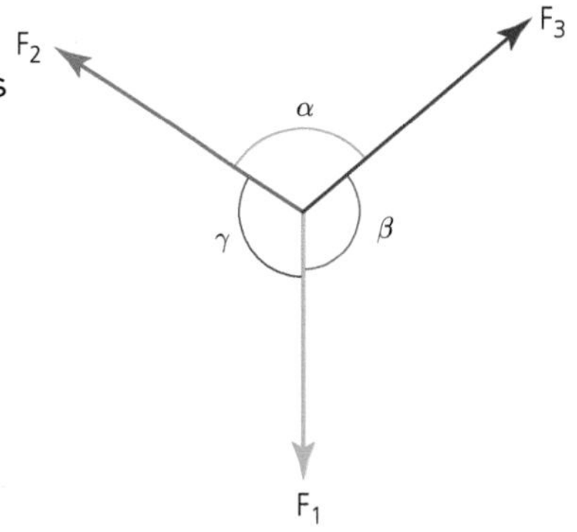

Figure 2.52

Example 2.12

Two husky dogs are pulling a sledge. They both exert forces of 60 N but at different angles to the line of the sledge, as shown in Figure 2.53. The sledge is moving straight forwards.

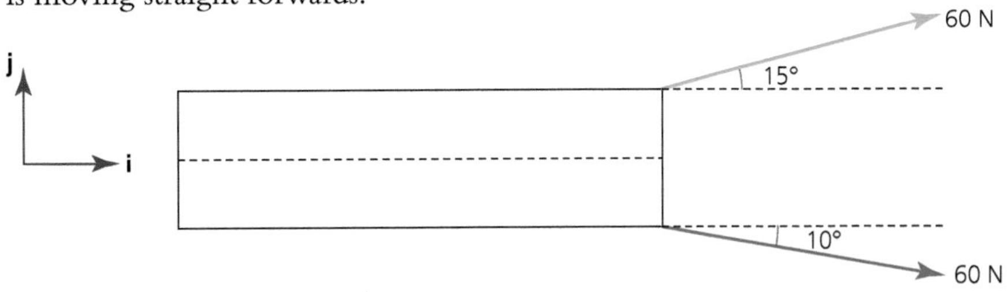

Figure 2.53

(i) Resolve the two forces into components parallel and perpendicular to the line of the sledge.

(ii) Find the overall forward force from the dogs and the overall sideways force.

The resistance to motion is 20 N along the line of the sledge and up to 400 N perpendicular to it.

(iii) Find the magnitude and direction of the overall horizontal force on the sledge.

(iv) How much force is lost due to the dogs not pulling straight forwards?

Solution

(i) Taking unit vectors **i** along the line of the sledge and **j** perpendicular to the line of the sledge.

The forces exerted by the two dogs are

$$60\cos 15°\ \mathbf{i} + 60\sin 15°\ \mathbf{j}$$

$$= 57.95\ldots\mathbf{i} + 15.52\ldots\mathbf{j}$$

and $60\cos 10°\mathbf{i} - 60\sin 10°\mathbf{j}$

$$= 59.08\ldots\ \mathbf{i} - 10.41\ldots\mathbf{j}$$

(ii) The overall forward force is equal to

$$60\cos 15^\circ + 60\cos 10^\circ = 117.04\ldots$$

The overall sideways force is equal to

$$60\sin 15^\circ - 60\sin 10^\circ = 5.11\ldots$$

(iii) The sideways force is cancelled by the resistance force opposing it.

The forward force is reduced by an amount 20 N from the resistance to motion.

So the overall forward force is 97 N and the overall sideways force is 0.

The magnitude of the overall force on the sledge is thus 97 N in the direction of motion.

(iv) If the dogs were pulling straight, the overall force on the sledge would be 100 N, so the amount of force lost due to the dogs not pulling straight is thus 3 N.

100 − 97.04...

60 + 60 − 20 (60 N from each dog less 20 N from the resistance)

Exercise 2.3

① The following sets of forces are in equilibrium. Find the values of p and q in each case.

(i) $\begin{pmatrix} 24 \\ 18 \end{pmatrix}$ N, $\begin{pmatrix} 25 \\ 60 \end{pmatrix}$ N and $\begin{pmatrix} p \\ q \end{pmatrix}$ N

(ii) $\begin{pmatrix} p \\ -2 \end{pmatrix}$ N, $\begin{pmatrix} -3 \\ 4 \end{pmatrix}$ N and $\begin{pmatrix} 2 \\ -q \end{pmatrix}$ N

(iii) $\begin{pmatrix} 2p \\ 5 \end{pmatrix}$ N, $\begin{pmatrix} q \\ 4p \end{pmatrix}$ N, $\begin{pmatrix} p \\ -3 \end{pmatrix}$ N and $\begin{pmatrix} 5 \\ -q \end{pmatrix}$ N.

② A brick of mass 2 kg is resting on a rough plane inclined at 40° to the horizontal.

(i) Draw a diagram showing all the forces acting on the brick.

(ii) Find the normal contact force of the plane on the brick.

(iii) Find the frictional force acting on the brick.

③ A particle is in equilibrium under the three forces shown in Figure 2.54. Find the magnitude of the force F and the angle θ.

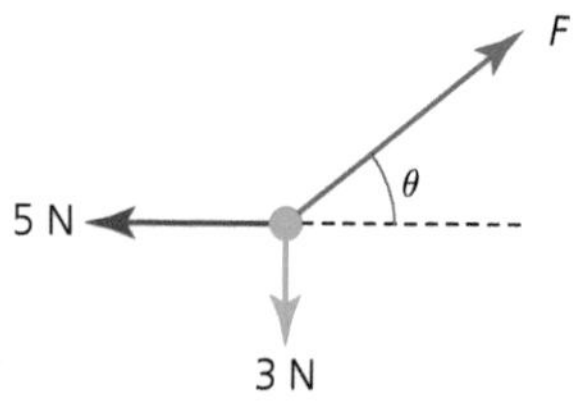

Figure 2.54

④ A box of mass 10 kg is at rest on a horizontal floor.

(i) Find the value of the normal contact force of the floor on the box.

The box remains at rest on the floor when a force of 30 N is applied to it at an angle of 25° to the upward vertical as shown in Figure 2.55.

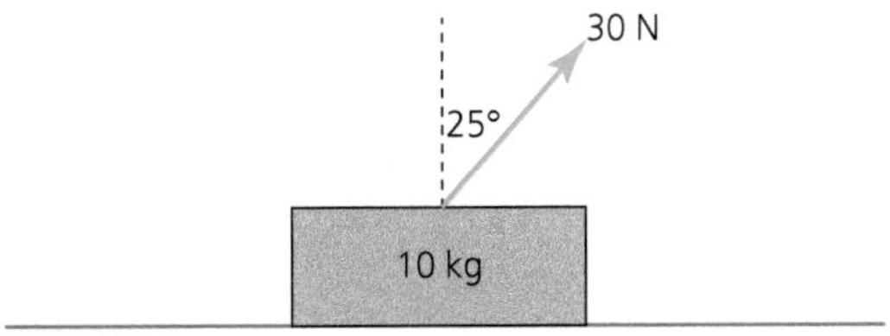

Figure 2.55

(i) Draw a diagram showing all the forces acting on the box.

(ii) Calculate the new value of the normal contact force of the floor on the box and also the frictional force.

⑤ A block of weight 100 N is on a rough plane that is inclined at 30° to the horizontal. The block is in equilibrium with a force of 35 N acting on it, in the direction of the plane as shown in Figure 2.56.

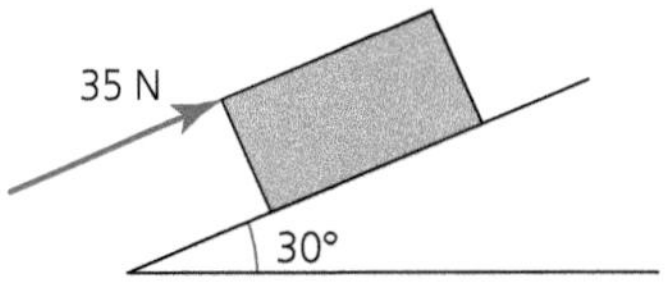

Figure 2.56

Calculate the frictional force acting on the block.

⑥ A crate of mass 10 kg is being pulled across rough horizontal ground by a rope making an angle θ with the horizontal. The tension in the rope is 60 N and the frictional force between the crate and the ground is 35 N. The crate is in equilibrium.

(i) Draw a labelled diagram showing all the forces acting on the crate.

(ii) Find the angle θ.

(iii) Find the normal contact force between the floor and the crate.

⑦ Each of three light strings has a block attached to one of its ends. The other ends of the strings are tied together at a point A. The strings are in equilibrium with two of them passing over fixed smooth pulleys and with the blocks hanging freely.

The weights of the blocks, and the angles between the sloping parts of the strings and the vertical, are as shown in Figure 2.57. Find the values of W_1 and W_2.

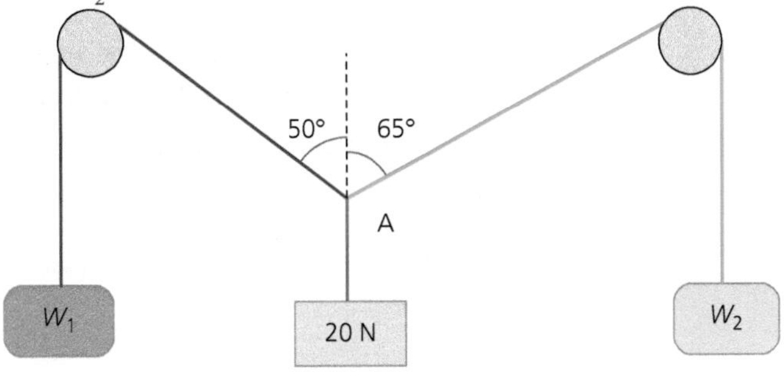

Figure 2.57

⑧ A block of mass 10 kg rests in equilibrium on a smooth plane inclined at 30° to the horizontal. It is held by a light string making an angle of 15° with the line of greatest slope of the plane.

(i) Draw a labelled diagram showing all the forces acting on the block.

(ii) Find the tension in the string and the normal contact force of the plane on the block.

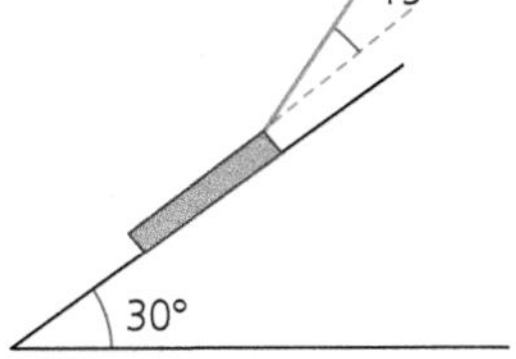

Figure 2.58

⑨ A particle A of mass 3 kg is at rest in equilibrium on horizontal rough ground. A is attached to two light, inextensible strings making angles of 20° and 50° with the vertical. The tensions in the two strings are 10 N and 20 N, as shown in Figure 2.59.

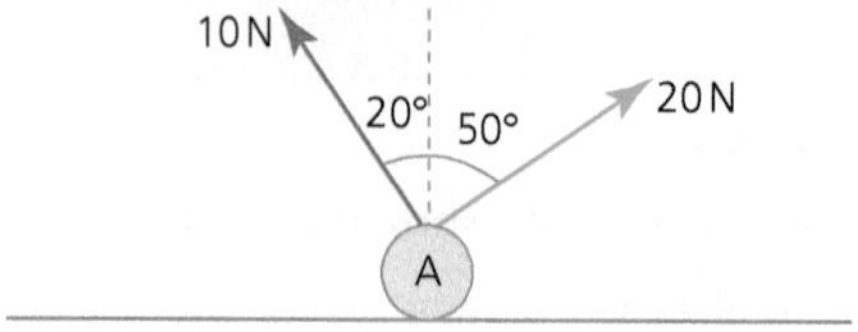

Figure 2.59

(i) Draw a diagram showing all the forces acting on A.

(ii) Find the normal contact force between the ground and A.

(iii) Find the magnitude of the frictional force, indicating the direction in which it is acting.

⑩ Four wires, all of them horizontal, are attached to the top of a telegraph pole as shown in this plan view. There is no overall force on the pole and tensions in the wires are as shown.

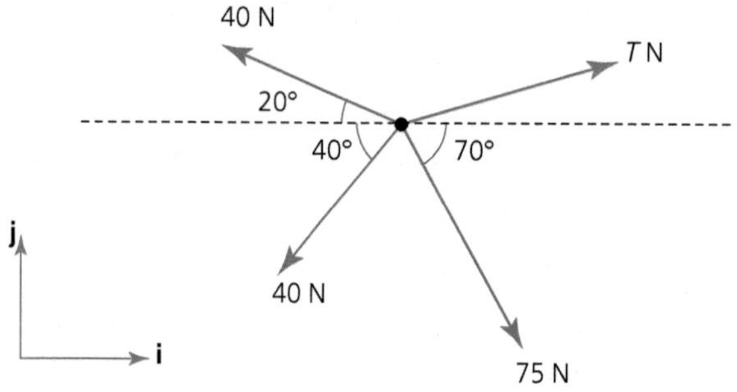

Figure 2.60

(i) Using perpendicular directions as shown in Figure 2.61, show that the force of 75 N may be written as $(25.7\mathbf{i} - 70.5\mathbf{j})$ N (to 3 significant figures).

(ii) Find T in both component form and magnitude and direction form.

(iii) The force T is changed to $(40\mathbf{i} + 50\mathbf{j})$ N. Show that there is now a resultant force on the pole and find its magnitude and direction.

⑪ A ship is being towed by two tugs. They exert forces on the ship as indicated.

There is also a drag force on the ship.

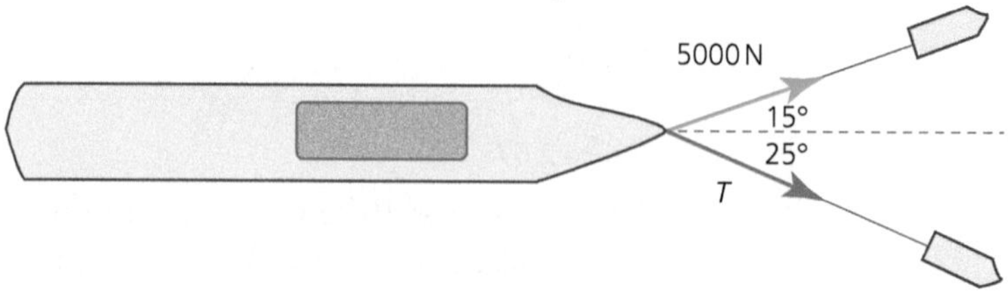

Figure 2.61

(i) Write down the components of the tensions in the towing cables along and perpendicular to the line of motion, l, of the ship.

(ii) There is no resultant force perpendicular to the line l. Find T.

(iii) The ship is travelling with constant velocity along the line l. Find the magnitude of the drag force acting on it.

⑫ A suitcase of mass 3 kg slides down a rough slope inclined at 35° to the horizontal.

(i) Draw a diagram showing the forces acting on the suitcase.

(ii) Resolve these forces into components up the slope and perpendicularly away from the slope.

(iii) The suitcase moves at constant speed. Find the magnitudes of the frictional force and of the normal contact force on the suitcase.

(iv) The suitcase is pulled back to the top of the slope at constant speed by a rope parallel to the slope. Assuming that the frictional force is the same as before, calculate the tension in the rope.

⑬ Figure 2.62 shows a block of mass 10 kg on a rough inclined plane. The block is attached to a 7 kg weight by a light string which passes over a smooth pulley; it is on the point of sliding up the slope.

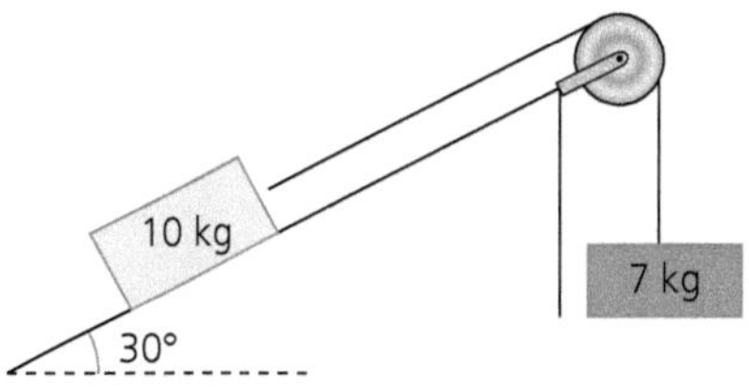

Figure 2.62

(i) Draw a diagram showing the forces acting on the block.

(ii) Resolve these forces into components parallel and perpendicular to the slope.

(iii) Find the force of resistance to the block's motion.

The 7 kg mass is replaced by one of mass m kg.

(iv) Find the value of m for which the block is on the point of sliding down the slope, assuming the resistance to motion is the same as before.

⑭ Figure 2.63 shows a sign attached to a point A by a light rigid rod AB. It is supported by two light rigid rods AC and AD. AC is horizontal and AD makes an angle θ with the horizontal with $\tan\theta = 0.75$. The mass of the sign is 20 kg.

Find the forces in the rods AB, AC and AD stating whether they are in tension or compression.

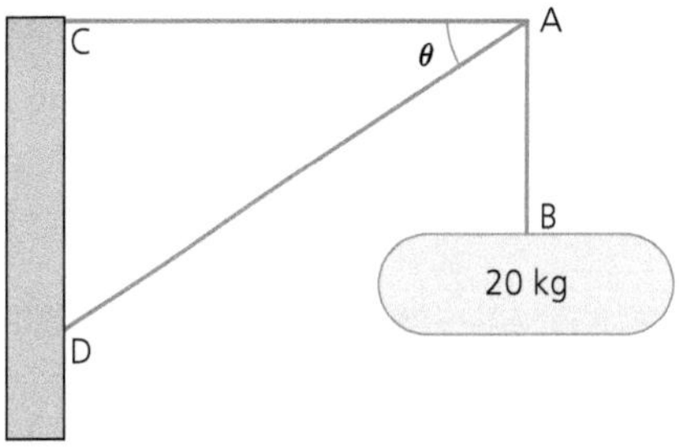

Figure 2.63

⑮ A block of mass 75 kg is in equilibrium on smooth horizontal ground with one end of a light string attached to its upper edge. The string passes over a smooth pulley, with a block of mass m kg attached at the other end.

The part of the string between the pulley and the block makes an angle of 65° with the horizontal. A horizontal force F is also acting on the block.

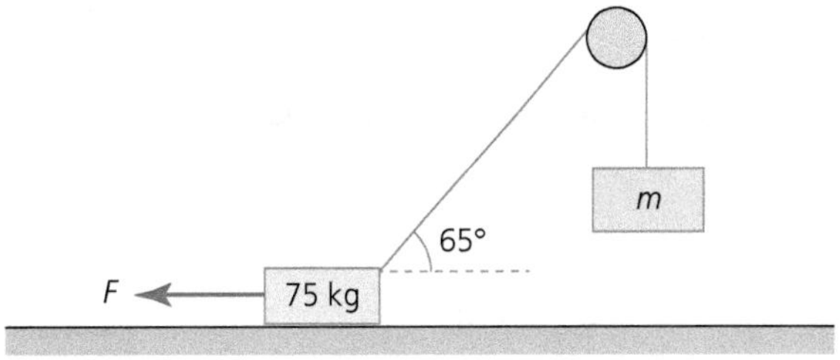

Figure 2.64

(i) Find a relationship between T, the tension in the string, and R, the normal contact force between the block and the ground.

The block is on the point of lifting off the ground.

(ii) Find T and m.

(iii) Find F.

⑯ Two boxes of masses 15 kg and 12 kg are held by light strings AB, BC and CD. As shown in the figure, AB makes an angle α with the horizontal and is fixed at A.

Angle α is such that $\sin \alpha = 0.28$. BC is horizontal and CD makes an angle β with the horizontal.

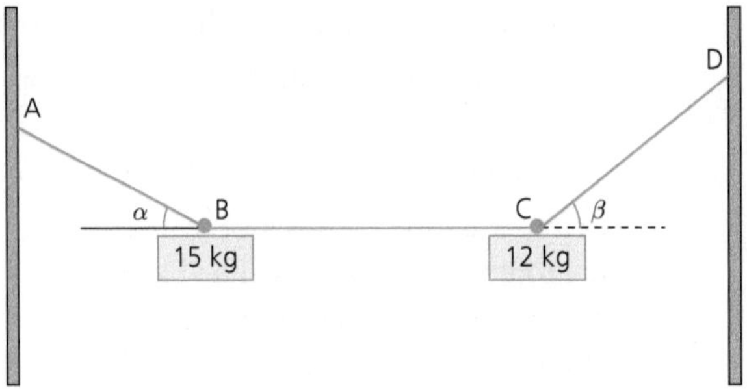

Figure 2.65

(i) By considering the equilibrium of point B, find the tension in string AB and show that the tension in string BC is 504 N.

(ii) Find β and the tension in CD.

4 Finding resultant forces

When forces are in equilibrium their resultant is zero; however, forces are not always in equilibrium. The next example shows you how to find the resultant of forces that are not in equilibrium. You know from Newton's second law that the acceleration of the body will be in the same direction as the resultant force; remember that force and acceleration are both vector quantities.

Example 2.13

A sledge is being pulled up a smooth slope inclined at an angle of 15° to the horizontal by a rope which makes an angle of 30° with the slope. The mass of the sledge is 5 kg and the tension in the rope is 40 N.

(i) Draw a diagram to show the forces acting on the sledge.

(ii) Find the resultant of these forces.

(iii) Find the acceleration of the sledge.

Solution

(i) Here is the force diagram (Figure 2.66).

(ii) ***Method 1***

Resolve the forces into components parallel and perpendicular to the slope.

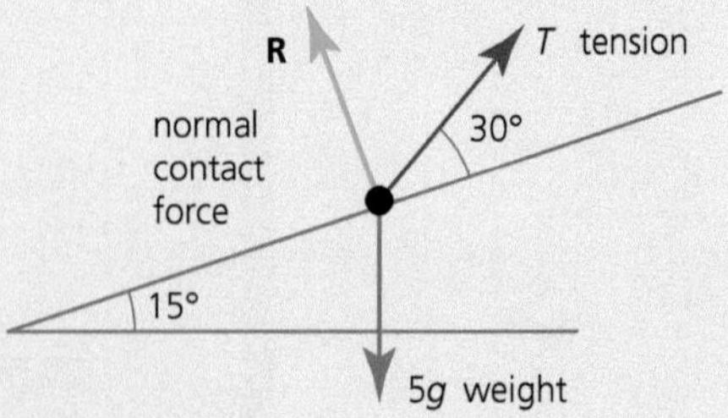

Figure 2.66

Note

When the sledge is modelled as a particle, all the forces can be assumed to be acting at a point.

Note

There is no friction force because the slope is smooth.

Hint

Notice that although the sledge is moving up the slope this does not mean that the resultant force is up the slope. Its direction depends on the acceleration of the sledge which may be up or down the slope, or zero if the sledge is moving at constant speed.

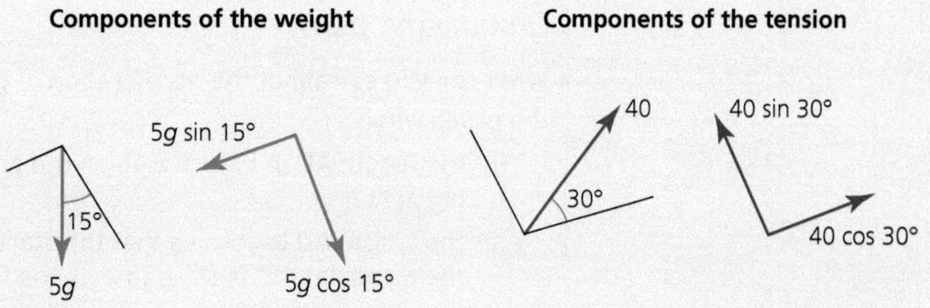

Figure 2.67

Resolve parallel to the slope:

The resultant is $F = 40\cos 30° - 5g\sin 15°$
$= 21.959\ldots$

> The force **R** is perpendicular to the slope so it has no component in this direction.

Resolve perpendicular to the slope:

$$\mathbf{R} + 40\sin 30° - 5g\cos 15° = 0$$

$$\mathbf{R} = 5g\cos 15° - 40\sin 30° = 27.33$$

> There is no resultant in this direction because the motion is parallel to the slope.

To 3 significant figures, the normal contact force is 27.3 N and the resultant is 22.0 N up the slope.

Method 2

Alternatively, you could have worked in column vectors as follows.

$$\begin{pmatrix} 0 \\ \mathbf{R} \end{pmatrix} + \begin{pmatrix} 40\cos 30° \\ 40\sin 30° \end{pmatrix} + \begin{pmatrix} -5g\sin 15° \\ -5g\cos 15° \end{pmatrix} = \begin{pmatrix} F \\ 0 \end{pmatrix}$$

> Parallel to slope

> Perpendicular to slope

Normal contact force + Tension + Weight = Resultant

Discussion point

Try resolving horizontally and vertically. You will obtain 2 equations in the two unknowns F and **R**. It is perfectly possible to solve these equations, but it is quite a lot of work. How can you decide which directions will be easiest to work with?

(iii) Once you know the resultant force you can work out the acceleration of the sledge using Newton's second law.

$$F = ma$$

$$21.959\ldots = 5a$$

$$a = \frac{21.959\ldots}{5} = 4.392\ldots$$

The acceleration is $4.4\,\text{m s}^{-2}$ (correct to 1 d.p.).

> The resultant force is in the direction of motion and so must be parallel to the slope.

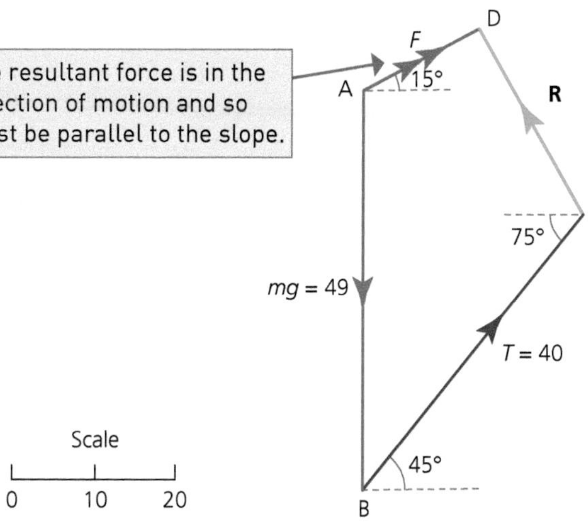

Figure 2.68

An alternative way of approaching the previous example is to draw a scale diagram with the three forces represented by three of the sides of a quadrilateral taken in order (with the arrows following each other, $\overrightarrow{AB}$, $\overrightarrow{BC}$ and $\overrightarrow{CD}$) as shown in Figure 2.68. The resultant is represented by the fourth side AD.

From the diagram you can estimate the normal contact force to be about 30 N and the resultant 20 N.

Discussion point

In what order would you draw the lines in Figure 2.68?

Discussion point

What can you say about the acceleration of the sledge in the cases when

(i) the length AD in Figure 2.68 on the previous page is not zero?

(ii) the length AD is zero so that the starting point on the quadrilateral is the same as the finishing point?

(iii) BC is so short that the point D is to the left of A as shown in Figure 2.69?

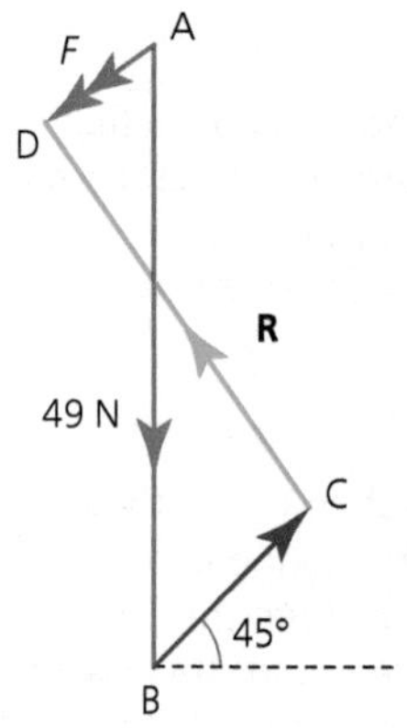

Figure 2.69

Example 2.14

Two forces **P** and **Q** act at a point O on a particle of mass 2 kg. Force **P** has magnitude 50 N and acts along a bearing of 030°. Force **Q** has magnitude of 30 N and acts along a bearing of 315°.

(i) Find the magnitude and bearing of the resultant force **P** + **Q**.

(ii) Find the acceleration of the particle.

Solution

(i) Forces **P** and **Q** are illustrated below.

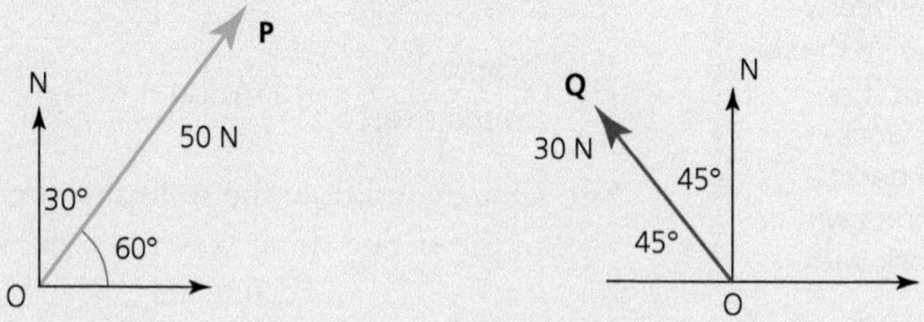

Figure 2.70

Note

Notice that **P** and **Q** are written as vectors.

$$\mathbf{P} = \begin{pmatrix} 50\cos 60° \\ 50\sin 60° \end{pmatrix}$$

$$= \begin{pmatrix} 25 \\ 43.30\ldots \end{pmatrix}$$

$$\mathbf{Q} = \begin{pmatrix} -30\cos 45° \\ 30\sin 45° \end{pmatrix}$$

$$= \begin{pmatrix} -21.21\ldots \\ 21.21\ldots \end{pmatrix}$$

$$\mathbf{P}+\mathbf{Q} = \begin{pmatrix} 25 \\ 43.30\ldots \end{pmatrix} + \begin{pmatrix} -21.21\ldots \\ 21.21\ldots \end{pmatrix}$$

$$= \begin{pmatrix} 3.78\ldots \\ 64.51\ldots \end{pmatrix}$$

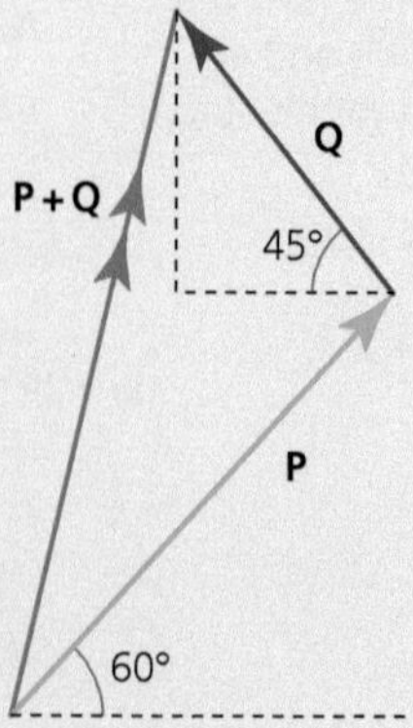

Figure 2.71

The resultant is shown in Figure 2.72.

Magnitude $|\mathbf{P}+\mathbf{Q}| = \sqrt{3.78...^2 + 64.51...^2}$

$= 64.62$

Direction $\tan\theta = \dfrac{64.51...}{3.78...}$

$\theta = 86.64...°$

The bearing is $90° - 86.64...° = 3.36...°$

The force $\mathbf{P} + \mathbf{Q}$ has magnitude 65 N and bearing 003°.

(ii) The acceleration of the particle is given by

$$\mathbf{a} = \frac{1}{2}(\mathbf{P}+\mathbf{Q}) = \frac{1}{2}\begin{pmatrix} 3.78... \\ 64.51... \end{pmatrix} = \begin{pmatrix} 1.89 \\ 32.3 \end{pmatrix}$$

$m = 2$ kg

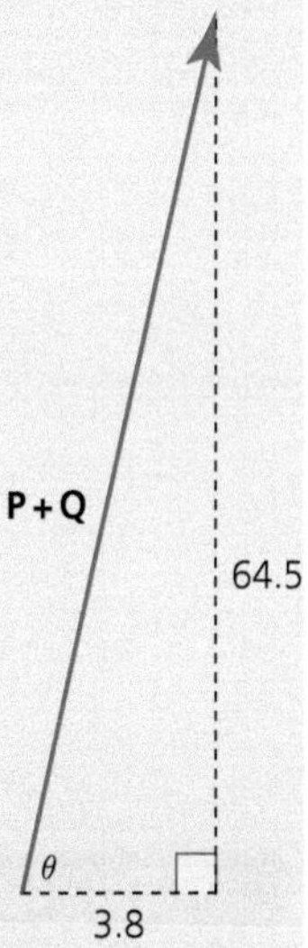

Figure 2.72

The magnitude of the acceleration is $\sqrt{1.89^2 + 32.3^2} = 32.4$.

The bearing is $\arctan\left(\dfrac{1.89}{32.3}\right) = 3.35°$.

P and **Q** give the particle an acceleration of 32.3 m s^{-2} on a bearing of 003°.

Sometimes, as in the next example, it is just as easy to work with the trigonometry of the diagram as with the components of the forces.

Example 2.15

The angle between the lines of action of two forces **X** and **Y** is θ. Find the magnitude and direction of the resultant.

Solution

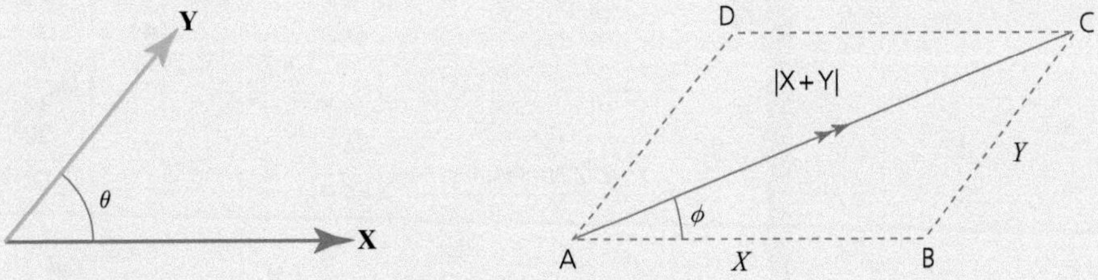

Figure 2.73

Use the cosine rule in triangle ABC. The magnitude of the resultant is F.

$$F = |\mathbf{X}+\mathbf{Y}| = \sqrt{AB^2 + BC^2 - 2AB \times BC \times \cos(\widehat{ABC})}$$

$$= \sqrt{X^2 + Y^2 - 2XY\cos(180° - \theta)}$$

$$= \sqrt{X^2 + Y^2 + 2XY\cos\theta}$$

Use the sine rule in triangle ABC. The resultant makes an angle ϕ with the **X** force.

$$\frac{\sin\widehat{CAB}}{BC}=\frac{\sin\widehat{ABC}}{AC}$$

$$\frac{\sin\phi}{Y}=\frac{\sin(180°-\theta)}{F}$$

$$\sin\phi=\frac{Y}{F}\sin\theta$$

$$\phi=\arcsin(\frac{Y}{F}\sin\theta)$$

The resultant of the two forces **X** and **Y** inclined at θ has magnitude $F=\sqrt{X^2+Y^2+2XY\cos\theta}$ and makes an angle $\arcsin(\frac{Y}{F}\sin\theta)$ with the **X** force.

Exercise 2.4

For questions 1–6, carry out the following steps. All forces are in newtons.

(i) Draw a scale diagram to show the forces and their resultant for Figure 2.74.

(ii) State whether you think the forces are in equilibrium and, if not, estimate the magnitude and direction of the resultant.

(iii) Write the forces in component form, using the directions indicated and so obtain the components of the resultant. Hence find the magnitude and direction of the resultant.

(iv) Compare your answers to parts (ii) and (iii).

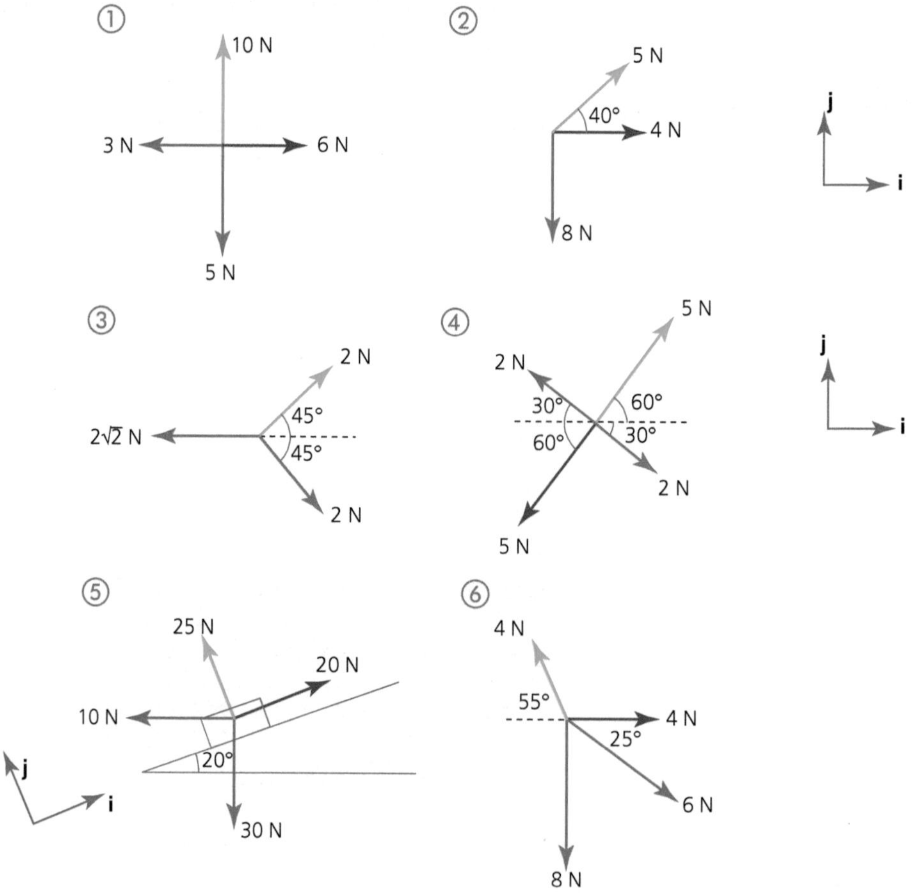

Figure 2.74

⑦ Four horizontal wires are attached to a telephone post and exert the following tensions on it: 25 N in the north direction, 30 N in the east direction, 45 N in the north-west direction and 50 N in the south-west direction. Calculate the resultant tension on the post and find its direction.

⑧ Forces of magnitude 7 N, 10 N and 15 N act on a particle of mass 1.5 kg in the directions shown in Figure 2.75.

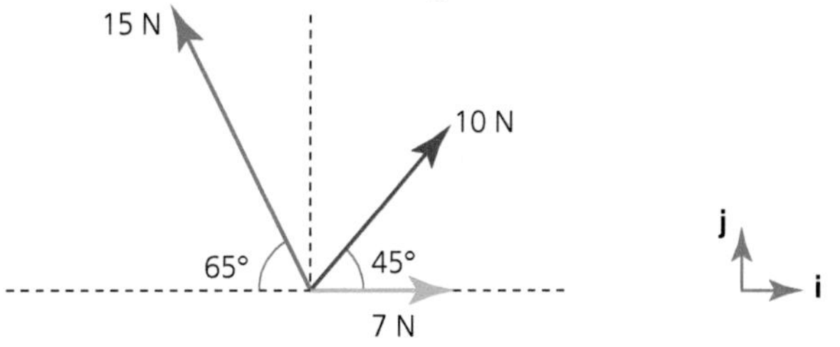

Figure 2.75

(i) Find the components of the resultant of the three forces in the **i** and **j** directions.

(ii) Find the magnitude and direction of the resultant.

(iii) Find the acceleration of the particle.

⑨ (i) Find the resultant of the set of 6 forces whose magnitudes and directions are shown in Figure 2.76.

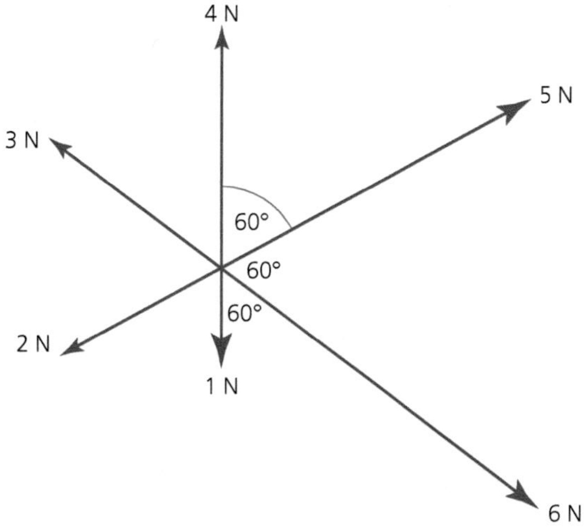

Figure 2.76

The forces are acting on a particle P of mass 5 kg which is initially at rest at O.

(ii) How fast is P moving after 3 s and how far from O is it now?

⑩ A force **P** of magnitude 5 N makes an angle of 60° with a force **Q** of magnitude 4 N. Find the magnitude of the resultant force and the angle it makes with the **P** force.

⑪ Two forces **P** and **Q** are at right angles to each other. The resultant has magnitude 20 N and makes an angle 60° with **P**. Find the magnitude of **P** and **Q**.

⑫ The resultant of two forces **P** and **Q** acting on a particle has magnitude $P = |\mathbf{P}|$. The resultant of the two forces 3**P** and 2**Q** acting in the same directions as before has magnitude $2P$. Find the magnitude of **Q** and the angle between **P** and **Q**.

KEY POINTS

1 Newton's laws of motion
- Every object continues in a state of rest or uniform motion in a straight line unless it is acted on by an external force.
- Resultant force = mass × acceleration or $\mathbf{F} = m\mathbf{a}$
- When one object exerts a force on another there is always a reaction force which is equal and opposite in direction to the acting force.

2 Force is a vector. It may be represented in either magnitude–direction form or in component form

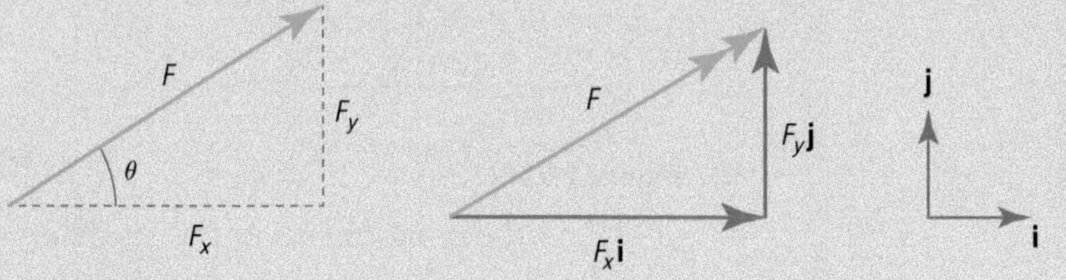

Figure 2.77

Magnitude of $\mathbf{F} = |\mathbf{F}| = \sqrt{F_x^2 + F_y^2}$ $\quad \mathbf{F} = F_x\mathbf{i} + F_y\mathbf{j} = \begin{pmatrix} F_x \\ F_y \end{pmatrix}$

Direction of **F** $\quad \theta = \arctan\left(\frac{F_y}{F_x}\right)$

3 Resolving forces

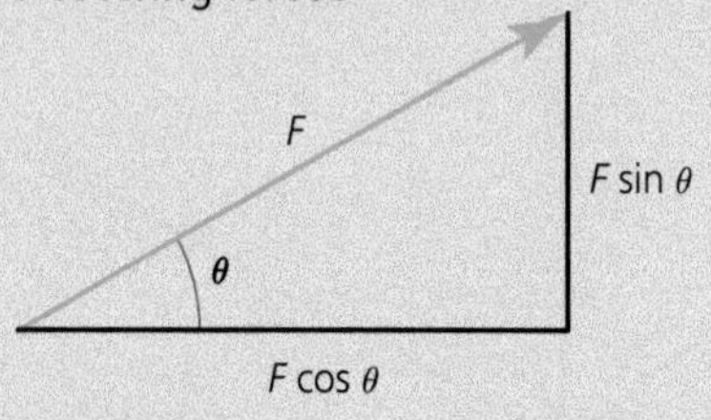

Figure 2.78

$$\mathbf{F} = F\cos\theta\mathbf{i} + F\sin\theta\mathbf{j} = \begin{pmatrix} F\cos\theta \\ F\sin\theta \end{pmatrix}$$

4 Resultant forces

$$\mathbf{R} = \mathbf{F} + \mathbf{G} + \mathbf{H} = \begin{pmatrix} F_x \\ F_y \end{pmatrix} + \begin{pmatrix} G_x \\ G_y \end{pmatrix} + \begin{pmatrix} H_x \\ H_y \end{pmatrix}$$

$$\mathbf{R} = \begin{pmatrix} X \\ Y \end{pmatrix}; X = F_x + G_x + H_x, Y = F_y + G_y + H_y$$

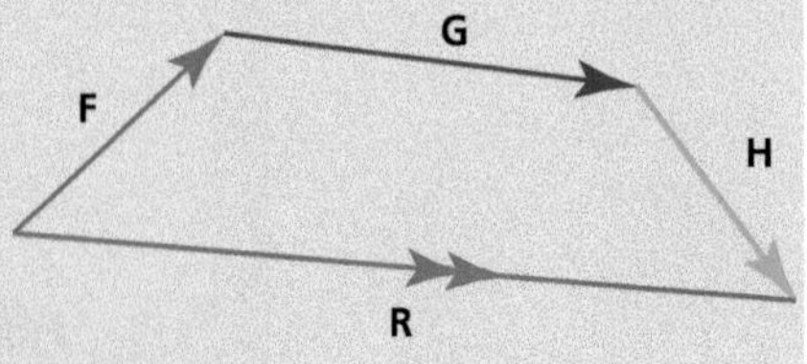

Figure 2.79

Magnitude of $\mathbf{R} = \sqrt{X^2 + Y^2}$ $\quad$ Direction of **R** $\theta = \arctan\left(\frac{Y}{X}\right)$

5 Equilibrium

When the resultant is zero, the forces are in equilibrium.

6 Triangle of forces

If an object is in equilibrium under three non-parallel forces, their lines of action are concurrent and they can be represented by a triangle.

LEARNING OUTCOMES

When you have finished this chapter, you should be able to

- draw a diagram showing the forces acting on a body
- apply Newton's laws of motion to problems in one or more dimensions
- resolve a force into components having selected suitable directions for resolution
- find the resultant of several concurrent forces
- realise that a particle is in equilibrium under a set of concurrent forces if and only if the resultant is zero
- know that a closed polygon may be drawn to represent the forces acting on a particle in equilibrium
- formulate equations for equilibrium by resolving forces in suitable directions
- formulate the equation of motion of a particle which is being acted on by several forces
- know that contact between two surfaces is lost when the normal contact force becomes zero.

3 A model for friction

A gem cannot be polished without friction, nor a man perfected without trials

Lucius Annaeus Seneca

Discussion point

Would mountain goats survive without friction?

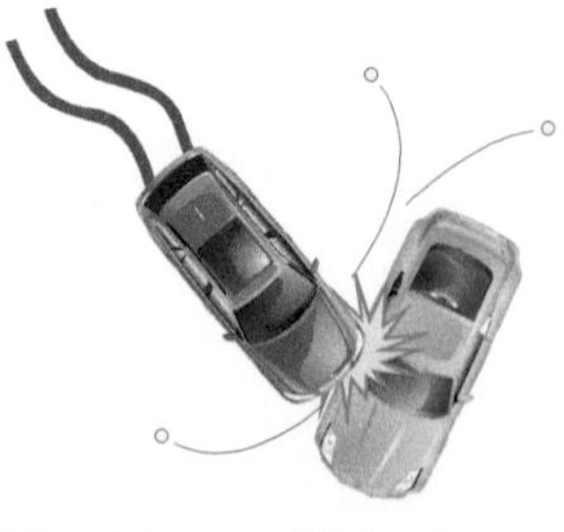

Figure 3.1 When an accident involving a collision happens, skid marks are sometimes left on the roadway by a vehicle that has locked its brakes. By measuring the skid marks and applying mechanics, it is possible to estimate the speed of the vehicle, prior to collision.

Discussion point

In Figure 3.1 the driver of the red car left a 10 metre skid mark on the road. He claimed that this showed he was driving within the speed limit of 30 mph.

It is the duty of a court to decide whether the driver of the red car was innocent or guilty. Is it possible to deduce his speed from the skid mark, and what important factors do you need to consider when modelling this situation?

1 A model for friction

Clearly the key information about the accident involving the red car is provided by the skid marks. To interpret it, you need a model for how friction works; in this case between the car's tyres and the road.

As a result of experimental work, Coulomb formulated a model for friction between two surfaces. The following laws are usually attributed to him.

1 Friction always opposes relative motion between two surfaces in contact.
2 Friction is independent of the relative speed of the surfaces.
3 The magnitude of the frictional force has a maximum which depends on the normal contact force between the surfaces and on the roughness of the surfaces in contact.
4 If there is no sliding between the surfaces

$$F \leq \mu R$$

where F is the magnitude of the force due to friction and R is the magnitude of the normal contact force. μ is called the **coefficient of friction**.
5 When sliding is just about to occur, friction is said to be **limiting** and $F = \mu R$.
6 When sliding occurs $F = \mu R$.

According to Coulomb's model, μ is a constant for any pair of surfaces. Typical values and ranges of values for the coefficient of friction μ are given in the table.

Surfaces in contact	μ
Wood sliding on wood	0.2–0.6
Metal sliding on metal	0.15–0.3
Normal tyres on dry road	0.8
Racing tyres on dry road	1.0
Sandpaper on sandpaper	2.0
Skis on snow	0.02

How fast was the driver of the red car going?

You can proceed with the problem. As an initial model, the driver of the red car made the following assumptions:

1 that the road was level
2 that his car was travelling at $2\,\mathrm{m\,s^{-1}}$ when it hit the orange car (this was consistent with the damage to the cars)
3 that the car and driver could be treated as a particle, subject to Coulomb's laws of friction with $\mu = 0.8$ (i.e. dry road conditions).

Discussion point

How good is this model and would you be confident in offering the answer as evidence in your defence in court? Look carefully at the three assumptions. What effect do they have on the estimate of the initial speed?

Taking the direction of travel as positive, let the car and driver have acceleration $a\,\mathrm{m\,s^{-2}}$ and mass $m\,\mathrm{kg}$. You have probably realised that the acceleration will be negative. The forces (in N) and acceleration are shown in Figure 3.2.

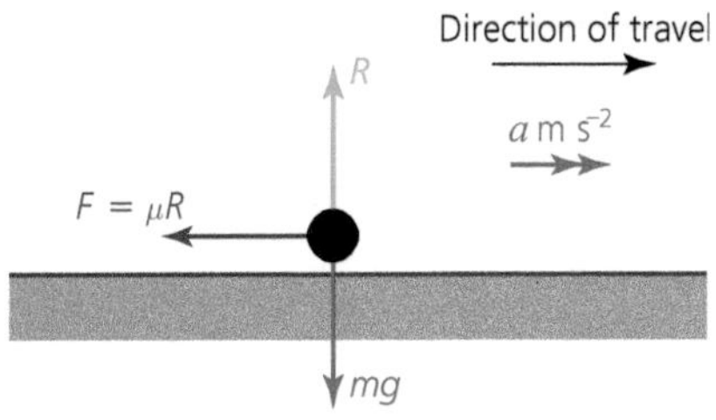

Figure 3.2

Apply Newton's second law:

perpendicular to the road $R - mg = 0$ ①

parallel to the road $-\mu R = ma$ ②

Solving for a gives

$$a = -\frac{\mu R}{m} = -\frac{\mu mg}{m} = -\mu g$$

Taking $\mu = 0.8$ and $g = 9.8\,\text{m}\,\text{s}^{-2}$ gives $a = -7.84\,\text{m}\,\text{s}^{-2}$.

There is no vertical acceleration.

There is a constant force $-\mu R = ma$ from friction.

From ① $R = mg$

The constant acceleration formula

$$v^2 = u^2 + 2as$$

can be used to calculate the initial speed of the red car. Substituting $s = 10$, $v = 2$ and $a = -7.84$ gives

$$u = \sqrt{2^2 + 2 \times 7.84 \times 10} = 12.68\,\text{m}\,\text{s}^{-1}$$

Convert this figure to miles per hour.

$$\text{Speed} = \frac{12.68 \times 3600}{1600}$$

$$= 28.5\,\text{mph}$$

1 hour is 60×60 seconds.

1 mile is approx. 1600 m.

So the model suggests that the red car was travelling at a speed of just under 30 mph before skidding began.

Discussion point

In this example the brakes were locked. What happens when you slow down in normal driving? Where does friction act?

Modelling with friction

While there is always some frictional force between two sliding surfaces its magnitude is often so small as to be negligible. In such cases the surfaces are described as **smooth**.

In situations where frictional forces cannot be ignored, the surface(s) are described as **rough**. Coulomb's law is the standard model for dealing with such cases.

Frictional forces are essential in many ways. For example, a ladder leaning against a wall would always slide if there were no friction between the foot of the ladder and the ground. The absence of friction in icy conditions causes difficulties for road users: pedestrians slip over, cars and motorcycles skid.

Remember that friction always opposes sliding motion.

Discussion point

In what direction is the frictional force between the back wheel of a cycle and the road?

Example 3.1

A stone slides in a straight line across a frozen pond. It starts to move with a speed of $8\,\text{m}\,\text{s}^{-1}$ and slides for 40 m before coming to rest. Calculate the coefficient of friction between the stone and the pond.

Solution

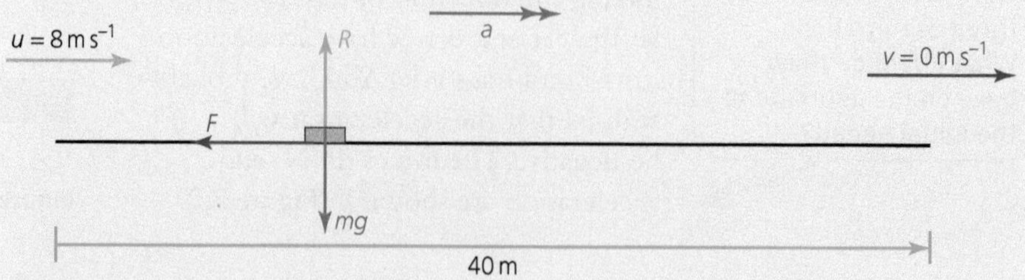

Figure 3.3

The only force acting on the stone in the direction of motion is the frictional force F, which is uniform, thus giving rise to a constant acceleration a. In order to find a, use the constant acceleration formula

$v^2 = u^2 + 2as$

$0 = 8^2 + 2 \times 40 \times a$

$a = -\frac{64}{80} = -0.8$

Use Newton's second law to give

$-F = -0.8m$

$-\mu mg = -0.8m$

$\mu = \frac{0.8}{9.8} = 0.0816\ldots$

Since the stone is in motion: $F = \mu R$

Vertical equilibrium means $R = mg$

The coefficient of friction between the stone and the pond is 0.082.

Example 3.2

A box of mass 2 kg rests on rough horizontal ground. The coefficient of friction between the box and the ground is 0.4. A light inextensible string is attached to the box in order to pull it along. If the tension in the string is T N, find the value that T must exceed if the box is to accelerate when the string is

(i) horizontal

(ii) 30° above the horizontal

(iii) 30° below the horizontal.

Solution

(i) The forces acting on the box are shown in Figure 3.4.

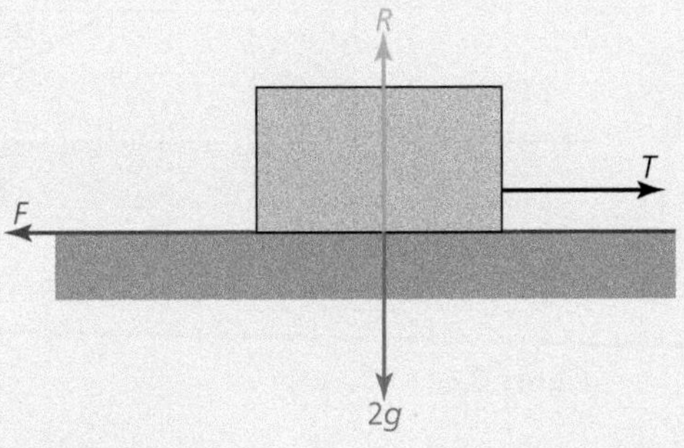

Figure 3.4

Horizontal forces: $T > F$

This is the condition for the box to accelerate.

Vertical forces: $R = 2g$

$R = 2 \times 9.8 = 19.6$

The law of friction states that for a moving object

$F = \mu R$

So in this case

$F = 0.4 \times 19.6$

$F = 7.84\,\text{N}$

T must exceed 7.84 N for the box to accelerate.

(ii) The forces acting on the box are shown in Figure 3.5.

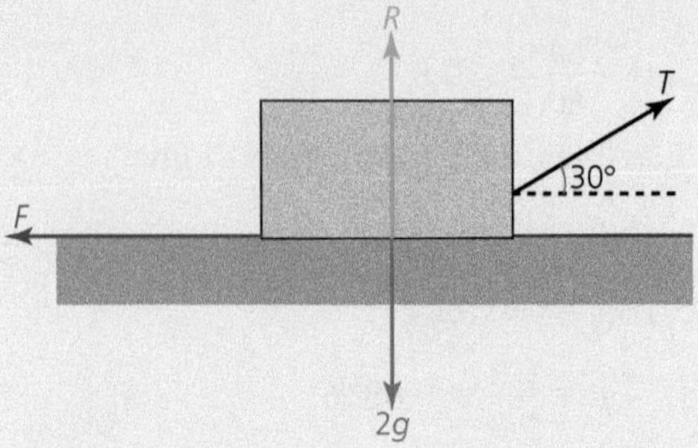

Figure 3.5

Resolving horizontally: $T \cos 30° > F$ ①

This is the condition for the box to accelerate.

vertically: $R + T \sin 30° = 2g$

So that $R = 2g - T \sin 30°$

This equation shows that in this situation the magnitude of R is less than $2g$.

When motion occurs $F = \mu R = 0.4(2g - T \sin 30°)$

Substituting in ① $T \cos 30° > 0.4(2g - T \sin 30°)$

Rearranging $T(\cos 30° + 0.4 \sin 30°) > 0.8g$

$$T > \frac{0.8 \times 9.8}{(\cos 30° + 0.4 \sin 30°)} = \frac{7.84}{1.066} = 7.35\ \ldots$$

T must exceed 7.35 N for the box to accelerate.

(iii) The forces acting on the box are shown in Figure 3.6.

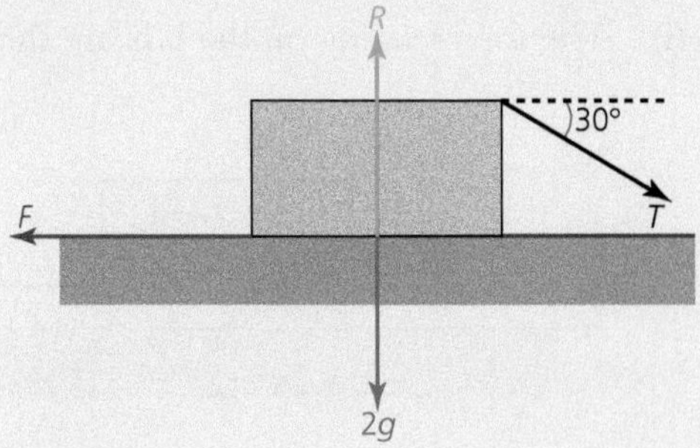

Figure 3.6

Resolving horizontally: $T \cos 30° > F$

vertically: $R = T \sin 30° + 2g$

When motion occurs $F = 0.4R = 0.4\,(T \sin 30° + 2g)$

So that $T \cos 30° > 0.4\,(T \sin 30° + 2g)$

$$T > \frac{7.84}{(\cos 30° - 0.4 \sin 30°)} = \frac{7.84}{0.666}$$

$T > 11.77\ \ldots$

T must exceed 11.8 N for the box to accelerate.

Note

It is clear from the example that the force required to move the box is largest when the force from the string is pointing downwards. The component of the force in the downward direction increases the normal contact force, which in turn increases the frictional force.

Example 3.3

Figure 3.7 shows a block of mass 5 kg resting on a rough table and connected by a light inextensible string passing over a smooth pulley to a block of mass 4 kg. The coefficient of friction between the 5 kg block and the table is 0.4.

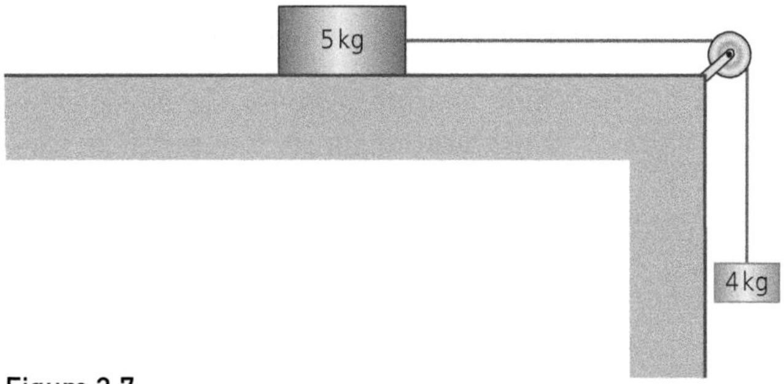

Figure 3.7

(i) Draw diagrams showing the forces acting on each block and the direction of the system's acceleration.

(ii) Show that acceleration does take place.

(iii) Find the acceleration of the system and the tension in the string.

Solution

(i)

> The 5 kg block has no vertical acceleration. $R = 5g$

> The directions of the acceleration of the blocks are clearly as shown here.

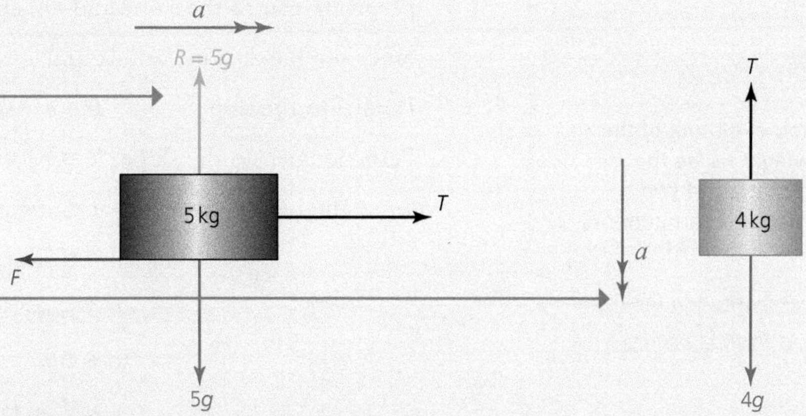

Figure 3.8

(ii) The equations of motion of the blocks are

The 4 kg block $4g - T = 4a$ ①

The 5 kg block $T - F = 5a$ ②

Adding ① and ② $4g - F = 9a$ ③

> You need to show that $a > 0$.

The maximum possible value of F is $\mu R = 0.4 \times 5g = 2g$

So in the left hand side of ③, $4g - F > 0$

Therefore $a > 0$ and sliding occurs.

(iii) When sliding occurs, you can replace F by $\mu R = 2g$

Then ③ gives $2g = 9a$

$$a = \frac{2}{9}g = 2.17$$

Substituting in ① gives $T = 4(g - a) = 4 \times \frac{7}{9}g = 30.5$ (1 d.p.)

The acceleration of the system is $2.2\,\text{ms}^{-2}$ and the tension in the string is 30.5 N.

Example 3.4

A block of mass m is placed on a slope inclined at an angle θ to the horizontal. The coefficient of friction between the block and the slope is 0.4.

(i) Find the values of θ for which the block would be at rest.

The angle of the slope is actually 30°.

(ii) Find the time taken for the block to slide a distance of 1.5 m down the slope, assuming it starts at rest.

Solution

(i) The forces acting on the block are shown in Figure 3.9.

> **Note**
>
> In a situation like this where an object is on a slope, it is almost always easier to work with directions perpendicular and parallel to the slope rather than vertical and horizontal.

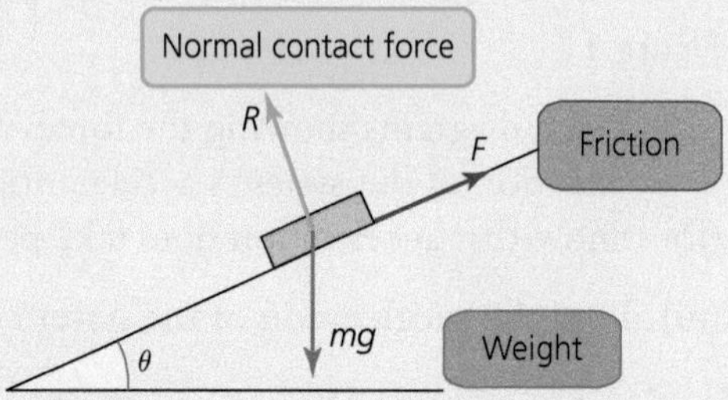

Figure 3.9

The weight mg can be resolved into components $mg\cos\theta$ perpendicular to the slope and $mg\sin\theta$ parallel to the slope.

> **Note**
>
> You can think of the weight mg as the resultant of two resolved components.

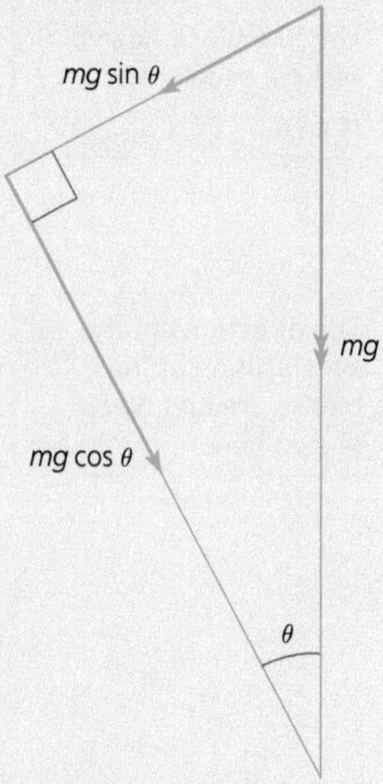

Figure 3.10

Since the block is in equilibrium

Parallel to the slope: $F = mg\sin\theta$ ①

Perpendicular to the slope: $R = mg\cos\theta$ ②

Since the block is at rest: $F \leq \mu R$

> Substituting for F and R from ① and ②

$$mg\sin\theta \leq \mu mg\cos\theta$$

$$\Rightarrow \sin\theta \leq \mu\cos\theta$$

$$\Rightarrow \tan\theta \leq \mu$$

$$\theta \leq \arctan\mu$$

In this case $\mu = 0.4$, so $\tan\theta \leq 0.4$ and $\theta \leq 21.8°$.

The block is at rest for values of θ less than 21.8°.

(ii)

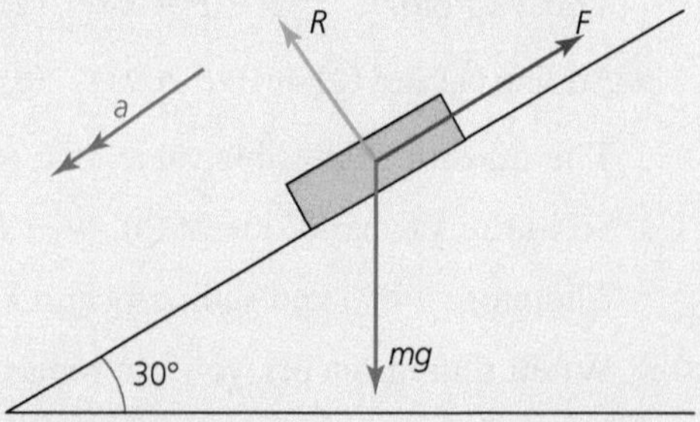

Figure 3.11

The block is now sliding down the plane. It has an acceleration, a.

The equation of motion for the block is

$$ma = mg\sin 30° - F \quad ③$$

Since the block is moving

$$F = \mu R = 0.4mg \cos 30° \quad ④$$

Substituting ④ into ③

$$ma = mg \sin 30° - 0.4mg \cos 30°$$

Dividing through by m

$$a = g(\sin 30° - 0.4 \cos 30°)$$
$$= 9.8 \times (0.5 - 0.4 \times 0.866\ldots)$$
$$= 1.505\ldots$$

Using the constant acceleration formula $s = ut + \frac{1}{2}at^2$ with $u = 0$, $s = 1.5$ and $a = 1.505\ldots$

$$1.5 = 0.5 \times 1.505\ldots \times t^2$$

$$\Rightarrow t = \sqrt{\frac{1.5}{0.5 \times 1.505\ldots}} = 1.41\ldots$$

The block takes 1.4 s to slide down the slope.

Historical note

Charles Augustin de Coulomb was born in Angoulême in France in 1736 and is best remembered for his work on electricity rather than that on friction. Coulomb's law concerns the forces on charged particles and was determined using a torsion balance. The unit for electric charge is named after him. Coulomb worked in many fields, including the elasticity of metal, silk fibres and the design of windmills. He died in Paris in 1806.

Note

1 The result is independent of the mass of the block. This is often found when simple models are applied to mechanics problems. For example, two objects of different mass fall to the ground with the same acceleration. However, when such models are refined, for example, to take account of air resistance, mass is often found to have some effect on the result.

2 The angle for which the block is about to slide down the slope is called the *angle of friction*. The angle of friction is often denoted by λ (lambda) and is defined by $\tan \lambda = \mu$.

When the angle of the slope is equal to the angle of the friction, it is just possible for the block to stay on the slope without sliding. If the slope is slightly steeper, the block will start to slide.

Exercise 3.1

① A block of mass 25 kg is resting on a horizontal surface. It is being pulled by a horizontal force T N, and is on the point of sliding. Draw a diagram showing the forces acting and find the coefficient of friction when

(i) $T = 20$

(ii) $T = 5$

② A box of mass 25 kg is resting on rough horizontal ground. The box can just be moved by a horizontal force of 60 N. Find the coefficient of friction between the box and the ground.

③ A stone is sliding across a frozen pond. It travels a distance of 12 m before coming to rest from an initial speed of $4\,\text{m}\,\text{s}^{-1}$.

Find the coefficient of friction between the stone and the pond.

④ A parcel drops out of a van travelling at $20\,\text{m}\,\text{s}^{-1}$. The parcel slides a distance of 30 m before coming to rest. Calculate the coefficient of friction between the parcel and the road.

⑤ In each of the following situations find, in any order, the acceleration of the system, the tension(s) in the string(s) and the magnitude of the frictional force.

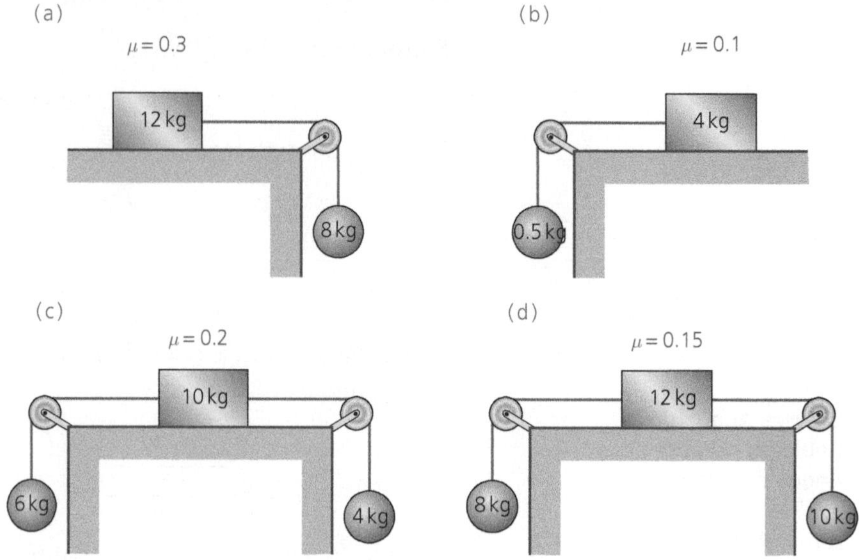

Figure 3.12

⑥ A block of mass 5 kg is about to move up a rough plane inclined at 30° to the horizontal, under the application of a force of 50 N parallel to the slope, as shown in Figure 3.13.

Find the value of the coefficient of friction between the block and the plane.

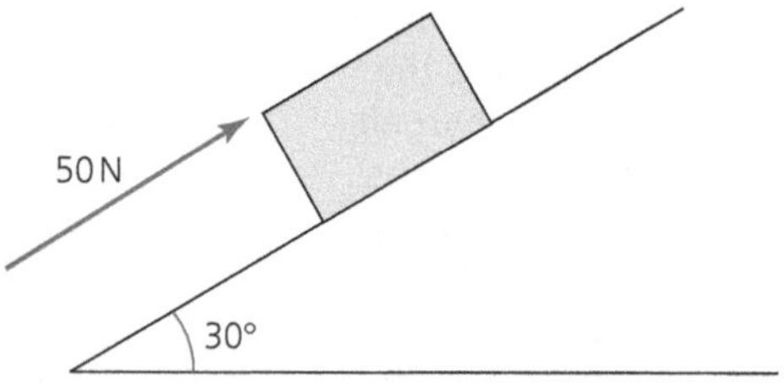

Figure 3.13

⑦ An ice hockey player is sliding a puck of mass 50 g across the ice rink. The initial speed of the puck is $8\,\mathrm{m\,s^{-1}}$ and it takes it 40 m to come to rest.

(i) Find the deceleration of the puck.

(ii) Find the frictional force acting on the puck.

(iii) Find the coefficient of friction between the puck and the ice rink.

(iv) How far will a 60 g puck travel if it, too, is given an initial speed of $8\,\mathrm{m\,s^{-1}}$?

⑧ A car of mass 1200 kg is travelling at $30\,\mathrm{m\,s^{-1}}$ when it is forced to perform an emergency stop. Its wheels lock as soon as the brakes are applied so that they slide along the road without rotating. For the first 40 m the coefficient of friction between the wheels and the road is 0.75 but then the road surface changes and the coefficient of friction becomes 0.8.

(i) Find the deceleration of the car immediately after the brakes are applied.

(ii) Find the speed of the car when it comes to the change of road surface.

(iii) Find the total distance the car travels before it comes to rest.

⑨ A girl, whose mass is 25 kg, is sitting on a sledge of mass 10 kg which is being pulled at constant speed along horizontal ground by her brother. The coefficient of friction between the sledge and the snow-covered ground is 0.1. Find the tension in the rope from the boy's hand to the sledge when

(i) the rope is horizontal

(ii) the rope makes an angle of 20° with the horizontal.

⑩ A particle of mass 5 kg is projected upwards along a plane that is inclined at an angle of 25° to the horizontal, with a speed of $10\,\text{m s}^{-1}$. The particle comes to rest after 10 m.

(i) Find the deceleration of the particle.

(ii) Find the frictional force F and the normal contact force R, and hence deduce the coefficient of friction between the particle and the plane.

The particle then starts to move down the plane with acceleration $a\ \text{m s}^{-2}$.

(iii) Find a and the speed of the particle as it passes its starting point.

⑪ A playground slide consists of a sloping part and a horizontal part. The sloping part is 5 m long and makes an angle α to the horizontal, where $\tan\alpha = 0.75$. A child starts at the top of the slide with zero speed and slides down. The coefficient of friction between the child and the slide is 0.3. No speed is lost at the point where the sloping part changes to the horizontal part, and the child comes to rest before reaching the end of the horizontal part.

Find the smallest possible length of the horizontal part.

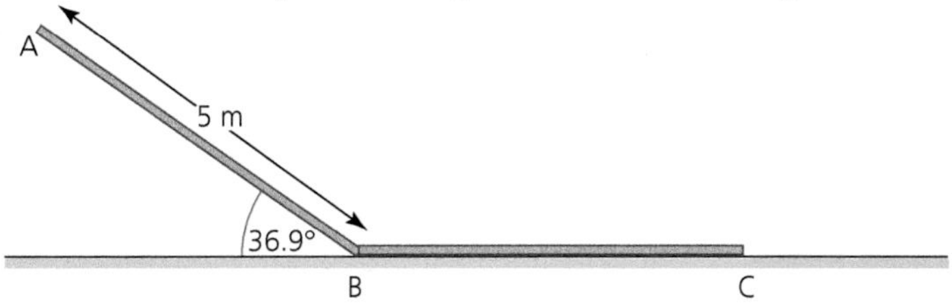

Figure 3.14

⑫ A 10 kg block lies on a rough horizontal table. The coefficient of friction between the block and the table is 0.15. The block is attached, by a light inextensible string which passes over a smooth pulley, to a mass of 2 kg hanging freely. The 10 kg block is 1.2 m from the pulley and the 2 kg mass is 1 m from the floor. The system is released from rest. Find

(i) the acceleration of the system

(ii) the time taken for the 2 kg mass to reach the floor

(iii) the velocity with which the 10 kg mass hits the pulley.

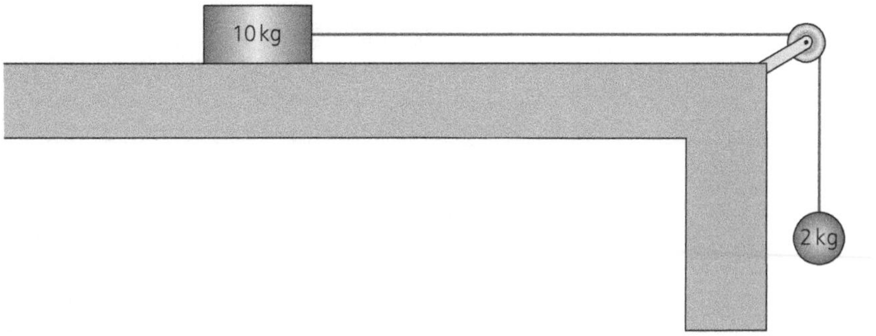

Figure 3.15

⑬ A box of mass 250 kg is placed on a rough inclined plane of slope $\arcsin\left(\frac{7}{25}\right)$ and coefficient of friction $\frac{1}{4}$. A rope is attached to the box and the direction of the rope makes an angle $\arcsin\left(\frac{3}{5}\right)$ with the upper surface of the plane. If the tension in the rope is T N, find the limiting values of T for which the box remains in equilibrium.

⑭ A box of weight 200 N is pulled at a steady speed across a rough horizontal surface by a rope which makes an angle α with the horizontal. The coefficient of friction between the box and the surface is 0.5. Assume that the box slides on its underside and does not tip up.

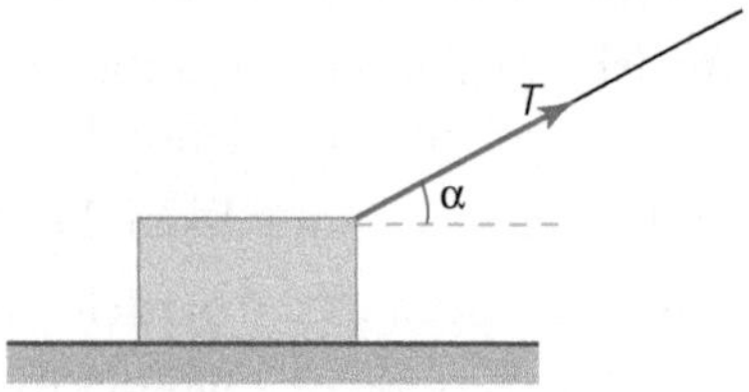

Figure 3.16

(i) Find an expression for the value of T for any angle α.

(ii) For what value of α is T a minimum and what is the value of that minimum?

⑮ A block of mass 10 kg is lying on a rough plane inclined at 30° to the horizontal. A horizontal force P is applied to the block as shown in Figure 3.17. The coefficient of friction between the block and the plane is 0.5.

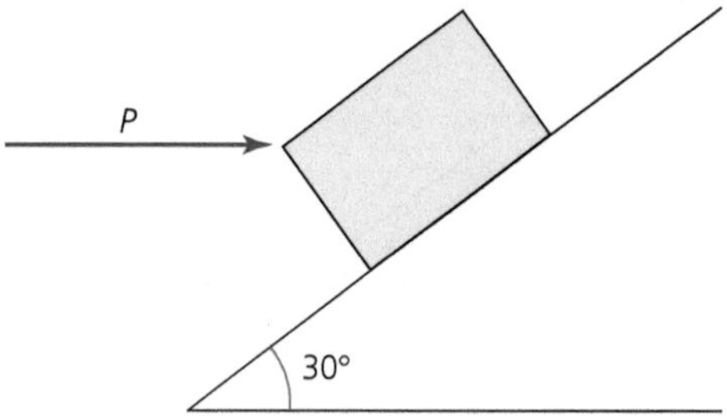

Figure 3.17

(i) Find the least force P necessary to start the block sliding up the plane.

(ii) Find the least force P necessary to stop the block from sliding down the plane.

⑯ A block of mass m is on the point of slipping down a plane inclined at an angle α to the horizontal. The same plane is raised so that it is now inclined at an angle β to the horizontal, with $\beta > \alpha$. Show that the least force P parallel to the plane which is required to keep the block in equilibrium is

$$mg \sin(\beta - \alpha) \sec \alpha$$

KEY POINTS

1. The total contact force between two surfaces may be expressed in terms of a frictional force and a normal contact force (also called a normal reaction).
2. The magnitude of the frictional force, F, between two surfaces is given by:
   $F < \mu R$ when there is no sliding except in limiting equilibrium
   $F = \mu R$ in limiting equilibrium
   $F = \mu R$ when sliding occurs
   where R is the magnitude of the normal contact force of one surface on the other and μ is the coefficient of friction between the surfaces.
3. The frictional force always acts in the direction to oppose sliding.
4. The magnitude of the normal contact force is affected by any force which has a component perpendicular to the direction of sliding.

LEARNING OUTCOMES

When you have completed this chapter, you should

- understand that the total contact force between surfaces may be expressed in terms of a frictional force and a normal contact force
- be able to draw a force diagram to represent a situation involving friction
- understand that a frictional force may be modelled by $F \leq \mu R$
- know that a frictional force acts in the direction to oppose sliding
- be able to model friction using $F = \mu R$ when sliding occurs
- know how to apply Newton's laws of motion to situations involving friction
- be able to derive and use the result that a body on a rough slope inclined at angle α to the horizontal is on the point of slipping if $\mu = \tan \alpha$.

4 Moments of forces

A system is in equilibrium when the forces constituting it are arranged in such a way as to compensate each other, like two weights pulling at the arms of a pair of scales.
Rudolf Arnheim

→ The photograph shows a mobile tower crane, consisting of the main vertical section housing the engine, winding gear and controls and the boom which supports the load and the counterweight. The counterweight is at a fixed distance from the centre line and the load is at a variable distance from the centre line. Why is the counterweight needed?

1 Introduction to moments

The operation of the crane depends on turning effects or *moments* of forces. To understand these you might find it helpful to look at a simpler situation.

Two children sit on a simple see-saw, made of a plank balanced on a fulcrum as in Figure 4.1. Will the see-saw balance?

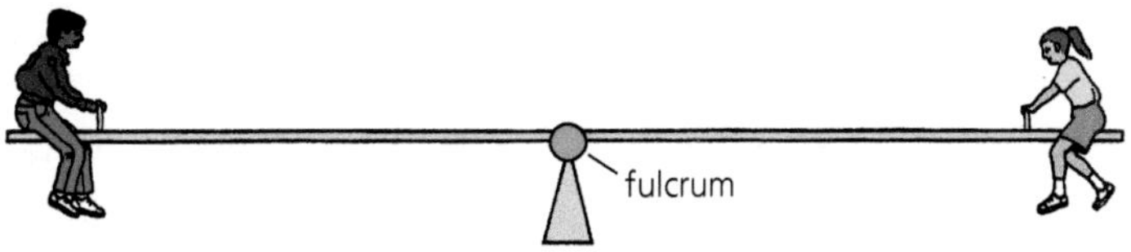

Figure 4.1

If both children have the same mass and sit the same distance from the fulcrum, then you expect to see the see-saw balance.

Now consider possible changes to this situation:

(i) If one child is heavier than the other, then you expect the heavier one to go down.

(ii) If one child moves nearer to the centre, you expect that child to go up.

You can see that both the weights of the children and their distances from the fulcrum are important.

What about this case? Both children now sit on one side of the see-saw and their father is on the other side. The father has a mass of 84 kg and sits 1.25 m from the fulcrum. The children of mass 25 kg and 35 kg sit 2.1 m and 1.5 m from the fulcrum on the other side.

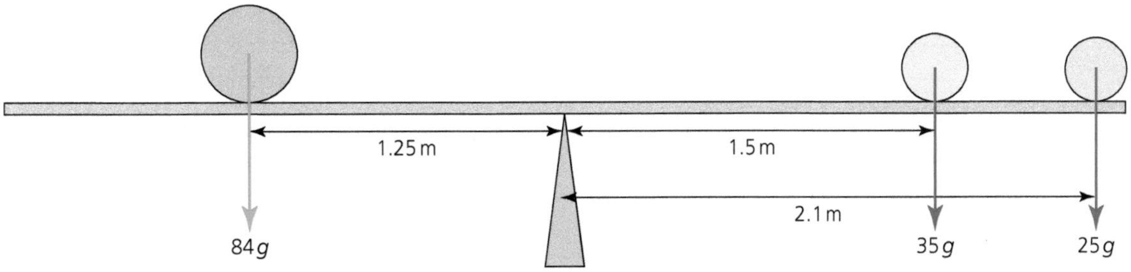

Figure 4.2

Taking the products of their weights and their distances from the fulcrum, gives

Father: $84g \times 1.25 = 105g$

Child A: $25g \times 2.1 = 52.5g$

Child B: $35g \times 1.5 = 52.5g$

Both children: $52.5g + 52.5g = 105g$

So you might expect the see-saw to balance, and this indeed is what would happen.

Rigid bodies

Until now the particle model has provided a reasonable basis for the analysis of the situations you have met. In an example like the see-saw, however, where turning is important, this model is inadequate because the forces do not all act through the same point.

In such cases you need the **rigid body model** in which an object, or **body**, is recognised as having size and shape, but is assumed not to be deformed when forces act on it.

Suppose that you push a tray lying on a smooth table with one finger so that the force acts parallel to one edge and through the centre of mass (Figure 4.3).

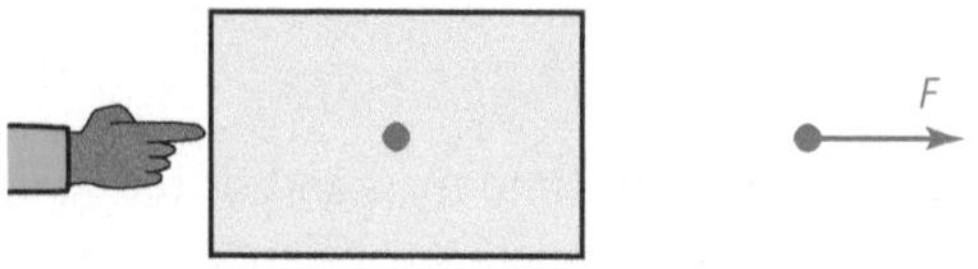

Figure 4.3

The particle model is adequate here: the tray travels in a straight line in the direction of the applied force.

If you push the tray equally hard with two fingers, as in Figure 4.4, symmetrically either side of the centre of mass, the particle model is still adequate.

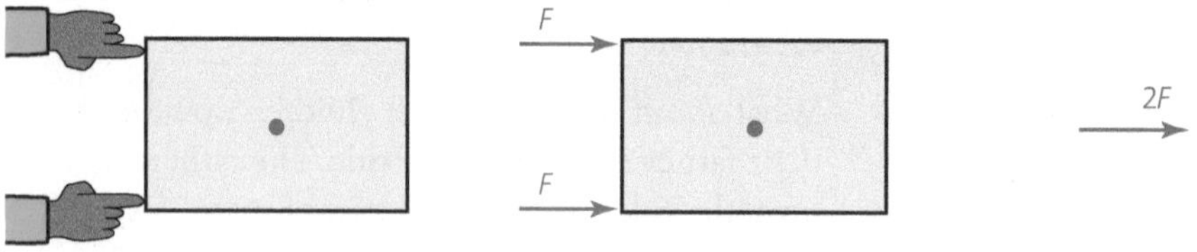

Figure 4.4

However, if the two forces are not equal or are not symmetrically placed, or, as in Figure 4.5, are in different directions, the particle model cannot be used.

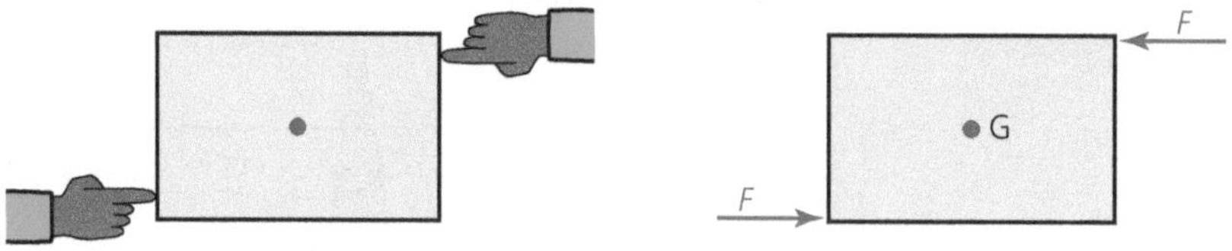

Figure 4.5

The resultant force in Figure 4.5 is zero, since the individual forces are equal in magnitude but opposite in direction. What happens to the tray? Experience tells you that it starts to rotate about G. How fast it starts to rotate depends, among other things, on the magnitude of the forces and the width of the tray. The rigid body model allows you to analyse the situation.

Moments

The example of the see-saw involved the product of each force and its distance from a fixed point. This product is called the **moment** of the force about the point.

The see-saw balances because the moments of the forces on either side of the fulcrum are of the same magnitude and act in opposite directions. One would tend to make the see-saw turn clockwise, the other anticlockwise. By contrast, the moments about G of the forces on the tray in the last situation do not balance. They both tend to turn it anticlockwise, so rotation occurs.

Conventions and units

The moment of a force F about a point O is defined by

$$\text{moment} = Fd$$

where d is the perpendicular distance from the point O to the line of action of the force (Figure 4.6).

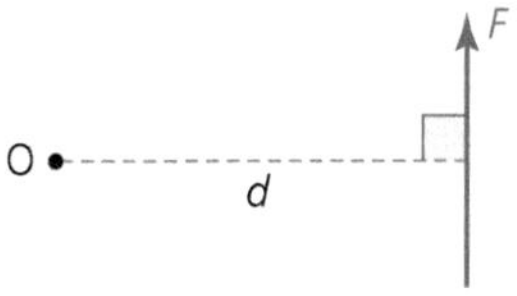

Figure 4.6

Hint

The line of the force and its perpendicular make a T (for 'turning')

In two dimensions, the sense of a moment is described as either positive (anticlockwise) or negative (clockwise), as shown in Figure 4.7.

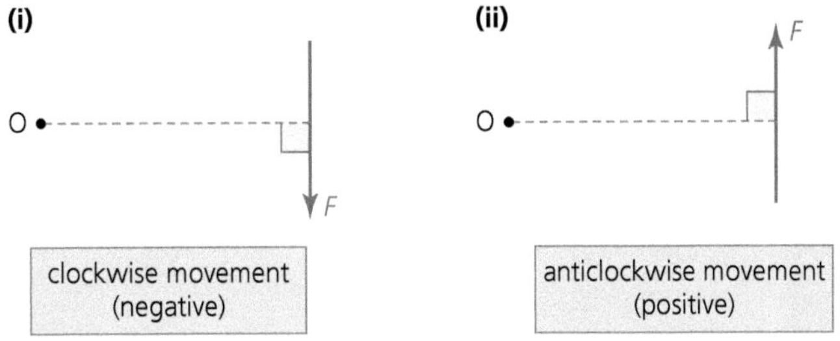

Figure 4.7

If you imagine putting a pin at O and pushing along the line of F, your page would turn clockwise for **(i)** and anticlockwise for **(ii)**.

In the S.I. system, the unit for moment is the newton metre (N m), because a moment is the product of a force, the unit of which is the newton, and distance, the unit of which is the metre. Remember that moments are always taken about a point and you must always specify which point. A force acting through the point will have no moment about that point because in that case $d = 0$.

Discussion point

Figure 4.8 shows two tools used for tightening nuts. Discuss the advantages and disadvantages of each.

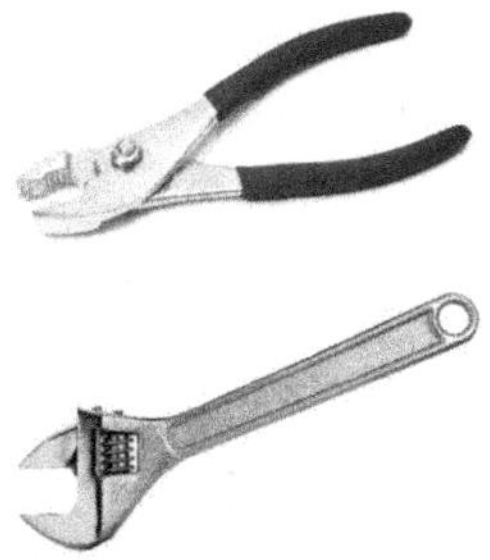

Figure 4.8

Couples

Whenever two forces of the same magnitude act in opposite directions along different lines, they have a zero resultant force, but do have a turning effect. In fact, the moment will be Fd about any point, where d is the perpendicular distance between the forces. This is demonstrated in Figure 4.9.

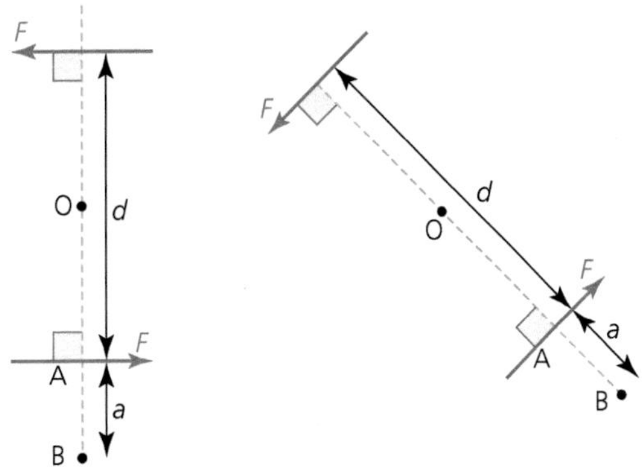

Figure 4.9

In each of these situations:

Moment about O $\quad F\frac{d}{2} + F\frac{d}{2} = Fd$ ← Anticlockwise is positive.

Moment about A $\quad 0 + Fd = Fd$

Moment about B $\quad -aF + (a + d)F = Fd$

Any set of forces like these with a zero resultant force but a non-zero total moment is known as a **couple**. The effect of a couple on a rigid body is to cause rotation.

Equilibrium revisited

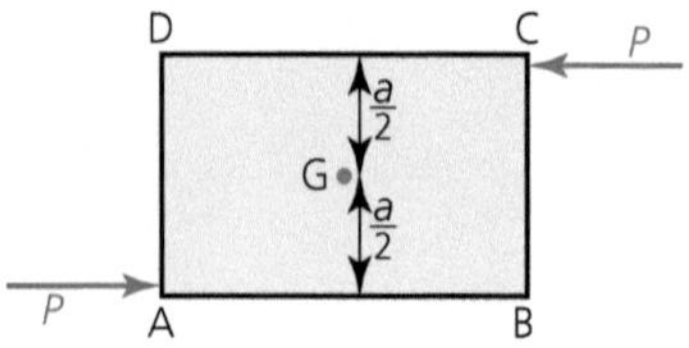

Figure 4.10

In Chapter 2 you saw that an object is in equilibrium if the resultant force on the object is zero. This definition is adequate provided all the forces act through the same point on the object. However, when the forces act at different points, there may be an overall moment even though their resultant is zero. Figure 4.10 shows a tray on a smooth surface being pushed equally hard at opposite corners.

The resultant force on the tray is clearly zero, but the resultant moment about its centre point, G, is

$$P \times \frac{a}{2} + P \times \frac{a}{2} = Pa$$

Note

You could have taken moments about any of the corners, A, B, C or D, or any other point in the plane of the paper and the answer would have been the same, *Pa* anticlockwise.

The tray will start to rotate about its centre and so it is clearly not in equilibrium.

So you now need to tighten the mathematical definition of equilibrium to include moments. For an object to remain at rest (or moving at constant velocity) when a system of forces is applied, both the resultant force and the total moment must be zero.

To check that an object is in equilibrium under the action of a system of forces, you need to check two things:

(i) that the resultant force is zero

(ii) that the resultant moment about any point is zero. (You only need to check one point.)

Another way of saying the resultant moment is zero is clockwise moments = anticlockwise moments.

Example 4.1

A three metre uniform rod AB of mass 10 kg is hinged at one end to a vertical wall. The other end is attached to a vertical cable. A block of mass 15 kg is resting on the rod 2 m from the wall.

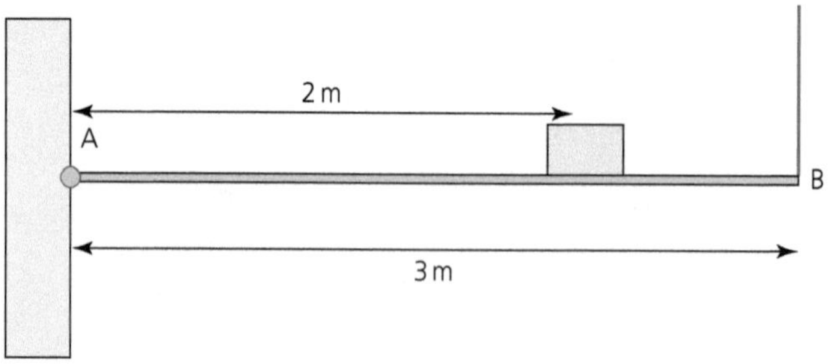

Figure 4.11

(i) Find the tension in the cable.

(ii) Find the magnitude and direction of the force exerted by the hinge on the rod.

Solution

(i) The forces acting on the rod are shown in Figure 4.12.

The force exerted by the hinge could be in any direction.

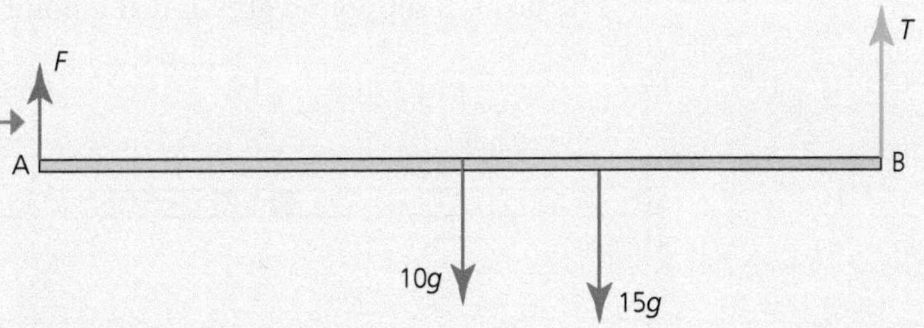

Figure 4.12

The rod is in equilibrium, so the total moment about any point is zero.

Choose A to eliminate F from the moment equation.

Take moments about A.

$$F \times 0 + 10g \times 1.5 + 15g \times 2 - T \times 3 = 0$$

As F goes through A

The rod is uniform so the mass is at the centre of the rod.

This gives

$$15g + 30g - 3T = 0$$

$$\Rightarrow \quad T = 15g = 147\,\text{N}$$

The tension in the cable is 147 N.

(ii) The rod is in equilibrium so the resultant of the forces acting on it is zero. This means that the force exerted by the hinge must be vertically upwards.

$$F + T - 10g - 15g = 0$$

$$F = 25g - T$$

Substituting for T now gives

$$F = 25g - 15g = 10g$$

$$= 98\,\text{N}$$

The force at the hinge has magnitude 98 N and is in same direction as T.

Note

The reaction force at a hinge may act in any direction, according to the forces elsewhere in the system. A hinge can be visualised in cross-section, as shown in Figure 4.13. If the hinge is well oiled, and the friction between the inner and outer parts is negligible, the hinge cannot exert any moment. In this situation the rod is said to be 'freely hinged'.

Contact may occur anywhere inside this circle.

Figure 4.13

Example 4.2

A uniform plank AB of length 1.2 m and mass 5 kg carries 2 particles. One is of mass 2 kg and lies at C, 40 cm from A. The other is at B and is of mass 1 kg.

The plank is supported at A and at a point D, 20 cm from B.

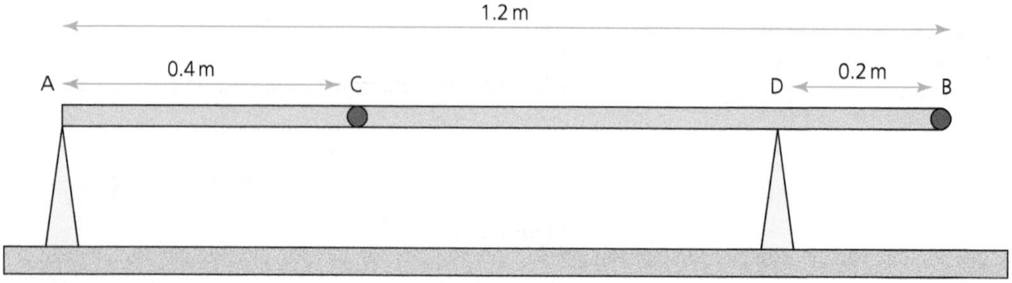

Figure 4.14

Find the reaction forces acting on the plank.

Solution

Figure 4.15 shows the forces acting on the plank.

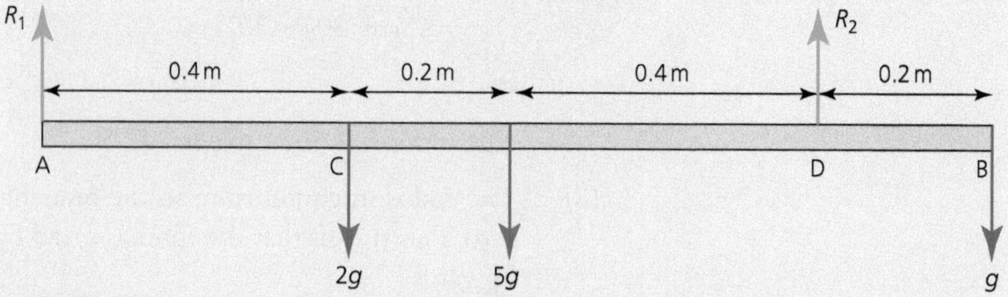

Figure 4.15

For the plank to be in equilibrium, both the resultant force and the total moment about any point must be zero.

All the forces act vertically.

$2g + 5g + g$

$$R_1 + R_2 - 8g = 0 \quad ①$$

A is chosen so that the number of unknowns in the equation is minimised.

Taking moments about the point A gives

R_1 passes through A.

$$R_1 \times 0 + 2g \times 0.4 + 5g \times 0.6 - R_2 \times 1 + g \times 1.2 = 0 \quad ②$$

The plank is uniform so the mass is at its centre.

② reduces to $0.8g + 3g - R_2 + 1.2g = 0$

$\Rightarrow$ $R_2 = 5g = 49\,\text{N}$

Substitute in ① to give

$$R_1 = 8g - R_2 = 3g$$

$$= 29.4\,\text{N}$$

The reaction forces on the plank at A and D are 29.4 N and 49 N.

Note

1. You cannot solve this problem without taking moments.
2. You can take moments about any point and can, for example, show that by taking moments about B you get the same answer.
3. The whole weight of the plank is being considered to act at its centre.
4. When a force acts through the point about which moments are being taken, its moment about that point is zero.

Levers

A lever can be used to lift or move a heavy object using a relatively small force. Levers depend on moments for their action.

Two common lever configurations are shown in Figures 4.16 and 4.17. In both cases, a load W is being lifted by an applied force F, using a lever of length l. The calculations assume equilibrium.

Case 1

The fulcrum is within the lever, Figure 4.16.

Note

This is a class 1 lever.

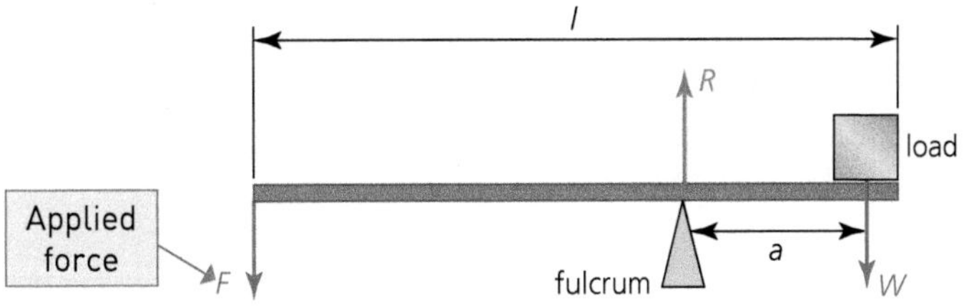

Figure 4.16

Taking moments about the fulcrum:

$$F \times (l - a) - W \times a = 0$$

$$F = W \times \frac{a}{l-a}$$

Provided that the fulcrum is nearer the end with the load, the applied force is less than the load.

Examples of class 1 levers are see-saws, crowbars and scissors.

Case 2

The fulcrum is at one end of the lever, Figure 4.17.

Note

This is a class 2 lever.

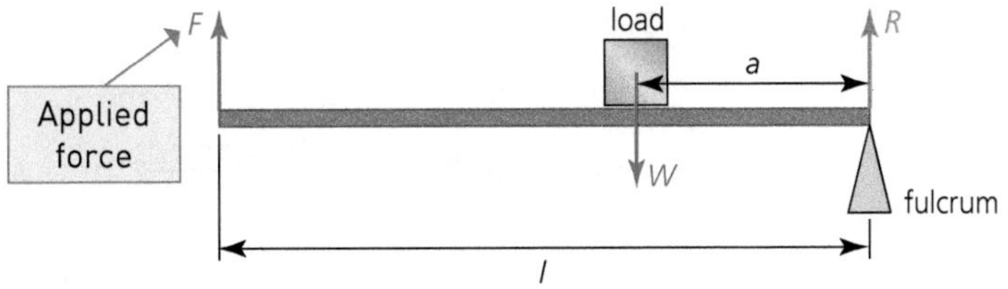

Figure 4.17

Taking moments about the fulcrum:

$$F \times l - W \times a = 0$$

$$F = W \times \frac{a}{l}$$

Since a is much smaller than l, the applied force F is much smaller than the load W.

Examples of class 2 levers include wheelbarrows, nutcrackers or bottle openers.

These examples also indicate how to find a single force equivalent to two parallel forces. The force equivalent to F and W should be equal and opposite to R and with the same line of action.

Example 4.3

Describe the single force equivalent to P and Q in each of these cases.

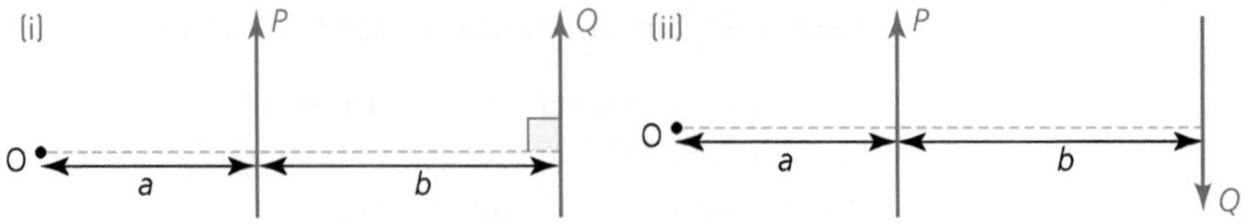

Figure 4.18

In each case state its magnitude and line of action.

Solution

The resultant of the two forces P and Q is a force of magnitude $P + Q$ pointing upwards.

The total moment about O of P and Q is equal to $P \times a + Q \times (a+b)$.

Replacing P and Q by a single force $(P + Q)$ requires placing it at a distance x from O, such that $(P+Q)x = Pa + Q(a+b)$ leading to $x = \frac{Pa + Q(a+b)}{P+Q}$.

(i)

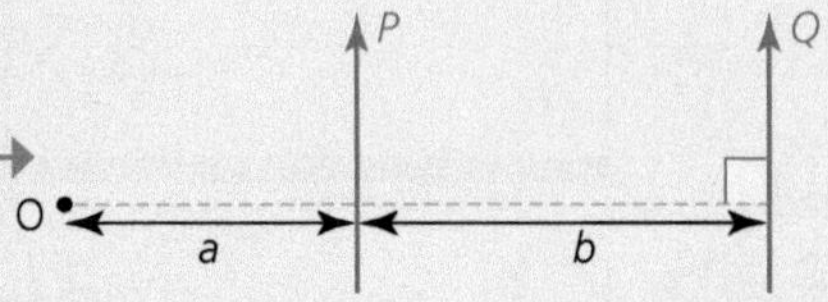

Figure 4.19

The single force equivalent to P and Q is shown in Figure 4.20.

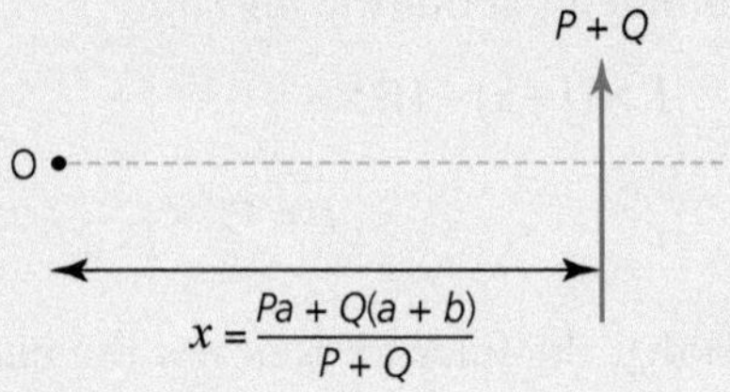

Figure 4.20

(ii)

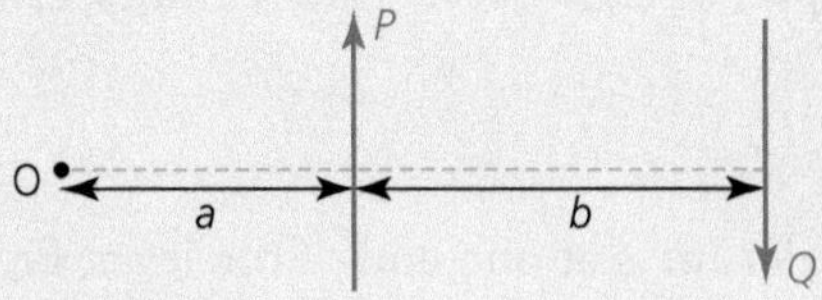

Figure 4.21

The magnitude of the resultant of the two forces P and Q is $(P-Q)$. If $P > Q$ the resultant acts upwards; if $P < Q$ it acts downwards.

Replacing P and Q by a single force $P - Q$ requires placing it at distance y from O such that $(P-Q)y = Pa - Q(a+b)$

The single force equivalent to P and Q is the force $P - Q$ pointing upwards and distance $\frac{Pa - Q(a+b)}{P-Q}$ from O.

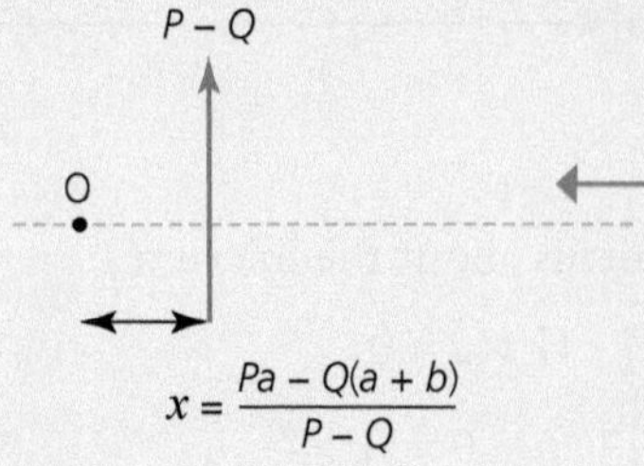

Figure 4.22

Notice that if $x < 0$, the line of action of the single resultant force is to the left of O.

Discussion point

The stays on a sailing boat are taut wires fastened to the top of the mast(s) and the hull of the boat. Why are they needed?

Figure 4.23

Exercise 4.1

① In each of the situations shown here, find the moment of the force about the point and state whether it is positive (anticlockwise) or negative (clockwise).

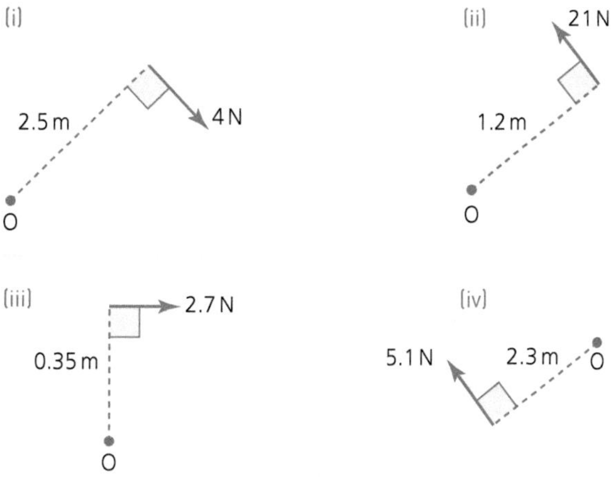

Figure 4.24

② The situations below involve several forces acting on each object. For each one, find the total moment.

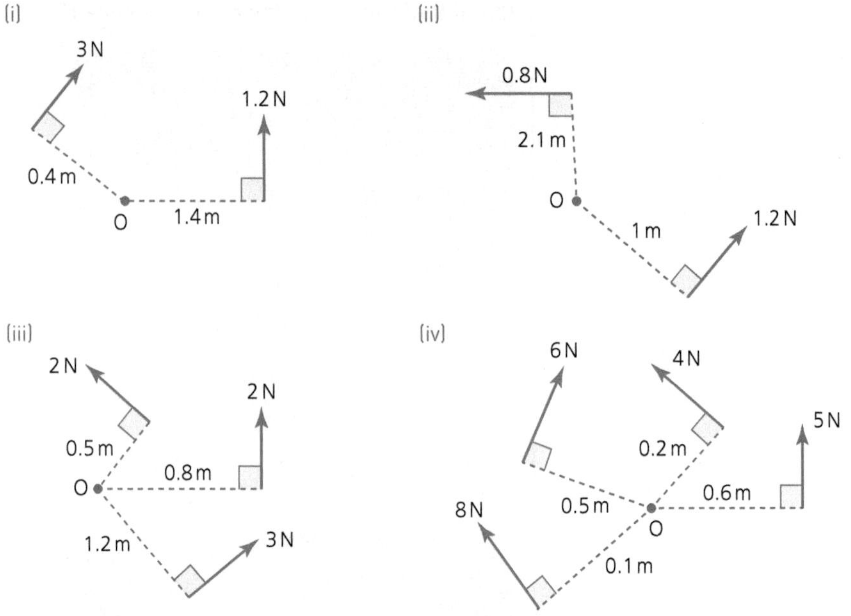

Figure 4.25

③ Each situation shows a uniform beam, of weight 50 N and length 4 m, held in equilibrium by two light inextensible strings. Find the tension in each string.

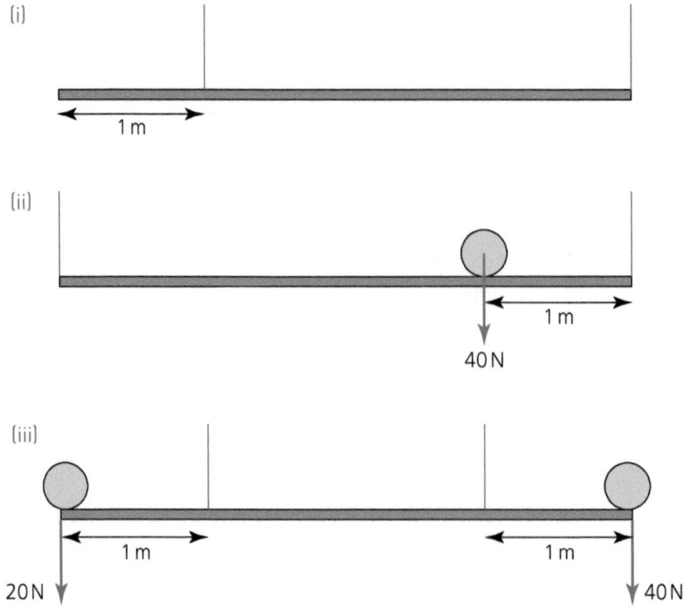

Figure 4.26

④ A uniform plank has length 6 m and mass 40 kg. It is placed on horizontal ground at the edge of a vertical river bank, so that 1.5 m of the plank is projecting over the edge, as shown in Figure 4.26.

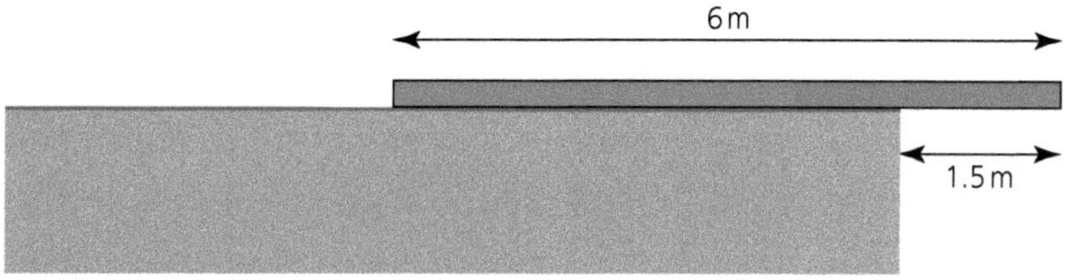

Figure 4.27

How far can a man of mass 70 kg walk along the plank without tipping it?

⑤ Two young children of mass 30 kg and 35 kg sit at the ends of a see-saw. Each child is 2.5 m from the fulcrum. Their father whose mass is 75 kg joins them. Where must he sit in order for the see-saw to balance?

⑥ A light rod, 2 m long, is hanging horizontally supported by vertical strings at each end. The maximum tension which the strings can exert is 80 N.

Along what range of positions on the rod is it safe to hang a 10 kg mass?

⑦ A sign consists of a uniform rectangular lamina of weight 50 N. It is suspended in equilibrium in a vertical plane by vertical light chains attached to the sign at the points A and B as shown in Figure 4.28.

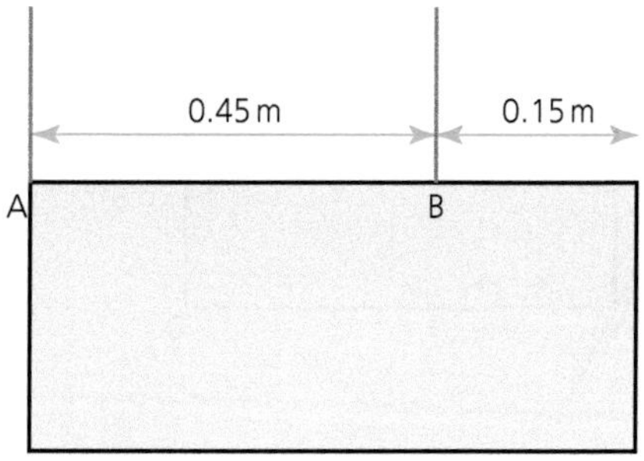

Figure 4.28

(i) Draw a diagram showing all the forces acting on the sign.

(ii) Find the tensions in the chains.

⑧ A non-uniform beam AB of length 1.6 m and weight 20 N has its centre of mass at a point 0.6 m from A. The rod is suspended by two light inextensible strings, one attached to A and the other to B. The rod is in equilibrium in a horizontal position with the strings vertical. Find the tensions in the strings.

⑨ AB represents a uniform shelf of weight 30 N which is supported at X and Y. Blocks are placed along the shelf as shown in Figure 4.29.

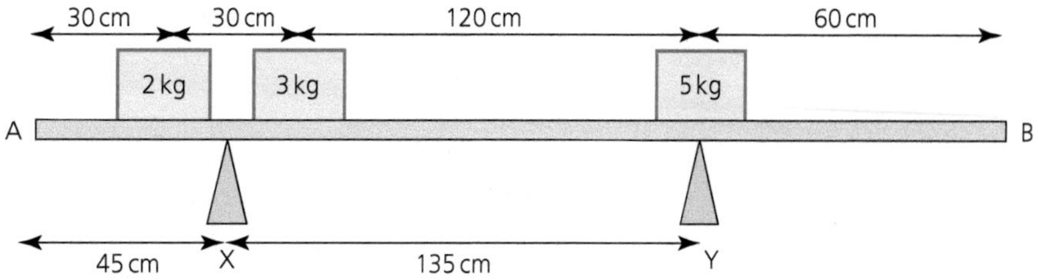

Figure 4.29

(i) Find the reaction forces of the supports on the shelf at X and Y.

(ii) What is the greatest mass of an object which can be placed at B without the shelf tipping?

⑩ A uniform plank 9 m long of mass 80 kg is horizontal. It is supported by vertical strings attached at 1 m and 8 m from one end.

What is the mass of an object which should be placed on one end, so that

(i) the tension in one string just vanishes

(ii) the tension in one string is double the tension in the other?

⑪ In Figure 4.30, Y is the resultant force of the 2 forces X N and 4 N acting at P and Q respectively. Find X and Y.

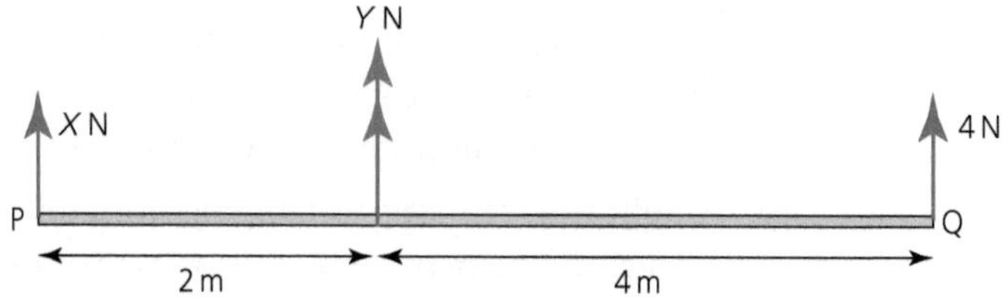

Figure 4.30

⑫ A sign consists of a uniform rectangular lamina ABCD of mass 30 kg. It is freely hinged to a sloping wall at A and kept in equilibrium in a vertical plane by a horizontal rod at B, as shown in Figure 4.31.

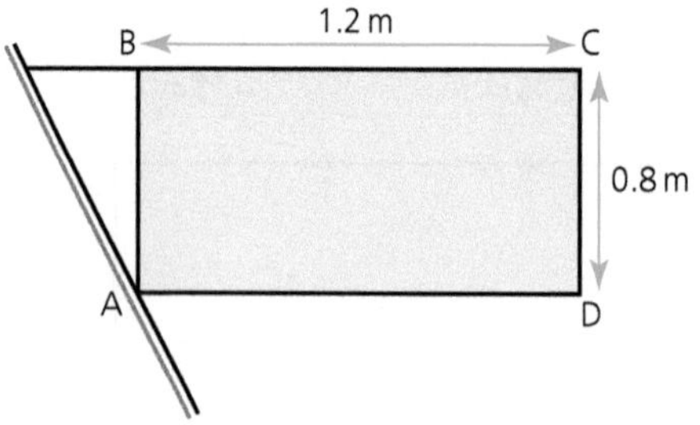

Figure 4.31

(i) Find the tension in the rod.

(ii) A basket of flowers of mass 5 kg is hung vertically from the sign at D. Find the new value of the tension in the rod.

⑬ Find the magnitude, direction and line of action of the resultant of this system of forces.

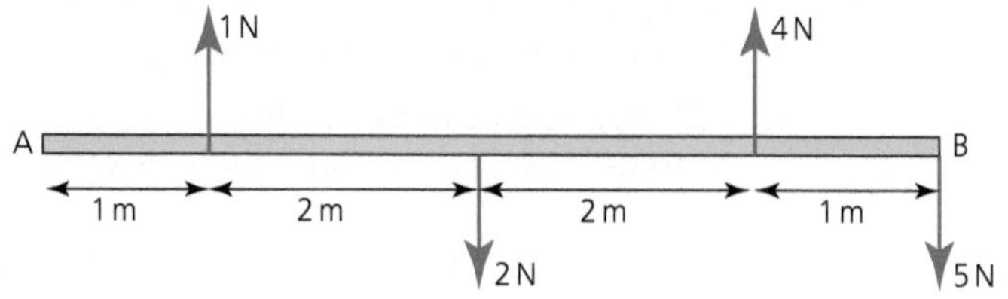

Figure 4.32

⑭ A rigid rod AB, of mass 10 kg and length 3 m, whose centre of mass is 125 cm from A, is suspended horizontally by two vertical strings attached to points C and D, 50 cm from each end. Each string could just support the weight of the rod. Particles of mass m_1 kg and m_2 kg are placed at A and B respectively.

(i) Show that the tension in one of the strings is

$(15 - m_1 + 5m_2)\frac{g}{4}$ and find the tension in the other string.

(ii) Find the values of m_1 and m_2 when both the strings are on the point of breaking.

2 The moment of a force which acts at an angle

Note that this content (pages 83–93) relates to the year 2 A Level specification

EXPERIMENT

Set up the apparatus shown in Figure 4.33 and experiment with two or more weights in different positions. Record your results in a table showing weights, distances from O and moments about O.

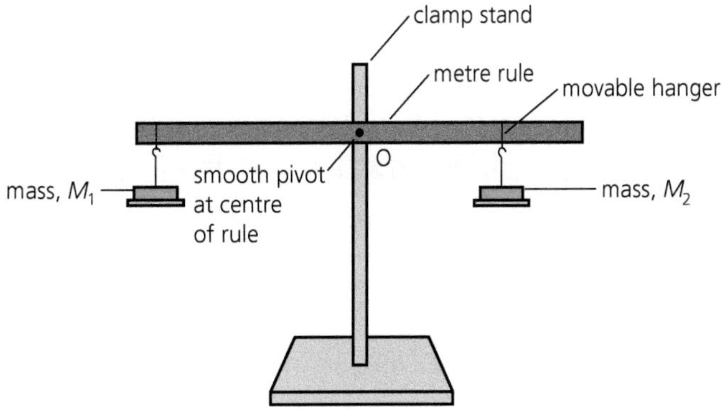

Figure 4.33

Two masses are suspended from the rule in such a way that the rule balances in a horizontal position. What happens when the rule is then moved to an incline position and released?

Now attach a pulley, as in Figure 4.34. Start with equal weights and measured d and l. Then try different weights and pulley positions.

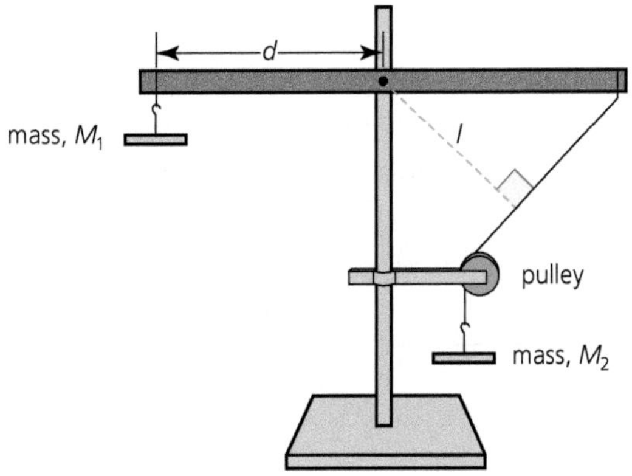

Figure 4.34

From the experiment, you will have seen that the moment of a force about the pivot depends on the **perpendicular distance** from the pivot to the line of the force.

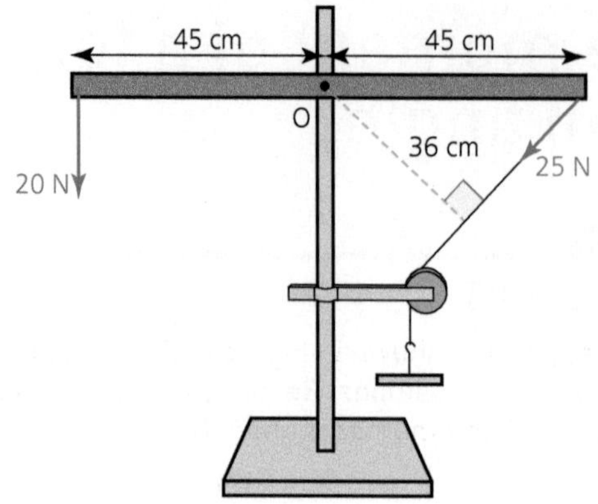

Figure 4.35

In Figure 4.35, where the system remains at rest, the moment about O of the 20 N force is $20 \times 0.45 = 9$ N m. The moment about O of the 25 N force is $-25 \times 0.36 = -9$ N m. The system is in equilibrium even though unequal forces act at equal distances from the pivot.

The magnitude of the moment of the force F about O in Figure 4.36 is given by

$$F \times l = Fd \sin \alpha$$

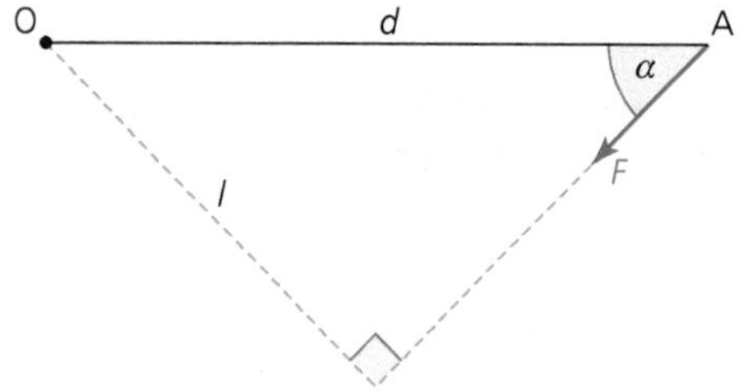

Figure 4.36

Alternatively, the moment can be found by noting that the force F can be resolved into components $F \cos \alpha$ parallel to AO and $F \sin \alpha$ perpendicular to AO, both acting through A (Figure 4.37). The moment of each component can be found and then summed to give the total moment.

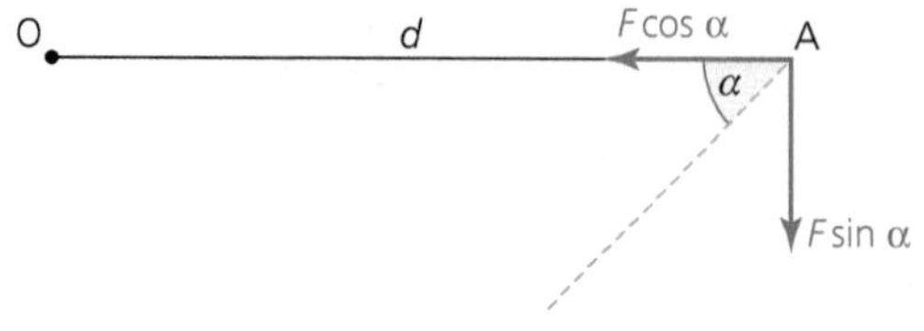

Figure 4.37

The moment of the component along AO is zero because it acts through O. The magnitude of the moment of the perpendicular component is $F \sin \alpha \times d$ so the total moment is $Fd \sin \alpha$, as expected.

Example 4.4

A force of 40 N is exerted on a rod as shown. Find the moment of the force about the point marked O.

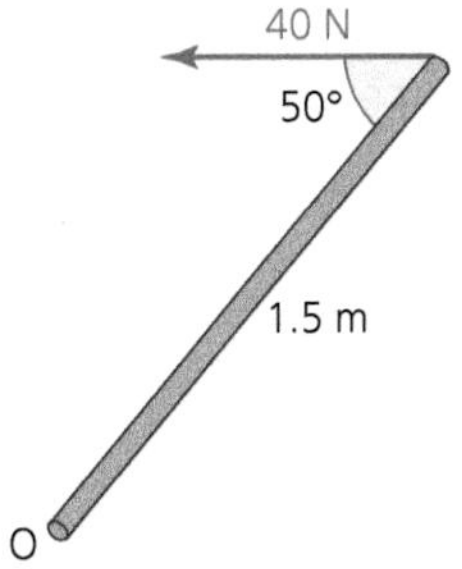

Figure 4.38

Solution

In order to calculate the moment, the perpendicular distance between O and the line of action of the force must be found. This is shown on Figure 4.39.

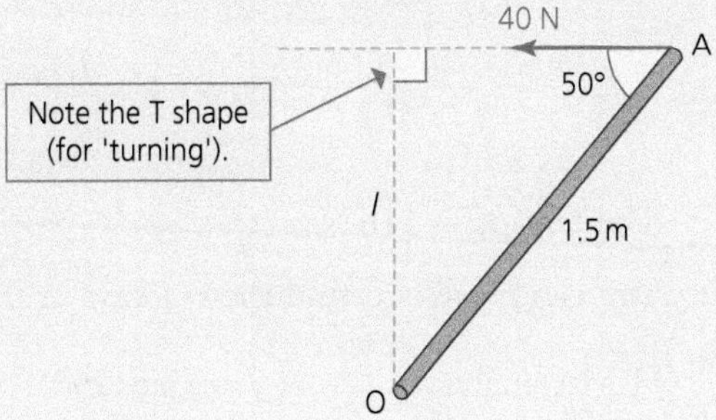

Figure 4.39

Here $l = 1.5 \times \sin 50°$.

So the moment about O is

$$F \times l = 40 \times (1.5 \times \sin 50°)$$

$$= 46.0\,\text{N m}$$

Alternatively, you can resolve the 40 N force into components as in Figure 4.40.

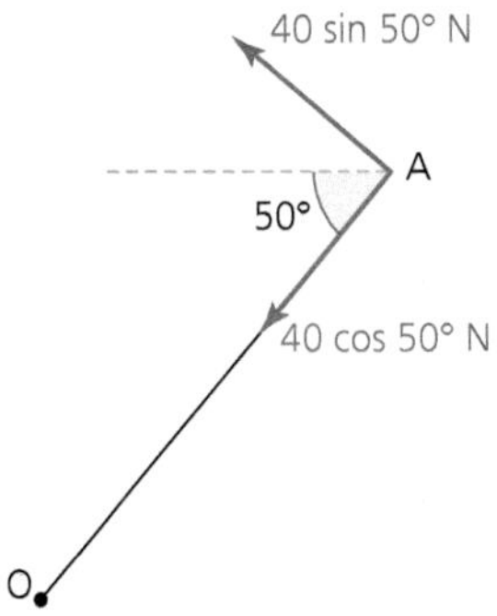

Figure 4.40

The component of the force parallel to AO is $40 \cos 50°$ N. The component perpendicular to AO is N (or $40 \cos 40°$ N).

So the moment about O is

$$40 \sin 50° \times 1.5 = 60 \sin 50°$$

$$= 46.0\,\text{N m}$$

Example 4.5

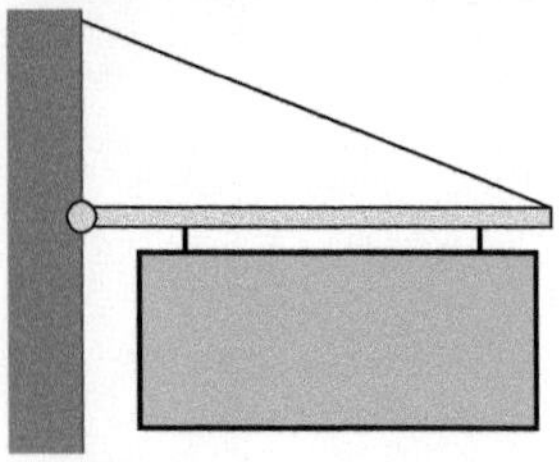

Figure 4.41

A sign is attached to a light rod of length 1 m which is freely hinged to the wall and supported in a vertical plane by a light string, as in Figure 4.41.

The sign is assumed to be a uniform rectangle of mass 10 kg. The angle of the string to the horizontal is 25°.

(i) Find the tension in the string.

(ii) Find the magnitude and direction of the reaction force of the hinge on the sign.

You can see that R_H must point to the right by considering horizontal components of force, and you can see that R_V must be upwards by considering moments about A. However, if you get the direction wrong, it does not greatly matter – you will simply get a negative answer.

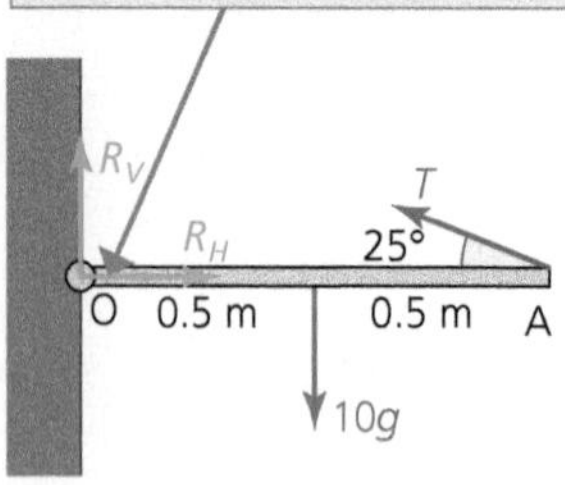

Figure 4.42

Discussion point

In Figure 4.42 the vertical component of the force at O has been marked as upwards. Why has this been done?

Discussion point

Is it by chance that R and T have the same magnitude and act at the same angle to the horizontal?

Solution

(i) Figure 4.42 shows the forces acting on the rod OA, where R_H and R_V are the magnitudes of the horizontal and vertical components of the reaction **R** on the rod at the wall.

Taking moments about O:

$$0 \times R_V + 0 \times R_H - 10g \times 0.5 + T\sin 25° \times 1 = 0$$

$$\Rightarrow \quad T\sin 25° = 5g$$

$$T = 116 \text{ (to 3 s.f.)}$$

The tension is 116 N.

(ii) You can resolve to find the reaction at the wall.

Horizontally: $R_H = T\cos 25°$

$$\Rightarrow \quad R_H = 105$$

Vertically: $R_V + T\sin 25° = 10g$

$$\Rightarrow \quad R_V = 10g - 5g = 49$$

$$R = \sqrt{105^2 + 49^2}$$

$$= 116$$

$$\tan\theta = \frac{49}{105}$$

$\theta = 25°$ (to the nearest degree)

The reaction at the hinge has magnitude 116 N and acts at 25° above the horizontal.

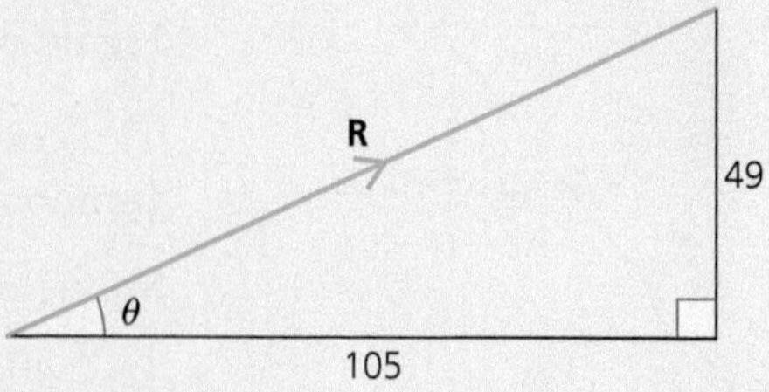

Figure 4.43

Example 4.6

A uniform ladder is standing on rough ground and leaning against a smooth wall at an angle of 60° to the ground. The ladder has length 4 m and mass 15 kg. Find the normal contact forces at the wall and ground and the friction force at the ground.

Solution

Figure 4.44 shows the forces acting on the ladder. The forces are in newtons.

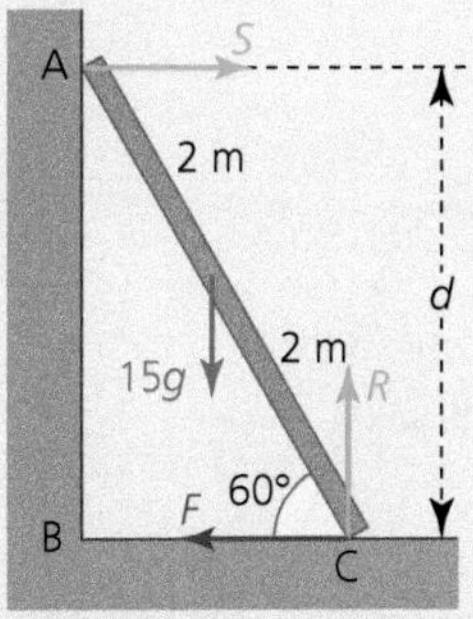

$d = AB = 4 \sin 60°$ m
$BC = 4 \cos 60°$ m
$\frac{1}{2}BC = 2 \cos 60°$ m

Figure 4.44

The diagram shows that there are three unknown forces S, R and F so you need three equations from which to find them. If the ladder remains at rest (in equilibrium), then the resultant force is zero and the resultant moment is zero.

These two conditions provide the three necessary equations.

Equilibrium of horizontal components: $S - F = 0$ ①

Equilibrium of vertical components: $R - 15g = 0$ ②

Taking moments about the foot of the ladder means that there are only two moments to consider because the forces F and R both act through the foot of the ladder and so have zero moment.

Moments about the foot of the ladder:

$$R \times 0 + F \times 0 + 15g \times 2\cos 60° - S \times 4 \sin 60° = 0$$

$$\Rightarrow \quad 147 - 4S \sin 60° = 0$$

$$\Rightarrow \quad S = \frac{147}{4 \sin 60°} = 42.4 \text{ (to 3 s.f.)}$$

From ① $F = S = 42.4$

From ② $R = 147$

The force at the wall is 42.4 N, and those at the ground are 42.4 N horizontally and 147 N vertically.

Exercise 4.2

① Find the moment about O of each of the forces illustrated below.

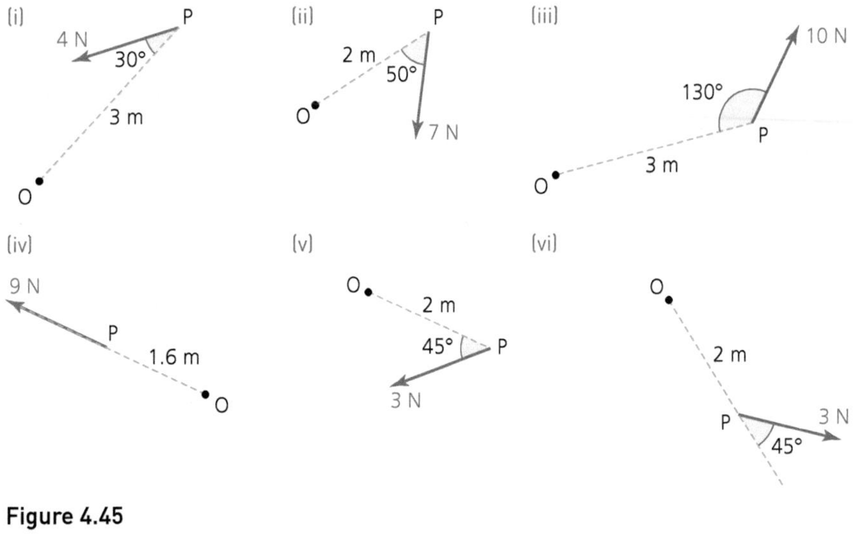

Figure 4.45

② Figure 4.46 shows three children pushing a playground roundabout. Hannah and David want it to go one way but Rabina wants it to go the other way. Who wins?

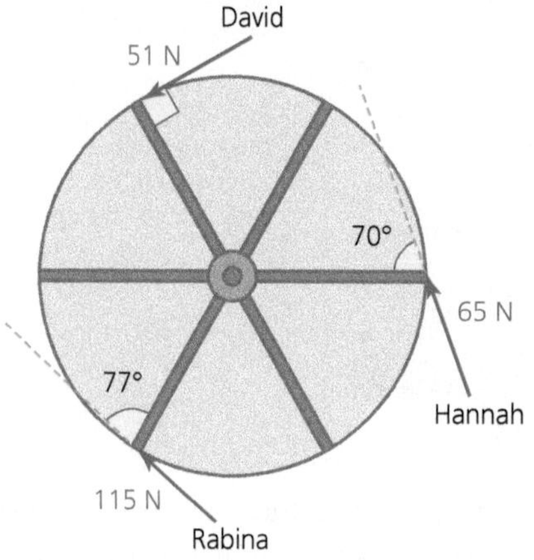

Figure 4.46

③ The operating instructions for a small crane specify that when the jib is at an angle of 25° above the horizontal, the maximum safe load for the crane is 5000 kg. Assuming that this maximum load is determined by the maximum moment that the pivot can support, what is the maximum safe load when the angle between the jib and the horizontal is

(i) 40°

(ii) an angle θ?

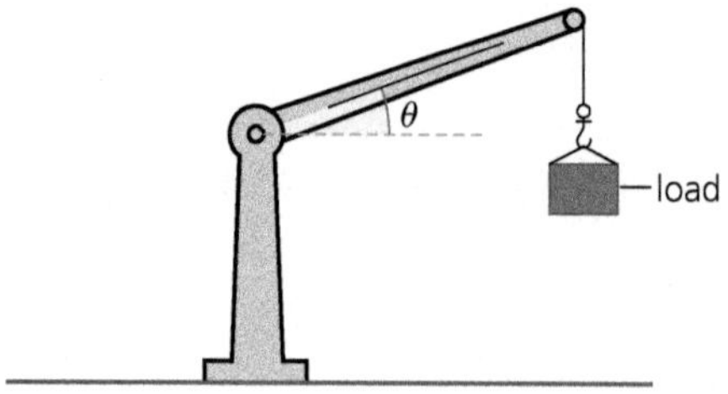

Figure 4.47

④ In each of these diagrams within Figure 4.48, a uniform beam of mass 5 kg and length 4 m, freely hinged at one end, A, is in equilibrium. Find the magnitude of the force T in each case.

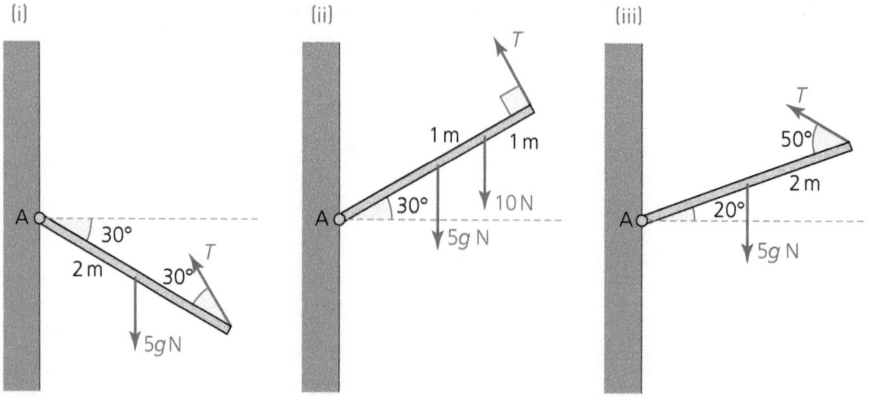

Figure 4.48

⑤ Figure 4.49 shows a uniform rectangular sign ABCD, 3 m × 2 m, of weight 20 N. It is freely hinged at A and supported by the string CE, which makes an angle of 30° with the horizontal. The tension in the string is T (in N).

(i) Resolve the tension T into horizontal and vertical components.

(ii) Hence show that the moment of the tension in the string about A is given by $2T\cos 30° + 3T\sin 30°$.

(iii) Write down the moment of the sign's weight about A.

(iv) Hence show that $T = 9.28$.

(v) Hence find the horizontal and vertical components of the reaction on the sign at the hinge, A.

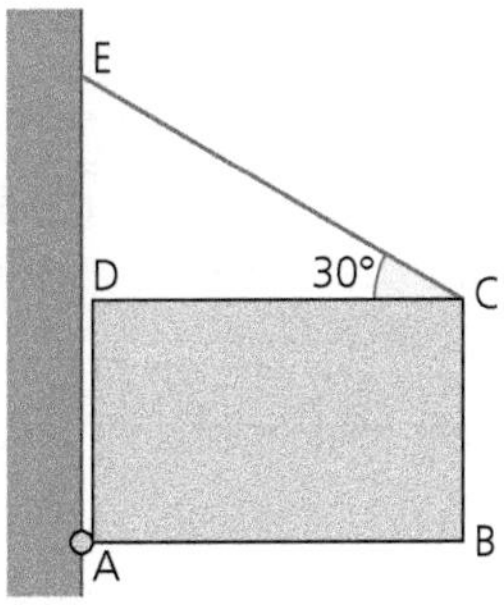

Figure 4.49

You can also find the moment of the tension in the string about A as $d \times T$, where d is the length of AF as shown in Figure 4.50.

(vi) Find

(a) the angle ACD

(b) the length d.

(vii) Show that you get the same value for T when it is calculated in this way.

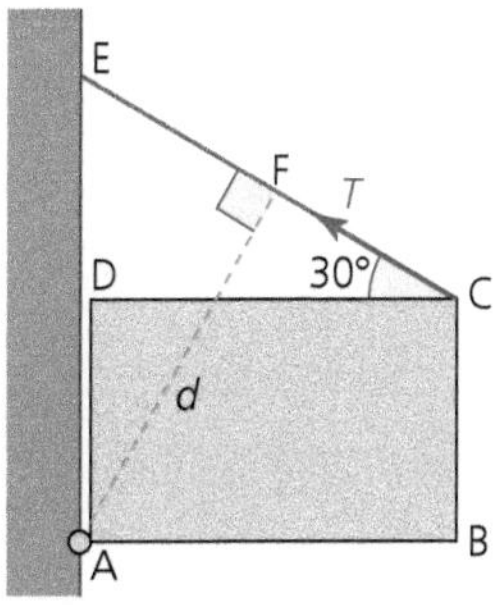

Figure 4.50

⑥ Figure 4.51 shows a simple crane supporting a 50 kg mass. The weight of the jib (AB) may be ignored. The crane is in equilibrium in the position shown.

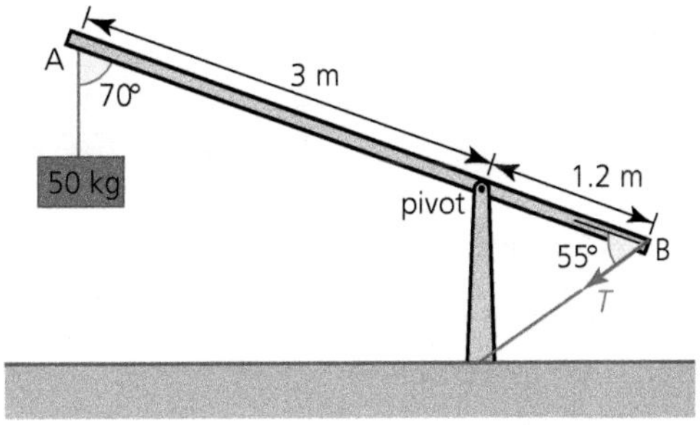

Figure 4.51

(i) By taking moments about the pivot, find the magnitude of the tension T (in N).

(ii) Find the reaction of the pivot on the jib in the form of components parallel and perpendicular to the jib.

Chapter 4 Moments of forces

(iii) Show that the total moment about the end A of the forces acting on the jib is zero.

(iv) What would happen if

(a) the rope holding the 50 kg mass snapped?

(b) the rope with tension T snapped?

⑦ A uniform plank, AB, of mass 50 kg and length 6 m is in equilibrium leaning against a smooth wall at an angle of 60° to the horizontal. The lower end, A, is on rough horizontal ground.

(i) Draw a diagram showing all the forces acting on the plank.

(ii) Write down the total moment about A of all the forces acting on the plank.

(iii) Find the normal contact force of the wall on the plank at point B.

(iv) Find the frictional force on the foot of the plank. What can you deduce about the coefficient of friction between the ground and the plank?

(v) Show that the total moment about B of all the forces acting on the plank is zero.

⑧ A uniform ladder of mass 20 kg and length $2l$ rests in equilibrium with its upper end against a smooth vertical wall and its lower end on a rough horizontal floor. The coefficient of friction between the ladder and the floor is μ. The normal contact force at the wall is S, the frictional force at the ground is F and the normal contact force at the ground is R. The ladder makes an angle α with the horizontal.

(i) Draw a diagram showing the forces acting on the ladder.

For each of the cases

(a) $\alpha = 60°$ (b) $\alpha = 45°$

(ii) find the magnitudes of S, F and R

(iii) find the least possible value of μ.

⑨ Figure 4.52 shows a car's handbrake. The force F is exerted by the hand in operating the brake, and this creates a tension T in the brake cable. The handbrake is freely pivoted at point B and is assumed to be light.

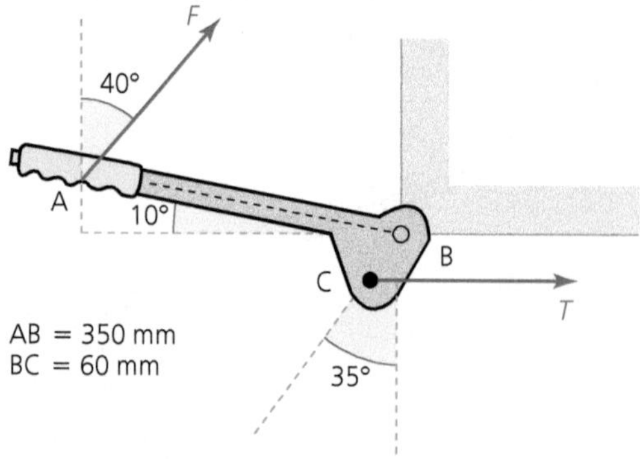

Figure 4.52

(i) Draw a diagram showing all the forces acting on the handbrake.

(ii) What is the required magnitude of force F if the tension in the brake cable is to be 1000 N?

(iii) A child applies the handbrake with a force of 10 N. What is the tension in the brake cable?

⑩ Figure 4.53 shows four tugs manoeuvring a ship. A and C are pushing it, B and D are pulling it.

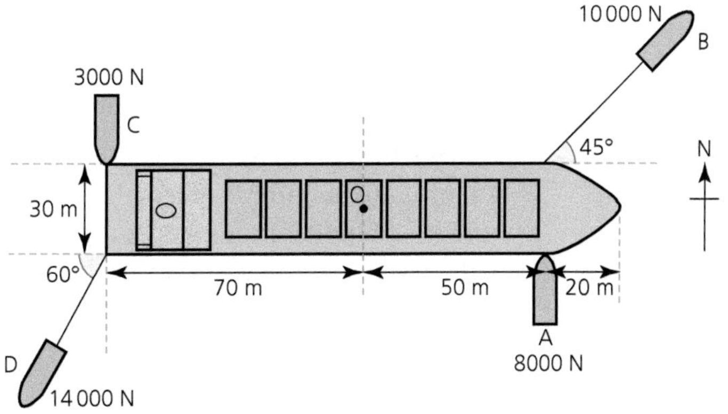

Figure 4.53

(i) Show that the resultant force on the ship is less than 100 N.

(ii) Find the overall turning moment on the ship about its centre point, O.

A breeze starts to blow from the south, causing a total force of 2000 N to act uniformly along the length of the ship, at right angles to it.

(iii) Assuming B and D continue to apply the same forces, how tugs A and C counteract the sideways force on the ship by altering the forces with which they are pushing, while maintaining the same overall moment about the centre of the ship?

⑪ Jules is cleaning windows. Her ladder is uniform and stands on rough ground at an angle of 60° to the horizontal and with the top resting on the edge of a smooth window sill. The ladder has a mass 12 kg and length 2.8 m and Jules has mass 56 kg.

(i) Draw a diagram to show the forces on the ladder when nobody is standing on it. Show that the reaction at the sill is then $3g$ N.

(ii) Find the friction and normal contact forces at the foot of the ladder.

Jules needs to be sure that the ladder will not slip however high she climbs.

(iii) Find the least possible value of μ for the ladder to be safe at 60° to the horizontal.

(iv) The value of μ is in fact 0.4. How far up the ladder can Jules stand before it begins to slip?

⑫ A uniform horizontal beam AB of length 2 m and mass 8 kg is attached to a vertical wall at A. It is supported by a light strut CM which is attached to the middle of the beam M and to the wall at C below the beam, as shown in Figure 4.54. The strut makes an angle of 45° with the beam.

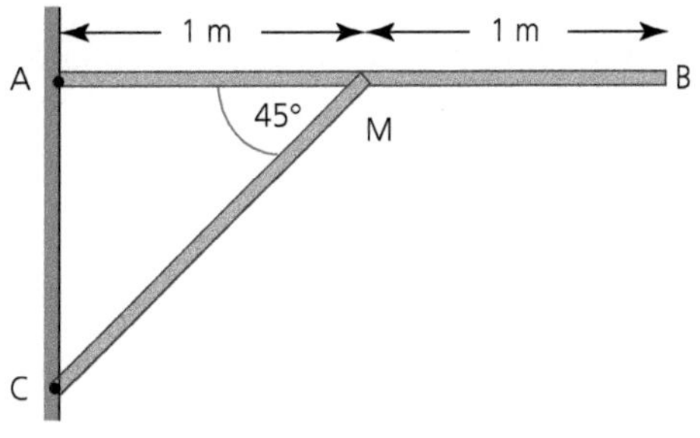

Figure 4.54

(i) Draw a diagram showing all the forces acting on the beam.

(ii) Find the magnitude of the force in the strut.

The beam is now loaded with an object of mass of 50 kg which hangs vertically from B. In this new situation, calculate

(iii) the magnitude of the force in the strut,

(iv) the magnitude and direction of the force on the beam at A.

⑬ A non-uniform rod AB of length 1.6 m and weight 20 N has its centre of mass at a point 0.6 m from A. It rests in equilibrium in a horizontal position with end A against a rough vertical wall. It is kept in equilibrium by a light inextensible string attached to B which makes an angle of 30° with the horizontal, as shown in Figure 4.55.

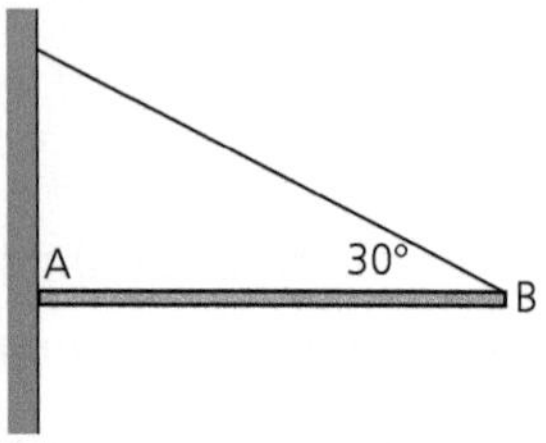

Figure 4.55

(i) Find the tension in the string.

(ii) Find the minimum value of the coefficient of friction between the rod and the wall for equilibrium to be possible.

⑭ A uniform rod AB of length 6 m and weight 2000 N is hung from a point O by two light wires, each of length 5 m, attached to each end of the rod. A weight of 500 N is placed at a point C, 2 m from B. The tension in wire AO is T_1 and that in wire BO is T_2. The rod rests in equilibrium at an angle θ to the horizontal. The point X is directly below O and M is the midpoint of the rod.

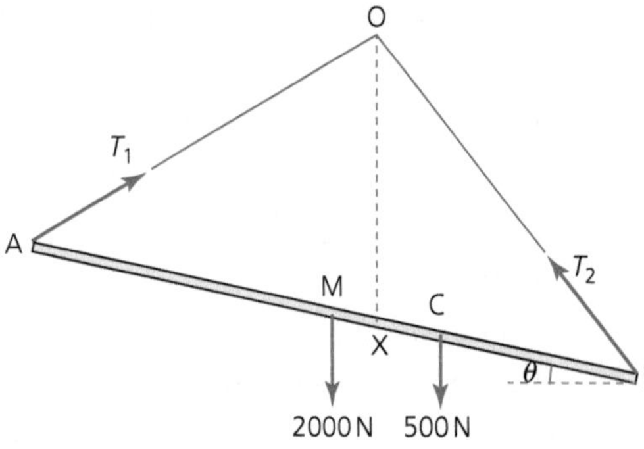

Figure 4.56

(i) By taking moments about O, find the distances MX and XC.

(ii) Find the angle θ.

(iii) By taking moments about each end of the rod, show that the ratio of the tensions in the wires is $T_1 : T_2 = 7:8$ and use this to find T_1 and T_2.

⑮ Figure 4.57 shows a uniform ladder AB of mass m and length $2l$ resting in equilibrium with its upper end A against a smooth vertical wall and its lower end B on a smooth inclined plane. The inclined plane makes an angle θ with the horizontal and the ladder makes an angle ϕ with the wall. What is the relationship between θ and ϕ?

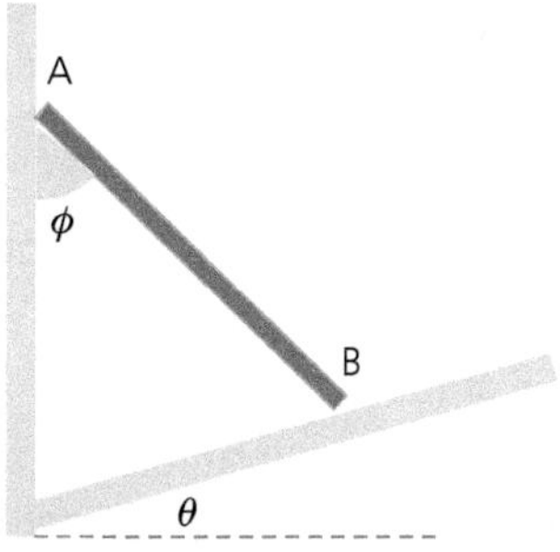

Figure 4.57

⑯ A uniform ladder of length 8 m and weight 180 N rests against a smooth, vertical wall and stands on a rough, horizontal surface. A woman of weight 720 N stands on the ladder so that her weight acts at a distance x m from its lower end as shown in Figure 4.58. The system is in equilibrium with the ladder at 20° to the vertical.

(i) Show that the frictional force between the ladder and the horizontal surface is F N, where

$$F = 90(1+x)\tan 20°$$

(ii) Deduce that F increases as x increases and hence find the values of the coefficient of friction between the ladder and the surface for which the woman can stand anywhere on the ladder without it slipping.

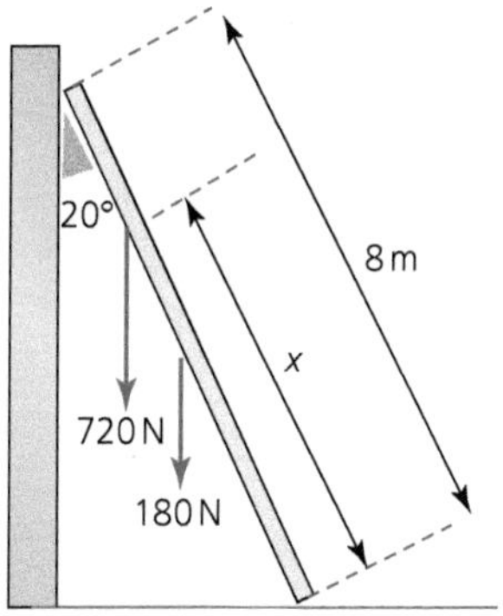

Figure 4.58

KEY POINTS

1 The moment of a force F about a point O is given by the product Fd where d is the perpendicular distance from O to the line of action of the force.

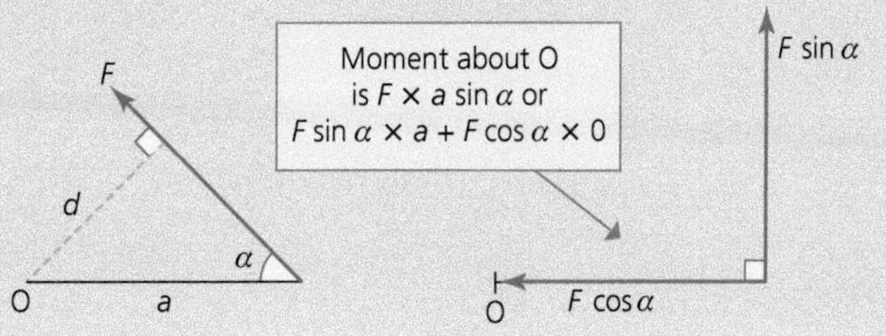

Figure 4.59

2 The S.I. unit for moment is the newton metre (N m).
3 Anticlockwise moments are usually called positive, clockwise negative.
4 If a body is in equilibrium the resultant force is zero and the sum of the moments of the forces acting on it, about any point, is zero.

LEARNING OUTCOMES

When you have completed this chapter, you should

- be able to calculate the moment about a fixed point O of a force acting on a body as the product of the force and the perpendicular distance of O from the line of action of the force or by first resolving the force into components and then finding the product of that component which does not go through O and its distance from O
- be able to find the resultant of a set of parallel forces
- know how different types of lever work
- know the meaning of the word couple
- know that an object is in equilibrium if the resultant of all the applied forces acting on it is zero and the sum of their moments about any point is also zero.

5 Work, energy and power

I like work: it fascinates me. I can sit and look at it for hours.

Jerome K. Jerome

Discussion point

Figure 5.1 shows the tidal power station at Annapolis in Nova Scotia, Canada. Where does the energy it produces come from?

Figure 5.1

1 Energy and momentum

When describing the motion of objects in everyday language the words **energy** and **momentum** are often used quite loosely and sometimes no distinction is made between them. In mechanics they must be defined precisely.

For an object of mass m moving with velocity $\mathbf{v}$:

- Kinetic energy $= \frac{1}{2}mv^2$ (this is the energy it has due to its motion)
- Momentum $= m\mathbf{v}$

v is the speed, the magnitude of the velocity; $v = |\mathbf{v}|$.

Notice that kinetic energy is a scalar quantity with magnitude only, but momentum is a vector in the same direction as the velocity.

Both the kinetic energy and the momentum are liable to change when a force acts on a body and you will learn more about how the energy is changed in this chapter. You will meet momentum again in Chapter 6.

Work and energy

In everyday life you encounter many forms of energy such as heat, light, electricity and sound. You are familiar with the conversion of one form of energy to another: from chemical energy stored in wood to heat energy when you burn it; from electrical energy to the energy of a train's motion, and so on. The S.I. unit for energy is the joule, J.

Mechanical energy and work

In mechanics, two forms of energy are particularly important.

- **Kinetic energy** is the energy which a body possesses because of its motion. The kinetic energy of a moving object equals $\frac{1}{2} \times$ mass $\times$ (speed)^2.
- **Potential energy** is the energy which a body possesses because of its position. It may be thought of as stored energy which can be converted into kinetic energy or other forms of energy. You will meet this again later in this chapter.
- The energy of an object is usually changed when it is acted on by a force. When a force is applied to an object which moves in the direction of its line of action, the force is said to do *work*.
  The work done by a constant force is equal to force $\times$ distance moved in the direction of the force.

The following examples illustrate how to use these ideas.

Example 5.1

A brick, initially at rest, is raised by a force averaging 40 N to a height of 5 m above the ground, where it is left stationary. How much work is done by the force?

Solution

The work done by the force in raising the brick is given by

$$\begin{aligned}\text{work done} &= \text{force} \times \text{distance}\\ &= 40 \times 5\\ &= 200\text{ J}\end{aligned}$$

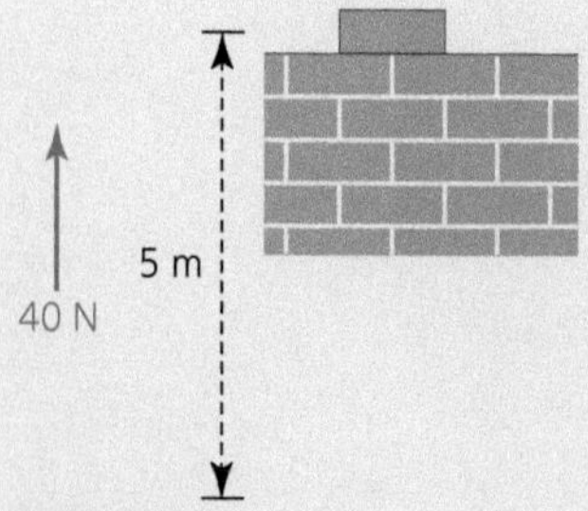

Figure 5.2

Examples 5.2 and 5.3 show how the work done by a force can be related to the change in kinetic energy of an object.

Example 5.2

A train travelling on level ground is subject to a resistive force (from the brakes and air resistance) of 250 kN for a distance of 5 km. How much kinetic energy does the train lose?

Note

Work and energy have the same units.

Solution

The forward force is −250 000 N.

The work done by it is −250 000 × 5000 = −1 250 000 000 J.

So −1 250 000 000 J of kinetic energy are gained by the train. In other words, +1 250 000 000 J of kinetic energy are lost and the train slows down. This energy is converted to other forms such as heat and perhaps a little sound.

Example 5.3

A car of mass m kg is travelling at $u\,\text{m s}^{-1}$ when the driver applies a constant driving force F N. The ground is level and the road is straight and resistance to motion can be ignored. The speed of the car increases to $v\,\text{m s}^{-1}$ in a period of t s over a distance of s m. Show that the change in kinetic energy of the car is equal to the work done by the driving force.

Solution

Treating the car as a particle and applying Newton's second law:

$$F = ma$$

$$a = \frac{F}{m}$$

Since F is assumed constant, the acceleration is constant also. So, using the constant acceleration equation $v^2 = u^2 + 2as$:

$$v^2 = u^2 + \frac{2Fs}{m}$$

$$\Rightarrow \frac{1}{2}mv^2 = \frac{1}{2}mu^2 + Fs$$

$$Fs = \frac{1}{2}mv^2 - \frac{1}{2}mu^2$$

change in kinetic energy

⇒ work done by force = final kinetic energy − initial kinetic energy of the car.

Note

This is an important result given in symbols and in words.

The work–energy principle

Examples 5.4 and 5.5 illustrate the **work–energy principle** which states that:

> The total work done by the forces acting on a body is equal to the increase in the kinetic energy of the body.

Example 5.4

A sledge of total mass 30 kg, initially moving at $2\,\mathrm{m\,s^{-1}}$, is pulled 14 m across smooth horizontal ice by a horizontal rope in which there is a constant tension of 45 N. Find its final velocity.

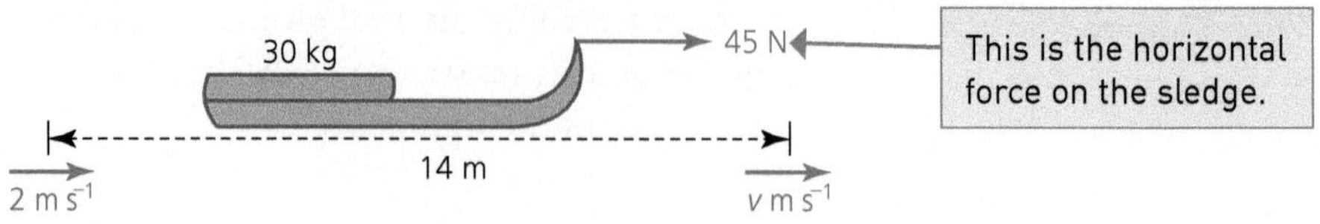

Figure 5.3

Solution

Since the ice is smooth, the work done by the force is all converted into kinetic energy and the final velocity can be found by using

work done by force = final kinetic energy − initial kinetic energy

$$45 \times 14 = \frac{1}{2} \times 30 \times v^2 - \frac{1}{2} \times 30 \times 2^2$$

So $v^2 = 46$ and the final velocity of the sledge is $6.8\,\mathrm{m\,s^{-1}}$ (to 2 s.f.).

Example 5.5

The combined mass of a cyclist and her bicycle is 65 kg. She accelerates from rest to $8\,\mathrm{m\,s^{-1}}$ in 80 m along a horizontal road.

(i) Calculate the work done by the net force in accelerating the cyclist and her bicycle.

(ii) Hence calculate the net forward force (assuming the force to be constant).

Solution

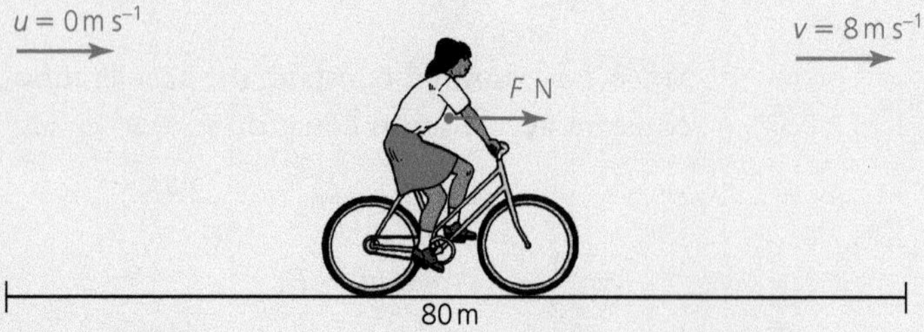

Figure 5.4

(i) The work done by the net force F is given by

work = final K.E. − initial K.E.

$$= \frac{1}{2}mv^2 - \frac{1}{2}mu^2$$

$$= \frac{1}{2} \times 65 \times 8^2 - 0$$

$$= 2080\,\mathrm{J}$$

The work done is 2080 J.

(ii) Work done $= Fs$

$$= F \times 80$$

So $80F = 2080$

$$F = 26$$

The net forward force is 26 N.

Work

It is important to realise that:

- work is done by a force
- work is only done when there is movement
- a force only does work on an object when it has a component in the direction of motion of the object.

Notice that if you stand holding a brick stationary above your head, painful though it may be, the force you are exerting on it is doing no work. Nor is the vertical force doing any work if you walk round the room holding the brick at the same height. However, once you start climbing the stairs, a component of the brick's movement is in the direction of the upward force that you are exerting on it, so the force is now doing some work.

When applying the work–energy principle, you have to be careful to include all the forces acting on the body. In the example of a brick of weight 40 N being raised 5 m vertically, starting and ending at rest, the change in kinetic energy is clearly 0.

This seems paradoxical when it is clear that the force which raised the brick has done $40 \times 5 = 200$ J of work. However, the brick was subject to another force, namely its weight, which did $-40 \times 5 = -200$ J of work on it, giving a total of $200 + (-200) = 0$ J.

Conservation of mechanical energy

The net forward force on the cyclist in Example 5.5 is her driving force minus resistive forces such as air resistance and friction in the bearings. In the absence of such resistive forces, she would gain more kinetic energy. Also the work she does against them is lost; it is dissipated as heat and sound. Contrast this with the work a cyclist does against gravity when going uphill. This work can be recovered as kinetic energy on a downhill run. The work done against the force of gravity is conserved and gives the cyclist potential energy.

Forces such as friction which result in the dissipation of mechanical energy are called **dissipative forces**. Forces which conserve mechanical energy are called **conservative forces**. The force of gravity is a conservative force and so is the tension in an elastic string; you can test this using an elastic band.

The mechanical energy of a system is the sum of its potential energy and its kinetic energy. If there are no dissipative forces, the mechanical energy of the system is conserved.

Example 5.6

A bullet of mass 25 g is fired at a wooden barrier 3 cm thick. When it hits the barrier it is travelling at $200\,\text{m s}^{-1}$. The barrier exerts a constant resistive force of 5000 N on the bullet.

(i) Does the bullet pass through the barrier and, if so, with what speed does it emerge?

(ii) Is energy conserved in this situation?

Solution

(i) The work done **by** the force is defined as the product of the force and the distance moved **in the direction of the force.** Since the bullet is moving in the direction opposite to the net resistive force, the work done by this force is negative.

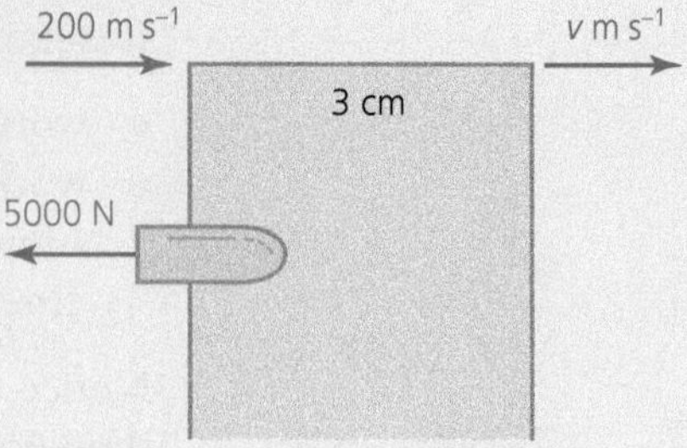

Figure 5.5

Work done $= -5000 \times 0.03$

$= -150\text{J}$

3 cm = 0.03 m

The initial kinetic energy of the bullet is

Initial K. E. $= \frac{1}{2}mu^2$

$= \frac{1}{2} \times 0.025 \times 200^2$

$= 500\text{J}$

25 g = 0.025 kg

A loss in energy of 150J will not reduce kinetic energy to zero, so the bullet will still be moving on exit.

Since the work done is equal to the change in kinetic energy,

$$-150 = \frac{1}{2}mv^2 - 500$$

Solving for v

$$\frac{1}{2}mv^2 = 500 - 150$$

$$v^2 = \frac{2 \times (500 - 150)}{0.025}$$

$$v = 167 \text{ (to nearest whole number)}$$

So the bullet emerges from the barrier with a speed of 167 m s^{-1}.

(ii) Total energy is conserved but there is a loss of mechanical energy of $\frac{1}{2}mu^2 - \frac{1}{2}mv^2 = 150\text{J}$. This energy is converted into non-mechanical forms such as heat and sound.

Example 5.7

An aircraft of mass m kg is flying at a constant velocity v m s^{-1} horizontally. Its engines are providing a horizontal driving force FN.

(i) (a) Draw a diagram showing the driving force, the lift force LN, the air resistance (drag force) RN and the weight of the aircraft.

(b) State which of these forces are equal in magnitude.

(c) State which of the forces are doing no work.

(ii) In the case when $m = 100\,000$, $v = 270$ and $F = 350\,000$ find the work done in a 10-second period by those forces which are doing work, and show that the work-energy principle holds in this case.

At a later time the pilot increases the thrust of the aircraft's engines to 400 000 N. When the aircraft has travelled a distance of 30 km, its speed has increased to 300 m s^{-1}.

(iii) Find the work done against air resistance during this period, and the average, resistive force.

Solution

(i) (a)

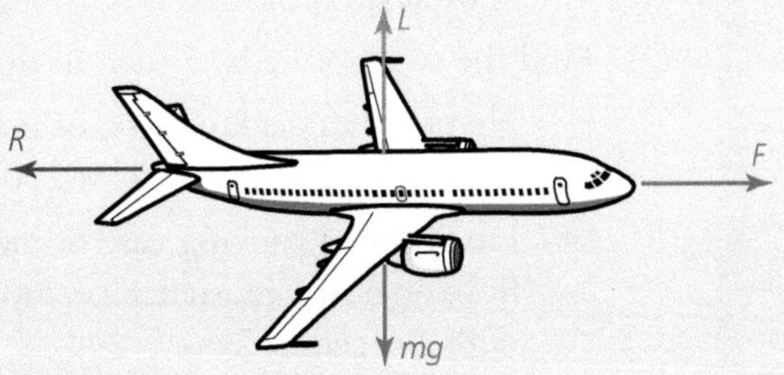

Figure 5.6

(b) Since the aircraft is travelling at constant velocity it is in equilibrium.

Horizontal forces: $F = R$

Vertical forces: $L = mg$

(c) Since the aircraft's velocity has no vertical component, the vertical forces, L and mg, are doing no work.

(ii) In 10 s at 270 m s^{-1} the aircraft travels 2700 m.

Work done by driving force $F = 350000 \times 2700 = 945000000$ J

Work done by resistance force $R = 350000 \times -2700 = -945000000$ J

The work–energy principle states that in this situation

work done by F + work done by R = change in kinetic energy

Now work done by F + work done by R = (945 000 000 − 945 000 000) = 0 J, and change in kinetic energy = 0 (since velocity is constant), so the work-energy principle does indeed hold in this case.

(iii) Final K.E. − initial K.E. $= \frac{1}{2}mv^2 - \frac{1}{2}mu^2$

$= \frac{1}{2} \times 100000 \times 300^2 - \frac{1}{2} \times 100000 \times 270^2$

$= 855 \times 10^6$ J

Work done by driving force $= 400000 \times 30000$

$= 12000 \times 10^6$ J

Total work done = K.E. gained

Work done by resistive force $+ 12000 \times 10^6 = 855 \times 10^6$

Work done by resistive force $= -11145 \times 10^6$ J

Average force × distance = Work done by force

Average force $\times 30000 = 11145 \times 10^6$

$\Rightarrow$ The average resistive force is 371 500 N (in the negative direction).

Note

When an aircraft is in flight, most of the work done by the, resistive force results in air currents and the generation of heat. A typical large jet cruising at 35 000 feet has a body temperature about 30°C above the surrounding air temperature. For supersonic flight the temperature difference is much greater. Concorde used to fly with a skin temperature more than 200°C above that of the surrounding air.

Exercise 5.1

① Find the kinetic energy of the following objects.

(i) An ice skater of mass 50 kg travelling with speed $10\,\mathrm{m\,s^{-1}}$.

(ii) An elephant of mass 5 tonnes moving with speed $4\,\mathrm{m\,s^{-1}}$.

(iii) A train of mass 7000 tonnes travelling with speed $40\,\mathrm{m\,s^{-1}}$.

(iv) The Moon of mass 7.4×10^{22} kg, travelling at $1000\,\mathrm{m\,s^{-1}}$ in its orbit around the Earth.

(v) A bacterium of mass 2×10^{-16} g which has a speed of $1\,\mathrm{mm\,s^{-1}}$.

② Find the work done by a man in the following situations.

(i) He pushes a packing case of mass 35 kg a distance of 5 m across a rough floor against a resistance of 200 N. The case starts and finishes at rest.

(ii) He pushes a packing case of mass 35 kg a distance of 5 m across a rough floor against a resistance of 200 N. The case starts at rest and finishes with a speed of $2\,\mathrm{m\,s^{-1}}$.

(iii) He pushes a packing case of mass 35 kg a distance of 5 m across a rough floor against a resistance of 200 N. Initially the case has speed $2\,\mathrm{m\,s^{-1}}$ but it ends at rest.

(iv) He is handed a packing case of mass 35 kg. He holds it stationary, at the same height, for 20 s and then someone else takes it away from him.

③ A sprinter of mass 60 kg is at rest at the beginning of a race and accelerates to $12\,\mathrm{m\,s^{-1}}$ in a distance of 30 m. Assume air resistance is negligible.

(i) Calculate the kinetic energy of the sprinter at the end of the 30 m.

(ii) Write down the work done by the sprinter over this distance.

(iii) Calculate the forward force exerted by the sprinter, assuming it to be constant, using work = force × distance.

(iv) Using force = mass × acceleration and the constant acceleration formulae, show that this force is consistent with the sprinter having a speed of $12\,\mathrm{m\,s^{-1}}$ after 30 m.

④ A sports car of mass 1.2 tonnes accelerates from rest to $30\,\mathrm{m\,s^{-1}}$ in a distance of 150 m. Assume air resistance to be negligible.

(i) Calculate the work done in accelerating the car. Does your answer depend on an assumption that the driving force is constant?

(ii) If the driving force is in fact constant, what is its magnitude?

(iii) Is it reasonable to assume that air resistance is negligible?

⑤ A car of mass 1600 kg is travelling at a speed of $25\,\mathrm{m\,s^{-1}}$ when the brakes are applied so that it stops after moving a further 75 m. Assuming that other resistive forces can be neglected, find

(i) the work done by the brakes

(ii) the retarding force from the brakes, assuming that it is constant.

⑥ The forces acting on a hot air balloon of mass 500 kg are its weight and the total uplift force.

(i) Find the total work done when the vertical speed of the balloon changes from

(a) $2\,\mathrm{m\,s^{-1}}$ to $5\,\mathrm{m\,s^{-1}}$ (b) $8\,\mathrm{m\,s^{-1}}$ to $3\,\mathrm{m\,s^{-1}}$.

(ii) If the balloon rises 100 m vertically while its speed changes calculate in each case the work done by the uplift force.

⑦ A bullet of mass 20 g, found at the scene of a police investigation, had penetrated 16 cm into a wooden post. The speed for that type of bullet is known to be $80\,\mathrm{m\,s^{-1}}$.

(i) Find the kinetic energy of the bullet before it entered the post.

(ii) What happened to this energy when the bullet entered the wooden post?

(iii) Write down the work done in stopping the bullet

(iv) Calculate the resistive force on the bullet, assuming it to be constant.

Another bullet of the same mass and shape had clearly been fired from a different and unknown type of gun. This bullet had penetrated 20 cm into the post.

(v) Estimate the speed of this bullet before it hit the post.

⑧ The highway code gives the braking distance for a car travelling at $22\,\mathrm{m\,s^{-1}}$ (50 mph) to be 38 m (125 ft). A car of mass 1300 kg is brought to rest in just this distance. It may be assumed that the only resistance forces come from the car's brakes.

(i) Find the work done by the brakes.

(ii) Find the average force exerted by the brakes.

(iii) What happened to the kinetic energy of the car?

(iv) What happens when you drive a car with the handbrake on ?

⑨ A car of mass 1200 kg experiences a constant resistance force of 600 N. The driving force from the engine depends upon the gear, as shown in the table.

Gear	1	2	3	4
Force (N)	2800	2100	1400	1000

Starting from rest, the car is driven 20 m in first gear, 40 m in second, 80 m in third and 100 m in fourth. How fast is the car travelling at the end?

⑩ In this question take g to be $10\,\mathrm{m\,s^{-1}}$. A chest of mass 60 kg is resting on a rough horizontal floor. The coefficient of friction between the floor and the chest is 0.4. A woman pushes the chest in such a way that its speed–time graph is as shown below.

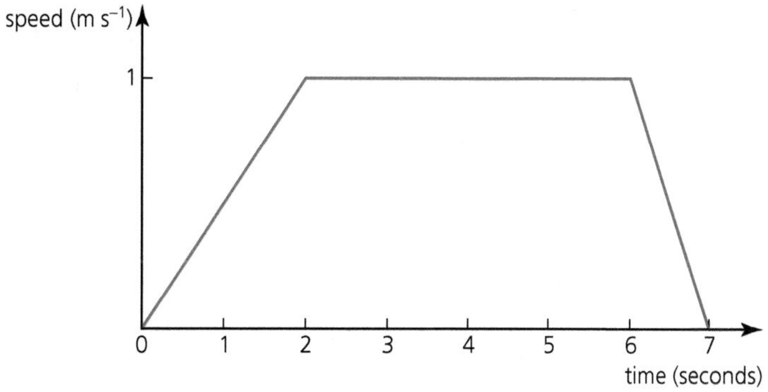

Figure 5.7

(i) Find the force of frictional resistance acting on the chest when it moves.

(ii) Use the speed–time graph to find the total distance travelled by the chest.

(iii) Find the total work done by the woman.

(iv) Find the acceleration of the chest in the first 2 seconds of its motion and hence the force exerted by the woman during this time, and the work done.

(v) In the same way find the work done by the woman during the time intervals 2 to 6 seconds, and 6 to 7 seconds.

(vi) Show that your answers to parts (iv) and (v) are consistent with your answer to part (iii).

2 Gravitational potential energy

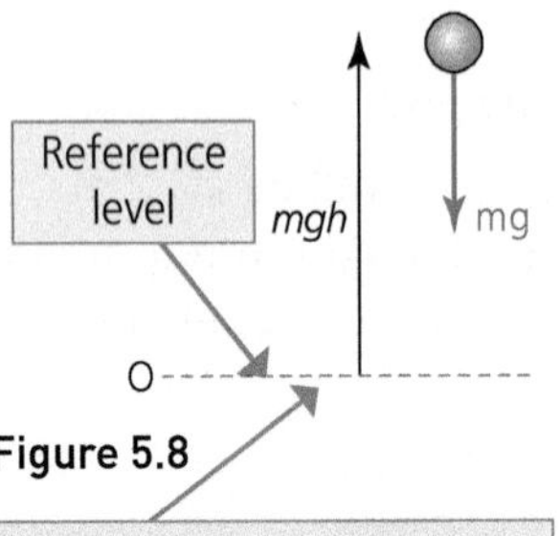

Figure 5.8

You will often have to choose the reference level for a particular situation. It could be ground level, the top of a building or the height of an aircraft. There is no right answer but choosing a suitable level can make your calculations easier.

As you have seen, kinetic energy (K.E.) is the energy that an object has because of its motion. Potential energy (P.E.) is the energy an object has because of its position. The units of potential energy are the same as those of kinetic energy or any other form of energy, namely, joules.

One form of potential energy is **gravitational potential energy**. The gravitational potential energy of the object in Figure 5.8 of mass, m kg, at height, h m, above a particular reference level, 0, is mgh J. If it falls to the reference level, the force of gravity does mgh J of work and the body loses mgh J of potential energy.

A loss in gravitational potential energy is an alternative way of accounting for the work done by the force of gravity.

If a mass m kg is **raised** through a distance h m, the gravitational potential energy **increases** by mgh J. If a mass, m kg, is **lowered** through a distance, h m, the gravitational potential energy **decreases** by mgh J.

Example 5.8

Calculate the gravitational potential energy, relative to the ground, of a ball of mass 0.15 kg at a height of 2 m above the ground.

Solution

Mass $m = 0.15$, height $h = 2$.

$$\text{Gravitational potential energy} = mgh$$
$$= 0.15 \times 9.8 \times 2$$
$$= 2.94\,\text{J}$$

Note

Assuming no air resistance, the gain in K.E. is 2.94 J so that the maximum theoretical speed of the ball when it hits the ground is $\sqrt{\frac{2 \times 2.94}{0.15}} = 6.26\,\text{m s}^{-1}$.

In reality there would be air resistance, so the ball's speed would be less than this.

Note

If the ball falls:

loss in P.E. = work done by gravity

= gain in K.E.

There is no change in the total energy (P.E. + K.E.) of the ball.

Using conservation of mechanical energy

When gravity is the only force which does work on a body, mechanical energy is conserved. When this is the case, many problems are easily solved using energy. This is possible even when the acceleration is not constant.

Example 5.9

A skier starts from rest and slides down a ski slope 400 m long which is at an angle of 30° to the horizontal. The slope is smooth and air resistance can be neglected.

(i) Find the speed of the skier when he reaches the bottom of the slope.

At the foot of the slope the ground becomes horizontal and is made rough in order to help skiers stop. The coefficient of friction between his skis and the ground is $\frac{1}{4}$.

(ii) Find how far the skier travels before coming to rest.

(iii) In what way is your model unrealistic?

Solution

(i) The skier is modelled as a particle.

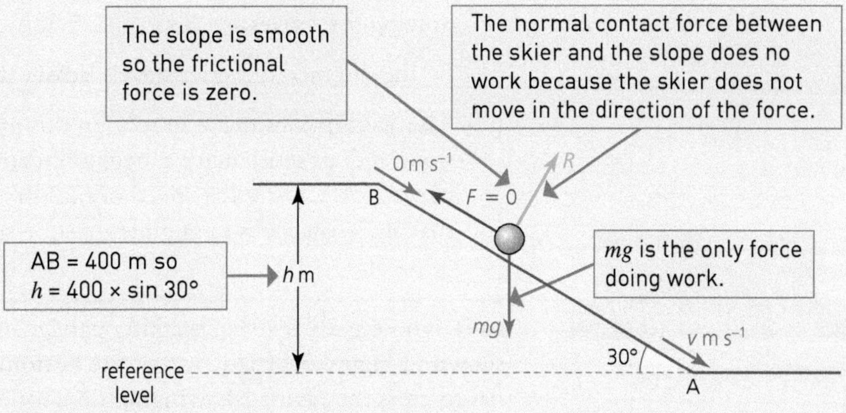

Figure 5.9

Mechanical energy is conserved.

$$\text{Total mechanical energy at B} = mgh + \frac{1}{2}mu^2$$
$$= m \times 9.8 \times 400 \sin 30° + 0$$
$$= 1960\, m \text{ J}$$

$$\text{Total mechanical energy at A} = \left(0 + \frac{1}{2}mv^2\right)\text{J}$$

Since mechanical energy is conserved.

$$\frac{1}{2}mv^2 = 1960m$$
$$v^2 = 3920$$
$$v = 62.6\ldots..$$

Notice that the mass of the skier cancels out. In this model all skiers should arrive at the bottom of the slope with the same speed.

The slope could be curved and the model would give the same speed so long as the total height lost is the same.

The skier's speed at the bottom of the slope is 62.6 m s⁻¹ (to 3 s.f.).

(ii) For the horizontal part there is some friction. Suppose the skier travels a further distance s m before stopping.

Note

An alternative approach to this problem is to use the constant acceleration formulae. Make sure you are comfortable with both approaches.

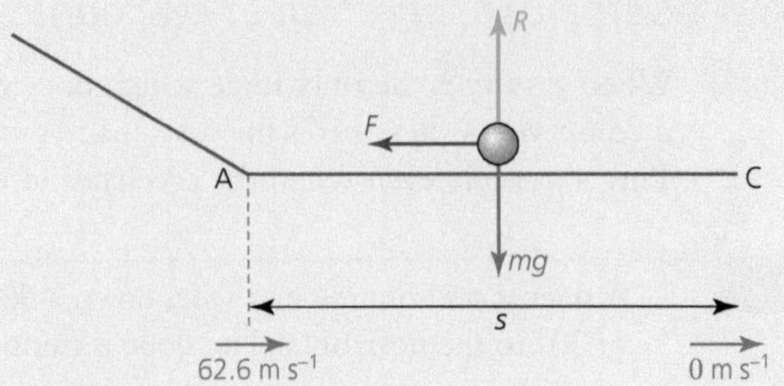

Figure 5.10

The frictional force is $F = \mu R = \frac{1}{4}R$.

There is no vertical acceleration, so $R = mg$

and so $F = \frac{1}{4}mg$.

Negative because the force is in the opposite direction to the motion.

Work done by the friction force $= -F \times s = -\frac{1}{4}mgs$

The increase in kinetic energy between A and C $= \left(0 - \frac{1}{2}mv^2\right)$ J.

$-\frac{1}{4}mgs = -\frac{1}{2}mv^2 = -1960m$ from ①

The increase in kinetic energy $0 - \frac{1}{2}mv^2$ = work done

Solving for s gives $s = 800$.

So the distance the skier travels before stopping is 800 m.

(iii) The assumptions made in solving this problem are that friction on the slope and air resistance are negligible, and that the slope ends in a smooth curve at A. Clearly the speed of 62.6 m s^{-1} is very high, so the assumption that air resistance is negligible must be suspect.

Example 5.10

Ama, whose mass is 40 kg, is taking part in an assault course. The obstacle shown in Figure 5.11 is a river at the bottom of a ravine that is 8 m wide. She has to cross the ravine by swinging on a rope 5 m long secured to a point on the branch of a tree, immediately above the centre of the ravine.

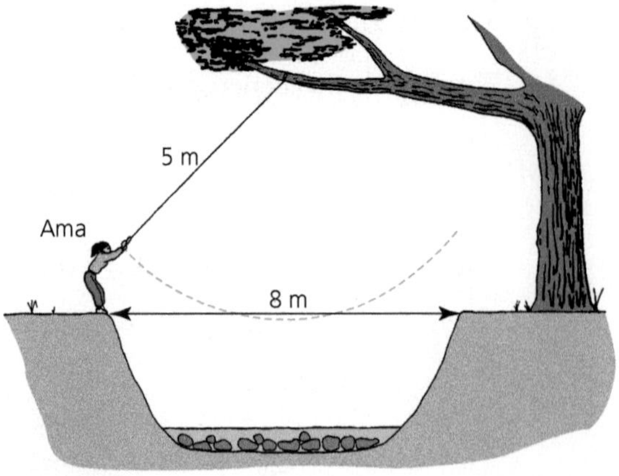

Figure 5.11

(i) Find how fast Ama is travelling at the lowest point of her crossing

(a) if she starts from rest

(b) if she launches herself off at a speed of 1 m s^{-1}.

(ii) Will her speed be 1 m s^{-1} faster throughout her crossing?

Solution

(i) (a) The vertical height Ama loses is HB in Figure 5.12.

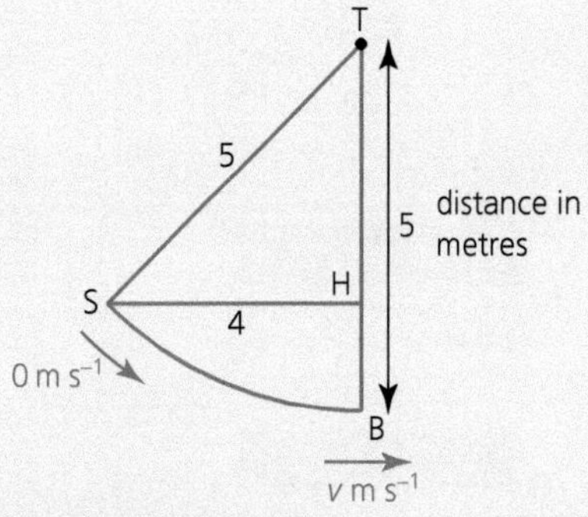

Figure 5.12

Using Pythagoras' theorem in triangle TSH.

$TH = \sqrt{5^2 - 4^2} = 3$

$HB = 5 - 3 = 2$

P.E. lost $= mgh$

$= 40 \times 9.8 \times 2 = 784$

K.E. gained $= \frac{1}{2}mv^2 - 0$

$= \frac{1}{2} \times 40 \times v^2 = 20v^2$

Conservation of mechanical energy, K.E. gained = P.E. lost

$20v^2 = 784$

$v = \sqrt{39.2} = 6.26$

Ama is travelling at $6.26\,\text{m}\,\text{s}^{-1}$.

(b) If she has initial speed $1\,\text{m}\,\text{s}^{-1}$ at S and speed $v\,\text{m}\,\text{s}^{-1}$ at B, her initial K.E. is $\frac{1}{2} \times 40 \times 1^2$ and her K.E. at B is $\frac{1}{2} \times 40 \times v^2$.

Using conservation of mechanical energy,

$\frac{1}{2} \times 40 \times v^2 - \frac{1}{2} \times 40 \times 1^2 = 40 \times 9.8 \times 2$

$20v^2 - 20 = 784$

$v = 6.34$

Ama is travelling at $6.34\,\text{m}\,\text{s}^{-1}$.

(ii) Ama's speed at the lowest point is only $0.08\,\text{m}\,\text{s}^{-1}$ faster in part (i) (b) compared with that in part (i) (a), so she clearly will not travel $1\,\text{m}\,\text{s}^{-1}$ faster throughout the crossing in part (i) (b).

Exercise 5.2

① Calculate the gravitational potential energy, relative to the reference level OA, for each of the objects shown.

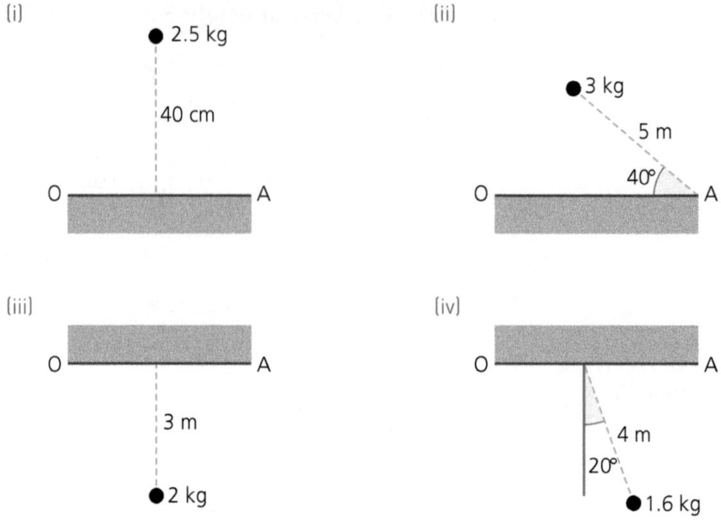

Figure 5.13

② Calculate the change in gravitational potential energy when each object moves from A to B in the situations shown below. State whether the change is an increase or a decrease.

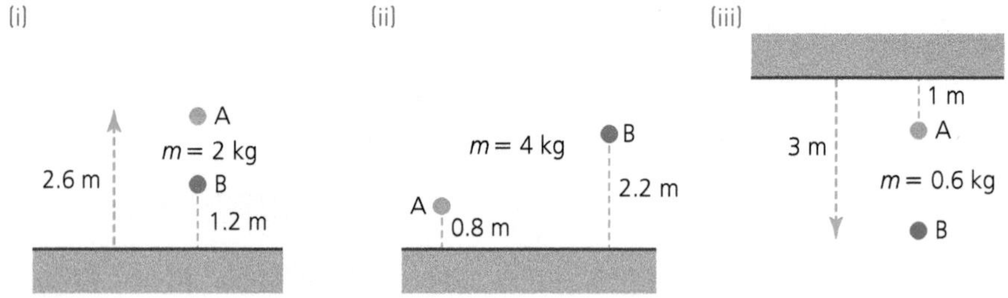

Figure 5.14

③ A vase of mass 1.2 kg is lifted from ground level and placed on a shelf at a height of 1.5 m. Find the work done against the force of gravity.

④ Find the increase in gravitational potential energy of a woman of mass 60 kg who climbs to the twelfth floor of a block of flats. The distance between the floors is 3.3 m.

⑤ A sledge of mass 10 kg is being pulled across level ground by a rope which makes an angle of 20° with the horizontal. The tension in the rope is 80 N and there is a resistance force of 14 N.

(i) Find the work done while the sledge moves a distance of 20 m by

(a) the tension in the rope

(b) the resistance force.

(ii) Find the speed of the sledge after it has moved 20 m

(a) if it starts at rest

(b) if it starts at $4\,\mathrm{m\,s^{-1}}$.

⑥ A bricklayer carries a hod of bricks of mass 25 kg up a ladder of length 10 m inclined at an angle of 60° to the horizontal.

(i) Calculate the increase in the gravitational potential energy of the bricks.

(ii) If instead he had raised the bricks vertically to the same height, using a rope and pulleys, would the increase in potential energy be less, the same, or more than in part (i)?

7. A bead of mass 0.03 kg is threaded on a smooth wire which forms a fixed circle of radius 20 cm in a vertical plane.

   (i) The bead is placed at the top of the circle and given a small displacement, so that it slides round the circle to the bottom. Find the speed of the bead when it reaches the bottom of the circle.

   (ii) The bead is placed at the bottom of the circle and given a velocity of $3\ \mathrm{m\,s^{-1}}$ in the direction of the tangent to the circle. Show that it moves in a complete circle.

8. A small iron ball of mass 1.1 kg is attached to one end of a light inextensible string of length 90 cm. The other end of the string is fixed to a support so that the system can swing freely to either side. Initially the ball hangs in equilibrium.

Find the smallest initial speed that the ball can be given so that in the subsequent motion the string reaches the horizontal.

9. A conker of mass 0.07 kg is fixed to one end of a light extensible string of length 10 cm, and the other end of the string is fixed to the ceiling of a room.

   (i) The conker is held so that the string is taut and makes an angle of 30° with the downward vertical, and it is then released. Find the speed of the conker when it reaches its lowest point.

   (ii) The conker hangs in equilibrium with the string taut, and it is then given a horizontal speed of $0.6\ \mathrm{m\,s^{-1}}$. Find the maximum angle between the string and the vertical in the subsequent motion.

10. Tarzan swings on one end of a light inextensible rope of length 6 m. The other end is tied to a convenient tree. Initially the rope makes an angle of 60° with the downward vertical, and Tarzan, yelling loudly, starts from rest and moves in a circular path.

   (i) Find Tarzan's speed v when he reaches the lowest point of his circular path.

At the bottom of the circular path Tarzan catches hold of Jane and the two continue to move in a circle together, with a combined speed of $0.6v$.

   (ii) Find the horizontal distance that Tarzan and Jane travel together before they come to a halt.

11. A simple pendulum is modelled as a light inextensible string of length l m, with a particle of mass m kg attached to one end acting as the "bob". The other end is fixed.

   (i) The bob hangs in equilibrium and is then given a horizontal velocity $u\ \mathrm{m\,s^{-1}}$. Ignoring air resistance, find an expression for the greatest angle θ_0 that the string makes with the downward vertical in the subsequent motion.

The bob is now held to one side of the downward vertical and is then released. On its first complete swing the bob travels through a total distance of 20 cm before returning to its original position. Because of air resistance the total distance travelled by the bob on each subsequent swing is 0.99 times the total distance on the previous swing. The time for each complete swing of the pendulum is a constant T.

   (ii) Find how long it takes, in terms of T, before the distance travelled by the bob on one complete swing is less than 5 cm.

3 Work and kinetic energy for two-dimensional motion

Historical note

James Joule was born in Salford in Lancashire on Christmas Eve 1818. He studied at Manchester University at the same time as the famous chemist, John Dalton.

Joule spent much of his life conducting experiments to measure the equivalence of heat and mechanical forms of energy to ever increasing degrees of accuracy. Working with Lord Kelvin he also made the discovery that when a gas is allowed to expand without doing work against external forces it cools. It was this discovery that paved the way for the development of refrigerators. Joule died in 1889; his contribution to science is remembered with the S.I. unit for energy named after him.

Discussion point

Imagine that you are cycling along a level winding road in a strong wind. Suppose that the strength and direction of the wind are constant, but, because the road is winding, sometimes the wind is directly against you but at other times it is from your side or even behind you.

How does the work you do in travelling a certain distance, say 1 m, change with your direction?

Work done by a force at an angle to the direction of motion

You have probably decided that as a cyclist you would do work against the component of the wind force that is directly against you. The sideways component does not resist your forward progress.

Suppose you are cycling along the straight bit of the horizontal road OP shown (seen from above) in Figure 5.15. The force of the wind on you is F N. In a certain time you travel a distance s m along the road. The component of this distance in the direction of F is d m, as shown in Figure 5.15.

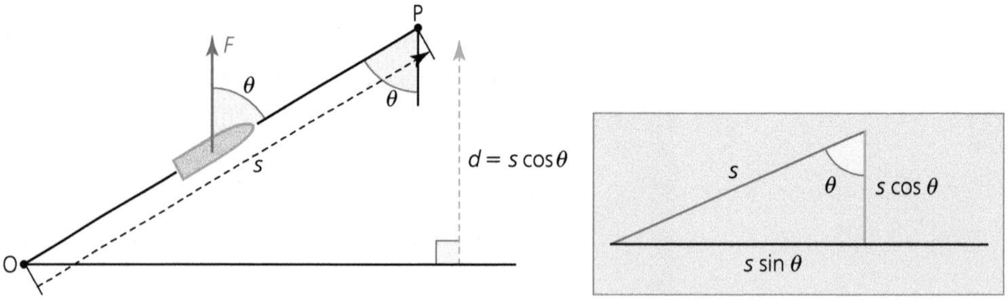

Figure 5.15

Work done by $F = Fd$

The work done by the force F is $Fs \cos \theta$. This can also be written as the product of the component of F along OP, $F \cos \theta$, and the distance moved along OP, s.

$$F \times s \cos \theta = F \cos \theta \times s$$

Example 5.11

As a car of mass m kg drives up a slope at an angle α to the horizontal. It experiences a constant resistive force F N and a driving force D N.

(i) Draw a diagram showing the forces acting on the car.

(ii) State what can be said about the work done by each of the forces as the car moves a distance d up the slope.

(iii) What can be deduced about the work done by the force D when

(a) the car moves at constant speed?

(b) the car slows down?

(c) the car gains speed?

The initial and final speeds of the car are denoted by u m s^{-1} and v m s^{-1}, respectively.

(iv) Write v^2 in terms of the other variables.

Solution

(i)

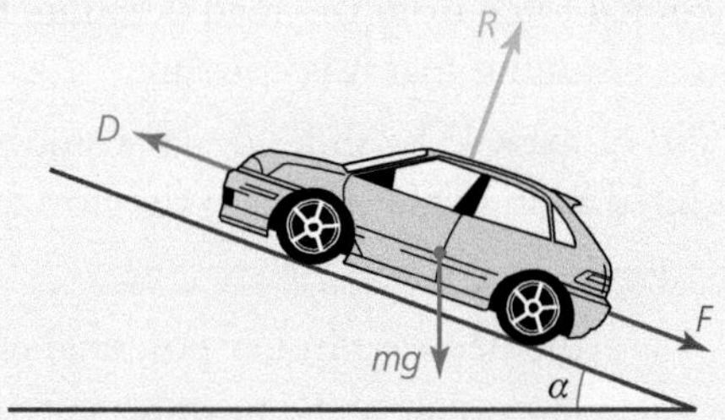

Figure 5.16

(ii)

Force	**Work done**
Resistance F	$-Fd$
Normal contact force	0
Force of gravity mg	$-mgd\sin\alpha$
Driving force D	Dd
Total work done	$Dd - Fd - mgd\sin\alpha$

(iii) (a) If the car moves at a constant speed, there is no change in kinetic energy so the total work done is zero, giving

work done by D is

$$Dd = Fd + mgd\sin\alpha$$

(b) If the car slows down, the total work done by the forces is negative, and hence work done by D is

$$Dd < Fd + mgd\ sin\ \alpha$$

(c) If the car gains speed, the total work done by the forces is positive so work done by D is

$$Dd > Fd + mgd\sin\alpha$$

(iv) Total work done = Final K.E. – initial K.E.

$$\Rightarrow \quad Dd - Fd - mgd\sin\alpha = \frac{1}{2}mv^2 - \frac{1}{2}mu^2$$

Multiplying by $\frac{2}{m}$

$$\Rightarrow \quad v^2 = u^2 + \frac{2d}{m}(D - F) - 2gd\sin\alpha$$

Exercise 5.3

① A force of 24 N acting on a particle produces a displacement of 12 m in a straight line. The angle between the force and the displacement is 20°.

(i) Find the work done by the force.

(ii) The particle has mass 3 kg and starts from rest. Find its final speed.

② A bead slides along a straight smooth horizontal wire. It is acted on by a force of 15 N making an angle of 120° with its velocity.

(i) Find the work done against the force when the particle moves 6 m.

(ii) The mass of the particle is 0.05 kg and its initial speed is 4.5 m s^{-1}. Find the distance in cm needed for the bead to come to rest.

③ A car of mass 800 kg travelling at 15 $\mathrm{m\,s^{-1}}$ skids to a halt. In skidding it moves for 20 m in a straight line at 170° to the direction in which the frictional force from the road is acting. Find the magnitude of the frictional force, assuming that it is constant.

④ A girl of mass 45 kg slides down a smooth water chute of length 6 m inclined at an angle of 40° to the horizontal.

(i) Find

(a) the decrease in her potential energy

(b) her speed at the bottom.

(ii) How are answers to part (i) affected if the slide is not smooth?

⑤ A gymnast of mass 50 kg swings on a rope of length 10 m. Initially the rope makes an angle of 50° with the vertical.

(i) Find the decrease in her potential energy when the rope has reached the vertical.

(ii) Find her kinetic energy and hence her speed when the rope is vertical, assuming that air resistance may be neglected.

(iii) The gymnast continues to swing. What angle will the rope make with the vertical when she is next temporarily at rest?

(iv) Explain why the tension in the rope does no work.

⑥ A car of mass 0.9 tonnes is driven 200 m up a slope inclined at 5° to the horizontal. There is a resistance force of 100 N.

(i) Find the work done by the car against gravity.

(ii) Find the work done against the resistance force.

(iii) When asked to work out the total work done by the car, a student replied '$(900g + 100) \times 200$ J'. Explain the error in this answer.

(iv) If the car slows down from 12 $\mathrm{m\,s^{-1}}$ to 8 $\mathrm{m\,s^{-1}}$, what is the total work done by the engine?

⑦ A stone of mass 0.2 kg is dropped from the top of a building 80 m high. After t s it has fallen a distance x m and has speed v $\mathrm{m\,s^{-1}}$. Air resistance may be neglected.

(i) What is the gravitational potential energy of the stone relative to ground level when it is at the top of the building?

(ii) What is the potential energy of the stone t s later?

(iii) Show that, for certain values of t, $v^2 = 19.6x$ and state the range of values of t for which it is true.

(iv) Find the speed of the stone when its kinetic energy is 10 J.

(v) Find the kinetic energy of the stone when its gravitational potential energy relative to the ground is 66.8 J.

⑧ Wesley, whose mass is 70 kg, inadvertently steps off a bridge 50 m above water. When he hits the water, Wesley is travelling at 25 $\mathrm{m\,s^{-1}}$.

(i) Calculate the potential energy Wesley has lost and the kinetic energy he has gained.

(ii) Find the size of the resistance force acting on Wesley while he is in the air, assuming it to be constant.

Wesley descends to a depth of 5 m below the water surface, then returns to the surface.

(iii) Find the total upthrust (assumed constant) acting on him while he is moving downwards in the water.

⑨ A hockey ball of mass 0.15 kg is hit from the centre of the pitch. Its position vector (in m) t s later is modelled by

$$\boldsymbol{r} = 10t\ \mathbf{i} + \left(10t - 4.9t^2\right)\mathbf{j}$$

where the unit vectors **i** and **j** are in the directions along the line of the pitch and vertically upwards.

(i) What value of g is used in this model?

(ii) Find an expression for the gravitational potential energy of the ball at time t. For what values of t is your answer valid?

(iii) What is the maximum height of the ball? What is its velocity at that instant?

(iv) Find the initial velocity, speed and kinetic energy of the ball.

(v) Show that according to this model mechanical energy is conserved and state what modelling assumption is implied by this. Is it reasonable in this context?

⑩ A ski-run starts at altitude 2471 m and ends at 1863 m.

(i) If all resistance forces could be ignored, what would the speed of a skier be at the end of the run?

A particular skier of mass 70 kg actually attains a speed of $42\,\mathrm{m\,s^{-1}}$. The length of the run is 3.1 km.

(ii) Find the average force of resistance acting on a skier.

Two skiers are equally skilful.

(iii) Which would you expect to be travelling faster by the end of the run, the heavier or the lighter?

⑪ A tennis ball of mass 0.06 kg is hit vertically upwards with speed $20\,\mathrm{m\,s^{-1}}$ from a point 1.1 m above the ground. It reaches a height of 16 m.

(i) Find the initial kinetic energy of the ball, and its potential energy when it is at its highest point.

(ii) Calculate the loss of mechanical energy due to air resistance.

(iii) Find the magnitude of the air resistance force on the ball, assuming it to be constant while the ball is moving.

(iv) With what speed does the ball land?

⑫ Akosua draws water from a well 12 m below the ground. Her bucket holds 5 kg of water and by the time she has pulled it to the top of the well it is travelling at $1.2\,\mathrm{m\,s^{-1}}$.

(i) How much work does Akosua do in drawing the bucket of water?

On an average day 150 people in the village each draw 6 such buckets of water. One day a new electric pump is installed that takes water from the well and fills an overhead tank 5 m above ground level every morning. The flow rate through the pump is such that the water has speed $2\,\mathrm{m\,s^{-1}}$ on arriving in the tank.

(ii) Assuming that the villagers' demand for water remains unaltered, how much work does the pump do in one day?

⑬ A block of mass 20 kg is pulled up a slope passing through points A and B with speeds $10\,\mathrm{m\,s^{-1}}$ and $2\,\mathrm{m\,s^{-1}}$ respectively. The distance between A and B is 100 m and B is 12 m higher than A. For the motion of the block from A to B, find

(i) the loss in kinetic energy of the block

(ii) the gain in potential energy of the block.

The resistance to motion of the block has magnitude 10 N.

(iii) Find the work done by the pulling force acting on the block.

The pulling force acting on the block has constant magnitude 25 N and acts at an angle α upwards from the slope.

(iv) Find the value of α.

4 Power

Figure 5.17

It is claimed that a motorcycle engine can develop a maximum **power** of 26.5 kW at a top **speed** of $165\,\mathrm{km\,h^{-1}}$. This suggests that power is related to speed and this is indeed the case.

Power is the rate at which work is being done. A powerful car does work at a greater rate than a less powerful one.

Think of a force, F, acting for a very short time t over a small distance, s. Assume F to be constant over this short time.

Power is the rate of working so

$$\text{power} = \frac{\text{work}}{\text{time}}$$

$$= \frac{Fs}{t}$$

$$= Fv$$

> **Note**
>
> This gives you the power at an *instant* of time. The result is true whether or not F is constant.

The power of a vehicle moving at speed v under a driving force F is given by Fv.

For a motor vehicle the power is produced by the engine, whereas for a bicycle it is produced by the cyclist. They both make the wheels turn, and the friction between the rotating wheels and the ground produces a forward force on the machine.

The unit of power is the watt (W), named after James Watt. The power produced by a force of 1 N acting on an object that is moving at $1\,\text{m}\,\text{s}^{-1}$ is 1 W. Because the watt is such a small unit, you will probably use kilowatts more often (1 kW = 1000 W).

Example 5.12

A car of mass 1000 kg can produce a maximum power of 45 kW. Its driver wishes to overtake another vehicle. Ignoring air resistance, find the maximum acceleration of the car when it is travelling at

(i) $12\,\text{m}\,\text{s}^{-1}$

(ii) $28\,\text{m}\,\text{s}^{-1}$

Solution

(i) Power = force × velocity

The driving force at $12\,\text{m}\,\text{s}^{-1}$ is F_1 N where

$$45\,000 = F_1 \times 12$$

$$\Rightarrow \quad F_1 = 3750$$

By Newton's second law $F = ma$

$$\Rightarrow \quad \text{acceleration} = \frac{3750}{1000} = 3.75\,\text{m}\,\text{s}^{-2}$$

(ii) Now the driving force F_2 is given by

$$45\,000 = F_2 \times 28$$

$$\Rightarrow \quad F_2 = 1607$$

$$\Rightarrow \quad \text{acceleration} = \frac{1607}{1000} = 1.61\,\text{m}\,\text{s}^{-2}.$$

This example shows why it is easier to overtake a slow moving vehicle.

Example 5.13

A car of mass 900 kg produces a power of 45 kW when moving at a constant speed. It experiences a resistance of 1700 N.

(i) What is its speed?

(ii) The car comes to a downhill stretch inclined at 2° to the horizontal. What is its maximum speed downhill if the power and resistance remain unchanged?

Solution

(i) As the car is travelling at a constant speed, there is no resultant force on the car. In this case, the forward force of the engine must have the same magnitude as the resistance forces, i.e. 1700 N.

Denoting the speed of the car by $v\,\text{m}\,\text{s}^{-1}$, $P = Fv$ gives

$$v = \frac{P}{F} = \frac{45\,000}{1700} = 26.5$$

The speed of the car is 26.5 m s^{-1} (which is approximately 60 mph).

(ii) Figure 5.18 shows the forces acting.

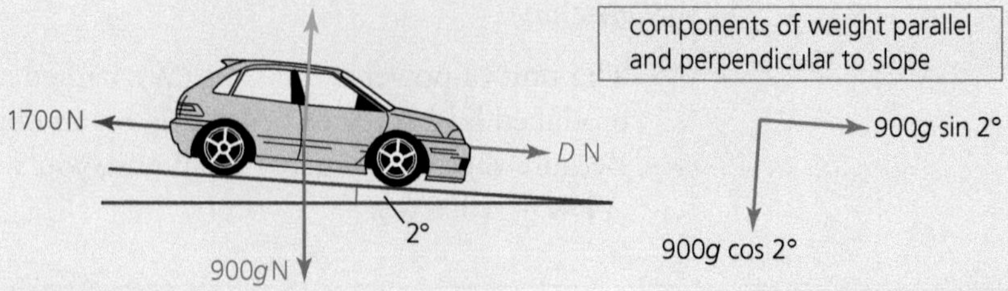

Figure 5.18

At maximum speed there is no acceleration so the resultant force down the slope is zero.

When the driving force is D N

$$D + 900g \sin 2° - 1700 = 0$$

$$\Rightarrow \quad D = 1392$$

But power is Dv so $45\,000 = 1392v$

$$\Rightarrow \quad v = \frac{45\,000}{1392}$$

The maximum speed is 32.3 m s^{-1} (about 73 mph).

Sometimes you will want to calculate the **average power**. You calculate this by finding the total work done and dividing it by the total time taken.

Example 5.14

A porter carries a total of 160 kg of luggage up a height of 9 m. He takes 10 minutes to complete the task. Calculate the average power at which he is working.

Solution

Work done = change in energy

= gravitational potential energy gained

$= 160g \times 9$

$= 14\,112$ J.

> If the porter cannot carry all the luggage at once he will not be working at the same rate throughout the task, so it is sensible to calculate the *average* power.

The time taken is $10 \times 60 = 600$ seconds.

$\Rightarrow$ average power $= 14\,112 \div 60$

$= 23.52$ watts

The porter is working at an average rate of 23.5 watts.

Historical note

James Watt was born in 1736 in Greenock in Scotland, the son of a house- and ship-builder. As a boy James was frail and he was taught by his mother rather than going to school. This allowed him to spend time in his father's workshop where he developed practical and inventive skills.

As a young man he manufactured mathematical instruments: quadrants, scales, compasses and so on. One day, he was repairing a model steam engine for a friend and noticed that its design was very wasteful of steam. He proposed an alternative arrangement, which was to become standard on later steam engines.

This was the first of many engineering inventions which made possible the subsequent industrial revolution. James Watt died in 1819, a well-known and highly respected man. His name lives on as the S.I. unit for power.

Example 5.15

A car of mass 1000 kg travels along a horizontal straight road. The power provided by the car's engine is constant and equal to 20 kW. The resistance to the car's motion is constant and equal to 800 N. The car passes two points A and B with speed 15 m s^{-1} and 25 m s^{-1} respectively and takes 40 seconds to travel from A to B. Find the distance AB.

Solution

The work done by the engine in travelling from A to B is

$$20\,000 \times 40 = 800\,000 \text{ J}$$

The work done against the resistance is

$$800 \times \text{AB J}$$

The increase in the kinetic energy of the car is

$$\tfrac{1}{2} \times 1000 \times 25^2 - \tfrac{1}{2} \times 1000 \times 15^2 = 200\,000 \text{J}$$

Using the work-energy principle:

$$800\,000 - 800\text{AB} = 200\,000$$

$$\text{AB} = \frac{600\,000}{800} = 750 \text{ m}$$

The distance AB is 750 m.

Example 5.16

A car of mass 1200 kg is travelling at a constant speed of 15 m s^{-1}, climbing for 30 s along a uniform slope of elevation arcsin (0.05) against a constant resistance of 900 N.

Calculate the power generated by the driving force.

Solution

The distance travelled by the car along the slope is $15 \times 30 = 450$ m

The work done against the, resistive force is thus $900 \times 450 = 405\,000$ J

The vertical height gained by the car is $450 \times 0.05 = 22.5$ m

The gravitational potential energy gained by the car is therefore

$$1200 \times 9.8 \times 22.5 = 264\,600 \text{ J}$$

The total work done by the driving force is

$$405\,000 + 264\,600 = 669\,600 \text{ J}$$

This work is produced in 30 s, thus the rate of doing work is equal to

$$669\,600 \div 30 = 22\,320 \text{ W}$$

The power generated by the driving force is 22 320 W.

Exercise 5.4

① A builder hoists bricks up to the top of the house he is building. Each brick weighs 3.5 kg and the house is 9 m high. In the course of one hour the builder raises 120 bricks from ground level to the top of the house, where they are unloaded by his assistant.

(i) Find the increase in gravitational potential energy of one brick when it is raised in this way.

(ii) Find the total work done by the builder in one hour of raising bricks.

(iii) Find the average power with which he is working.

② A weightlifter takes 2 seconds to lift 120 kg from the floor to a position 2 m above it, where the weight has to be held stationary.

(i) Calculate the work done by the weightlifter.

(ii) Calculate the average power developed by the weightlifter.

The weightlifter is using the 'clean and jerk' technique. This means that in the first stage of the lift he raises the weight 0.8 m from the floor in 0.5 s. He then holds it stationary for 1 s before lifting it up to the final position in another 0.5 s.

(iii) Find the average power developed by the weightlifter during each of the stages of the lift.

③ A winch is used to pull a crate of mass 180 kg up a rough slope of angle 30° against a frictional force of 450 N. The crate moves at a steady speed of $1.2\,\text{m}\,\text{s}^{-1}$.

(i) Calculate the gravitational potential energy given to the crate during 30 s.

(ii) Calculate the work done against friction during this time.

(iii) Calculate the total work done per second by the winch.

The cable from the winch to the crate runs parallel to the slope.

(iv) Calculate the tension, T, in the cable.

(v) What information is given by the product of T and the speed of the crate?

④ The power output from the engine of a car of mass 850 kg which is travelling along level ground at a constant speed of $33\,\mathrm{m\,s^{-1}}$ is 23 200 W.

(i) Find the total resistance on the car under these conditions.

(ii) You were given one piece of unnecessary information. Which is it?

⑤ A motorcycle has a maximum power output of 26.5 kW and a top speed of 103 mph (about $46\,\mathrm{m\,s^{-1}}$). Find the force exerted by the motorcycle engine when the motorcycle is travelling at top speed.

⑥ A crane is raising a load of 500 tonnes at a steady rate of $5\,\mathrm{cm\,s^{-1}}$. What power is the engine of the crane producing? (Assume that there are no forces from friction or air resistance.)

⑦ A cyclist, travelling at a constant speed of $8\,\mathrm{m\,s^{-1}}$ along a level road, experiences a total resistance of 70 N.

(i) Find the power which the cyclist is producing.

(ii) Find the work done by the cyclist in 5 minutes under these conditions.

⑧ A mouse of mass 15 g is stationary 2 m below its hole when it sees a cat. It runs to its hole, arriving 1.5 seconds later with a speed of $3\,\mathrm{m\,s^{-1}}$.

(i) Show that the acceleration of the mouse is not constant.

(ii) Calculate the average power of the mouse.

⑨ A train consists of a diesel shunter of mass 100 tonnes pulling a truck of mass 25 tonnes along a level track. The engine is working at a rate of 125 kW. The resistance to motion of the truck and shunter is 50 N per tonne.

(i) Calculate the constant speed of the train.

While travelling at this constant speed, the truck becomes uncoupled. The shunter engine continues to produce the same power.

(ii) Find the acceleration of the shunter immediately after this happens.

(iii) Find the greatest speed the shunter can now reach.

⑩ A supertanker of mass 4×10^8 kg is steaming at a constant speed of $8\,\mathrm{m\,s^{-1}}$. The resistance force is 2×10^6 N.

(i) What power is being produced by the ship's engines?

One of the ship's two engines suddenly fails but the other continues to work at the same rate.

(ii) Find the deceleration of the ship immediately after the failure.

The resistance force is directly proportional to the speed of the ship.

(iii) Find the eventual steady speed of the ship under one engine only, assuming that the single engine maintains constant power output.

⑪ A car of mass 850 kg has a maximum speed of $50\,\mathrm{m\,s^{-1}}$ and a maximum power output of 40 kW. The resistance force R N at speed $v\,\mathrm{m\,s^{-1}}$ is modelled by $R = kv$.

(i) Find the value of k.

(ii) Find the resistance force when the car's speed is $20\,\mathrm{m\,s^{-1}}$.

(iii) Find the power needed to travel at a constant speed of $20\,\mathrm{m\,s^{-1}}$ along a level road.

(iv) Find the maximum acceleration of the car when it is travelling at $20\,\mathrm{m\,s^{-1}}$

(a) along a level road

(b) up a hill at 5° to the horizontal.

⑫ A car of mass 1500 kg travels along a straight horizontal road. The resistance to the motion of the car is $kv^{\frac{1}{2}}$ N, where $v\,\mathrm{m\,s^{-1}}$ is the speed of the car and k is a constant. At the instant when the engine produces a power of 15000 W, the car has speed $15\,\mathrm{m\,s^{-1}}$ and is accelerating at $0.4\,\mathrm{m\,s^{-2}}$.

(i) Find the value of k.

It is given that the greatest steady speed of the car on this road is $30\,\mathrm{m\,s^{-1}}$.

(ii) Find the greatest power that the engine can produce.

⑬ (i) A car of mass 800 kg is moving at a constant speed of $20\,\mathrm{m\,s^{-1}}$ on a straight road down a hill inclined at an angle α to the horizontal. The engine of the car works at a constant rate of 10 kW and there is a resistance to motion of 1300 N. Show that $\sin\alpha = \frac{5}{49}$.

(ii) The car now travels up the same hill and its engine now works at a constant rate of 20 kW. The resistance to motion remains 1300 N. The car starts from rest and its speed is $8\,\mathrm{m\,s^{-1}}$ after it has travelled a distance of 22.1 m. Calculate the time taken by the car to travel this distance.

⑭ A tractor and its plough have a combined mass of 6000 kg. When developing a power of 5 kW, the tractor is travelling at a steady speed of $2.5\,\mathrm{m\,s^{-1}}$ along a horizontal field.

(i) Calculate the resistance to the motion.

The tractor comes to a patch of wet ground where the resistance to motion is different. The power developed by the tractor during the next 10 seconds has an average value of 8 kW over this time. During this time, the tractor accelerates uniformly from $2.5\,\mathrm{m\,s^{-1}}$ to $3\,\mathrm{m\,s^{-1}}$.

(ii) Show that the work done against the resistance to motion during the 10 seconds is 71 750 J. Assuming that the resistance to the motion is constant, calculate its value.

The tractor now comes to a slope at $\arcsin\left(\frac{1}{20}\right)$ to the horizontal. The non-gravitational resistance to motion on this slope is 2000 N. The tractor accelerates uniformly from $3\,\mathrm{m\,s^{-1}}$ to $3.25\,\mathrm{m\,s^{-1}}$ over a distance of 100 m while climbing the slope.

(iii) Calculate the time taken to travel this distance of 100 m and the average power required over this time period.

⑮ A car of mass 1250 kg has a maximum power of 50 kW. Resistive forces have a constant magnitude of 1500 N.

(i) Find the maximum speed of the car on level ground.

The car is now ascending a hill with inclination θ and $\sin\theta = 0.1$.

(ii) Calculate the maximum steady speed of the car when ascending the hill.

(iii) Calculate the acceleration of the car when it is descending the hill at $20\,\mathrm{m\,s^{-1}}$ working at half the maximum power.

⑯ A car of mass 1000 kg travels along a horizontal straight road. The power provided by the car's engine is a constant 15 kW. The resistance to the car's motion is a constant 400 N. The car passes through two points A and B with speeds $10\,\mathrm{m\,s^{-1}}$ and $20\,\mathrm{m\,s^{-1}}$ respectively. The car takes 30 seconds to travel from A to B.

(i) Find the acceleration at A.

(ii) Find the distance AB.

KEY POINTS

1. The work done by a constant force F is given by Fs where s is the distance moved in the direction of the force.
2. The kinetic energy (K.E.) of a body of mass m moving with speed v is given by $\frac{1}{2}mv^2$. Kinetic energy is the energy a body possesses on account of its motion.
3. The work–energy principle states that the total work done by all the forces acting on a body is equal to the increase in the kinetic energy of the body.
4. The gravitational potential energy of a body of mass m at a height h above a given reference level is given by mgh. It is the work done against the force of gravity in raising the body.
5. Mechanical energy (kinetic energy + gravitational potential energy) is conserved when no forces other than gravity do work.
6. Power is the rate of doing work, and is given by Fv.
7. Average power = total work done ÷ total time taken
8. The S.I. unit for energy is the joule and for power is the watt.

LEARNING OUTCOMES

When you have completed this chapter, you should be able to

- understand the language relating to work, energy and power
- calculate the work done by a force which moves either along its line of action or at an angle to it
- calculate kinetic energy and gravitational potential energy
- understand and use the principle of conservation of energy
- use energy considerations to calculate the speed of a particle at a given point on a circular path
- understand and use the work–energy principle
- understand and use the concept of power.

PRACTICE QUESTIONS: SET 1

① A train starts from rest and accelerates uniformly for 4 minutes, by which time it has gained a speed of $36\,\text{km}\,\text{h}^{-1}$. It runs at this speed for 5 minutes and then decelerates uniformly, coming to rest in 2 minutes.

(i) Draw the speed–time graph using consistent units on the two axes. [4 marks]

(ii) Find the total distance travelled. [3 marks]

② A particle is moving in a straight line. The position s of the particle at time t is given by

$$s = 18 - 24t + 9t^2 - t^3, \quad 0 \le t \le 5$$

(i) Find the velocity v at time t and the values of t for which $v = 0$. [4 marks]

(ii) Find the position of the particle at those times. [2 marks]

(iii) Find the total distance travelled by the particle in the interval $0 \le t \le 5$. [5 marks]

③ A skier of mass 60 kg is skiing down a slope inclined at 20° to the horizontal.

(i) Draw a diagram showing the forces acting on the skier. [3 marks]

(ii) Resolve these forces into components parallel and perpendicular to the slope. [2 marks]

(iii) The skier is travelling at constant speed. Find the normal reaction of the slope on the skier and the resistive force on her. [3 marks]

The skier later returns to the top of the slope by being pulled up it at a constant speed of $8\,\text{m}\,\text{s}^{-1}$ by a rope parallel to the slope.

(iv) Assuming the resistance on the skier is the same as before, calculate the tension in the rope. [2 marks]

(v) The rope suddenly breaks. How far does the skier travel before coming to rest? [4 marks]

④ Two forces **P** and **Q** act in the directions of the unit vectors **i** and **j**. The resultant has magnitude 20 N and makes an angle of 60° with the direction of **i**.

(i) Find the magnitude of **P** and the magnitude of **Q**. [3 marks]

(ii) Find the magnitude and direction of a force of $-3\mathbf{P} + \sqrt{3}\mathbf{Q}$. [3 marks]

⑤ Overhead cables for a tramway are supported by uniform, rigid, horizontal beams of weight 1500 N and length 5 m that each support two cables which may be modelled by vertical loads of 1000 N, one 1.5 m from A and the other at 1 m from B.

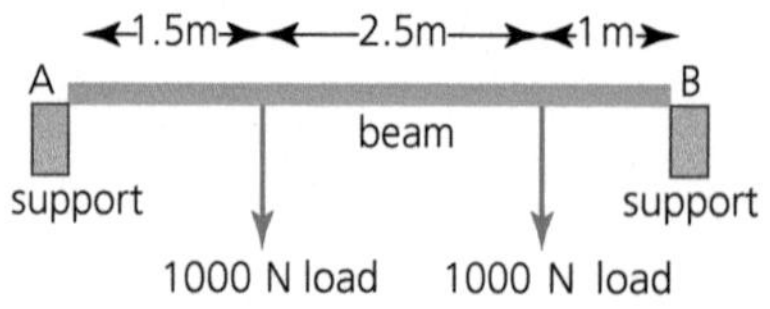

Figure 1

(i) The beam is held in equilibrium by resting on small horizontal supports at A and B, as in Figure 1. Find the magnitudes of the vertical forces acting on the beam at

(a) A, [2 marks]

(b) B. [1 mark]

The support at B is replaced by a thin rigid rod BC that makes an angle of 30° with the horizontal, as in Figure 2.

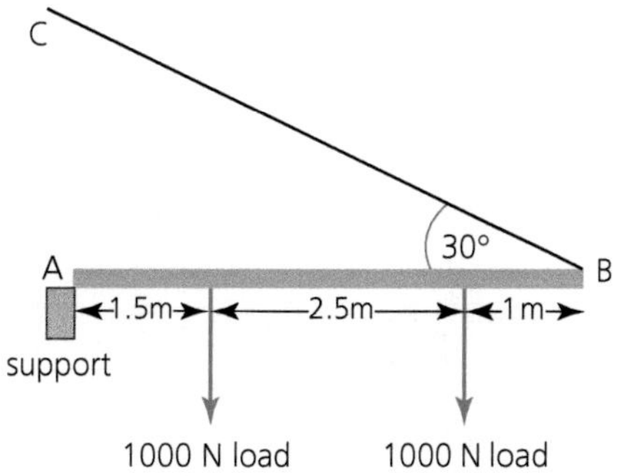

Figure 2

(ii) Find the tension in the rod BC. [4 marks]

⑥

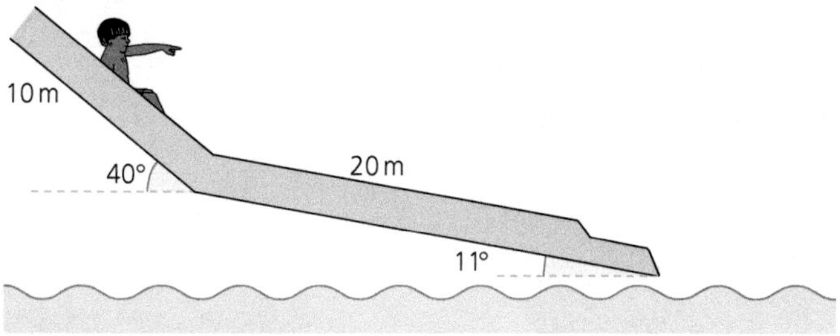

Figure 3

A chute at a water sports centre has been designed so that swimmers first slide down a steep part which is 10 m long and at an angle of 40° to the horizontal. They then come to a 20 m section with a gentler slope, 11° to the horizontal, where they travel at constant speed.

(i) Find the coefficient of friction between a swimmer and the chute. [4 marks]

(ii) Find the acceleration of a swimmer on the steeper part. [4 marks]

(iii) Find the speed of a swimmer at the end of the chute. (You may assume that no speed is lost at the point where the slope changes). [3 marks]

An alternative design of chute is made out of the same material. It has the same starting and finishing points but has a constant gradient.

(iv) With what speed do swimmers arrive at the end of this chute? [4 marks]

6 Impulse and momentum

I collided with a stationary truck coming the other way.

Statement on an insurance form reported in the Toronto News

→ The karate expert in the photograph has just broken a pile of wooden planks with a single blow from his hand. Forces in excess of 3000 N have been measured during karate chops. How is this possible?

1 Impulse

Although the karate expert produces a very large force, it acts for only a short time. This is often the case in situations where impacts occur, as in the following example involving a tennis player.

Example 6.1

A tennis player hits the ball as it is travelling towards her at $10\,\text{m s}^{-1}$ horizontally. Immediately after she hits it, the ball is travelling away from her at $20\,\text{m s}^{-1}$ horizontally. The mass of the ball is 0.06 kg. What force does the tennis player apply to the ball?

Solution

You cannot tell unless you know how long the impact lasts, and that will vary from one shot to another.

Discussion point

Show that the average force she applies to the ball in the cases where the impact lasts 0.1 s and 0.015 s are 18 N and 120 N, respectively. What does 'average' mean in this context?

Although you cannot calculate the force unless you know the time for which it acts, you can work out the product force × time. This is called the **impulse**. An impulse is usually denoted by **I** and its magnitude by *I*.

When a constant force acts for a time *t* the impulse of the force is defined as

$$\text{impulse} = \text{force} \times \text{time}$$

The impulse is a vector in the direction of the force. Impulse is often used when force and time cannot be known separately but their combined effect is known, as in the case of the tennis ball. The S.I. unit for impulse is the newton second (N s).

Discussion point

The magnitude of the momentum of an object is often thought of as its resistance to being stopped. Compare the momentum and kinetic energy of a cricket ball of mass 0.15 kg bowled very fast at $40\,\text{m s}^{-1}$ and a 20 tonne railway truck moving at the very slow speed of 1 cm per second.

Which would you rather be hit by, an object with high momentum and low energy, or one with high energy and low momentum?

Impulse and momentum

When the motion is in one dimension and the velocity of an object of mass *m* is changed from *u* to *v* by a constant force *F*, you can use Newton's second law and the equations for motion with constant acceleration.

$$F = ma$$

and $$v = u + at$$

$$\Rightarrow \quad mv = mu + mat$$

Substituting *F* for *ma* gives $$mv = mu + Ft$$

$$\Rightarrow \quad Ft = mv - mu \qquad ①$$

The quantity 'mass × velocity' is defined as the **momentum** of the moving object.

The equation ① can be written as

$$\text{impulse of force} = \text{final momentum} - \text{initial momentum} \qquad ②$$

So impulse = change in momentum

This equation also holds for any large force acting for a short time even when it cannot be assumed to be constant. The force on the tennis ball will increase as it embeds itself into the strings and then decrease as it is catapulted away, but you can calculate the impulse of the tennis racket on the ball as

$$0.06 \times 20 - 0.06 \times (-10) = 1.8\,\text{N s}$$

final momentum

initial momentum

impulse

The −10 takes account of the change in direction.

Equation ② is also true for a variable force. It is also true, but less often used, when a longer time is involved.

Example 6.2

A ball of mass 50 g hits the ground with a speed of 4 m s^{-1} and rebounds with an initial speed of 3 m s^{-1}. The situation is modelled by assuming that the ball is in contact with the ground for 0.01 s and that during this time the reaction force on it is constant.

(i) Find the average force exerted on the ball.

(ii) Find the loss in kinetic energy during the impact.

(iii) Which of the answers to parts (i) and (ii) would be affected by a change in the modelling assumption that the ball is only in contact with the ground for 0.01 s?

Solution

(i) The impulse is given by:

$$I = mv - mu$$
$$= 0.05 \times 3 - 0.05 \times (-4)$$
$$= 0.35$$

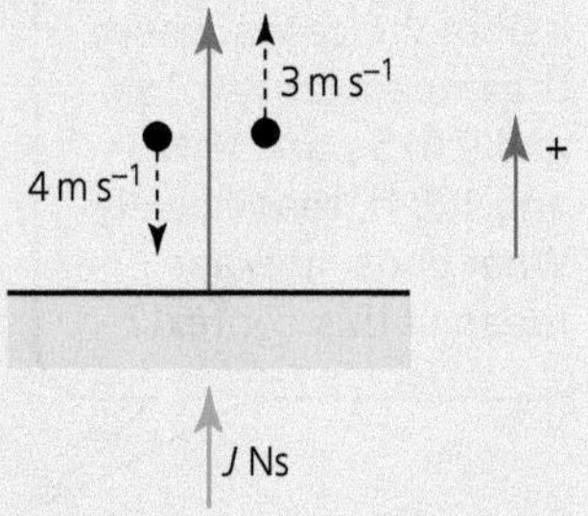

Figure 6.1

The impulse is also given by

$$I = Ft$$

where F is the average force, i.e. the constant force which, acting for the same time interval, would have the same effect as the variable force which actually acted.

$$\therefore \quad 0.35 = F \times 0.01$$
$$F = 35$$

So the ground exerts an average upward force of 35 N.

(ii) Initial K.E. $= \frac{1}{2} \times 0.05 \times 4^2$

$= 0.400$ joules

Final K.E. $= \frac{1}{2} \times 0.05 \times 3^2$

$= 0.225$ joules

Loss in K.E. $= 0.175$ joules

(This is converted into heat and sound.)

(iii) A change in the model will affect the answer to part (i), but not part (ii).

Note

Example 6.2 demonstrates the important point that mechanical energy is not conserved during an impact.

Although the force of gravity acts during the impact, its impulse is negligible over such a short time.

Example 6.3

A car of mass 800 kg is pushed with a constant force of magnitude 200 N for 10 s. The car starts from rest. Resistance to motion may be ignored.

(i) Find its speed at the end of the ten-second interval by using

(a) the impulse on the car (b) Newton's second law.

(ii) Comment on your answers to part (i).

Solution

(i) (a) The force of 200 N acts for 10 s, so the impulse on the car is

The impulse is in the direction of the force.

$$I = 200 \times 10 = 2000\,\text{N s}$$

Hence the change in momentum (in N s) is

$$mv = 2000$$

$$\therefore \quad v = \frac{2000}{800} = 2.5$$

The speed at the end of the time interval is $2.5\,\text{m s}^{-1}$.

Since the force is assumed to be a constant, so is the acceleration and so you can use the constant acceleration formulae.

(b) Newton's second law

$F = ma$

$200 = 800a$

$a = 0.25\,\text{m s}^{-2}$

$v = u + at$

$v = 0 + 0.25 \times 10 = 2.5\,\text{m s}^{-1}$

(ii) Both methods give the same answer but the method based on Newton's second law and the constant acceleration formulae only works because the force is constant.

Consider a variable force $F(t)$ acting on an object in the interval of time $0 \le t \le T$ which changes its velocity from U to V.

At any instant, Newton's second law gives

$$F = ma = m\frac{dv}{dt}$$

and so the overall effect is given by

$$\int_0^T F\,\mathrm{d}t = m\int_{v=U}^{v=V} \frac{\mathrm{d}v}{\mathrm{d}t}\mathrm{d}t = m\int_U^V \mathrm{d}v$$

$$= mV - mU$$

This is the impulse–momentum equation.

Exercise 6.1

① Find the momentum of the following objects, assuming each of them to be travelling in a straight line.

(i) An ice skater of mass 50 kg travelling with speed $10\,\text{m s}^{-1}$.

(ii) An elephant of mass 5 tonnes moving at $4\,\text{m s}^{-1}$.

(iii) A train of mass 7000 tonnes travelling at $40\,\text{m s}^{-1}$.

(iv) A bacterium of mass 2×10^{-16} g moving with speed $1\,\text{mm s}^{-1}$.

② Calculate the impulse required in each of these situations:

(i) to stop a car of mass 1.3 tonnes travelling at $14\,\text{m s}^{-1}$

(ii) to putt a golf ball of mass 1.5 g with speed $1.5\,\text{m s}^{-1}$

(iii) to stop a cricket ball of mass 0.15 kg travelling at $20\,\text{m s}^{-1}$

(iv) to fire a bullet of mass 25 g with speed $400\,\text{m s}^{-1}$.

③ A stone of mass 1.5 kg is dropped from rest. After a time interval t s, it has fallen a distance s m and has velocity v m s^{-1}.

Take g to be 10 m s^{-2} and neglect air resistance.

(i) Write down the force F (in N) acting on the stone.

(ii) Find s when $t = 2$.

(iii) Find v when $t = 2$.

(iv) Write down the value, units and meaning of Fs and explain why this has the same value as $\frac{1}{2} \times 1.5v^2$.

(v) Write down the value, units and meaning of Ft and explain why this has the same value as $1.5v$.

④ A ball of mass 200 g is moving in a straight line with a speed of 5 m s^{-1} when a force of 20 N is applied to it for 0.1 s in the direction of motion. Find the final speed of the ball

(i) using the impulse–momentum equation

(ii) using Newton's second law and the constant acceleration formulae.

(iii) Compare the methods.

⑤ A girl throws a ball of mass 0.06 kg vertically upwards with initial speed 20 m s^{-1}.
Take g to be 10 m s^{-2} and neglect air resistance.

(i) What is the initial momentum of the ball?

(ii) How long does it take for the ball to reach the top of its flight?

(iii) What is the momentum of the ball when it is at the top of its flight?

(iv) What impulse acted on the ball over the period between its being thrown and its reaching maximum height?

⑥ A netball of mass 425 g is moving horizontally with speed 5 m s^{-1} when it is caught.

(i) Find the impulse needed to stop the ball.

(ii) Find the average force needed to stop the ball if it takes

(a) 0.1 s (b) 0.05 s.

(iii) Why does the action of taking a ball into your body make it easier to catch?

⑦ A car of mass 0.9 tonnes is travelling at 13.2 m s^{-1} when it crashes head-on into a wall. The car is brought to rest in a time of 0.12 s.
Taking g to be 10 m s^{-2}, find

(i) the impulse acting on the car

(ii) the average force acting on the car

(iii) the average deceleration of the car in terms of g.

(iv) Explain why many cars are designed with crumple zones rather than with completely rigid construction.

⑧ Boris is sleeping on a bunk-bed at a height of 1.5 m when he rolls over and falls out. His mass is 20 kg.

(i) Find the speed with which he hits the floor.

(ii) Find the impulse that the floor has exerted on him when he has come to rest.

(iii) Find the impulse he has exerted on the floor.

It takes Boris 0.2 s to come to rest.

(iv) Find the average force acting on him during this time.

⑨ A railway truck of mass 10 tonnes is travelling at $3\,\text{m}\,\text{s}^{-1}$ along a siding when it hits some buffers. After the impact it is travelling at $1.5\,\text{m}\,\text{s}^{-1}$ in the opposite direction.

(i) Find the initial momentum of the truck.

(ii) Find the momentum of the truck after it has left the buffers.

(iii) Find the impulse that has acted on the truck.

During the impact the force F N that the buffers exert on the truck varies as shown in this graph.

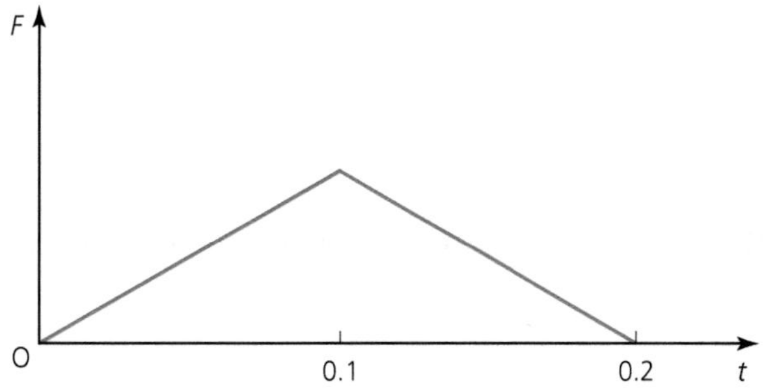

Figure 6.2

(iv) State what information is given by the area under the graph.

(v) What is the greatest value of the force F.

⑩ A van of mass 2500 kg starts from rest. In the first 4 seconds after starting, the driving force on its engine follows the relationship $F(t) = 2400t - 300t^2$.

(i) Find the total impulse on the van over the 4 seconds.

(ii) Find the speed of the van, ignoring the effect of air resistance.

2 Conservation of momentum

Collisions

In an experiment to investigate car design, two vehicles were made to collide head-on. How would you investigate this situation? What is the relationship between the change in momentum of the van and that of the car?

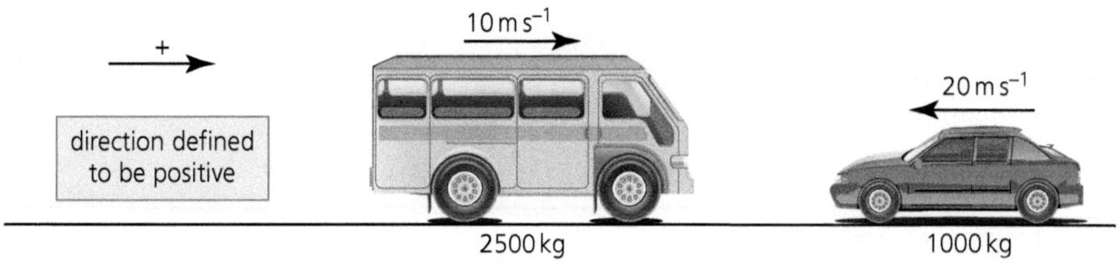

Figure 6.3

Remember Newton's third law. The force that body A exerts on body B is equal to the force that B exerts on A, but in the opposite direction.

Suppose that once the van is in contact with the car, it exerts a force F on the car for a time t. Newton's third law tells us that the car also exerts a force F on the van for a time t. (This applies whether F is constant or variable.) So both vehicles receive equal impulses, but in opposite directions. Consequently, the increase in momentum of the car in the positive direction is exactly equal to the increase in momentum of the van in the negative direction. For the two vehicles together, the total change in momentum is zero.

This example illustrates the **law of conservation of momentum.**

It is important to remember that although momentum is conserved in a collision, mechanical energy is not conserved. Some of the work done by the forces is converted into heat and sound.

The law of conservation of momentum states that when there are no external influences on a system, the total momentum of the system is constant.

Since momentum is a vector quantity, this applies to the magnitude of the momentum in any direction.

For a collision you can say

total momentum before collision = total momentum after collision

Example 6.4

The two vehicles in the previous discussion collide head-on, and, as a result, the van comes to rest.

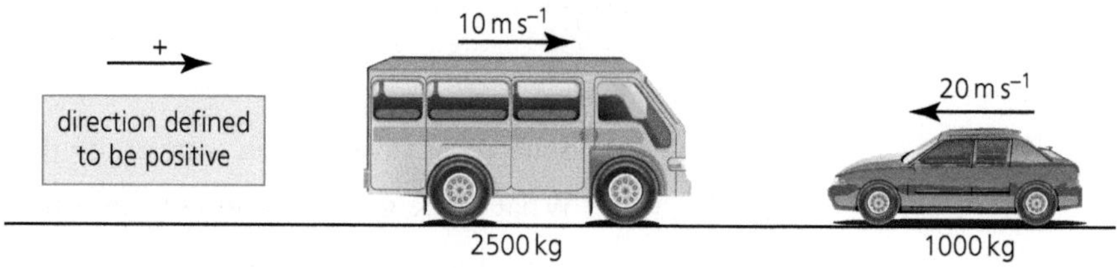

Figure 6.4

(i) Draw diagrams showing the situation before and after the collision.

(ii) Find the final velocity of the car, $v\,\text{m s}^{-1}$.

(iii) Find the impulse on each vehicle.

(iv) Find the kinetic energy lost.

(v) In modelling the collision, it is assumed that the impact lasts for one-twentieth of a second. Find the average force on each vehicle and the acceleration of each vehicle.

Note

When you are solving an impact problem, always draw a 'before' and 'after' diagram like in Figure 6.5.

All relevant information on the masses and velocities of the two vehicles is given on it.

Solution

(i) The vehicles are modelled as particles in Figure 6.5.

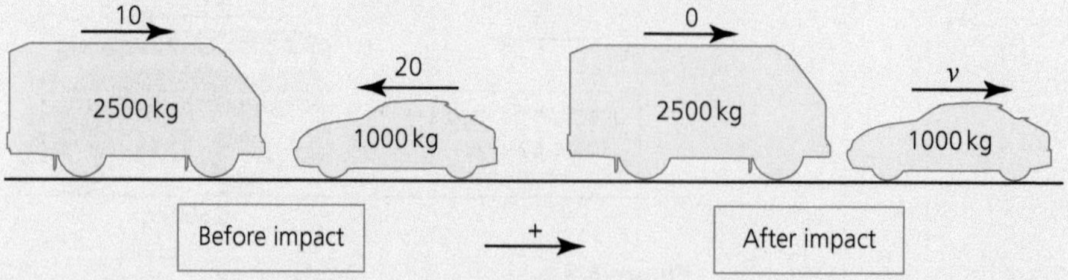

Figure 6.5

Note

The vehicles experience equal and opposite impulses.

(ii) Using conservation of momentum, and taking the positive direction as being to the right:

$$2500 \times 10 + 1000 \times (-20) = 2500 \times 0 + 1000 \times v$$
$$5000 = 1000\,v$$
$$v = 5$$

The final velocity of the car is $5\,\text{m s}^{-1}$ in the positive direction (i.e. the car travels backwards).

(iii) Impulse = final momentum − initial momentum

For the van, impulse $= 2500 \times 0 - 2500 \times 10$

$= -25\,000$ N s

For the car, impulse $= 1000 \times 5 - 1000 \times (-20)$

$= +25\,000$ N s

The van experiences an impulse of 25 000 N s in the negative direction, the car 25 000 N s in the positive direction.

(iv) Total initial K.E. $= \frac{1}{2} \times 2500 \times 10^2 + \frac{1}{2} \times 1000 \times 20^2$

$= 325\,000$ joules

Total final K.E. $= \frac{1}{2} \times 2500 \times 0^2 + \frac{1}{2} \times 1000 \times 5^2$

$= 12\,500$ joules

Loss in K.E. $= 312\,500$ joules

(v) The impulse is equal to the average force × time. If F is the average force, then

$$25\,000 = F \times \frac{1}{20}$$

$$F = 500\,000\,\text{N}$$

The average force on the car is 500 000 N to the right and that on the van is 500 000 N to the left.

Using $F = ma$ on each vehicle gives an average acceleration of $500\,\text{m s}^{-2}$ for the car and $-200\,\text{m s}^{-2}$ for the van.

This is over $50g$ and most people black out at less than $10g$.

Discussion point

These accelerations ($500\,\text{m s}^{-2}$ and $-200\,\text{m s}^{-2}$) seem very high. Are they realistic for a head-on collision?

Work out the distance each car travels during the time interval of one-twentieth of a second between impact and separation. This will give you an idea of the amount of damage there would be.

Is it better for cars to be made strong so that there is little damage, or to be designed to crumple under impact?

Example 6.5

In an experiment on lorry bumper design, the Transport Research Laboratory arranged for a car and a lorry, of masses 1 and 3.5 tonnes, to travel towards each other, both with speed $9\,\text{m s}^{-1}$.

After colliding, both vehicles moved together. What was their combined velocity after the collision?

Solution

The situation before and after the collision is illustrated below.

The vehicles are treated as particles and all relevant information is in Figure 6.6.

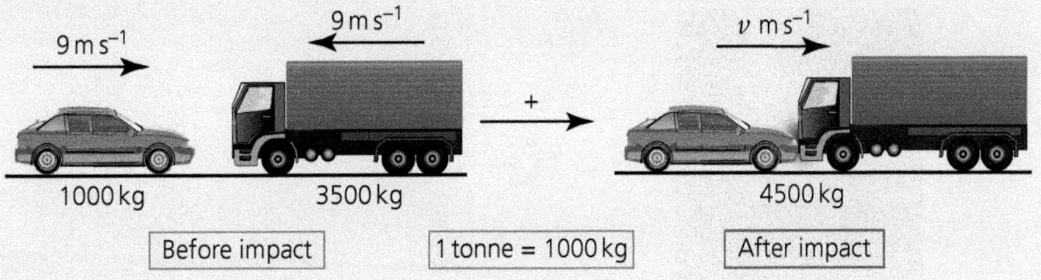

Figure 6.6

Taking the positive direction to be to the right, before the collision

momentum of the car in N s: $1000 \times 9 = 9000$

momentum of the lorry in N s: $3500 \times (-9) = -31\,500$

total momentum in N s: $9000 - 31\,500 = -22\,500$

After the collision, assume that they move as a single object of mass 4.5 tonnes with velocity $v\,\text{m s}^{-1}$ in the positive direction so that the total momentum is now $4500v$ N s.

Momentum is conserved so $4500v = -22\,500$

$v = -5$

The car and lorry move at $5\,\text{m s}^{-1}$ in the direction in which the lorry was moving.

Example 6.6

A child of mass 30 kg running through a supermarket at $4\,\text{m s}^{-1}$ leaps on to a stationary shopping trolley of mass 15 kg. Find the speed of the child and trolley together, assuming that the trolley is free to move easily.

Solution

Figure 6.7 shows the situation before the child hits the trolley

Before impact

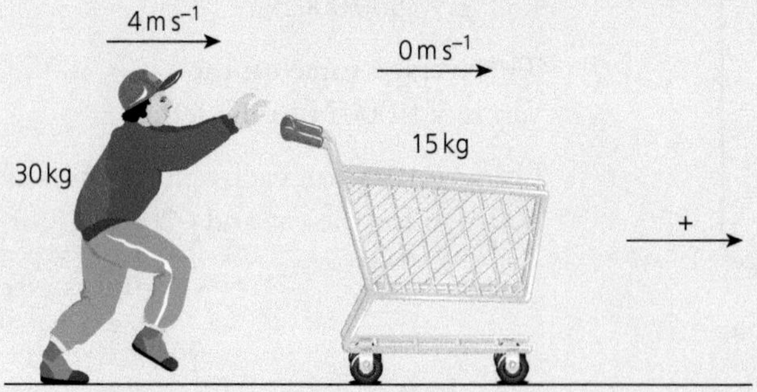

Figure 6.7

Taking the direction of the child's velocity as positive, the total momentum before impact is equal to $4 \times 30 + 0 \times 15 = 120$ N s.

The situation after impact is shown below.

After impact

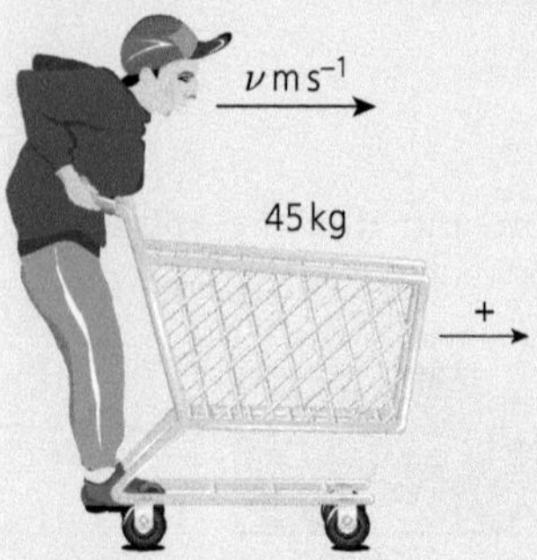

Figure 6.8

The total mass of child and trolley is 45 kg, so the total momentum after is $45v$ N s.

Conservation of momentum gives:

$$45v = 120$$

$$v = 2\frac{2}{3}$$

The child and the trolley together move at $2\frac{2}{3}$ m s^{-1}.

Explosions

Conservation of momentum also applies when explosions take place provided there are no external forces – for example when a bullet is fired from a rifle, or a rocket is launched.

Example 6.7

A rifle of mass 8 kg is used to fire a bullet of mass 80 g at a speed of 200 m s^{-1}. Calculate the initial recoil speed of the rifle.

Solution

Before the bullet is fired, the total momentum of the system is zero.

Before explosion

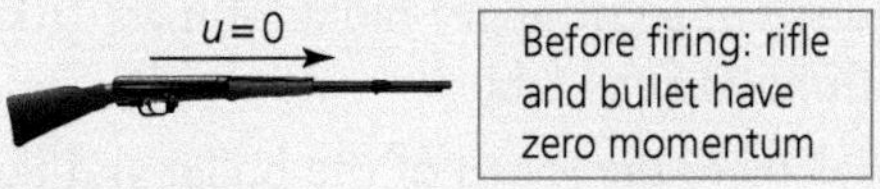

Figure 6.9

After firing, the situation is as illustrated below.

After explosion

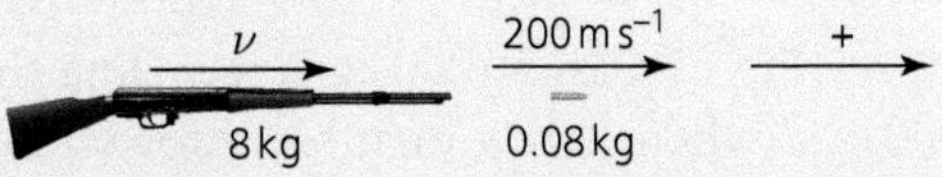

Figure 6.10

The total momentum in the positive direction after the firing is $8v + 0.08 \times 200$.

For momentum to be conserved,

$$8v + 0.08 \times 200 = 0$$

so that

You have probably realised that v would turn out to be negative.

$$v = \frac{-0.08 \times 200}{8} = -2$$

The recoil speed of the rifle is 2 m s^{-1}.

Exercise 6.2

① A spaceship of mass 50 000 kg travelling with speed 200 m s^{-1} docks with a space station of mass 500 000 kg travelling in the same direction with speed 195 m s^{-1}. What is their speed after the docking is completed?

② A railway truck of mass 20 tonnes is shunted with speed 3 m s^{-1} towards a stationary truck of mass 10 tonnes. What is the speed after impact

(i) if the two trucks remain in contact

(ii) if the second truck now moves at 3 m s^{-1}?

③ The driver of a car of mass 1000 kg falls asleep while it is travelling at 30 m s^{-1}. The car runs into the back of the car in front which has mass 800 kg and is travelling in the same direction at 20 m s^{-1}. The bumpers of the two cars become locked together and they continue as one vehicle.

(i) What is the speed of the cars immediately after impact?

(ii) What impulse does the larger car give to the smaller one?

(iii) What impulse does the smaller car give to the larger one?

④ A lorry of mass 5 tonnes is about to tow a car of mass 1 tonne. Initially the tow rope is slack and the car stationary. As the rope becomes taut the lorry is travelling at 2 m s^{-1}.

(i) Find the speed of the car once it is being towed.

(ii) Find the magnitude of the impulse transmitted by the tow rope and state the direction of the impulse on each vehicle.

⑤ A bullet of mass 50 g is moving horizontally at 200 m s^{-1} when it becomes embedded in a stationary block of mass 16 kg which is free to slide on a smooth horizontal table.

(i) Calculate the speed of the bullet and the block after the impact.

(ii) Find the impulse from the bullet on the block.

The bullet takes 0.01 s to come to rest relative to the block.

(iii) What is the average force acting on the bullet while it is decelerating?

⑥ A spaceship of mass 50 000 kg is travelling through space with speed 5000 m s^{-1} when a crew member throws a box of mass 5 kg out of the back with speed 10 m s^{-1} relative to the spaceship.

(i) What is the absolute speed of the box?

(ii) What is the speed of the spaceship after the box has been thrown out?

⑦ A gun of mass 500 kg fires a shell of mass 5 kg horizontally with muzzle speed 300 m s^{-1}.

(i) Calculate the recoil speed of the gun.

An army commander would like soldiers to be able to fire such a shell from a rifle held against their shoulders (so they can attack armoured vehicles).

(ii) Explain why such an idea has no hope of success.

⑧ Manoj (mass 70 kg) and Alka (mass 50 kg) are standing stationary facing each other on a smooth ice rink. They then push against each other with a force of 35 N for 1.5 s. The direction in which Manoj faces is taken as positive.

(i) What is their total momentum before they start pushing?

(ii) Find the velocity of each of them after they have finished pushing.

(iii) Find the momentum of each of them after they have finished pushing.

(iv) What is their total momentum after they have finished pushing?

⑨ A truck P of mass 2000 kg starts from rest and moves down an incline from A to B as illustrated in Figure 6.11 The distance from A to B is 50 m and $\sin\alpha = 0.05$. CBDE is horizontal.

Figure 6.11

Neglecting resistance to motion, calculate

(i) the potential energy lost by the truck P as it moves from A to B

(ii) the speed of the truck P at B.

Truck P then continues from B without loss of speed towards a second truck Q of mass 1500 kg at rest at D. The two trucks collide and move on towards E together. Still neglecting resistances to motion, calculate

(iii) the common speed of the two trucks just after they become coupled together

(iv) the percentage loss of kinetic energy in the collision.

⑩ A pile-driver has a block of mass 2 tonnes which is dropped from a height of 5 m on to a pile of mass 600 kg which it is driving vertically into the ground. The block rebounds with a speed of $2\,\mathrm{m\,s^{-1}}$ immediately after the impact. Taking g to be $10\,\mathrm{m\,s^{-2}}$, find

(i) the speed of the block immediately before the impact

(ii) the impulse acting on the block

(iii) the impulse acting on the pile.

From the moment of impact the pile takes 0.025 s to come to rest.

(iv) Calculate the force of resistance on the pile, assuming it to be constant.

(v) How far does the pile move?

⑪ Katherine (mass 40 kg) and Elizabeth (mass 30 kg) are on a sledge (mass 10 kg) which is travelling across smooth horizontal ice at $5\,\mathrm{m\,s^{-1}}$. Katherine jumps off the back of the sledge with speed $4\,\mathrm{m\,s^{-1}}$ backwards relative to the sledge.

(i) What is Katherine's absolute speed when she jumps off?

(ii) With what speed does Elizabeth, still on the sledge, then go?

Elizabeth then jumps off in the same manner, also with speed $4\,\mathrm{m\,s^{-1}}$ relative to the sledge.

(iii) What is the speed of the sledge now?

(iv) What would the final speed of the sledge have been if Katherine and Elizabeth had both jumped off at the same time, with speed $4\,\mathrm{m\,s^{-1}}$ backwards relative to the sledge?

⑫ A sledge of mass 5 kg is initially at rest on a smooth, horizontal surface. All resistances to motion may be neglected. Give all answers correct to three significant figures.

(i) A snowball of mass 0.1 kg is thrown at the sledge, strikes it horizontally at $10\,\mathrm{m\,s^{-1}}$ and coalesces with it. At what speed does the sledge move off?

(ii) If a second identical snowball is thrown in the same way, what will the new speed of the sledge be?

(iii) After n identical snowballs have been thrown in the same way show that the speed of the sledge, $v\,\text{m s}^{-1}$, is given by $v = \frac{n}{5+0.1n}$.

(iv) Show that the expression in (iii) may be written as $v = 10 - \frac{50}{5+0.1n}$ and hence sketch a graph of the relationship between v and n. How does the velocity of the sledge change as n increases?

(v) If the snowball were replaced by a rubber ball of the same mass as in (i), so that it bounced back off the sledge, would the speed of the sledge be greater, the same or less? Give brief reasons for your answer.

⑬ Ben, whose mass is 80 kg, is standing at the front of a sledge of length 5 m and mass 40 kg. The sledge is initially stationary and on smooth ice. Ben then walks towards the back with speed $1\,\text{m s}^{-1}$ relative to the sledge.

(i) Find the velocity of the sledge while Ben is walking towards the back of it.

(ii) Show that, throughout his walk, the combined centre of mass of Ben and the sledge does not move.

(iii) Investigate whether the result of part (ii) is true in general for this type of situation, or just a fluke depending on the particular values of the variables involved.

Discussion point

If you drop two different balls, say a tennis ball and a cricket ball, from the same height, will they both rebound to the same height? How will the heights of the second bounces compare with the heights of the first ones?

3 Newton's law of impact

Your own experience probably tells you that different balls will rebound to different heights.

For example, a tennis ball will rebound to a greater height than a cricket ball. Furthermore, the surface on which the ball is dropped will affect the bounce. A tennis ball dropped onto a concrete floor will rebound higher than if dropped onto a carpeted floor. The following experiment allows you to look at this situation more closely.

EXPERIMENT

The aim of this experiment is to investigate what happens when balls bounce. Make out a table to record your results.

1. Drop a ball from a variety of heights and record the heights of release h_a and rebound h_s. Repeat several times for each height.
2. Use your values of h_a and h_s to calculate v_a and v_s, the speeds on impact and rebound. Enter your results in your table.
3. Calculate the ratio $\frac{v_s}{v_a}$ for each pair of readings of h_a and h_s and enter the results in your table.
4. What do you notice about these ratios?
5. Repeat the experiment with different types of ball.

Coefficient of restitution

Newton's experiments on collisions led him to formulate a simple law relating to the speeds before and after a direct collision between two bodies, called **Newton's law of impact**.

$$\frac{\text{speed of separation}}{\text{speed of approach}} = \text{constant}$$

This can be written as

speed of separation = constant × speed of approach

This constant is called the **coefficient of restitution** and is conventionally denoted by the letter e. For two particular surfaces, e is a constant between 0 and 1. It does not have any units, being the ratio of two speeds.

For very bouncy balls, e is close to 1, and for balls that do not bounce, e is close to 0. A collision for which $e = 1$ is called **perfectly elastic**, and a collision for which $e = 0$ is called **perfectly inelastic**. For perfectly elastic collisions there is no energy loss. For perfectly inelastic collisions the objects coalesce and the energy loss is the largest it can be.

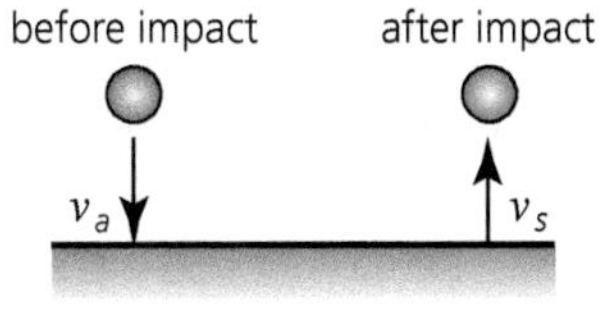

Figure 6.12

Direct impact with a fixed surface

The value of e for the ball you used in the experiment is given by $\frac{v_s}{v_a}$, and you should have found that this had approximately the same value each time for any particular ball. When a moving object hits a fixed surface which is perpendicular to its motion, it rebounds in the opposite direction. If the speed of approach is v_a and the speed of separation is v_s, Newton's law of impact gives

$$\frac{v_s}{v_a} = e$$

$$\Rightarrow \quad v_s = ev_a$$

Collisions between bodies moving in the same straight line

Figure 6.13 shows two objects that collide while moving along a straight line. Object A is catching up with B, and after the collision either B moves away from A or they continue together.

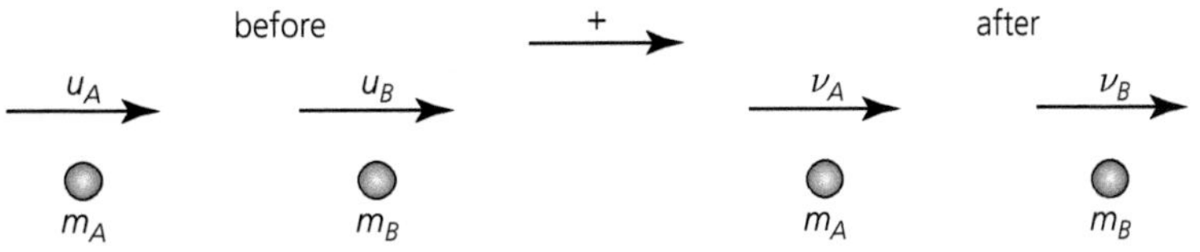

Figure 6.13

$u_A > u_B$ for the collision to occur

$v_B \geq v_A$ as B moves away from A

If the particles coalesce then $v_A = v_B$

Speed of approach: $u_A - u_B$

Speed of separation: $v_B - v_A$

By Newton's law

speed of separation = e × speed of approach

$$\Rightarrow \quad v_B - v_A = e(u_A - u_B) \quad ①$$

The law of conservation of momentum gives a second equation relating the velocities before and after impact.

momentum after collision = momentum before collision

$$m_A v_A + m_B v_B = m_A u_A + m_B u_B \qquad ②$$

These two equations, ① and ②, allow you to calculate the final velocities, v_A and v_B, after any collision as shown in the next two examples.

Example 6.8

A direct collision takes place between two snooker balls. The white cue ball travelling at $2\,\mathrm{m\,s^{-1}}$ hits a stationary red ball. After the collision, the red ball moves in the direction in which the cue ball was moving before the collision. The balls have equal mass and the coefficient of restitution between the two balls is 0.6. Predict the velocities of the two balls after the collision.

Solution

Let the mass of each ball be m. Before the collision, their velocities are u_W and u_R. After the collision, their velocities are v_W and v_R.

The situation is summarised in Figure 6.14.

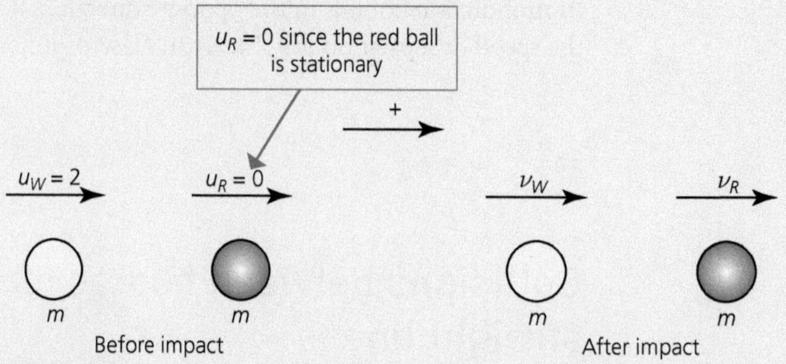

Figure 6.14

By Newton's law of impact

Speed of approach = 2 − 0 = 2

Speed of separation = $v_R - v_W$

Speed of separation = $e \times$ Speed of approach

$\Rightarrow \quad v_R - v_W = 0.6 \times 2$

$\Rightarrow \quad v_R - v_W = 1.2 \qquad ①$

Conservation of momentum

$$mv_W + mv_R = mu_W + mu_R$$

Dividing through by m, and substituting $u_W = 2$, $u_R = 0$, this becomes

$$v_W + v_R = 2 \qquad ②$$

Adding ① + ② gives $2v_R = 3.2$

so $v_R = 1.6$, and from equation ②, $v_W = 0.4$.

After the collision both balls move in the original direction of the white cue ball, the red ball at a speed of $1.6\,\mathrm{m\,s^{-1}}$ and the cue ball at a speed of $0.4\,\mathrm{m\,s^{-1}}$.

Example 6.9

An object A of mass m moving with speed $2u$ hits an object B of mass $2m$ moving with speed u in the opposite direction to A. The coefficient of restitution is e.

(i) Show that the ratio of speeds remains unchanged whatever the value of e.

(ii) Find the loss of kinetic energy in terms of m, u and e.

Solution

(i) Let the velocities of A and B after the collision be v_A and v_B, respectively.

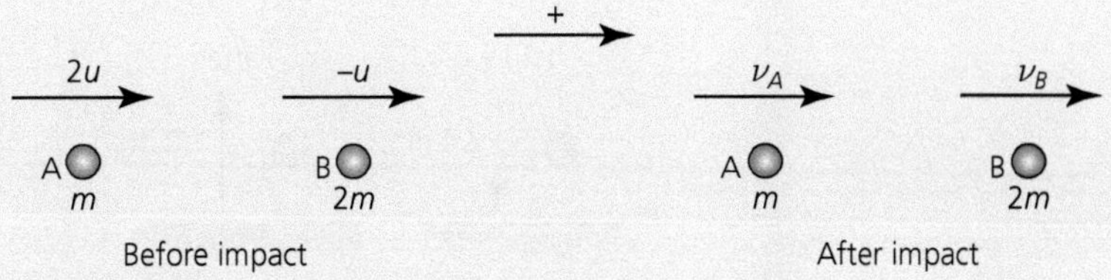

Figure 6.15

$$\text{Speed of approach} = 2u - (-u) = 3u$$
$$\text{Speed of separation} = v_B - v_A$$

Using Newton's law of impact

$$\text{speed of separation} = e \times \text{speed of approach}$$
$$v_B - v_A = e \times 3u \quad ①$$

Conservation of momentum gives

$$mv_A + 2mv_B = m(2u) + 2m(-u)$$

Dividing by m gives

$$v_A + 2v_B = 0 \quad ②$$

Equation ① is $\quad v_B - v_A = 3eu$

Adding ① + ② $\quad 3v_B = 3eu$

$$v_B = eu$$

From ②, $\quad v_A = -2eu$

The ratio of speeds was initially $2u : u$ and finally $2eu : eu$ so the ratio of speeds is unchanged at $2 : 1$ (providing $e \neq 0$).

(ii)

Initial K.E. of A	$\frac{1}{2}m \times (2u)^2 = 2mu^2$
Initial K.E. of B	$\frac{1}{2}(2m) \times u^2 = mu^2$
Total K.E before impact	$3mu^2$
Final K.E. of A	$\frac{1}{2}m \times 4e^2u^2 = 2me^2u^2$
Final K.E. of B	$\frac{1}{2}(2m) \times e^2u^2 = me^2u^2$
Total K.E. after impact	$3me^2u^2$
Loss of K.E.	$3mu^2(1 - e^2)$

Note

In this case, A and B lose *all* their energy when $e = 0$, but this is not true in general. Only when $e = 1$ is there no loss in K.E. Kinetic energy is lost in any collision in which the coefficient of restitution is not equal to 1.

Exercise 6.3

You will find it helpful to draw diagrams when answering these questions.

① In each of the situations shown in Figure 6.16, find the unknown quantity, either the initial speed u, the final speed v or the coefficient of restitution e.

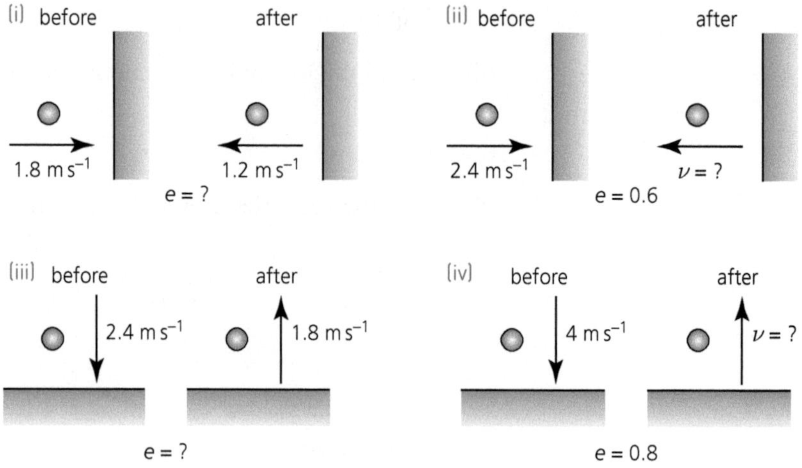

Figure 6.16

② Find the coefficient of restitution in the following situations.

(i) A football hits the goalpost at $10\,\text{m}\,\text{s}^{-1}$ and rebounds in the opposite direction with speed $3\,\text{m}\,\text{s}^{-1}$.

(ii) A beanbag is thrown against a wall with speed $5\,\text{m}\,\text{s}^{-1}$ and falls straight down to the ground.

(iii) A superball is dropped onto the ground, landing with speed $8\,\text{m}\,\text{s}^{-1}$ and rebounds with speed $7.6\,\text{m}\,\text{s}^{-1}$.

(iv) A photon approaches a mirror along a line normal to its surface with speed $3 \times 10^8\,\text{m}\,\text{s}^{-1}$ and leaves it along the same line with speed $3 \times 10^8\,\text{m}\,\text{s}^{-1}$.

③ A tennis ball of mass 60 g is hit against a practice wall. At the moment of impact it is travelling horizontally with speed $15\,\text{m}\,\text{s}^{-1}$. Just after the impact its speed is $12\,\text{m}\,\text{s}^{-1}$, also horizontally. Find

(i) the coefficient of restitution between the ball and the wall

(ii) the impulse acting on the ball

(iii) the loss of kinetic energy during the impact.

④ A ball of mass 80 g is dropped from a height of 1 m onto a level floor and bounces back to a height of 0.81 m. Find

(i) the speed of the ball just before it hits the floor

(ii) the speed of the ball just after it has hit the floor

(iii) the coefficient of restitution

(iv) the change in the kinetic energy of the ball from just before it hits the floor to just after it leaves the floor

(v) the change in the potential energy of the ball from the moment when it was dropped to the moment when it reaches the top of its first bounce

(vi) the height of the ball's next bounce.

⑤ In each of the situations in Figure 6.17, a collision is about to occur. Masses are given in kilograms, speeds are in metres per second. In each case

(i) Draw diagrams showing the situation before and after impact, including known velocities and the symbols you are using for velocities that are not yet known.

(ii) Use the equations corresponding to the law of conservation of momentum and to Newton's law of impact to find the final velocities.

(iii) Find the loss of kinetic energy during the collision.

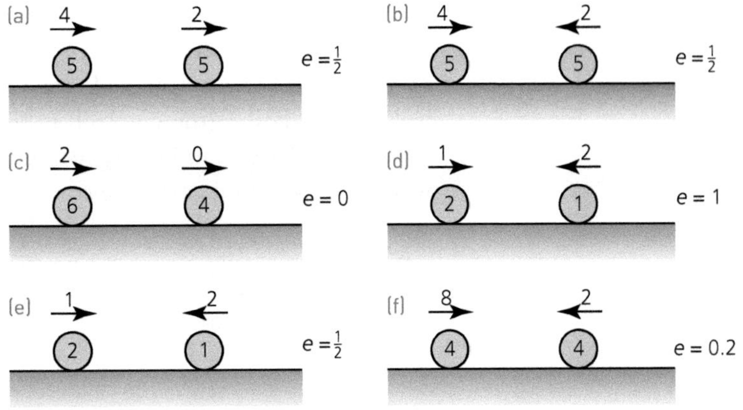

Figure 6.17

⑥ Two children drive dodgems straight at each other, and collide head-on. Both dodgems have the same mass (including their drivers) of 150 kg. Isobel is driving at $3\,\mathrm{m\,s^{-1}}$, Stuart at $2\,\mathrm{m\,s^{-1}}$. After the collision Isobel is stationary. Find

(i) Stuart's velocity after the collision

(ii) the coefficient of restitution between the cars

(iii) the impulse acting on Stuart's car

(iv) the kinetic energy lost in the collision.

⑦ A trapeze artist of mass 50 kg falls from a height of 20 m into a safety net.

(i) Find the speed with which she hits the net. (You may ignore air resistance.)

Her speed on leaving the net is $15\,\mathrm{m\,s^{-1}}$.

(ii) What is the coefficient of restitution between her and the net?

(iii) What impulse does the trapeze artist receive?

(iv) How much mechanical energy is absorbed in the impact?

(v) If you were a trapeze artist would you prefer a safety net with a high coefficient of restitution or a low one?

⑧ Two spheres of equal mass, m, are travelling towards each other along the same straight line when they collide. Both have speed v just before the collision and the coefficient of restitution between them is e. Your answers should be given in terms of m, v and e.

(i) Draw diagrams to show the situation before and after the collision.

(ii) Find the velocities of the spheres after the collision.

(iii) Show that the kinetic energy lost in the collision is given by $mv^2(1 - e^2)$.

(iv) Explain why the result in part (iii) shows that e cannot have a value greater than 1.

⑨ Three identical spheres are lying in the same straight line. The coefficient of restitution between any pair of spheres is $\frac{1}{2}$. Initially the left-hand sphere has a velocity of $2\,\text{m s}^{-1}$ towards the other two which are both stationary. What are the final velocities of all three, when no more collisions can occur?

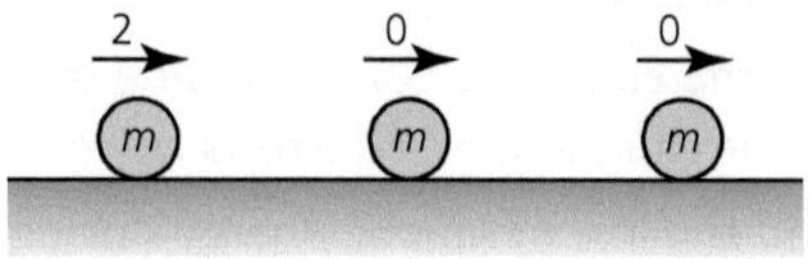

Figure 6.18

⑩ Figure 6.19 shows two snooker balls and one edge cushion. The coefficient of restitution between the balls and the cushion is 0.5 and that between the balls is 0.75. Ball A (the cue ball) is hit directly towards the stationary ball B with speed $8\,\text{m s}^{-1}$. Find the speed and directions of the two balls after their second impact with each other.

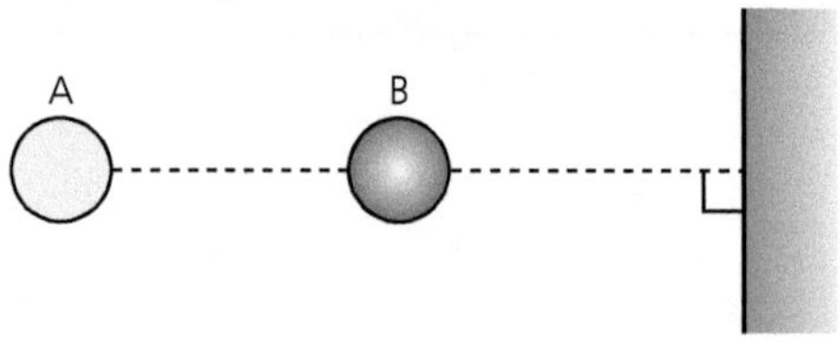

Figure 6.19

⑪ A ball of mass 0.1 kg rolls along a smooth table with speed $6\,\text{m s}^{-1}$. It hits a stationary ball of mass 0.2 kg. After the collision the speed of the first ball is $v\,\text{m s}^{-1}$. The coefficient of restitution between the two balls is e. The two balls move in the same straight line.

(i) Show that $v = 2(1 - 2e)$.

(ii) Find the range of possible values of v.

⑫ Two spheres A and B, of masses 0.5 kg and 0.3 kg respectively, are suspended by light inextensible strings from the ceiling. Sphere A hangs at rest and sphere B falls towards it so that the speed of B directly before impact is $4\,\text{m s}^{-1}$. The impact is direct, so that the velocities of the spheres before and after impact are along the same straight line. Find the speed of A immediately after the impact if

(i) the loss of kinetic energy in the impact is as great as possible

(ii) there is no loss of kinetic energy in the collision.

⑬ A spacecraft has two parts which may separate in flight, the body with mass 15 000 kg and the nose-cone with mass 5000 kg. They rejoin by means of a 'docking' procedure which requires the nose-cone and body to approach along the axis shown in Figure 6.20 with a speed of approach of no more than $3\,\text{m s}^{-1}$. If the speed of approach is too great, the linking mechanism will not engage and the two parts will bounce off each other with a speed of separation which is $\frac{1}{4}$ of the speed of approach (i.e. a coefficient of restitution of 0.25). At all times both parts may be taken as travelling in a straight line.

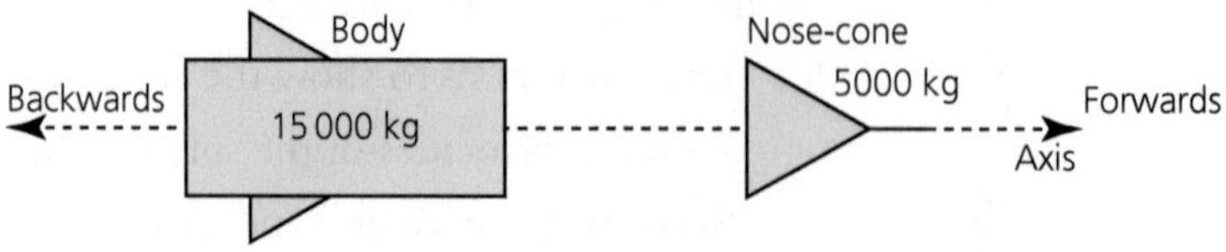

Figure 6.20

On one occasion the body is travelling forwards at $105\,\text{m}\,\text{s}^{-1}$ and the nose-cone at $103\,\text{m}\,\text{s}^{-1}$.

(i) Draw diagrams showing the velocities of the parts before and after docking.

(ii) Calculate the final velocity of the spacecraft.

On another occasion the nose-cone is moving backwards at $5.5\,\text{m}\,\text{s}^{-1}$ and the body forwards at $2.5\,\text{m}\,\text{s}^{-1}$.

(iii) Show that the body comes to rest and find the direction and speed of the nose-cone.

After this has happened, before a further attempt to dock is made, the speed of the body is changed in its line of motion by expelling a mass m kg of fuel. The fuel is expelled at a speed of $2000\,\text{m}\,\text{s}^{-1}$ and you may assume that all the fuel is expelled instantaneously (i.e. before the body changes speed).

(iv) What value of m would cause the body to have a forward speed of $2.5\,\text{m}\,\text{s}^{-1}$ after the fuel is expelled?

14 Two particles A and B, of masses 20 kg and m kg respectively, are initially at rest. A force of 15 N acts for 12 s on particle A.

(i) Calculate the magnitude of the impulse given to particle A. Show that the speed of the particle at the end of the 12 s is $9\,\text{m}\,\text{s}^{-1}$.

Particle A now collides with particle B. Except during the collision, the forces acting on the particles are negligible.

(ii) Explain why the linear momentum of the pair of particles is conserved in the collision but the linear momentum of each individual particle is not.

Immediately after the collision, particles A and B have speeds of $3\,\text{m}\,\text{s}^{-1}$ and $5\,\text{m}\,\text{s}^{-1}$, respectively, in the original direction of motion of particle A.

(iii) Find the coefficient of restitution between the particles in the collision.

(iv) Calculate the value of m. Calculate also the impulse given to particle A in the collision.

Figure 6.21 shows a new situation in which particle C collides with particle D. Particle C has mass 20 kg and speed $8\,\text{m}\,\text{s}^{-1}$. Particle D has mass M kg and speed $13\,\text{m}\,\text{s}^{-1}$. The coefficient of restitution is $\frac{1}{3}$.

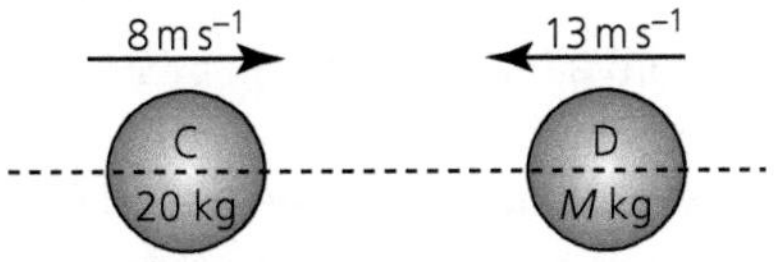

Figure 6.21

(v) If particle C is brought to rest in the collision, find M. What would happen to particle C after the collision if the mass of particle D were greater than this value?

15 A disc A of mass 2 kg is sliding with speed $u\,\text{m}\,\text{s}^{-1}$ over a smooth horizontal table when it makes direct contact with disc B of mass 3 kg which is initially at rest. The coefficient of restitution in the collision is e.

(i) Draw a diagram indicating the velocities of the discs before and after the collision.

(ii) Write down two equations involving the velocities of the discs before and after the collision.

Solve the equations to show that after the collision disc A has a speed of $\frac{u}{5}(2-3e)$ in the original direction of its motion, and find the velocity of disc B.

(iii) For what values of e will the direction of the motion of disc A change in the collision?

(iv) Find the value of e for which disc A moves off after the collision with speed $\frac{u}{10}$ in the opposite direction to its original motion. Find an expression for the kinetic energy lost in the collision in this case.

16 The coefficient of restitution between a ball and the floor is e. The ball is dropped from a height h. Air resistance may be neglected, and your answers should be given in terms of e, h, g and n, the number of bounces.

(i) Find the time it takes the ball to reach the ground and its speed when it arrives there.

(ii) Find the ball's height at the top of its first bounce.

(iii) Find the height of the ball at the top of its nth bounce.

(iv) Find the time that has elapsed when the ball hits the ground for the second time, and for the nth time.

(v) Show that according to this model the ball comes to rest within a finite time having completed an infinite number of bounces.

(vi) What distance does the ball travel before coming to rest?

17 Two spheres which are travelling at the same speed in opposite directions collide directly. Immediately after the collision they move in the same direction with equal momenta. If the coefficient of restitution between the spheres is $\frac{1}{2}$, show that the ratio of the masses of the spheres is $(2+\sqrt{3}):1$.

18 Three identical smooth spheres A, B and C lie at rest on a smooth horizontal table with their centres in a straight line and B lying between A and C. A is projected towards B with speed u. If the coefficient of restitution at each collision is e, where $0 < e < 1$, find the velocity of each of the spheres just after C is set in motion. Show that A strikes B a second time whatever the value of e and that B strikes C a second time if e is less than $3-2\sqrt{2}$.

KEY POINTS

1 The impulse from a force $\mathbf{F}$ is given by $\mathbf{F}t$ where t is the time for which the force acts.

2 Impulse is conventionally denoted by $\mathbf{I}$. It is a vector quantity.

3 The momentum of a body of mass m travelling with velocity $\mathbf{v}$ is given by $m\mathbf{v}$. Momentum is a vector quantity.

4 The S.I. unit of impulse and momentum is the newton second (N s).

5 The impulse-momentum equation is

$$\text{impulse} = \text{final momentum} - \text{initial momentum}$$

6 The law of conservation of momentum states that when no external forces are acting on a system, the total momentum of the system is constant. Since momentum is a vector quantity this applies to the magnitude of the momentum in any direction.

7 Newton's law of impact:

$$\text{coefficient of restitution } e = \frac{\text{speed of separation}}{\text{speed of approach}}$$

$$\text{speed of separation} = e \times \text{speed of approach}$$

LEARNING OUTCOMES

When you have completed this chapter, you should

- know how to apply the principle of conservation of momentum to direct impacts
- understand Newton's law of impact and know the meaning of coefficient of restitution
- know and use the fact that $0 \le e \le 1$
- understand the implications of values of 0 and 1 for the coefficient of restitution
- understand that when the coefficient of restitution is less than 1, energy is not conserved during an impact
- be able to find the loss of kinetic energy during a direct impact
- know that for perfectly elastic collisions there is no energy loss
- know that for perfectly inelastic collisions the energy loss is the largest it can be.

7 Dimensional analysis

But whatever his weight in pounds, shillings and ounces,
He always seems bigger because of his bounces.
The house at Pooh Corner,
A.A. Milne

→ What makes the rhyme on the left about Tigger sound so ridiculous?
Look at the units in the line of the rhyme. Pounds can be units of either money or mass, shillings are units of money and ounces are units of mass. You can see at once that not only is there a mixture of units, but also of the underlying quantities which they are measuring.

1 Dimensional analysis

In this chapter, you will look at the quantities that you will meet in mechanics and classify them according to their **dimensions**. The dimensions of a quantity are closely related to the units in which it is measured.

All of the quantities you will meet in this book can be described in terms of three fundamental quantities, Mass, Length and Time. Take, for example, the quantity **area**; there are many familiar ways of finding area, depending on the shape involved (see Figure 7.1).

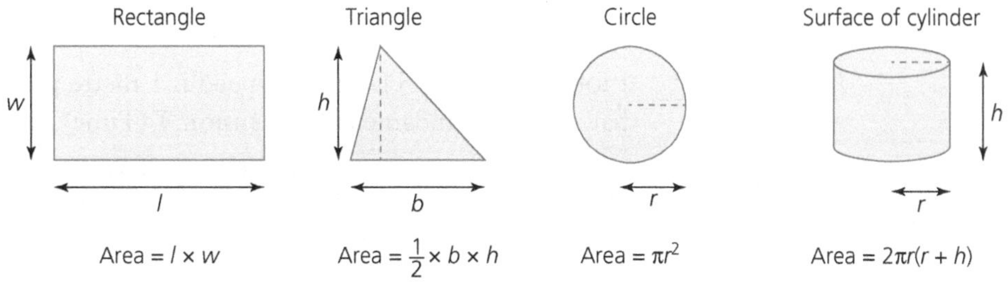

Figure 7.1

All of these formulae have essentially the same form

area = number × length × length

In the case of the rectangle, the 'number' is 1 and the two 'lengths' are the length and width of the shape. For the circle, the two 'lengths' are the same, namely, the radius and the 'number' is π. For the surface area of the cylinder, one of the 'lengths' is a sum of 2 lengths: the radius of the base and the height of the cylinder. However, the structure of the formula is the same for all four shapes, and, indeed, for any other area formula you can think of (for example, the area of a trapezium or the surface area of a cone).

The dimensions of the quantity Area can therefore be summarised using the formula

$$[\text{Area}] = L^2$$

The square brackets [ ] mean the **dimensions of**, and the letter L represents the quantity Length. So the whole statement reads

The dimensions of area are Length squared.

There are two important points to notice about this.

1 The numbers at the start of the formulae (in the four cases above, they are 1, $\frac{1}{2}$, π and 2π) do not feature in the dimensions of the quantity because they are dimensionless.
2 The units in which a quantity is measured are derived directly from its dimensions. In the S.I. system, the unit of length is 1 metre. Since the dimensions of area are L^2, it follows that the S.I. unit for area is 1 metre-squared, usually written m^2.

Note

The area under a curve is often found by calculus methods, using the formula

Area = $\int y\,dx$

In this case, both y and the infinitesimal quantity dx represent lengths and so the integral has dimensions L^2, as must be the case since it represents an area.

> **Discussion point**
> How many formulae can you find for the volumes of objects?
> Show that all your formulae for volume involve multiplying three lengths together so that
> [Volume] = L^3

The dimensions of further quantities

So far the quantities discussed, area and volume, have only involved lengths. What are the dimensions of speed (or velocity) and of acceleration?

To find the dimensions of any quantity, start by writing down a simple formula which you might use to calculate it. For example, to calculate speed you might use

$$\text{Speed} = \frac{\text{Distance}}{\text{Time}}$$

The dimensions follow immediately from this. A distance is clearly a length, so

$$[\text{Speed}] = \frac{[\text{Distance}]}{[\text{Time}]} = \frac{\text{L}}{\text{T}} = \text{LT}^{-1}$$

It follows that the S.I. unit for speed is 1 metre per second, written m s^{-1}. Notice that a second fundamental dimension, T (Time), is now involved.

Similarly $\quad \text{Acceleration} = \dfrac{\text{Change in velocity}}{\text{Time taken}}$

and so

$$[\text{Acceleration}] = \frac{[\text{Speed}]}{[\text{Time}]} = \frac{\text{LT}^{-1}}{\text{T}} = \text{LT}^{-2}$$

The corresponding S.I. unit is therefore $1\,\text{m s}^{-2}$.

Exactly the same procedure allows you to find the dimensions of force.

$$\text{Force} = \text{Mass} \times \text{Acceleration}$$

$$[\text{Force}] = [\text{Mass}] \times [\text{Acceleration}] = \text{M} \times \text{LT}^{-2} = \text{MLT}^{-2}$$

Therefore the S.I. unit for force is 1 kilogram metre per second squared. Because force is an important concept, and this unit would be such a mouthful, it is given a name of its own, the newton (N).

$$1\text{N} = 1\,\text{kg m s}^{-2}$$

Notice that now all three of the basic dimensions M, L and T are being used.

Example 7.1

(i) Find the dimensions of

(a) kinetic energy

(b) gravitational potential energy

(c) work.

(ii) Comment on the significance of your answers.

Solution

(i) (a) Kinetic energy $= \frac{1}{2}mv^2$

$$[\text{K.E.}] = \text{M} \times (\text{LT}^{-1})^2$$
$$= \text{ML}^2\text{T}^{-2}$$

(b) Gravitational potential energy $= mgh$

g is an acceleration so it has dimensions LT^{-2}.

$$[\text{G.P.E}] = \text{M} \times \text{LT}^{-2} \times \text{L}$$
$$= \text{ML}^2\text{T}^{-2}$$

(c) Work = Force × Distance

$$= \text{MLT}^{-2} \times \text{L}$$
$$= \text{ML}^2\text{T}^{-2}$$

(ii) All three have the same dimensions because they are examples of the same underlying quantity, energy. The S.I. unit could be written as $1\,\text{kg}\,\text{m}^2\,\text{s}^{-2}$ but is actually given the special name of 1 joule (J).

Dimensionless quantities

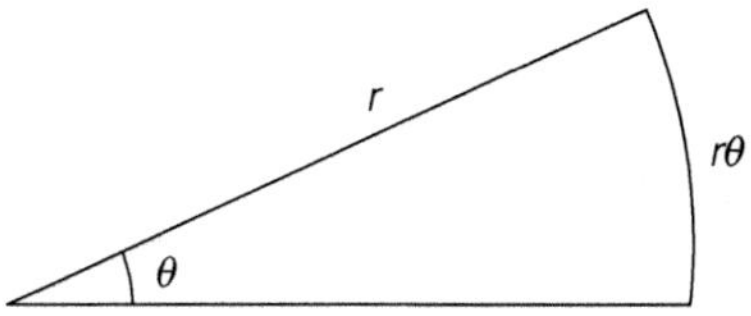

Figure 7.2

Some quantities have no dimensions. For example, angles are dimensionless. The angle θ in radians in Figure 7.2 is defined as

$$\theta = \frac{\text{arc length}}{\text{radius}}$$

Consequently, $[\theta] = \frac{\text{L}}{\text{L}}$ and θ is dimensionless.

Notice that although, in this case, the formula used gave θ in radians, the same result would have been obtained for θ in degrees, using

$$\theta = 360 \times \frac{\text{arc length}}{2\pi \times \text{radius}}$$

The dimensions of a quantity cannot be altered by changing the units in which it is measured.

All numbers are dimensionless, including the trigonometrical ratios, for example $\sin\theta, \cos\theta, \tan\theta$, and irrational numbers such as π and e. This is the reason why you ignore any numbers in a formula when considering its dimensions: numbers, being dimensionless, cannot be included in this analysis.

Dimensionless quantities may be ratios of two lengths, such as $\pi = \frac{\text{circumference}}{\text{diameter}}$ or the golden ratio $\phi = \frac{1+\sqrt{5}}{2}$, or ratios of two forces, such as the coefficient of friction between two surfaces in contact $\mu = \frac{F}{R}$, or even ratios of two speeds such as the coefficient of restitution: $e = \frac{\text{speed of separation}}{\text{speed of approach}}$.

Other systems of units

The units used in this book are almost entirely S.I. units. There are other self-consistent sets of units, such as the 'cgs' system (centimetre, gram, second) or the imperial system (foot, pound, second). Knowing the dimensions of a quantity allows you to find the appropriate unit within any system.

The set of dimensions may also be extended to include quantities that arise in electricity and magnetism. For example, Q represents the dimension of electrical charge.

Change of units

It is helpful to know the dimensions of a quantity when you are changing the units in which it is to be measured, as in the following example.

Example 7.2

The energy of a body is 5000 foot poundals (imperial units based on feet, pounds and seconds). Write this in S.I. units, i.e. joules.

(To 3 s.f. 1 pound (lb) = 0.454 kg and 1 foot = 0.305 m)

Solution

The dimensions of energy are $ML^2T^{-2} = \frac{ML^2}{T^2}$

So
$$1 \text{ foot poundal} = \frac{1 \text{ lb} \times (1 \text{ foot})^2}{(1 \text{ second})^2}$$
$$= \frac{0.454 \text{ kg} \times (0.305 \text{ m})^2}{(1 \text{ second})^2}$$
$$= 0.0422 \text{ J}$$

and
$$5000 \text{ foot poundals} = 5000 \times 0.0422 \text{ J}$$
$$= 211 \text{ J (to 3 s.f.)}$$

ACTIVITY 7.1

Draw up a table like this one and, having copied the first two lines, extend it to cover the other quantities.

Quantity	Formula	Dimensions	S.I. unit
Area	$l \times w$	L^2	m^2
Volume	$l \times w \times h$	L^3	m^3
Speed			
Acceleration			
g			
Force (= mass × acceleration)			
Weight			
Kinetic energy			
Gravitational potential energy			
Work			

Quantity	Formula	Dimensions	S.I. unit
Power			
Impulse			
Momentum			
Pressure (= force/area)			
Density			
Moment			
Angle			
Gravitational constant (G)			
Coefficient of friction			
Coefficient of restitution			

Copy the table and use these blank lines for other quantities as you come across them.

You may find it helpful to keep the completed table somewhere handy for reference.

Dimensional consistency

In any equation or formula, all the terms must have the same dimensions. If that is the case, the equation is said to be **dimensionally consistent**. If not, for example, if force and area are being added or subtracted, or if a mass is being equated to a velocity, the equation is said to be **dimensionally inconsistent**.

Any statement that is dimensionally inconsistent **must** be wrong. In the quotation at the start of this chapter, the phrase '*his weight in pounds, shillings and ounces*' is nonsense because it is **dimensionally inconsistent**.

Example 7.3

Show that the formula

$$s = ut + \frac{1}{2}at^2$$

is dimensionally consistent.

Solution

There are three terms, with dimensions as follows:

$$[s] = \mathrm{L}$$

$$[ut] = \mathrm{LT^{-1}} \times \mathrm{T} = \mathrm{L}$$

$$\left[\frac{1}{2}at^2\right] = \mathrm{LT^{-2}} \times \mathrm{T^2} = \mathrm{L}$$

All three terms have the same dimensions, and so the formula is dimensionally consistent.

The fact that a formula is dimensionally consistent does not mean it is necessarily right, but if it is dimensionally inconsistent it is certainly wrong.

Good mathematicians develop the habit of automatically checking the dimensional consistency of anything they write. A consequence of this is that they tend to leave everything written in symbols until the final calculation. You know, for example, that g has dimensions LT^{-2} but if it is replaced by an approximate value, e.g. 10, its dimensions are no longer evident: $h = \frac{1}{2}gt^2$ is dimensionally correct but $h = 5t^2$ seems not to be.

Example 7.4

A mathematician writes down the equation

$$\frac{1}{2}m_1v_1^2 = m_2gh + m_2v_2$$

Show that it must be wrong.

Solution

Checking for dimensional consistency:

$$\left[\frac{1}{2}m_1v_1^2\right] = M \times (LT^{-1})^2 = ML^2T^{-2}$$

$$[m_2gh] = M \times LT^{-2} \times L = ML^2T^{-2}$$

$$[m_2v_2] = M \times LT^{-1} = MLT^{-1}$$

The third term is dimensionally different from the other two and so the equation is incorrect.

Finding the form of a relationship

It is sometimes possible to determine the form of a relationship just by looking at the dimensions of the quantities likely to be involved. Consider this example.

A pendulum consists of a light string of length l with a bob of mass m attached to the end. You would expect that the period, t, might depend in some way on the variables l and m and also on the value of g.

This can be expressed in the form

$$t = kl^{\alpha}m^{\beta}g^{\gamma}$$

where k is dimensionless and the powers α, β and γ are to be found.

Writing down the dimensions of each side gives

$$T = L^{\alpha} \times M^{\beta} \times (LT^{-2})^{\gamma}$$

$$T = L^{\alpha+\gamma}M^{\beta}T^{-2\gamma}$$

The left-hand side of the equation, T, may be written as $L^0M^0T^1$ and so

$$L^0M^0T^1 = L^{\alpha+\gamma}M^{\beta}T^{-2\gamma}$$

Equating the powers of L, M and T gives:

L: $0 = \alpha + \gamma$

M: $0 = \beta$

T: $1 = -2\gamma$

Solving these gives $\alpha = \frac{1}{2}$, $\beta = 0$ and $\gamma = -\frac{1}{2}$ and so the relationship is

$$t = k\sqrt{\frac{l}{g}}$$

Simple harmonic motion is studied in the Further Pure Mathematics book. If you are taking that course you will then be equipped to find that the value of k is 2π, so the complete formula is

$$t = 2\pi\sqrt{\frac{l}{g}}$$

In the method used here, all you had to do was to think about the dimensions, a very beautiful piece of mathematics. Of course, the dimensions method does not tell you that the value of k is 2π, but it does provide the correct form of the relationship.

Notice that the mass of the pendulum bob, m, does not feature in the formula for the period. This is found to be the case in practice: a heavier bob makes no difference to the period.

What about the angle of swing of the pendulum, θ? Since angles are dimensionless it cannot feature in this argument. You may like to think of its effect as being included within the dimensionless k. In fact, the value of k is approximately constant (equal to 2π) for small values of θ, but it does vary with θ for larger swings.

In the next example, the work is taken a step further. First, the form of a relationship is proposed, then data are used to determine the constant involved. The resulting formula is used to predict the outcome of a future experiment. Notice that the units look after themselves providing you are consistent with their use; in this case, they happen to be in the cgs system.

Example 7.5

In an experiment, small spheres are dropped into a container of liquid which is sufficiently deep for them to attain terminal velocity. For any sphere, the terminal velocity, V, is thought to depend on its radius, r, its weight mg and the viscosity of the liquid, η (the Greek letter 'eta'). (Viscosity is a measure of the 'stickiness' of a liquid and has dimensions $ML^{-1}T^{-1}$.)

(i) Write down a formula for V as the product of unknown powers of r, mg, η and a dimensionless constant k.

(ii) Find the powers of r, mg and η, and write down the formula for V with these values substituted in.

In a particular liquid it is found that a sphere of mass 0.02 g and radius 0.1 cm has a terminal velocity $5\,\text{cm}\,\text{s}^{-1}$.

(iii) Find the value of $\frac{k}{\eta}$ taking g to be $1000\,\text{cm}\,\text{s}^{-2}$.

(iv) Find, using these values, the terminal velocity of a sphere of mass 0.03 g and radius 0.2 cm.

Note

At terminal velocity the force of resistance is equal to the weight of the sphere, so its acceleration is zero and it does not go any faster.

Solution

(i) $V = kr^{\alpha}(mg)^{\beta}\eta^{\gamma}$

(ii) Taking dimensions of both sides of the equation gives

$$LT^{-1} = L^{\alpha} \times (MLT^{-2})^{\beta} \times (ML^{-1}T^{-1})^{\gamma}$$

$$M^0L^1T^{-1} = M^{\beta+\gamma}L^{\alpha+\beta-\gamma}T^{-2\beta-\gamma}$$

Equating powers: M: $0 = \beta + \gamma$

L: $1 = \alpha + \beta - \gamma$

T: $-1 = -2\beta - \gamma$

Solving these gives $\alpha = -1$, $\beta = 1$ and $\gamma = -1$ and so the formula is

$$V = \frac{kmg}{r\eta} \qquad ①$$

(iii) Substituting $m = 0.02$, $r = 0.1$, $g = 1000$ and $V = 5$ gives

$$5 = \frac{k \times 0.02 \times 1000}{0.1 \times \eta}$$

$$\frac{k}{\eta} = 0.025 \quad \text{(in cgs units)}$$

(iv) Substituting $m = 0.03$, $r = 0.2$, $g = 1000$ and $\frac{k}{\eta} = 0.025$ in ① gives

$$V = \frac{0.025 \times 0.03 \times 1000}{0.2}$$

$$= 3.75$$

The terminal velocity of this sphere is $3.75\,\text{cm}\,\text{s}^{-1}$.

The method of dimensions

This method for finding the form of a proposed formula is sometimes called **the method of dimensions**; at other times it is simply referred to as **dimensional analysis**. There are a number of points which you should realise when using it.

1 In mechanics, relationships are based on three fundamental quantities, Mass, Length and Time, and so the right-hand side of the formula can involve no more than three independent quantities. Otherwise you will end up with three equations to find four or more unknown powers. (The last example actually involved four quantities, m, g, r and η, but the first two of these were tied together as the weight, mg, and were not therefore independent.)

2 The method requires you to make modelling assumptions about which quantities are going to be important and which can be ignored. You must always be prepared to review these assumptions.

3 This method can only be used when a quantity can be written as a product of powers of other quantities. There are many situations which cannot be modelled by this type of formula and for these situations this method is not appropriate. For example, the formula $s = ut + \frac{1}{2}at^2$ has two separate terms which are added together on the right-hand side. The form of this relationship could not be predicted using the method of dimensions.

Exercise 7.1

① Check the dimensional consistency of each of the formulae below and hence state whether it could be correct or is definitely wrong. You may assume that all letters have their conventional meanings.

(i) $v^2 - u^2 = 2as$

(ii) $x = \dfrac{(m_1x_1 + m_2x_2)}{m_1 + m_2}$

(iii) $F - mg = ma$

(iv) $T_1 - T_2 = \frac{1}{2}mv^2$ (T_1 and T_2 are tensions)

(v) $Fs = mv - mu$

(vi) $mg\sin\alpha - \mu mg\cos\alpha = ma$

(vii) $m_1gd_1 - m_2gd_2 = (m_1 + m_2)a$

(viii) $\frac{1}{2}mv^2 = \frac{1}{2}mu^2 + mgh\sin\theta$

(ix) $\frac{1}{2}F(u+v) = \dfrac{(v^2 - u^2)}{2t}$

② Find the dimensions of quantities measured in the following units:

(i) kg m s^{-2}

(ii) N m s^{-1}

(iii) J s^2

③ A scientist thinks that the speed, v, of a wave travelling along the surface of an ocean depends on the depth of the ocean, h, the density of the water in the ocean, ρ (the Greek letter 'rho'), and g.

(i) Write down the dimensions of each of the quantities v, h, ρ and g.

The scientist expresses his idea using the formula

$v = kh^{\alpha}\rho^{\beta}g^{\gamma}$ where k is dimensionless.

(ii) Use dimensional analysis to find the values of α, β and γ and write out the formula with these values substituted in.

(iii) Do waves travel faster in deep water or shallow water?

(iv) Do waves travel faster in winter (when the water density is greater) or in summer?

④ A water container has a hole in the bottom. When it is filled to a depth d it takes time t for the water to run out. The time t may be modelled as the product of powers of d and g and a dimensionless constant k.

(i) Write down a formula for t.

(ii) Use dimensional analysis to find the powers of d and g in the formula.

When the container is filled to a depth of 0.4 m it takes 30 s to empty.

(iii) Taking g to be $10\,\text{m s}^{-2}$, find the value of k.

(iv) How long does it take the container to empty when it is filled to a depth of 60 cm?

⑤ A plane uniform circular disc of radius a and mass m hangs at rest in a vertical plane from a pivot at a point on its circumference about which it can freely rotate. It is believed that the periodic time T of small oscillations of the disc about its rest position might depend upon a, m and the local gravitational acceleration g through a relationship of the form

$$T = km^{\alpha}a^{\beta}g^{\gamma}$$

where k is a dimensionless constant.

(i) Use a dimensional argument to show that T does not depend on m.

(ii) Find an expression for T in terms of a and g.

A number of careful observations of the small oscillations of a disc of radius 0.50 m in a local gravitational acceleration of 9.8 m s^{-2} shows that they have a period of 1.74 s.

(iii) Determine the numerical value of the dimensionless constant k suggested by these observations.

⑥ A ball of mass m travelling with velocity v vertically downwards hits a horizontal surface and bounces back up, rising to a height h. The coefficient of restitution between the ball and the surface is e.

(i) Use the definition of coefficient of restitution to show that e is dimensionless.

It is believed that h depends on a product of powers of v, m, g and a dimensionless constant, so a formula is proposed of the form

$$h = kv^{\alpha}m^{\beta}g^{\gamma}$$

where k is dimensionless.

(ii) Use dimensional analysis to find the values of α, β and γ, and write down the formula with these values substituted in.

(iii) Two balls, identical in all respects except that one is heavier than the other, fall with equal speeds. Explain how your answer to part (ii) allows you to decide which (if either) bounces higher.

(iv) The height h clearly does also depend on e. Why was it not considered useful to include it in the formula?

(v) Use your knowledge of mechanics to find a formula for h in terms of v, m, g and e.

(vi) Explain the relationship between k in the answer to part (ii) and e.

⑦ The volume rate of flow R (in m^3 s^{-1}) of a liquid with a viscosity η (in kg m^{-1} s^{-1}) through a cylindrical pipe of length a (in m) and an internal radius r (in m) is believed to be of the form

$$R = k\eta^{w}a^{x}r^{y}p^{z}$$

where k is a non-dimensional constant and p (in N m^{-2}) is the pressure difference between the ends of the pipe.

Using dimensional considerations

(i) show that $w = -1$ and $z = 1$

(ii) find the relationship between x and y.

Observations of a water supply provided at constant pressure and viscosity produced the following recordings:

Pipe length, a (m)	100	200
Internal radius, r (m)	0.050	0.050
Flow rate, R (m^3 s^{-1})	0.420	0.210

(iii) Derive a formula for R in terms of a and r for such a supply.

(iv) Find the rate of flow of water through 1000 m of pipe with an internal radius of 0.075 m under the same pressure and with the same viscosity.

⑧ In an investigation into viscosity, small spheres are allowed to fall from rest through a column of viscous liquid and their terminal speeds are measured. It is believed that the terminal speed V of a sphere depends upon a product of powers of its weight mg, its radius r and the viscosity η of the liquid and a dimensionless constant.

(i) Given that the dimensions of viscosity are $ML^{-1}T^{-1}$ use the method of dimensions to establish the form of the relationship for V in terms of m, r, η and g.

(ii) The mass m of the sphere may be written in terms of its radius r and its density ρ. Write down this relationship.

(iii) Using (i) and (ii) write down a relationship for V in terms of ρ, r, η and g.

(iv) A steel sphere of radius 0.15 cm and density 7.8 g cm^{-1} falls through a column of a viscous liquid and is found to have a terminal speed of 6.0 cm s^{-1}. A lead sphere of density 11.4 g cm^{-3} falling through the same liquid is found to have a terminal speed of 5.0 cm s^{-1}. Determine the radius of the lead sphere.

⑨ (i) Define π and hence find its dimensions.

(ii) Newton's law of universal gravitation states that the magnitude of the force F on a point mass m_1 due to the presence of a point mass m_2 at a distance r is given by

$$F = \frac{Gm_1m_2}{r^2}$$

Find the dimensions of G.

(iii) The constant G has a value 6.67×10^{-11} in S.I. units. An astronomer proposes a system of units based upon the mass of the Earth, M_E, its radius, R_E, and the time it takes for one revolution about the Sun, T_E. Given that $M_E = 5.98 \times 10^{24}$ kg, $R_E = 6.37 \times 10^6$ m and $T_E = 3.16 \times 10^7$ s, find the value of G in terms of these Earth units.

(iv) Comment briefly upon the different natures of the constants π and G.

⑩ Newton's law of universal gravitation states that the magnitude of the force F on a point mass m_1 due to the presence of a point mass m_2 at a distance r is given by

$$F = \frac{Gm_1m_2}{r^2}$$

(i) Find the dimensions of G.

Consider the case of a point mass (m) at the surface of a much larger spherical mass (M) of radius (R). The acceleration due to gravity of the mass m is thus given by

$$g = \frac{GM}{R^2}$$

(ii) The universal constant G has a value of 6.674×10^{-11} in S.I. units. An astronomer proposes a system of units based upon the mass of the Earth ($M_E = 5.976 \times 10^{24}$ kg), the radius of the Earth ($R_E = 6.371 \times 10^6$ m) and the acceleration due to gravity at the surface of the Earth ($g_E = 9.807$ m s^{-2}). Find the value of G in these Earth units.

(iii) The mass of the Moon is 7.346×10^{22} kg and the mean radius is 1.738×10^6 m. Express these in terms of Earth units and use your results to find the acceleration due to gravity on the Moon's surface.

(iv) The corresponding data for Mars are $M = 6.417 \times 10^{23}$ kg and $R = 3.396 \times 10^6$ m. Find g for Mars, in terms of g_E.

⑪ For a wave travelling with speed c, the wavelength is denoted by λ and the frequency, which is the number of complete oscillations per second, by f.

(i) Verify that the relation $c = \lambda f$ is dimensionally consistent.

For a sound wave travelling in either air or water, the frequency, f, depends on the wavelength, λ, the density, ρ, and the pressure, P. [Pressure is force per unit area.]

(ii) State the dimensions of P and ρ.

(iii) Assuming a relation of the form $f = K\lambda^{\alpha}P^{\beta}\rho^{\gamma}$, find the value of α, β and γ given that K is a dimensionless constant with a different value for air and water. How can the value of K be found?

The speed of propagation, c, of a sound wave is known to be given by

$c = \sqrt{\frac{AP}{\rho}}$ where $A = 1.4$ for air.

(iv) By using this expression for c and the equation in (i), find the value of K for sound waves in air.

(v) It is observed that the density of water is much greater than the density of air and that the speed of sound in water is much greater than in air. What does this imply about the value of A for water? Explain your answer.

⑫ The magnitude of the force of gravitational attraction, F, between two objects of mass m_1 and m_2 at a distance d apart is given by

$$F = \frac{Gm_1m_2}{d^2}$$

where G is the universal constant of gravitation.

(i) Find the dimensions of G.

An astronomer proposes a model in which the lifetime t of a star depends on a product of powers of its mass m, its initial radius r_0, G and a dimensionless constant.

(ii) Use the method of dimensions to find the resulting formula for t.

Observation shows that the larger the initial radius, the longer the lifetime of the star, but that the larger the mass, the shorter the lifetime of the star.

(iii) Is the model consistent with these observations?

(iv) Show that the model can be expressed more simply if the initial density, ρ_0, of the star is used as one of the variables.

⑬ In the early seventeenth century, Mersenne (1588–1648) conducted experiments with long lengths of rope and so obtained the law for the frequency of transverse vibrations of strings.

Assume that the frequency depends on products of powers of T, the tension in the rope, l, the length of the rope, and m, the mass per unit length of the rope.

(i) Find, by dimensional analysis, the form of the relationship.

A rope of length 24 m and mass 0.5 kg m^{-1} under tension of 72 N is found to vibrate with a frequency of $\frac{1}{4}$ of a cycle per second.

(ii) State the exact relationship between the frequency, T, l and m.

(iii) Find the frequency of vibration of a string of length 20 cm and mass 0.005 g cm^{-1} under a tension of 8×10^5 dynes. (The dyne is the cgs unit of force: 1 dyne is the force required to give a mass of 1 g an acceleration of 1 cm s^{-2}.)

⑭ An artillery officer is conducting a series of experiments to find the maximum range, R, of a gun which fires shells from ground level across level ground.

(i) Show, by considering the shell as a projectile with initial velocity u at an angle α to the horizontal and ignoring air resistance, that

$$R = \frac{u^2}{g}\sin 2\alpha$$

and that this has a maximum value, R_M, when α is 45°.

(ii) Show that the expression for R in part (i) is dimensionally consistent.

The officer finds that the shells fall some distance short of their predicted range. Deciding that this must be due to air resistance, he proposes a model in which the magnitude of the force of resistance, F, is proportional to the speed of the shell, v;

$$F = cv$$

(iii) Show that the constant c is not dimensionless and write down its dimensions.

The officer then suggests that a better model for the range of the shell, when fired at 45° to the horizontal, is given by

$$R = R_M(1 - \varepsilon)$$

where ε (epsilon) is a number less than 1 representing the proportion of the range which is lost.

(iv) State the dimensions of ε.

The officer believes that ε depends on a product of powers of the speed of projection, u, the constant c, g and the mass m of the shell.

(v) Use dimensional analysis to find an expression for ε in which the power of u is 1. Express the improved model as a formula for R.

It is suggested that a more accurate and more general model still would have the form

$$R = R_M\left(1 + a_1\varepsilon + a_2\varepsilon^2 + a_3\varepsilon^3 + \ldots\right)$$

where a_1, a_2, a_3,... are dimensionless coefficients, taking into account (among other things) the angle of projection. (Clearly, a_1 would be negative.)

(vi) Show that such a model is dimensionally consistent.

⑮ Kepler's third law of planetary motion compares the orbital period and the radius of the orbit of a planet around the Sun. The comparison being made is that the ratio of the square of the periods to the cube of the average distances from the Sun is the same for every one of the planets. If T is the period of the planet and R the average distance from the Sun then

$$T^2 = KR^3$$

(i) Find the dimension of K.

The average distance of the Earth from the Sun is 1.4957×10^{11} m. This is known as an astronomical unit (1 a.u.).

The orbital period of the Earth around the Sun is one year or 3.156×10^{7} s.

(ii) Find the value of K in S.I. units.

The distances of the planets from the sun are given in the table below.

Planet	Mercury	Venus	Earth	Mars	Jupiter	Saturn	Uranus	Neptune
Distance (a.u.)	0.387	0.723	1	1.52	5.21	9.55	19.2	30.1
Period (year)			1					

(iii) Find the periods of the planets.

KEY POINTS

1. Any quantity in mechanics may be expressed in terms of the three fundamental dimensions: mass, M; length, L; time, T.
2. The dimension of a quantity d is denoted by $[d]$.
3. The unit for any quantity is derived from the three fundamental dimensions.
4. Numbers are dimensionless.
5. All formulae and equations must be dimensionally consistent.
6. Using dimensional analysis you can sometimes find the form of a relationship as the product of powers of the quantities involved and a dimensionless constant.

LEARNING OUTCOMES

When you have completed this chapter, you should be able to

- find the dimensions of a quantity in terms of M, L and T
- use the dimensions of a quantity to determine its units
- change the units in which a quantity is given
- understand that some quantities are dimensionless
- use dimensional analysis to check a relationship for consistency
- use dimensional analysis to determine unknown indices in a proposed formula
- use a model based on dimensional analysis.

8 Circular motion 1

Whirlpools and storms his circling arm invest;
With all the might of gravitation blest.
Alexander Pope

Discussion point

→ These photographs show some objects that move in circular paths. What other examples can you think of?

→ What makes objects move in circles?

→ Why does the Moon circle the Earth?

→ What happens to the hammer when the athlete lets it go?

→ Do the pilots of the planes need to be strapped into their seats at the top of a loop in order not to fall out?

1 Introduction to circular motion

The answers to the questions on the previous page lie in the nature of circular motion. Even if an object is moving at constant speed in a circle, its velocity keeps changing because its direction of motion keeps changing. Consequently the object is accelerating and so, according to Newton's first law, there must be a force acting on it. The force required to keep an object moving in a circle can be provided in many ways.

Without the Earth's gravitational force, the Moon would move off at constant speed in a straight line into space. The wire attached to the athlete's hammer provides a tension force which keeps the ball moving in a circle. When the athlete lets go, the ball flies off at a tangent because the tension has disappeared.

Although it would be sensible for the pilot to be strapped in, no upward force is necessary to stop him falling out of the plane because his weight contributes to the force required for motion in a circle.

In this chapter, these effects are explained.

Notation

To describe circular motion (or indeed any other topic) mathematically you need a suitable notation. It will be helpful in this chapter to use the notation (attributed to Newton) for differentiation with respect to time in which, for example, $\frac{ds}{dt}$ is written as $\dot{s}$, and $\frac{d^2\theta}{dt^2}$ as $\ddot{\theta}$.

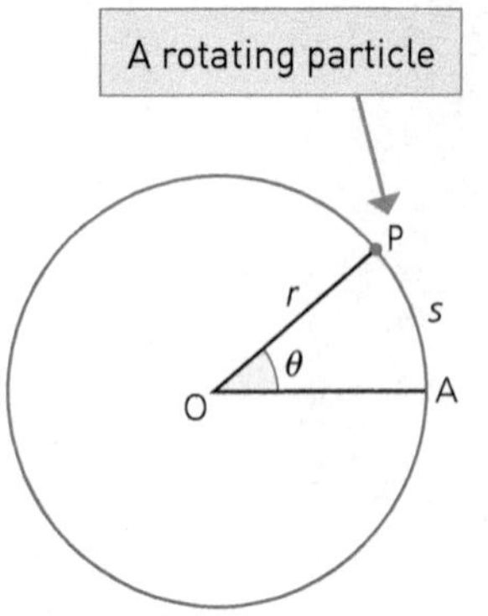

Figure 8.1

Figure 8.1 shows a particle P moving round the circumference of a circle of radius r, centre O. At time t, the position vector OP of the particle makes an angle θ (in radians) with the fixed direction OA. The arc length AP is denoted by s.

Angular speed

Using this notation,

$$s = r\theta$$

Differentiating with respect to time using the product rule gives

$$\frac{ds}{dt} = r\frac{d\theta}{dt} + \theta\frac{dr}{dt}$$

Since r is constant for a circle, $\frac{dr}{dt} = 0$, so the rate at which the arc length increases is

$$\frac{ds}{dt} = r\frac{d\theta}{dt} \text{ or } \dot{s} = r\dot{\theta}$$

In this equation, $\dot{s}$ is the speed at which P is moving round the circle (often denoted by v), and $\dot{\theta}$ is the rate at which the angle θ is increasing, i.e. the rate at which the position vector $\overrightarrow{OP}$ is rotating.

The quantity $\frac{d\theta}{dt}$, or $\dot{\theta}$, can be called the **angular velocity** or the **angular speed** of P.

In more advanced work, angular velocity is treated as a vector, whose direction is taken to be that of the axis of rotation. In this book, $\frac{d\theta}{dt}$ is often referred to as angular speed, but is given a sign: positive for an anticlockwise rotation and negative for a clockwise rotation.

Note

It is common practice to give angular speed as multiples of π.

Angular speed is often denoted by ω, the Greek letter omega. So the equation $\dot{s} = r\dot{\theta}$ may be written as

$$v = r\omega$$

Notice that for this equation to hold, θ must be measured in radians, so the angular speed is measured in radians per second or rad s^{-1}.

Figure 8.2 shows a disc rotating about its centre, O, with angular speed ω. The line OP represents any radius.

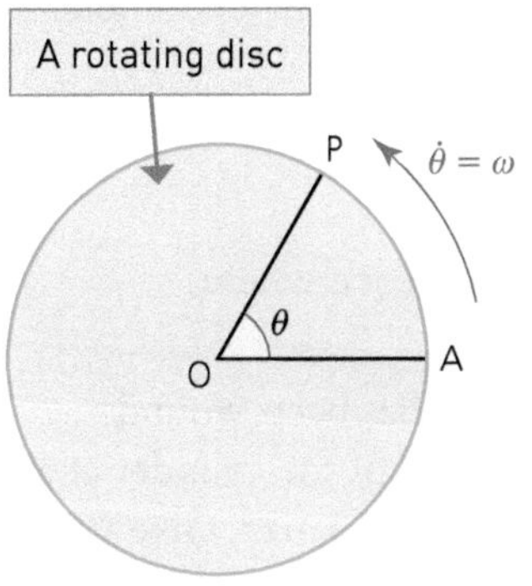

Figure 8.2

Every point on the disc describes a circular path, and all the points have the same angular speed. However, the actual speed of any point depends on its distance from the centre: increasing r in the equation $v = r\omega$ increases v. You will appreciate this if you have ever been at the end of a rotating line of people in a dance or watched a body of marching soldiers wheeling round a corner.

Angular speeds are sometimes measured in revolutions per second or revolutions per minute (rpm) where one revolution is equal to 2π radians. For example, a computer hard disc might spin at 7200 rpm or more; at cruising speeds, crankshafts in car engines typically rotate at 3000 to 4000 rpm.

Example 8.1

A police car drives at 40 mph around a circular bend of radius 16 m. A second car moves so that it has the same angular speed as the police car but in a circle of radius 12 m. Is the second car breaking the 30 mph speed limit? (Use the approximation 1 mile = $\frac{8}{5}$ km.)

Notes

1 Notice that working in fractions gives an exact answer.

2 A quicker way to do this question would be to notice that, because the cars have the same angular speed, the actual speeds of the cars are proportional to the radii of the circles in which they are moving. Using this method it is possible to stay in mph. The ratio of the two radii is $\frac{12}{16}$ so the speed of the second car is $\frac{12}{16} \times 40$ mph = 30 mph.

Solution

Converting miles per hour to metres per second gives:

$$\begin{aligned} 40 \text{ mph} &= 40 \times \frac{8}{5} \text{km h}^{-1} \\ &= \frac{40 \times 8 \times 1000}{5 \times 3600} \text{ m s}^{-1} \\ &= \frac{160}{9} \text{ m s}^{-1} \end{aligned}$$

Using $v = r\omega$

$$\begin{aligned} \omega &= \frac{160}{9 \times 16} \text{ rad s}^{-1} \\ &= \frac{10}{9} \text{ rad s}^{-1} \end{aligned}$$

The speed of the second car is:

$$\begin{aligned} v &= 12\omega \\ &= \frac{10}{9} \times 12 \text{ m s}^{-1} \\ &= \frac{120 \times 5 \times 3600}{9 \times 8 \times 1000} \text{ mph} \\ &= 30 \text{ mph} \end{aligned}$$

The second car is just on the speed limit.

Exercise 8.1

① Find the angular speed in radians per second to one decimal place, of antique records rotating at

(i) 78 rpm (ii) 45 rpm (iii) $33\frac{1}{3}$ rpm.

② A flywheel is rotating at $300\,\text{rad}\,\text{s}^{-1}$. Express this angular speed in rpm, correct to the nearest whole number.

③ The London Eye observation wheel has a diameter of 135 m and completes one revolution in 30 minutes.

(i) Calculate its angular speed in

(a) rpm (b) radians per second.

(ii) Calculate the speed of the point on the circumference where passengers board the moving wheel.

④ A lawnmower engine is started by pulling a rope that has been wound round a cylinder of radius 4 cm. Find the angular speed of the cylinder at a moment when the rope is being pulled with a speed of $1.3\,\text{m}\,\text{s}^{-1}$. Give your answer in radians per second, correct to one decimal place.

⑤ The wheels of a car have radius 20 cm. What is the angular speed, in radians per second, correct to one decimal place, of a wheel when the car is travelling at

(i) $10\,\text{m}\,\text{s}^{-1}$ (ii) $30\,\text{m}\,\text{s}^{-1}$?

⑥ The angular speed of an audio CD changes continuously so that a laser can read the data at a constant speed of $12\,\text{m}\,\text{s}^{-1}$. Find the angular speed (in rpm) when the distance of the laser from the centre is

(i) 30 mm (ii) 55 mm.

⑦ What is the average angular speed of the Earth in radians per second as it

(i) orbits the Sun

(ii) rotates about its own axis?

The radius of the Earth is 6400 km.

(iii) At what speed is someone on the equator travelling relative to the centre of the Earth?

(iv) At what speed are you travelling relative to the centre of the Earth?

⑧ A tractor has front wheels of diameter 70 cm and back wheels of diameter 1.6 m.

What is the ratio of their angular speeds when the tractor is being driven along a straight road?

⑨ (i) Find the kinetic energy of a 50 kg person riding a big wheel with radius 5 m when the ride is rotating at 3 rpm. You should assume that the person can be modelled as a particle.

(ii) Explain why this modelling assumption is necessary.

⑩ The minute hand of a clock is 1.2 m long and the hour hand is 0.8 m long.

(i) Find the speeds of the tips of the hands.

(ii) Find the ratio of the speeds of the tips of the hands and explain why this is not the same as the ratio of the angular speeds of the hands.

⑪ Figure 8.3 represents a 'Chairoplane' ride at a fair. It completes one revolution every 2.5 seconds.

(i) Find the radius of the circular path which a rider follows.

(ii) Find the speed of a rider.

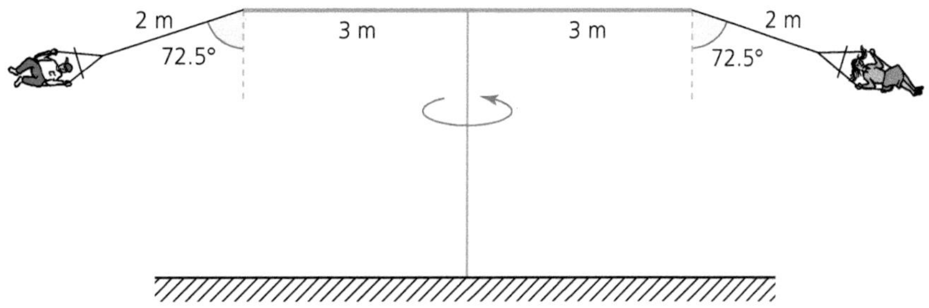

Figure 8.3

⑫ The position vector of a rider on a helter-skelter is given by

$$\mathbf{r} = 2\sin t\ \mathbf{i} + 2\cos t\ \mathbf{j} + \left(8 - \tfrac{1}{2}t\right)\mathbf{k}$$

where the units are in metres and seconds. The unit vector $\mathbf{k}$ is vertically upwards.

(i) Find an expression for the velocity of the rider at time t.

(ii) Find the speed of the rider at time $t = \frac{\pi}{4}$.

(iii) Find the magnitude and direction of the rider's acceleration when $t = \frac{\pi}{4}$.

Velocity and acceleration

Velocity and acceleration are both vector quantities. They can be expressed either in magnitude–direction form, or in components. When describing circular motion or other orbits, it is most convenient to take components in directions along the radius (*radial* direction) and at right angles to it (*tangential* direction).

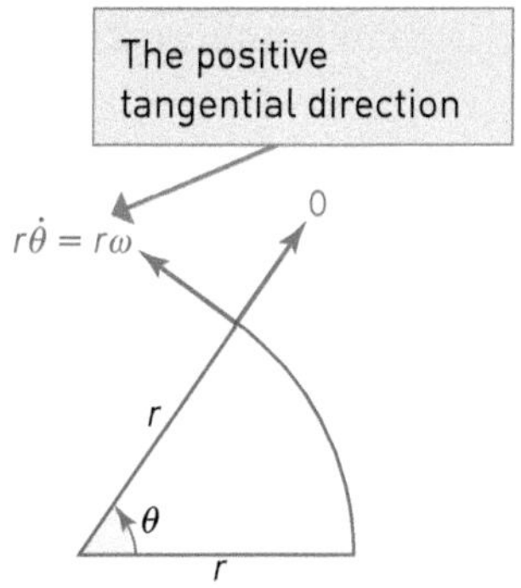

Figure 8.4 Velocity

For a particle moving round a circle of radius r, the velocity has:

radial component: 0

tangential component: $r\dot{\theta}$ or $r\omega$.

The acceleration of a particle moving round a circle of radius r has:

radial component: $-r\dot{\theta}^2$ or $-r\omega^2$

tangential component: $r\ddot{\theta}$ or $r\dot{\omega}$.

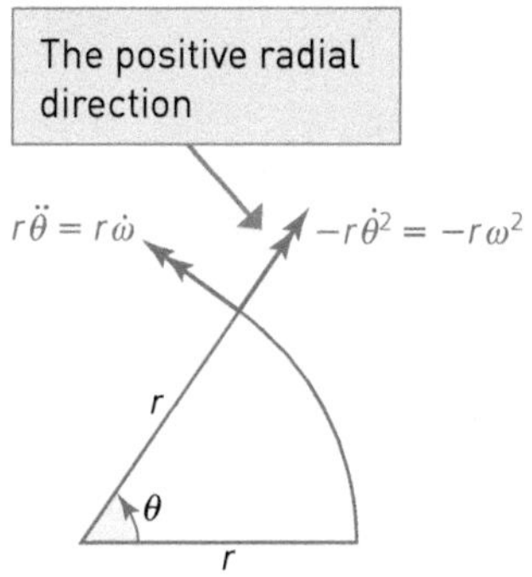

Figure 8.5 Acceleration

The tangential component is just what you would expect, the radius multiplied by the angular acceleration, $\ddot{\theta}$. If the particle has constant angular speed, its angular acceleration is zero and so the tangential component of its acceleration is also zero.

In contrast, the radial component of the acceleration, $-r\omega^2$, is almost certainly not a result you would have expected intuitively. It tells you that a particle travelling in a circle is always accelerating towards the centre of the circle, but without getting any closer to the centre. If this seems a strange idea, you may find it helpful to remember that circular motion is not a natural state; left to itself a particle will travel in a straight line. To keep a particle in the unnatural state of circular motion it must be given an acceleration at right angles to its motion, i.e. towards the centre of the circle.

The derivation of these expressions for the acceleration of a particle in a circular motion is complicated by the fact that the radial and tangential directions are themselves changing as the particle moves round the circle, in contrast to the fixed x and y directions in the Cartesian system. The derivation is given in a mathematical note on page 249. At first reading you may prefer to accept the results, but make sure that at a later stage you work through and understand the derivation.

2 Circular motion with constant speed

In this section, the circular motion is assumed to be uniform and so has no tangential component of acceleration. In a later chapter, situations are considered in which the angular speed varies.

Problems involving circular motion often refer to the actual speed of the object, rather than its angular speed. It is easy to convert one into the other using the relationship $v = r\omega$. The relationship can also be used to express the magnitude of the acceleration in terms of v and r.

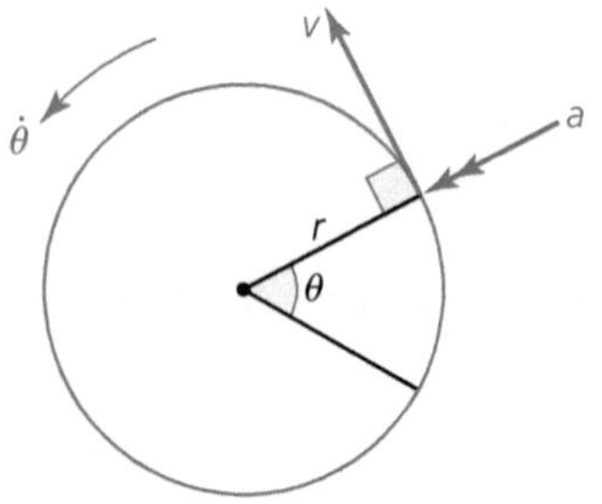

Figure 8.6

$$\omega = \frac{v}{r}$$

$$a = r\omega^2 = r\left(\frac{v}{r}\right)^2 = v\omega$$

$$\Rightarrow a = \frac{v^2}{r} \text{ towards the centre}$$

Velocity $v = r\omega$

Angular speed $\dot{\theta} = \omega$

Acceleration has magnitude $a = r\omega^2 = \frac{v^2}{r}$ and is directed towards the centre

Example 8.2

A turntable is rotating at 45 rpm. A fly is standing on it, 8 cm from its centre.

Find

(i) the angular speed of the fly in radians per second

(ii) the speed of the fly in metres per second

(iii) the acceleration of the fly.

Hint

One revolution is 2π radians.

Solution

(i) $45\,\text{rpm} = 45 \times 2\pi\,\text{rad}\,\text{min}^{-1}$

$$= \frac{45 \times 2\pi}{60}\,\text{rad}\,\text{s}^{-1}$$

$$= \frac{3\pi}{2}\,\text{rad}\,\text{s}^{-1}.$$

(ii) v can be found using

$$v = r\omega$$

$$= 0.08 \times \frac{3\pi}{2}$$

$$= 0.376...$$

So the speed of the fly is $0.38\,\text{m}\,\text{s}^{-1}$ (to 2 d.p.).

(iii) The acceleration of the fly is given by

$$r\omega^2 = 0.08 \times \left(\frac{3\pi}{2}\right)^2 \text{m}\,\text{s}^{-2}$$

$$= 1.78\,\text{m}\,\text{s}^{-2}$$

It is directed towards the centre of the turntable.

The forces required for circular motion

Newton's first law of motion states that a body will continue in a state of rest or uniform motion in a straight line unless acted upon by an external force. Any object moving in a circle, such as the police car and the fly in Examples 8.1 and 8.2, must therefore be acted upon by a resultant force in order to produce the required acceleration towards the centre.

A force towards the centre is called a **centripetal** (centre-seeking) force. A resultant centripetal force is necessary for a particle to move in a circular path.

Examples of circular motion

You are now in a position to use Newton's second law to determine theoretical answers to some of the questions which were posed at the beginning of this chapter. These will, as usual, be obtained using models of the true motion which will be based on simplifying assumptions, for example zero air resistance.

Example 8.3

A coin is placed on a rotating horizontal turntable, 5 cm from the centre of rotation. The coefficient of friction between the coin and the turntable is 0.5.

(i) The speed of rotation of the turntable is gradually increased. At what angular speed will the coin begin to slide?

(ii) What happens next?

Solution

(i) Because the speed of the turntable is increased only gradually, the coin will not slip tangentially.

Figure 8.7 shows the forces acting on the coin, and its acceleration.

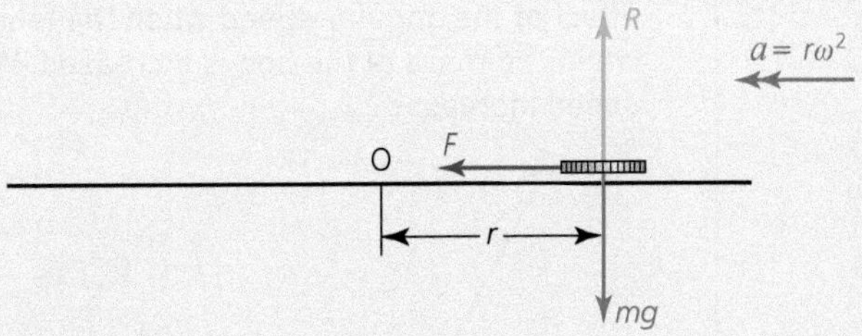

Figure 8.7

The acceleration is towards the centre of the circular path, O, so there must be a frictional force F in that direction.

There is no vertical component of acceleration, so the resultant force acting on the coin has no vertical component.

Therefore

$$R - mg = 0$$

$$R = mg \qquad ①$$

By Newton's second law towards the centre of the circle:

$$\text{Force } F = ma = mr\omega^2$$

The coin will not slide so long as $F \leq \mu R$. ②

Substituting from ① and ② this gives

$$mr\omega^2 \le \mu mg$$

$$\Rightarrow \quad r\omega^2 \le \mu g$$

Notice that the mass, m, has been eliminated at this stage, so the answer does not depend upon it.

Taking g in m s^{-2} as 9.8 and substituting $r = 0.05$ and $\mu = 0.5$

$$\omega^2 \le 98$$

$$\omega \le \sqrt{98}$$

$$\omega \le 9.89...$$

The coin will move in a circle provided the angular speed is less than about $10\,\text{rad s}^{-1}$ and the speed is independent of the mass of the coin.

(ii) In general, at radius r the coin will slip if $\omega > \sqrt{\frac{\mu g}{r}}$. When the angular speed increases beyond this, the coin slips to a new position. The value of r has increased, so in the new position it will not continue to slip. But if the angular speed continues to increase, it will slip once more, and eventually it will fly off the turntable in the direction of the tangent.

The conical pendulum

A conical pendulum consists of a small bob tied to one end of a string. The other end of the string is fixed and the bob is made to rotate in a horizontal circle below the fixed point so that the string describes a cone, as in Figure 8.8.

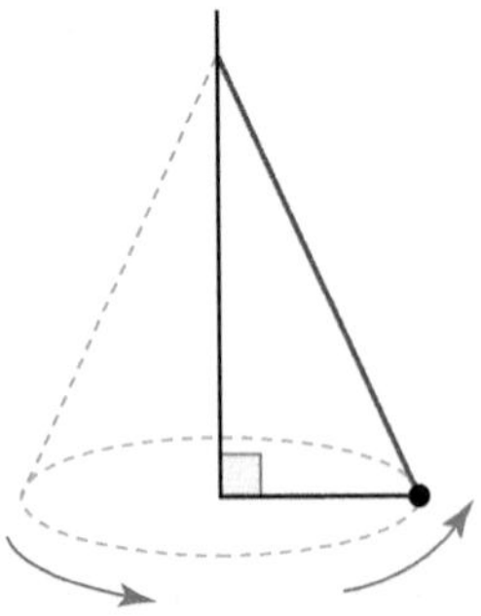

Figure 8.8

EXPERIMENT

1 Draw a diagram showing the magnitude and direction of the acceleration of the bob and the forces acting on it.

2 In the case that the radius of the circle remains constant, try to predict the effect of the angular speed when the length of the string is increased or when the mass of the bob is increased. What might happen when the angular speed increases?

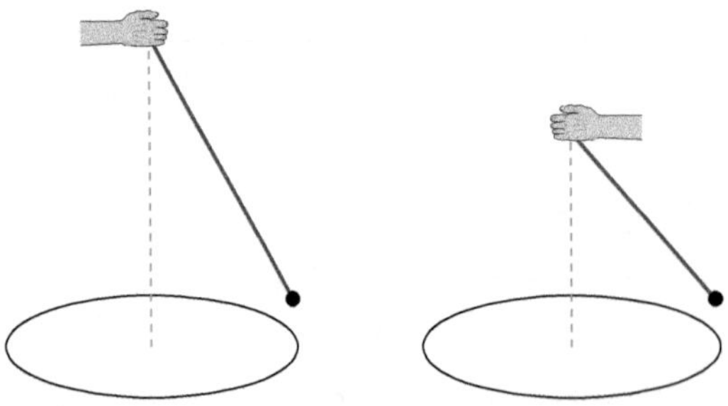

Figure 8.9

3 Draw two circles of equal diameter on horizontal surfaces so that two people can make the bobs of two conical pendulums rotate in circles of the same radius.

(i) Compare pendulums of different lengths with bobs of equal mass.

(ii) Compare pendulums of the same length but with bobs of different masses.

Does the angular speed depend on the length of the pendulum or the mass of the bob?

4 What happens when somebody makes the speed of the bob increase?

5 Can the bob be made to rotate with the string horizontal?

Theoretical model for the conical pendulum

A conical pendulum may be modelled as a particle of mass m attached to a light, inextensible string of length l. The mass is rotating in a horizontal circle with angular speed ω and the string makes an angle α with the downward vertical. The radius of the circle is r and the tension in the string is T, all in consistent units (e.g. S.I. units). The situation is shown in Figure 8.10.

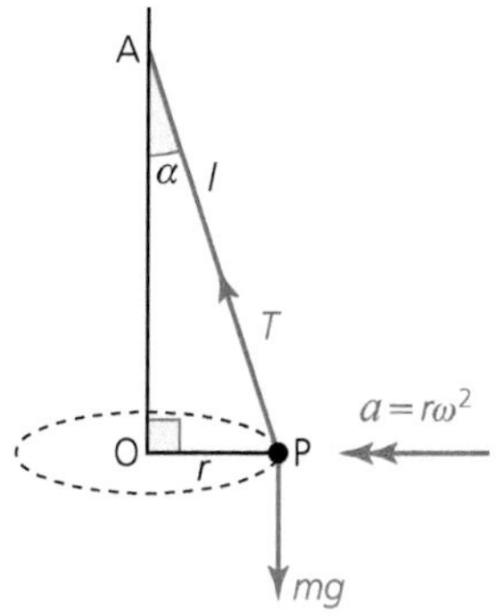

Figure 8.10

The magnitude of the acceleration is $r\omega^2$. The acceleration acts in a horizontal direction towards the centre of the circle. This means that there must be a resultant force acting towards the centre of the circle.

There are two forces acting on this particle, its weight mg and the tension T in the string.

As the acceleration of the particle has no vertical component, the resultant force has no vertical component, so

$$T\cos\alpha - mg = 0 \qquad ①$$

Using Newton's second law towards the centre, O, of the circle

$$T\sin\alpha = ma = mr\omega^2 \qquad ②$$

In triangle AOP $\quad r = l\sin\alpha$

Substituting for r in ② gives $\quad T\sin\alpha = m(l\sin\alpha)\,\omega^2$

$\Rightarrow \quad T = ml\omega^2$

Substituting this in ① gives

$$ml\omega^2\cos\alpha - mg = 0$$

$$\Rightarrow \quad l\cos\alpha = \frac{g}{\omega^2} \qquad ③$$

This equation provides sufficient information to give theoretical answers to the questions in the experiment.

- When r is kept constant and the length of the string is increased, the length AO $= l\cos\alpha$ increases. Equation ③ indicates that the value of $\frac{g}{\omega^2}$ increases and so the angular speed ω decreases. Conversely, the angular speed increases when the string is shortened.
- The mass of the particle does not appear in equation ③, so it has no effect on the angular speed, ω.
- When the length of the pendulum is unchanged, but the angular speed is increased, $\cos\alpha$ decreases, leading to an increase in the angle α and hence in r.
- If $\alpha \geq 90°$, $\cos\alpha \leq 0$, so $\frac{g}{\omega^2} \leq 0$, which is impossible. You can see from Figure 8.10 that the tension in the string must have a vertical component to balance the weight of the particle.

Example 8.4

The diagram on the right of Figure 8.11 represents one of several arms of a fairground ride shown on the left. The arms rotate about an axis and riders sit in chairs linked to the arms by chains.

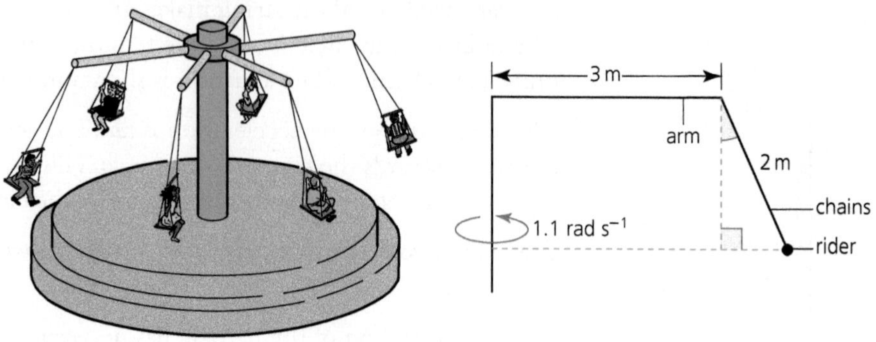

Figure 8.11

The chains are 2 m long and the arms are 3 m long. Find the angle that the chains make with the vertical when the rider rotates at 1.1 rad s^{-1}.

Solution

Let T be the resultant tension in the chains holding a chair and let m kg be the mass of the chair and rider.

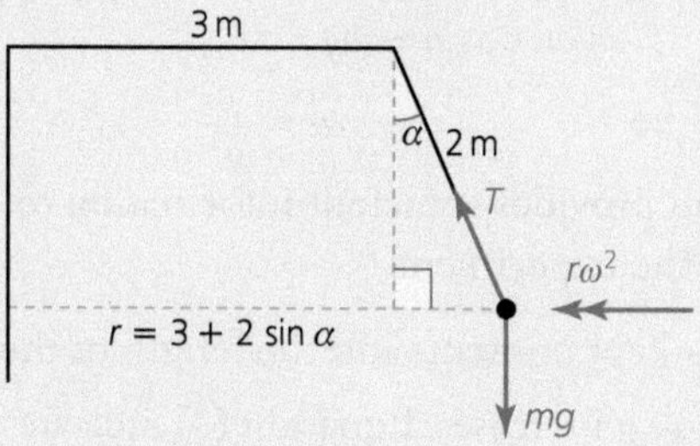

Figure 8.12

If the chains make an angle α with the vertical, the motion is in a horizontal circle with radius given by

$$r = 3 + 2\sin\alpha$$

The magnitude of the acceleration is given by

$$r\omega^2 = (3 + 2\sin\alpha)\,1.1^2$$

It is in a horizontal direction towards the centre of the circle. Using Newton's second law in this direction gives

$$\text{Force} = mr\omega^2$$

$$\Rightarrow \quad T\sin\alpha = m(3 + 2\sin\alpha)1.1^2 \qquad ①$$

$$= 1.21\,m(3 + 2\sin\alpha)$$

Vertically $T\cos\alpha - mg = 0$

$$\Rightarrow \quad T = \frac{mg}{\cos\alpha}$$

> **Note**
>
> Since the answer does not depend on the mass of the rider and chair, when riders of different masses, or even no riders, are on the equipment all the chains should make the same angle with the vertical.

Substituting for T in equation ①:

$$\frac{mg}{\cos\alpha}\sin\alpha = 1.21\,m(3+2\sin\alpha)$$

$$\Rightarrow \quad 9.8\tan\alpha = 3.63 + 2.42\sin\alpha$$

Since m cancels out at this stage, the angle does not depend on the mass of the rider.

This equation cannot be solved directly, but a numerical method will give you the solution 25.5° correct to three significant figures. You might like to solve the equation yourself or check that this solution does in fact satisfy the equation.

Banked tracks

> **Note**
>
> Keep away from other people and breakable objects when carrying out this activity.

ACTIVITY 8.1

Place a coin on a piece of stiff A4 card and hold it horizontally at arm's length with the coin near your hand.

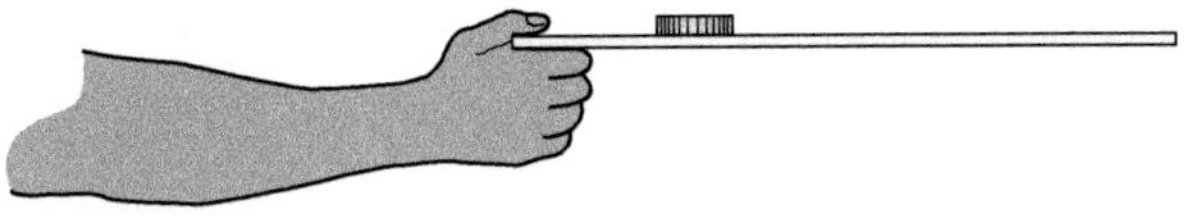

Figure 8.13

Turn round slowly so that your hand moves in a horizontal circle. Now gradually speed up. The outcome will probably not surprise you.
What happens though if you tilt the card?

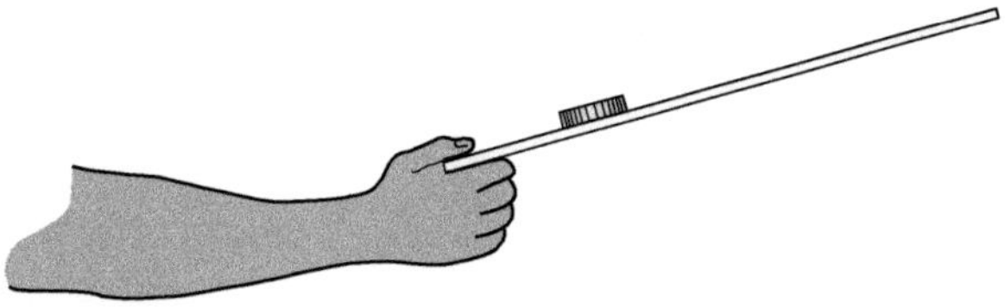

Figure 8.14

Figure 8.15

You may have noticed that when they curve round bends, most roads are banked so that the edge at the outside of the bend is slightly higher than that at the inside. For the same reason, the outer rail of a railway track is slightly higher than the inner rail when it goes round the bend. On bobsleigh tracks the bends are almost bowl shaped, with a much greater gradient on the outside.

Figure 8.16 shows a car rounding a bend on a road which is banked so that the cross-section makes an angle α with the horizontal.

Figure 8.16

In modelling such situations, it is usual to treat the bend as part of a horizontal circle whose radius is large compared to the width of the car. In this case, the radius of the circle is taken to be r metres, and the speed of the car constant at v metres per second.

Discussion point

The direction of the frictional force F will be up or down the slope depending on whether the car has a tendency to slip sideways towards the inside or outside of the bend.

Under what conditions do you think each of these will occur?

The car is modelled as a particle which has an acceleration of $\frac{v^2}{r}$ m s^{-2} in a horizontal direction towards the centre of the circle. The forces and acceleration are shown in Figure 8.17.

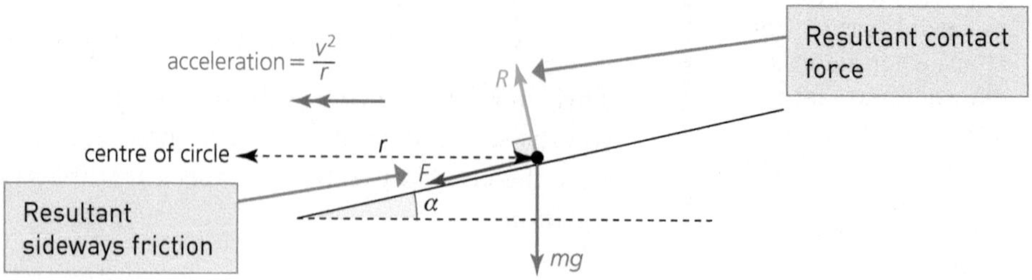

Figure 8.17

Example 8.5

A car is rounding a bend of radius 100 m which is banked at an angle of 10° to the horizontal. At what speed must the car travel to ensure that it has no tendency to slip sideways?

Solution

When there is no tendency to slip there is no frictional force, so, in the plane perpendicular to the direction of motion of the car, the forces and acceleration are as shown in Figure 8.18. The only horizontal force is provided by the horizontal component of the normal contact force of the road on the car.

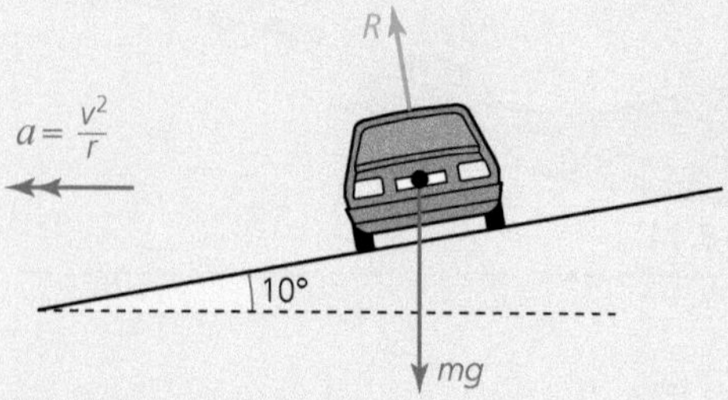

Figure 8.18

Note

The normal contact force R is resolved into components

$R \sin 10°$ horizontally ←

$R \cos 10°$ vertically ↑

Vertically there is no acceleration so there is no resultant force:

$$R\cos 10° - mg = 0$$

$$\Rightarrow \quad R = \frac{mg}{\cos 10°} \quad ①$$

By Newton's second law in the horizontal direction towards the centre of the circle:

$$R\sin 10° = ma = \frac{mv^2}{r}$$

$$= \frac{mv^2}{100}$$

Substituting for R from ①

$$\left(\frac{mg}{\cos 10^\circ}\right)\sin 10^\circ = \frac{mv^2}{100}$$

$$\Rightarrow \qquad v^2 = 100g\tan 10^\circ$$

$$\Rightarrow \qquad v = 13.14\ldots$$

The mass, m, cancels out at this stage, so the answer does not depend on it.

The speed of the car must be about $13.1\,\mathrm{m\,s^{-1}}$ or 30 mph.

There are two important points to notice in this example.

- The speed is the same whatever the mass of the car.
- The example looks at the situation when the car does not tend to slide, and finds the speed at which this is the case. At this speed, the car does not depend on friction to keep it from sliding and, indeed, it could travel safely round the bend at this speed even in very icy conditions. However, at other speeds there is a tendency to slide, and friction actually helps the car to follow its intended path.

Safe speeds on a bend

What would happen in the previous example if the car travelled either more slowly than $13.1\,\mathrm{m\,s^{-1}}$ or more quickly?

The answer is that there would be a frictional force acting so as to prevent the car from sliding across the road.

There are two possible directions for the frictional force. When the vehicle is stationary or travelling slowly, there is a tendency to slide down the slope and the friction acts up the slope to prevent this. When it is travelling quickly round the bend, the car is more likely to slide up the slope, so the friction acts down the slope.

Fortunately, under most road conditions, the coefficient of friction between tyres and the road is large, typically about 0.8. This means that there is a range of speeds that are safe for negotiating any particular bend.

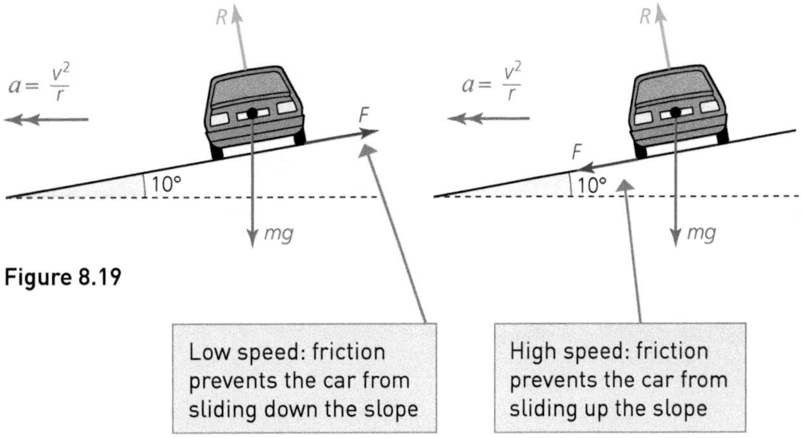

Figure 8.19

Discussion points

1 Using a particle model for the car, show that it will not slide up or down the slope provided

$$\sqrt{rg\frac{(\sin\alpha-\mu\cos\alpha)}{(\cos\alpha+\mu\sin\alpha)}} < v < \sqrt{rg\frac{(\sin\alpha+\mu\cos\alpha)}{(\cos\alpha-\mu\sin\alpha)}}$$

If $r = 100$ and $\alpha = 10°$ (so that tan $\alpha = 0.176$) the minimum and maximum safe speeds (in mph) for different values of μ are given in the following table.

μ	0	0.1	0.2	0.3	0.4	0.5	0.6	0.7	0.8	0.9	1.0	1.1	1.2
Minimum safe speed	30	19	0	0	0	0	0	0	0	0	0	0	0
Maximum safe speed	30	37	44	50	55	61	66	70	75	80	84	89	93

2 Would you regard this bend as safe? How, by changing the values of r and α, could you make it safer?

Example 8.6

A bend on a railway track has a radius of 500 m and is to be banked so that a train can negotiate it at 60 mph without the need for a lateral force between its wheels and the rail. The distance between the rails is 1.43 m.

How much higher should the outside rail be than the inside one?

Solution

There is very little friction between the track and the wheels of a train. Any sideways force required is provided by the 'lateral thrust' between the wheels and the rail. The ideal speed for the bend is such that the lateral thrust is zero.

Figure 8.20 shows the forces acting on the train and its acceleration when the track is banked at an angle α to the horizontal.

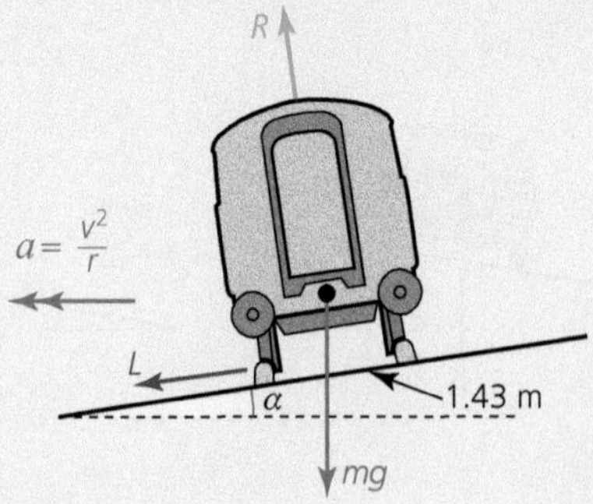

Figure 8.20

When there is no lateral thrust, $L = 0$.

Horizontally: $R\sin\alpha = \frac{mv^2}{r}$ ①

Vertically: $R\cos\alpha = mg$ ②

Dividing ① by ② gives $\tan\alpha = \frac{v^2}{rg}$

Using the fact that 60 mph = 26.8 m s^{-1} this becomes

$\tan\alpha = 0.147$

$\Rightarrow \quad \alpha = 8.4°$ (to 2 s.f.)

The outside rail should be raised by 1.43 $\sin\alpha$ metres, i.e. about 21 cm.

Motion in a vertical circle

Unless some driving or resistive force is present, the speed of an object moving in a vertical circle varies from its lowest at the top to its highest at the bottom. Finding the speed at a given point on the circle is most easily done by considering energy, and this has already been covered in Chapter 5, on pages 106 to 114. A fuller treatment of motion in a vertical circle is given in Chapter 11.

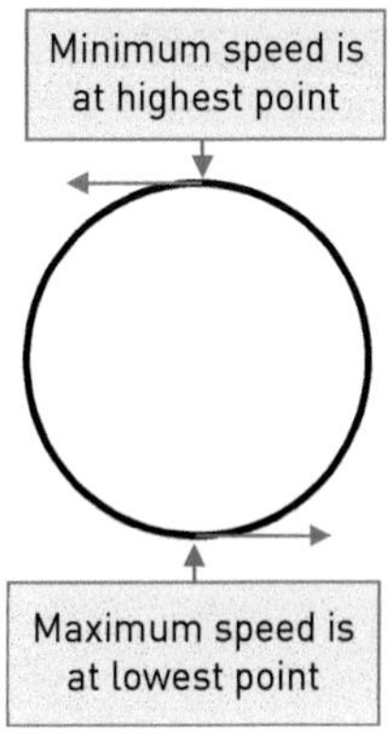

Figure 8.21

Exercise 8.2

① Figure 8.22 shows two cars A and B, travelling at constant speeds in different lanes (radii 24 m and 20 m) round a circular traffic island. Car A has speed 18 m s^{-1} and car B has speed 15 m s^{-1}.

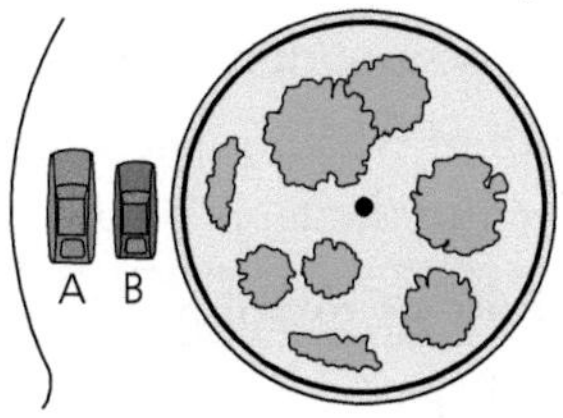

Figure 8.22

Answer the following questions, giving reasons for your answers.

(i) Which car has the greater angular speed?

(ii) Is one car overtaking the other?

(iii) Find the magnitude of the acceleration of each car.

(iv) In which direction is the resultant force on each car acting?

② A bead of mass 0.06 kg moves with constant speed v m s^{-1}, angular velocity ω rad s^{-1}, in a horizontal circle of radius r. Find the acceleration of the bead if

(i) $r = 0.2$ and $\omega = 6$

(ii) $r = 0.25$ and $v = 2$

(iii) $v = 4$ and $\omega = 1.2$.

③ Two coins are placed on a horizontal turntable. Coin A has mass 15 g and is placed 5 cm from the centre; coin B has mass 10 g and is placed 7.5 cm from the centre. The coefficient of friction between each coin and the turntable is 0.4.

(i) Describe what happens to the coins when the turntable turns at

(a) $6\,\text{rad}\,\text{s}^{-1}$ (b) $8\,\text{rad}\,\text{s}^{-1}$ (c) $10\,\text{rad}\,\text{s}^{-1}$.

(ii) What would happen if the coins were interchanged?

④ A car is travelling at a steady speed of $15\,\text{m}\,\text{s}^{-1}$ round a roundabout of radius 20 m on a flat horizontal road.

(i) Criticise this false argument:

The car is travelling at a steady speed and so its speed is neither increasing nor decreasing and therefore the car has no acceleration.

(ii) Calculate the magnitude of the acceleration of the car.

(iii) The car has mass 800 kg. Calculate the sideways force on each wheel assuming it to be the same for all four wheels.

(iv) Is the assumption in part (iii) realistic?

⑤ A fairground ride has seats at 3 m and at 4.5 m from the centre of rotation. Each rider travels in a horizontal circle. Say whether each of the following statements is TRUE or FALSE, giving your reasons.

(i) Riders in the two positions have the same angular speed at any time.

(ii) Riders in the two positions have the same speed at any time.

(iii) Riders in the two positions have the same magnitude of acceleration at any time.

⑥ A skater of mass 60 kg follows a circular path of radius 4 m, moving at $2\,\text{m}\,\text{s}^{-1}$.

(i) Calculate:

(a) the angular speed of the skater

(b) the magnitude of the acceleration of the skater

(c) the resultant force acting on the skater.

(ii) What modelling assumptions have you made?

⑦ Two spin driers, both of which rotate about a vertical axis, have different specifications as given in the table below.

Model	Rate of rotation	Drum diameter
A	600 rpm	60 cm
B	800 rpm	40 cm

State with reasons, which model you would expect to be the more effective.

⑧ A satellite of mass M_s is in a circular orbit around the Earth, with a radius of r metres. The force of attraction between the Earth and the satellite is given by

$$F = \frac{GM_eM_s}{r^2}$$

where $G = 6.67 \times 10^{-11}$ in S.I. units. The mass of the Earth M_e is 5.97×10^{24} kg.

(i) Find, in terms of r, expressions for

(a) the speed of the satellite, $v\,\text{m}\,\text{s}^{-1}$

(b) the time, T s, it takes to complete one revolution.

Note

The law found in part (ii) was discovered experimentally by Johannes Kepler (1571–1630) to hold true for the planets as they orbit the Sun, and is commonly known as Kepler's third law.

(ii) Hence show that, for all satellites, T^2 is proportional to r^3.

A geostationary satellite orbits the Earth so that it is always above the same place on the equator.

(iii) How far is it from the centre of the Earth?

⑨ A rotary lawn mower uses a piece of light nylon string with a small metal sphere on the end to cut the grass. The string is 20 cm in length and the mass of the sphere is 30 g.

(i) Find the tension in the string when the sphere is rotating at 2000 rpm assuming that the string is horizontal.

(ii) Explain why it is reasonable to assume that the string is horizontal.

(iii) Find the speed of the sphere when the tension in the string is 80 N.

⑩ In this question, you should assume that the orbit of the Earth around the Sun is circular, with radius 1.44×10^{11} m, and that the Sun is fixed.

(i) Find the magnitude of the acceleration of the Earth as it orbits the Sun.

The force of attraction between the Earth and the Sun is given by

$$F = \frac{GM_e M_s}{r^2}$$

where M_e is the mass of the Earth, M_s is the mass of the Sun, r is the radius of the Earth's orbit and G the universal constant of gravitation (6.67×10^{-11} S.I. units).

(ii) Calculate the mass of the Sun.

(iii) Comment on the significance of the fact that you cannot calculate the mass of the Earth from the radius of its orbit.

⑪ Sarah ties a model aeroplane of mass 180 g to the end of a piece of string 80 cm long and then swings it round so that the plane travels in a horizontal circle.

The aeroplane is not designed to fly and there is no lift force acting on its wings.

(i) Explain why it is not possible for the string to be horizontal.

Sarah gives the aeroplane an angular speed of 120 rpm.

(ii) What is the angular speed in radians per second?

(iii) Copy Figure 8.23 and mark the tension in the string, the weight of the aeroplane and the direction of the acceleration.

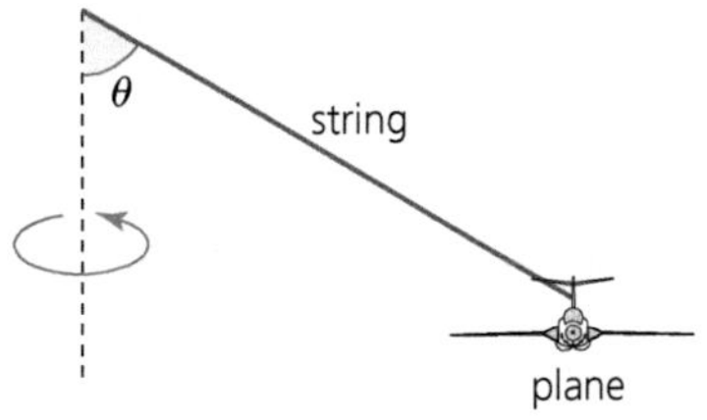

Figure 8.23

(iv) Write down the horizontal radial equation of motion for the aeroplane and the vertical equilibrium equation in terms of the angle θ.

(v) Show that, under these conditions, θ has a value between 85° and 86°.

(vi) Find the tension in the string.

⑫ Experiments carried out by the police accident investigation department suggest that a typical value for a coefficient of friction between the tyres of a car and a road surface is 0.8.

(i) Using this information, find the maximum safe speed on a level circular motorway slip road of radius 50 m.

(ii) How much faster could cars travel if the road were banked at an angle of 5° to the horizontal?

⑬ The coefficient of friction between the tyres of a car and the road is 0.8. The mass of the car and its passengers is 800 kg. Model the car as a particle.

(i) Find the maximum frictional force that the road can exert on the car and describe what might be happening when this maximum force is acting

(a) at right angles to the line of motion

(b) along the line of motion.

(ii) What is the maximum speed that the car can travel without skidding on level ground round a circular bend of radius 120 m?

Figure 8.24 shows the car now travelling around a bend of radius 120 m on a road banked at an angle α to the horizontal. The car's speed is such that there is no sideways force (up or down the slope) exerted on its tyres by the road.

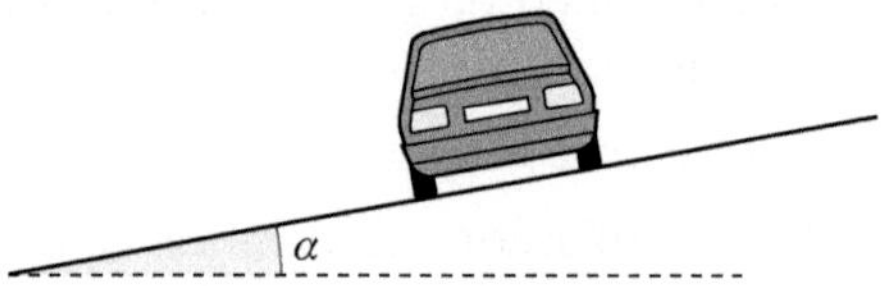

Figure 8.24

(iii) Draw a diagram showing the weight of the car, the normal contact force of the road on it and the direction of its acceleration.

(iv) Resolve the forces in the horizontal radial and vertical directions and write down the horizontal equation of motion and the vertical equilibrium equation.

(v) Show that $\tan\alpha = \frac{v^2}{120g}$ where v is the speed of the car in metres per second.

(vi) On this particular bend, vehicles are expected to travel at $15\,\text{m}\,\text{s}^{-1}$. At what angle, α, should the road be banked?

⑭ A big wheel at a fairground is rotating in a vertical circle at a constant rate of one revolution per minute.

(i) Calculate the angular speed of the wheel in radians per second.

(ii) Calculate the linear speed of a point 10 m from the axis of rotation.

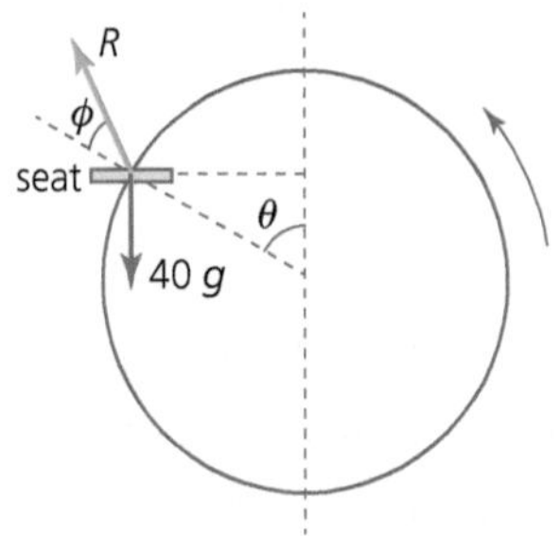

Figure 8.25

A child of mass 40 kg is sitting 10 m from the axis of rotation on a seat on the wheel.

The situation may be modelled by assuming that there is negligible distance between the seat and the child's centre of mass and that the seat remains horizontal at all times. When the radius joining the seat to the axis is inclined at θ to the upward vertical, the reaction R of the seat on the child is inclined at ϕ to that radius, as shown in Figure 8.25

(iii) By resolving the forces acting on the child in a direction perpendicular to the radius, explain why

$$R \sin \phi = 40g \sin \theta$$

(iv) Write down the equation of motion of the child in the radial direction.

(v) Given that $\theta = \frac{\pi}{6}$, find R and ϕ.

⑮ A light inextensible string of length 0.8 m is threaded through a smooth ring and carries a particle at each end. Particle A of mass m kg is at rest at a distance of 0.3 m below the ring. The other particle, B, of mass M kg is rotating in a horizontal circle whose centre is A.

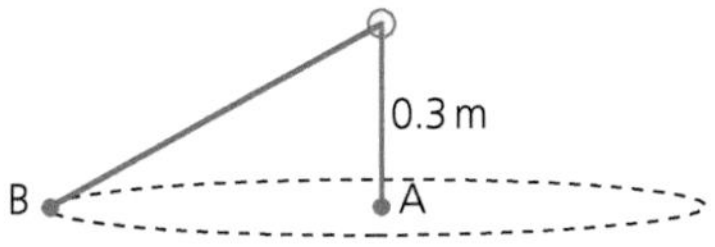

Figure 8.26

(i) Express M in terms of m.

(ii) Find the angular velocity of B.

⑯ A particle of mass 0.2 kg is moving on the smooth inside surface of a fixed hollow sphere of radius 0.75 m. The particle moves in a horizontal circle whose centre is 0.45 m below the centre of the sphere (see Figure 8.27).

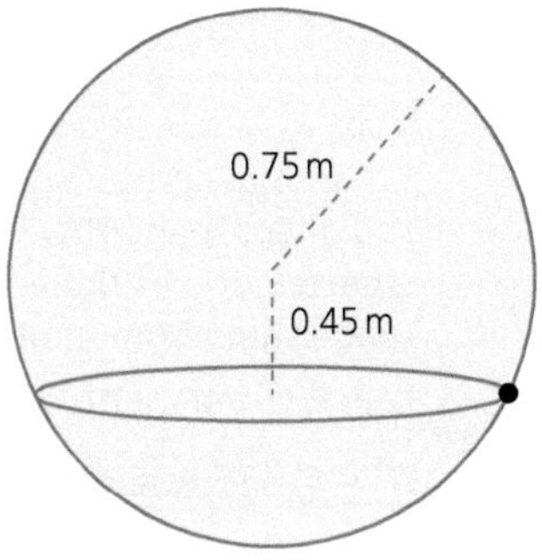

Figure 8.27

(i) Show that the force exerted by the sphere on the particle has magnitude $\frac{1}{3}g$.

(ii) Find the speed of the particle.

(iii) Find the time taken for the particle to complete one revolution.

⑰ A particle P of mass 0.25 kg is attached to one end of each of two inextensible strings which are both taut. The other end of the longer string is attached to a fixed point A, and the other end of the shorter string is attached to a fixed point B, which is vertically below A.

String AP is 0.2 m long and string BP is 0.15 m long. P moves in a horizontal circle of radius 0.12 m with constant angular speed 10 rad s^{-1}. Both strings are taut: T_1 is the tension in AP and T_2 is the tension in BP.

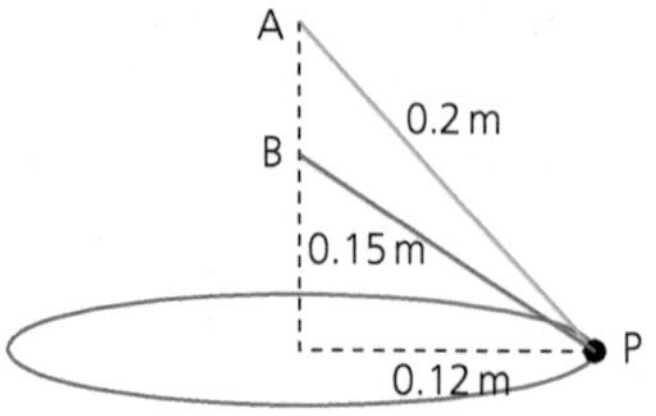

Figure 8.28

(i) Resolve vertically to show that $8T_1 + 6T_2 = 2.5g$.

(ii) Find another equation connecting T_1 and T_2 and hence calculate T_1 and T_2.

KEY POINTS

1 Position, velocity and acceleration of a particle moving on a circle of radius r.

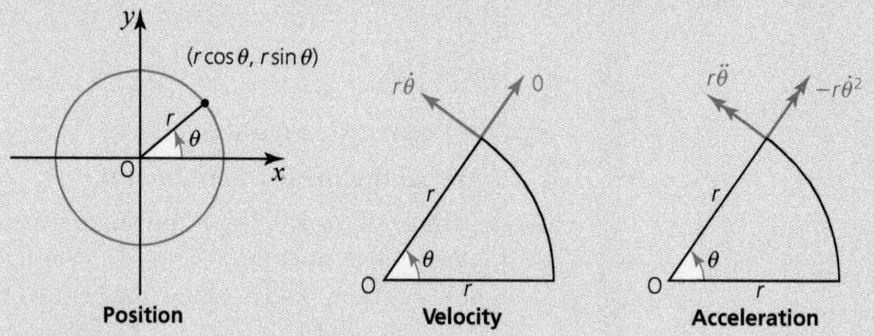

Figure 8.29

2
- position: $(r\cos\theta, r\sin\theta)$
- velocity: tangential component: $v = r\dot{\theta} = r\omega$
  radial component: 0
  where $\dot{\theta}$ or ω is the angular velocity of the particle.
- acceleration: tangential component: $r\ddot{\theta} = r\dot{\omega}$
  radial component: $r\dot{\theta}^2 = r\omega = \frac{v^2}{r} = r\omega$
  where $\ddot{\theta}$ or $\dot{\omega}$ is the angular acceleration of the particle.

LEARNING OUTCOMES

When you have finished this chapter, you should be able to

- understand the language and notation associated with circular motion
- identify the forces acting on a body in circular motion
- calculate acceleration towards the centre of circular motion
- model situations involving circular motion with uniform speed in a horizontal plane

① Most of the world outside of the UK expresses the fuel consumption of cars in litres per 100 kilometres.

What are the dimensions of this measure of fuel consumption?

Express 1 litre per 100 kilometres in S.I. base units. [3 marks]

M ② A suitcase of mass 5 kg is pulled up a rough inclined plane by a rope. The plane makes an angle of 10° to the horizontal and the rope makes an angle of 30° to the plane (see Figure 1).

The tension in the rope is 32 N and the coefficient of friction between the the suitcase and the plane is 0.4. Find the acceleration of the suitcase. [4 marks]

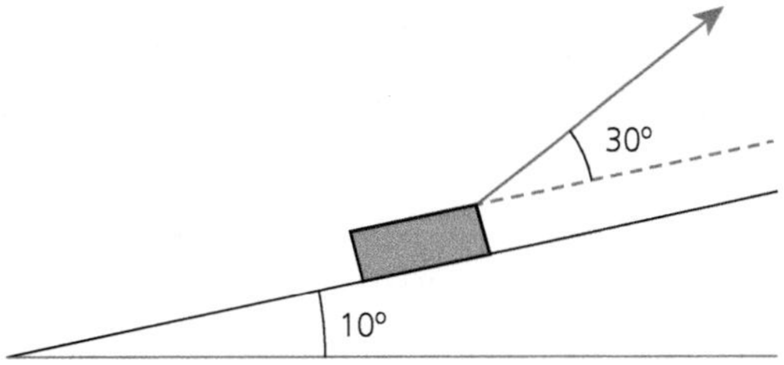

Figure 1

P PS M ③ Three small circular discs are on a smooth horizontal surface. The centres of the discs initially lie on a straight line and all the motion takes place on this line. Discs A, B and C have masses $2m$, m and m. Initially, B is at rest. A is travelling towards B with speed $U\,\mathrm{m\,s^{-1}}$ and C is travelling towards B from the other side with speed $kU\,\mathrm{m\,s^{-1}}$, where $k > 0$. This situation is shown in Figure 2.

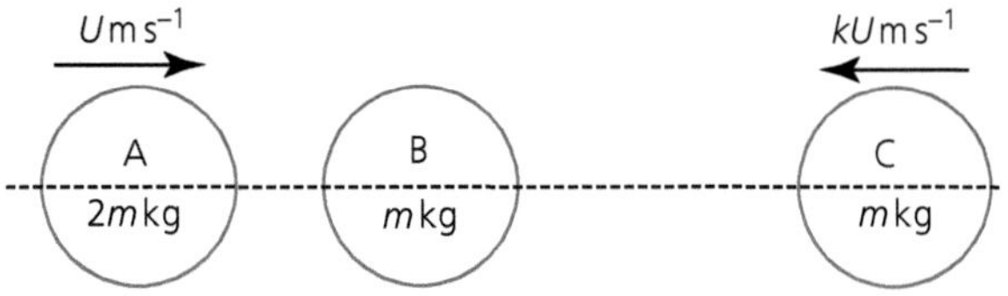

Figure 2

The first collision is between A and B. The coefficient of restitution is e.

(i) Find an expression in terms of U and e for the speed of B after the collision. Show that the speed of A is $\frac{U}{3}(2-e)$. [6 marks]

B now collides with C and the discs coalesce to form the body D.

(ii) Find an expression in terms of k, U and e for the speed of D. [3 marks]

(iii) Show that A will collide with D if $k > \frac{2}{3}(2e-1)$. [3 marks]

Suppose A collides with D and they coalesce to form the body E.

(iv) Show that the speed of E is independent of e.

Find the speed of E in terms of U in the case $k = \frac{4}{9}$. [4 marks]

PS M ④ A car of mass 1200 kg is travelling at $15\,\mathrm{m\,s^{-1}}$ with acceleration $0.7\,\mathrm{m\,s^{-2}}$ up a uniform slope at an angle α with the horizontal, where $\sin\alpha = 0.1$. At this speed, the air resistance to its motion is 250 N. Other resistances to the motion of the car are negligible.

(i) Calculate the power of the driving force on the car. [5 marks]

The driver of the car sees an obstruction, removes the driving force and presses the brake pedal so hard that the wheels stop rotating and the car slides until it comes to rest.

You are given the following information:

- the car starts sliding when its speed is $12\,\text{m}\,\text{s}^{-1}$
- the coefficient of friction between the car's tyres and the road is 0.4
- the total work done against air resistance while the car is sliding is 1500 J.

(ii) Using an energy method, calculate the distance the car travels while it is sliding. [5 marks]

(iii) State a modelling assumption that is necessary in order to calculate the frictional force between the road and the sliding car. [1 mark]

P M PS

⑤ A thin rigid uniform rectangular plank AB has weight W N and length 5 m. End A of the plank rests on a rough horizontal floor; a light string is attached to end B.

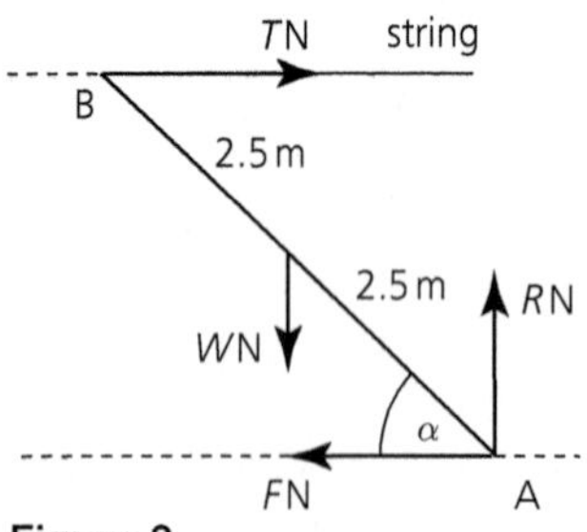

Figure 3

In one situation, the plank is in equilibrium at an angle α with the floor with the string horizontal and in tension. Figure 3 shows this information and the forces acting: W N is the weight of the plank; T N is the tension in the string; R N is the normal contact force of the floor on the plank; F N is the frictional force between the plank and the floor. The plank is on the point of slipping.

(i) Show that the coefficient of friction between the plank and the floor is $\dfrac{1}{2\tan\alpha}$. [5 marks]

In another situation, shown in Figure 4, the plank is in equilibrium with $\cos\alpha = \dfrac{3}{5}$ and the string at an angle β to the horizontal where $\alpha + \beta = 90°$.

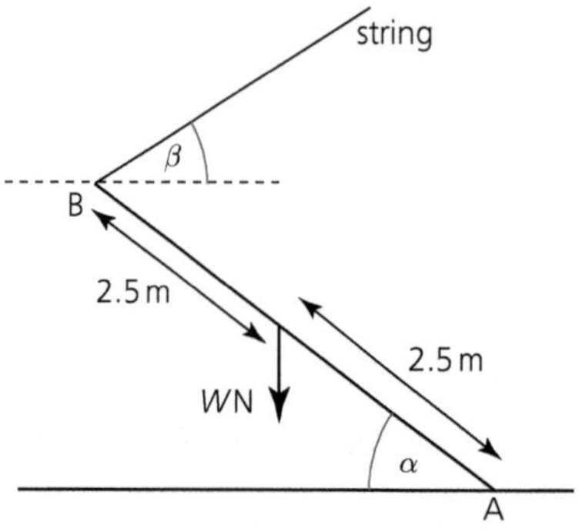

Figure 4

(ii) Draw a diagram showing the forces acting and find an expression for the range of values of the coefficient of friction between the plank and the floor. [9 marks]

⑥ A light inextensible string of length 0.8 m is attached to two points A and C, with A 0.4 m vertically above C. A smooth bead B of mass 10 grams is threaded on the string. B rotates in a circle of radius 0.3 m with the string taut and BC horizontal (see Figure 5).

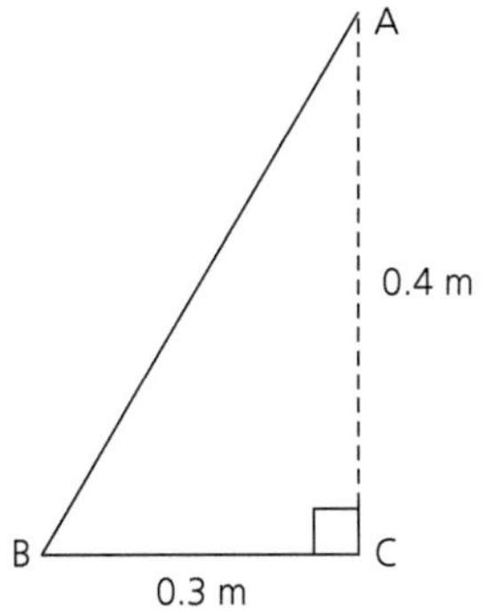

Figure 5

(i) Calculate the tension in the string. [4 marks]

(ii) Calculate the time taken for B to make one complete revolution. [3 marks]

P M T ⑦ Figure 6 shows a rod OA of length 2 m and mass 0.25 kg with its centre of mass at G which is 1.6 m from O. The rod is attached to a hinge at O and moves only in a vertical plane. One end of a string is attached to end A of the rod. This string passes over a pulley at B and an object of mass m kg hangs from the other end of the string. OB is vertical and the distance OB is 2 m.

The angle AOB is θ and the angle OAB is ϕ.

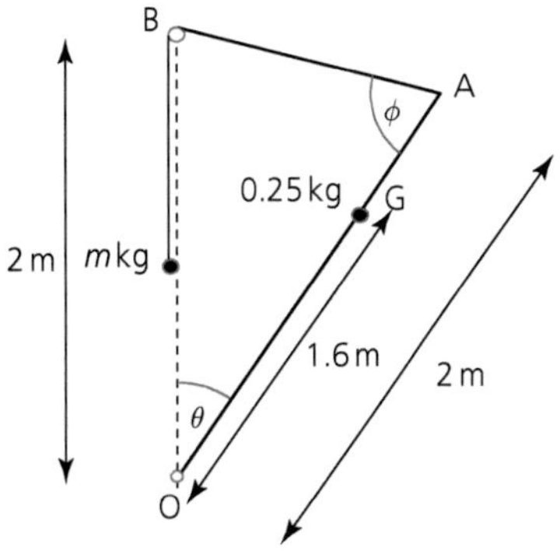

Figure 6

Table 1

θ rad	c.w. moment	a.c. moment
1.1	3.493 532 851	4.177 370 158
1.15	3.578 034 646	4.112 042 282
1.2	3.653 593 217	4.044 144 513
1.25	3.720 019 708	3.973 719 286
1.3	3.777 148 087	3.900 810 613
1.35	3.824 835 563	3.825 464 061
1.4	3.862 962 942	3.747 726 718
1.45	3.891 434 925	3.667 647 168
1.5	3.910 180 347	3.585 275 457
1.55	3.919 152 356	3.500 663 067
1.6	3.918 328 524	3.413 862 876

A number of modelling assumptions are made: the rod is thin and rigid; the rod moves freely about the hinge; the string is light; the pulley is small and smooth; the object is a particle and hangs freely.

(i) Show that, for all θ such that $0 \le \theta < \pi$, the clockwise (c.w.) moment about O is $0.4g \sin\theta$ and the anti-clockwise (a.c.) moment is $2mg \sin\phi$. [2 marks]

The system is set up with $m = 0.25$.

The values of the clockwise and anticlockwise moments of the forces acting on the rod predicted by the model for some values of θ are shown in Table 1.

(ii) Estimate the value of θ predicted by the model for which the system is in equilibrium. [1 mark]

The system is to be released from rest with $\theta = 1.3$.

(iii) Using the values in the table, state what the model predicts will happen. [1 mark]

When the experiment is carried out it is found that the system does not move.

(iv) What does this tell you about the model? [1 mark]

9 Centre of mass 1

Let man then contemplate the whole of nature in her full and grand mystery.... It is an infinite sphere, the centre of which is everywhere, the circumference nowhere.

Blaise Pascal

Discussion point

Figure 9.1, which is drawn to scale, shows a mobile suspended from the point P. The horizontal rods and the strings are light but the geometrically shaped pieces are made of uniform heavy card. Does the mobile balance? If it does, what can you say about the position of its centre of mass?

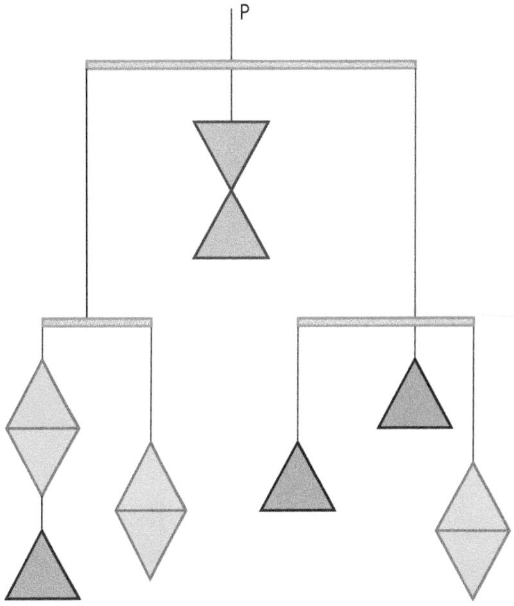

Figure 9.1

1 The centre of mass

In this chapter, you meet the concept of centre of mass in the context of two general models.

The particle model
The centre of mass is the single point at which the whole mass of the body may be taken to be situated.

The rigid body model
The centre of mass is the balance point of a body with size and shape.

The following examples show how to calculate the position of the centre of mass of a body.

Centre of mass of one-dimensional bodies

Example 9.1

An object consists of three point masses 8 kg, 5 kg and 4 kg attached to a rigid light rod, as shown.

Figure 9.2

Calculate the distance of the centre of mass of the object from O. (Ignore the mass of the rod.)

Solution

Suppose the centre of mass C is $\bar{x}$ m from O.

If a pivot were at this position, the rod would balance.

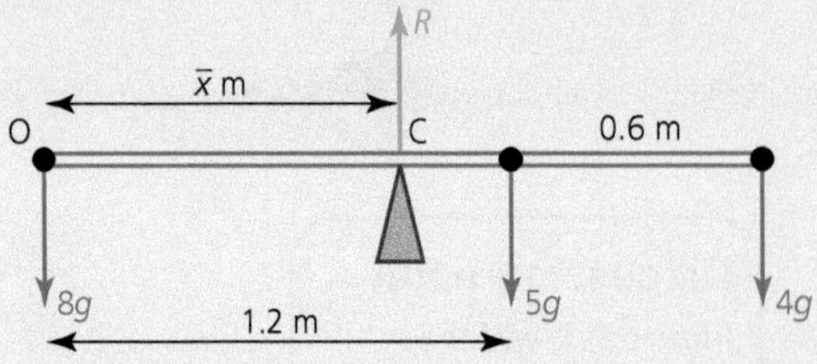

Figure 9.3

For equilibrium $\quad R = 8g + 5g + 4g = 17g$

Taking moments of the forces about O gives:

Total clockwise moment $= (8g \times 0) + (5g \times 1.2) + (4g \times 1.8)$
$= 13.2g\,\text{N m}$

Total anticlockwise moment $= R\bar{x}$
$= 17g\bar{x}\,\text{N m}$

The overall moment must be zero for the rod to be in balance, so

$$17g\bar{x} - 13.2g = 0$$

$$\Rightarrow \quad 17\bar{x} = 13.2$$

$$\Rightarrow \quad \bar{x} = \frac{13.2}{17} = 0.776 \text{ (to 3 s.f.)}$$

The centre of mass is 0.776 m from the end O of the rod.

Note

Although g was included in the calculation, it cancelled out. The answer depends only on the masses and their distances from the origin and not on the value of g.

This example can be generalised to give a method for finding the position of a centre of mass. In the first place, consider a set of n point masses $m_1, m_2, \ldots, m_n$ attached to a rigid light rod (whose mass is neglected) at positions $x_1, x_2, \ldots, x_n$ from one end O. The situation is shown in Figure 9.4.

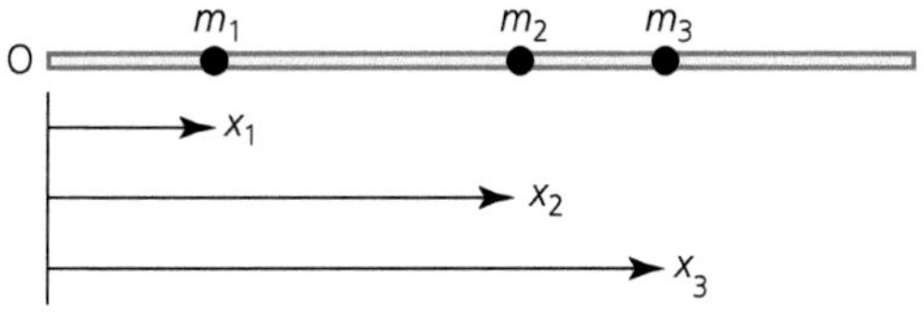

Figure 9.4

The position, $\bar{x}$, of the centre of mass relative to O is defined by the equation:

moment of whole mass at centre of mass = sum of moments of individual masses

$$(m_1 + m_2 + m_3 + \cdots)\bar{x} = m_1x_1 + m_2x_2 + m_3x_3 + \cdots$$

or

$$M\bar{x} = \sum_{i=1}^{n} m_i x_i$$

where M is the total mass (or Σm_i).

> The symbol Σ (sigma) means 'the sum of'.

Example 9.2

A uniform rod of length 2 m has mass 5 kg. Masses of 4 kg and 6 kg are fixed at each end of the rod. Find the centre of mass of the rod.

Solution

Since the rod is uniform, it can be treated as a point mass at its centre.

Figure 9.5 illustrates this situation.

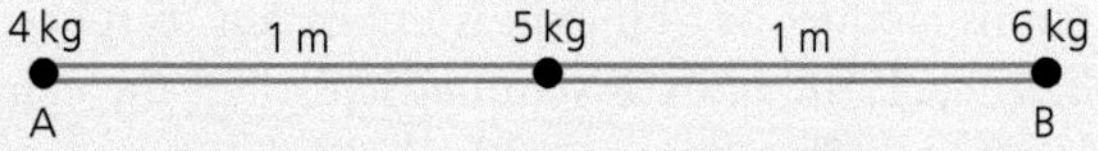

Figure 9.5

Taking the end A as the origin

$$M\bar{x} = \sum m_i x_i$$
$$(4+5+6)\bar{x} = 4\times 0 + 5\times 1 + 6\times 2$$
$$15\bar{x} = 17$$
$$\bar{x} = \frac{17}{15} = 1\frac{2}{15}$$

So the centre of mass is 1.133 m from the 4 kg point mass.

> **Discussion point**
> Check that the rod would balance about a pivot $1\frac{2}{15}$ m from A.

Example 9.3

A rod of mass 1.1 kg and length 1.2 m has its centre of mass 0.48 m from the end A. What mass should be attached to the end B to ensure that the centre of mass is at the midpoint of the rod?

Solution

Let the extra mass be m kg.

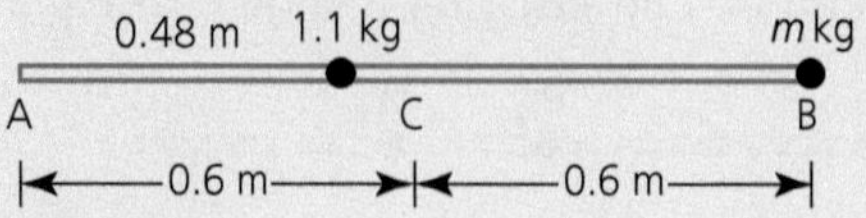

Figure 9.6

Method 1

Refer to the midpoint, C, as origin, so $\bar{x} = 0$. Then

$$(1.1 + m) \times 0 = 1.1 \times (-0.12) + m \times 0.6$$

$$\Rightarrow \quad 0.6m = 1.1 \times 0.12$$

$$\Rightarrow \quad m = 0.22$$

The 1.1 kg mass has negative x referred to C.

A mass of 220 grams should be attached to B.

Method 2

Refer to the end A as origin, so $\bar{x} = 0.6$. Then

$$(1.1 + m) \times 0.6 = 1.1 \times 0.48 + m \times 1.2$$

$$\Rightarrow \quad 0.66 + 0.6m = 0.528 + 1.2m$$

$$\Rightarrow \quad 0.132 = 0.6m$$

$$\Rightarrow \quad m = 0.22 \text{ as before}$$

Composite bodies

The position of the centre of mass of a composite body such as a cricket bat, tennis racquet or golf club is important to sports people who like to feel its balance. If the body is symmetrical, then the centre of mass will be on the axis of symmetry. The next example shows how to model a composite body as a system of point masses so that the methods of the previous section can be used to find the centre of mass.

Example 9.4

A squash racquet of mass 200 g and total length 70 cm consists of a handle of mass 150 g, whose centre of mass is 20 cm from the end, and a frame of mass 50 g, whose centre of mass is 55 cm from the end of the handle.

Find the distance of the centre of mass from the end of the handle.

Solution

Figure 9.7 shows the squash racquet and its dimensions.

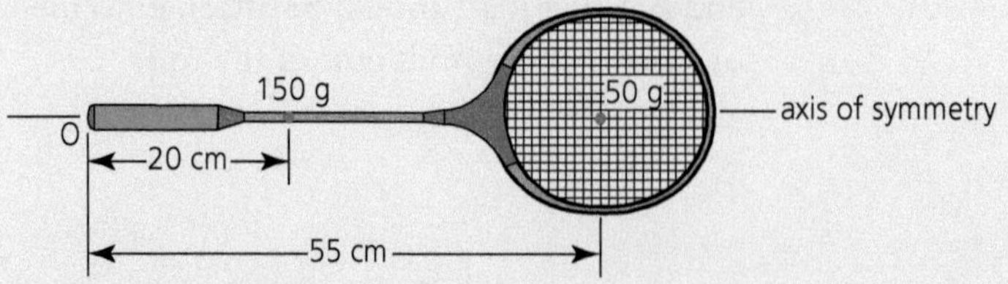

Figure 9.7

The centre of mass lies on the axis of symmetry. Model the handle as a point mass of 0.15 kg at a distance 0.2 m from O and the frame as a point mass of 0.05 kg a distance 0.55 m from the end O.

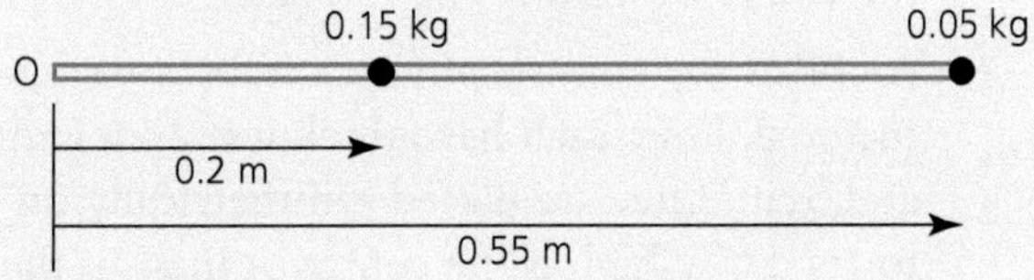

Figure 9.8

The distance $\bar{x}$ of the centre of mass from O is given by

$$(0.15 + 0.05)\bar{x} = (0.15 \times 0.2) + (0.05 \times 0.55)$$

$$\bar{x} = 0.2875$$

The centre of mass of the squash racquet is 28.75 cm from the end of the handle.

Exercise 9.1

① Figure 9.9 show point masses attached to rigid light rods. In each case calculate the position of the centre of mass relative to the point O.

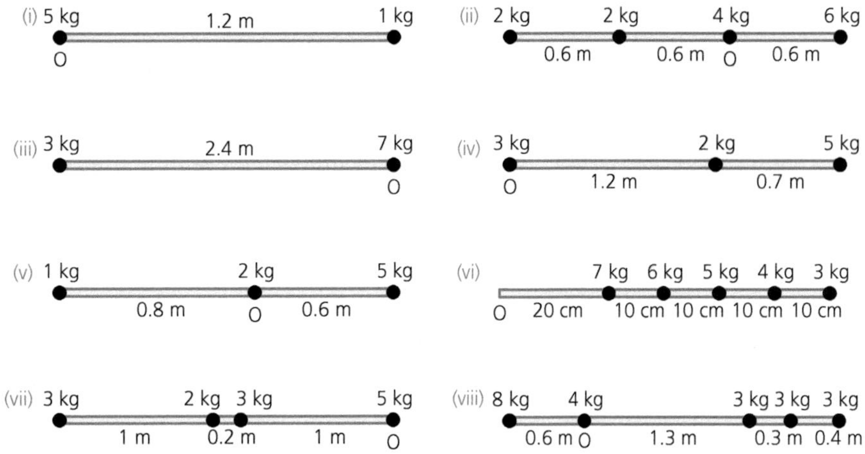

Figure 9.9

② A see-saw consists of a uniform plank 4 m long of mass 10 kg. Calculate the centre of mass when two children, of masses 20 kg and 25 kg, sit, one on each end.

③ A weightlifter's bar in a competition has mass 10 kg and length 1 m. By mistake, 50 kg is placed on one end and 60 kg on the other end. How far is the centre of mass of the bar from the centre of the bar itself?

④ The masses of the Earth and the Moon are 5.98×10^{24} kg and 7.38×10^{22} kg, and the distance between their centres is 3.84×10^{5} km. How far from the centre of the Earth is the centre of mass of the Earth–Moon system?

⑤ A school crossing supervisor carries a sign which consists of a uniform rod of length 1.5 m, and mass 1 kg, on top of which is a circular disc of radius 0.25 m and mass 0.2 kg. Find the distance of the centre of mass from the free end of the stick.

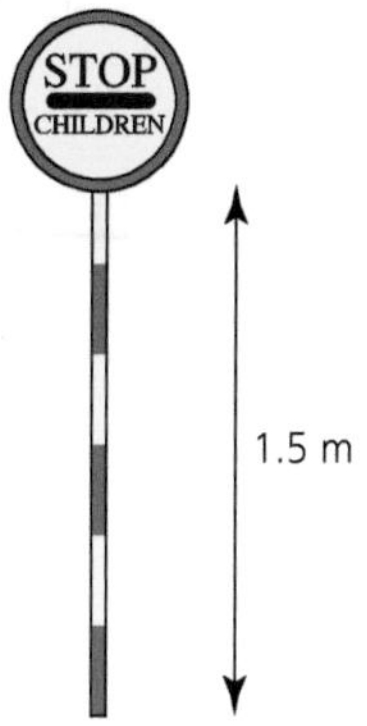

Figure 9.10

⑥ A rod has length 2 m and mass 3 kg. The centre of mass should be in the middle but due to a fault in the manufacturing process it is not. This error is corrected by placing a 200 g mass 5 cm from the centre of the rod. Where is the centre of mass of the rod itself?

⑦ A child's toy consists of four uniform discs, all made out of the same material. They each have thickness 2 cm and their radii are 6 cm, 5 cm, 4 cm and 3 cm. They are placed symmetrically on top of each other to form a tower. How high is the centre of mass of the tower?

⑧ A standard lamp consists of a uniform heavy metal base of thickness 4 cm, attached to which is a uniform metal rod of length 1.75 m and mass 0.25 kg.

What is the minimum mass for the base if the centre of mass of the lamp is no more than 12 cm from the ground?

⑨ A uniform scaffold pole of length 5 m has brackets bolted to it, as shown in Figure 9.11 below. The mass of each bracket is 1 kg.

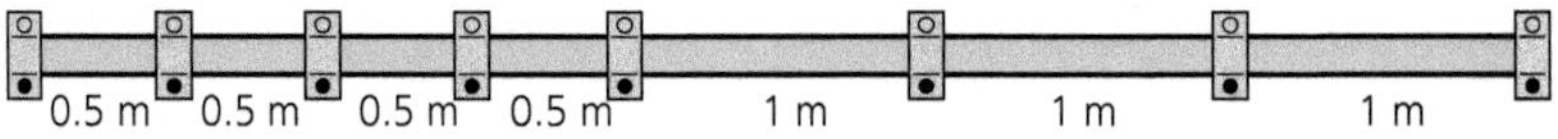

Figure 9.11

The centre of mass is 2.44 m from the left-hand end. What is the mass of the pole?

⑩ An object of mass m_1 is placed at one end of a light rod of length l. An object of mass m_2 is placed at the other end. Find the position of the centre of mass.

⑪ Figure 9.12 illustrates a mobile tower crane. It consists of the main vertical section (mass M tonnes), housing the engine, winding gears and controls, and the boom. The centre of mass of the main section is on its centre line. The boom, which has negligible mass, supports the load (L tonnes) and the counterweight (C tonnes). The main section stands on supports at P and Q, distance $2d$ m apart. The counterweight is held at a fixed distance a m from the centre line of the main section and the load at a variable distance l m.

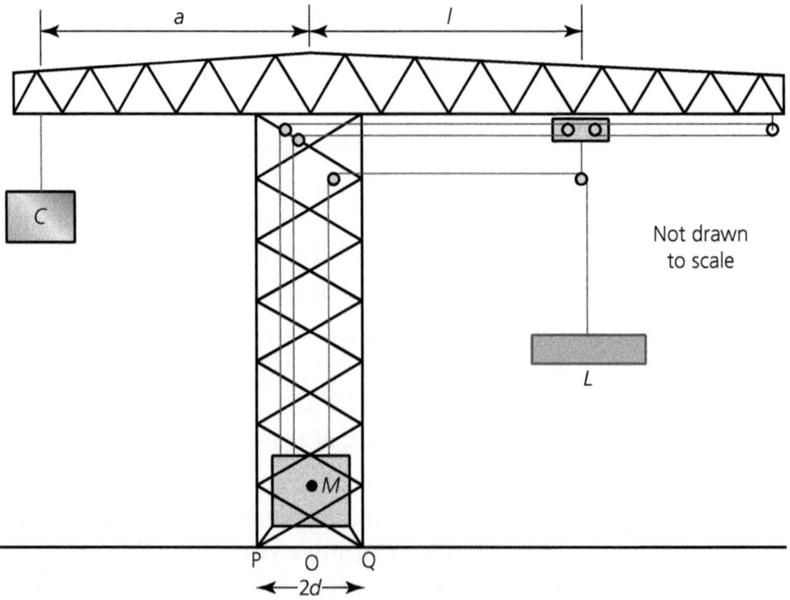

Figure 9.12

(i) In the case when $C = 3, M = 10, L = 7, a = 8, d = 2$ and $l = 13$, find the horizontal position of the centre of mass and say what happens to the crane.

(ii) Show that for these values of C, M, a, d and l the crane will not fall over when it has no load, and find the maximum safe load that it can carry.

(iii) Formulate two inequalities in terms of C, M, L, a, d and l that must hold if the crane is to be safe loaded or unloaded.

(iv) Find, in terms of M, a, d and l, the maximum load that the crane can carry.

2 Centre of mass of two- and three-dimensional bodies

The techniques developed for finding the centre of mass using moments can be extended in two and three dimensions.

If a two-dimensional body consists of a set of n point masses $m_1, m_2, \ldots, m_n$ located at positions $(x_1, y_1), (x_2, y_2), \ldots, (x_n, y_n)$, as in Figure 9.13, then the position of the centre of mass of the body $(\bar{x}, \bar{y})$ is given by

$$M\bar{x} = \sum m_i x_i \text{ and } M\bar{y} = \sum m_i y_i$$

where $M\left(= \sum m_i\right)$ is the total mass of the body.

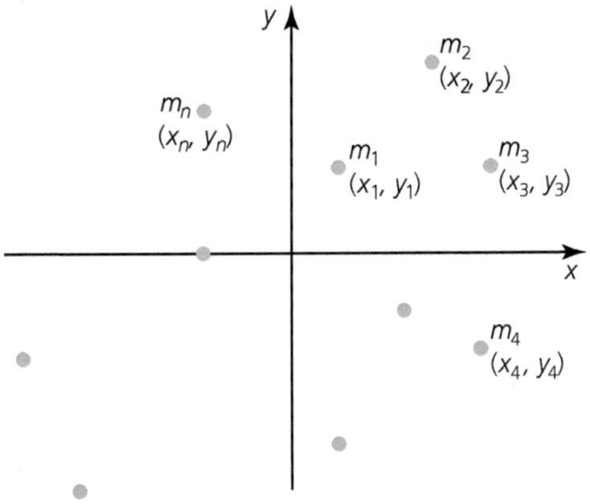

Figure 9.13

In three dimensions, the z coordinates are also included; to find $\bar{z}$ use

$$M\bar{z} = \sum m_i z_i$$

The centre of mass of any composite body in two or three dimensions can be found by replacing each component by a point mass at its centre of mass.

Example 9.5

Joanna makes herself a pendant in the shape of a letter J made up of uniform rectangular shapes, as shown in Figure 9.14.

(i) Find the position of the centre of mass of the pendant relative to the coordinate system shown in Figure 9.14.

(ii) Find the angle that AB makes with the horizontal if she hangs the pendant from a point M in the middle of AB.

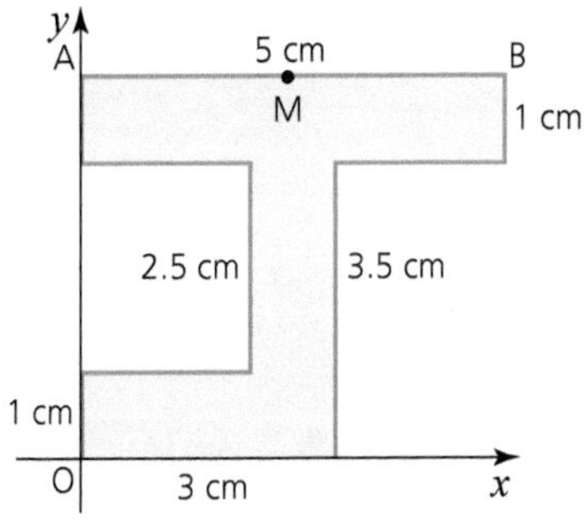

Figure 9.14

She wishes to hang the pendant so that AB is horizontal.

(iii) How far along AB should she place the ring that the suspending chain will pass through?

Solution

(i) The first step is to split the pendant into three rectangles.

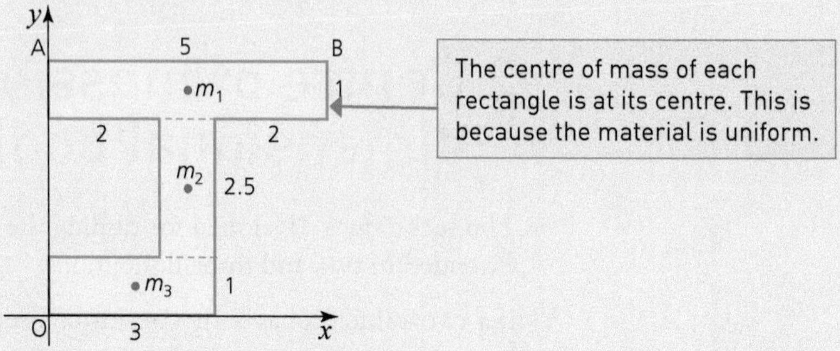

Figure 9.15

You can model the pendant as three point masses m_1, m_2 and m_3 which are proportional to the areas of the rectangular shapes. Since the areas are 5 cm², 2.5 cm² and 3 cm², the masses in suitable units are 5, 2.5 and 3, and the total mass is 5 + 2.5 + 3 = 10.5 (in the same units).

The table below gives the mass and position of m_1, m_2 and m_3.

Mass	m_1	m_2	m_3	M
Mass units	5	2.5	3	10.5
Position of centre of mass x	2.5	2.5	1.5	$\bar{x}$
y	4	2.25	0.5	$\bar{y}$

Now it is possible to find $\bar{x}$:

$$M\bar{x} = \sum m_i x_i$$

$$10.5\bar{x} = 5 \times 2.5 + 2.5 \times 2.5 + 3 \times 1.5$$

$$\bar{x} = \frac{23.25}{10.5} = 2.2\,\text{cm}$$

Similarly for $\bar{y}$:

$$M\bar{y} = \sum m_i y_i$$

$$10.5\bar{y} = 5 \times 4 + 2.5 \times 2.25 + 3 \times 0.5$$

$$\bar{y} = \frac{27.125}{10.5} = 2.6\,\text{cm}$$

The centre of mass is at (2.2, 2.6).

(ii) When the pendant is suspended from M, the centre of mass, G, is vertically below M, as shown in Figure 9.16.

The pendant hangs like in Figure 9.15 but you might find it easier to draw your own diagram like the second.

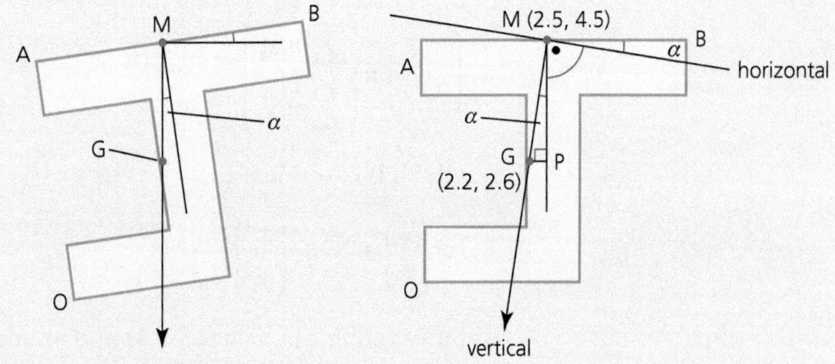

Figure 9.16

$$GP = 2.5 - 2.2 = 0.3$$

$$MP = 4.5 - 2.6 = 1.9$$

$$\therefore \quad \tan\alpha = \frac{0.3}{1.9} \Rightarrow \alpha = 9^\circ$$

AB makes an angle of 9° with the horizontal (or 8.5° working with unrounded figures).

(iii) For AB to be horizontal the point of suspension must be directly above the centre of mass, and so it is 2.2 cm from A.

Example 9.6

Find the centre of mass of a body consisting of a uniform square plate of mass 3 kg and side length 2 m, with small objects of mass 1 kg, 2 kg, 4 kg and 5 kg at the corners of the square.

Solution

Figure 9.17 shows the square plate, with the origin taken at the corner at which the 1 kg mass is located. The mass of the plate is represented by a 3 kg point mass at its centre.

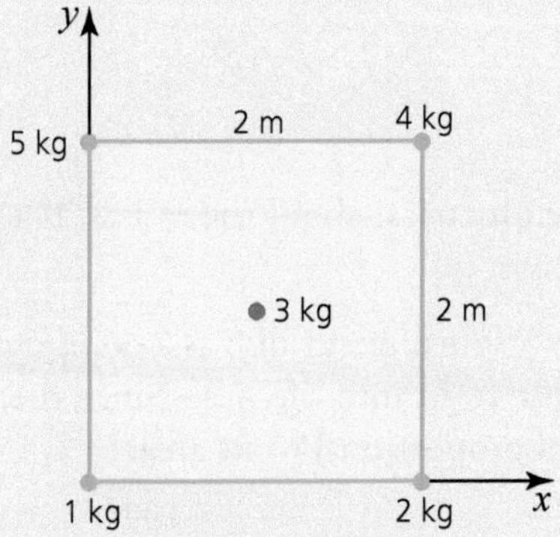

Figure 9.17

In this example, the total mass M (in kilograms) is 1 + 2 + 4 + 5 + 3 = 15.

The two formulae for $\bar{x}$ and $\bar{y}$ can be combined into one using column vector notation:

$$\begin{pmatrix} M\bar{x} \\ M\bar{y} \end{pmatrix} = \begin{pmatrix} \sum m_i x_i \\ \sum m_i y_i \end{pmatrix}$$

which is equivalent to

$$M\begin{pmatrix} \bar{x} \\ \bar{y} \end{pmatrix} = \sum m_i \begin{pmatrix} x_i \\ y_i \end{pmatrix}$$

Substituting our values for M and m_i and x_i and y_i

$$15\begin{pmatrix} \bar{x} \\ \bar{y} \end{pmatrix} = 1\begin{pmatrix} 0 \\ 0 \end{pmatrix} + 2\begin{pmatrix} 2 \\ 0 \end{pmatrix} + 4\begin{pmatrix} 2 \\ 2 \end{pmatrix} + 5\begin{pmatrix} 0 \\ 2 \end{pmatrix} + 3\begin{pmatrix} 1 \\ 1 \end{pmatrix}$$

$$15\begin{pmatrix} \bar{x} \\ \bar{y} \end{pmatrix} = \begin{pmatrix} 15 \\ 21 \end{pmatrix}$$

$$\begin{pmatrix} \bar{x} \\ \bar{y} \end{pmatrix} = \begin{pmatrix} 1 \\ 1.4 \end{pmatrix}$$

The centre of mass is the point (1, 1.4).

Example 9.7

A metal disc of radius 15 cm has a hole of radius 5 cm cut in it, as shown in Figure 9.18. Find the centre of mass of the disc. Coordinate axes are defined with origin O as shown in Figure 9.18.

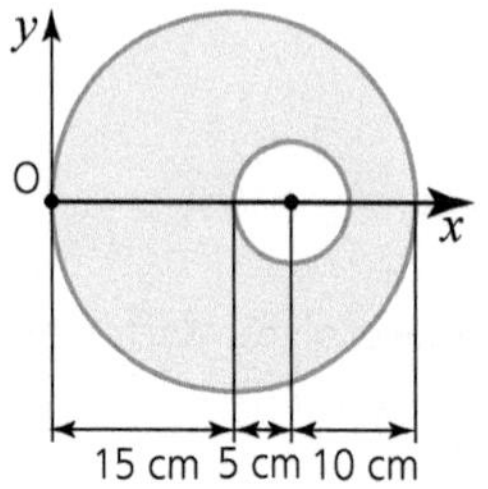

Figure 9.18

Solution

The disc is symmetrical about the x-axis. The centre of mass must therefore be on the x-axis.

Think of the original uncut disc as a composite body made up of the final body and a disc to fit into the hole. Since the material is uniform, the mass of each part is proportional to its area.

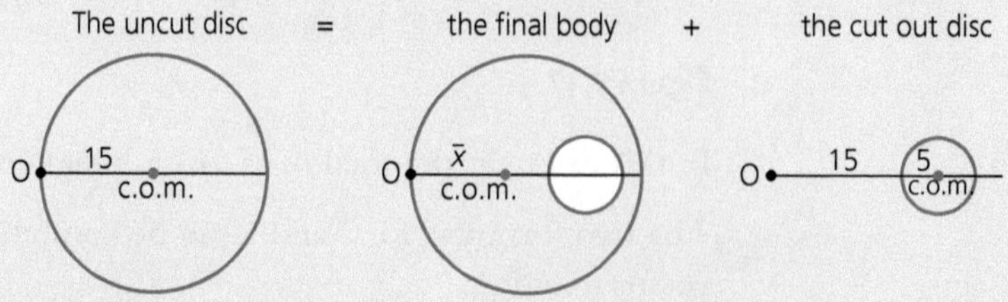

Figure 9.19

	Uncut disc	Final body	Cut out disc
Area	$15^2\pi = 225\pi$	$15^2\pi - 5^2\pi = 200\pi$	$5^2\pi = 25\pi$
Distance from O to centre of mass	15 cm	$\bar{x}$ cm	20 cm

Taking moments about O:

$$225\pi \times 15 = 200\pi \times \bar{x} + 25\pi \times 20$$ ← Divide by π

$$\Rightarrow \quad \bar{x} = \frac{225 \times 15 - 25 \times 20}{200}$$

$$= 14.375$$

The centre of mass is 14.4 cm from O; that is, 0.6 cm to the left of the centre of the disc.

Centre of mass of a triangle

The triangle in Figure 9.20 is divided up into thin strips parallel to the side AB.

The centre of mass of each strip lies in the middle of the strip, at the points C_1, C_2, C_3, …

When these points are joined they form the median of the triangle drawn from C. Similarly, the centre of mass also lies on the medians from A and B. Therefore, the centre of mass lies at the intersection of the three medians; this is the **centroid** of the triangle. This point is $\frac{2}{3}$ of the distance along the median from the vertex.

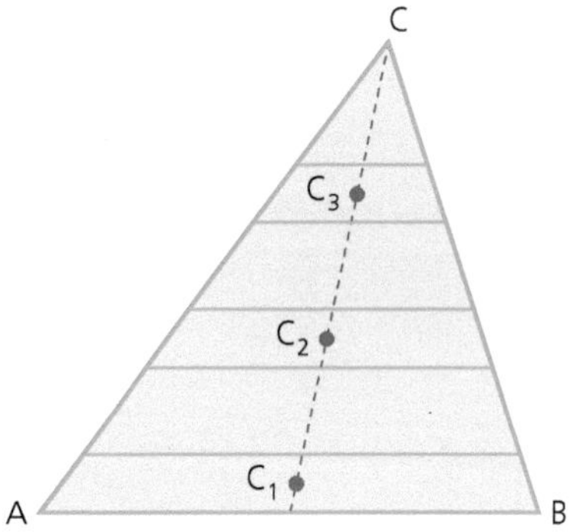

Figure 9.20

Note

The median of a triangle joins a vertex to the midpoint of the opposite side.

Example 9.8

Find the coordinates of the centre of mass of a uniform triangular lamina with vertices at A (4, 4), B (1, 1) and C (5, 1).

If the lamina is suspended from A, find the angle that the line BC makes with the horizontal.

Solution

The midpoint of BC is at M with coordinates (3, 1). The centre of mass G is $\frac{2}{3}$ of the way down the median AM.

G has x coordinate: $4 - \frac{2}{3} \times (4 - 3) = 3\frac{1}{3}$

and y coordinate: $4 - \frac{2}{3} \times (4 - 1) = 2$

The centre of mass G of the lamina is at $\left(3\frac{1}{3}, 2\right)$

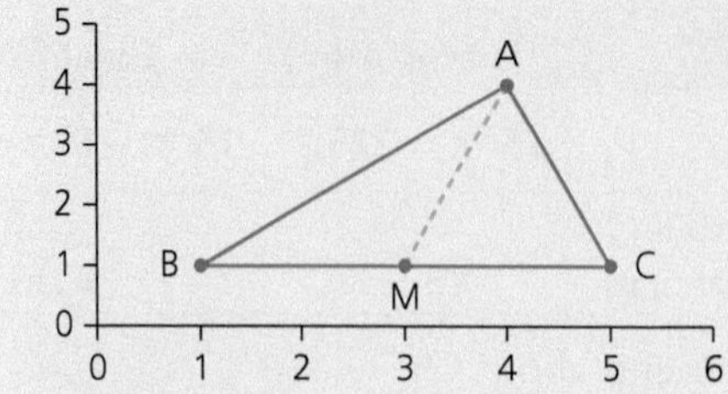

Figure 9.21

The lamina is suspended from A. G will be directly below A. The line AG and also the median AM will be along the vertical. The horizontal through M makes an angle θ with BC. The same angle θ is shown in the triangle AMH, from which you can derive

$$\tan\theta = \frac{\text{MH}}{\text{AH}} = \frac{4-3}{4-1} = \frac{1}{3} \Rightarrow \theta = 18.4°$$

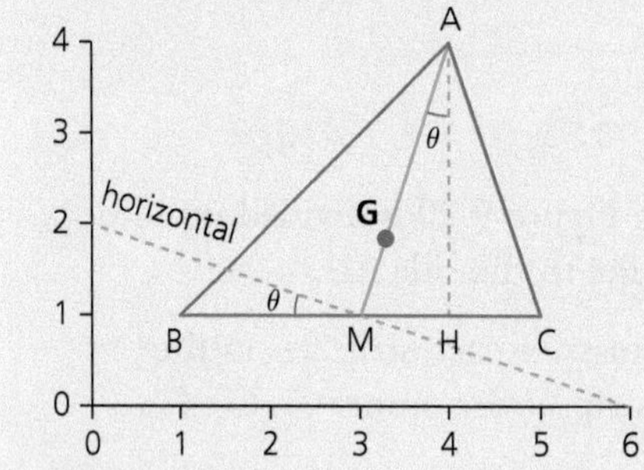

Figure 9.22

The line BC makes an angle 18.4° with the horizontal when the lamina is suspended from A.

Centres of mass of other shapes

The table below gives the position of the centre of mass of some uniform objects which you may encounter or wish to include within models of composite bodies.

The centre of mass for each of these shapes lies on its line of symmetry.

These standard results may be obtained using calculus methods which are introduced in Chapter 13.

Body	Position of centre of mass	Diagram
Solid cone or pyramid	$\frac{1}{4}h$ from base	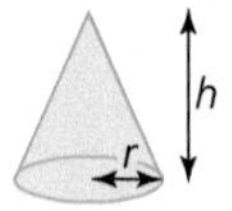
Hollow cone or pyramid	$\frac{1}{3}h$ from base	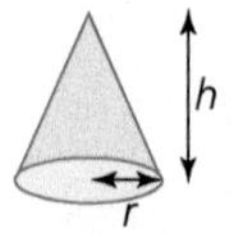
Solid hemisphere	$\frac{3}{8}r$ from base	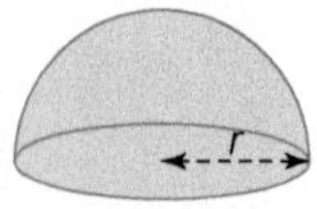

Body	Position of centre of mass	Diagram
Hollow hemisphere	$\frac{1}{2}r$ from base	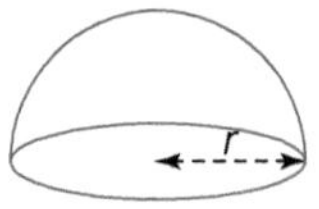
Semicircular lamina	$\frac{4r}{3\pi}$ from base	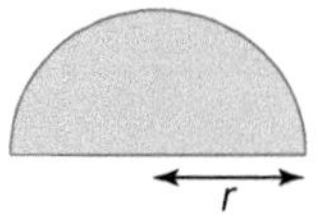

Example 9.9

Find the centre of mass of the uniform lamina illustrated in Figure 9.23.

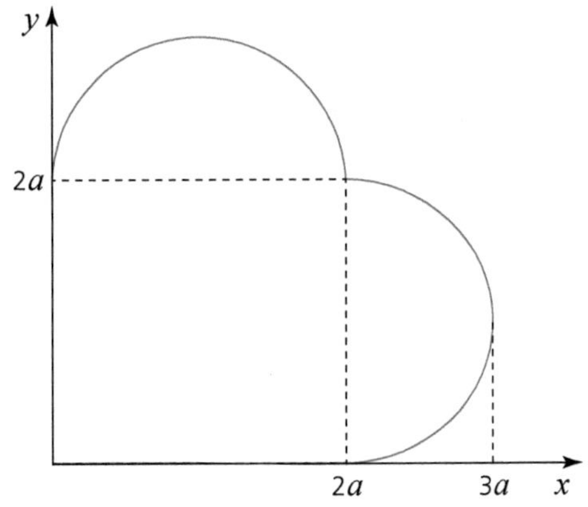

Figure 9.23

Solution

The shape is symmetrical about the line $y = x$. It thus follows that the centre of mass lies on that line. In other words, you need only find one of the coordinates. The shape is made up of a square of side $2a$ with two semicircles of radius a added on at the edges. The square has centre of mass at (a, a). The semicircles have centre of mass at $\left(a,\ 2a+\frac{4a}{3\pi}\right)$ and $\left(2a+\frac{4a}{3\pi},\ a\right)$.

The mass of each shape is proportional to its area: $4a^2$ for the square and $\frac{1}{2}\pi a^2$ for the semicircles. This gives rise to the moments equation

$$(4a^2+\frac{1}{2}\pi a^2+\frac{1}{2}\pi a^2)\bar{x} = 4a^2\times a+\frac{1}{2}\pi a^2\times a+\frac{1}{2}\pi a^2\times\left(2a+\frac{4a}{3\pi}\right)$$

$$\bar{x}\left(4a^2+\pi a^2\right)=\frac{14}{3}a^3+\frac{3\pi}{2}a^3$$

$$\Rightarrow \qquad \bar{x}=\frac{a}{6}\left(\frac{28+9\pi}{4+\pi}\right)=1.313\ldots a$$

The centre of mass is at $(1.31a, 1.31a)$.

Exercise 9.2

① Find the centre of mass of the following sets of point masses.

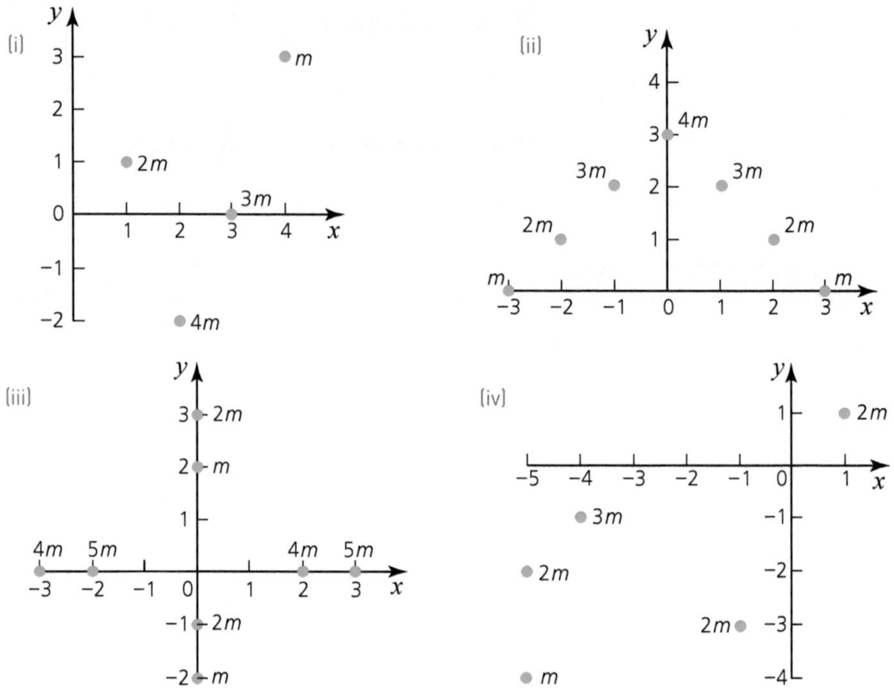

Figure 9.24

② Masses of 1, 2, 3 and 4 grams are placed at the corners A, B, C and D of a square piece of uniform cardboard of side 10 cm and mass 5 g. Find the position of the centre of mass relative to axes through AB and AD.

③ As part of an illuminated display, letters are produced by mounting bulbs in holders 30 cm apart on light wire frames. The combined mass of a bulb and its holder is 200 g. Find the position of the centre of mass for each of the letters shown below, in terms of its horizontal and vertical displacement from the bottom left-hand corner of the letter.

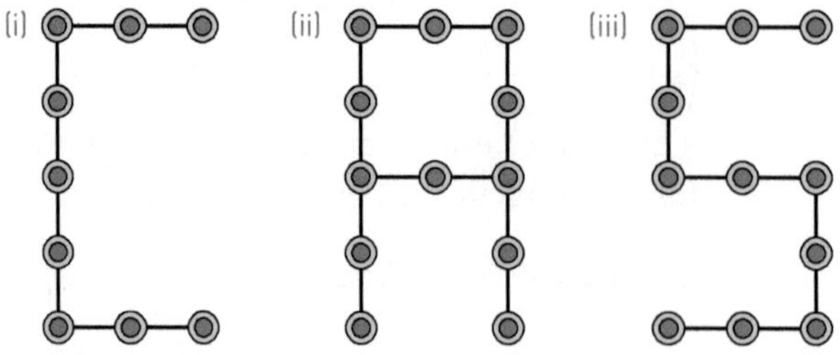

Figure 9.25

④ Four people of masses 60 kg, 65 kg, 62 kg and 75 kg sit on the four seats of the fairground ride shown in Figure 9.26. The seat and the connecting arms are light. Find the radius of the circle described by the centre of mass when the ride rotates about O.

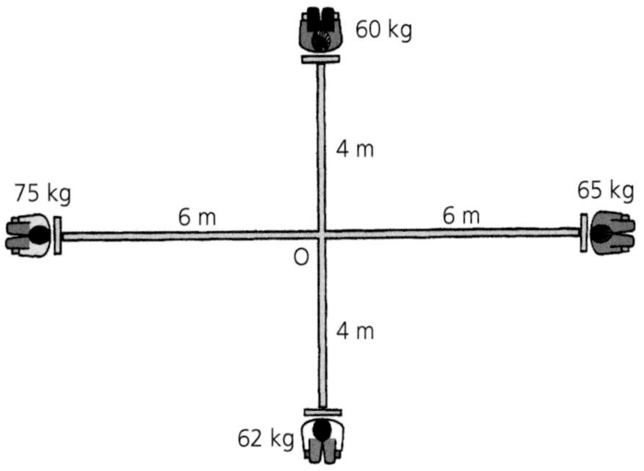

Figure 9.26

⑤ Find the coordinates of the centre of mass of each of these uniform laminae.

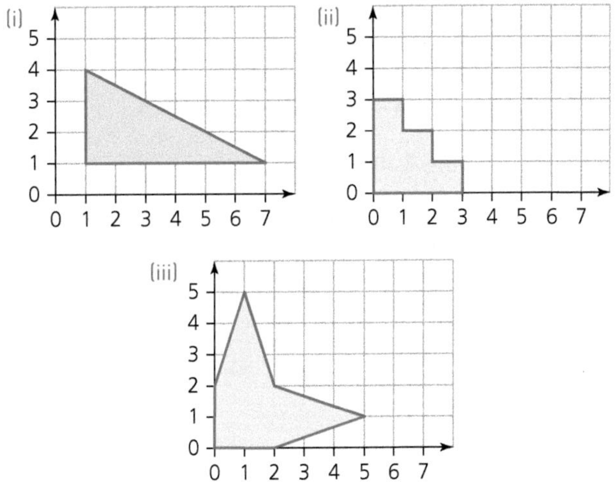

Figure 9.27

⑥ The following shapes are made of uniform card.

For each shape find the coordinates of the centre of mass relative to O.

Figure 9.28

⑦ A pendant is made from a uniform circular disc of mass $4m$ and radius 2 cm with a decorative edging of mass m as shown. The centre of mass of the decoration is 1 cm below the centre, O, of the disc. The pendant is symmetrical about the diameter AB.

(i) Find the position of the centre of mass of the pendant.

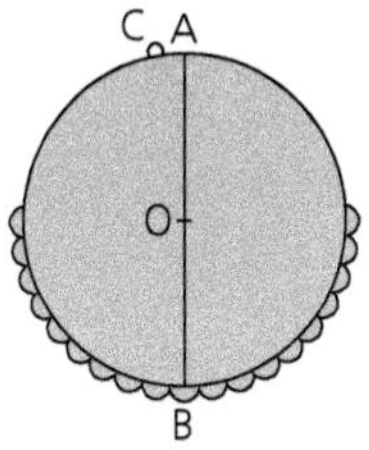

Figure 9.29

The pendant should be hung from A but the light ring for hanging it is attached at C where angle AOC is 10°.

(ii) Find the angle between AB and the vertical when the pendant is hung from C.

⑧ ABCD is a rectangular plate, with AB = 5 cm and AD = 8 cm. E is the midpoint of BC. The triangular portion ABE is removed and the remainder is suspended from A.

Find the angle that AD makes with the vertical.

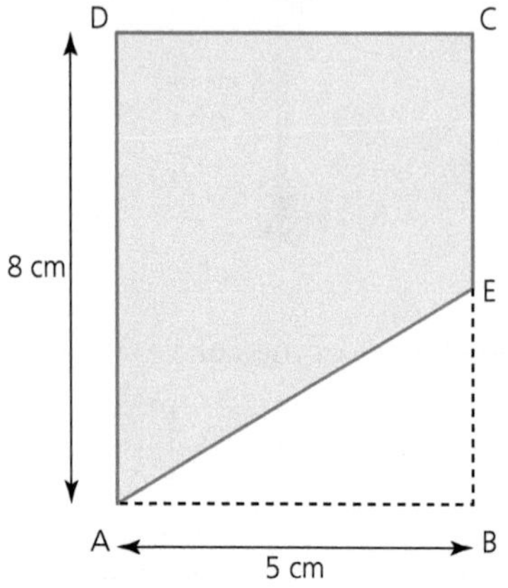

Figure 9.30

⑨ Some years ago a textbook included the following incorrect worked example.

Example

Given that $\mathbf{u} = \mathbf{0}$, $\mathbf{a} = 4\mathbf{i} + 2\mathbf{j} - \mathbf{k}$ and $\mathbf{v} = 4\mathbf{i} - 2\mathbf{j} + 3\mathbf{k}$, find $\mathbf{s}$.

Solution

Let $\mathbf{s} = x\mathbf{i} + y\mathbf{j} + z\mathbf{k}$.

Using $v^2 = u^2 + 2as$:

$x \quad 4^2 = 0^2 + 2 \times 4 \times x \qquad$ so $x = 2$

$y \quad (-2)^2 = 0^2 + 2 \times 2 \times y \qquad$ so $y = 1$

$z \quad 3^2 = 0^2 + 2 \times (-1) \times z \qquad$ so $z = -4.5$

Therefore, $\mathbf{s} = 2\mathbf{i} + \mathbf{j} - 4.5\mathbf{k}$.

(i) Show that the given values of $\mathbf{u}$, $\mathbf{v}$ and $\mathbf{a}$ are incompatible.

(ii) What does this tell you about the use of the equation $\mathbf{v} \cdot \mathbf{v} = \mathbf{u} \cdot \mathbf{u} + 2\mathbf{a} \cdot \mathbf{s}$?

⑩ A uniform rectangular lamina, ABCD, where AB is of length a and BC of length $2a$, has a mass $10m$. Further point masses m, $2m$, $3m$ and $4m$ are fixed to the points A, B, C and D respectively.

(i) Find the centre of mass of the system relative to x and y axes along AB and AD respectively.

(ii) If the lamina is suspended from the point A find the angle that the diagonal AC makes with the vertical.

(iii) To what must the mass at the point D be altered if this diagonal is to hang vertically? [MEI]

⑪ A vase is made from a uniform solid cylinder of height 25 cm and radius 10 cm by removing a smaller cylinder of height 22 cm and radius 9 cm from it so that there is an axis of symmetry vertically through the centre of the base.

Find the centre of mass of the vase.

Figure 9.31

⑫ A filing cabinet has the dimensions shown in Figure 9.32. The body of the cabinet has mass 20 kg and its construction is such that its centre of mass is at a height of 60 cm, and is 25 cm from the back of the cabinet. The mass of a drawer and its contents may be taken to be 10 kg and its centre of mass to be 10 cm above its base and 30 cm from its front face.

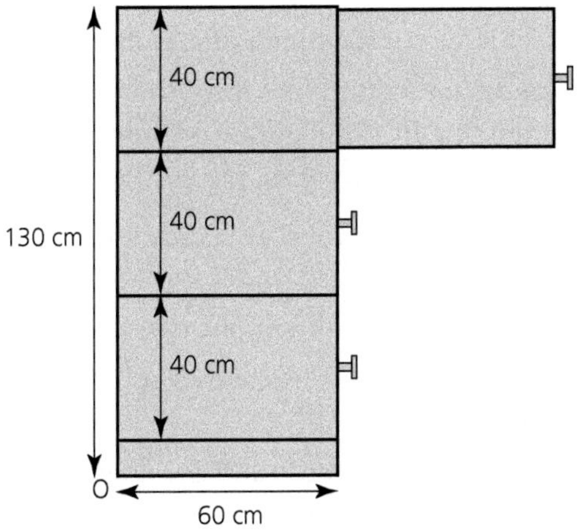

Figure 9.32

(i) Find the position of the centre of mass when all the drawers are closed.

(ii) Find the position of the centre of mass when the two top drawers are fully open.

(iii) Show that when all three drawers are fully opened the filing cabinet will tip over.

(iv) Two drawers are fully open. How far can the third drawer be opened without the cabinet tipping over?

⑬ Uniform wooden bricks have length 20 cm and height 5 cm. They are glued together as shown in Figure 9.33 with each brick 5 cm to the right of the one below it. The origin is taken to be at O.

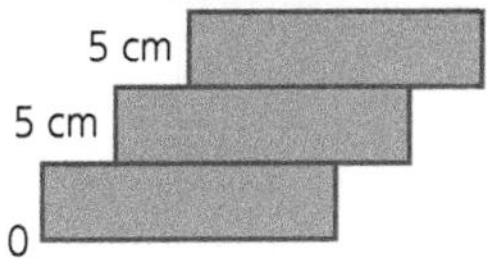

Figure 9.33

(i) Find the coordinates of the centre of mass for

(a) 1 (b) 2 (c) 3 (d) 4 (e) 5 bricks.

(ii) How many bricks is it possible to assemble in this way without them tipping over?

(iii) If the displacement were changed from 5 cm to 2 cm, find the coordinates of the centre of mass for n bricks. How many bricks can now be assembled without them tipping over?

(iv) If the displacement is $\frac{1}{2}$ cm, what is the maximum height possible for the centre of mass of such an assembly of bricks without them tipping over?

⑭ Figure 9.34 gives the dimensions of the design of a uniform metal plate.

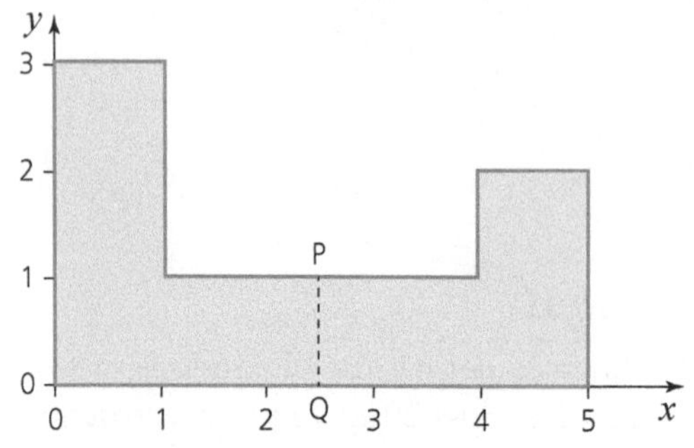

Figure 9.34

Use a coordinate system with O as origin, the x and y axes as shown and 1 metre as 1 unit.

(i) Show that the centre of mass has y coordinate 1 and find its x coordinate.

The design requires the plate to have its centre of mass half way across (i.e. on the line PQ in Figure 9.34) and in order to achieve this a circular hole centred on $\left(\frac{1}{2}, \frac{1}{2}\right)$ is considered.

(ii) Find the appropriate radius for such a hole and explain why this idea is not feasible.

It is then decided to cut out two holes of radius r, both centred on the line $x = \frac{1}{2}$. The first hole is centred at $\left(\frac{1}{2}, \frac{1}{2}\right)$ and the centre of mass of the plate is to be at P.

(iii) Find the value of r and the coordinates of the centre of the second hole. [MEI]

⑮ A toy consists of a solid hemisphere of radius R joined to a solid right cone of radius R and height H. The hemispherical base is made of a material which is twice as dense as the conical top.

Show that the centre of mass of the toy lies at a distance

$$\frac{H^2 - 6R^2}{4(H + 4R)}$$

from the common face of the two solids.

⑯ Find the centre of mass of the following uniform lamina.

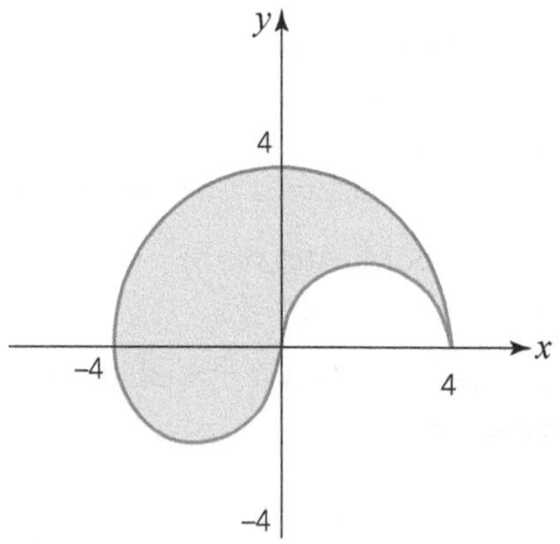

Figure 9.35

⑰ A drink can is symmetrical, with height h cm, and when empty its mass is m g. The drink that fills it has mass M g and can be taken to fill the can completely.

(i) Find the height of the centre of mass when the can is standing on a level table and

(a) it is half full

(b) a proportion, α, of the drink remains.

When the can is full, the centre of mass is clearly half way up it, at a height of $\frac{1}{2}h$. The same is true when it is completely empty. In between these two extremes, the centre of mass is below the middle.

(ii) Show that when the centre of mass is at its minimum height, α satisfies the equation $M\alpha^2 + 2\alpha m - m = 0$ and that the centre of mass lies on the surface of the drink.

KEY POINTS

1 The centre of mass of a body has the property that the moment, about any point, of the whole mass of the body taken at the centre of mass is equal to the sum of moments of the various particles comprising the body.

$M\bar{\mathbf{r}} = \sum m_i \mathbf{r}_i$ where $M = \sum m_i$

2 In one dimension

$M\bar{x} = \sum m_i x_i$

3 In two dimensions

$$M\begin{pmatrix}\bar{x}\\\bar{y}\end{pmatrix} = \sum m_i \begin{pmatrix}x_i\\y_i\end{pmatrix}$$

4 In three dimensions

$$M\begin{pmatrix}\bar{x}\\\bar{y}\\\bar{z}\end{pmatrix} = \sum m_i \begin{pmatrix}x_i\\y_i\\z_i\end{pmatrix}$$

LEARNING OUTCOMES

When you have finished this chapter, you should

- be able to find the centre of mass of a system of particles of given position and mass
- be able to find the centre of mass of a simple shape
- know how to use symmetry when finding a centre of mass
- know the positions of the centres of mass of simple shapes
- be able to find the centre of mass of a composite body
- be able to use centre of mass in problems involving the equilibrium of a rigid body.

10 Motion under a variable force

Evolution has ensured that our brains just aren't equipped to visualise 11 dimensions directly. However, from a purely mathematical point of view it is just as easy to think in 11 dimensions as it is to think in 3 or 4.

Steven Hawking

→ The Hubble space telescope floats against a background of Earth in this photograph from the service module used to repair it. How would you describe its motion?

1 Motion in more than one dimension

The first chapter of this book covers motion along a straight line. This is now extended to cover motion in 2 and 3 dimensions. The first step is to establish the notation and vocabulary.

Notation and vocabulary

Position

In 2 dimensions the position of a point is usually defined using standard x-y axes. Figure 10.1 shows a general point A with position (x, y).

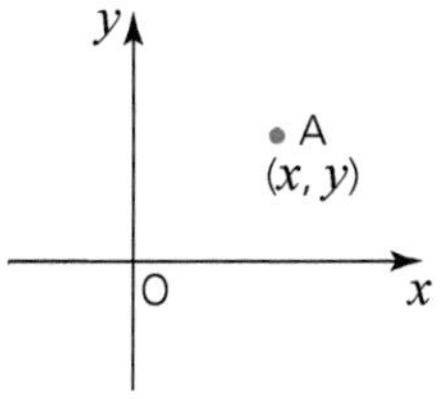

Figure 10.1

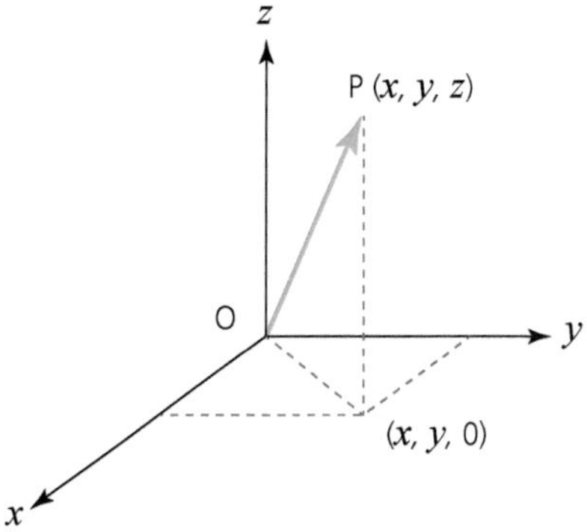

Figure 10.2

The equivalent in 3 dimensions is the general point P in Figure 10.2 with coordinates (x, y, z).

Position vector

The displacement of a point from the origin, in this case $\overrightarrow{OA}$ or $\overrightarrow{OP}$, is called its *position vector*. A position vector is often denoted by $\mathbf{r}$.

In 2 dimensions, this can be given in terms of unit vectors $\mathbf{i}$ and $\mathbf{j}$ parallel to the x- and y-axes, or as a column vector.

Thus $\overrightarrow{OA} = \mathbf{r} = x\mathbf{i} + y\mathbf{j} = \begin{pmatrix} x \\ y \end{pmatrix}$.

In 3 dimensions, the unit vectors are $\mathbf{i}, \mathbf{j}$ and $\mathbf{k}$.

$$\overrightarrow{OP} = \mathbf{r} = x\mathbf{i} + y\mathbf{j} + z\mathbf{k} = \begin{pmatrix} x \\ y \\ z \end{pmatrix}.$$

In 2 dimensions

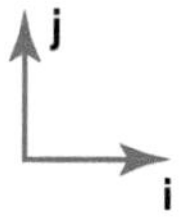

Figure 10.3

In 3 dimensions

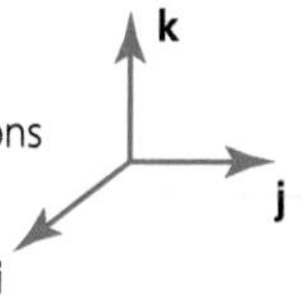

Figure 10.4

Note

Notice that vector quantities are always shown in bold type.

Displacement

The displacement of a point T from a point S is the vector $\overrightarrow{ST}$. The term can be used whatever the number of dimensions.

Distance

Distance is the length of the displacement. It is a scalar quantity. Thus the distance of the point A from the origin is $\sqrt{x^2 + y^2}$. The 3-dimensional equivalent for P is $\sqrt{x^2 + y^2 + z^2}$. This distance is denoted by r or $|\mathbf{r}|$.

Velocity

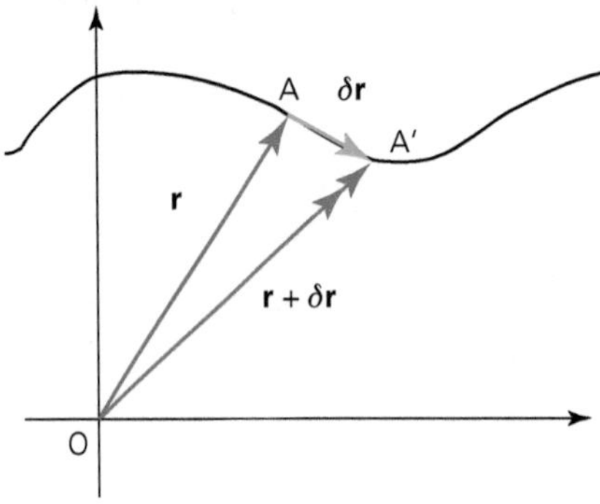

Figure 10.5

Figure 10.5 shows a particle moving in 2 dimensions from A at time t to A′ at time $t + \delta t$.

The displacement is $\overrightarrow{AA'} = \delta\mathbf{r}$, where $\delta\mathbf{r}$ is the vector $\delta x\mathbf{i} + \delta y\mathbf{j}$; δx and δy are small increments in the direction of the x- and y-axes.

The average velocity during the time interval δt is given by $\dfrac{\delta r}{\delta t} = \dfrac{\delta x}{\delta t}\mathbf{i} + \dfrac{\delta y}{\delta t}\mathbf{j}$.

As $\delta t \to 0$ and A′ approaches A, $\dfrac{\delta r}{\delta t}$ tends to the limiting vector $\dfrac{\mathrm{d}\mathbf{r}}{\mathrm{d}t}$, the derivative of $\mathbf{r}$ with respect to t.

The velocity of P is given by

$$\mathbf{v} = \frac{\mathrm{d}\mathbf{r}}{\mathrm{d}t} = \frac{\mathrm{d}x}{\mathrm{d}t}\mathbf{i} + \frac{\mathrm{d}y}{\mathrm{d}t}\mathbf{j}$$

Note

A dot placed above the variable means differentiation with respect to time.

This can also be written as $\mathbf{v} = \dot{x}\mathbf{i} + \dot{y}\mathbf{j} = \begin{pmatrix} \dot{x} \\ \dot{y} \end{pmatrix}$

The equivalent ways of writing velocity in 3 dimensions are

$$\mathbf{v} = \frac{\mathrm{d}\mathbf{r}}{\mathrm{d}t} = \frac{\mathrm{d}x}{\mathrm{d}t}\mathbf{i} + \frac{\mathrm{d}y}{\mathrm{d}t}\mathbf{j} + \frac{\mathrm{d}z}{\mathrm{d}t}\mathbf{k} = \dot{x}\mathbf{i} + \dot{y}\mathbf{j} + \dot{z}\mathbf{k} = \begin{pmatrix} \dot{x} \\ \dot{y} \\ \dot{z} \end{pmatrix}$$

Speed

Speed is a the magnitude of velocity, written v or $|\mathbf{v}|$, and so it is a scalar quantity.

In 2 dimensions it is given by $\sqrt{\dot{x}^2 + \dot{y}^2}$ (and equivalent forms) and in 3 dimensions by $\sqrt{\dot{x}^2 + \dot{y}^2 + \dot{z}^2}$.

The speed of P is then given by $|\mathbf{v}| = \sqrt{\dot{x}^2 + \dot{y}^2 + \dot{z}^2}$.

Acceleration

Acceleration is the rate of change of velocity. It is a vector quantity. So its derivation from velocity is similar to that of velocity from displacement and it is given by

$$\mathbf{a} = \frac{d\mathbf{v}}{dt} = \frac{d^2\mathbf{r}}{dt^2}$$

There are several equivalent ways of writing acceleration including the following.

2 dimensions	3 dimensions
$\mathbf{a} = \ddot{x}\mathbf{i} + \ddot{y}\mathbf{j} = \begin{pmatrix} \ddot{x} \\ \ddot{y} \end{pmatrix}$	$\mathbf{a} = \ddot{x}\mathbf{i} + \ddot{y}\mathbf{j} + \ddot{z}\mathbf{k} = \begin{pmatrix} \ddot{x} \\ \ddot{y} \\ \ddot{z} \end{pmatrix}$

Magnitude of acceleration

Magnitude of acceleration, denoted by a or $|\mathbf{a}|$, is given by $\sqrt{\ddot{x}^2 + \ddot{y}^2}$ or equivalent forms in 2 dimensions and by $\sqrt{\ddot{x}^2 + \ddot{y}^2 + \ddot{z}^2}$ in 3 dimensions. It is a scalar quantity.

Example 10.1

The position vector of a particle at time t seconds is given in metres by

$$\mathbf{r} = t^2\mathbf{i} - 5t\,\mathbf{j} + (t^2 - 1)\mathbf{k}$$

(i) Find expressions for its velocity $\mathbf{v}$ and acceleration $\mathbf{a}$.

(ii) Calculate the distance of the particle from the origin, its speed and the magnitude of its acceleration when $t = 2$.

Solution

(i) The velocity is the rate of change of the position vector.

$$\mathbf{v} = \frac{d\mathbf{r}}{dt} = 2t\mathbf{i} - 5\mathbf{j} + 2t\mathbf{k}$$

The acceleration is the rate of change of the velocity.

$$\mathbf{a} = \frac{d\mathbf{v}}{dt} = \frac{d^2\mathbf{r}}{dt^2} = 2\mathbf{i} + 2\mathbf{k}$$

(ii) When $t = 2$, $\mathbf{r} = \begin{pmatrix} 4 \\ -10 \\ 3 \end{pmatrix}$

So the distance of the particle from the origin is

$\sqrt{4^2 + (-10)^2 + 3^2} = \sqrt{125} = 11.18\ldots$ m

It is moving with velocity $\begin{pmatrix} 4 \\ -5 \\ 4 \end{pmatrix}$.

So its speed is $\sqrt{4^2+(-5)^2+4^2} = \sqrt{57} = 7.54\ldots \text{ ms}^{-1}$

Its acceleration is $\begin{pmatrix} 2 \\ 0 \\ 2 \end{pmatrix}$.

So the magnitude of its acceleration is $\sqrt{2^2+2^2} = 2.82\ldots \text{ ms}^{-2}$

You have seen how successive differentiation allows you to use an expression for a position vector in terms of time to find expressions for velocity and acceleration. Similarly, you may use the same process in reverse and use integration with respect to time to find the velocity and position vector of a point from its acceleration.

$$\mathbf{v} = \int \mathbf{a}\,\mathrm{d}t \text{ and } \mathbf{r} = \int \mathbf{v}\,\mathrm{d}t$$

These results are summarised in the table below.

	→ differentiate		→ differentiate	
Position		**Velocity**		**Acceleration**
	← integrate		← integrate	

The next example illustrates the use of integration in this way.

Example 10.2

A particle of mass 5 kg is initially at rest at a point (2, 3). It is acted on by a force

$$\mathbf{F} = 20t\mathbf{i} + (30 - 10t)\mathbf{j} \text{ N}$$

where t is the time in seconds.

Find, when $t = 5$,

(i) the magnitude of the acceleration

(ii) the speed

(iii) the distance of the particle from the origin.

Solution

(i) By Newton's second law, $\mathbf{F} = m\mathbf{a}$

$$\text{So } \mathbf{a} = \frac{\mathbf{F}}{m} = \frac{(20t\mathbf{i} + (30-10t)\mathbf{j}}{5}$$
$$= 4t\mathbf{i} + (6 - 2t)\mathbf{j}$$

When $t = 5$, $\mathbf{a} = 20\mathbf{i} - 4\mathbf{j}$

and $a = |\mathbf{a}| = \sqrt{20^2 + (-4)^2} = 20.4$, in ms^{-2}.

c_1 and c_2 are constants of integration, one for each component.

Both components of **v** must be zero if $\mathbf{v} = \mathbf{0}$.

This comes from using $\mathbf{r} = \int \mathbf{v}\,dt$.

(ii) Integrating **a** with respect to t gives

$$\mathbf{v} = \left(2t^2 + c_1\right)\mathbf{i} + \left(6t - t^2 + c_2\right)\mathbf{j}$$

Initially, the particle is at rest, so $\mathbf{v} = \mathbf{0}$ at $t = 0$

$$\Rightarrow c_1 = c_2 = 0.$$

$$\mathbf{v} = 2t^2\mathbf{i} + \left(6t - t^2\right)\mathbf{j}$$

When $t = 5$, $\mathbf{v} = 50\mathbf{i} + 5\mathbf{j}$ and $v = |\mathbf{v}| = \sqrt{50^2 + 5^2} = 50.2$, in $\mathrm{ms^{-1}}$.

(iii) Integrating again gives

$$\mathbf{r} = \left(\frac{2}{3}t^3 + k_1\right)\mathbf{i} + \left(3t^2 - \frac{1}{3}t^3 + k_2\right)\mathbf{j}$$

Substituting the initial condition, that $\mathbf{r} = 2\mathbf{i} + 3\mathbf{j}$ when $t = 0$, gives $k_1 = 2$ and $k_2 = 3$.

Therefore $\mathbf{r} = \left(\frac{2}{3}t^3 + 2\right)\mathbf{i} + \left(3t^2 - \frac{1}{3}t^3 + 3\right)\mathbf{j}$

When $t = 5$, $\mathbf{r} = \frac{256}{3}\mathbf{i} + \frac{109}{3}\mathbf{j}$ and $r = |\mathbf{r}| = 92.7$, in m.

The constant acceleration formulae

You can use integration to obtain the constant acceleration formulae.

When the acceleration **a** is a constant vector, then $\mathbf{v} = \int \mathbf{a}\,dt = \mathbf{a}t + \mathbf{c}$.

If the initial velocity is **u**, then $\mathbf{v} = \mathbf{u}$ when $t = 0$, leading to $\mathbf{c} = \mathbf{u}$ and

$$\mathbf{v} = \mathbf{u} + \mathbf{a}t \qquad ①$$

Integrating again gives $\mathbf{r} = \int \mathbf{v}\,dt = \int (\mathbf{u} + \mathbf{a}t)\,dt$

$$\mathbf{r} = \mathbf{u}t + \frac{1}{2}\mathbf{a}t^2 + \mathbf{n}$$

Initially $\mathbf{r} = \mathbf{r}_0$ so $\mathbf{r}_0 = \mathbf{k}$ and $\mathbf{r} = \mathbf{u}t + \frac{1}{2}\mathbf{a}t^2 + \mathbf{r}_0$ ②

Rearrange ① to give you $\mathbf{a}t = \mathbf{v} - \mathbf{u}$, which is substituted in ② to give

$$\mathbf{r} = \mathbf{u}t + \frac{1}{2}(\mathbf{v} - \mathbf{u})t + \mathbf{r}_0$$

$$\mathbf{r} = \frac{1}{2}(\mathbf{u} + \mathbf{v})t + \mathbf{r}_0 \qquad ③$$

Rearrange ① to give you $\mathbf{u} = \mathbf{v} - \mathbf{a}t$, and substitute in ② to give

$$\mathbf{r} = (\mathbf{v} - \mathbf{a}t)t + \frac{1}{2}\mathbf{a}t^2 + \mathbf{r}_0$$

$$\mathbf{r} = \mathbf{v}t - \frac{1}{2}\mathbf{a}t^2 + \mathbf{r}_0 \qquad ④$$

Equations ①–④ are the vector equivalents of the constant acceleration formulae used for motion in one dimension found in Chapter 1.

Motion in one dimension	Vector form
$v = u + at$	$\mathbf{v} = \mathbf{u} + \mathbf{a}t$
$s = ut + \frac{1}{2}at^2 + s_0$	$\mathbf{r} = \mathbf{u}t + \frac{1}{2}\mathbf{a}t^2 + \mathbf{r}_0$
$s = \frac{1}{2}(u + v)t + s_0$	$\mathbf{r} = \frac{1}{2}(\mathbf{u} + \mathbf{v})t + \mathbf{r}_0$
$s = vt - \frac{1}{2}at^2 + s_0$	$\mathbf{r} = \mathbf{v}t - \frac{1}{2}\mathbf{a}t^2 + \mathbf{r}_0$

In the case of one dimension, there is a fifth equation $[v^2 = u^2 + 2a(s - s_0)]$. There is a vector form of this equation which can be found by use of the scalar product between two vectors.

The scalar product between two vectors **A** and **B** is defined as

$$\mathbf{A} \cdot \mathbf{B} = \begin{pmatrix} A_x \\ A_y \\ A_z \end{pmatrix} \cdot \begin{pmatrix} B_x \\ B_y \\ B_z \end{pmatrix} = A_x B_x + A_y B_y + A_z B_z$$

From equation ③: $\mathbf{r} - \mathbf{r}_0 = \frac{1}{2}(\mathbf{u} + \mathbf{v})t$

From equation ①: $\mathbf{a} = \dfrac{\mathbf{v} - \mathbf{u}}{t}$

$$\Rightarrow \quad 2\mathbf{a} \cdot (\mathbf{r} - \mathbf{r}_0) = 2\left(\frac{\mathbf{v} - \mathbf{u}}{t}\right) \cdot \frac{1}{2}(\mathbf{u} + \mathbf{v})t$$

$$= (\mathbf{v} - \mathbf{u}) \cdot (\mathbf{u} + \mathbf{v})$$

$$= \mathbf{v} \cdot \mathbf{v} - \mathbf{u} \cdot \mathbf{u} = v^2 - u^2$$

$$\Rightarrow \quad 2\mathbf{a} \cdot (\mathbf{r} - \mathbf{r}_0) = v^2 - u^2 \qquad ⑤$$

The magnitude of any vector, say **p**, is denoted by p or $|\mathbf{p}|$. This is given by

$p = \sqrt{p_x^2 + p_y^2 + p_z^2}$ and so

$p^2 = p_x^2 + p_y^2 + p_z^2 = \mathbf{p} \cdot \mathbf{p}$.

In this case $\mathbf{v} \cdot \mathbf{v} = v^2$ and $\mathbf{u} \cdot \mathbf{u} = u^2$.

This is the vector form of the fifth constant acceleration equation.

Example 10.3

A particle is moving with constant acceleration $\mathbf{a} = \begin{pmatrix} 3 \\ -5 \end{pmatrix}$. It passes O at $t = 0$ with initial velocity $\mathbf{u} = \begin{pmatrix} -1 \\ 3 \end{pmatrix}$. The unit vectors $\begin{pmatrix} 1 \\ 0 \end{pmatrix}$ and $\begin{pmatrix} 0 \\ 1 \end{pmatrix}$ are in the directions due east and due north, respectively.

(i) Show that after 1 s the particle is moving south-east and find its speed.

(ii) Calculate the bearing of the particle from O after it has been moving for 2.5 s.

Solution

(i) Use the formula $\mathbf{v} = \mathbf{u} + \mathbf{a}t$.

a is constant so you can use the constant acceleration formulae.

$$\mathbf{v} = \begin{pmatrix} -1 \\ 3 \end{pmatrix} + \begin{pmatrix} 3 \\ -5 \end{pmatrix} t$$

$$= \begin{pmatrix} -1 + 3t \\ 3 - 5t \end{pmatrix}$$

After 1 s $\quad \mathbf{v} = \begin{pmatrix} 2 \\ -2 \end{pmatrix}$

The bearing of the motion is $(90° + \theta)$

$$\theta = \arctan 1 = 45°$$

So that the bearing is $90° + 45° = 135°$.

The angle θ is shown in Figure 10.6.

The speed of the particle is

$\sqrt{2^2 + 2^2} = \sqrt{8} = 2.82 \text{ m s}^{-1}$.

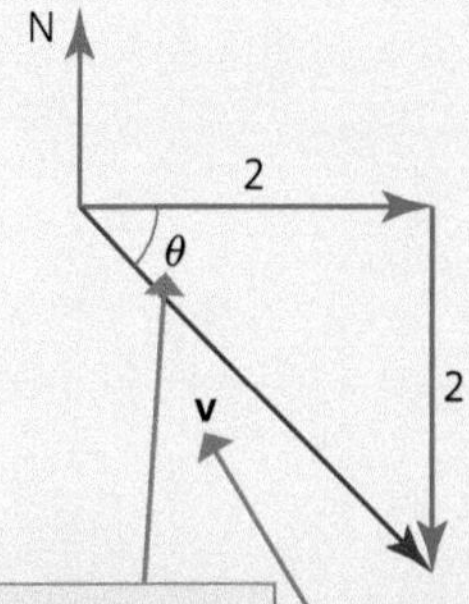

Figure 10.6

The particle is moving south-east with speed 2.82 m s^{-1}.

The direction of motion is the direction of **v**.

(ii) Use the formula $\mathbf{r} = \mathbf{u}t + \frac{1}{2}\mathbf{a}t^2$.

Substituting $t = 2.5$ gives:

$$\mathbf{r} = \begin{pmatrix} -1 \\ 3 \end{pmatrix} \times 2.5 + 0.5 \times \begin{pmatrix} 3 \\ -5 \end{pmatrix} \times 6.25$$

$$= \begin{pmatrix} -2.5 \\ 7.5 \end{pmatrix} + \begin{pmatrix} 9.375 \\ -15.625 \end{pmatrix}$$

$$= \begin{pmatrix} 6.875 \\ -8.125 \end{pmatrix}$$

$$\phi = \arctan\left(\frac{8.125}{6.875}\right) = 49.76°$$

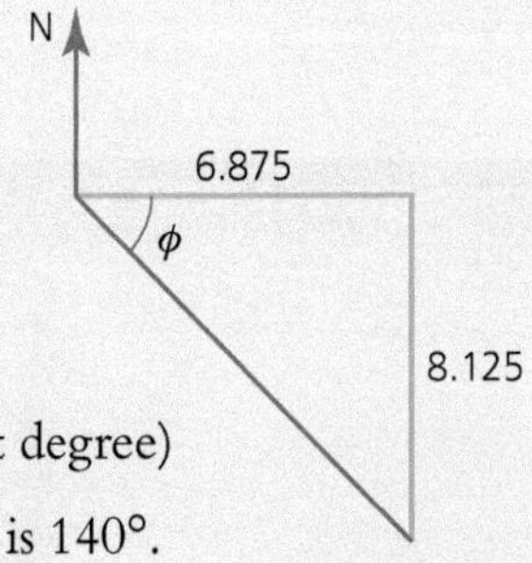

Figure 10.7

The position of the particle **r** determines its bearing.

So the bearing is $90° + 49.46° = 140°$ (nearest degree)

The bearing of the particle from O after 2.5 s is 140°.

Motion of a Projectile

The usual model of projectile motion involves the following assumptions:

- The projectile is a particle
- Acceleration is constant in magnitude and always acts vertically downwards
- Resistive forces are ignored.

Using this model for a particle projected from the origin with initial speed u at an angle of α to the horizontal gives $\mathbf{u} = u\begin{pmatrix} \cos\alpha \\ \sin\alpha \end{pmatrix}$ and $\mathbf{a} = \begin{pmatrix} 0 \\ -g \end{pmatrix}$.

Then

$$\mathbf{r} = \mathbf{u}t + \frac{1}{2}\mathbf{a}t^2 = u\begin{pmatrix} \cos\alpha \\ \sin\alpha \end{pmatrix} t - \frac{1}{2}\begin{pmatrix} 0 \\ -g \end{pmatrix} t^2$$

$$\mathbf{v} = \mathbf{u} + \mathbf{a}t = u\begin{pmatrix}\cos\alpha \\ \sin\alpha\end{pmatrix} - \begin{pmatrix}0 \\ -g\end{pmatrix}t$$

so that

$x = ut\cos\alpha$

$y = ut\sin\alpha - \frac{1}{2}gt^2$

$v_x = u\cos\alpha$

$v_y = u\sin\alpha - gt$

Eliminating t between the equations for x and y gives the **trajectory equation**

$$y = x\tan\alpha - \frac{gx^2}{2u^2}(1 + \tan^2\alpha)$$

This equation shows that the path taken by the projectile is a parabola:

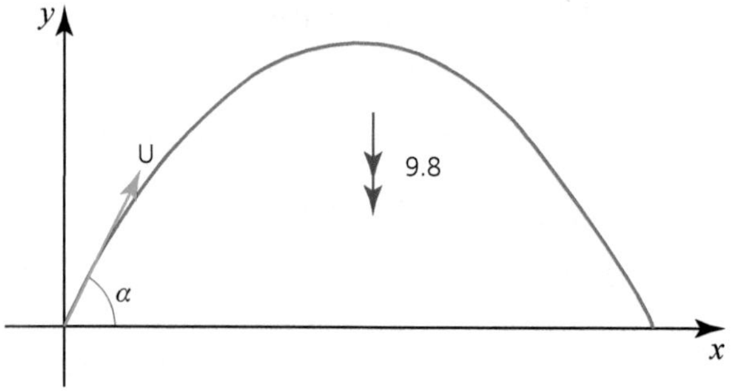

Figure 10.8

The trajectory equation can be used, for example, to find the angle required for a projectile to reach a given point.

Exercise 10.1

① The position vector of a moving point P at time t seconds is given by

$$\mathbf{r} = 4t\mathbf{i} + 3t^2\mathbf{j}$$

Find the speed of P at time $t = 2$.

② At time t seconds a particle has position vector

$$\mathbf{r} = 2t^3\mathbf{i} + (t^2 - 5)\mathbf{j}$$

$\mathbf{i}$ and $\mathbf{j}$ are unit vectors in the directions east and north.

Find the speed of the particle and its direction of motion when $t = 1$.

③ A particle P of mass m kg is at the point with position vector

$$\mathbf{r} = \begin{pmatrix}2t^3 + t \\ 3t \\ 5t^2 - 2\end{pmatrix}$$

at time t. Find the acceleration of P at time t and the force required to produce this acceleration.

④ A particle P of mass 2 kg is acted on by a force $\mathbf{F}(t) = \begin{pmatrix} 5t \\ 2t \\ 3 \end{pmatrix}$. Initially P is at a point (0, 1, 3) and is moving with velocity $\begin{pmatrix} 2 \\ 0 \\ 5 \end{pmatrix}$. Find the position vector of P at time t.

⑤ A particle moves with constant acceleration so that its velocity at time t is given by $\mathbf{v} = (5 - 0.1t)\mathbf{i} + (3 + 0.2t)\mathbf{j}$ where $\mathbf{i}$ and $\mathbf{j}$ are unit vectors in directions east and north.

(i) Write down $\mathbf{a}$ and $\mathbf{u}$.

(ii) Find the time t when the particle is travelling in the north-east direction and find its speed.

(iii) Find the distance and bearing of the particle from its starting point at that time.

⑥ A stone is thrown from a point on horizontal ground with a speed of 15 m s^{-1} at 40° to the horizontal. Find

(i) the time taken before the stone hits the ground again.

(ii) the maximum height above ground level.

⑦ A stone is thrown with speed 14.7 m s^{-1} at an angle of 20° below the horizontal from the top of a vertical cliff of height 68.6 m. At the foot of the cliff is the sea. Find how far from the foot of the cliff the stone hits the sea.

⑧ A shell is fired from a cannon with an initial speed of 100 m s^{-1} at an angle of 60° above the horizontal.

(i) A tower of height 80 m is situated 120 m from the cannon and in the line of fire. Show that the shell clears the top of the tower by about 100 m.

(ii) Assume that the shell does not hit anything before it reaches the ground again. Find its range (i.e. the distance it travels on the horizontal plane from which it was fired).

⑨ Sarah throws a basketball with speed 8 m s^{-1} at an angle of θ above the horizontal. The ball reaches a net placed 1 metre above the point at which she releases the ball and 1.6 m horizontally from that point. Find the two possible values of θ.

⑩ A particle has position vector $\mathbf{r} = 3t^2\mathbf{i} - 4t\mathbf{j}$ at time t. Find the angle between its position vector and its direction of motion at time $t = 2$.

⑪ Two forces $\mathbf{F}_1 = \begin{pmatrix} 5 \\ -8 \\ 6 \end{pmatrix}$ and $\mathbf{F}_2 = \begin{pmatrix} 3 \\ 2 \\ -2 \end{pmatrix}$ are acting on a particle of mass 2 kg.

(i) Find the resultant force acting on the particle and hence the acceleration of the particle.

When $t = 10$ seconds, the velocity of the particle is given by $\mathbf{v} = \begin{pmatrix} 10 \\ -15 \\ 30 \end{pmatrix}$.

(ii) Find the initial velocity $\mathbf{u}$.

(iii) Find when the speed of the particle is $10\sqrt{5}$.

⑫ Calculate the magnitude and direction of the acceleration of a particle that moves so that its position vector in metres is given by

$$\mathbf{r} = (3 + 5t - 6t^2)\mathbf{i} + (8 - 3t - 2.5t^2)\mathbf{j}$$

where t is the time in seconds and **i** and **j** are unit vectors in the directions east and north.

⑬ A particle is initially at rest at the origin. It experiences an acceleration given by $\mathbf{a} = 4t\mathbf{i} + (6 - 2t)\mathbf{j}$ where **i** and **j** are unit vectors in the directions east and north.

(i) Find expressions for the velocity and position of the particle at time t.

(ii) At what time is the particle moving north-east and what is its speed?

(iii) How far is the particle from O when $t = 2$? What is its bearing from O?

⑭ A speed boat is initially moving at $5\,\text{m}\,\text{s}^{-1}$ on a bearing of 120°.

(i) Express the initial velocity as a vector in terms of **i** and **j**, which are unit vectors east and north respectively.

The boat then begins to accelerate with an acceleration modelled by $\mathbf{a} = 0.2t\mathbf{i} + 0.1t\mathbf{j}$ in $\text{m}\,\text{s}^{-2}$.

(ii) Find the velocity of the boat 10 seconds after it begins to accelerate and its displacement over the 10 second period.

⑮ At time t, a particle has position vector, with respect to an origin O, given by $\mathbf{r} = \begin{pmatrix} 20t+12 \\ 15t^2 - t^3 \end{pmatrix}$; $\begin{pmatrix} 1 \\ 0 \end{pmatrix}$ and $\begin{pmatrix} 0 \\ 1 \end{pmatrix}$ are unit vectors in the east and north directions respectively.

(i) When $t = 2$ the particle is at P. Find the distance and bearing of P from O.

(ii) Find the velocity of the particle at time t and show that it is never 0.

(iii) Determine the value of t when the acceleration is zero.

(iv) Find the maximum speed of the particle.

⑯ A rock of mass 6 kg is acted on by two forces, $-60\mathbf{k}$ N and $(-\mathbf{i} + 12\mathbf{j} + 54\mathbf{k})$ N, where **i** and **j** are perpendicular unit vectors in a horizontal plane and **k** is a unit vector vertically upward.

(i) Show that the acceleration of the rock is $-\frac{1}{6}\mathbf{i}+2\mathbf{j}-\mathbf{k}\,\text{m}\,\text{s}^{-2}$.

The rock passes through the origin O, with velocity $(\mathbf{i} - 6\mathbf{j} + 4\mathbf{k})\,\text{m}\,\text{s}^{-1}$; 6 seconds later, it passes through A.

(ii) Find the position vector of A.

(iii) Find the distance OA.

(iv) Find the angle that OA makes with the horizontal.

⑰ A force $\mathbf{F} = (9\mathbf{i} + 12\mathbf{j})$N acts on a particle P of mass 5 kg which is free to move in a horizontal plane.

(i) Calculate the magnitude of the acceleration of P.

Initially the particle passes through a fixed point A with speed $2\,\text{m}\,\text{s}^{-1}$ in the same direction as **F**.

(ii) Show that the velocity of the particle at time t is $\mathbf{v} = \left(\frac{2}{3}+t\right)(1.8\mathbf{i}+2.4\mathbf{j})$.

(iii) Find the vector $\overrightarrow{AP}$ at time t.

(iv) A is the point (30, 25). Find the vector $\overrightarrow{OP}$ at time $t = 5$.

⑱ At time t s, a particle of mass m kg has a position vector $\mathbf{r}$ relative to a fixed origin where $\mathbf{r} = \cos(\lambda t^2)\mathbf{i} + \sin(\lambda t^2)\mathbf{j} + \lambda t^2\mathbf{k}$.

(i) Find expressions for the velocity and acceleration of the particle at time t.

(ii) Show that the particle is initially at rest and that the acceleration has magnitude $2\sqrt{2}\lambda$.

(iii) Find in terms of m, λ and t, an expression for the kinetic energy T of the particle.

(iv) Show that $T = c\mathbf{k}\cdot\mathbf{r}$ where c is a constant to be found.

2 Acceleration dependent upon velocity

When you studied the motion of projectiles you used a simple model which ignored air resistance. It is well known that air resistance is by no means negligible, especially for fast-moving objects. It is thus often important to incorporate an element of velocity dependence for the air resistance term. In this type of question you often use $a = \frac{dv}{dt}$ and you may need to solve a differential equation.

Example 10.4

A ball of mass 0.2 kg is thrown vertically upwards with initial speed $10\,\text{m s}^{-1}$. Modelling the air resistance as a force opposing the motion of magnitude $0.01v$ N, where v is the speed, find the time taken to reach the maximum height.

Solution

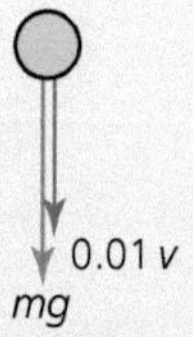

Figure 10.8

The equation of motion is $0.2\frac{dv}{dt} = -0.2g - 0.01v$

$$\Rightarrow \quad \frac{dv}{dt} = -(9.8 + 0.05v)$$

Take upwards as positive

$$\Rightarrow \quad \int \frac{dv}{9.8 + 0.05v} = -\int dt$$

Separate the variables

$$\Rightarrow \quad \frac{1}{0.05}\ln(9.8 + 0.05v) = -t + c$$

Use the initial condition to find c.

When $t = 0$, $v = 10$, so

$$\frac{1}{0.05}\ln(9.8 + 0.5) = c$$

$$\Rightarrow \quad c = \frac{1}{0.05}\ln(10.3)$$

$v = 0$ when

$$\frac{1}{0.05}\ln(9.8) = -t + c$$

$$\Rightarrow \quad t = \frac{1}{0.05}\ln(10.3) - \frac{1}{0.05}\ln(9.8) = \frac{1}{0.05}\ln\left(\frac{10.3}{9.8}\right)$$

$$= 0.99523\ldots$$

The time to reach the maximum height is 0.995 seconds (3 s.f.).

Sometimes you will need to use the integrating factor method to solve the differential equation.

Example 10.5

The motion of a particle is modelled by the differential equation

$$\frac{\mathrm{d}v}{\mathrm{d}t} + \frac{v}{t} = \mathrm{e}^{-0.1t}$$

Solve this equation, given that $v = 0$ when $t = 10$.

Solution

Write the equation as $\frac{\mathrm{d}v}{\mathrm{d}t} + \frac{1}{t}v = \mathrm{e}^{-0.1t}$

The integrating factor is $\mathrm{e}^{\int \frac{1}{t}\mathrm{d}t} = \mathrm{e}^{\ln t} = t$.

> The integrating factor for the equation $\frac{\mathrm{d}v}{\mathrm{d}t} + vf(t) = g(t)$ is $\mathrm{e}^{\int f(t)\mathrm{d}t}$.

$$\Rightarrow \quad t\frac{\mathrm{d}v}{\mathrm{d}t} + v = t\mathrm{e}^{-0.1t}$$

$$\Rightarrow \quad \frac{\mathrm{d}}{\mathrm{d}t}(tv) = t\mathrm{e}^{-0.1t}$$

$$tv = \int t\mathrm{e}^{-0.1t}\,\mathrm{d}t$$

This integral required the technique of integration by parts, expressed by the formula

$\int u\frac{\mathrm{d}v}{\mathrm{d}x}\mathrm{d}x = uv - \int v\frac{\mathrm{d}u}{\mathrm{d}x}\mathrm{d}x$, with t rather than x as the variable of integration.

To find $\int t\mathrm{e}^{-0.1t}\mathrm{d}t$

let $\quad u = t \quad \Rightarrow \quad \frac{\mathrm{d}u}{\mathrm{d}t} = 1$

and let $\frac{\mathrm{d}v}{\mathrm{d}t} = \mathrm{e}^{-0.1t} \quad \Rightarrow \quad v = -\frac{1}{0.1}\mathrm{e}^{-0.1t} = -10\mathrm{e}^{-0.1t}$.

$$\Rightarrow \quad tv = -10t\mathrm{e}^{-0.1t} + \int 10\mathrm{e}^{-0.1t}\mathrm{d}t$$

$$= -10t\mathrm{e}^{-0.1t} - 100\mathrm{e}^{-0.1t} + c$$

$$\Rightarrow \quad v = -10\mathrm{e}^{-0.1t} - \frac{100}{t}\mathrm{e}^{-0.1t} + c$$

> Don't forget the constant of integration

$t = 10, v = 0$:

$$0 = -10\mathrm{e}^{-1} - 10\mathrm{e}^{-1} + c$$

$$\Rightarrow \quad c = 20\mathrm{e}^{-1}$$

$$\Rightarrow \quad v = 20\mathrm{e}^{-1} - \left(10 + \frac{100}{t}\right)\mathrm{e}^{-0.1t}$$

Acceleration dependent on position

In the next example, the acceleration is dependent on the position. This is a situation that you will meet in Chapter 12 of this book, on Hooke's law, in the chapter on simple harmonic motion in the Further Pure Mathematics book, and elsewhere.

For this form of dependence there are two different sorts of differential equations that you may need to use.

- Connecting s (or x or y) and t. Acceleration is written in the form:

$$a = \frac{d^2s}{dt^2}\left(\text{or } \frac{d^2x}{dt^2} \text{ or } \frac{d^2y}{dt^2}\right).$$

  Questions involving second derivatives are not dealt with in this book, but they can be found in the Further Pure Mathematics book.

- Connecting v and s (or x or y). Acceleration is written in the form $a = v\frac{dv}{ds}$.

This form for acceleration is based on the chain rule.
$v\frac{dv}{ds} = \frac{ds}{dt} \times \frac{dv}{ds}$
$= \frac{dv}{dt}$
$= a$

The second of these is the subject of the next example, which uses the form $a = v\frac{dv}{dx}$ to solve a problem involving resisted motion in the x direction.

Example 10.6

A particle moves along the x-axis. It is initially at the origin and moving with speed $6\,\text{m s}^{-1}$ in the positive direction. When its displacement is x its acceleration is given by $a = -4x$ in m s^{-2}.

(i) Write down a differential equation connecting the velocity $v\,\text{m s}^{-1}$ of the particle with x.

(ii) Solve the differential equation subject to the initial conditions to give v as a function of x.

(iii) Write your answer to part (ii) as a differential equation connecting x and t.

(iv) Solve this equation.

Solution

(i) The differential equation is $\quad v\frac{dv}{dx} = -4x$

(ii) Separating variables gives $\quad \int v\,dv = -4\int x\,dx$

$$\frac{v^2}{2} = -2x^2 + c$$

Initial conditions, $v = 6$ when $x = 0 \Rightarrow c = 18$

$$\Rightarrow \quad v = \pm\sqrt{36 - 4x^2}$$

(iii) $\frac{dx}{dt} = \pm 2\sqrt{9 - x^2}$

(iv) Separating variables $\quad \pm\int \frac{dx}{\sqrt{9 - x^2}} = 2\int dt$

The left-hand side is a standard integral:

$$\pm\arcsin\left(\frac{x}{3}\right) + c = 2t$$

Initial conditions: $v > 0$ when $t = 0 \quad \Rightarrow \quad$ use positive sign

$x = 0$ when $t = 0 \quad \Rightarrow \quad c = 0$

The solution is $x = 3\sin 2t$.

Note

$\int \frac{dx}{\sqrt{a^2 - x^2}} = \pm\arcsin\left(\frac{x}{a}\right) + c$

In this case $a = 3$.

You may have noticed that the last example involved the same acceleration as the x-component of the one before. In the x-direction, the acceleration was given by $a = -4x$ and the initial conditions were the same.

However, the approach to solving it was quite different.

Using $a = v\frac{dv}{dx}$ is particularly helpful when you are dealing with stretched strings. In the simplest cases, Newton's second law and Hooke's law (which you will meet in Chapter 12) lead to the relationship $ma = -kx$ and to the differential equation $mv\frac{dv}{dx} = -kx$.

The solution of this is $\frac{1}{2}mv^2 = -\frac{1}{2}kx^2 + c$ and this is a very useful energy equation. Parts (iii) and (iv) went a stage further, providing the solution for x in terms of t.

However, to find x in terms of t, it would be more usual to use $\frac{d^2x}{dt^2}$ for the acceleration and solve the resulting second-order differential equation using the auxiliary equation method. Examples of this are given in the Further Pure Mathematics book.

Exercise 10.2

① In each of the following cases a particle of mass 1 kg is under the influence of a single force F N in a constant direction, but with a variable magnitude given as a function of

- either velocity v m s^{-1}
- or displacement x m
- or time t s.

The particle is initially at rest at the origin.

In each case, write down the equation of motion and solve it to supply the required information.

(i) $F = 5t + 1$; find v when $t = 2$.

(ii) $F = \frac{2}{5+x}$; find v when $x = 5$.

(iii) $F = \frac{2}{(1+x)^2}$; find v when $x = 1$.

(iv) $F = 9 - v^2$; find t when $v = 1$.

(v) $F = 1 + v^2$; find x when $v = 1$.

(vi) $F = 1 + v^2$; find t when $v = 1$.

(vii) $F = \frac{2}{(2+x)^3}$; find v when $x = 1$.

(viii) $F = 2\sin 3t$; find v when $t = \frac{\pi}{2}$.

② A particle moves with initial velocity $\begin{pmatrix} 10 \\ 20 \end{pmatrix}$ under the acceleration $\begin{pmatrix} -2 \\ -10 \end{pmatrix}$.

(i) Give expressions for the velocity and position vectors of the moving point.

(ii) Sketch the curve of the path followed by the particle.

(iii) Find the coordinates of the highest point of the path.

③ (i) Write the velocity v as an integral with respect to t when the acceleration is given by

(a) $\frac{v}{t}$ (b) $\frac{v}{t}+2t^2e^{-t^2}$

(ii) Write the velocity v as an integral with respect to the displacement s when the acceleration is given by

(a) $\frac{1+v^2}{2s}$ (b) $-2v(vs+e^{-s^2-2s})$

④ A ball P of mass 0.25 kg is projected vertically upwards from ground level with an initial speed of 20 m s^{-1}. A resisting force of magnitude $0.05v$ N acts on P during its ascent, where v m s^{-1} is the speed and x m is the displacement of the ball at time t s after it starts to move .

(i) Show that $\frac{dv}{dt}=-0.2(49+v)$.

(ii) Find an expression for v as a function of t.

(iii) Find the displacement x as a function of t.

(iv) Find the greatest height reached by the ball.

⑤ A particle starts from O and moves in a straight line. When the displacement is x m its velocity is v m s^{-1}and its acceleration is $\frac{2}{x+1}$.

(i) Given that $v = 3$ when $x = 0$ show that $v^2 = 4\ln|x + 1| + 9$.

(ii) Find the value of v when the acceleration is $\frac{2}{5}$.

⑥ The resistive force F acting on a particle of mass 10^{-20} kg moving in one dimension with speed v is modelled by $F = -2 \times 10^{-21}v - 5 \times 10^{-21} \times e^{-1.2t}$.

(i) Show that $\frac{dv}{dt}+0.2v=-0.5e^{-1.2t}$.

(ii) Use an integrating factor to solve this equation to give a formula for v in terms of t, given that when $t = 0$, $v = 10.5$.

⑦ A rocket of mass 1000 kg is launched from rest at ground level and travels vertically upwards. The mass of the rocket is constant and the only forces acting on it are its weight, a driving force of 20 000 N and a resistance force $5v$.

(i) Show that $\frac{dv}{dt}=10.2-0.005v$.

(ii) Find v in terms of t.

(iii) Find the distance travelled by the rocket in the first 5 seconds of its motion.

⑧ A cyclist and her bicycle have a combined mass of 64 kg. She starts from rest and rides in a straight line, exerting a constant force of 128 N. The motion is opposed by a resistance of magnitude $8v$ N, where v is the cyclist speed at time t s after starting.

(i) Show that $\frac{8}{16-v}\frac{dv}{dt}=1$.

(ii) Express v in terms of t.

(iii) Find the distance travelled by the cyclist in the first 8 seconds of the motion.

⑨ The motion of a particle is modelled by the equation $\frac{dv}{dt}+v\tan t=2\cos t$.

(i) Find a formula for v in terms of t, given that $v = 3$ when $t = 0$.

(ii) For what range of values of t is your formula valid?

(10) A particle is projected with speed U at time $t = 0$ and moves in a straight line. At time t, its velocity is v and the distance travelled is x. The acceleration of the particle is $-k\sqrt{v}$, where k is a constant.

(i) Show that the particle will come to rest when $t = \frac{2\sqrt{U}}{k}$.

(ii) Find in terms of k and U the distance travelled while the particle comes to rest.

(11) Take $g = 10\,\text{m s}^{-2}$ in this question.

A particle of mass 0.4 kg is projected vertically upwards with a speed of $20\,\text{m s}^{-1}$. The particle experiences a resistance of $0.5v$, where v is the velocity of the particle.

(i) Find the time taken for the particle to come to instantaneous rest.

(ii) Find the greatest height attained by the particle.

Having reached its highest point, the particle then drops down against a resistance of $0.5v$.

(iii) Show that $\frac{\mathrm{d}v}{\mathrm{d}t} = 1.25(8 - v)$ and use it to find an expression for v as a function of t.

(iv) Find the distance travelled as a function of t and hence show that the time taken for the particle to drop down to ground level is greater than the time taken to reach its highest point.

(12) A particle of mass 0.5 kg moves in a straight line on a smooth horizontal surface. A variable resisting force acts on the particle. At time t s, the displacement of the particle from a point O on the line is x m and its velocity is $(4 - x^2)\,\text{m s}^{-1}$. It is given that $x = 0$ when $t = 0$.

(i) Find the acceleration of the particle in terms of x and hence find the magnitude of the resisting force when $x = 1.5$ m.

(ii) Find an expression for x in terms of t.

(iii) How far from O can the particle ever get?

(13) A space probe of mass m enters a large cloud of gas with speed u. The gas provides a resistance force to the probe's motion; there is no other force acting on it.

When it has travelled a distance s in the cloud the probe's speed is $\frac{u}{2}$.

The distance across the gas cloud is $3s$.

Three models are considered for the resistance force, R, in terms of the probe's speed v.

In each case find

(i) the value of k in terms of m, u and s

(ii) the dimensions of k

(iii) the speed with which the probe leaves the gas cloud

(iv) the distance the probe travels inside the gas cloud.

(A) Model A, $R = k$

(B) Model B, $R = kv$

(C) Model C, $R = kv^2$

3 The work–energy equation in vector form

You will remember that the scalar (dot) product of two vectors **a** and **b** is defined as

$$\mathbf{a} \cdot \mathbf{b} = (\text{magnitude of } \mathbf{a}) \times (\text{magnitude of } \mathbf{b}) \times \cos(\text{angle between } \mathbf{a} \text{ and } \mathbf{b})$$

So, for a constant force **F** acting over a displacement **s**

Work done by **F** = (magnitude of **F**) × (magnitude of component of **s** in direction of **F**)

= (magnitude of **F**) × (magnitude of **s**) × cos (angle between **F** and **s**)

$= \mathbf{F} \cdot \mathbf{s}$

This is often an efficient way to calculate the work done by a force in 2 or 3 dimensions.

Likewise, a force **F** driving an object with velocity **v** is working with power $\mathbf{F} \cdot \mathbf{v}$.

Example 10.7

Calculate the work done by a force $\mathbf{F} = (3\mathbf{i} + 5\mathbf{j} - 2\mathbf{k})$ N when it acts over a displacement $\mathbf{s} = (2\mathbf{i} - \mathbf{j} - 5\mathbf{k})$ m.

Solution

$$\begin{aligned}\text{Work done} &= \mathbf{F} \cdot \mathbf{s} \\ &= (3\mathbf{i} + 5\mathbf{j} - 2\mathbf{k}) \cdot (2\mathbf{i} - \mathbf{j} - 5\mathbf{k}) \\ &= 3 \times 2 + 5 \times (-1) + (-2) \times (-5) \\ &= 6 - 5 + 10 \\ &= 11\text{ J}\end{aligned}$$

The work done by the force is 11 J.

The formula for the kinetic energy of a particle of mass m kg travelling with speed v m s^{-1} is $\frac{1}{2}mv^2$ J. How can you write this when the velocity **v** is given in vector form?

Suppose $\mathbf{v} = v_1\mathbf{i} + v_2\mathbf{j} + v_3\mathbf{k}$. The magnitude of this vector is $\sqrt{v_1^2 + v_2^2 + v_3^2}$. So this expression also gives the speed v of the particle, and $v^2 = v_1^2 + v_2^2 + v_3^2$.

This is the same expression as $\mathbf{v} \cdot \mathbf{v}$, which is often written simply as $\mathbf{v}^2$, so you can write

$$\text{Kinetic energy} = \frac{1}{2}mv^2 = \frac{1}{2}m\mathbf{v} \cdot \mathbf{v} = \frac{1}{2}m\mathbf{v}^2$$

> The magnitude of the vector **v** is often written as simply v, so the formula $\frac{1}{2}mv^2$ is unambiguous.

The work–energy principle states that

Change in kinetic energy = work done by external forces.

If the initial and final velocities are vectors **u** and **v** respectively, then this becomes

> **Discussion point**
> What is the link between this formula and the familiar equation $v^2 = u^2 + 2as$?

$$\frac{1}{2}m\mathbf{v}\cdot\mathbf{v} - \frac{1}{2}m\mathbf{u}\cdot\mathbf{u} = \text{work done by external forces}$$

If the external forces can be represented by a single constant force **F**, and **s** is the displacement, then the work-energy equation becomes

$$\frac{1}{2}m\mathbf{v}\cdot\mathbf{v} - \frac{1}{2}m\mathbf{u}\cdot\mathbf{u} = \mathbf{F}\cdot\mathbf{s}$$

You can use this equation to find the initial or final kinetic energy, or the work done, but you *cannot* 'undot' the equation to find any of the vectors separately.

> **Discussion point**
> Consider the following question.
> A particle of mass 1 kg is acted on by a force $\mathbf{F} = 3\mathbf{i} + 2\mathbf{j} - \mathbf{k}$. It starts from rest and moves through a displacement $\mathbf{s} = 6\mathbf{i} + 4\mathbf{j} - 2\mathbf{k}$. What can be said about its final velocity **v**?
> (i) Find the correct answer to the question.
> (ii) Sam gives the following solution. Discuss what he has done wrong.
>
> Using $\frac{1}{2}m\mathbf{v}\cdot\mathbf{v} - \frac{1}{2}m\mathbf{u}\cdot\mathbf{u} = \mathbf{F}\cdot\mathbf{s}$
>
> $$\frac{1}{2}\times 1\times\begin{pmatrix} v_x \\ v_y \\ v_z \end{pmatrix}^2 - \frac{1}{2}\times 1\times\begin{pmatrix} 0 \\ 0 \\ 0 \end{pmatrix}^2 = \begin{pmatrix} 3 \\ 2 \\ -1 \end{pmatrix}\cdot\begin{pmatrix} 6 \\ 4 \\ -2 \end{pmatrix}$$
>
> $\Rightarrow$ $\frac{1}{2}v_x^2 = 3 \times 6$
> $\frac{1}{2}v_y^2 = 2 \times 4$
> $\frac{1}{2}v_z^2 = -1 \times -2$
>
> $$\Rightarrow \quad \begin{pmatrix} v_x \\ v_y \\ v_z \end{pmatrix} = \begin{pmatrix} 36 \\ 16 \\ 4 \end{pmatrix}. \qquad ✗$$

Example 10.8

A particle of mass 5 kg moving with kinetic energy 15 J has an acceleration $\mathbf{a} = 3\mathbf{i} - 2\mathbf{j} + \mathbf{k}$ as it moves through a displacement $\mathbf{s} = 2\mathbf{j} + 5\mathbf{k}$. Find its final kinetic energy.

Solution

Initial K.E. = 15

$\Rightarrow \frac{1}{2}m\,\mathbf{u}\cdot\mathbf{u} = 15$

$\Rightarrow \quad \mathbf{u}\cdot\mathbf{u} = 6$

$$\mathbf{v} \cdot \mathbf{v} = \mathbf{u} \cdot \mathbf{u} + 2\mathbf{a} \cdot \mathbf{x}$$

$$\Rightarrow \mathbf{v} \cdot \mathbf{v} = 6 + 2 \times \begin{pmatrix} 3 \\ -2 \\ 1 \end{pmatrix} \cdot \begin{pmatrix} 2 \\ 0 \\ 5 \end{pmatrix}$$

$$= 6 + 22$$

$$= 28$$

Hence final K.E. $= \frac{1}{2} m \, \mathbf{v} \cdot \mathbf{v}$

$$= \frac{1}{2} \times 5 \times 28$$

$$= 70\text{J}$$

The final kinetic energy is 70J.

Forces that vary with displacement or time

So far most of the forces you have looked at have been constant. What happens when the force depends on the displacement, or the time?

Suppose δs is a displacement sufficiently small for the force F to stay roughly constant. Then the work done by the force is $F\delta s$, and the total work done over a series of such displacements is approximately $\Sigma F\delta s$. If you take smaller and smaller displacements, you get a more and more accurate answer. Taking the limit of this process, the sum $\Sigma F\delta s$ turns into the integral $\int F \, \mathrm{d}s$ and this formula gives an exact value for the total work done.

Example 10.9

A particle of mass 0.12 kg moves along the x-axis and is acted on by a variable force F with magnitude $8x^3$ in the positive x direction, where x is the displacement of the particle. At $x = 1$ the speed of the particle is $4\,\text{m}\,\text{s}^{-1}$. Find the speed of the particle when $x = 2$.

Solution

The work done by F is $\int F \, \mathrm{d}s = \int_1^2 8x^3 \, \mathrm{d}x$

$$= \left[2x^4\right]_1^2$$

$$= 32 - 2$$

$$= 30\text{ J}$$

> The displacement is along the x-axis, so you can replace ds by dx.

Work done = change in kinetic energy:

$$30 = \frac{1}{2} \times 0.12 \times v^2 - \frac{1}{2} \times 0.12 \times 4^2$$

$$\Rightarrow \quad 0.06v^2 = 30 + 0.96$$

$$\Rightarrow \quad v^2 = 516$$

$$\Rightarrow \quad v = 22.7156\ldots$$

The speed of the particle is $22.7\,\text{m}\,\text{s}^{-1}$ (3 s.f.).

This method works if you are given a formula for force in terms of **displacement**. If you are given a formula for force in terms of **time** you have to use the impulse–momentum equation.

Suppose δt is a time interval sufficiently small for the force F to stay roughly constant. Then the impulse exerted by the force is approximately $F\delta t$, and the total impulse over a series of such intervals is approximately $\Sigma F\delta t$. If you take smaller and smaller intervals, you get a more and more accurate answer. Taking the limit of this process, the sum $\Sigma F\delta t$ turns into the integral $\int F\,\mathrm{d}t$ and this formula gives an exact value for the total impulse.

Example 10.10

A particle of mass 0.12 kg moves in a straight line and is acted on by a variable force F with magnitude $8t^3$ at time t seconds. The force acts in the direction of motion of the particle. At $t = 1$ the speed of the particle is $4\,\mathrm{m\,s^{-1}}$. Find the speed of the particle when $t = 2$.

Solution

$$\begin{aligned}\text{Total impulse} &= \int F\,\mathrm{d}t \\ &= \int_1^2 8t^3\,\mathrm{d}t \\ &= \left[2t^4\right]_1^2 \\ &= 32 - 2 \\ &= 30\,\mathrm{kg\,m\,s^{-1}}\end{aligned}$$

Impulse = change in momentum:

$\Rightarrow \quad 30 = 0.12 \times v - 0.12 \times 4$

$\Rightarrow \quad 0.12v = 34.8$

$\Rightarrow \quad v = 254$

The speed of the particle is $254\,\mathrm{m\,s^{-1}}$.

Exercise 10.3

① Calculate the work done when a particle moves through a displacement of $4\mathbf{i} + 5\mathbf{j} - \mathbf{k}$ m under the action of a force $6\mathbf{i} - 2\mathbf{j} + 5\mathbf{k}$ N.

② A motor boat is sailing with constant velocity $32\mathbf{i} + 21\mathbf{j}\,\mathrm{m\,s^{-1}}$. The motor is producing a force $25\mathbf{i} + 20\mathbf{j}$ N. Find the power at which the motor is working.

③ Find the work required to change the velocity of a sphere of mass 0.8 kg from $\begin{pmatrix}1\\-2\\4\end{pmatrix}\mathrm{m\,s^{-1}}$ to $\begin{pmatrix}3\\5\\-2\end{pmatrix}\mathrm{m\,s^{-1}}$.

Historical note

In the sixteenth and seventeenth centuries there was much controversy as to whether momentum or kinetic energy was the fundamental measure of motion. Isaac Newton resolved the controversy by showing that both were associated with conservation laws and showed how the laws could be used with different types of force.

④ A charged particle of mass 1×10^{-23} kg and initial velocity $\begin{pmatrix} 2 \\ 4 \\ 3 \end{pmatrix} \times 10^4 \text{ m s}^{-1}$ is acted on by a force $\begin{pmatrix} 8 \\ -3 \\ 6 \end{pmatrix}$ N and is displaced through **s** m. Find its final speed when

(i) $\mathbf{s} = \begin{pmatrix} 4 \\ -2 \\ -2 \end{pmatrix} \times 10^{-15}$ m

(ii) $\mathbf{s} = \begin{pmatrix} 3 \\ -2 \\ -5 \end{pmatrix} \times 10^{-15}$ m

⑤ A particle of mass 0.7 kg is given an acceleration $\mathbf{a} = 7\mathbf{i} + 3\mathbf{j} - 2\mathbf{k}$ through a displacement $\mathbf{i} + 6\mathbf{j} + \mathbf{k}$. Its initial kinetic energy is 9.1 J. Use the equation $\mathbf{v} \bullet \mathbf{v} = \mathbf{u} \bullet \mathbf{u} + 2\,\mathbf{a} \bullet \mathbf{x}$ to find its final kinetic energy.

⑥ A particle of mass 0.2 kg has initial kinetic energy 0.003 J. It is given an acceleration $\mathbf{a} = 0.04\mathbf{i} + 0.05\mathbf{j} - 0.02\mathbf{k}$ through a displacement $0.1\mathbf{i} - 0.1\mathbf{j} + z\mathbf{k}$, and its final kinetic energy is 0.0016 J. Find the value of z.

⑦ A particle moves in the direction of the vector $x\mathbf{i} + 3\mathbf{j} - 7\mathbf{k}$. The force $\mathbf{F} = \mathbf{i} + 2\mathbf{j} + 3\mathbf{k}$ is the only force acting on the particle. The speed of the particle remains constant. Find the value of x.

⑧ A particle of mass 0.08 kg moves along the x-axis. At time $t = 0$ it is stationary at the origin, and it is acted on by a force F in the positive x-direction.

(i) Given that $F = 0.6x^2$, find the speed of the particle at $x = 5$.

(ii) Given that $F = 0.6t^2$, find the speed of the particle at $t = 2$.

⑨ A bead of mass 0.025 kg is threaded on a smooth wire which constrains it to move in a direction parallel to the vector $6\mathbf{i} + 3\mathbf{j} + 2\mathbf{k}$. The bead is initially at rest and is acted on by a force $(5\mathbf{i} + 3\mathbf{k})$ N. Find the speed of the bead when it has moved 1.4 m.

⑩ A particle moves from the origin O to the point A (1, 0) under a force with x-component given by $(x^2 - 3x)$ N. From there it moves to the point B (1, 1) under a force whose y-component is $(y^3 - 4y)$ N. All distances are in metres.

(i) Find the total work done by the force as the particle moves from O to B via A.

(ii) Show that, if the forces remain the same, you obtain the same answer if the particle moves from O to B via C (0, 1).

KEY POINTS

1 Relationships between the variables describing motion

Position	Velocity	Acceleration
⟶	differentiate	⟶
$\mathbf{r} = x\mathbf{i} + y\mathbf{j} + z\mathbf{k}$	$\mathbf{v} = \frac{d\mathbf{r}}{dt} = v_x\mathbf{i} + v_y\mathbf{j} + v_z\mathbf{k}$	$a = \frac{d\mathbf{v}}{dt} = \frac{d^2\mathbf{r}}{dt^2} = a_x\mathbf{i} + a_y\mathbf{j} + a_y\mathbf{k}$
$\mathbf{r} = \begin{pmatrix} x \\ y \\ z \end{pmatrix}$	$\mathbf{v} = \begin{pmatrix} v_x \\ v_y \\ v_z \end{pmatrix} = \begin{pmatrix} \dot{x} \\ \dot{y} \\ \dot{z} \end{pmatrix}$	$a = \begin{pmatrix} \frac{dv_x}{dt} \\ \frac{dv_y}{dt} \\ \frac{dv_z}{dt} \end{pmatrix} = \begin{pmatrix} \ddot{x} \\ \ddot{y} \\ \ddot{z} \end{pmatrix}$
Distance from O $\sqrt{x^2 + y^2 + z^2}$	**Speed** $\sqrt{\dot{x}^2 + \dot{y}^2 + \dot{z}^2}$	**Magnitude of acceleration** $\sqrt{\ddot{x}^2 + \ddot{y}^2 + \ddot{z}^2}$

Acceleration	Velocity	Position
⟶	integrate	⟶
$a = \begin{pmatrix} a_x \\ a_y \\ a_z \end{pmatrix}$	$\mathbf{v} = \int a\,dt$	$\mathbf{r} = \int \mathbf{v}\,dt$
	$\mathbf{v} = \int \begin{pmatrix} a_x \\ a_y \\ a_z \end{pmatrix} dt$	$\mathbf{r} = \int \begin{pmatrix} v_x \\ v_y \\ v_z \end{pmatrix} dt$

2 Acceleration may be due to a change in direction.

3 For constant acceleration

$$\mathbf{v} = \mathbf{u} + a t \qquad \mathbf{r} = \mathbf{r}_0 + \mathbf{u}t + \frac{1}{2}at^2$$

$$\mathbf{r} = \mathbf{r}_0 + \frac{1}{2}(\mathbf{u} + \mathbf{v})t \qquad \mathbf{r} = \mathbf{r}_0 + \mathbf{v}t - \frac{1}{2}at^2$$

4 Newton's second law, using vectors

$$\mathbf{F} = m\mathbf{a}$$

5 Differential equations may be used to model resisted motion. Acceleration may be expressed in a number of different ways and these give rise to different types of differential equations.

- Connecting v and t: $a = \frac{dv}{dt}$
- Connecting s and t: $a = \frac{d^2s}{dt^2}$
- Connecting v and s: $a = v\frac{dv}{ds}$

6 To verify the solution of a differential equation you must
- check that the function satisfies the differential equation
- check that it is consistent with the initial or boundary conditions.

7 For a constant force **F** acting over a displacement **s** and driving an object with velocity **v**:
- Work done = **F** • **s**
- Power = **F** • **v**.

8 The work done by a variable one-dimensional force F which depends on displacement s is $\int F\,ds$.

9 The impulse exerted by a variable one-dimensional force F which depends on time t is $\int F\,dt$.

LEARNING OUTCOMES

When you have completed this chapter, you should
- be able to extend the scope of techniques from motion in one dimension to that in two and three dimensions by using vectors
- be able to find the acceleration, velocity and position vector subject to a constant or varying force
- be able to use acceleration, velocity and position vectors of a particle to solve problems
- be able to formulate differential equations for motion under variable acceleration and solve them using separation of variables or an integrating factor
- know the different ways in which acceleration may be expressed
- be able to verify the solution of a differential equation
- be able to use the work–energy principle in the case of a constant force given as a vector **F**, and find the power exerted
- be able to use the equation **v** • **v** = **u** • **u** + 2**a** • **x** to solve problems
- be able to use the work–energy equation for a variable one-dimensional force which depends on displacement
- be able to use the impulse–momentum equation for a variable one-dimensional force which depends on time.

11 Circular motion 2

What makes planets go round the sun? At the time of Kepler, some people answered this problem by saying that there were angels behind them beating their wings and pushing the planets around an orbit. As you will see the answer is not far from the truth. The only difference is that the angels sit in a different direction and their wings push inwards.

Richard Feynman (Nobel prize winner in Physics, 1965).

Discussion point

- The diameter of the London Eye is about 120 metres, and it takes about half an hour to go round once. It does not slow down or stop for people to get on or off. Imagine that you are on the Eye, standing still in your pod.
- Estimate the percentage difference in the contact force the pod exerts on you when it is at its highest point compared to that when you have just got on.
- What can you say about the magnitude of the contact force when the pod is half way up?

1 Circular motion with variable speed

You have already met the general expressions for the acceleration of a particle in circular motion:

- the **tangential component of acceleration** is $r\dot{\omega}$ or $r\ddot{\theta}$ along the tangent
- the **radial component of acceleration** is $-r\omega^2$ or $-r\dot{\theta}^2$ along the radius.

For circular motion with variable speed, the radial component, $-r\dot{\theta}^2$, is the same as that for circular motion with constant speed. The effect of the varying speed appears in the tangential component, $r\ddot{\theta}$.

You may remember that the speed was found by differentiating $s = r\theta$ with respect to time to give $\dot{s} = r\dot{\theta}$. The tangential component of acceleration for circular motion is found by differentiating again: $\ddot{s} = r\ddot{\theta}$.

The symbols $\ddot{\theta}$ and $\dot{\omega}$ denote the rate of change of angular velocity, or the **angular acceleration**. This quantity is measured in radians per second squared (rad s^{-2}).

In the next two sections, you will be studying two types of circular motion with variable speed:

1 motion with constant angular acceleration
2 unforced motion in a vertical circle.

Circular motion with constant acceleration

When the angular acceleration of an object moving in a circle is constant, it is convenient to use the standard notation

$$\ddot{\theta} = \alpha$$

You can find the angular speed and the angular displacement by integrating this with respect to time:

$$\dot{\theta} = \alpha t + c \text{ for some constant } c$$

It is usual to call the initial angular speed ω_0. In this case, $\dot{\theta} = \omega_0$ when $t = 0$, so $c = \omega_0$.

This gives

$$\dot{\theta} = \omega_0 + \alpha t \text{ or } \omega = \omega_0 + \alpha t.$$

Integrating again and assuming that $\theta = 0$ when $t = 0$:

$$\theta = \omega_0 t + \frac{1}{2}\alpha t^2$$

These two equations may look familiar to you. They are very much like the equations for motion in a straight line with constant acceleration:

$$v = u + at$$

and $$s = ut + \frac{1}{2}at^2$$

There is a direct correspondence between the variables.

Motion in a straight line with constant acceleration	s	u	v	a
Circular motion with constant angular acceleration	θ	ω_0	$\omega\ (=\dot{\theta})$	α

In fact, it can be shown that each equation for motion in a straight line with constant acceleration corresponds to an equation for circular motion with constant angular acceleration.

$$v = u + at \quad \leftrightarrow \quad \omega = \omega_0 + \alpha t$$

$$s = ut + \frac{1}{2}at^2 \quad \leftrightarrow \quad \theta = \omega_0 t + \frac{1}{2}\alpha t^2$$

$$s = \frac{1}{2}(u+v)t \quad \leftrightarrow \quad \theta = \frac{1}{2}(\omega_0 + \omega)t$$

$$s = vt - \frac{1}{2}at^2 \quad \leftrightarrow \quad \theta = \omega t - \frac{1}{2}\alpha t^2$$

$$v^2 = u^2 + 2as \quad \leftrightarrow \quad \omega^2 = \omega_0^2 + 2\alpha\theta$$

Example 11.1

Oliver is standing on a playground roundabout at a distance of 2 m from the centre.

Imogen pushes the roundabout with constant angular acceleration for 2 s and in this time the angular speed increases from 0.3 rad s^{-1} to 1.5 rad s^{-1}. Find

(i) the angular acceleration of the roundabout

(ii) the magnitude and direction of the resultant horizontal force acting on Oliver just before Imogen stops pushing the roundabout. (Oliver's mass is 40 kg.)

Solution

(i) Using standard notation: $\omega_0 = 0.3$, $\omega = 1.5$, $t = 2$. To find α the required equation is:

$$\omega = \omega_0 + \alpha t$$

$$\Rightarrow 1.5 = 0.3 + 2\alpha$$

$$\Rightarrow \quad \alpha = 0.6$$

The angular acceleration is 0.6 rad s^{-2}

(ii)

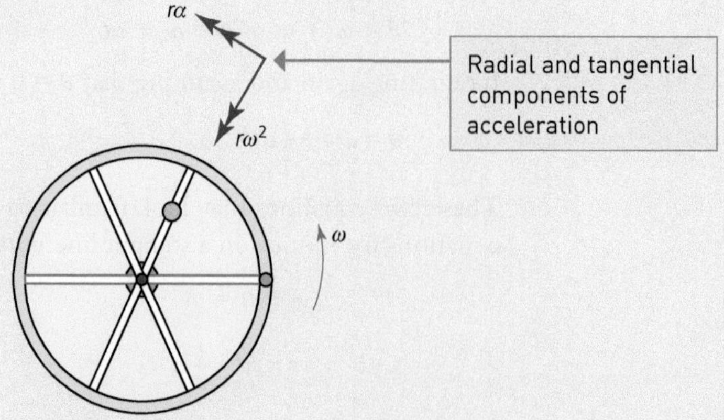

Figure 11.1

Just before Imogen stops pushing, Oliver's acceleration has two horizontal components.

Tangential motion: $r\ddot{\theta} = r\alpha$

$= 2 \times 0.6$

$= 1.2\,\text{m s}^{-2}$

Radial motion towards the centre: $r\dot{\theta}^2 = r\omega^2$

$= 2 \times 1.5^2$

$= 4.5\,\text{m s}^{-2}$

The resultant acceleration has two perpendicular components $1.2\,\text{m s}^{-2}$ and $4.5\,\text{m s}^{-2}$. Its magnitude is $\sqrt{1.2^2 + 4.5^2} = 4.657\ldots$ or $4.66\,\text{m s}^{-2}$ (3 s.f.) and it makes an angle $\arctan\left(\frac{4.5}{1.2}\right) = 75.068\ldots$ or $75°$ (to the nearest degree) with the tangential direction shown.

By Newton's second law, the resultant horizontal force is given by

$F = ma$

$= 40 \times 4.657\ldots$

So the resultant force is 186 N (to 3 s.f.) at 75° to the tangential direction.

Exercise 11.1

① A flywheel is initially rotating at $6\,\text{rad s}^{-1}$. After 5 minutes it comes to rest. Find

(i) the angular deceleration of the flywheel (assumed constant)

(ii) the total angle through which it turns before coming to rest.

② A skater spins at 1 revolution per second with her arms out sideways horizontally. She then takes 2 s to lower her arms and increases her angular speed to 3 revolutions per second. Find

(i) the angular acceleration in rad s^{-2} (assumed constant)

(ii) the number of complete revolutions she makes during the 2 s while she is lowering her arms.

③ A small stone slides round a horizontal circular track of radius 2 m. Its initial speed is $8\,\text{m s}^{-1}$ and it has a constant tangential deceleration of $0.001\,\text{m s}^{-2}$.

(i) Calculate the initial angular velocity of the stone.

(ii) Calculate the angular deceleration of the stone.

(iii) Calculate the total angle through which the stone travels before coming to rest.

(iv) Calculate the distance travelled by the stone before it comes to rest.

④ In a model of a discus throw, the discus is rotated in a horizontal circle of radius 0.75 m with steadily increasing angular speed up to the moment of release. The athlete starts from rest and takes 1.5 seconds to do 1.5 revolutions before releasing the discus. With what speed is it thrown?

⑤ Figure 11.2 shows the big wheel at a fairground. It has a radius of 3 m. Once it is loaded with passengers, it is given a uniform angular acceleration for 20 s and then runs at uniform angular speed for 2 minutes. It then slows down at a uniform rate over a further 10 s. During the main part of the ride, the wheel completes 1 revolution every 10 s.

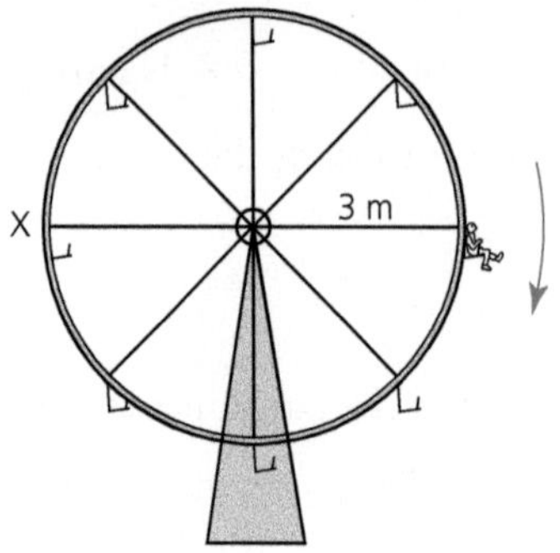

Figure 11.2

(i) Draw a graph showing the angular speed of the wheel against time and state what information is given by the area under the graph.

(ii) Find the total angle through which a passenger moves and the distance the passenger travels.

(iii) Find the magnitude of the acceleration of a passenger at the top of the ride when it is travelling at maximum speed. Draw a force diagram to show the forces on a passenger of mass 20 kg at the highest point of the ride.

(iv) Describe the acceleration vector of a passenger who is at point X where the wheel is half-way through its acceleration phase.

2 Motion in a vertical circle

Figure 11.3 shows the forces acting on a particle of mass m undergoing free circular motion in a vertical plane. For free motion it is assumed that there is no tangential force.

Note

The weight, mg, is resolved into components
Radial $mg \cos\theta$
Tangential $mg \sin\theta$

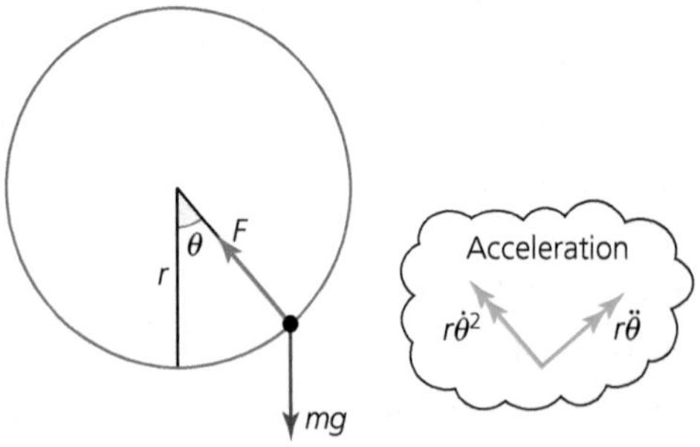

Figure 11.3

For circular motion to take place, there must be a resultant force acting on the particle towards the centre of the circle, as you have seen. This is denoted by F.

When the circle is vertical, the force of gravity also acts in this plane, and is therefore relevant to the motion. When the particle is in the position shown in Figure 11.3, Newton's second law gives the following equations.

Towards the centre $\quad F - mg\cos\theta = mr\dot{\theta}^2 \quad$ ①

Tangential motion $\quad -mg\sin\theta = mr\ddot{\theta} \quad$ ②

The force, F, in the first equation might be the tension in a string or the normal contact force from a surface. This force will vary with θ and so equation ① is not helpful in describing how θ varies with time. The second equation, however, does not involve F and may be written as

$$\frac{d^2\theta}{dt^2} = -\frac{g}{r}\sin\theta$$

This differential equation can be solved, using suitable calculus techniques, to obtain an expression for θ in terms of t. The work is beyond the scope of this book.

Using conservation of energy

A different (and at this stage more profitable) approach is to consider the energy of the particle. Since there is no motion in the radial direction, and no force in the tangential direction, the principle of conservation of mechanical energy can be applied.

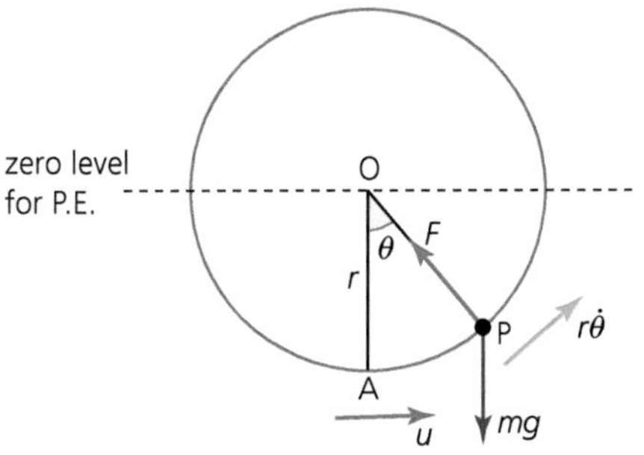

Figure 11.4

Take u to be the speed of the particle at A, the lowest point of the circle, and take the zero level of gravitational potential energy to be that through the centre of the circle, O, as shown in Figure 11.4.

The total energy at A is $\frac{1}{2}mu^2 - mgr$
(K.E.) (P.E.)

The total energy at P is $\frac{1}{2}m(r\dot{\theta})^2 - mgr\cos\theta$
(K.E.) (P.E.)

By the principle of conservation of energy

$$\frac{1}{2}m(r\dot{\theta})^2 - mgr\cos\theta = \frac{1}{2}mu^2 - mgr$$

$$\Rightarrow \quad r\dot{\theta}^2 = \frac{u^2}{r} - 2g(1-\cos\theta)$$

This tells you the angular speed, $\dot{\theta}$, of the particle when OP is at an angle θ to OA.

The next two examples show how conservation of energy may be applied to theoretical models of problems involving motion in a vertical circle.

Example 11.2

A particle of mass 0.03 kg is attached to the end, P, of a light rod OP of length 0.5 m which is free to rotate in a vertical circle with centre O. The particle is set in motion starting at the lowest point of the circle.

The initial speed of the particle is $2\,\text{m s}^{-1}$.

(i) Find the initial kinetic energy of the particle.

(ii) Find an expression for the potential energy gained when the rod has turned through an angle θ.

(iii) Find the value of θ when the particle first comes to rest.

(iv) Find the stress in the rod at this point, stating whether it is a tension or a thrust.

(v) Repeat parts (i) to (iv) using an initial speed of $4\,\text{m s}^{-1}$.

(vi) Why is it possible for the first motion (when $v_0 = 2$) to take place if the rod is replaced by a string, but not in the second (when $v_0 = 4$)?

Solution

(i) Kinetic energy $= \frac{1}{2}mv^2$

$$= \frac{1}{2} \times 0.03 \times 2^2$$

$$= 0.06$$

The initial kinetic energy is 0.06 J.

(ii) Figure 11.5 shows the position of the particle when the rod has rotated through an angle θ.

It has risen a distance AN where

$$\text{AN} = \text{OA} - \text{ON}$$

$$= 0.5 - 0.5\cos\theta$$

$$= 0.5(1 - \cos\theta)$$

The gain in potential energy at P is therefore

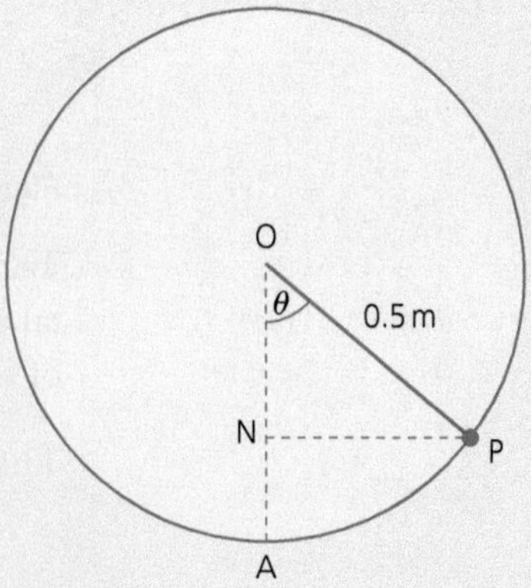

Figure 11.5

$$0.03g \times 0.5(1 - \cos\theta) = 0.015g(1 - \cos\theta)\,\text{J}$$

(iii) When the particle first comes to rest, the kinetic energy is zero, so by the principle of conservation of energy:

$$0.015g(1 - \cos\theta) = 0.06$$

$$1 - \cos\theta = \frac{0.06}{0.015g}$$

$$= 0.408\ldots$$

$$\Rightarrow \quad \cos\theta = 0.591\ldots$$

$$\Rightarrow \quad \theta = 53.7°.$$

(iv) The forces acting on the particle and its acceleration are as shown in Figure 11.6

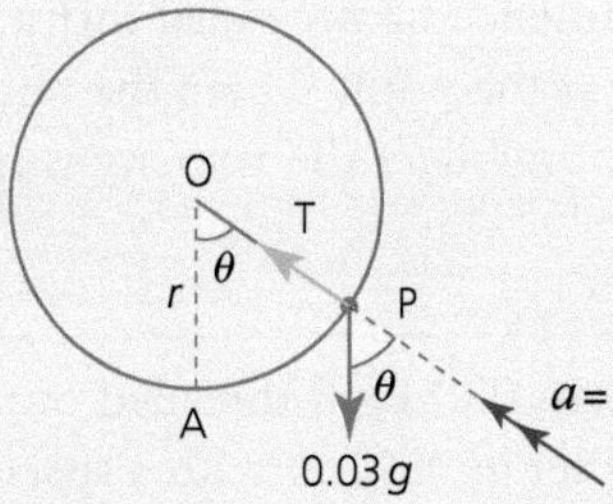

Figure 11.6

The component of the acceleration towards the centre of the circle is $r\dot{\theta}^2$ which equals zero when the angular speed is zero. Resolving towards the centre:

$$T - 0.03g\cos\theta = 0 \quad ①$$

$$T = 0.03 \times 9.8 \times \cos 53.7° = 0.174$$

Since this is positive, the stress in the rod is a tension. Its magnitude is 0.174 N.

(v) When the initial speed is $4\,\mathrm{m\,s^{-1}}$, the initial kinetic energy is

$\frac{1}{2} \times 0.03 \times 4^2 = 0.24$ J.

The gain in potential energy at P, as shown in part (ii),

$= 0.015g(1 - \cos\theta)$ J.

When the particle first comes to rest, the kinetic energy is zero, so by the principle of conservation of energy:

$$0.015g(1 - \cos\theta) = 0.24$$

$$\cos\theta = 1 - \frac{0.24}{0.015 \times 9.8} = -0.632\ldots$$

$$\theta = 129°$$

Now equation ① gives the tension in the rod as

$$T = 0.03g\cos\theta = -0.186$$

The negative tension means that the stress is in fact a thrust of magnitude 0.186 N.

Figure 11.7 illustrates the forces acting in this position.

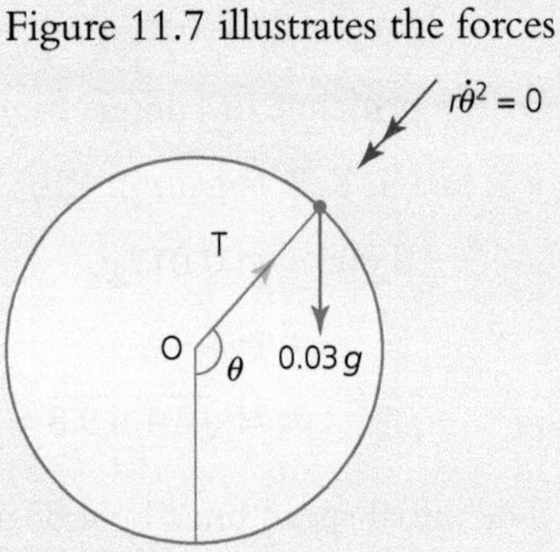

Figure 11.7

(vi) A string cannot exert a thrust so, although the rod could be replaced by a string in the first case, it would be impossible in the second. In the absence of any radial thrust, the particle would leave its circular path at the point where the tension is zero and before reaching the position where the velocity is zero.

Example 11.3

Hint

When a bead is threaded on a wire it can't fall off.

A bead of mass 0.01 kg is threaded onto a smooth circular wire of radius 0.6 m and is set in motion with a speed of $u\,\mathrm{m\,s^{-1}}$ at the bottom of the circle. This just enables the bead to reach the top of the wire.

(i) Find the value of u.

(ii) What is the direction of the force of the wire on the bead when the bead is at the top of the circle?

Solution

(i) The initial kinetic energy is

$$\frac{1}{2}\times 0.01\,u^2 = 0.005\,u^2$$

If the bead just reaches the top, the speed there is zero. If this is the case, the kinetic energy at the top will also be zero.

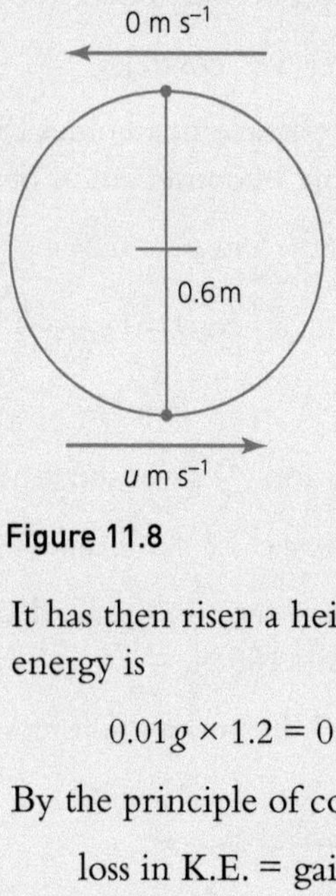

Figure 11.8

It has then risen a height of $2 \times 0.6 = 1.2\,\mathrm{m}$, so its gain in potential energy is

$$0.01g \times 1.2 = 0.012g$$

By the principle of conservation of energy,

$$\text{loss in K.E.} = \text{gain in P.E.}$$

$$0.005\,u^2 = 0.012g$$

$$u^2 = 2.4g$$

$$u = \sqrt{2.4 \times 9.8} = 4.849\ldots$$

The initial speed must be $4.85\,\mathrm{m\,s^{-1}}$ (to 2 d.p.).

(ii) The force of the wire on the bead could be directed either towards the centre of the circle or away from it. The bead has zero angular speed at the top, so the component of its acceleration, and therefore the resultant force, towards the centre is zero. The force must be outwards, as shown in Figure 11.9, and equal to $0.01g$ N.

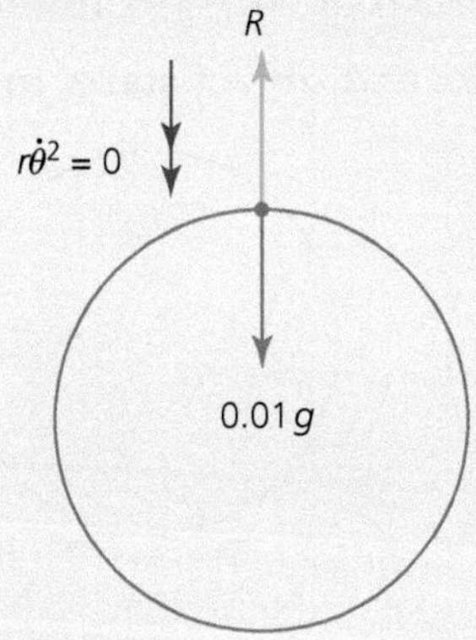

The mass of the bead is 0.01 kg.

Figure 11.9

Discussion point

Would this motion be possible if the bead were tied to the end of a string instead of being threaded on a wire?

The breakdown of circular motion

ACTIVITY 11.1

Tie a small object to the end of a piece of strong thread and tie the other end loosely (to minimise friction) round a smooth knitting needle (or a smooth rod with a cork on one end).

Hold the pointed end of the needle and make the object move in a vertical circle, as shown in Figure 11.10.

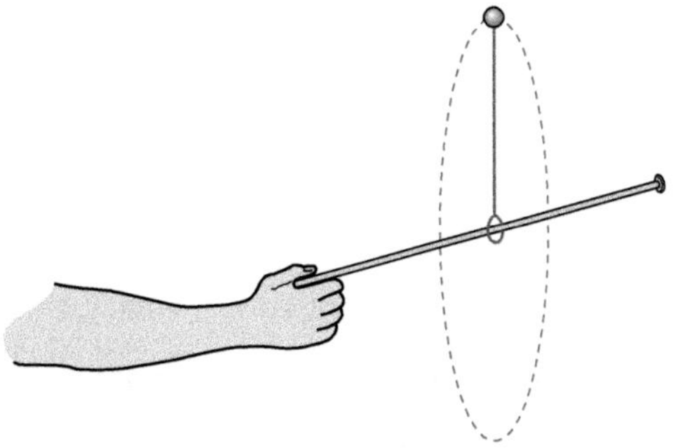

Figure 11.10

Demonstrate these three types of motion.

1 The object travels in complete circles.
2 The object swings like a pendulum.
3 The object rises above the level of the needle but then fails to complete a full circle.

What would happen if the string broke?
What would happen if a rod were used rather than a string?

Note

When carrying out this activity, keep well away from other people and breakable objects.

The three different types of motion mentioned in the Activity, and the case in which the string breaks, are illustrated in the following diagrams of Figure 11.11.

(a) **Object oscillates in complete circles**

(b) **Object oscillates backwards and forwards**

(c) **Object leaves circle at some point and falls inwards**

(d) **String breaks and object starts to move away along a tangent**

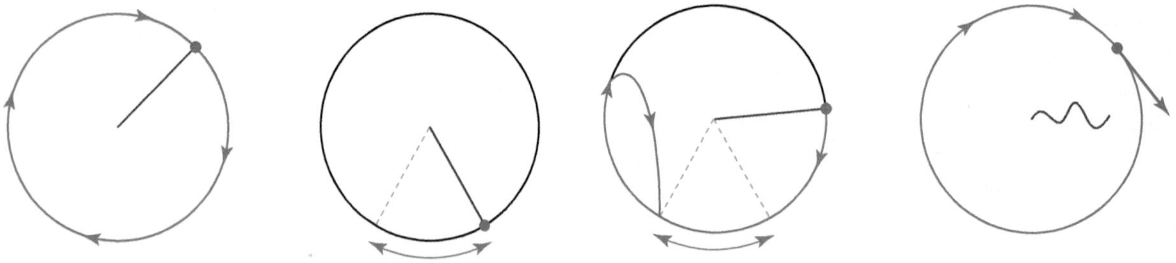

Figure 11.11

Modelling the breakdown of circular motion

For what reasons might something depart from motion in a circle? For example, under what conditions will a particle attached to a string and moving in a vertical circle fall out of the circle? Under what conditions will a bicycle travelling over a speed bump with circular cross-section leave the road?

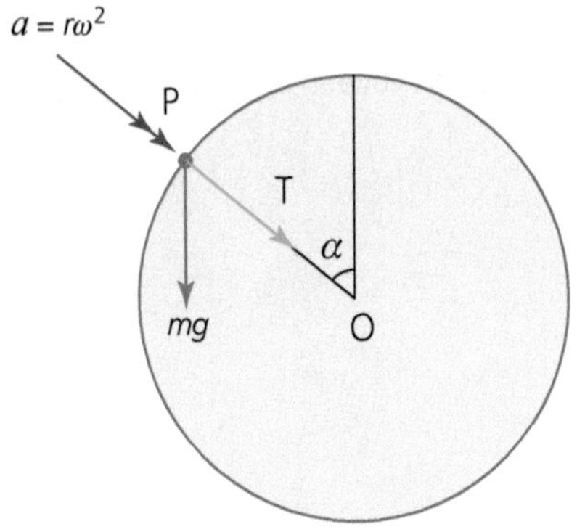

Figure 11.12

A particle on a string

Figure 11.12 shows a particle P of mass m attached to a string of length r, rotating with angular speed ω in a vertical circle, centre O.

There are two forces acting on the particle, its weight, mg, and the tension, T, in the string. The acceleration of the particle is $r\omega^2$ towards the centre of the circle.

Applying Newton's second law towards the centre gives

$$T + mg\cos\alpha = mr\omega^2 \quad ①$$

where α is the angle shown in Figure 11.12.

While the particle is in circular motion, the string is taut and so $T > 0$. At the instant it starts to leave the circle, the string goes slack and $T = 0$.

Substituting $T = 0$ in ① gives $\quad mg\cos\alpha = mr\omega^2$

$$\Rightarrow \qquad \cos\alpha = \frac{r\omega^2}{g}$$

The equation $\cos\alpha = \frac{r\omega^2}{g}$ allows you to find the angle α at which the particle leaves the circle, if it does.

The greatest possible value for $\cos\alpha$ is 1, so if $\frac{r\omega^2}{g}$ is greater than 1 throughout the motion, the equation has no solution and this means that the particle never leaves the circle. Thus the condition for the particle to stay in circular motion is that $\omega^2 \geq \frac{g}{r}$ throughout.

In this example of a particle on a string, ω varies throughout the motion. As you saw earlier, the value of ω at any instant is given by the energy equation which in this case is

$$\frac{1}{2}mr^2\omega^2 + mgr(1+\cos\alpha) = \frac{1}{2}mu^2$$

where u is the speed of the particle at the lowest point.

A particle moving on the inside of a vertical circle

The same analysis applies to a particle sliding around the inside of a smooth circle. The only difference is that, in this case, the tension, T, is replaced by the normal force, R, of the surface on the particle (see Figure 11.14). When $R = 0$, the particle leaves the surface.

Figure 11.13

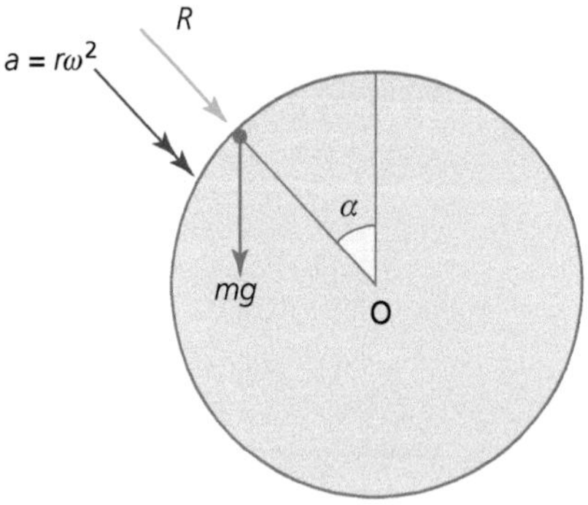

Figure 11.14

A particle moving on the outside of a vertical circle

The forces acting on a particle moving on the outside of a vertical circle, such as a car going over a hump-backed bridge, are the normal force, R, acting outwards and the weight of the particle, as shown in Figure 11.15.

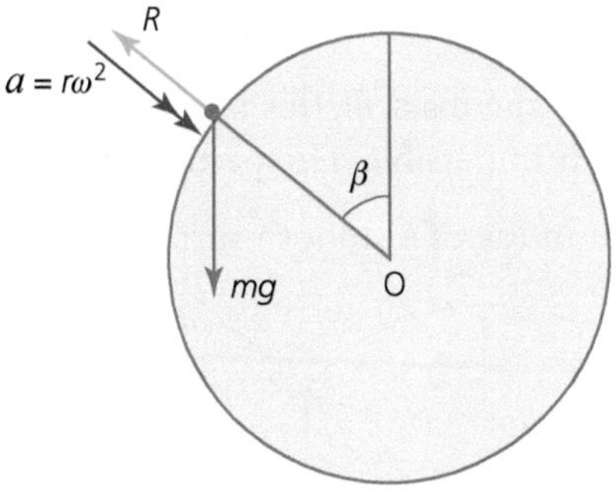

Figure 11.15

Applying Newton's second law towards the centre gives

$$mg\cos\beta - R = mr\omega^2 \quad ②$$

where β is the angle shown.

If the normal force is zero, it means there is no force between the particle and the surface and so the particle is leaving the surface.

Substituting $R = 0$ in ② gives $\quad mg\cos\beta = mr\omega^2$

$$\Rightarrow \qquad \cos\beta = \frac{r\omega^2}{g}$$

> **Discussion point**
>
> The conditions for the breakdown of circular motion seem to be the same in the cases of a particle on the end of a string and a particle on the outside of a circle.
>
> However, everyday experience tells you that circular motion on the end of a string is only possible if the angular speed is large enough whereas a particle will only stay on the outside of a circle if the angular speed is small enough.
>
> How do the conditions $T > 0$ and $R > 0$ explain this difference?

Example 11.4

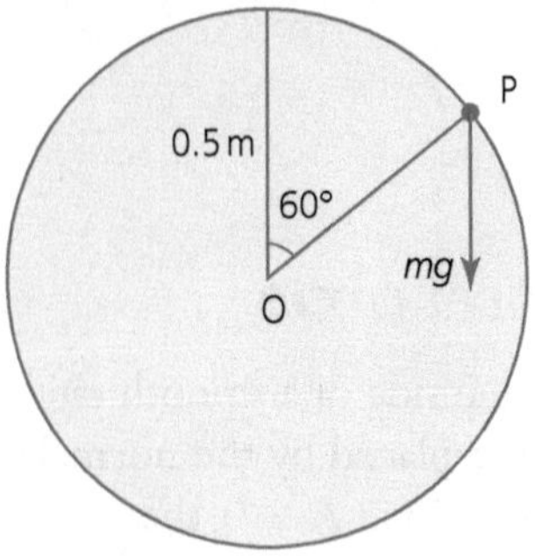

Figure 11.16

Determine whether it is possible for a particle, P, of mass m kg to be in the position shown in Figure 11.16 moving round a vertical circle of radius 0.5 m with an angular speed of $4\,\text{rad}\,\text{s}^{-1}$ when it is

4 rad s^{-1}

(i) sliding on the outside of a smooth surface

(ii) sliding on the inside of a smooth surface

(iii) attached to the end of a string OP

(iv) threaded on a smooth vertical ring.

Solution

(i) On the outside of a smooth surface:

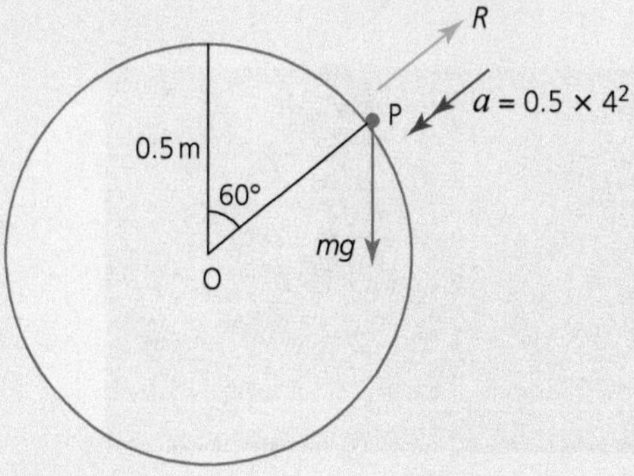

Figure 11.17

The normal force R N of the surface on the particle must be acting outwards, so Newton's second law towards the centre gives

$$mg\cos 60° - R = m \times 0.5 \times 4^2$$

$$\Rightarrow \quad R = mg\cos 60° - 8m$$

$$= -3.1m$$

Whatever the mass, m, this negative value of R is impossible, so the motion is impossible. The particle will already have left the surface.

(ii) On the inside of a smooth surface:

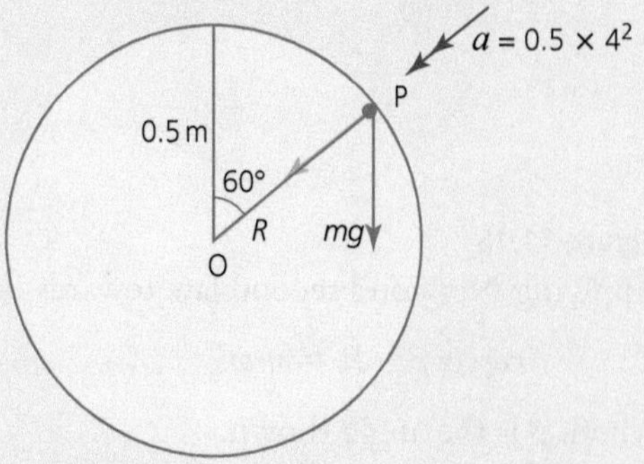

Figure 11.18

The normal force of the surface on the particle will now be acting towards the centre and so

$$R + mg\cos 60° = m \times 0.5 \times 4^2$$

$$\Rightarrow \quad R = +3.1m$$

This is possible.

(iii) Attached to the end of a string:

This situation is like that in part (ii) since the tension acts towards the centre, so the motion is possible.

Discussion point

Which of the situations in Example 11.4 are possible when the angular speed is $3\,\text{m}\,\text{s}^{-1}$?

(iv) Threaded on a smooth ring:

If the particle is threaded on a ring the normal force can act inwards or outwards so the motion can take place whatever the angular speed. This is also the case when a particle is attached to the centre by a light rod. The rod will exert a tension or a thrust as required.

Example 11.5

Eddie, a skier of mass m kg, is skiing down a hillside when he reaches a smooth hump in the form of an arc AB of a circle with centre O and radius 8 m, as shown in Figure 11.19. O, A and B lie in a vertical plane and OA and OB make angles of 20° and 40° with the vertical, respectively. Eddie's speed at A is $7\,\text{m}\,\text{s}^{-1}$. Determine whether Eddie will lose contact with the ground before reaching the point B.

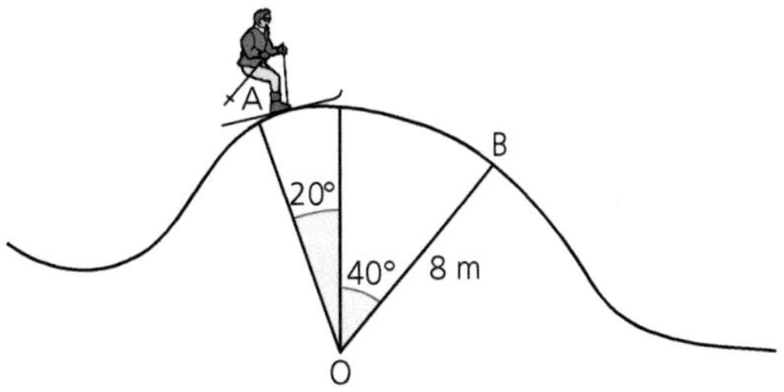

Figure 11.19

Solution

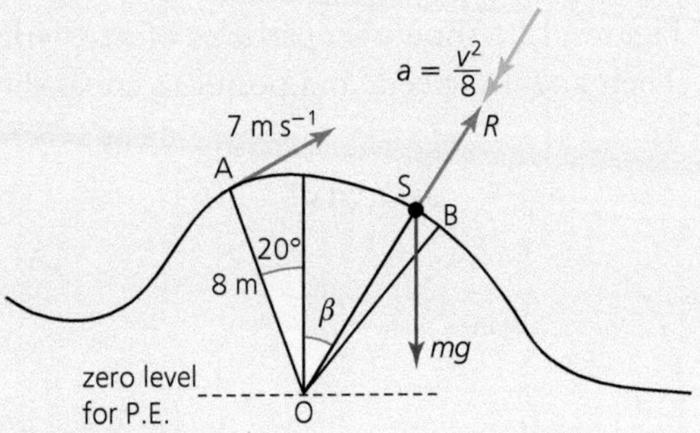

Figure 11.20

Note

S is a general point on the surface of the arc of the circle.

Taking the zero level for potential energy to be a horizontal line through O, the initial energy at A is

$$\frac{1}{2}m\times 7^2 + mg\times 8\cos 20°$$

The energy at point S is

$$\frac{1}{2}mv^2 + mg\times 8\cos\beta$$

By the principle of conservation of energy these are equal.

$$\frac{1}{2}mv^2 + mg\times 8\cos\beta = \frac{1}{2}m\times 7^2 + mg\times 8\cos 20°$$

$$\Rightarrow \quad v^2 + 16g\cos\beta = 49 + 147.34\ldots$$

$$\Rightarrow \quad v^2 = 196.34\ldots - 16g\cos\beta \qquad ①$$

Using Newton's second law towards the centre of the circle

$$mg\cos\beta - R = m\frac{v^2}{8}$$

$$\Rightarrow \quad R = m\left(g\cos\beta - \frac{v^2}{8}\right)$$

If Eddie leaves the circle at point S, then $R = 0$

$$\Rightarrow \quad v^2 = 8g\cos\beta$$

Substituting in ①

$$8g\cos\beta = 196.34\ldots - 16g\cos\beta$$

$$\Rightarrow \quad 24g\cos\beta = 196.34\ldots$$

$$\Rightarrow \quad \cos\beta = \frac{196.34\ldots}{24\times 9.8} = 0.834\ldots$$

$$\Rightarrow \quad \beta = 33.4°$$

This gives $\beta = 33.4°$, which is less than 40°, so Eddie will lose contact with the ground before he reaches the point B.

Exercise 11.2

① Figure 11.21 show two particles of mass m kg moving in vertical circles. Their angular speeds and positions are as shown.

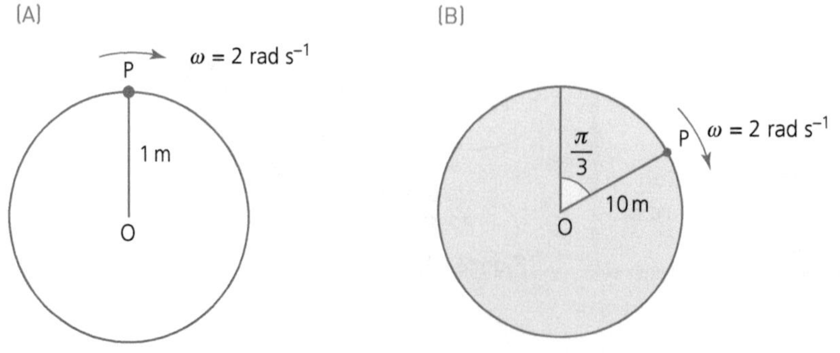

Figure 11.21

(i) Write down the components of their acceleration along PO.

(ii) By considering the forces acting on the particle, determine, in each case, whether it is possible for it to be moving with this speed in this position when it is:

(a) sliding on the outside of a smooth surface

(b) sliding on the inside of a smooth surface

(c) attached to the end of a string OP

(d) threaded on a smooth ring in a vertical plane.

② Each of the following diagrams in Figure 11.22 shows a particle of mass m which is constrained to move in a vertical circle. Initially, it is in the position shown and moving with the given speed.

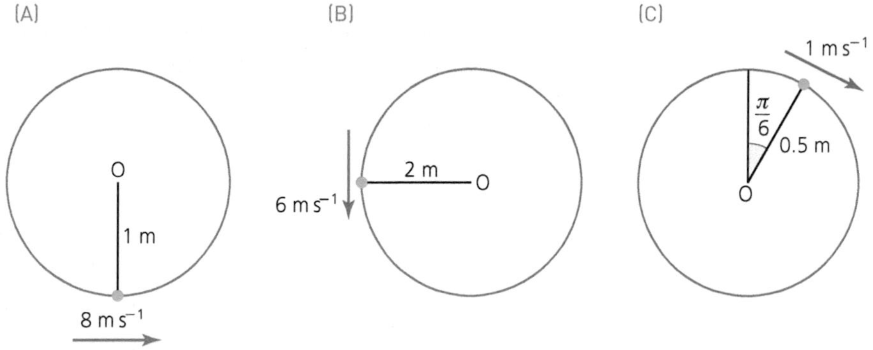

Figure 11.22

In each case:

(i) Using the horizontal through the centre of the circle as the zero level for potential energy, write down the total initial mechanical energy of the particle.

(ii) Decide whether the particle will make complete revolutions or whether it will come to rest below the highest point. If it makes complete revolutions, determine the speed at the top. Otherwise find the height above the centre when it comes to rest.

(iii) Assuming that the particle is moving under the action of its weight and a radial force only, find the magnitude and direction of the radial force

(a) initially

(b) when it reaches the top or comes to rest.

③ A smooth hemispherical bowl of radius r, with lowest point A, is fixed with its rim uppermost and horizontal. A particle of mass m is projected along the inner surface of the bowl with a speed $\sqrt{gr}$ towards A, from a point at a vertical height $\frac{1}{2}r$ above A, so that its motion is in a vertical plane through A.

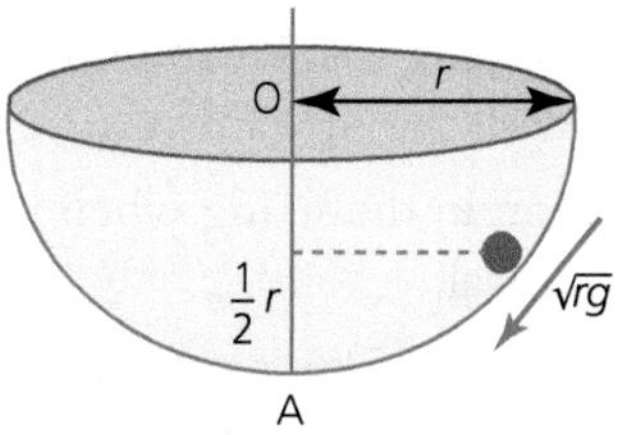

Figure 11.23

(i) Show that the particle will just reach the top of the bowl.

(ii) Find the reaction between the particle and the bowl when it is at a height $\frac{1}{3}r$ above A.

④ A bead B of mass m is threaded onto a fixed smooth circular wire, with centre O and radius a, whose plane is vertical. When the bead is at the lowest point of the wire, it is projected horizontally with velocity u and, in the subsequent motion, B reaches a maximum vertical height of $\frac{1}{2}a$ above O.

(i) Show that $u^2 = 3ga$.

(ii) If θ is the angle which OB makes with the downward vertical, prove that the reaction R of B on the wire is given by

$$R = mg(1 + 3\cos\theta).$$

⑤ Figure 11.24 shows a model car track. You may assume that all parts of the track lie in the same vertical plane.

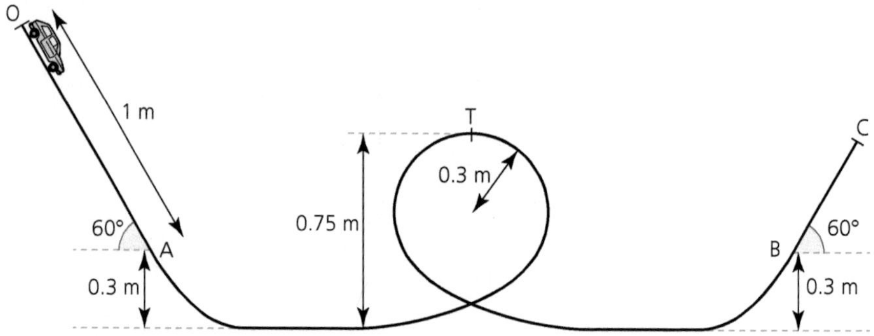

Figure 11.24

Between A and B the track is symmetrical about a vertical line through T; its length from A to T is 2.1 m. OA and BC are straight and the top of the loop is an arc of a circle of radius 0.3 m. For a car of mass m kg there is a frictional resistance of $0.06mg$ N.

The car starts from rest at the point O.

(i) Find the work done against friction between O and T.

(ii) Use the work–energy principle to show that the kinetic energy at T is $0.230mg$ J.

(iii) By considering circular motion at T, show that the car will move right round the loop in contact with the track.

(iv) The car stops at C before returning. Find the length BC.

(v) Will the car reach T on the return journey?

⑥ A particle of mass m hangs by a string of length a from a fixed point. The particle is given a horizontal velocity of $\sqrt{\frac{7}{2}ga}$.

(i) Show that the string will be about to become slack when it makes an angle of 60° with the upward vertical.

(ii) Find the tension in the string when it makes an angle of 60° with the downward vertical.

⑦ A metal sphere of mass 0.5 kg is moving in a vertical circle of radius 0.8 m at the end of a light, inelastic string. At the top of the circle the sphere has speed $3\,\text{m s}^{-1}$.

(i) Calculate the gravitational potential energy lost by the sphere when it reaches the bottom of the circle and hence calculate its speed at this point.

(ii) Find an expression for the speed of the sphere when the string makes an angle, θ, with the upward vertical.

(iii) Find the tension in the string when the sphere is

(a) at the top of the circle

(b) at the bottom of the circle.

(iv) Draw a diagram showing the forces acting on the sphere when the string makes an angle θ with the upward vertical. Find expressions for the tension in the string and the tangential component of the sphere's acceleration at this instant.

⑧ A glider is travelling horizontally until the pilot executes a loop-the-loop manoeuvre, as shown in Figure 11.25. The loop may be modelled as a vertical circle. The glider is initially at a height of 700 m, travelling at $30\,\mathrm{m\,s^{-1}}$. The bottom of the loop is at a height 400 m and the radius of the loop is 100 m.

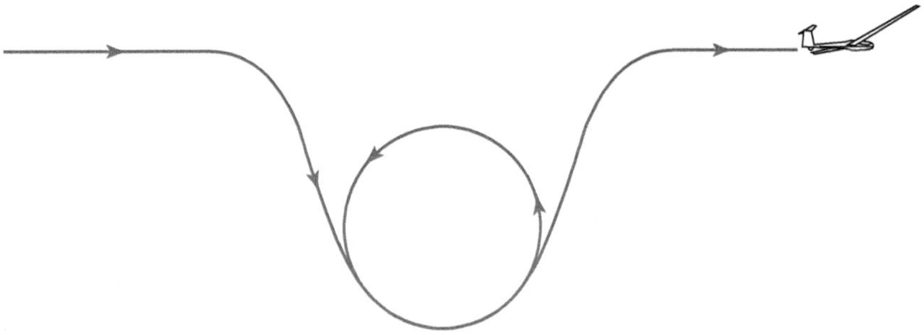

Figure 11.25

Assuming that the mechanical energy is conserved, calculate:

(i) the speed of the glider at the lowest and highest points of the loop

(ii) the magnitude of the acceleration of the glider at the lowest and highest points of the loop.

The mass of the pilot is 70 kg.

(iii) Draw diagrams to show the forces acting on him at the lowest and highest points of the loop and state their magnitudes.

(iv) What would happen if he attempted a loop of radius 150 m, starting from the same lowest point?

(v) What is the maximum radius for a successful loop from this point?

⑨ As a challenge, a girl is required to swing a bucket of water in a vertical circular arc above her head. If the bucket is not moving fast enough, she will get wet. This may be modelled by taking the girl's arm to be 55 cm long and the bucket 35 cm from base to handle. The handle is taken to be rigidly attached to the bucket and is held firmly so that her arm is always in line with the centre of the base. Assume that the water behaves as a solid block.

The girl considers three possible depths of water in the bucket: 5 cm, 10 cm and 15 cm.

(i) For which depth does she need to give the bucket the highest angular speed?

In the event, she is forced to have 15 cm of water in the bucket.

(ii) Find the minimum angular speed at the top of the arc for the water to stay in the bucket.

(iii) Deduce the average angular acceleration the girl must give the bucket, assuming that it is at rest at the lowest point.

One girl, doing this for real, ended with the bucket as well as the water hitting her head.

(iv) How could you model this situation?

⑩ Figure 11.26 shows a ride at an amusement park. The loop is, to a good approximation, a circle of radius 8 m, in a vertical plane.

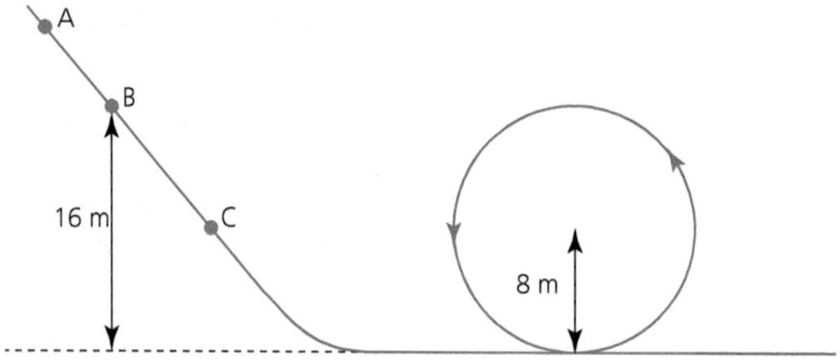

Figure 11.26

In answering the following questions, you should assume that no energy is lost to forces such as friction and air resistance, and that the car starts from rest.

(i) Explain why a car which starts just above point B, 16 m above ground level, will not complete the loop.

(ii) For a car to complete the loop successfully, it must start at or above point A. What is the height of A?

(iii) On 'Kiddie days' the organisers start the car below point C. Describe what happens to the car and state the maximum height of point C for it to be safe.

⑪ Figure 11.27 illustrates an old road bridge over a river. The road surface follows an approximately circular arc with radius 15 m.

A car is being driven across the bridge and you should model it as a particle.

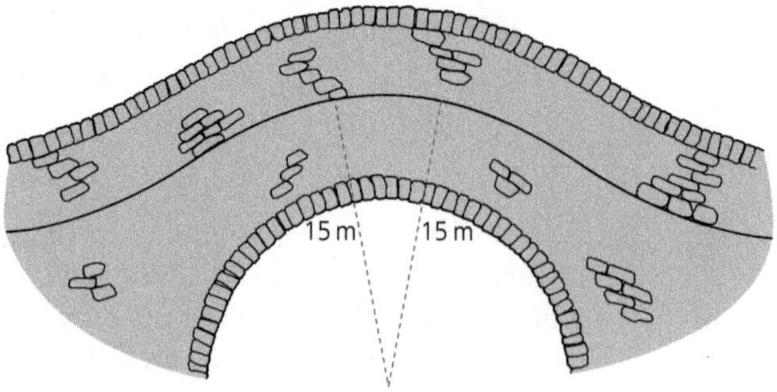

Figure 11.27

(i) Calculate the greatest constant speed at which it is possible to drive the car across the bridge without it leaving the road, giving your answer both in $m\,s^{-1}$ and in mph.

(ii) Comment on the fact that the bridge is old.

(iii) How is it possible to improve the design of the bridge?

⑫ A car of mass 200 kg travels along the track of a roller-coaster. In one section of the track, the car travels around the inside of a vertical circle of radius 10 m, as shown in Figure 11.28.

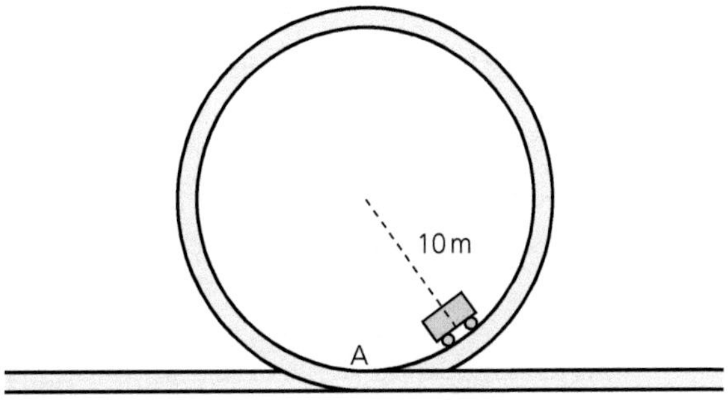

Figure 11.28

The car is attached to the track so that it can move freely along it, but cannot leave the circular path. While the car is travelling around the circle, there is no driving force present. Friction and air resistance may be neglected.

The car enters the circle at its lowest point, A, with a speed of $21\,\mathrm{m\,s^{-1}}$.

(i) Show that the speed of the car at the highest point is $7\,\mathrm{m\,s^{-1}}$.

(ii) Find the radial acceleration at the highest point. Hence calculate the force that the track exerts on the car at this point. Could the roller-coaster operate if the car was not attached to the track?

Explain your answer briefly.

(iii) Calculate the radial and tangential components of acceleration when the car has travelled through 120° round the circle from A. Show that the resultant acceleration at this point is directed towards A. [MEI]

⑬ A particle of mass m is attached to one end, A, of a light, inelastic string of length, l. The other end, B, of the string is attached to a ceiling so that the particle is free to swing in a vertical plane; the angle between the string and the downward vertical is θ radians. You may assume that the air resistance on the particle is negligible.

Initially, $\theta = \frac{\pi}{3}$ and the particle is released from rest.

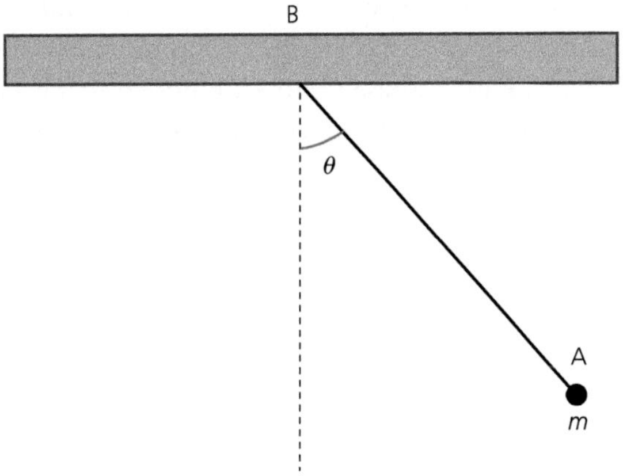

Figure 11.29

(i) Show that the potential energy lost by the particle since leaving its initial position is $\frac{mgl}{2}(2\cos\theta - 1)$. Hence find an expression for v^2, where v is the linear speed of the particle, in terms of l, g and θ.

(ii) Show that the tension in the string at any point of the motion is $mg(3\cos\theta - 1)$.

(iii) Find the greatest tension in the string. What is the position of the particle when the tension in the string is greatest?

Before its release with $\theta = \frac{\pi}{3}$, the particle is held in position by means of a second light string inclined at an acute angle, α, to the downward vertical, as shown in Figure 11.30. The second string is cut to allow the particle to swing.

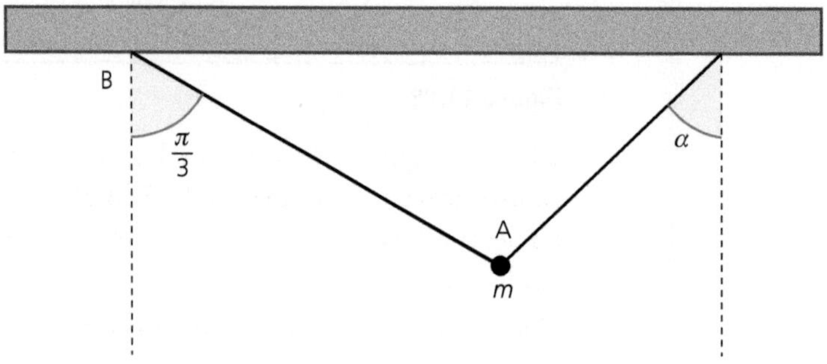

Figure 11.30

(iv) What is the direction of the acceleration of the particle just after the string is cut?

You are given that the tension in the string AB when the particle is being supported is

$$\frac{2mg}{1+\sqrt{3}\cot\alpha}$$

(v) Calculate the value of α for which the tension in AB remains unchanged when the string is cut. [MEI]

Velocity and acceleration for motion in a circle

When a particle moves in a circle, it is convenient for the velocity and acceleration to be expressed in the radial and tangential directions. For this reason, unit vectors $\hat{\boldsymbol{r}}$ and $\hat{\boldsymbol{\theta}}$ are defined in these two directions. However, unlike the unit vectors **i** and **j**, these vectors are not constant. Their magnitudes are constant and equal to 1 but their directions change as the particle moves round the circle.

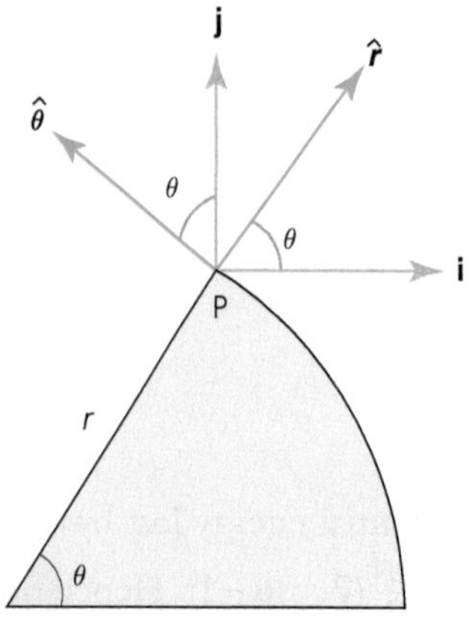

Figure 11.31

When the particle P is at a general position, as shown in Figure 11.31, $\hat{\boldsymbol{r}}$ and $\hat{\theta}$ are given by the following expressions:

$$\hat{\boldsymbol{r}} = \cos\theta\mathbf{i} + \sin\theta\mathbf{j}$$

and $$\hat{\theta} = -\sin\theta\mathbf{i} + \cos\theta\mathbf{j}$$

Differentiating $\hat{\boldsymbol{r}}$ with respect to time,

$$\begin{aligned}\frac{d\hat{\boldsymbol{r}}}{dt} &= \frac{d}{dt}(\cos\theta)\mathbf{i} + \frac{d}{dt}(\sin\theta)\mathbf{j} \\ &= -\sin\theta\frac{d\theta}{dt}\mathbf{i} + \cos\theta\frac{d\theta}{dt}\mathbf{j} \\ &= (-\sin\theta\mathbf{i} + \cos\theta\mathbf{j})\dot{\theta} \quad \text{where } \dot{\theta} = \frac{d\theta}{dt}.\end{aligned}$$

Note

These two results $\frac{d\hat{r}}{dt} = \dot{\theta}\hat{\theta}$ and $\frac{d\hat{\theta}}{dt} = -\dot{\theta}\hat{r}$ apply to all motion described in polar coordinates, not just circular motion.

You will recognise that the vector in brackets $(-\sin\theta\mathbf{i} + \cos\theta\mathbf{j})$ is the same as $\hat{\theta}$, the unit vector in the tangential direction. Consequently

$$\frac{d\hat{\boldsymbol{r}}}{dt} = \dot{\theta}\hat{\theta}$$

Similarly,

$$\begin{aligned}\frac{d\hat{\theta}}{dt} &= -\cos\theta\,\dot{\theta}\mathbf{i} - \sin\theta\,\dot{\theta}\mathbf{j} \\ &= -(\cos\theta\mathbf{i} + \sin\theta\mathbf{j})\dot{\theta}\end{aligned}$$

i.e. $$\frac{d\hat{\theta}}{dt} = -\dot{\theta}\hat{\boldsymbol{r}}.$$

In the case of circular motion with radius r, the displacement from the centre at any time is given by

$$\text{displacement} = r\hat{\boldsymbol{r}} \qquad \text{(the displacement is in the radial direction)}$$

Differentiating this with respect to time, you obtain

$$\begin{aligned}\text{velocity} &= \frac{dr}{dt}\hat{\boldsymbol{r}} + r\frac{d\hat{\boldsymbol{r}}}{dt} \\ &= 0 + r\dot{\theta}\hat{\theta} \qquad \text{(since } r \text{ is constant)} \\ &= r\dot{\theta}\hat{\theta} \qquad \text{(the velocity is in the tangential direction).}\end{aligned}$$

Differentiating again you obtain

$$\begin{aligned}\text{acceleration} &= \frac{dr}{dt}\dot{\theta}\hat{\theta} + r\frac{d\dot{\theta}}{dt}\hat{\theta} + r\dot{\theta}\frac{d\hat{\theta}}{dt} \\ &= 0 + r\ddot{\theta}\hat{\theta} - r\dot{\theta}^2\hat{\boldsymbol{r}} \\ &= r\ddot{\theta}\hat{\theta} - r\dot{\theta}^2\hat{\boldsymbol{r}}\end{aligned}$$

Thus the acceleration has two components:

a tangential component: $r\ddot{\theta}$

and a radial component: $-r\dot{\theta}^2$.

KEY POINTS

1 The equations for circular motion with constant acceleration α are

- $\omega = \omega_0 + \alpha t$
- $\theta = \frac{1}{2}[\omega + \omega_0]t$
- $\theta = \omega_0 t + \frac{1}{2}\alpha t^2$
- $\theta = \omega t - \frac{1}{2}\alpha t^2$
- $\omega^2 = \omega_0^2 + 2\alpha\theta$

where ω_0 is the initial angular speed.

2 Problems involving free motion in a vertical circle can be solved using the conservation of energy principle

P. E. + K.E. = constant

in conjunction with Newton's second law.

3 Circular motion breaks down when the available force towards the centre is $< mr\omega^2$.

LEARNING OUTCOMES

When you have finished this chapter, you should be able to

- model situations involving motion in a vertical circle
- calculate the radial and tangential components of acceleration for motion in a circle with variable acceleration
- identify the conditions under which a particle departs from circular motion, and calculate the path of the subsequent motion
- solve problems involving the motion of a particle on a string moving in a vertical circle and then as a projectile.

12 Hooke's law

The only way of finding the limits of the possible is by going beyond them into the impossible.
Arthur C. Clarke

- The photographs show people bungee jumping.
- Bungee jumping is a dangerous sport which originated in the South Sea Islands where creepers were used instead of ropes. In the more modern version, a person jumps off a high bridge or crane to which they are attached by an elastic rope around their ankles or with a harness.

Discussion point

If somebody bungee jumping from a bridge wants the excitement of just reaching the surface of the water below, how would you calculate the length of rope required?

The answer to this question clearly depends on the height of the bridge, the mass of the person jumping and the elasticity of the rope. All ropes are elastic to some extent, but it would be extremely dangerous to use an ordinary rope for this sport because the impulse necessary to stop somebody falling would involve a very large tension acting in the rope for a short time and this would provide too great a shock to the system. A bungee is a strong elastic rope, similar to those used to secure loads on cycles, cars or lorries, with the essential property for this sport that it allows the impulse to act over a much longer time so that the rope exerts a smaller force on the jumper.

Generally in mechanics, the word **string** is used to represent such things as ropes which can be in tension but not in compression. In contrast, a **spring** can be compressed as well as stretched. So a spring can be in compression or in tension. In this book, it is assumed that springs are open coiled.

In this chapter, you will be studying some of the properties of elastic strings and springs and will return to the problem of the bungee jumper as a final investigation.

1 Strings and springs

So far, in situations involving strings, it has been assumed that they do not stretch when they are under tension. Such strings are called **inextensible**. For some materials this is a good assumption, but for others the length of the string increases significantly under tension. Strings and springs which stretch are said to be **elastic**.

The length of a string or spring when there is no force applied to it is called its **natural length**. If it is stretched, the increase in length is called its **extension**, and if a spring is compressed, it is said to have a **negative extension** or **compression**.

When stretched, a spring exerts an inward force, or *tension,* on whatever is attached to its ends (Figure 12.1(b)). When compressed, it exerts an outward force, or **thrust,** on its ends (Figure 12.1(c)). An elastic string exerts a tension when stretched, but when slack exerts no force.

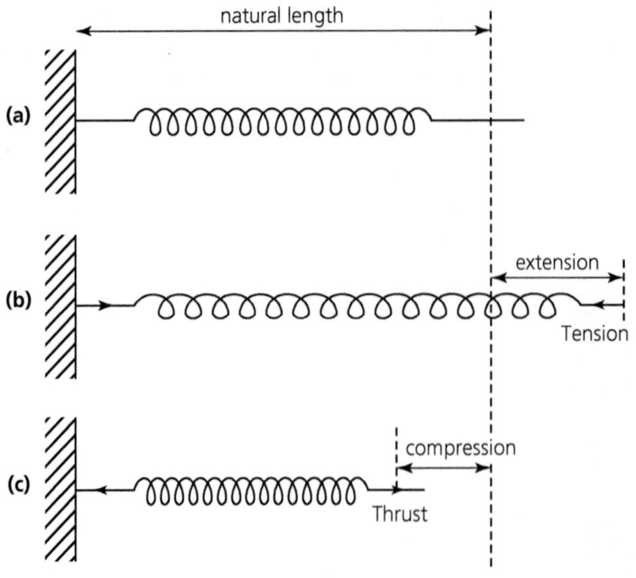

Figure 12.1

Here are some questions for you to think about.

1 How are the extension of a string and the weight of an object hung from it related?
2 If a string of the same material but twice the natural length has the same weight attached, how does the extension change?
3 Does the string return to its original length when unloaded
   (i) if the weight of the object is small?
   (ii) if the weight of the object is large?

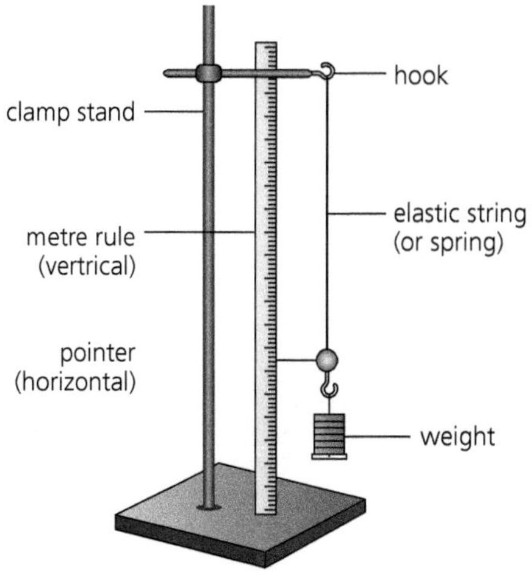

Figure 12.2

You may choose to carry out experiments to help you answer these questions. If you do you will need some elastic strings, some open coiled springs, some weights and a support stand. Set up the apparatus as shown in Figure 12.2.

You can use the same equipment to find the period of oscillation of an object hanging on an elastic string or spring.

Now, for each string, plot a graph of tension, i.e. the weight of the object (vertical axis), against the extension (horizontal axis) to help you to answer these questions.

Design and carry out an experiment which will investigate the relationship between the thrust in an open coiled spring and the decrease in its length.

If you carry out these experiments, you should make the following observations:

- Each string or spring returns to its original length once the object is removed, up to a certain limit.
- The graph of tension or thrust against extension for each string or spring is a straight line for all or part of the data.
- The gradient of the linear part of the graph is roughly halved when the string is doubled in length.
- If you keep increasing the weight, the string or spring may stop stretching or may stretch without returning to its original length. In this case, the graph is no longer a straight line: the material has passed its **elastic limit**.
- During your experiment using an open coiled spring you may have found it necessary to prevent the spring from buckling. You may also have found that there comes a point when the coils are completely closed and a further decrease in length is impossible.

Strings or springs which exhibit this linear behaviour are said to be *perfectly elastic*.

Hooke's law

In 1678, Robert Hooke formulated a **rule or law of nature in every springing body** which, for small extensions relative to the length of the string or spring, can be stated as follows:

> The tension in an elastic spring or string is proportional to the extension. If a spring is compressed the thrust is proportional to the decrease in length of the spring.

When a string or spring is described as elastic, it means that it is reasonable to apply the modelling assumption that it obeys Hooke's law. A further assumption, that it is light (i.e. has zero mass), is usual and is made in this book.

There are three ways in which Hooke's law is commonly expressed for a string. Which one you use depends on the extent to which you are interested in the string itself rather than just its overall properties. Denoting the natural length of the string by l_0 and its area of cross-section by A, the different forms are as follows.

- $T = \frac{EA}{l_0}x$ In this form, E is called **Young's modulus** and is a property of the material out of which the string is formed. This form is commonly used in physics and engineering, subjects in which properties of materials are studied. It is rarely used in mathematics. The S.I. unit for Young's modulus is $\mathrm{N\,m^{-2}}$.
- $T = \frac{\lambda}{l_0}x$ The constant λ is called the **modulus of elasticity** of the string and will be the same for any string of a given cross-section made out of the same material. Many situations require knowledge of the natural length of a string and this form may well be the most appropriate in such cases. The S.I. unit for the modulus of elasticity is N.
- $T = kx$ In this simplest form, k is called the **stiffness** of the string. It is a property of the string as a whole. You may choose to use this form if neither the natural length nor the cross-sectional area of the string is relevant to the situation. The S.I. unit for stiffness is $\mathrm{N\,m^{-1}}$.

Notice that $k = \frac{\lambda}{l_0} = \frac{EA}{l_0}$.

In this book, only the form using modulus of elasticity is used, and this can be applied to springs as well as strings.

Example 12.1

A light elastic string of natural length 0.7 m and modulus of elasticity 50 N has one end fixed and a particle of mass 1.4 kg attached to the other. The system hangs vertically in equilibrium. Find the extension of the string.

Solution

The forces acting on the particle are the tension, T N, upwards and the weight, $1.4g$ N, downwards.

Since the particle is in equilibrium

$$T = 1.4g$$

Using Hooke's law: $T = \frac{\lambda}{l_0}x$

$$\Rightarrow \quad 1.4g = \frac{50}{0.7}x$$

$$\Rightarrow \quad x = \frac{0.7 \times 1.4g}{50}$$

$$= 0.192$$

The extension in the string is 0.19 m (to 2 s.f.).

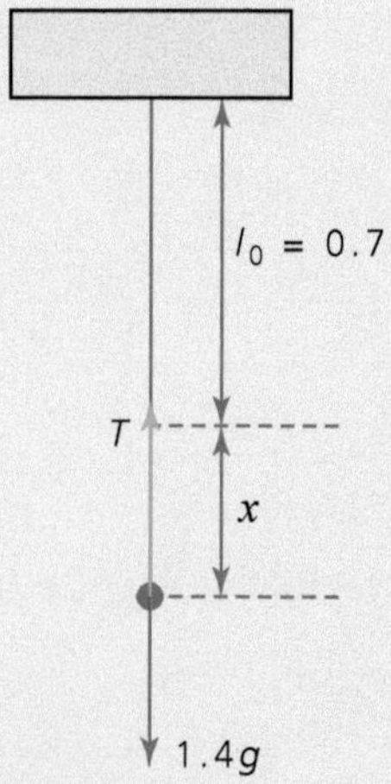

Figure 12.3

Example 12.2

The mechanism of a set of kitchen scales consists of a light scale pan supported on a spring of natural length 8 cm. When measuring 1.5 kg of flour, the spring is compressed by 7 mm. Find

(i) the modulus of elasticity of the spring
(ii) the mass of the heaviest object that can be measured if it is impossible to compress the spring by more than 15 mm.

Solution

(i) The forces on the scale pan with its load of flour are the weight, $1.5g$ N, downwards, and the thrust of the spring, T N, upwards.

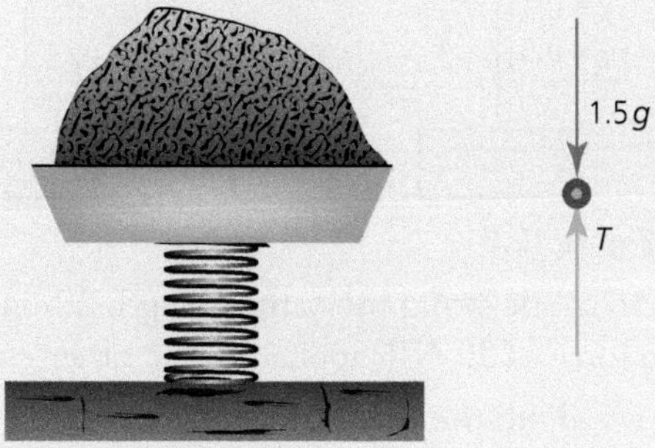

Figure 12.4

Since it is in equilibrium

$$T = 1.5g$$

Applying Hooke's law with modulus of elasticity λN and natural length 0.08 m:

$$T = \frac{\lambda}{0.08} \times 0.007$$

$$1.5g = 0.0875\lambda$$

$$\Rightarrow \quad \lambda = 168$$

The modulus of elasticity of the spring is 168 N.

(ii) Let the mass of the heaviest object be M kg, so the maximum thrust is Mg N. Then Hooke's law for a compression of 15 mm gives:

$$Mg = \frac{168}{0.08} \times 0.015$$

$$\Rightarrow \quad M = 3.214...$$

The mass of the heaviest object that can be measured is 3.21 kg (to 3 s.f.).

Note

These scales would probably be calibrated to a maximum of 3 kg.

Exercise 12.1

① In each of these diagrams in Figure 12.5 an object is suspended by a light elastic string. The top of the string is attached to a fixed ceiling. The object is in equilibrium.

In each diagram, information is provided about the mass of the object and two out of the natural length l_0 m, the length l m and the extension x m.

In each case, find

(a) the tension in the string

(b) the modulus of elasticity of the string.

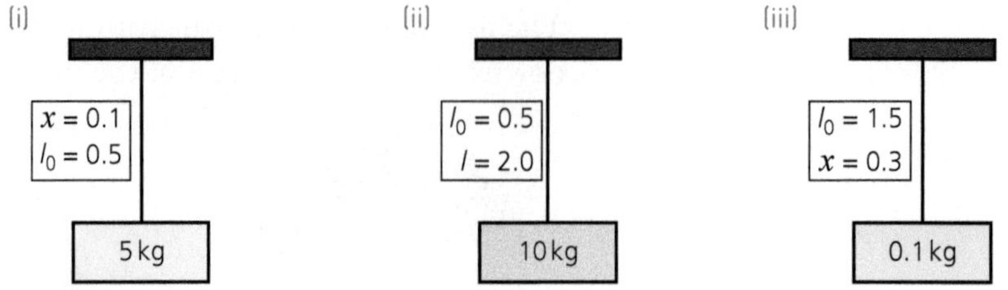

Figure 12.5

② An elastic string has natural length 20 cm. The string is fixed at one end. When a force of 20 N is applied to the other end the string doubles in length.

(i) Find the modulus of elasticity.

Another elastic string also has natural length 20 cm. When a force of 20 N is applied to each end the string doubles in length.

(ii) Find the modulus of elasticity.

(iii) Explain the connection between the answers to parts (i) and (ii).

③ A light elastic spring of modulus of elasticity λ and natural length 1.6 m is attached to a ceiling. A block of mass m kg hangs in equilibrium, attached to the other end of the spring.

(i) Draw a diagram showing the forces acting on the block.

The mass of the block is 0.25 kg and the extension of the spring is 0.4 m.

(ii) Find the value of λ in S.I. units.

④ An object of mass 0.5 kg is attached to an elastic string and causes an extension of 8 cm when the system hangs vertically in equilibrium.

(i) What is the tension in the string?

(ii) What is the mass of an object which causes an extension of 10 cm?

The modulus of elasticity of the string is 73.5 N.

(iii) What is the natural length of the string?

⑤ In this question take the value of g to be $10\,\mathrm{m\,s^{-2}}$. Figure 12.6 shows a spring of natural length 60 cm which is being compressed under the weight of a block of mass m kg. Smooth supports constrain the block to move only in the vertical direction.

The modulus of elasticity of the spring is 180 N. The system is in equilibrium and the length of the spring is 50 cm. Find

(i) the thrust in the spring

(ii) the value of m.

More blocks are piled on.

(iii) Describe the situation when there are seven blocks in total, all identical to the first one.

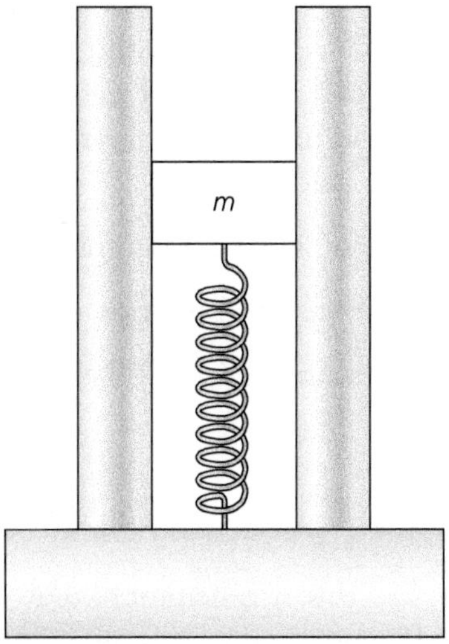

Figure 12.6

⑥ An open coiled spring has natural length 30 cm and modulus of elasticity 80 N.

The spring is fully compressed when its length is 15 cm.

If the spring is extended to twice its natural length it passes its elastic limit and can no longer return to its natural length.

Find the limits of the applied force for which Hooke's law may be used as a model for this spring.

⑦ A light spring has modulus of elasticity 0.75 N. One end is attached to a ceiling, the other to a particle of weight 0.03 N which hangs in equilibrium below the ceiling. In this situation, the length of the spring is 49 cm.

(i) Find the tension in the spring.

(ii) Find the natural length of the spring.

The particle is removed and replaced with one of weight w N. When this hangs in equilibrium the total length of the spring is 63 cm.

(iii) What is the value of w?

⑧ A light spring has modulus of elasticity λ N and natural length l m. One end is attached to a ceiling, the other to a particle of weight w N which hangs in equilibrium below the ceiling. In this situation the total length of the string is L m. When $w = 0.03$, $L = 0.49$, and when $w = 0.06$, $L = 0.53$.

(i) Find the value of l and the value of λ.

(ii) Find the value of w when $L = 0.6$.

2 Using Hooke's law with more than one spring or string

Hooke's law allows you to investigate situations involving two or more springs or strings in various configurations.

Example 12.3

A particle of mass 0.4 kg is attached to the midpoint of a light elastic string of natural length 1 m and modulus of elasticity λ N. The string is then stretched between a point A at the top of a doorway and a point B which is on the floor 2 m vertically below A.

(i) Find, in terms of λ, the extensions of the two parts of the string.

(ii) Calculate their values in the case when $\lambda = 9.8$.

(iii) Find the minimum value of λ that will ensure that the lower half of the string is not slack.

Solution

For a question like this, it is helpful to draw two diagrams, one showing the relevant natural lengths and extensions, and the other showing the forces acting on the particle.

Since the force of gravity acts downwards on the particle, its equilibrium position will be below the midpoint of AB. This is also shown in Figure 12.7.

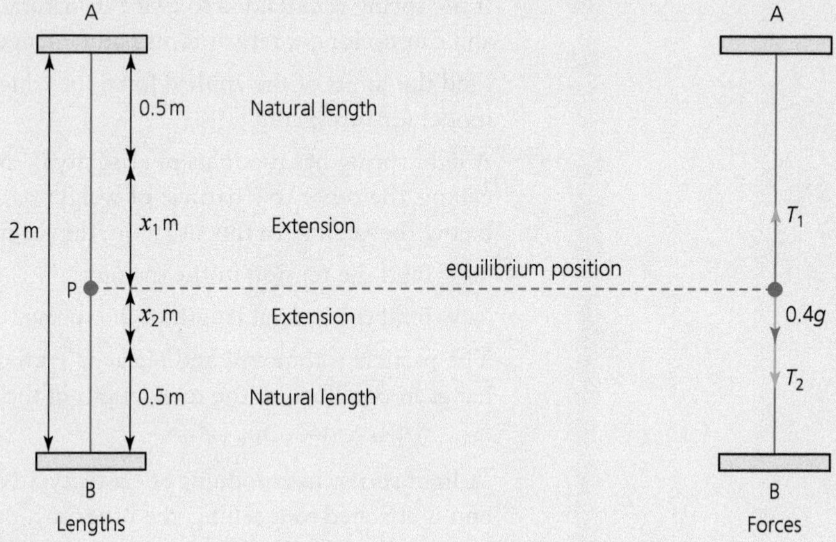

Figure 12.7

(i) The particle is in equilibrium, so the resultant vertical force acting on it is zero.

Therefore $\quad T_1 = T_2 + 0.4g \quad$ ①

Hooke's law can be applied to each part of the string.

For AP: $\quad T_1 = \dfrac{\lambda}{0.5}x_1 \quad$ ②

For BP: $\quad T_2 = \dfrac{\lambda}{0.5}x_2 \quad$ ③

Substituting these expressions in equation ① gives:

$$\frac{\lambda}{0.5}x_1 = \frac{\lambda}{0.5}x_2 + 0.4g$$

$$\Rightarrow \lambda(x_1 - x_2) = 0.5 \times 0.4g$$

$$\Rightarrow x_1 - x_2 = 0.2\frac{g}{\lambda} \quad (4)$$

But from the first diagram in Figure 12.7 it can be seen that:

$$x_1 + x_2 = 1 \quad (5)$$

Adding (4) and (5) gives:

$$2x_1 = 1 + 0.2\frac{g}{\lambda}$$

$$\Rightarrow \quad x_1 = 0.5 + 0.1\frac{g}{\lambda}$$

Similarly subtracting (4) from (5) gives:

$$x_2 = 0.5 - 0.1\frac{g}{\lambda} \quad (6)$$

(ii) Since $\lambda = 9.8$, the extensions are 0.6 m and 0.4 m.

(iii) The lower part of the string will not become slack providing $x_2 > 0$. It follows from equation (6) that:

$$0.5 - 0.1\frac{g}{\lambda} > 0$$

$$\Rightarrow \quad 0.5 > 0.1\frac{g}{\lambda}$$

$$\Rightarrow \quad \lambda > 0.2g$$

The minimum value of λ for which the lower part of the string is not slack is 1.96 N, and in this case BP has zero tension.

Historical note

If you search for Robert Hooke (1635–1703) on the internet, you will find that he was a man of many parts. He was one of a talented group of polymaths (which included his rival Newton) who have had an enormous impact on scientific thought and practice. Among other things, he designed and built Robert Boyle's air pump, discovered the red spot on Jupiter and invented the balanced spring mechanism for watches. His work on microscopy led to his becoming the father of microbiology and he was the first to use the term 'cell' with respect to living things. Hooke worked closely with his friend Sir Christopher Wren in the rebuilding of the City of London after the Great Fire, and was responsible for the realisation of many of his designs including the Royal Greenwich Observatory. Both Hooke and Wren were astronomers and architects and they designed the Monument to the Fire with a trapdoor at the top and a laboratory in the basement so that it could be used as an enormous 62 m telescope. Hooke, the great practical man, also used the column for experiments on air pressure and pendulums.

Exercise 12.2

① Figure 12.8 shows a uniform plank of weight 120 N symmetrically suspended in equilibrium by two identical elastic strings, each of natural length 0.8 m and modulus of elasticity 1200 N.

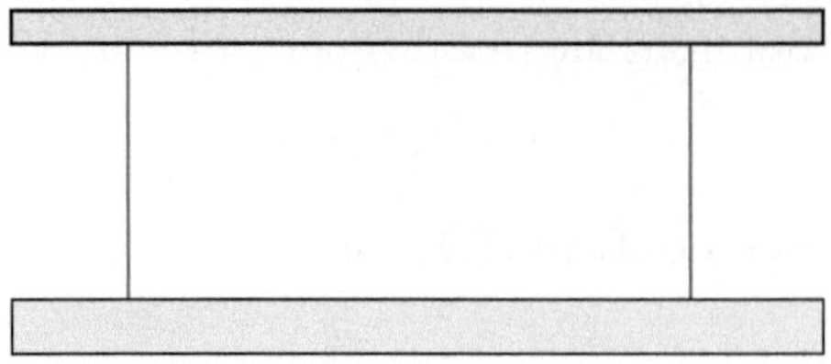

Figure 12.8

Find:

(i) the tension in each string

(ii) the extension of each string.

The two strings are replaced by a single string, also of natural length 0.8 m, attached to the middle of the plank. The plank is in the same position.

(iii) Find the modulus of elasticity of this string and comment on its relationship to that of the original strings.

② The manufacturer of a sports car specifies the coil spring for the front suspension as a spring of 10 coils with a natural length 0.3 m and a compression 0.1 m when under a load of 4000 N.

(i) Calculate the modulus of elasticity of the spring.

(ii) If the spring were cut into two equal parts, what would be the stiffness of each part?

The weight of a car is 8000 N and half of this weight is taken by two such 10-coil front springs so that each bears a load of 2000 N.

(iii) Find the compression of each spring.

(iv) Two people each of weight 800 N get into the front of the car. How much further are the springs compressed? (Assume that their weight is carried equally by the front springs.)

③ The coach of an impoverished rugby club decides to construct a scrummaging machine as illustrated in Figure 12.9. It is to consist of a vertical board, supported in horizontal runners at the top and bottom of each end. The board is held away from the wall by springs, as shown, and the players push the board with their shoulders, against the thrust of the springs.

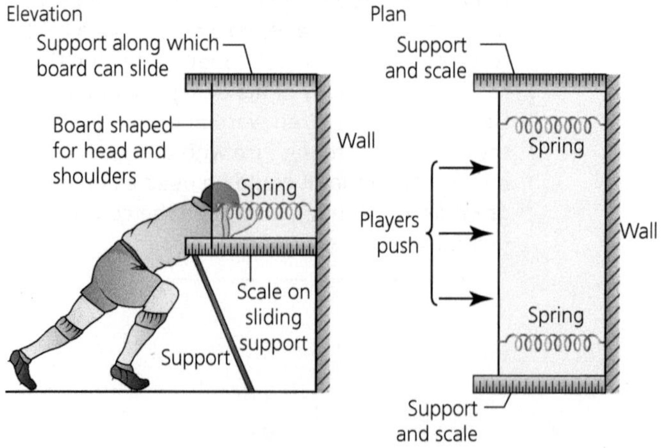

Figure 12.9

The coach has one spring of length 1.4 m and modulus of elasticity 7000 N, which he cuts into two pieces of equal length.

(i) Find the modulus of elasticity of the original spring.

(ii) Find the modulus of elasticity and the stiffness of each of the half-length springs.

(iii) On one occasion, the coach observes that the players compress the springs by 20 cm. What total force do they produce in the forward direction?

④ Figure 12.10 shows the rear view of a load of weight 300 N in the back of a pickup truck of width 2 m.

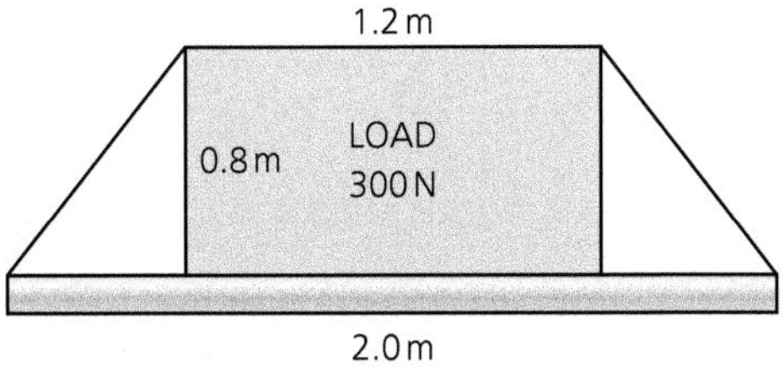

Figure 12.10

The load is 1.2 m wide, 0.8 m high and is situated centrally on the truck. The coefficient of friction between the load and the truck is 0.4. The load is held down by an elastic rope of natural length 2 m and modulus of elasticity 400 N which may be assumed to pass smoothly over the corners and across the top of the load. The rope is secured at the edges of the truck platform.

Find:

(i) the tension in the rope

(ii) the normal contact force of the truck on the load

(iii) the percentage by which the maximum possible frictional force is increased by using the rope

(iv) the shortest stopping distance for which the load does not slide, given that the truck is travelling at $30\,\mathrm{m\,s^{-1}}$ initially. (Assume constant deceleration and use 10 for g.)

⑤ Two springs of modulus of elasticity λ_1 and λ_2 and equal natural length l_0 are connected in series as shown and a force F is applied to each end.

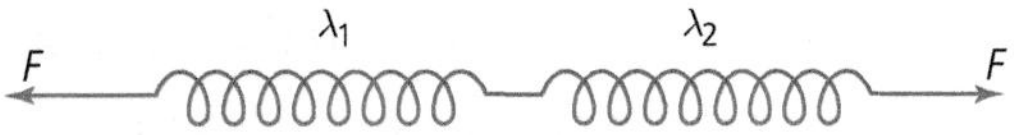

Figure 12.11

(i) Write down the tension in each spring and find expressions for their extensions in terms of F, l_0 and λ_1 or λ_2.

(ii) If these two springs are equivalent to one spring of modulus of elasticity λ and length l_0 show that

$$\frac{1}{\lambda} = \frac{1}{\lambda_1} + \frac{1}{\lambda_2}$$

The two springs are now connected in parallel, and held so that their extensions are equal.

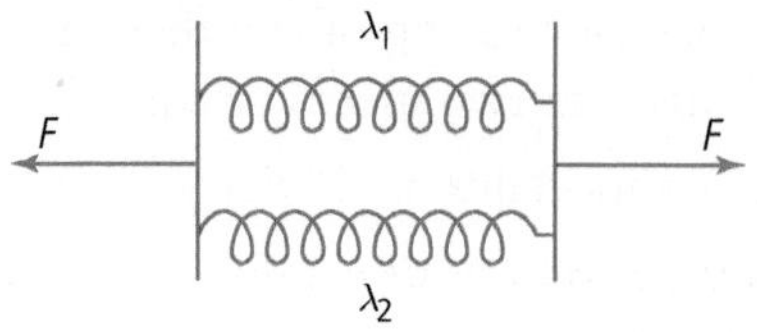

Figure 12.12

(iii) Show that they are now equivalent to a spring of length l_0 and with modulus of elasticity $\lambda_1 + \lambda_2$.

⑥ Figure 12.13 shows two light springs, AP and BP, connected at P. The ends A and B are secured firmly and the system is in equilibrium.

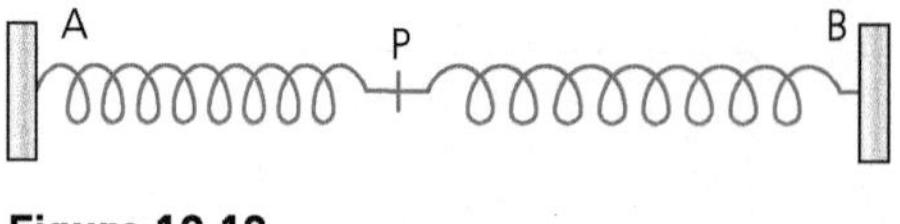

Figure 12.13

The spring AP has natural length 1 m and modulus of elasticity 16 N.

The spring BP has natural length 1.2 m and modulus of elasticity 30 N.

The distance AB is 2.5 m and the extension of the string AP is x m.

(i) Write down an expression, in terms of x, for the extension of the spring BP.

(ii) Find expressions, in terms of x, for the tensions in both springs.

(iii) Find the value of x.

⑦ Figure 12.14 shows two light springs, CQ and DQ, connected to a particle, Q, of weight 20 N. The ends C and D are secured firmly and the system is in equilibrium, lying in a vertical line.

The spring CQ has natural length 0.8 m and modulus of elasticity 16 N; DQ has natural length 1.2 m and modulus of elasticity 36 N. The distance CD is 3 m and QD is h m.

(i) Write down expressions, in terms of h, for the extensions of the two springs.

(ii) Find expressions, in terms of h, for the tensions in the two springs.

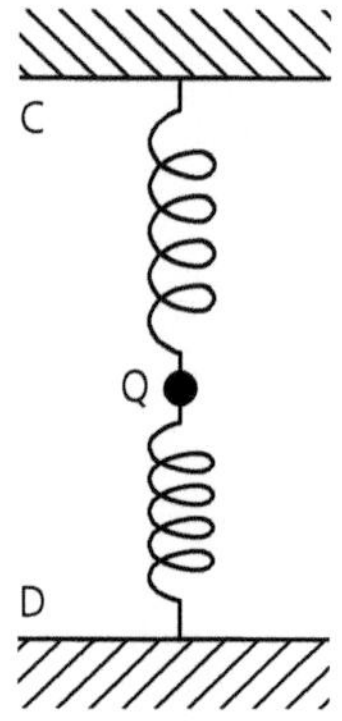

Figure 12.14

(iii) Use these results to find the value of h.

(iv) Find the forces the system exerts at C and at D.

⑧ Figure 12.15 shows a block of wood of mass m lying on a plane inclined at an angle α to the horizontal. The block is attached to a fixed peg by means of a light elastic string of natural length l_0 and modulus of elasticity λ; the string lies parallel to the line of greatest slope. The block is in equilibrium.

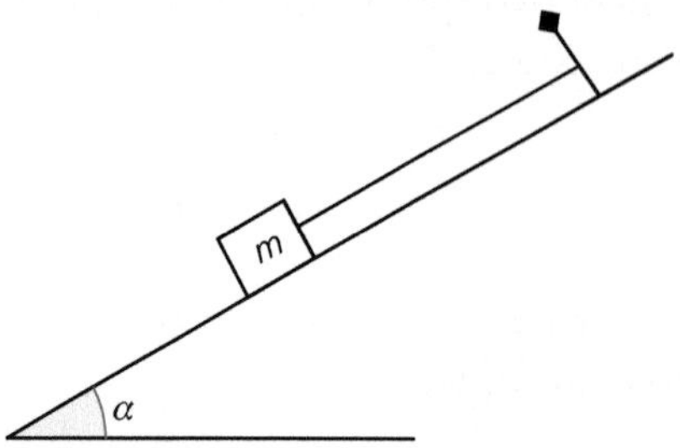

Figure 12.15

Find the extension of the string in the following cases.

(i) The plane is smooth.

(ii) The coefficient of friction between the plane and the block is μ ($\mu \neq 0$) and the block is about to slide (a) up the plane (b) down the plane.

⑨ In this question take g to be $10\,\text{m}\,\text{s}^{-2}$. A baby bouncer consists of a light, inextensible harness attached to a spring. It is suspended in a doorway on the end of a chain so that the baby's feet just touch the floor. The baby can then use its feet to bounce up and down. A harness, with a spring of natural length 20 cm, is set up for Emily (who has mass 10 kg). Before Emily is put into the harness (i.e. when the spring is not extended) the bottom of the harness is 17 cm from the ground. When she sits in the harness with her feet off the ground, the bottom of the harness is 15 cm above the ground.

(i) Find the modulus of elasticity of the spring.

Figure 12.16

The baby bouncer is also used by Charlotte and its height is not adjusted for her. Charlotte's mass is 12 kg (the limit recommended for the bouncer).

(ii) What is the extension of the spring when Charlotte sits in the bouncer with her feet off the ground?

(iii) Find an expression for the reaction R N, between Charlotte's feet and the ground in terms of the height, h cm, of the harness above the ground, assuming her to be in equilibrium at the time.

⑩ A strong elastic band of natural length 1 m and of modulus of elasticity 12 N is stretched round two pegs P and Q which are in a horizontal line a distance 1 m apart (Figure 12.17). A bag of mass 1.5 kg is hooked onto the band at H and hangs in equilibrium so that PH and QH make angles of θ with the horizontal. Make the modelling assumptions that the elastic band is light and runs smoothly over the pegs.

(i) Use Hooke's law to show that the tension in the band is $12\sec\theta$.

(ii) Find the depth of the hook below the horizontal line PQ.

(iii) Is the modelling in this question realistic?

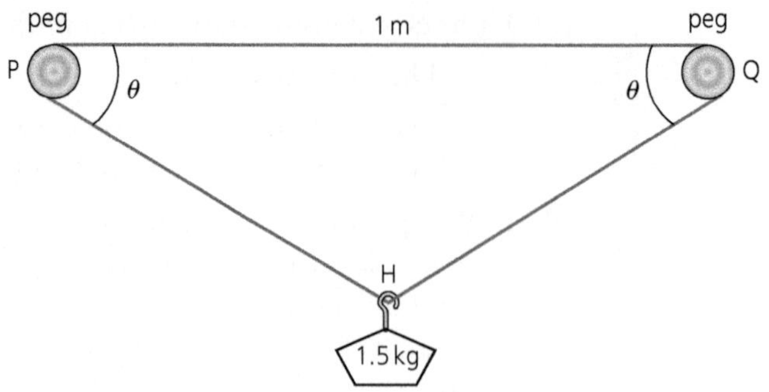

Figure 12.17

⑪ A light spring AB has natural length 0.8 m and modulus of elasticity 200 N. The end A is fixed and a small ball is attached at B. The ball hangs in equilibrium below A.

(i) Given that the length of the spring is 1 m, calculate the mass of the ball.

(ii) If, instead, the mass of the ball is 2 kg, calculate the length of the spring.

The end A of the spring is now fixed to a vertical wall and the end B is fixed to the midpoint of a light rod CD, of length 1.2 m, as shown in Figure 12.18. The end C of the rod is freely hinged to the wall vertically below A and a small ball of mass m kg is attached to the end D of the rod. The rod rests in equilibrium perpendicular to the spring and at an angle of 60° to the upward vertical.

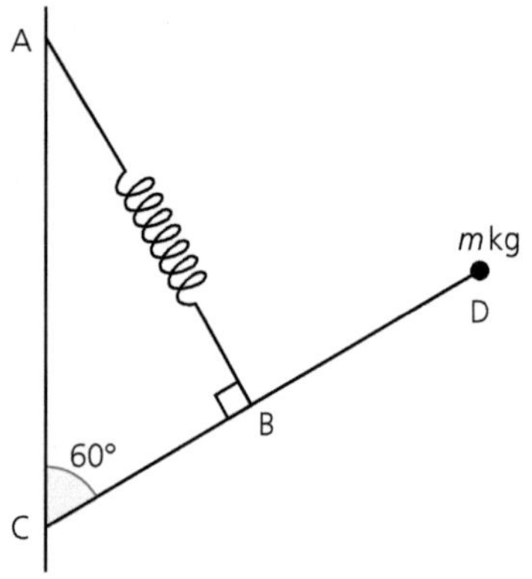

Figure 12.18

(iii) Show that the extension of the spring is 0.239 m (to 3 s.f.) and hence calculate the tension in the spring.

(iv) Calculate m.

The end A is now attached to a different point on the wall. In this position the rod rests horizontally in equilibrium and angle ABC = θ.

(v) Show that $3\tan\theta - 4\sin\theta = 1.37$ (to 3 s.f.).

⑫ Many cafeterias have a device for stacking plates where, for any number of plates in the stack, the top of the top plate is always at the counter level, as shown in Figure 12.19 on the left. This is achieved by standing the plates on a metal base which is supported by a number of springs which hang vertically as, shown in the diagram on the right. The base is shaped so that when there are no plates on the stack, the top of the base is level with the counter.

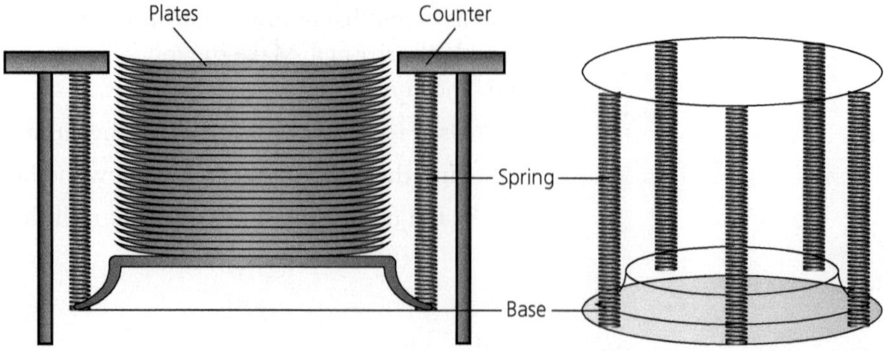

Figure 12.19

The situation may be modelled by assuming that each plate has a mass of 0.1 kg and raises the vertical height of the stack by 1.5 cm when placed on another plate (or the base). The springs have a natural length of 10 cm and a modulus of elasticity of 0.8 N. The springs may be assumed to be light and resistances to motion due to friction may be neglected.

(i) Suppose that n springs are attached.

(a) Show that the extension in each spring when a mass m kg is supported by the system is given by $\frac{mg}{8n}$ m.

(b) What is the further extension of each spring when one plate is added to the stack?

(ii) Show that nine springs are required if the addition of each plate allows the top of the plate to be as near to the counter level as possible but to be above, not below, the counter level.

(iii) Assuming that nine springs are used, approximately how many plates would be above the counter level if there were 40 plates in the stack?

The system can be adjusted so that the top of the plate is at counter level by reducing the natural length of the springs.

(iv) When eight springs are used, what should be the natural length of each spring, correct to three decimal places? [MEI]

⑬ A light elastic string, of natural length l_0, is hung at one end from a fixed point. When a particle of mass m is hung from the other end the string extends a distance d. Show that the modulus of elasticity of the string is $\frac{mgl_0}{d}$.
The particle is removed and attached to the midpoint of the string. The ends of the string are now tied to two points A and B, where B is vertically below A and AB > l_0. In the equilibrium position, the lower part of the string remains taut. Show that the displacement of the particle from the midpoint of AB is $\frac{d}{4}$.

⑭ Blocks A and B are attached to opposite ends of a light elastic string of natural length 2 m and modulus of elasticity 6 N. Block A is at rest on a rough horizontal table. The string passes over a small smooth pulley P at the edge of the table, with the part AP of the string horizontal and of length 1.2 m. The frictional force acting on A is 1.5 N and the system is in equilibrium. Find the distance PB.

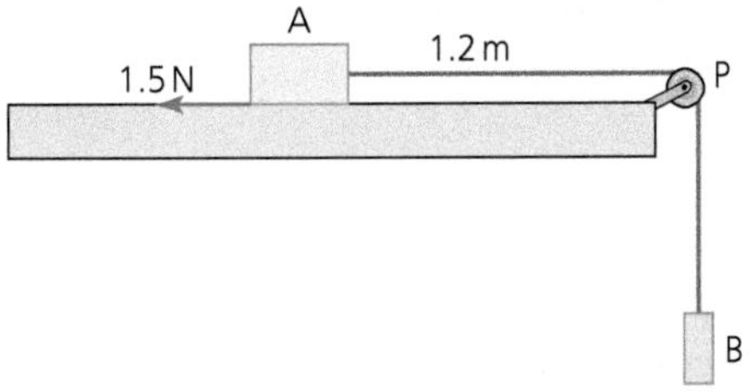

Figure 12.20

Figure 12.21

3 Work and energy

In order to stretch an elastic spring a force must do work on it. In the case of the muscle exerciser in Figure 12.21, this force is provided by the muscles working against the tension.

When the exerciser is pulled at constant speed, at any given time the force F applied at each end is equal to the tension in the spring; consequently, it changes as the spring stretches.

Suppose that one end of the spring is stationary and the extension is x, as in Figure 12.22.

By Hooke's law, the tension is given by:

$$T = \frac{\lambda}{l_0}x \text{ and so } F = \frac{\lambda}{l_0}x$$

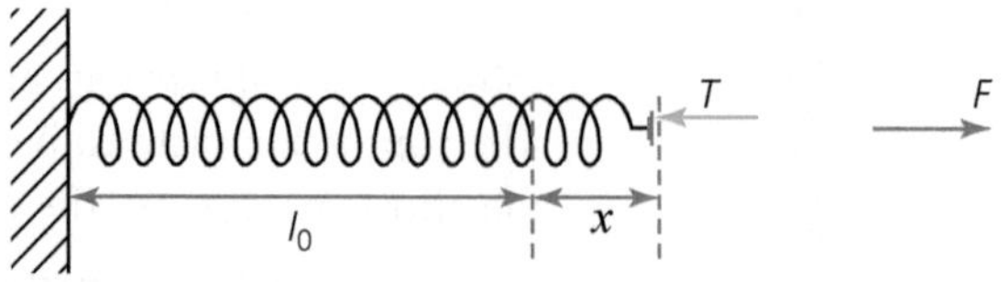

Figure 12.22

The work done by a **constant** force F in moving a distance d in its own direction is given by Fd. To find the work done by a variable force, the process has to be considered in small stages. Now imagine that the force extends the string a small distance δx. The work done is given by $F\delta x = kx\delta x$.

The work done in stretching the spring many small distances is:

$$\Sigma F\delta x = \Sigma kx\delta x$$

In the limit as $\delta x \to 0$, the work done is:

$$\int F\mathrm{d}x = \int \frac{\lambda}{l_0}x\,\mathrm{d}x$$

$$= \frac{\lambda}{2l_0}x^2 + c$$

When the extension $x = 0$, the work done is zero, so $c = 0$.

The total work done in stretching the spring an extension x from its natural length l_0 is therefore given by:

$$\frac{\lambda}{2l_0}x^2$$

The result is the same for the work done in compressing a spring.

> **Note**
>
> Notice that this is different from gravitational potential energy. Potential energy is energy which is available to be converted.

Elastic potential energy

The tensions and thrusts in perfectly elastic springs and strings are conservative forces, since any work done against them can be recovered in the form of kinetic energy. A catapult and a jack-in-a-box use this property.

The work done in stretching or compressing a string or spring can therefore be regarded as potential energy. It is known as **elastic potential energy**.

The elastic potential energy stored in a spring which is stretched or compressed by an amount x is given by:

> The elastic potential energy can also be written as $\frac{1}{2}kx^2$ where k is the stiffness of the string or spring.

$$\frac{1}{2}\frac{\lambda}{l_0}x^2$$

Figure 12.23

Example 12.4

An elastic rope of natural length 0.6 m is extended to a length of 0.8 m. The modulus of elasticity of the rope is 25 N. Find:

(i) the elastic potential energy in the rope

(ii) the further energy required to stretch it to a length of 1.65 m over a car roof-rack.

> **Note**
>
> In Example 12.4, the string is stretched so that its extension changes from x_1 to x_2. The work required to do this is:
>
> $\frac{\lambda}{2l_0}x_2^2 - \frac{\lambda}{2l_0}x_1^2$ or $\frac{\lambda}{2l_0}\left(x_2^2 - x_1^2\right)$.
>
> You can see by using algebra that this expression is *not* the same as $\frac{\lambda}{2l_0}\left(x_2 - x_1\right)^2$, so it is *not* possible to use the extra extension $(x_2 - x_1)$ directly in the energy expression to calculate the extra energy stored in the string.

Solution

(i) The extension of the elastic is (0.8 – 0.6) = 0.2 m.

The energy stored in the rope is $\frac{1}{2}\frac{\lambda}{l_0}x^2$

$= \frac{25}{2 \times 0.6} 0.2^2$

$= 0.83\text{J}$ (to 2 d.p.)

(ii) The extension of the elastic rope is now 1.65 – 0.6 = 1.05 m.

The elastic energy stored in the rope is $\frac{25}{2 \times 0.6} 1.05^2$

$= 22.97\text{J}$

The extra energy required to stretch the rope is 22.14 J (correct to 2 d.p.).

Example 12.5

A catapult has prongs which are 16 cm apart; the elastic string is 20 cm long. A marble of mass 70 g is placed in the centre of the elastic string and pulled back so that the string is just taut. The marble is then pulled back a further 9 cm and the force required to keep it in this position is 60 N. Find:

(i) the stretched length of the string

(ii) the tension in the string and its modulus of elasticity

(iii) the elastic potential energy stored in the string and the speed of the marble when the string regains its natural length, assuming they remain in contact.

Solution

> A and B are the ends of the elastic string and M_1 and M_2 are the two positions of the marble (before and after the string is stretched). D is the midpoint of AB.

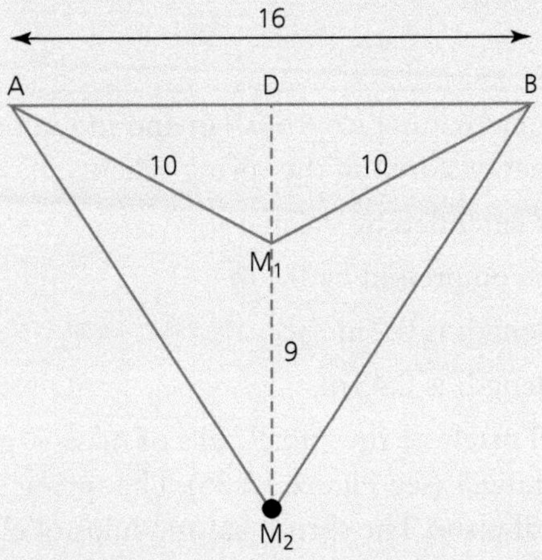

Figure 12.24

Note

You need to make these modelling assumptions.
- There is no elasticity in the frame of the catapult.
- The motion takes place in a horizontal plane.
- Air resistance is negligible.

(i) Using Pythagoras' theorem in triangle DBM_1 gives

$$DM_1 = \sqrt{10^2 - 8^2} = 6\,\text{cm}.$$

So

$$DM_2 = 9 + 6 = 15\,\text{cm}.$$

Using Pythagoras' theorem in triangle DBM_2 gives

$$BM_2 = \sqrt{15^2 + 8^2} = 17\,\text{cm}$$

The stretched length of the string is $2 \times 17 = 34$ cm.

(ii) Take the tension in the string to be T N.

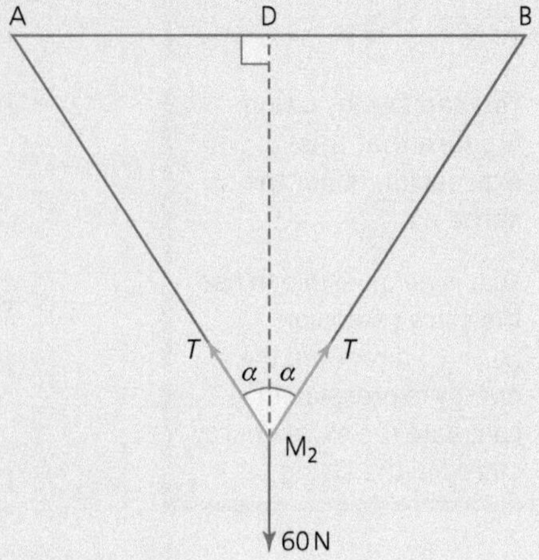

Figure 12.25

Resolving parallel to M_2D:

$$2T\cos\alpha = 60$$

Now $\cos\alpha = \dfrac{DM_2}{BM_2} = \dfrac{0.15}{0.17}$

So $T = \dfrac{60 \times 0.17}{2 \times 0.15} = 34$

The extension of the string is $(0.34 - 0.2) = 0.14$ m.

By Hooke's law the modulus of elasticity is given by $\lambda = \dfrac{Tl_0}{x}$.

$$\lambda = \frac{34 \times 0.2}{0.14} = 48.57\ldots$$

The modulus of elasticity is 49 N (to 2 s.f.).

(iii) The elastic potential energy stored in the string is:

$$\frac{\lambda}{2l_0}x^2 = \frac{48.57\ldots}{2 \times 0.2} \times 0.14^2 = 2.38\text{ J}$$

By the principle of conservation of energy, this is equal to the kinetic energy given to the marble. The mass of the marble is 0.07 kg, so

$$\tfrac{1}{2} \times 0.07v^2 = 2.38$$

$$\Rightarrow v = 8.246\ \ldots$$

The speed of the marble is 8.25 m s^{-1}.

Exercise 12.3

① A spring has natural length 0.4 m and modulus of elasticity 20 N. Find the elastic energy stored in the spring when:

(i) it is extended by 0.4 m

(ii) it is compressed by 0.1 m

(iii) its length is 0.2 m

(iv) its length is 0.45 m.

② A pinball machine fires small balls of mass 50 g by means of a spring and a light plunger (see Figure 12.26). The spring and the ball move in a horizontal plane. The spring has modulus of elasticity 72 N and natural length 12 cm and is compressed by 5 cm to fire a ball.

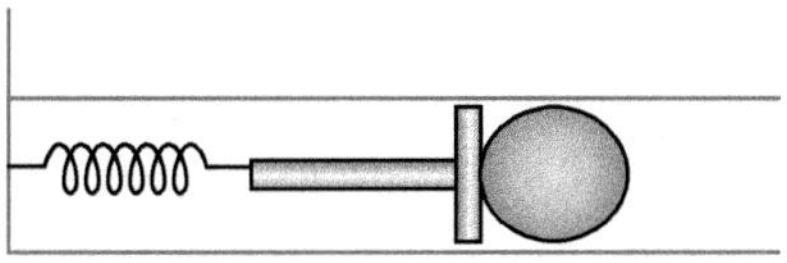

Figure 12.26

(i) Find the energy stored in the spring immediately before the ball is fired.

(ii) Find the speed of the ball when it is fired.

③ A catapult is made from elastic string with modulus of elasticity 5 N. The string is attached to two prongs which are 15 cm apart, and is just taut. A pebble of mass 40 g is placed in the centre of the string and is pulled back 4 cm and then released in a horizontal direction.

Figure 12.27

(i) Calculate the work done in stretching the string.

(ii) Calculate the speed of the pebble on leaving the catapult.

④ A simple mathematical model of a railway buffer consists of a horizontal open coiled spring attached to a fixed point. The modulus of elasticity of the spring is 2×10^5 N and its natural length is 2 m.

The buffer is designed to stop a railway truck before the spring is compressed to half its natural length, otherwise the truck will be damaged.

Figure 12.28

(i) Find the elastic energy stored in the spring when it is half its natural length.

(ii) Find the maximum speed at which a truck of mass 2 tonnes can approach the buffer safely. Neglect any other reasons for loss of energy of the truck.

A truck of mass 2 tonnes approaches the buffer at 5 m s^{-1}.

(iii) Calculate the minimum length of the spring during the subsequent period of contact.

(iv) Find the thrust in the spring and the acceleration of the truck when the spring is at its minimum length.

(v) What happens next?

⑤ Two identical springs are attached to a sphere of mass 0.5 kg that rests on a smooth horizontal surface, as shown. The other ends of the springs are attached to fixed points A and B.

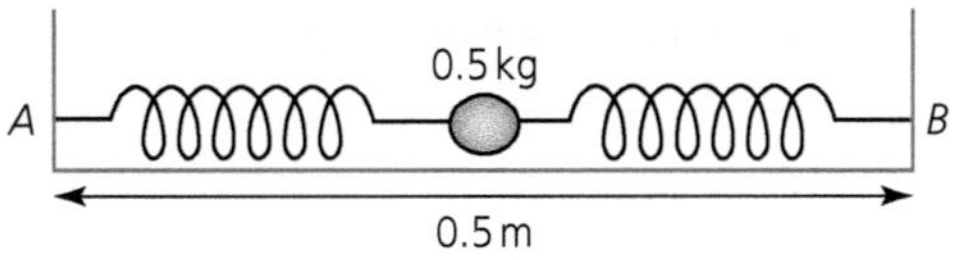

Figure 12.29

The springs each have modulus of elasticity 7.5 N and natural length 25 cm. The sphere is at rest at the midpoint when it is projected with speed $2\,m\,s^{-1}$ along the line of the springs towards B. Calculate the length of each spring when the sphere first comes to rest.

⑥ Two light springs are joined and stretched between two fixed points A and C which are 2 m apart, as shown in Figure 12.30. The spring AB has natural length 0.5 m and modulus of elasticity 10 N. The spring BC has natural length 0.6 m and modulus of elasticity 6 N. The system is in equilibrium.

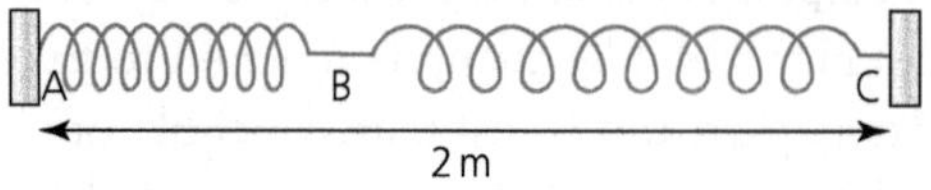

Figure 12.30

(i) Explain why the tensions in the two springs are the same.

(ii) Find the distance AB and the tension in each spring

(iii) How much work must be done to stretch the springs from their natural length to connect them as described above?

A small object of mass 0.012 kg is attached at B and is supported on a smooth horizontal table. A, B and C lie in a straight horizontal line and the mass is released from rest at the midpoint of AC.

(iv) What is the speed of the mass when it passes through the equilibrium position of the system? [MEI]

⑦

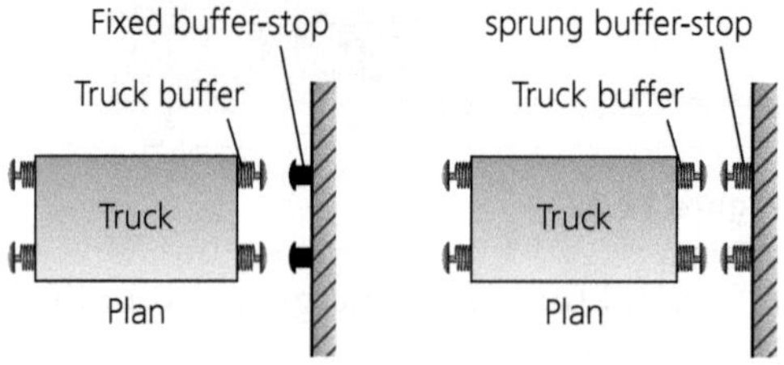

Figure 12.31

A railway truck of mass 4.5 tonnes, travelling with a speed of $0.5\,m\,s^{-1}$, collides with a **fixed** buffer-stop, as indicated in Figure 12.31.

The truck itself has, at each end, two buffers of negligible mass, each of which may be modelled as a spring of modulus of elasticity 10 000 N and natural length 40 cm. The truck comes momentarily to rest with the buffers compressed by a distance x cm and you may neglect the work done against any forces other than those in the buffers.

(i) Calculate the kinetic energy of the truck immediately before the impact.

(ii) Calculate the value of x.

The truck's buffers are designed to be compressed by 24 cm.

(iii) Calculate the greatest speed of the truck if it can be brought momentarily to rest by compression of the buffers.

On another occasion the same truck is travelling at $0.8\,m\,s^{-1}$ when it collides with a **sprung** buffer-stop, as indicated in the diagram on the right in Figure 12.31. The sprung buffer-stop has two buffers, each of which makes contact with a buffer on the truck. Each buffer on the buffer-stop has negligible mass and may be modelled by a spring of modulus of elasticity

10 000 N and natural length 50 cm. The truck is brought momentarily to rest when its buffers are compressed by a distance x_1 m and those of the stop by a distance x_2 m. You may assume that the forces of compression in each spring are equal in magnitude when the truck comes momentarily to rest.

(iv) Write down two equations involving x_1 and x_2 and hence determine their values.

⑧ One end of a light elastic string, of natural length 0.75 m and modulus of elasticity 44.1 N, is attached to a fixed point O. A particle P of mass 1.8 kg is attached to the other end of the string. P is released from rest at O and falls vertically. Assuming there is no air resistance, find

(i) the extension of the string when P is at its lowest position,

(ii) the acceleration of P at its lowest position.

⑨ The end A of a light elastic string AB is fixed to a smooth horizontal table. A small bead of mass 0.05 kg is attached to the end B. Also attached to the end B is another light elastic string BC. The end C is fixed to a point on the table so that the strings lie in a horizontal straight line with the bead resting in equilibrium on the table and with AC equal to 2.3 metres as shown in Figure 12.32.

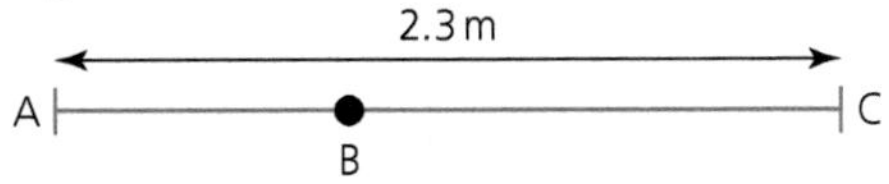

Figure 12.32

The string AB has natural length 0.4 m and modulus of elasticity 4 N. The string BC has natural length 0.5 m and modulus of elasticity 2 N.

(i) The extension in AB is x_1 m and the extension in BC is x_2 m. Show that $5x_1 = 2x_2$ and calculate x_1 and x_2.

The bead is held at A and released.

(ii) Determine whether the string BC goes slack.

(iii) Calculate the maximum extension of the string AB. [MEI]

4 Vertical motion involving elastic forces

There are two common approaches to the analysis of motion involving elastic strings and springs: using energy and using calculus. Both are covered in this section in the context of vertical motion.

Using energy

Example 12.6

A particle of mass m is attached to one end, A, of a light elastic string with natural length l_0 and modulus of elasticity λ. The other end of the string is attached to a fixed point O. The particle is released from O.

Initially it falls freely with the string slack but after some time it reaches a point P and the string becomes taut and exerts an upward force on the particle. At P, the particle has velocity u downwards. Air resistance is negligible.

(i) Draw a diagram illustrating the situation.

(ii) Find an expression for u at the instant when the string becomes taut.

(iii) Write down the energy equation of the system at a time when the extension of the string is x m and its velocity vertically downwards is v.

(iv) Obtain an equation for the value of x when the particle is at its lowest point.

Solution

(i)

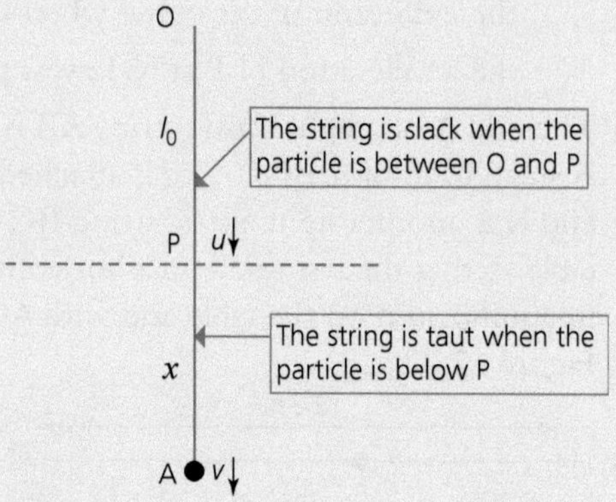

Figure 12.33

(ii) Between O and P the particle loses gravitational potential energy mgl_0 and gains kinetic energy $\frac{1}{2}mu^2$.

Using the law of conservation of energy, $\frac{1}{2}mu^2 = mgl_0$

$$\Rightarrow u = \sqrt{2gl_0}$$

(iii) When the particle has travelled a distance x m below P

Gravitational potential energy lost $= mgx$

Elastic potential energy stored in the string $= \frac{\lambda}{2l_0}x^2$

Kinetic energy gained $= \frac{1}{2}mv^2 - \frac{1}{2}mu^2$

Using conservation of energy:

$$\frac{1}{2}mv^2 - \frac{1}{2}mu^2 + \frac{\lambda}{2l_0}x^2 = mgx$$

(iv) At the lowest point, the particle is stationary so $v = 0$

$$\Rightarrow \quad \frac{\lambda}{2l_0}x^2 - mgx - \frac{1}{2}mu^2 = 0$$

and since $\frac{1}{2}mu^2 = mgl_0$, this equation can be written as:

$$\frac{\lambda}{2l_0}x^2 - mgx - mgl_0 = 0$$

Note

Notice that no units are given in this example. In such cases, you can assume that a consistent set of units is being applied to all the quantities.

Note

Notice that this is a quadratic equation and so will have two roots. One value is at the bottom of the particle's motion. The other would be at the top, but by then the string will have gone slack and so the model used in this example would no longer apply.

Using calculus

You can sometimes acquire more detailed information about the motion of an object by using calculus. The starting point is Newton's second law. This involves the acceleration of the body and there are three ways in which acceleration can be written.

- $\frac{dv}{dt}$ relates the velocity to the time taken.
- $v\frac{dv}{ds}$ relates the velocity to the distance travelled. (It is often written as $v\frac{dv}{dx}$.)
- $\frac{d^2x}{dt^2}$ gives rise to a second-order differential equation involving derivatives of x. It is not covered in this chapter but its use for simple harmonic motion is explained in the Further Pure Mathematics book.

The next example involves the first two of these forms. It involves exactly the same situation as the previous example but the approaches are different.

Example 12.7

A particle of mass m is attached to one end, A, of a light elastic string with natural length l_0 and modulus of elasticity λ. The other end of the string is attached to a fixed point O. The particle is released from O. Initially it falls freely with the string slack but after some time it reaches a point P and the string becomes taut and exerts an upward force on the particle. At P, the particle has velocity u downwards. Air resistance is negligible.

(i) Write down the equation of motion for the particle when the string is taut using $v\frac{dv}{dx}$ for the acceleration.

(ii) Solve this differential equation to find v in terms of x and interpret the solution.

(iii) Write the equation of motion for the particle when the string is taut using $\frac{dv}{dt}$ for the acceleration and comment on whether this is useful.

Solution

(i) Figure 12.34 shows the forces on the particle.

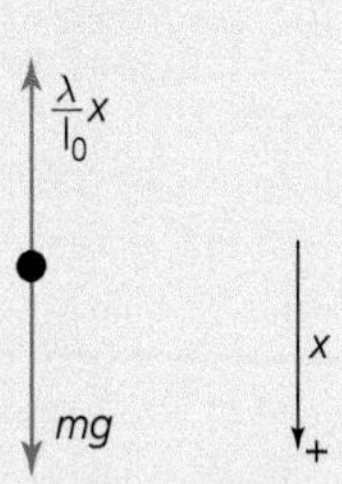

Figure 12.34

The equation of motion is $mg - \frac{\lambda}{l_0}x = ma$

or

$$v\frac{dv}{dx} = g - \frac{\lambda}{l_0 m}x$$

(ii) Separating variables gives $\int v\,dv = \int\left(g - \frac{\lambda}{l_0 m}x\right)dx$

and so $\frac{1}{2}v^2 = gx - \frac{\lambda}{2l_0 m}x^2 + c$

When $x = 0$, $v = u$, so $c = \frac{1}{2}u^2$

These are the boundary conditions. In this case, they are also the initial conditions and the solution is: $\frac{1}{2}v^2 = gx - \frac{\lambda}{2l_0 m}x^2 + \frac{1}{2}u^2$.

You can interpret this two in ways.

It gives an equation for v in terms of x, $v = \pm\sqrt{u^2 + 2gx - \frac{\lambda}{l_0 m}x^2}$ or

$v = \pm\sqrt{2g(l_0 + x) - \frac{\lambda}{l_0 m}x^2}$ ← Replacing u^2 by $2gl_0$

With a little rearrangement, it becomes the energy equation

$\frac{1}{2}mv^2 - \frac{1}{2}mu^2 + \frac{\lambda}{2l_0}x^2 = mgx$

(iii) The equation of motion can also be written as $\frac{dv}{dt} = g - \frac{\lambda}{l_0 m}x$.

This is not a useful form as it involves 3 variables, v, t and x, and so you cannot solve the differential equation.

ACTIVITY 12.1

The bungee jump

Figure 12.35

You may have noticed that the situation in the last two examples could be used to match the bungee jump described at the start of this chapter.

Typical parameters for a mobile crane bungee jump of the type usually done in Britain are:

Height of jump station: 55 m

Bottom safety space: 5 m

Static line length: 5 m (non-elastic straps etc.)

Unstretched elastic rope length: 12 m

Modulus of elasticity: 960 N

(i) Use these figures to decide on the right length of rope for a jumper. Does it depend on the person's mass?

(ii) Calculate the maximum deceleration of a jumper.

Exercise 12.4

① A particle of mass 0.2 kg is attached to one end of a light elastic spring of modulus of elasticity 0.8 N and natural length 0.08 m. The system hangs vertically and the particle is released from rest when the spring is at its natural length. The particle comes to rest when it has fallen a distance h m.

(i) Write down an expression in terms of h for the energy stored in the spring when the particle comes to rest at its lowest point.

(ii) Write down an expression in terms of h for the gravitational potential energy lost by the particle when it comes to rest at its lowest point.

(iii) Find the value of h.

② A particle of mass m is attached to one end of a light vertical spring of natural length l_0 and modulus of elasticity $2mg$. The particle is released from rest when the spring is at its natural length. Find, in terms of l_0, the maximum length of the spring in the subsequent motion.

③ A block of mass m is placed on a smooth plane inclined at 30° to the horizontal. The block is attached to the top of the plane by a spring of natural length l_0 and modulus of elasticity λ. The system is released from rest with the spring at its natural length. Find an expression for the maximum length of the spring in the subsequent motion.

④ A particle of mass 0.1 kg is attached to one end of a spring of natural length 0.3 m and modulus of elasticity 20 N. The other end is attached to a fixed point and the system hangs vertically. The particle is released from rest when the length of the spring is 0.2 m. In the subsequent motion the extension of the spring is denoted by x m.

(i) Show that $0.05\dot{x}^2+\frac{10}{0.3}(x^2-0.1^2)-0.98(x+0.1)=0$.

(ii) Find the maximum value of x.

⑤ A small apple of mass 0.1 kg is attached to one end of an elastic string of natural length 25 cm and modulus of elasticity 5 N. David is asleep under a tree and Sam fixes the free end of the string to the branch of the tree just above David's head. Sam releases the apple level with the branch and it just touches David's head in the subsequent motion. How high above his head is the branch?

⑥ A block of mass 0.5 kg lies on a light scale pan which is supported on a vertical spring of natural length 0.4 m and modulus of elasticity 40 N. Initially the spring is at its natural length and the block is moving downwards with a speed of $2\,\mathrm{m\,s^{-1}}$. Gravitational potential energy is measured relative to the initial position and g should be taken to be $10\,\mathrm{m\,s^{-2}}$.

(i) Find the initial mechanical energy of the system.

(ii) Show that the speed $v\,\mathrm{m\,s^{-1}}$ of the block when the compression of the spring is x m is given by $v=2\sqrt{1+5x-50x^2}$.

(iii) Find the minimum length of the spring during the oscillations.

⑦ A scale pan of mass 0.5 kg is suspended from a fixed point by a spring of modulus of elasticity 50 N and natural length 10 cm.

(i) Calculate the length of the spring when the scale pan is in equilibrium.

(ii) A bag of sugar of mass 1 kg is gently placed on the pan and the system is released from rest. Find the maximum length of the spring in the subsequent motion.

⑧ A bungee jump is carried out by a person of mass m kg using an elastic rope which can be taken to obey Hooke's law. The supervisor ensures that in any jump the total length of the rope will never exceed the limit of four times its original length. Prove that the tension in the rope is at most $\frac{8}{3}mg$ N.

⑨ A conical pendulum consists of a bob of mass m attached to an inextensible string of length l. The bob describes a circle of radius r with angular speed ω, and the string makes an angle θ with the vertical, as shown.

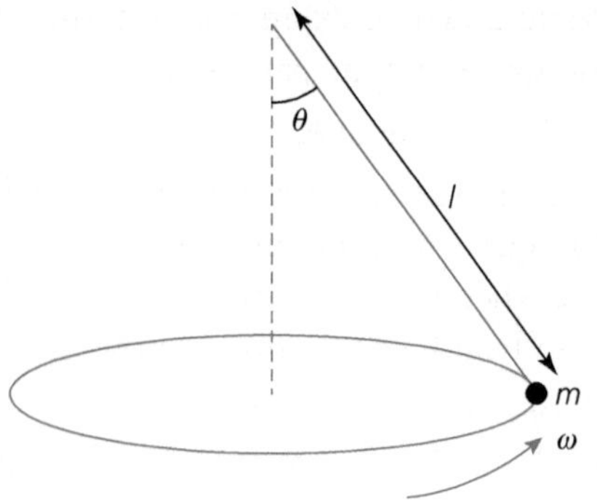

Figure 12.36

(i) Find an expression for θ in terms of ω, l and g.

The string is replaced with an elastic string of modulus of elasticity λ and natural length l_0.

(ii) Find an expression for the new value of θ in terms of ω, m, g, l_0 and λ.

⑩ A light, elastic string has natural length 0.5 m and modulus of elasticity 49 N. The end A is attached to a point on a ceiling. A small object of mass 3 kg is attached to the end B of the string and hangs in equilibrium.

(i) Calculate the length AB.

A second string, identical to the first one, is now attached to the object at B and to a point C on the floor, 2.5 m vertically below the point A. The system is in equilibrium with B a distance x m below A, as shown in Figure 12.37.

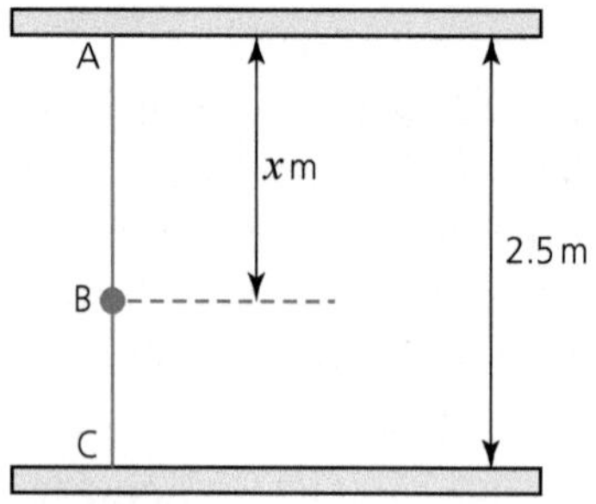

Figure 12.37

(ii) Find the tension in each of the strings in terms of x and hence show that $x = 1.4$.

(iii) Calculate the total elastic potential energy in the strings when the object hangs in equilibrium.

The object is now pulled down 0.1 m from its equilibrium position and released from rest.

(iv) Calculate the speed of the object when it passes through the equilibrium position. Any resistances to motion may be neglected. [MEI]

⑪ A light elastic string AB has modulus of elasticity λ and natural length l_0. The end A of the string is fixed to a vertical wall, and the end B to a block of mass M which is supported by a smooth horizontal plane. To the other side of the block is attached an inelastic light string which passes over a smooth pulley and is then tied to a particle of mass m at C which hangs freely at all times. The block is initially held against the wall and then is moved gently towards the pulley until it is in equilibrium. The elastic string and the part of the other string between the block and the pulley are horizontal, as shown in Figure 12.38.

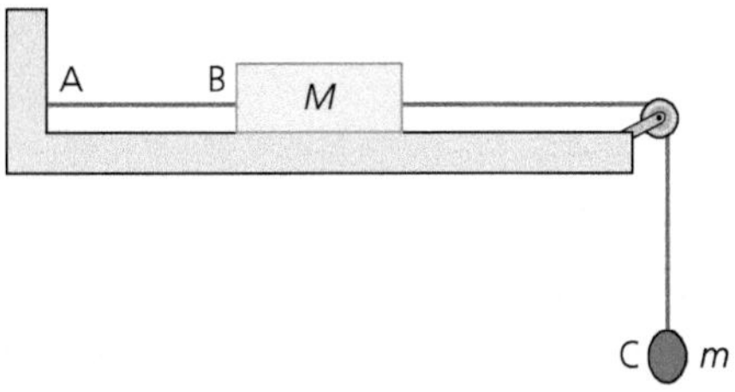

Figure 12.38

Find expressions for the following in terms of some or all of m, g, λ and l_0.

(i) The extension in the elastic string.

(ii) The potential energy lost by the hanging mass as the system is moved to its equilibrium position.

(iii) The energy stored in the elastic string.

(iv) Compare your answers to part (ii) and (iii). Why is energy not conserved?

(v) If the string supporting the hanging mass breaks when the system is in equilibrium, show that the block will hit the wall with a speed v given by $v^2 = \dfrac{m^2g^2l_0}{M\lambda}$. Find also an expression for the acceleration of the block immediately after the string breaks.

(vi) Show that the quantities v^2 and $\dfrac{m^2g^2l_0}{M\lambda}$ have the same dimensions. [MEI]

⑫ A man unloading 25 kg sacks drops each one 2 m, from rest, onto a light horizontal springboard which breaks the fall. The spring supporting the board is initially 50 cm long and compresses down to a minimum length of 15 cm under the impact of each falling sack, which is then removed by another man. Assuming that there is no energy loss on impact,

(i) show that the potential energy lost by the sack when it reaches its lowest point is about 576 J

(ii) show that the modulus of elasticity of the spring is 4700 N

(iii) find the maximum deceleration experienced by the falling sack. [MEI]

⑬ A light elastic string has one end fastened to a fixed point O and it hangs freely with a particle of mass m attached to the other end. In equilibrium, the length of the string is $\frac{5l}{3}$ where l is the natural length of the string. If the particle is raised to the point O and allowed to fall, show that the greatest length of string subsequently is $3l$. Find also the speed of the particle when it is passing through the equilibrium position.

⑭ A light elastic string of natural length 3.6 m and modulus of elasticity λ N has its ends attached to two points A and B, where AB = 3.6 m and AB is horizontal. A particle P of mass 0.5 kg is attached to the midpoint of the string. P rests in equilibrium at a distance of 0.75 m below the line AB, as shown in Figure 12.39.

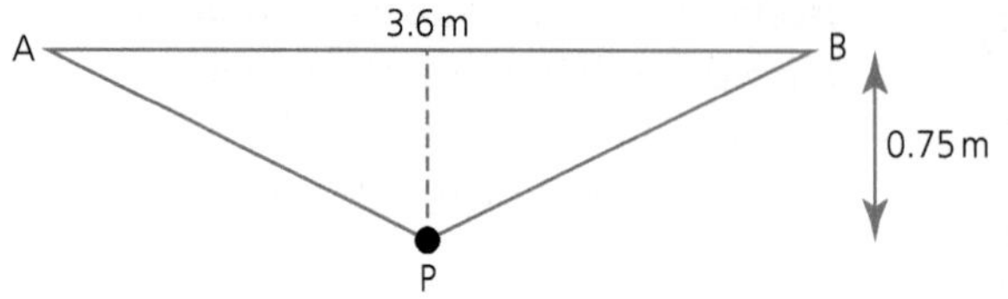

Figure 12.39

(i) Show that $\lambda = 76.44$ N.

The particle is pulled downwards from its equilibrium position until the total length of the elastic string is 6 m. The particle is released from rest.

(ii) Find the speed of P when it passes the line AB.

KEY POINTS

1 **Hooke's law**

The tension T in an elastic string or spring and its extension x are related by:

$$T = \frac{\lambda}{l_0} x$$

where λ is the modulus of elasticity and l_0 is the natural length of the string or spring.

2 When a spring is compressed, x is negative and the tension becomes a thrust.

3 **Elastic potential energy**

The elastic potential energy (E.P.E.) stored in a stretched spring or string, or in a compressed spring, is given by:

$$\text{E.P.E.} = \frac{1}{2}\frac{\lambda}{l_0} x^2$$

4 The tension or thrust in an elastic string or spring is a conservative force and so the elastic potential energy is recoverable.

5 When no frictional or other dissipative forces are involved, elastic potential energy can be used with kinetic energy and gravitational potential energy to form equations using the principle of conservation of energy.

LEARNING OUTCOMES

When you have completed this chapter, you should be able to

- understand the language associated with elasticity
- apply Hooke's law to strings and springs
- calculate stiffness and modulus of elasticity
- find the tension in a string or spring and the thrust in a spring
- find the equilibrium position of a system involving strings or springs
- calculate the energy stored in a string or spring
- use energy to model a system involving elastic strings or springs including determining extreme positions
- understand when Hooke's law is not applicable.

13 Centre of mass 2

Thou comest in such a questionable shape.

Hamlet, *William Shakespeare*

What do the shapes of the objects have in common? For each one, suggest a way of finding its volume.

How would you find the volume of:

- → an egg?
- → a table tennis ball?
- → the Moon?

1 Calculating volumes

One way of finding the volume of an irregular shape is to immerse it in water and measure the apparent increase in the volume of the water. This method is satisfactory for finding the volume of something small and dense like an egg, but you would find it difficult to use for a table tennis ball, and it would be impossible to find the volume of the Moon in this way.

You will be familiar with the formula $V = \frac{4}{3}\pi r^3$ for the volume of a sphere. The methods you meet in this chapter will enable you to prove this formula, and to calculate the volumes and the positions of the centre of mass of other solid shapes with **rotational symmetry** like those illustrated at the start of this chapter.

Volumes of revolution

If a set square (without a hole) is rotated through 360° about one of its shorter sides, its face will sweep out a solid cone (Figure 13.1(a)). A 60° set square will sweep out different cones depending on the side chosen. In the same way, a semicircular protractor will sweep out a sphere if it is rotated completely about its diameter as shown in Figure 13.1(b).

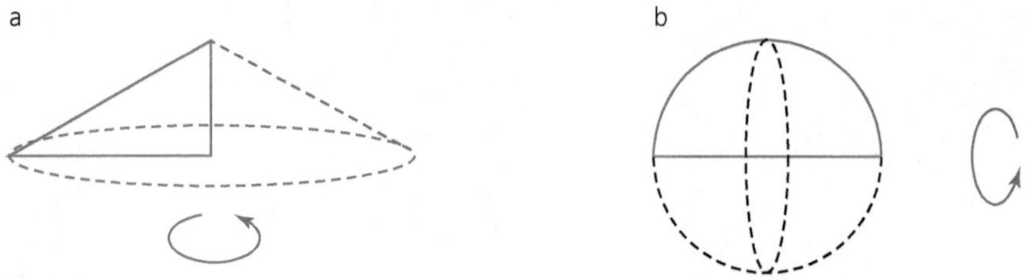

Figure 13.1

The cone and sphere are examples of **solids of revolution**. If any region of a plane is rotated completely about an axis in the plane, it will form a solid of revolution and any solid body with rotational symmetry can be formed in this way.

Imagine that such a solid is cut into thin slices perpendicular to the axis of rotation, just as a salami is sliced to make a pizza topping (Figure 13.2). Each slice will approximate to a thin disc, but the discs will vary in radius. The volume of the solid can be found by adding the volumes of these discs and then finding the limit of the volume as their thickness approaches zero. When thin discs are used to find a volume they are called elementary discs. (Similarly, when thin strips are used to find an area they are called elementary strips.)

Figure 13.2

Note

Thin slices are approximately cylindrical.

This is essentially the same procedure as that developed for finding the area under a curve, and so, as then, integration is required.

Volumes of revolution about the x-axis

Look at the solid formed by the rotation about the x-axis of the region under the graph of $y = f(x)$ between the values $x = a$ and $x = b$, as shown in Figure 13.3. (You should always start by drawing diagrams when finding areas and volumes.)

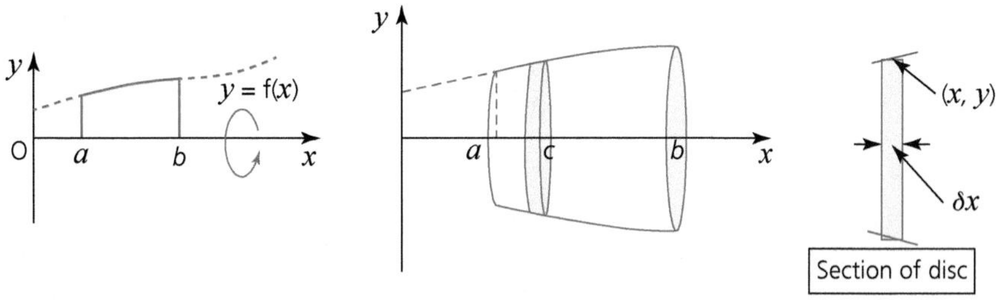

Figure 13.3

The volume of the solid of revolution (which is usually called the volume of revolution) can be found by imagining that it can be sliced into thin discs.

Each disc is a thin cylinder of radius y and thickness δx, so its volume is given by:

$$\delta V = \pi y^2 \delta x$$

The volume of the solid is the limit of the sum of all these elementary volumes as $\delta x \to 0$, i.e. the limit as $\delta x \to 0$ of

$$\underset{\text{Over all discs}}{\sum \delta V} = \sum_{x=a}^{x=b} \pi y^2 \delta x$$

In the limit as $\delta x \to 0$, the discs become infinitesimally thin and there are infinitely many of them.

The limiting values of sums such as these are integrals so:

$$V = \int_a^b \pi y^2 \, dx$$

In this new situation, δx is written as dx and Σ is replaced by the integral symbol, $\int$ (an elongated letter S).

The limits are a and b because x takes values from a to b.

It is essential to realise that this integral is written in terms of dx and so it cannot be evaluated unless the function y is also written in terms of x. For this reason the integral is sometimes written as:

$$V = \int_a^b \pi[f(x)]^2 \, dx$$

Example 13.1

Find the volume of revolution formed when the region between the curve $y = x^2 + 2$, the x-axis and the lines $x = 1$ and $x = 3$ is rotated completely about the x-axis.

Solution

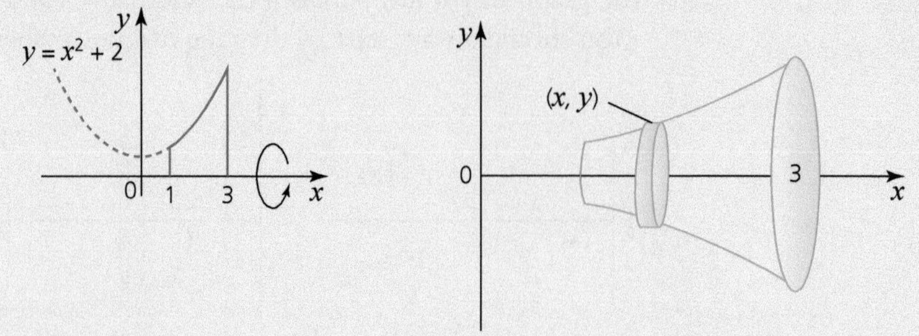

Figure 13.4

The volume is:

$$V = \int_a^b \pi[f(x)]^2 dx$$
$$= \int_1^3 \pi(x^2 + 2)^2 \, dx$$
$$= \int_1^3 \pi(x^4 + 4x^2 + 4) dx$$
$$= \left[\pi\left(\frac{1}{5}x^5 + \frac{4}{3}x^3 + 4x\right)\right]_1^3$$
$$= \pi\left[\left(\frac{3^5}{5} + 36 + 12\right) - \left(\frac{1}{5} + \frac{4}{3} + 4\right)\right]$$

The volume is $\frac{1366\pi}{15}$ cubic units or 286 cubic units correct to 3 significant figures.

Note

Unless a decimal answer is required, it is common practice to leave π in the answer, which is then exact.

Example 13.2

Find the volume of a spherical ball of radius 2 cm.

Solution

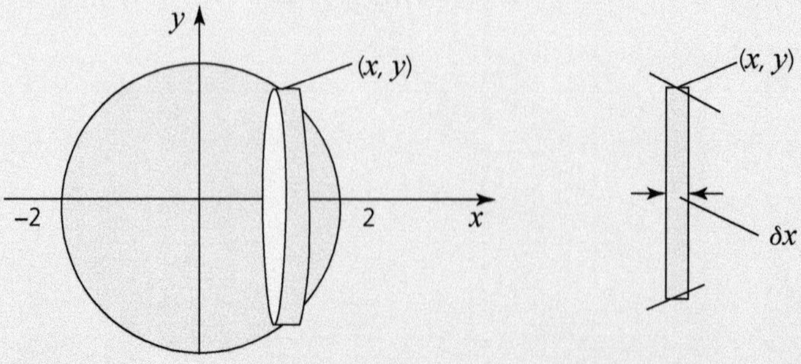

Figure 13.5

The volume of the sphere is found by using:

$$V = \int_a^b \pi y^2 \mathrm{d}x$$

The equation of a circle radius 2 centre (0, 0) is $x^2 + y^2 = 4$.

with limits $a = -2$ and $b = 2$.

Since $x^2 + y^2 = 4$, $y^2 = 4 - x^2$, and the integral may be written as:

$$V = \int_{-2}^{2} \pi\left(4 - x^2\right)\mathrm{d}x$$

The constant π can be taken outside the integral so:

$$V = \pi\left[4x - \frac{x^3}{3}\right]_{-2}^{2}$$

$$= \pi\left[\left(8 - \frac{8}{3}\right) - \left(-8 + \frac{8}{3}\right)\right]$$

$$= \frac{32\pi}{3} = 33.51\ldots$$

Notice that this is the same answer as you get from substituting $r = 2$ in the formula for the volume of a sphere, $V = \frac{4}{3}\pi r^3$.

The volume of a spherical ball with radius 2 cm is 33.5 cm^3 correct to 3 significant figures.

The volume of a sphere

The formula for the volume of a sphere of radius r can be found by following the same argument but using a circle of radius r rather than one of radius 2 cm. Its equation is $x^2 + y^2 = r^2$ and the limits of integration are $-r$ and r.

$$V = \int \pi y^2 \mathrm{d}x$$

$$= \int_{-r}^{r} \pi\left(r^2 - x^2\right)\mathrm{d}x$$

Therefore:

$$V = \pi\left[r^2 x - \frac{x^3}{3}\right]_{-r}^{r}$$

$$= \pi\left[\left(r^3 - \frac{r^3}{3}\right) - \left(-r^3 - \frac{-r^3}{3}\right)\right]$$

$$\Rightarrow \quad V = \frac{4}{3}\pi r^3$$

Volumes of revolution about the y-axis

In Example 13.1, a region under the curve $y = x^2 + 2$ was rotated about the x-axis. If the same portion of the curve $y = x^2 + 2$ were to be used to form a region which could be rotated about the y-axis, a very different solid would be obtained from that in Example 13.1. The region required would be that which lies between the curve and the y-axis and the limits $y = 3$ and $y = 11$, as shown in Figure 13.6.

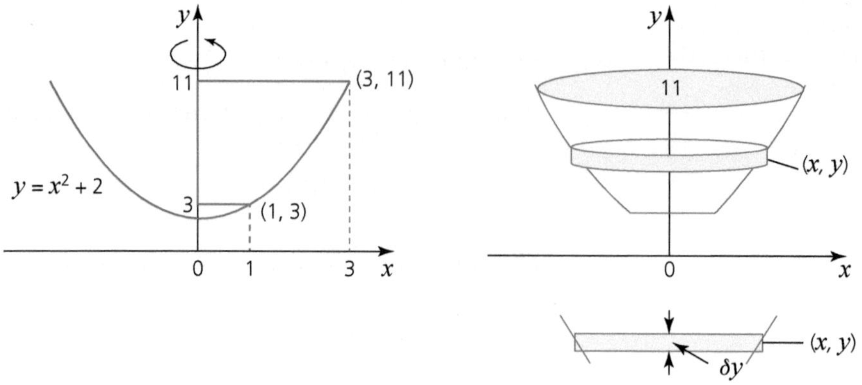

Figure 13.6

An elementary disc has an approximate volume $\delta V = \pi x^2 \delta y$ and the volume of revolution about the y-axis is given by:

$$V = \int \pi x^2 \mathrm{d}y$$

This time, it is necessary to write x^2 in terms of y. In this case, $x^2 = y - 2$ and so the final integral becomes:

$$V = \int_3^{11} \pi(y-2)\mathrm{d}y$$

$$V = \left[\pi\left(\frac{y^2}{2} - 2y\right)\right]_3^{11}$$

$$\Rightarrow \quad V = \pi\left[\left(\frac{11^2}{2} - 22\right) - \left(\frac{3^2}{2} - 6\right)\right] = 40\pi$$

The volume is 40π cubic units.

Exercise 13.1

① In each part of this question, a region is defined in terms of the lines which form its boundaries.

(a) Draw a sketch of the region.

(b) Find the volume of the solid obtained by rotating it through 360° about the x-axis.

(i) $y = 2x$, the x-axis and the lines $x = 1$ and $x = 3$.

(ii) $y = \sqrt{x}$, the x-axis and the line $x = 4$.

(iii) $y = 2x + 1$, the x-axis and the lines $x = 1$ and $x = 5$.

(iv) $y = \frac{1}{x}$, the x-axis and the lines $x = 1$ and $x = 3$.

(v) $y = 3e^x$, the x-axis, the y-axis and the line $x = 1.5$.

(vi) $y = \cos x$ (for $0 \le x \le \frac{\pi}{2}$), the x-axis and the y-axis.

Hint

$\cos^2 x = \frac{1}{2}(1 + \cos 2x)$

② In each part of the question, a region is defined in terms of the lines which form its boundaries.

(a) Draw a sketch of the region.

(b) Find the volume of the solid obtained by rotating it through 360° about the y-axis.

(i) $y = x^3$, the y-axis and the line $y = 8$.

(ii) $y = 2x - 1$, the y-axis and the line $y = 5$.

(iii) $x^2 + y^2 = 9$, the y-axis and the lines $y = 1$ and $y = 3$.

③ The triangle OAB shown in Figure 13.7 is rotated about the x-axis to form a solid cone.

(i) Find the equation of the line OB.

(ii) Hence show that the volume of a cone with radius r and height h is $\frac{1}{3}\pi r^2 h$.

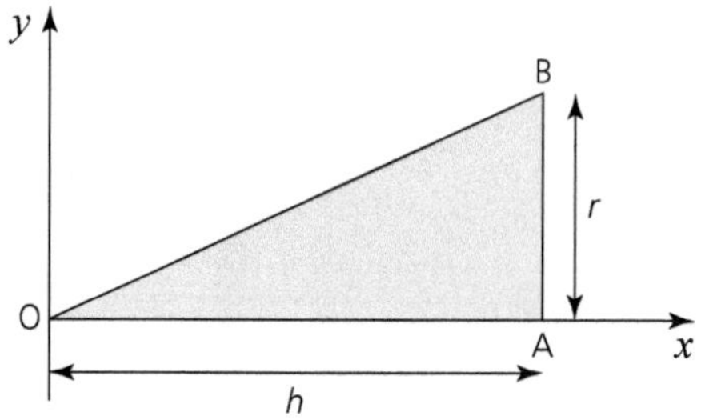

Figure 13.7

④ Find the volume generated when the area enclosed by the x-axis and the curve $y = x^2 - 4$ is rotated through 360° about the x-axis.

⑤ (i) Sketch the graph of $x^2 + y^2 = 36$.

(ii) A hemispherical bowl of internal radius 6 cm is filled with water to a depth of 4 cm. Find the volume of water in litres (1 litre = 1000 cm^3).

⑥ Figure 13.8 shows the ellipse $\frac{x^2}{a^2} + \frac{y^2}{b^2} = 1$, where $a > b$.

The region under this curve and above the x-axis is rotated through 360° about the x-axis to form an ellipsoid.

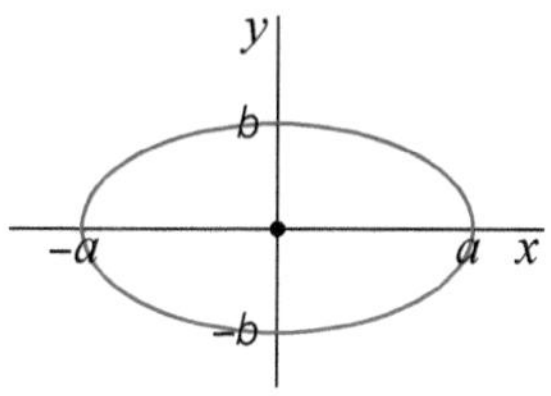

Figure 13.8

(i) Draw a diagram to illustrate the solid formed.

(ii) Show that the volume of this solid is $\frac{4}{3}\pi b^2 a$.

A mathematical model of an egg is that one end is a half ellipsoid of length a and greatest radius b and the other end is a hemisphere of radius b.

(iii) Find the volume of the egg in terms of a and b.

⑦ (i) Draw a diagram to illustrate the solid formed when the ellipse $\frac{x^2}{a^2} + \frac{y^2}{b^2} = 1$ $(a > b)$ is rotated about the y-axis.

Figure 13.9 shows the elliptical galaxy M87. This galaxy is estimated to have a maximum diameter of 10 000 light years.

Figure 13.9

(ii) Estimate its volume in m^3. (You will need to take measurements from the photograph. The speed of light is approximately 3×10^8 m s^{-1}.)

⑧ The area bounded by the curve $y^2 = 8x$ and the lines $x = 0$ and $y = 4$ is rotated through 360° about the y-axis. Show that the volume of the solid obtained is $\frac{16\pi}{5}$ and find the volume of the solid obtained by rotating the same region about the x-axis.

⑨ Find the volume generated when the region between the curve $y = 2x - x^2$ and the line $y = \frac{x}{2}$ is rotated through 360° about the x-axis.

⑩ Figure 13.10 shows the hyperbola $\frac{x^2}{a^2} - \frac{y^2}{b^2} = 1$.

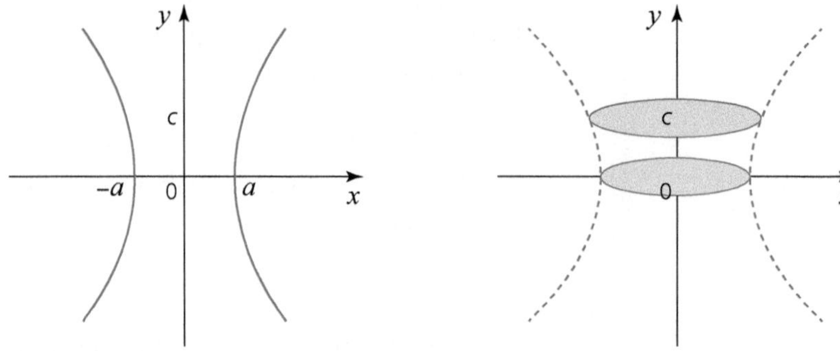

Figure 13.10

When it is rotated through 360° about the y-axis a hyperboloid is formed.

(i) Show that the volume enclosed by this hyperboloid between $y = 0$ and $y = c$ is given by

$$V = \frac{\pi a^2 c}{3b^2}\left(3b^2 + c^2\right)$$

The cooling towers of power stations can be modelled as hyperboloids and the dimensions of one such tower are shown in Figure 13.11.

Figure 13.11

(ii) Verify that the equation $\frac{x^2}{560} - \frac{y^2}{3600} = 1$ is a suitable mathematical model for the curve which is rotated to form the hyperboloid.

(iii) Use the formula above to find the volume occupied by the cooling tower, and show that the six towers of the power station occupy over 1.9 million cubic metres of space.

⑪ Figure 13.12 shows the ellipse $\frac{x^2}{a^2} + \frac{y^2}{b^2} = 1$.

When it is rotated through 360° about the y-axis an ellipsoid is formed.

(i) Show that the volume enclosed by this ellipsoid between $y = -c$ and $y = b$ is given by $V = \frac{\pi a^2}{3b^2}[2b^3 + c(3b^2 - c^2)$.

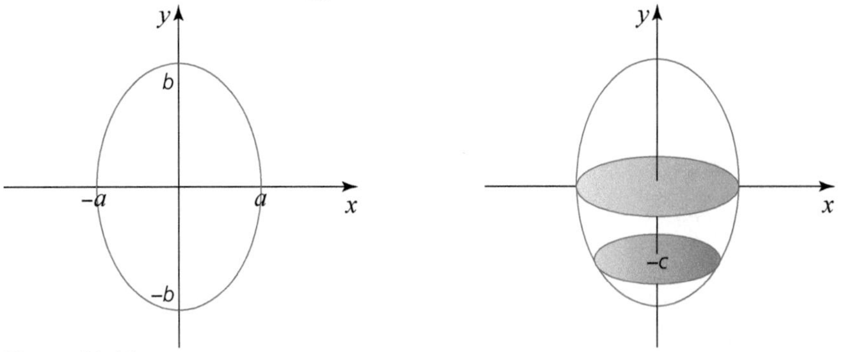

Figure 13.12

The London skyscraper the Gherkin can be modelled as an ellipsoid; the dimensions of this building are shown Figure 13.13.

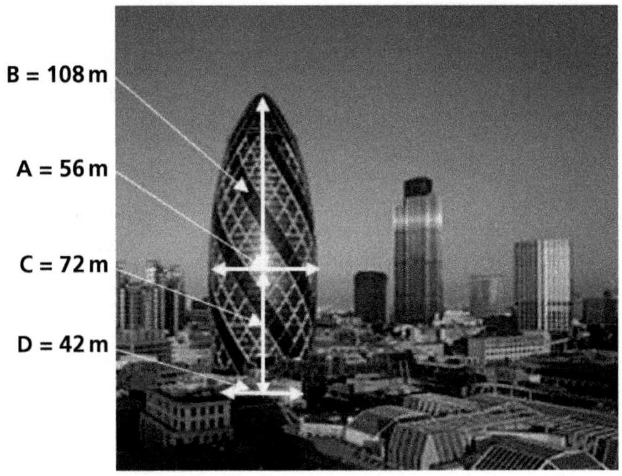

Figure 13.13

(ii) Verify that the equation $\frac{x^2}{28^2} + \frac{y^2}{108^2} = 1$ is a suitable mathematical model for the curve which is rotated to form the ellipsoid.

(iii) Use the formula above to find the volume occupied by the building.

12. A mathematical model for the curved surface of a measuring jug is obtained by rotating the part of the curve $y = 0.003x^4$ between $y = 1$ and $y = 10$ through 360° about the y-axis. It has a flat base. The units are centimetres.

    (i) Sketch the jug.

    (ii) Find the values of y for which marks must be placed on the side of the jug to indicate volumes of

    (a) 100 ml (b) 0.5 litre (c) 1 litre.

13. The circle $x^2 + (y + 1)^2 = 5$ meets the x-axis at the points A and B.

    The minor arc AB is rotated about the x-axis to form a solid of revolution which can be used to model a rugby ball.

    (i) Find the coordinates of A and B and show that

    $$y^2 = 6 - x^2 - 2\sqrt{5 - x^2}.$$

    (ii) Hence calculate the volume of the solid of revolution.

    (iii) A similar rugby ball is 30 cm long. Find its volume.

Figure 13.14

2 Centres of mass

The position of the centre of mass of a solid of revolution will affect its stability and the way it will roll. Some toys are designed so that they can never be knocked over. Many birds that live on cliffs lay pointed eggs which roll round in circles so that they do not fall over the cliff edge. The position of the centre of mass is also important in the design of some sporting equipment.

Using integration to find centres of mass

The calculus methods you have been using to determine the volumes of solids of revolution can be extended to find their centres of mass (assuming they are of uniform density).

Notice that, by symmetry, the centre of mass of a solid of revolution must lie on its axis, so provided you choose either the x-axis or the y-axis to be the axis of symmetry, there is only one coordinate to determine. For a solid of revolution about the x-axis, divide it into thin discs as before. An elementary disc situated at the point (x,y) on the curve, has a centre of mass at the point $(x,0)$ on the x-axis, as shown in Figure 13.15.

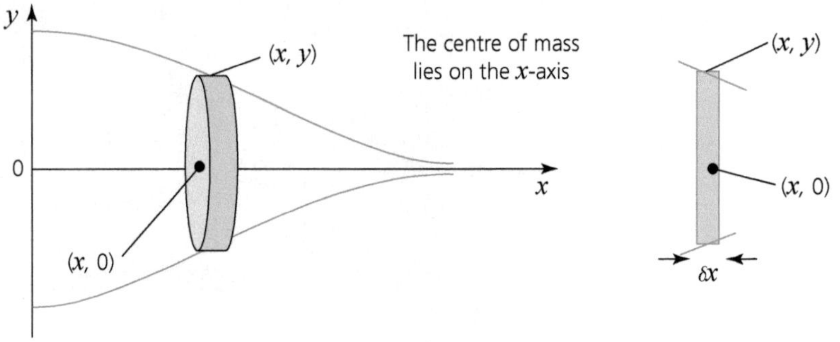

Figure 13.15

The volume of this disc is: $\delta V = \pi y^2 \delta x$

and so its mass is: $\delta M = \rho \pi y^2 \delta x$

where ρ is the density.

The sum of such discs forms a solid which approaches the original as $\delta x \to 0$ and the discs become thinner. Both the mass and the position of the centre of mass are known for each disc, so you can use the result from Chapter 9. For a composite body, the position, $\bar{x}$, of the centre of mass is given by:

moment of whole mass at centre of mass = sum of moments of individual masses

$$M\bar{x} = \sum m_i x_i$$

In this case,

$$\left(\sum_{\text{All discs}} \delta M\right)\bar{x} = \sum_{\text{All discs}} (\delta M x)$$

Substituting the expression for δM obtained above gives:

$$\left(\sum \rho\pi y^2 \delta x\right)\bar{x} = \sum \rho\pi y^2 x\,\delta x$$

In the limit as $\delta x \to 0$ these sums may be represented by integrals and so:

$$\left(\int \rho\pi y^2 \mathrm{d}x\right)\bar{x} = \int \rho\pi y^2 x\,\mathrm{d}x$$

Assuming that ρ is uniform, you can divide through by $\rho\pi$ to give:

$$\left(\int y^2 \mathrm{d}x\right)\bar{x} = \int y^2 x\,\mathrm{d}x \text{ or } \bar{x} = \frac{\int y^2 x\,\mathrm{d}x}{\int y^2\,\mathrm{d}x}$$

This result is valid for any solid of revolution of *uniform density* which is formed by rotation about the x-axis.

It may also be written as:

$$V\bar{x} = \int \pi y^2 x\,\mathrm{d}x$$

where V is the volume of the solid.

In the next example, the centre of mass of a solid hemisphere is found using the above result.

Example 13.3

Find the centre of mass of a solid hemisphere of radius r.

Note

With the hemisphere oriented as in Figure 13.16, the point (x, y) lies on the curve $x^2 + y^2 = r^2$ and the limits for the integration are $x = 0$ and $x = r$.

Note

You also know that the volume, V, is $\frac{3}{3}\pi r^3$ but the equations will look simpler if this is substituted later.

Solution

$$V\bar{x} = \int_0^r \pi y^2 x\,\mathrm{d}x$$

Substituting $y^2 = r^2 - x^2$ gives:

$$V\bar{x} = \int_0^r \pi(r^2 - x^2)x\,\mathrm{d}x$$

$$= \int_0^r \pi(r^2 x - x^3)\,\mathrm{d}x$$

$$= \pi\left[\frac{r^2x^2}{2} - \frac{x^4}{4}\right]_0^r$$

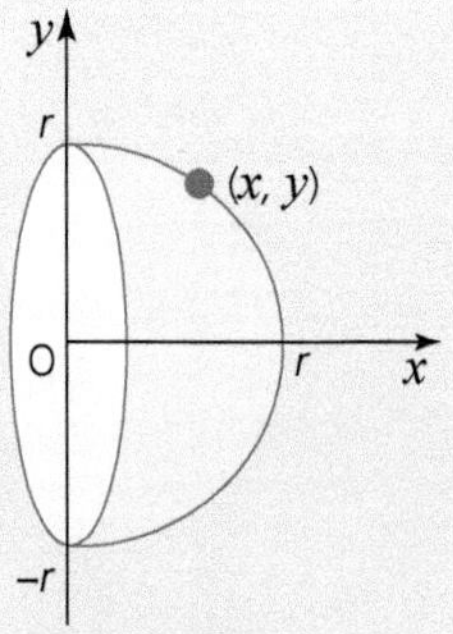

Figure 13.16

So $\qquad V\bar{x} = \frac{1}{4}\pi r^4$

Substituting for V gives: $\qquad \frac{2}{3}\pi r^3 \bar{x} = \frac{1}{4}\pi r^4$

$\Rightarrow \qquad \bar{x} = \frac{3}{8}r$

The centre of mass of a solid hemisphere is $\frac{3}{8}r$ from the centre of its base.

Chapter 13 Centre of mass 2

Example 13.4

Find the position of the centre of mass of the solid of revolution formed when the region between the curve $y = 2e^x$, the lines $x = 0$ and $x = 2$, and the x-axis is rotated through 360° about the x-axis.

Solution

Figure 13.17 show the region and the solid obtained.

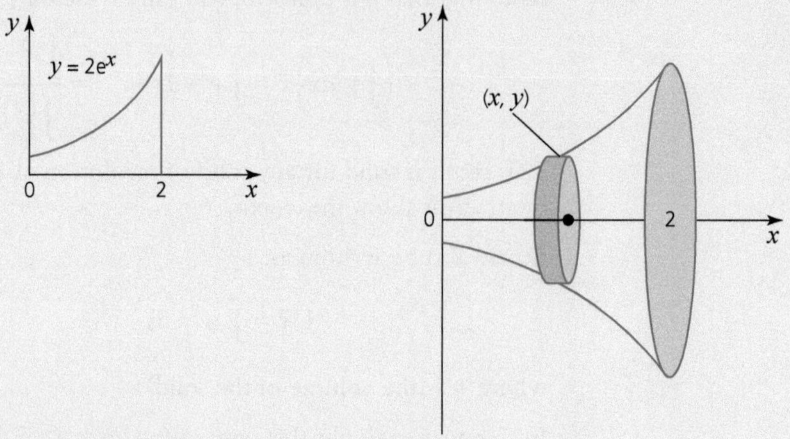

Figure 13.17

The volume V, of the solid is given by:

$$V = \int \pi y^2 dx$$

$$= \pi \int_0^2 (2e^x)^2 \, dx$$

$$V = 4\pi \int_0^2 e^{2x} dx$$

$$= 4\pi \left[\frac{e^{2x}}{2}\right]_0^2$$

$$= 2\pi(e^4 - 1)$$

By symmetry, the y coordinate of the centre of mass is 0. The x coordinate is given by $\bar{x}$ in

$$V\bar{x} = \int \pi y^2 x \, dx$$

$$= \pi \int_0^2 (2e^x)^2 x \, dx$$

Therefore: $$V\bar{x} = 4\pi \int_0^2 xe^{2x} dx \quad ①$$

This integral requires the technique of integration by parts, expressed by the general formula:

$$\int_a^b u\frac{dv}{dx}\,dx = [uv]_a^b - \int_a^b v\frac{du}{dx}\,dx$$

To find $\int xe^{2x}\,dx$

let $u = x \Rightarrow \frac{du}{dx} = 1,$

and let $\frac{dv}{dx} = e^{2x} \Rightarrow v = \frac{e^{2x}}{2}.$

The limits are $a = 0$ and $b = 2$.

Substituting these in the general formula, you obtain:

$$\int_0^2 xe^{2x}\,dx = \left[x\frac{e^{2x}}{2}\right]_0^2 - \int_0^2 \frac{e^{2x}}{2}\times 1\times dx$$

$$= \left[\frac{1}{2}xe^{2x}\right]_0^2 - \left[\frac{1}{4}e^{2x}\right]_0^2$$

$$= \left(e^4 - 0\right) - \left(\frac{1}{4}e^4 - \frac{1}{4}\right)$$

$$= \frac{1}{4}\left(3e^4 + 1\right)$$

Substituting this and $V = 2\pi(e^4 - 1)$ in ①

$$V\bar{x} = 4\pi\int_0^2 xe^{2x}\,dx$$

gives: $2\pi\left(e^4 - 1\right)\bar{x} = 4\pi \times \frac{1}{4}\left(3e^4 + 1\right)$

$$\bar{x} = \frac{\left(3e^4 + 1\right)}{2\left(e^4 - 1\right)}$$

$$= 1.54 \text{ (correct to 2 d.p.)}.$$

The centre of mass is at (1.54, 0).

Look at Figure 13.17 and check that this seems a reasonable answer.

Note

If the answer is required in decimal form, it is best to substitute the numerical value of constants such as e and π later rather than sooner. Notice that π cancels in this example.

Centres of mass of composite bodies

Once the positions of the centres of mass of standard solids have been found, it is possible to use these results to find the positions of the centres of mass of composite bodies. Some useful results are summarised in the following table.

Diagram	Body	Volume	Height of c.o.m. above base
	Solid sphere, radius r	$\frac{4}{3}\pi r^3$	r (above lower point)
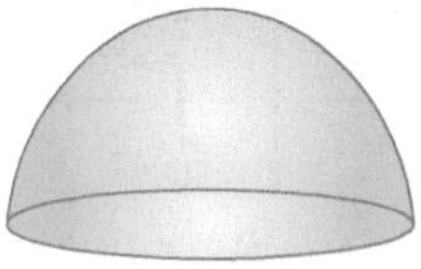	Solid hemisphere, radius r	$\frac{2}{3}\pi r^3$	$\frac{3}{8}r$
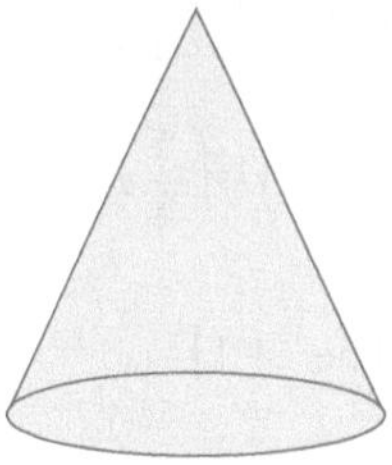	Solid cone, height h, radius r	$\frac{1}{3}\pi r^2 h$	$\frac{1}{4}h$

You may also find it helpful to know the position of the centre of mass for some shells (hollow bodies with negligible wall thickness), and these are given below.

Diagram	Body	Curved Surface area	Height of c.o.m. above base
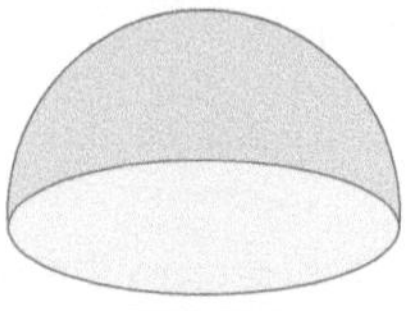	Hollow hemisphere, radius r	$2\pi r^2$	$\frac{1}{2}r$
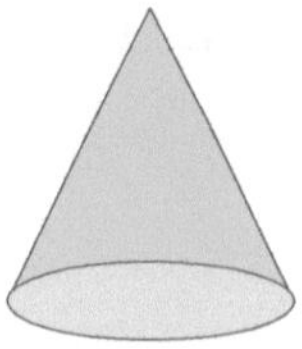	Hollow cone, height h, radius r	πrl $\left(l = \sqrt{r^2 + h^2}\right)$	$\frac{1}{3}h$

Example 13.5

(i) Find the position of the centre of mass of a uniform hemispherical bowl of thickness 1 cm and inside radius 9 cm.

(ii) A light handle AB of length 18 cm is attached to a point A on the rim of the bowl in such a way that the line AB passes through the centre of the hemisphere. What angle does AB make with the vertical when the bowl is hung from the end B?

Solution

(i) Think of the bowl as a solid hemisphere of radius 10 cm from which another solid hemisphere of radius 9 cm has been removed. Then the original 10 cm hemisphere can be treated as a composite body, consisting of the bowl and the 9 cm hemisphere.

You can put all the information in a table.

	The 10 cm hemisphere =	**the bowl +**	**the 9 cm hemisphere**
	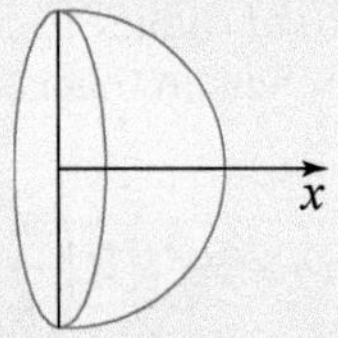 =	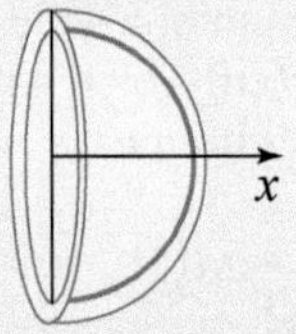 +	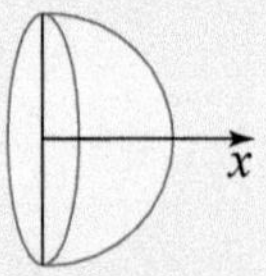
Mass	$\frac{2}{3}\pi\rho \times 10^3$	$\frac{2}{3}\pi\rho\left(10^3 - 9^3\right)$	$\frac{2}{3}\pi\rho \times 9^3$
Distance from O to c.o.m.	$\frac{3}{8} \times 10$	$\bar{x}$	$\frac{3}{8} \times 9$

Taking moments gives:

$$\left(\frac{2}{3}\pi\rho \times 10^3\right) \times \left(\frac{3}{8} \times 10\right) = \left(\frac{2}{3}\pi\rho\left(10^3 - 9^3\right) \times \bar{x}\right) + \left(\frac{2}{3}\pi\rho \times 9^3\right) \times \left(\frac{3}{8} \times 9\right)$$

This can be simplified by dividing through by $\frac{2}{3}\rho\pi$ to give:

$$\frac{3}{8} \times 10^4 = \left(10^3 - 9^3\right)\bar{x} + \frac{3}{8} \times 9^4$$

$$\bar{x} = \frac{3\left(10^4 - 9^4\right)}{8\left(10^3 - 9^3\right)}$$

$$= 4.76 \text{ (to 3 s.f.)}$$

(ii) The handle is light so the position of the centre of mass, G, is unchanged when it is attached. For equilibrium, G must be vertically below B and the angle required is the angle ABG = α.

Hint

To save time, you could rotate your page to look at the first diagram with BG vertical instead of drawing this.

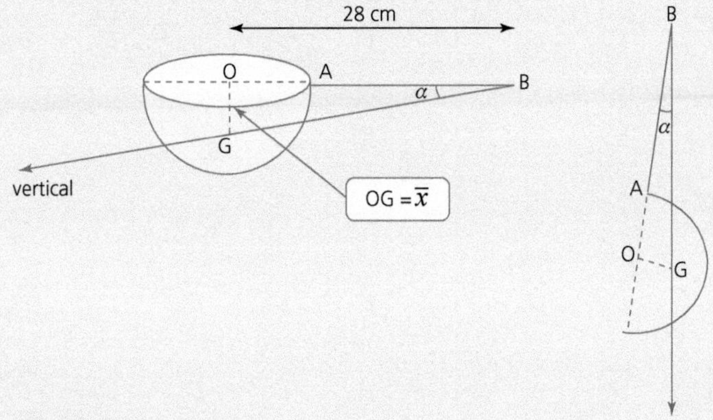

Figure 13.18

From the diagram

$$\tan\alpha = \frac{OG}{OB} = \frac{\bar{x}}{28}$$

$$\Rightarrow \qquad \alpha = 9.65°$$

The angle between AB and the vertical is about 10°.

Note

An alternative but equivalent method for finding $\bar{x}$ is to regard the bowl as the sum of a solid hemisphere of radius 10 cm and a solid hemisphere of radius 9 cm which has negative mass. In this case, the moments equation would be written as:

$$\frac{2}{3}\pi\rho\left(10^3 - 9^3\right)\bar{x} = \left(\frac{2}{3}\pi\rho \times 10^3\right) \times \left(\frac{3}{8} \times 10\right) + \left(-\frac{2}{3}\pi\rho \times 9^3\right) \times \left(\frac{3}{8} \times 9\right)$$

Example 13.6

A traffic cone is modelled as a hollow cone of height 45 cm standing on a heavy cylindrical disc of radius 20 cm and height 5 cm. The mass of the disc is twice that of the cone.

(i) Find the position of the centre of mass of the traffic cone.

(ii) What is the angle of the steepest slope on which it can be placed without toppling?

Solution

(i) You can put the information in a table.

	Cone	Disc	Together
Mass	m	$2m$	$3m$
Height of c.o.m. above O in cm	$\frac{1}{3} \times 45 + 5$	$\frac{1}{2} \times 5$	$\bar{y}$

Then $\quad 20m + 5m = 3m\bar{y}$

$$\Rightarrow \qquad \bar{y} = \frac{25}{3}$$

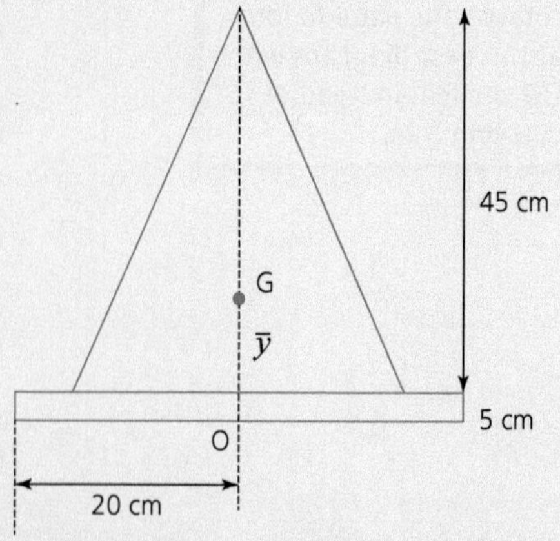

Figure 13.19

(ii) The cone begins to topple when the line GA is vertical.

Then $\tan\alpha = \frac{20}{\bar{y}} = \frac{20 \times 3}{25} = 2.4$

$\alpha = 67.4°$

The steepest slope is 67.4° to the horizontal.

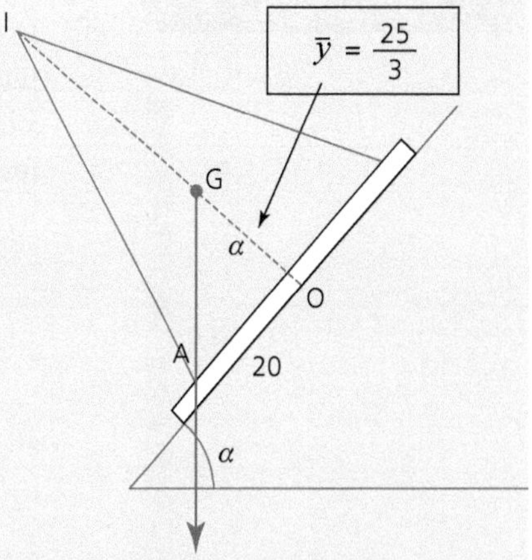

Figure 13.20

Suspended objects

Discussion point

Suppose you attach an object by a single point to the ceiling, using a string or a smooth hinge, so that it hangs in equilibrium. Where is the centre of mass of the object?

You should have agreed that the centre of mass is directly below the point of attachment. Otherwise the moment of the weight of the object about the point of attachment would not be zero, and there are no other forces with non-zero moments, so the object could not be in equilibrium.

Example 13.7

A uniform solid hemisphere of radius 5 cm is suspended from a point P on the circumference of the circular face. Find the angle between the circular face and the horizontal when the hemisphere is in equilibrium.

Solution

The centre of mass G will be vertically beneath the point of suspension P.

In equilibrium PG will be vertical.

If O is the centre of the circular face then the angle between the circular face and the vertical will be ∠OPG.

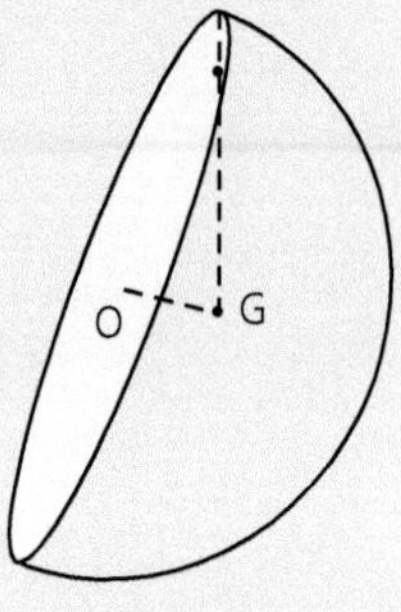

Figure 13.21

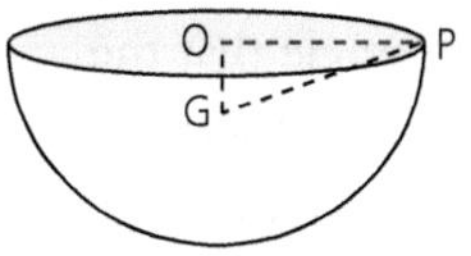

Figure 13.22

So the angle we need is $90 - O\hat{P}G = O\hat{G}P$

$OG = \frac{3}{8}r = \frac{3}{8} \times 5 = 1.875\,\text{cm}$

$OP = r = 5$

$\Rightarrow \quad O\hat{G}P = \arctan\left(\frac{5}{1.875}\right) = 69.44\ldots$

In equilibrium the angle between the circular face and the horizontal is 69.4° (3 s.f.).

It is easier to think of these angles when the shape is horizontally placed.

Exercise 13.2

① In Exercise 13.1 question 1, you found the volumes of several solids of revolution produced by rotating certain regions through 360° about the x-axis. These regions are described again below and the volumes of the resulting solids of revolution are given. In each case:

(a) draw a diagram of each solid showing an elementary disc at the point (x, y) on the curve

(b) determine the position of its centre of mass by equating $V\bar{x}$ to a suitable integral.

(i) $y = 2x$, the x-axis and the lines $x = 1$ and $= 3$ $\left(V = \frac{104\pi}{3}\right)$.

(ii) $y = \sqrt{x}$, the x-axis and the line $x = 4$ $(V = 8\pi)$.

(iii) $y = 2x + 1$, the x-axis and the lines $x = 1$ and $x = 5$ $\left(V = \frac{652\pi}{3}\right)$.

(iv) $y = \frac{1}{x}$, the x-axis and the lines $x = 1$ and $x = 3$ $\left(V = \frac{2\pi}{3}\right)$.

(v) $y = 3e^x$, the x-axis, the y-axis and the line $x = 1.5$ $\left(V = \frac{9\pi}{2}\left(e^3 - 1\right)\right)$.

(vi) $y = \cos x$ (from $x = 0$ to $\frac{\pi}{2}$), the x-axis and the y-axis $\left(V = \frac{\pi^2}{4}\right)$.

② In Exercise 13.1 question 2, you found the volumes of several solids of revolution produced by rotating certain regions through 360° about the y-axis. These are described again below and their volumes are given. In each case:

(a) draw a diagram of each solid showing an elementary disc at the point (x,y) on the curve

(b) determine the position of its centre of mass by equating $V\bar{y}$ to a suitable integral.

(i) $y = x^3$, the y-axis and the line $y = 8$ $\left(V = \frac{96\pi}{5}\right)$.

(ii) $y = 2x - 1$, the y-axis and the line $y = 5$ $(V = 18\pi)$.

(iii) $x^2 + y^2 = 9$, the y-axis and the lines $y = 1$ and $y = 3$ $\left(V = \frac{28\pi}{3}\right)$.

③ (i) Sketch the curve $y = x^2(2 - x)$.

(ii) Find the volume of the solid formed when the closed region between the curve and the x-axis is rotated about this axis.

(iii) Find the position of the centre of mass of this solid.

④ A uniform solid cone of base radius 5 cm and height 6 cm is suspended from a point on the circumference of the circular base. Find the angle that the circular face makes with the vertical when the cone is in equilibrium.

⑤ (i) Sketch the curve $y^2 = 4x$ (i.e. $y = \pm 2\sqrt{x}$) and shade the region between the curve, the x-axis and the lines $x = 1$ and $x = 4$.

(ii) Find the volume and the position of the centre of mass of the solid generated when the shaded region is rotated completely about the x-axis.

(iii) The region between the same portion of the curve and the y-axis is to be rotated through 360° about the y-axis. Find

(a) appropriate limits for y

(b) the volume of revolution so formed

(c) the position of the centre of mass of this new solid of revolution.

⑥ Water fills a light hemispherical bowl of radius 12 cm to a depth of 6 cm. Find the height of the centre of mass of the water above the base of the bowl.

⑦ (i) Sketch the ellipse $\frac{x^2}{9}+\frac{y^2}{4}=1$ and shade the region lying between the curve and the axes for positive values of x and y.

(ii) Find the volume and centre of mass of the solid obtained by rotating the shaded region through 360° about the x-axis.

⑧ The region bounded by the x-axis, the curve $y = x^2$ and the line $x = 2$ is rotated through 2π about the x-axis. The resulting solid is then suspended from a point on the circumference of the circular face so that the solid hangs freely in equilibrium. Find the angle between the circular face and the vertical.

⑨ A toy clown is modelled by a solid cone of radius r and height h, attached to a solid hemisphere of radius r and centre O as shown.

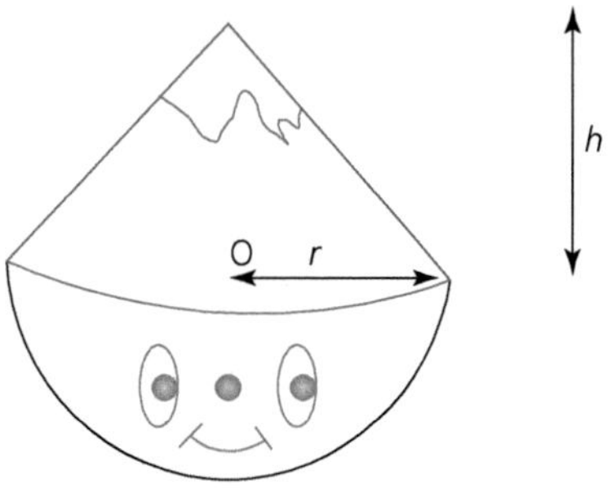

Figure 13.21

(i) Copy and complete the following table using the results above.

	Clown	Cone	Hemisphere
Mass			
Distance of c.o.m. above O	$\bar{y}$		

(ii) Write down an equation for finding $\bar{y}$. (Divide by any common factors.)

(iii) In the case when the centre of mass is at the centre of the hemisphere, use your equation to find the ratio of h to r.

(iv) In the case when the ratio of h to r is less than that obtained in part (iii), what position will the toy assume when placed with a point on the hemisphere in contact with the ground?

⑩ Figure 13.22 shows a container consisting of a hollow cylinder of radius 3 cm and height 18 cm with a circular base, centre O, topped by a hollow cone of the same radius and height 4 cm. The container is made of thin, uniform material. The origin O is at the centre of the base.

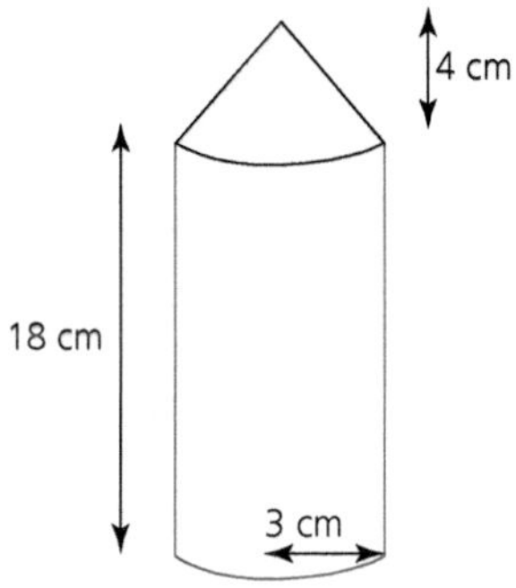

Figure 13.22

(i) Copy and complete the following table.

	Whole container	Cylinder base	Cylinder walls	Cone
Mass				
Distance of c.o.m. above O	$\bar{y}$			

(ii) Find the height of the centre of mass of the container above the base.

(iii) The container is placed with its circular base on a flat horizontal deck on a boat and is prevented from slipping. The boat heels (leans to one side) so that the deck makes an angle α to the horizontal.

Find the value of α at which the empty container will just topple over.

(iv) If the container is filled with liquid to the top of the cylinder, is it more or less likely to topple over than when it is empty? Give a reason for your answer.

⑪ The part of the curve with equation $y = (4 - x)\sqrt{x}$ between $x = 0$ and $x = 4$ is denoted by C. A solid S is formed by rotating the region of the plane bounded by C and the x-axis through 2π rad about the x-axis. The lengths are measured in centimetres.

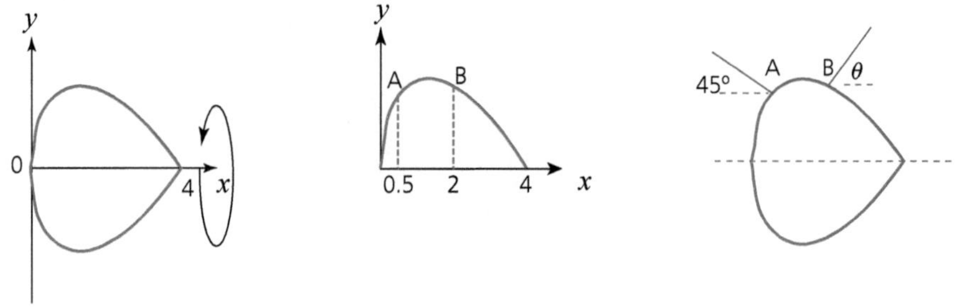

Figure 13.23

(i) Calculate the volume of S. (You may leave π in your answer.)

(ii) Calculate the position of the centre of mass of S.

The points A and B on the curve C have x coordinates 0.5 and 2, respectively, as shown in the middle diagram of Figure 13.23.

In preparation for a test in a wind tunnel, the solid S is suspended with its axis of symmetry horizontal by strings attached to the points A and B, as in the diagram on the right. The string attached to the point A is inclined at 45° to the horizontal.

(iii) Calculate the angle θ that the string attached to the point B makes with the horizontal. [MEI]

⑫ The shape of the bowl of a wine glass is produced by rotating the part of the curve $y = kx^2$ which lies between the origin and the line $y = h$ through 360° about the y-axis.

(i) Draw a diagram of the bowl and, by integration, find the volume of the solid of revolution contained within it.

(ii) Show that the centre of mass of this solid is at the point $\left(0, \frac{2}{3}h\right)$ and hence write down its distance below the top of the glass. (Notice that this is independent of the value of k.)

(iii) The bowl of the glass can be modelled as a solid block of depth 9 cm with another similar block of depth 8.8 cm scooped out. Show that the centre of mass of the bowl is 4.45 cm below the rim.

(iv) The complete wine glass can be modelled by a circular base of negligible thickness and radius 3 cm, a cylindrical stem of height 8 cm and the bowl (as above) of depth 9 cm. The masses of these three parts are in the ratio 1 : 1 : 2. Find the distance of the centre of mass of the whole glass from the circular base.

(v) If the glass is carried on a tray, what is the maximum angle to the horizontal that the tray can be held without the glass toppling over? You may assume that the glass does not slide.

⑬ The region in the x, y plane between the lines $x = h$, $y = 0$ and $y = kx$, shown in the diagram on the left of Figure 13.24, is rotated through 360° about the x-axis to form a right circular cone C.

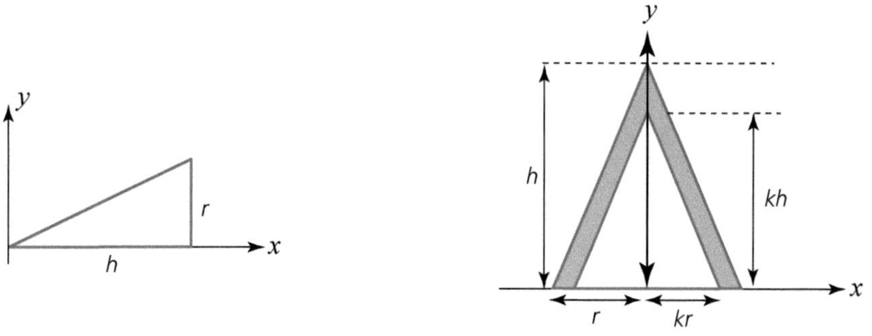

Figure 13.24

(i) Use calculus to prove that the volume of the cone C is $\frac{1}{3}\pi r^2 h$ and that the coordinates of the centre of mass are $\left(\frac{3h}{4}, 0\right)$.

A hollow cone B is formed by removing from C a similar smaller cone. The smaller cone removed has base radius kr and height kh, where $0 < k < 1$. This is shown in the diagram on the right with the cone B now standing upright with the centre of its base at the origin.

(ii) Show that the coordinates of the centre of mass of the hollow cone B are $\left(0, \frac{h(1-k^4)}{4(1-k^3)}\right)$.

For a cone of small thickness, k is close to 1 and so may be written as $k = 1 - \varepsilon$, where ε is small.

(iii) Show that $k^3 = 1 - 3\varepsilon$ when ε is very small, and find a similar expression for k^4 in terms of ε.

(iv) Hence show that for a hollow cone made of uniform material of negligible thickness, the centre of mass is one third of the way from the centre of the base to the vertex. [MEI]

3 Centres of mass of plane regions

ACTIVITY 13.1

Find the position of the centre of mass of a semicircular protractor by suspending it from one corner. In what ratio does it divide the axis of symmetry?

In Chapter 9 you found the centres of mass of some plane shapes made up from rectangles. In this section, that work is taken further to include shapes with curved edges, like the protractor in the Activity you have just done.

Vocabulary

- A thin plane surface, like a protractor, is called a **lamina** (plural laminae).
- The laminae considered in this chapter are all **uniform**; that is, they have the same mass per unit area, throughout. The letter σ (sigma) is often used to denote this area density.
- The **centroid** of a plane region is the centre of mass of a lamina of the same shape and negligible thickness.

Calculus methods for determining the centre of mass of a lamina

When a lamina or plane region is bounded by curves for which equations are known, you can use calculus methods to find the position of its centre of mass.

When a lamina occupies a region between a curve and x-axis, as shown in Figure 13.25, it can be divided into elementary strips of width δx and height y. One such strip, situated at the point (x, y) on the curve is shown. The dot indicates its centre of mass. The mass per unit area of the lamina is denoted by σ.

The height of the strip is y and its width is δx, so its mass δM is $\sigma y \delta x$.

The coordinates of the centre of mass of the strip are $\left(x, \frac{y}{2}\right)$ so $\bar{x}$ can be found using:

$$(\Sigma \delta M)\bar{x} = \Sigma(\delta M \times x)$$

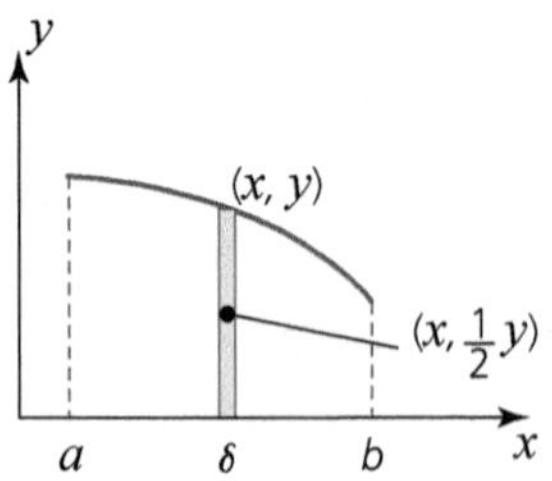

Figure 13.25

Substituting $\delta M = \sigma y \delta x$ in

$$(\Sigma \delta M)\bar{x} = \Sigma(\delta M x)$$

gives

$$(\Sigma \sigma y \delta x)\bar{x} = \Sigma(\sigma y \delta x \times x)$$

If the material is uniform, the mass per unit area is constant and so the equation can be divided through by σ. In that case,

$$(\Sigma\, y\delta x)\bar{x} = \Sigma(yx\delta x)$$

and in the limit as $\delta x \to 0$

$$\left(\int_a^b y \; \mathrm{d}x\right)\bar{x} = \int_a^b xy \; \mathrm{d}x \quad ①$$

Notice that the first integral gives the area of the lamina.

You can find $\bar{y}$ in a similar way. Using the y coordinate, $\frac{y}{2}$, of the centre of the strip and dividing by σ as before:

$$(\Sigma\, y\delta x)\,\bar{y} = \Sigma\left(y\delta x \times \frac{y}{2}\right)$$

In the limit as $\delta x \to 0$ this becomes:

$$\left(\int_a^b y \; \mathrm{d}x\right)\bar{y} = \int_a^b \frac{y^2}{2} \; \mathrm{d}x \quad ②$$

The equations ① and ② can be combined to give the coordinates of the centre of mass of the lamina in the form of a position vector:

$$A\begin{pmatrix} \bar{x} \\ \bar{y} \end{pmatrix} = \begin{pmatrix} \int_a^b xy \; \mathrm{d}x \\ \int_a^b \frac{y^2}{2}\,\mathrm{d}x \end{pmatrix}$$

where A is the total area of the lamina or $\int_a^b y \; \mathrm{d}x$.

Example 13.8

Find the position of the centre of mass of a uniform semicircular lamina of radius r.

Solution

Figure 13.26 shows the lamina.

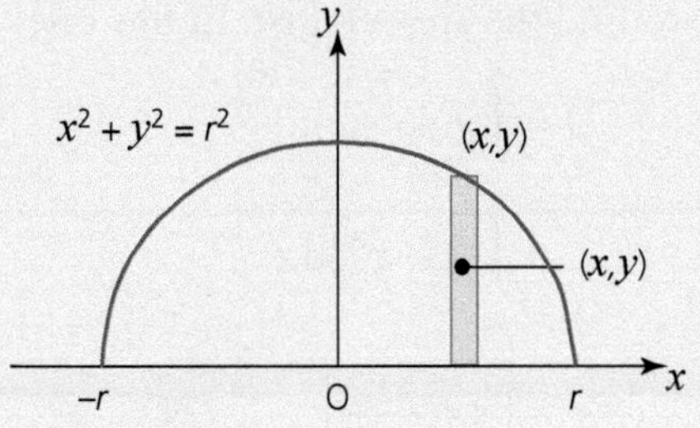

Figure 13.26

By symmetry, $\bar{x} = 0$.

To find $\bar{y}$, use $A\bar{y} = \int_a^b \frac{y^2}{2} \; \mathrm{d}x$.

In this case, $A = \frac{1}{2}\pi r^2$ (because the lamina is a semicircle), and the limits are $-r$ and $+r$.

Since the equation of the curve is $x^2 + y^2 = r^2$, you can write y^2 as $r^2 - x^2$.

This gives:

$$\frac{1}{2}\pi r^2 \bar{y} = \int_{-r}^{r} \frac{1}{2}(r^2 - x^2)\,dx$$

$$= \frac{1}{2}\left[r^2 x - \frac{x^3}{3}\right]_{-r}^{r}$$

$$\Rightarrow \frac{1}{2}\pi r^2 \bar{y} = \frac{1}{2}\left\{\left(r^3 - \frac{r^3}{3}\right) - \left(-r^3 - \frac{(-r)^3}{3}\right)\right\}$$

$$= \frac{2}{3}r^3$$

$$\Rightarrow \quad \bar{y} = \frac{4r}{3\pi}$$

This is the distance of the centre of mass of the semicircular lamina from its centre.

It is roughly 0.4 times the radius. How does this compare with your own measurements in Activity 13.1 on page 300.

Example 13.9

Find the coordinates of the centroid of the region between the curve $y = 4 - x^2$ and the positive x- and y-axes.

Solution

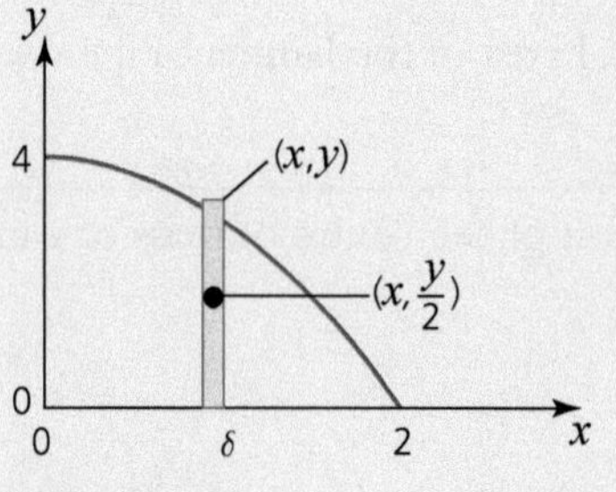

Figure 13.27

It is best to find the area, A, first. In this case:

$$A = \int y\,dx$$

$$= \int_0^2 (4 - x^2)\,dx$$

$$= \left[4x - \frac{x^3}{3}\right]_0^2$$

$$= \left(8 - \frac{8}{3}\right) - 0$$

$$= \frac{16}{3}$$

Then using $A\begin{pmatrix}\bar{x}\\\bar{y}\end{pmatrix}=\begin{pmatrix}\int_0^2 xy\,dx\\\int_0^2 \frac{y^2}{2}dx\end{pmatrix}$ to give:

$$A\bar{x}=\int_0^2 (4-x^2)x\ dx \qquad A\bar{y}=\int_0^2 \frac{(4-x^2)^2}{2}dx$$

$$=\int_0^2 (4x-x^3)dx \qquad =\int_0^2 \frac{16-8x^2+x^4}{2}\ dx$$

$$=\left[\frac{4x^2}{2}-\frac{x^4}{4}\right]_0^2 \qquad =\frac{1}{2}\left[16x-\frac{8x^3}{3}+\frac{x^5}{5}\right]_0^2$$

$$=4 \qquad =\frac{128}{15}$$

Substituting $A=\frac{16}{3}$ gives:

$$\bar{x}=4\times\frac{3}{16} \qquad \bar{y}=\frac{128}{15}\times\frac{3}{16}$$

$$\bar{x}=\frac{3}{4}=0.75 \qquad \bar{y}=\frac{8}{5}=1.6$$

The coordinates of the centroid are (0.75, 1.6).

Using strips parallel to the x-axis

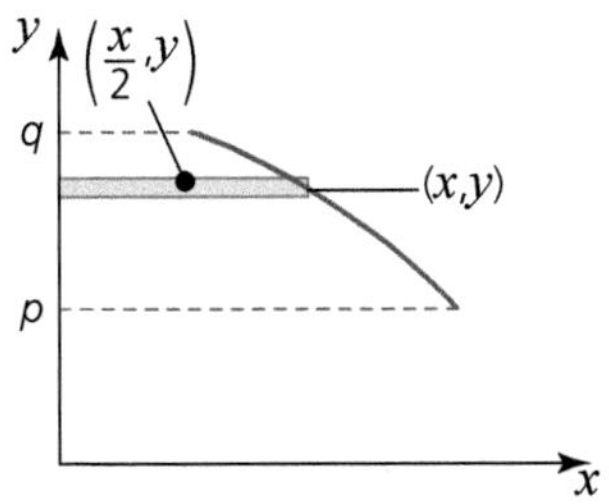

Figure 13.28

Sometimes it is necessary (or easier) to divide the region into strips parallel to the x-axis, as shown in Figure 13.28. The area A is then $\int_p^q x\ dy$ and

$$A\begin{pmatrix}\bar{x}\\\bar{y}\end{pmatrix}=\begin{pmatrix}\int_p^q \frac{x^2}{2}dy\\\int_p^q yx\ dy\end{pmatrix}$$

Note

In this case, the x in each integral should be written in terms of y. When there is a choice between methods, choose the one that gives the easier integral to evaluate.

Exercise 13.3

① The regions (a) to (d) below are all symmetrical about one axis and are defined in terms of the lines and curves which form their boundaries. For each region:

(i) Draw a sketch of the region and, using symmetry, write down one coordinate of the centroid G.

(ii) Show on your diagram an elementary strip parallel to the y-axis situated at the point (x, y) on the curve and mark a dot at its centre. Show the coordinates of this dot on your diagram.

(iii) Write down the area of the strip in terms of x and δx.

(iv) Use $A\bar{x} = \int xy \, dx$ or $A\bar{y} = \int \frac{y^2}{2} dx$, as appropriate, to find the other coordinate of G.

(a) The curve $y = 4 - x^2$ and the x-axis.

(b) The curves $y = e^x$ and $y = -e^x$, the y-axis and the line $x = 1$.

(c) The curve $y^2 = 4x$ (i.e. $y = \pm 2\sqrt{x}$) and the line $x = 4$. (Take care over the length of the strip.)

(d) The curve $y = \sin x$ between $x = 0$, $x = \pi$ and the x-axis.

② In Figure 13.29, OAB is a uniform right-angled triangular lamina. OA = 6 cm and OB = 12 cm.

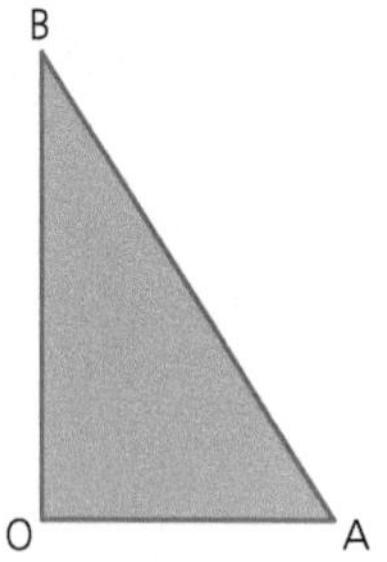

Figure 13.29

(i) Write down the area of the triangle.

(ii) Using OA as the x-axis and OB as the y-axis, find the equation of the line AB.

(iii) Find, by integration, the coordinates $(\bar{x}, \bar{y})$ of the centre of mass, G, of the triangle and verify that $\bar{x} = \frac{1}{3}$OA and $\bar{y} = \frac{1}{3}$OB.

③ A uniform rectangular wooden board of sides 3 m and 2 m hangs freely from one corner. Find the angle between one of the short sides and the horizontal.

④ A lamina is in the form of a right-angled triangle ABC with AB = 12 cm, AC = 9 cm and $\angle A = 90°$. The lamina is suspended from A so that it hangs freely. Find the angle between AB and the vertical.

⑤ Find the centroid of the region shown in Figure 13.30.
It is bounded by the curve $y = \frac{1}{x}$, the x-axis and the lines $x = \frac{1}{2}$ and $x = 2$.

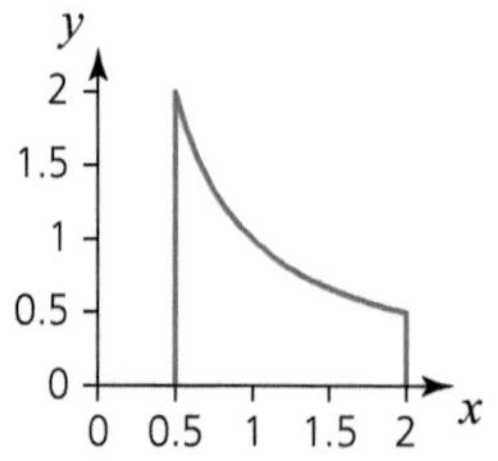

Figure 13.30

⑥ (i) Sketch the curve $y = x^2(3 - x)$.

(ii) Find the coordinates of the centroid of the region between this curve and the x-axis. (Note that this region is not symmetrical.)

⑦ (i) Draw a diagram showing the region R bounded by the curve $y^2 = 4x$ and the line $x = 4$. Mark on your diagram a strip parallel to the x-axis, passing through a general point (x, y) on the curve.

(ii) Write down the area of the strip and the x coordinate of its centroid.

(iii) Find by integrating with respect to y, the centre of mass of the region R.

⑧ Find the coordinates of the centre of mass of each of the following uniform laminae.

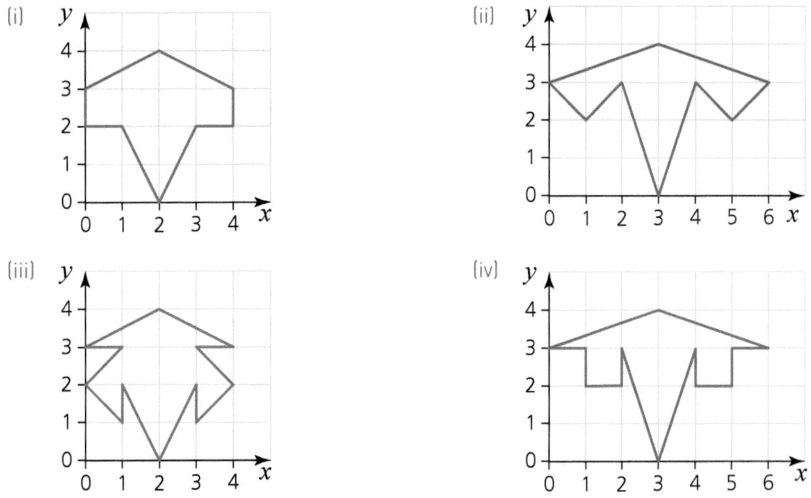

Figure 13.31

⑨ (i) The vertices of a uniform triangular lamina OAB are $(0, 0)$, $(a, 0)$ and $(0, b)$.

Write down the coordinates of its centre of mass.

Figure 13.32 shows another triangular lamina, PQR. It is divided into elementary strips parallel to QR, as shown.

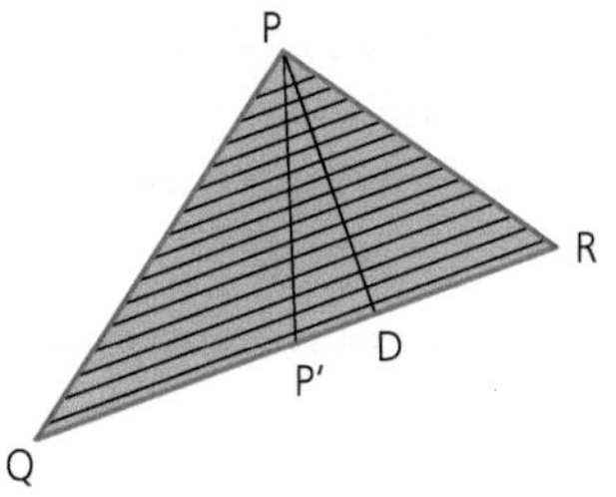

Figure 13.32

(ii) Explain why the centre of mass, G, of PQR lies on the median PP′.

(iii) PQR is made up of two right-angled triangles, PDQ and PDR.

Draw a diagram showing the positions of the centres of mass of PDQ and PDR. Hence show that PG and GP′ are in the ratio 2:1.

In questions 10–12 you can use the result for the position of the centre of mass of a semicircle found in Example 13.8. It is at a distance $\frac{4r}{3\pi}$ from the centre.

⑩ 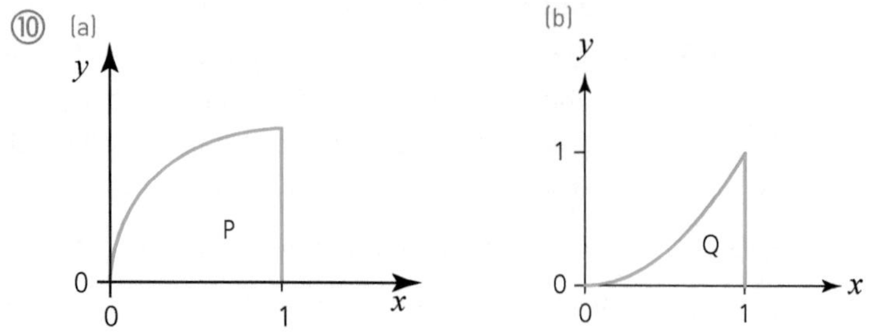

Figure 13.33

(i) The region P of a uniform lamina satisfies the inequalities $(x-1)^2 + y^2 \leq 1, 0 \leq x \leq 1$, and $y \geq 0$ (i.e. P is a quadrant of a circle of radius 1 and centre $(1, 0)$, as shown in Figure 13.33(a)). Find $\bar{y}$ for P and hence show that the coordinates of the centre of mass of P are $\left(\frac{3\pi-4}{3\pi}, \frac{4}{3\pi}\right)$.

(ii) The region Q of a uniform lamina satisfies the inequalities $y \leq x^2, 0 \leq x \leq 1$ and $y \geq 0$, as shown in Figure 13.33(b). Find the coordinates of the centre of mass of Q.

The uniform lamina R is obtained by taking the region P defined above and then removing the region Q, as shown in Figure 13.34.

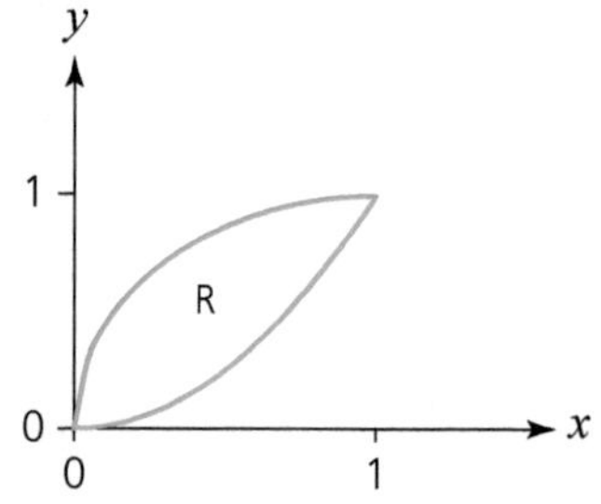

Figure 13.34

(iii) Find the coordinates of the centre of mass of R, referred to the axes shown in Figure 13.34, giving your answers to three decimal places. [MEI]

⑪ A letter P is made up from a rectangle and a semicircle with a smaller semicircle cut out as shown.

(i) Taking O as the origin, write down the areas of the component parts of the letter, and the coordinates of their centres of mass.

(ii) Find the coordinates of the centre of mass of the letter.

(iii) What angle will AO make with the vertical if the letter is hung from the corner A?

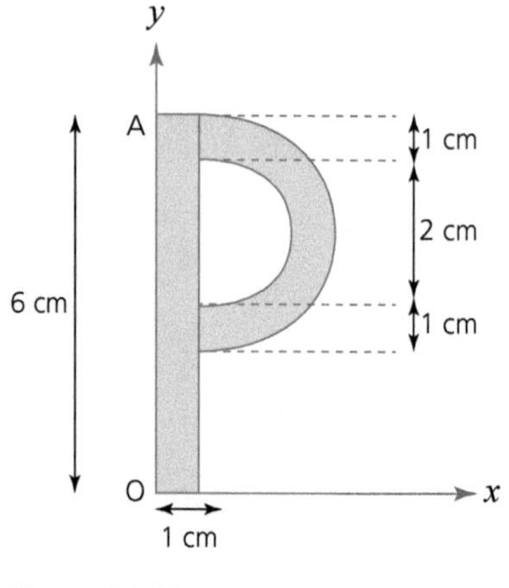

Figure 13.35

⑫ (i) Draw a diagram to show the circle $x^2 + y^2 = 4$ and the line $x = 1$.

(ii) Show that the area of the minor segment of the circle $x^2 + y^2 = 4$ which is cut off by the line $x = 1$ is

$$A = \frac{4\pi}{3} - \sqrt{3}$$

(iii) Find the x coordinate of the centre of mass of this segment by finding a suitable integral between the limits 1 and 2.

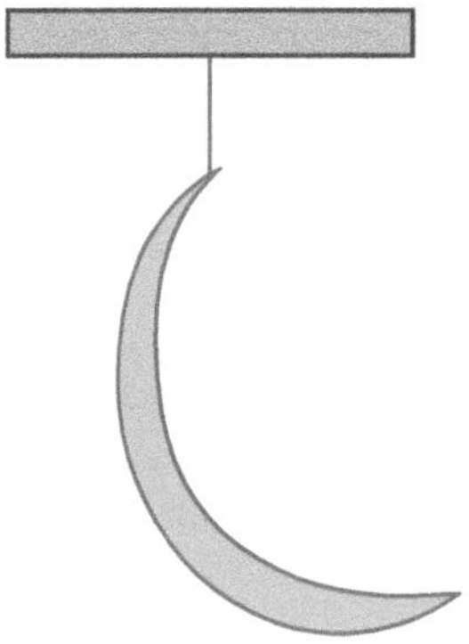

Figure 13.36

(iv) A crescent is formed by removing a segment of this shape from a semicircle of radius $\sqrt{3}$ units. Find the position of the centre of mass of this crescent.

(v) Find the angle between the diameter of the semicircle and the vertical when the crescent is hung from one end of this diameter.

⑬ (i) Find the position of the centre of mass of the region A defined by the inequalities $x^2 - 1 \leq y \leq 1 - x^2$; $0 \leq x \leq 1$.

(ii) Find the position of the centre of mass of the region B defined by the inequalities $0.25x^2 - 1 \leq y \leq 1 - 0.25x^2$; $0 \leq x \leq 2$.

A pendant C is made up from a uniform lamina in such a way that region A is removed from region B as shown in Figure 13.37.

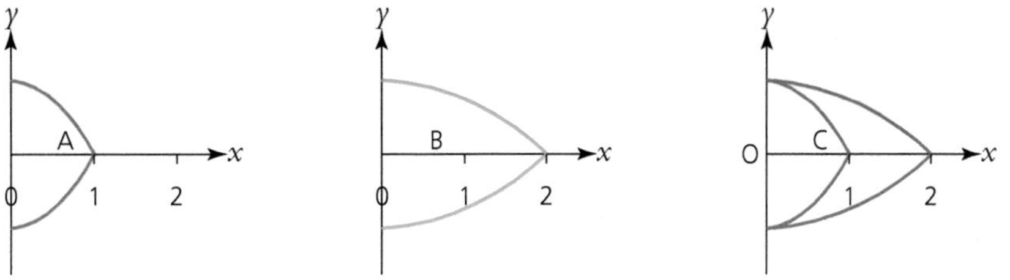

Figure 13.37

(iii) Find the position of the centre of mass of the pendant.

(iv) The pendant is suspended from a vertical string attached to the point Y with coordinates (0, 1). Find the angle that OY makes with the vertical.

⑭ Find the coordinates of the centre of mass of the uniform lamina made from the region between the curves $y = 4 - x^2$ and $y = x^2$ and the y-axis.

⑮ The region between the curve $y = 4 - x^2$ and the curves $y = 2x - x^2$ and $y = -2x - x^2$ is shown in Figure 13.38.

Find the position of the centre of mass of the region.

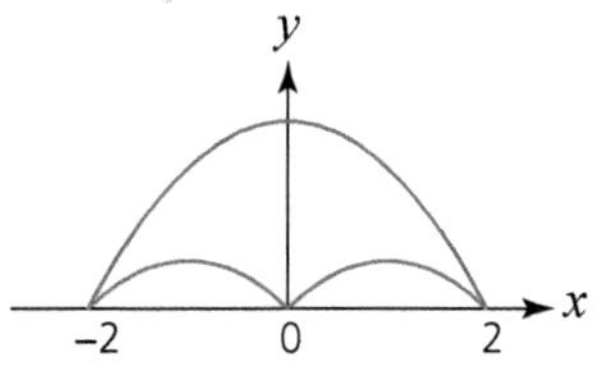

Figure 13.38

⑯ The figure below is composed of a semicircle of radius R from which two semicircles of radius r are removed and a semicircle of radius $R - 2r$ is added.

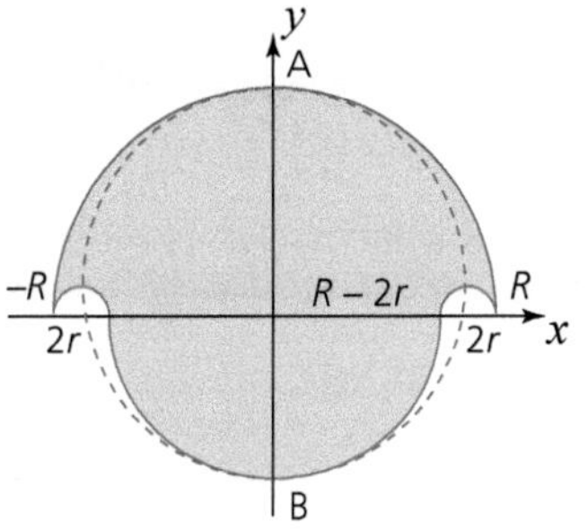

Figure 13.39

(i) Show that the area of the shape is the same as that of a circle centred at $(0, r)$ and of radius $R - r$.

(ii) Find the position of the centre of mass of the shape.

Note

Archimedes proved in his *Book of Lemmas* that this figure, which he called *salinon* (salt cellar), has an area equal to the circle with AB as diameter.

Historical note

Archimedes of Syracuse (287 BC–212 BC) was an ancient Greek mathematician. He anticipated modern calculus and analysis by applying concepts of infinitesimals and the method of exhaustion to derive and rigorously prove a range of geometrical theorems. He was able to apply mathematics to physical phenomena, thus founding hydrostatics and statics, including an explanation of the principle of the lever. He is credited with designing innovative machines such as the screw pump, compound pulleys and defensive war machines to protect his native Syracuse from invasion.

4 Sliding and toppling

Figure 13.40 shows a double decker bus on a test ramp. The angle of the ramp to the horizontal is slowly increased.

Figure 13.40

Discussion point

What happens to the bus? Would a loaded bus behave differently from the empty bus in Figure 13.40?

EXPERIMENT

Figure 13.41 show a force being applied to a cereal packet in different positions

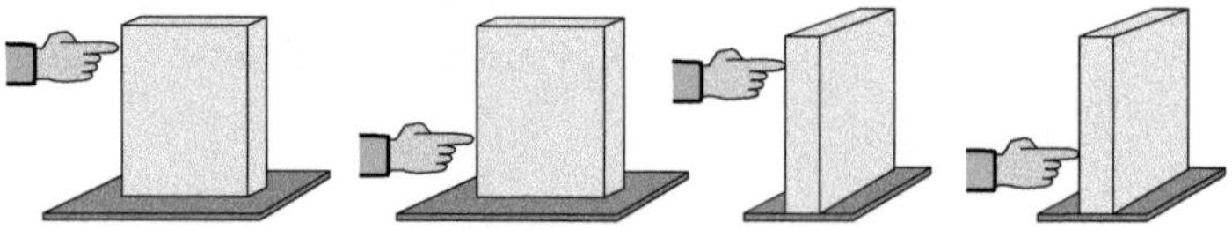

Figure 13.41

In which case do you think the packet is most likely to fall over? In which case is it most likely to slide? Investigate your answers practically, using boxes of different shapes.

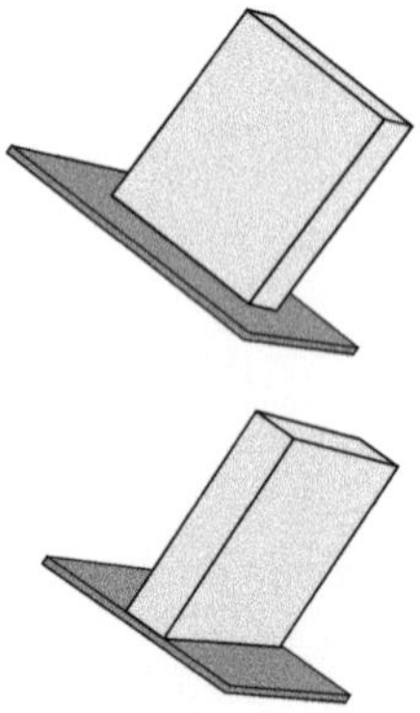

Figure 13.42

Discussion point

Figure 13.42 shows the cereal packet placed on a slope. Is the box more likely to topple or slide as the angle of the slope to the horizontal increases?

To what extent is this situation comparable to that of the bus on the test ramp?

Two critical cases

When an object stands on a surface, the only forces acting on it are its weight W and the **resultant** of all the contact forces between the surfaces, which must act through a point on both surfaces. This resultant contact force is often resolved into two components: the friction, F, parallel to any possible sliding and the normal contact force, R, perpendicular to F, as in Figures 13.43–13.45.

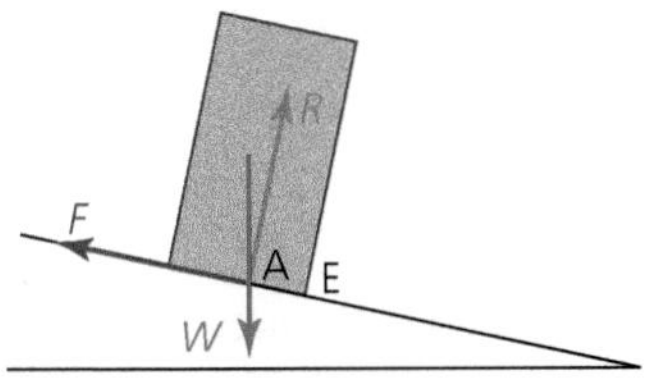

Figure 13.43

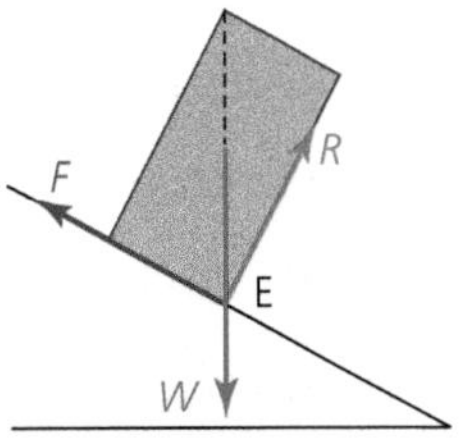

Figure 13.44

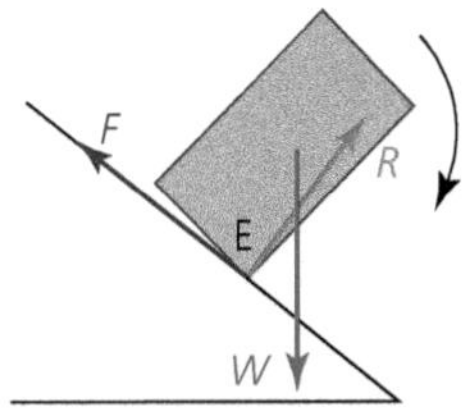

Figure 13.45

Equilibrium can be broken in two ways.

(i) **The object is on the point of sliding.** Then $F = \mu R$ according to the model.

(ii) **The object is on the point of toppling.** The pivot is at the lowest point of contact which is the point E in Figure 13.44. In this critical case:

- the centre of mass is directly above E so the weight acts vertically downwards through E
- the resultant reaction of the plane on the object acts through E, vertically upwards. This is the resultant of F and R.

When three non-parallel forces are in equilibrium, their lines of action must be concurrent (they must all pass through one point). Otherwise there is a resultant moment about the point where two of them meet, as in Figure 13.45.

> **Discussion point**
> Why does the object topple in Figure 13.45?

Example 13.10

An increasing force P newtons is applied to a block, as shown in Figure 13.46, until the block moves. The coefficient of friction between the block and the plane is 0.4.

Does the block slide or topple?

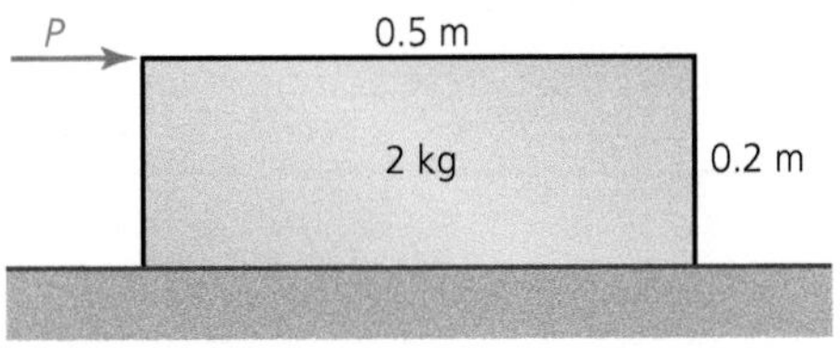

Figure 13.46

Solution

The forces acting are shown in Figure 13.47. The normal contact force may be thought of as a single force acting somewhere within the area of contact. When toppling occurs (or is about to occur), the line of action is through the edge about which it topples.

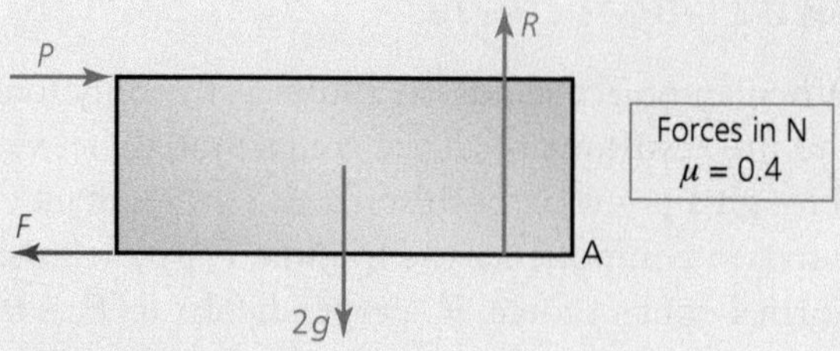

Figure 13.47

Until the block moves, it is in equilibrium.

Horizontally, $P = F$ ①

Vertically, $R = 2g$ ②

If *sliding* is about to occur, $F = \mu R$

From ① $P = \mu R = 0.4 \times 2g$

$= 7.84$

> **Hint**
>
> *R* acts through A.

If the block is about to topple, then A is the pivot point and the reaction of the plane on the block acts at A. Taking moments about A gives

$$[\text{anticlockwise}] \quad 2g \times 0.25 - P \times 0.2 = 0$$

$$P = 24.5$$

So in order to slide P needs to exceed 7.84 N but to topple it needs to exceed 24.5 N: the block will slide before it topples.

Example 13.11

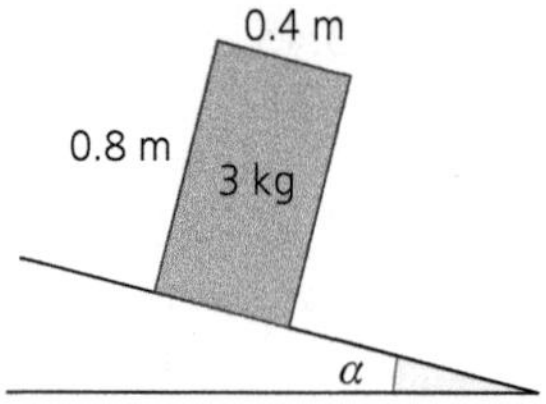

Figure 13.48

A rectangular block of mass 3 kg is placed on a slope as shown in Figure 13.48. The angle α is gradually increased.

What happens to the block given that the coefficient of friction between the block and the slope is 0.6?

Solution

Check for possible sliding.

Figure 13.49 shows the forces acting when the block is in equilibrium.

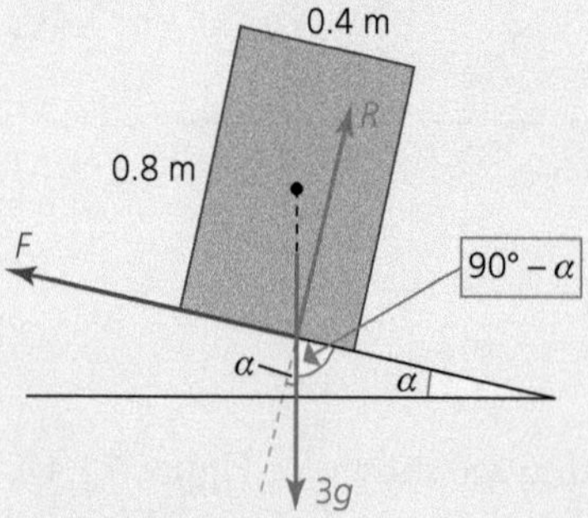

Figure 13.49

Resolve parallel to the slope $F = 3g \sin \alpha$

Perpendicular to the slope $R = 3g \cos \alpha$

When the block is on the point of sliding $F = \mu R$ so

$$3g \sin \alpha = \mu \times 3g \cos \alpha$$

$$\Rightarrow \quad \tan \alpha = \mu = 0.6$$

$$\Rightarrow \quad \alpha = 31.0°$$

The block is on the point of sliding when $\alpha = 31°$.

Check for possible toppling.

When the block is on the point of toppling about the edge E the centre of mass is vertically above E, as shown in Figure 13.50.

Then the angle α is given by

$$\tan \alpha = \frac{0.4}{0.8}$$

$$\alpha = \arctan(0.5) = 26.6°$$

The block topples when $\alpha = 26.6°$.

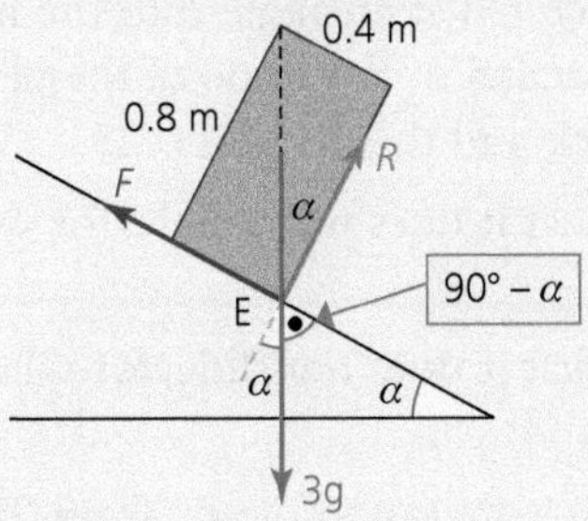

Figure 13.50

Discussion point

Is it possible for sliding and toppling to occur for the same angle?

The angle for sliding (31°) is greater than the angle for toppling (26.6°), so the block topples without sliding when $\alpha = 26.6°$.

Exercise 13.4

① A force of magnitude P newtons acts as shown on a block resting on a horizontal plane. The coefficient of friction between the block and the plane is 0.7.

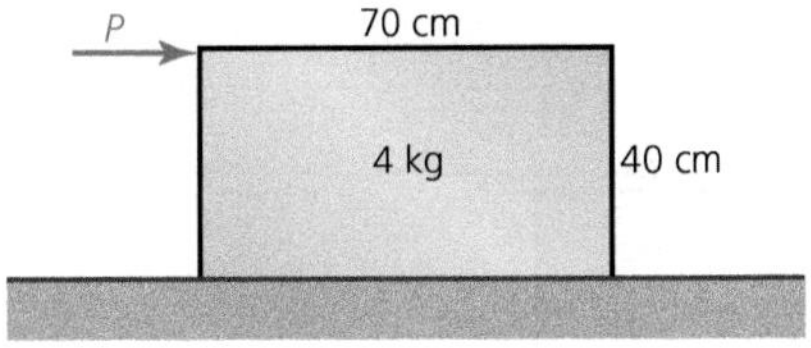

Figure 13.51

The magnitude of the force P is gradually increased from zero.

(i) Find the magnitude of P if the block is on the point of sliding, assuming it does not topple.

(ii) Find the magnitude of P if the block is on the point of toppling, assuming it does not slide.

(iii) Does the block slide or topple?

② A solid uniform cuboid is placed on a horizontal surface. A force is P is applied as shown in Figure 13.52.

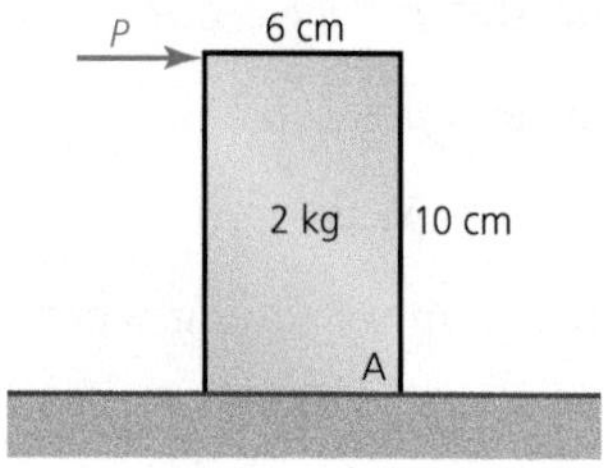

Figure 13.52

(i) If the block is on the point of sliding express P in terms of μ, the coefficient of friction between the block and the plane.

(ii) Find the magnitude of P if the block is on the point of toppling.

(iii) For what values of μ will the block slide before it topples?

(iv) For what values of μ will the block topple before it slides?

③ A uniform rectangular block of height 30 cm and width 10 cm is placed on a rough plane inclined at an angle α to the horizontal. The block lies with its shorter side parallel to the slope of the plane. The coefficient of friction between the block and the plane is 0.25.

(i) Assuming that it does not topple, for what value of α does the block just slide?

(ii) Assuming that it does not slide, for what value of α does the block just topple?

(iii) The angle α is increased slowly from 0°. Which happens first, sliding or toppling?

④ A horizontal force of increasing magnitude is applied to the middle of the face of a 50 cm uniform cube, at right angles to the face. The coefficient of friction between the cube and the surface is 0.4 and the cube is on a level surface. What happens to the cube?

⑤ A solid uniform cube of side 4 cm and weight 60 N is situated on a rough horizontal plane. The coefficient of friction between the cube and the plane is 0.4. A force P acts in the middle of one of the edges of the top of the cube, as shown in Figure 13.53.

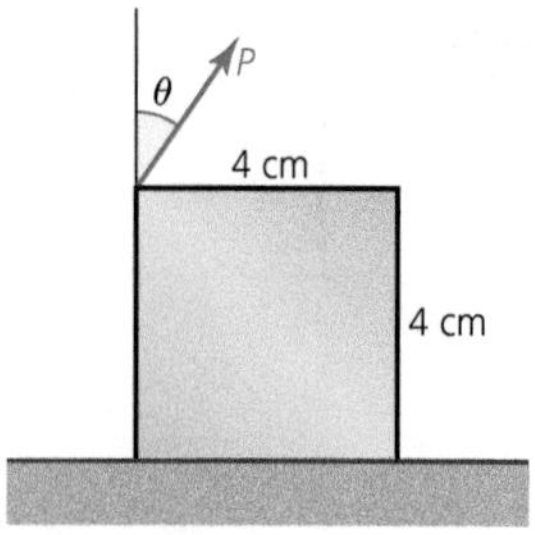

Figure 13.53

In the cases when the value of θ is (a) 60°, (b) 80°, find

(i) the force P needed to make the cube slide, assuming it does not topple

(ii) the force P needed to make the cube topple, assuming it does not slide

(iii) whether it first slides or topples as the force P is increased.

For what value of θ do toppling and sliding occur for the same value of P, and what is that value of P?

⑥ A solid uniform cuboid, 10 cm × 20 cm × 50 cm, is to stand on an inclined plane, which makes an angle α with the horizontal. One edge of the cuboid is to be parallel to the line of the slope. The coefficient of friction between the cuboid and the plane is μ.

(i) Which face of the cuboid should be placed on the slope to make it

(a) least likely and (b) most likely to topple?

(ii) How does the cuboid's orientation influence the likelihood of it sliding?

(iii) Find the range of possible values of μ in the situations where:

(a) it will slide whatever its orientation;

(b) it will topple whatever its orientation.

⑦ 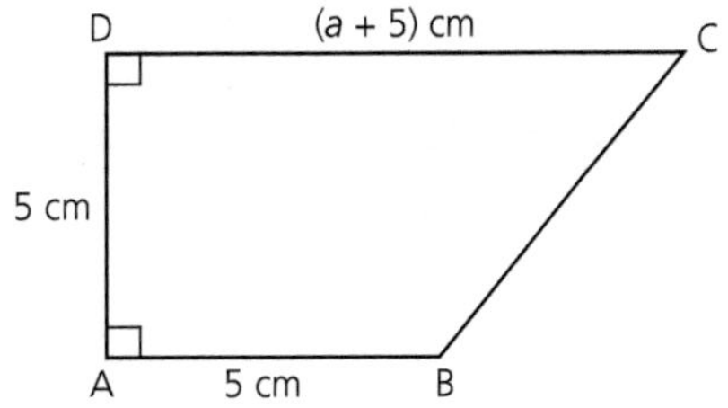

Figure 13.54

Figure 13.54 shows the cross-section through the centre of mass of a uniform solid prism. The cross-section is a trapezium ABCD with AB and CD perpendicular to AD. The lengths of AB and AD are each 5 cm and the length of CD is $(a + 5)$ cm.

(i) Show the distance of the centre of mass of the prism from AD is

$$\frac{a^2 + 15a + 75}{3(a + 10)}\text{ cm}$$

The prism is placed with the face containing AB in contact with a horizontal surface.

(ii) Find the greatest value of a for which the prism does not topple.

The prism is now placed on an inclined plane which makes an angle $\theta°$ with the horizontal. AB lies along a line of greatest slope with B higher than A.

(iii) Using the value for a found in part (ii), and assuming the prism does not slip down the plane, find the greatest value of θ for which the prism does not topple.

⑧ A cube of side 4 cm and mass 100 g is acted on by a force as shown in Figure 13.55.

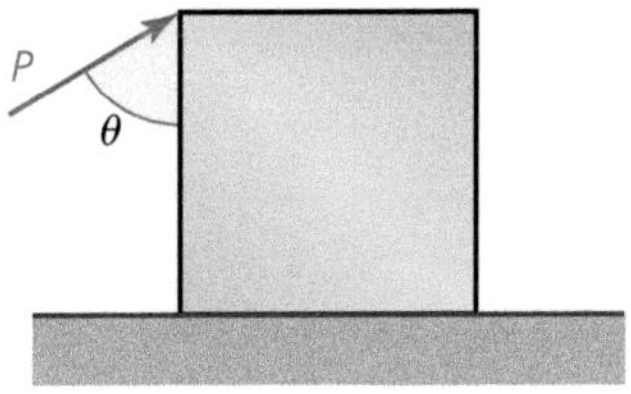

Figure 13.55

The coefficient of friction between the cube and the plane is 0.3. What happens to the cube if

(i) $\theta = 45°$ and $P = 0.3$ N

(ii) $\theta = 15°$ and $P = 0.45$ N?

⑨ A cube of side l and weight W is resting on a rough horizontal plane. A force of magnitude T is applied to a point P on the top edge of the cube. This force makes an angle θ with the horizontal such that $\tan\theta = \frac{3}{4}$ and the force is in the vertical plane containing P and the centre of the cube. The cube does not slip and is on the point of tipping.

Show that $T = 2.5W$.

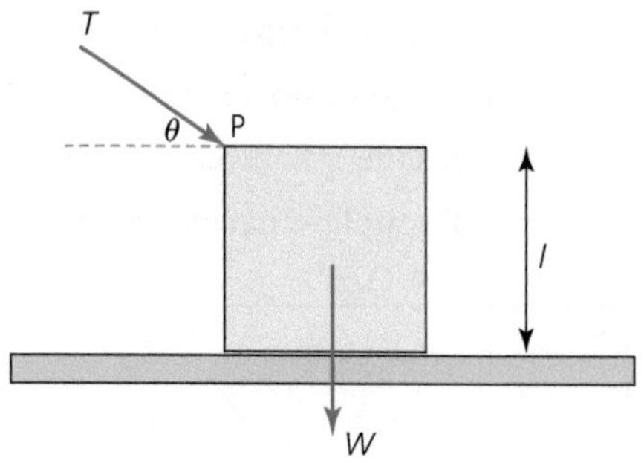

Figure 13.56

KEY POINTS

Volumes of revolution

1 About the x-axis:

$$V = \int_a^b \pi y^2 \, dx$$

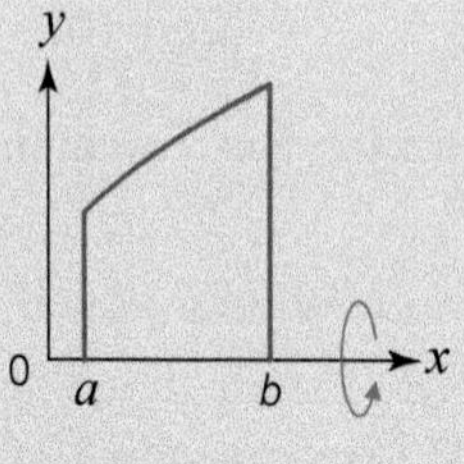

Figure 13.57

About the y-axis:

$$V = \int_p^q \pi x^2 \, dy$$

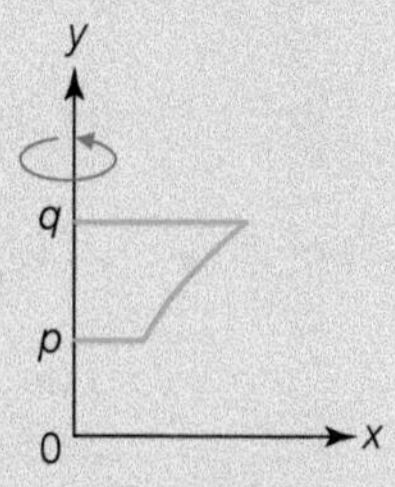

Figure 13.58

Centres of mass of uniform bodies

2 For a volume of revolution

About the x-axis:

$$\left(\int_a^b \pi y^2 \, dx\right)\bar{x} = \int_a^b \pi x y^2 \, dx$$

and $\bar{y} = 0$

About the y-axis:

$\bar{x} = 0$ and

$$\left(\int_p^q \pi x^2 \, dy\right)\bar{y} = \int_p^q \pi y x^2 \, dy$$

3 For a uniform plane lamina, area A, as shown in Figures 13.57 and 13.58.

$$A = \int_a^b y \, dx$$

$$A\begin{pmatrix}\bar{x}\\ \bar{y}\end{pmatrix} = \begin{pmatrix}\int_a^b xy \, dx \\ \int_a^b \frac{y^2}{2} \, dx\end{pmatrix}$$

$$A = \int_p^q x \, dy$$

$$A\begin{pmatrix}\bar{x}\\ \bar{y}\end{pmatrix} = \begin{pmatrix}\int_p^q \frac{x^2}{2} \, dy \\ \int_p^q yx \, dy\end{pmatrix}$$

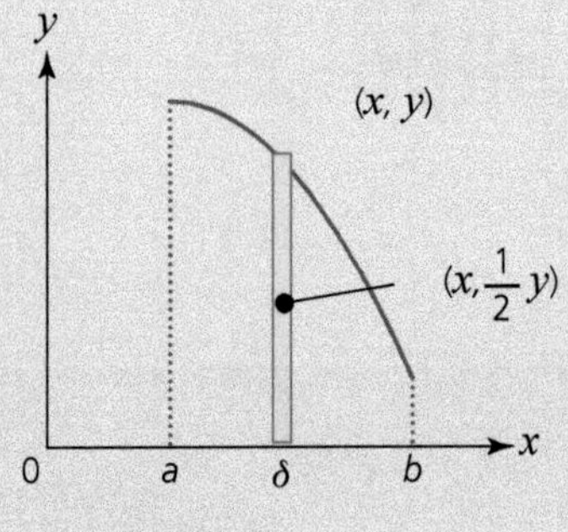

Figure 13.59

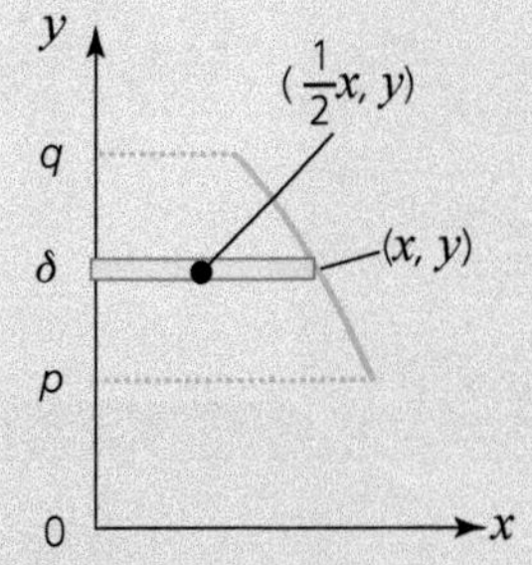

Figure 13.60

LEARNING OUTCOMES

When you have completed this chapter, you should be able to

- calculate the volume generated by rotating a plane region about an axis
- use calculus methods to calculate the centre of mass of a solid body formed by rotating a plane region about an axis
- find the centre of mass of a compound body, parts of which are solids of revolution
- use calculus methods to find the position of the centre of mass of a plane lamina
- find the position of the centre of mass of a compound shape made up of plane regions
- find the angle between part of an object and the horizontal or vertical when it is suspended in equilibrium
- be able to identify how equilibrium can be broken by sliding or toppling.

14 Oblique impact

Pray always for all the learned, the oblique, the delicate. Let them not be quite forgotten at the throne of God when the simple come into their kingdom.

Evelyn Waugh

Discussion point

In what direction should the white cue ball be struck for the blue ball to be potted? Is it possible to pot the red ball?

1 Impulse and momentum in more than one dimension

In Chapter 6 you met situations involving impact between objects moving along a straight line. This involved working with momentum and impulse. It is summed up by the equation

final momentum = initial momentum + impulse

In this chapter, these ideas are extended to motion in more than one direction.

Both impulse and momentum are vectors. The impulse of a force is in the direction of the force and the momentum of a moving object is in the direction of its velocity. So the equation above can be represented as the vector diagram in Figure 14.1.

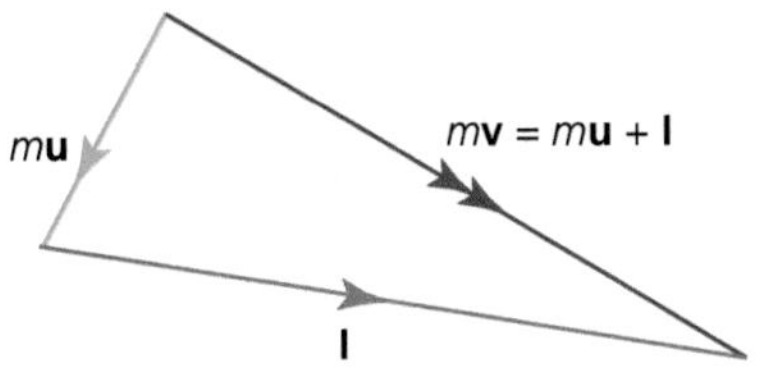

Figure 14.1

Written in symbols, the equation is:

$$m\mathbf{v} = m\mathbf{u} + \mathbf{I}$$

The quantities **u** and **v** can usually be measured but **I** cannot and has to be inferred, using the impulse-momentum equation in the form:

$$\mathbf{I} = m\mathbf{v} - m\mathbf{u}$$

Figure 14.2 shows how this applies to a ball which changes direction when it is hit by a bat.

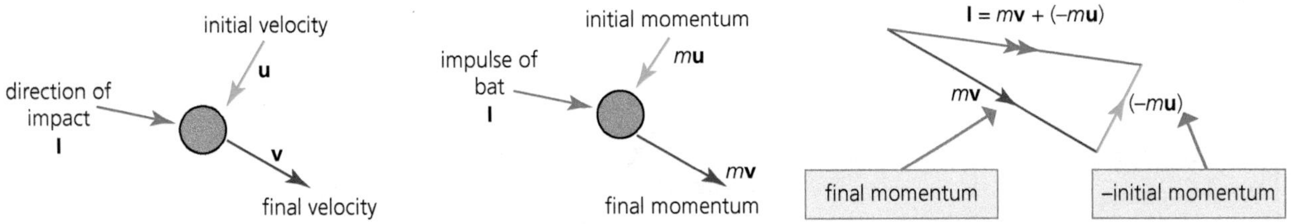

Figure 14.2

Example 14.1

In a game of snooker, the white cue ball of mass 0.2 kg is hit towards a stationary red ball at $0.8\,\mathrm{m\,s^{-1}}$. After the collision the cue ball is moving at $0.6\,\mathrm{m\,s^{-1}}$ having been deflected through 30°.

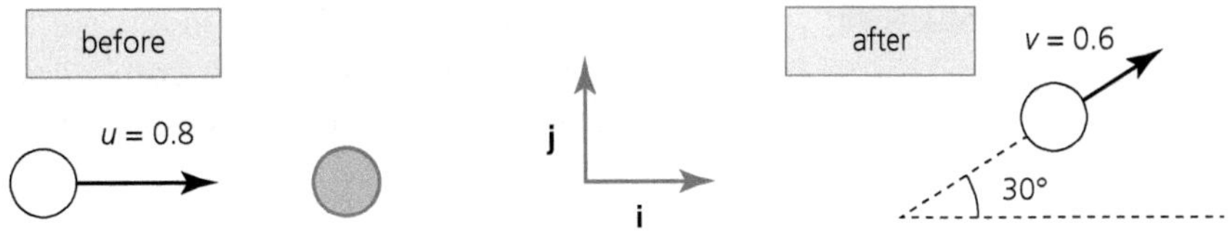

Figure 14.3

Find the impulse on the cue ball and show this in a vector diagram.

Solution

In terms of unit vectors **i** and **j** the velocities of the ball before and after the collision are given by:

$$\mathbf{u} = 0.8\mathbf{i}$$
$$\mathbf{v} = 0.6\cos 30°\,\mathbf{i} + 0.6\sin 30°\,\mathbf{j}$$

Then, using the impulse–momentum equation:

$$\begin{aligned} \mathrm{I} &= m\mathbf{v} - m\mathbf{u} \\ &= 0.2(0.6\cos 30°\mathbf{i} + 0.6\sin 30°\mathbf{j}) - 0.2(0.8\mathbf{i}) \\ &= -0.056\mathbf{i} + 0.06\mathbf{j} \end{aligned}$$

Magnitude of impulse: $\sqrt{0.056^2 + 0.06^2}$

$= 0.082$

Direction of impulse:

$$\tan\alpha = \frac{0.06}{0.056}$$
$$\alpha = 47°$$
$$\theta = 133°$$

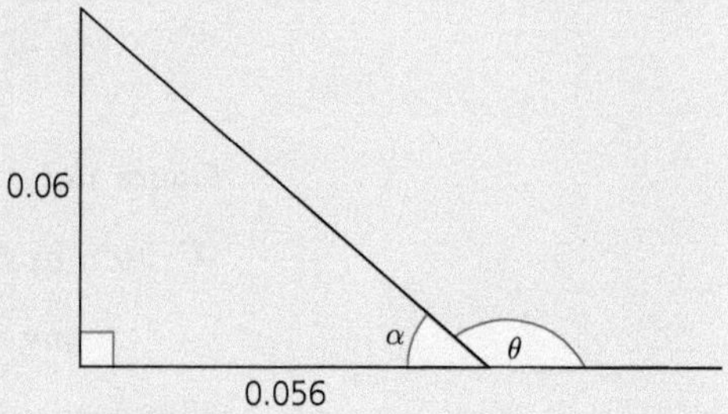

Figure 14.4

The impulse has magnitude 0.082 N s at an angle of 133° to the initial motion of the ball.

This is shown in the vector diagram, Figure 14.5. Note that the impulse–momentum equation shows the direction of the impulsive force acting on the cue ball.

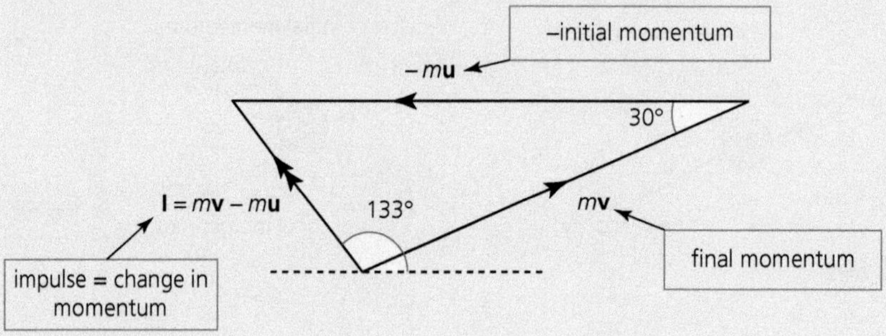

Figure 14.5

Discussion point
What happens to the red ball?

Example 14.2

A hockey ball of mass 0.15 kg is moving at 4 m s^{-1} parallel to the side of a pitch when it is struck by a blow from a hockey stick that exerts an impulse of 4 N s at an angle of 120° to its direction of motion. Find the final velocity of the ball.

Solution

Figure 14.6 shows the motion of the ball.

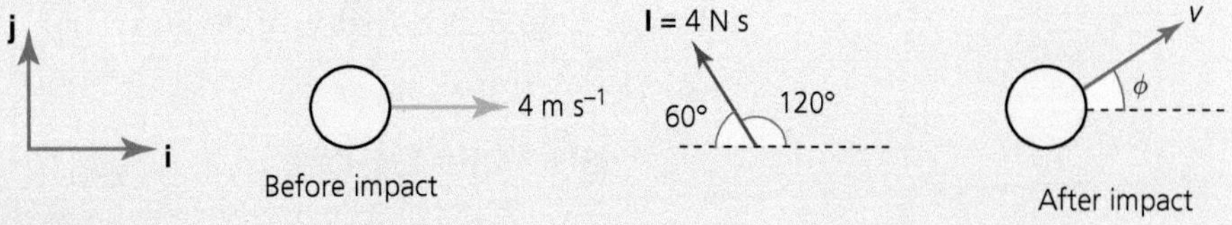

Figure 14.6

In terms of unit vectors $\mathbf{i}$ and $\mathbf{j}$:

$$\mathbf{u} = 4\mathbf{i}$$

and

$$\begin{aligned}\mathbf{I} &= -4\cos 60°\,\mathbf{i} + 4\sin 60°\,\mathbf{j}\\ &= -2\mathbf{i} + 3.46\mathbf{j}\end{aligned}$$

Using

$$\mathbf{I} = m\mathbf{v} - m\mathbf{u}$$

$$-2\mathbf{i} + 3.46\mathbf{j} = 0.15\mathbf{v} - 0.15 \times 4\mathbf{i}$$

$$\Rightarrow \quad 0.15\mathbf{v} = -2\mathbf{i} + 0.6\mathbf{i} + 3.46\mathbf{j}$$

$$\Rightarrow \quad 0.15\mathbf{v} = -1.4\mathbf{i} + 3.46\mathbf{j}$$

$$\Rightarrow \quad \mathbf{v} = -9.33\mathbf{i} + 23.1\mathbf{j}$$

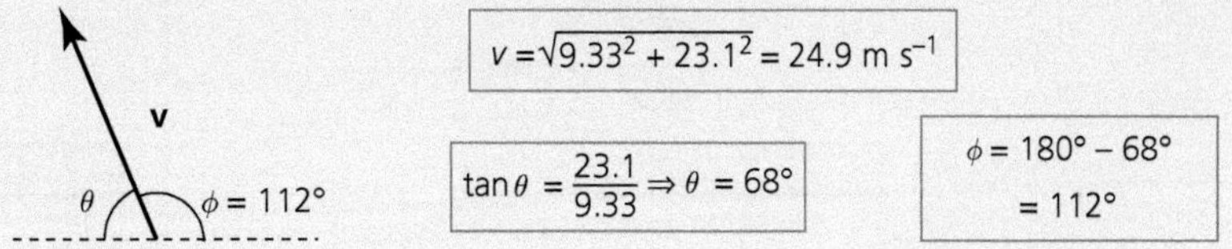

Figure 14.7

After the blow, the ball has a velocity of magnitude $24.9\,\mathrm{m\,s^{-1}}$ at an angle of 112° to the original direction of motion.

Conservation of momentum

The principle of conservation of momentum is equally valid in more than one dimension. In its vector form it can be expressed as follows.

If two particles, of masses m_1 and m_2, collide, their initial velocities $\mathbf{u}_1$ and $\mathbf{u}_2$, and their final velocities $\mathbf{v}_1$ and $\mathbf{v}_2$, satisfy the equation

$$m_1\mathbf{u}_1 + m_2\mathbf{u}_2 = m_1\mathbf{v}_1 + m_2\mathbf{v}_2.$$

Example 14.3

A body of mass 2 kg, moving with velocity $(3\mathbf{i} + 4\mathbf{j})\,\mathrm{m\,s^{-1}}$, collides with a body of mass 3 kg, moving with velocity $(-4\mathbf{i} + 5\mathbf{j})\,\mathrm{m\,s^{-1}}$. After the collision the two bodies coalesce. Find the common velocity of the combined body after the impact.

Solution

Let the common velocity after the impact be $u\mathbf{i} + v\mathbf{j}$.

$2 \times (3\mathbf{i} + 4\mathbf{j}) + 3 \times (-4\mathbf{i} + 5\mathbf{j}) = 5(u\mathbf{i} + v\mathbf{j})$.

$\Rightarrow \quad (6 - 12)\mathbf{i} = 5u\mathbf{i}$

$\quad\quad (8 + 15)\mathbf{j} = 5v\mathbf{j}$

$\Rightarrow \quad u = -1.2, v = 4.6$

The common velocity of the combined body after the impact is $(-1.2\mathbf{i} + 4.6\mathbf{j})\ \mathrm{m\,s^{-1}}$.

Oblique impact of a sphere on a plane

When an object hits a smooth plane there can be no impulse parallel to the plane so the component of momentum, and hence velocity, is unchanged in this direction. Perpendicular to the plane, the momentum is changed but Newton's law of impact still applies.

Figure 14.8 show the components of the velocity of a ball immediately before and after it hits a smooth plane with coefficient of restitution e.

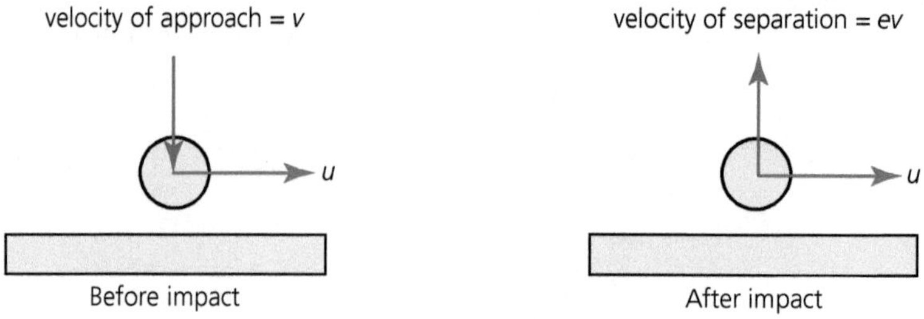

Figure 14.8

When the ball is travelling with speed U at an angle α to the plane, the components of the final velocity are $U \cos \alpha$ parallel to the plane and $eU \sin \alpha$ perpendicular to the plane.

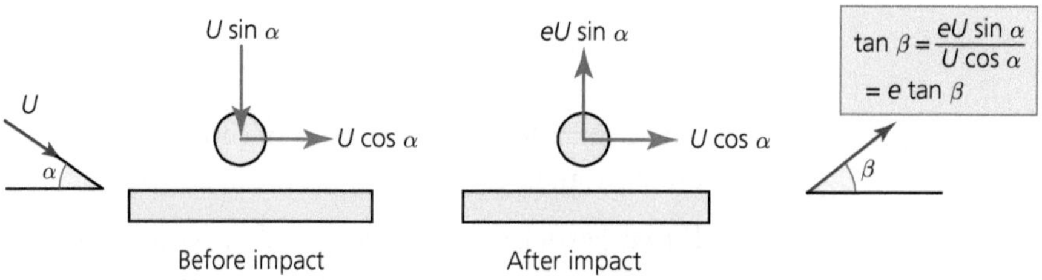

Figure 14.9

The *impulse* on the ball is equal to final momentum – initial momentum. This is perpendicular to the plane because there is no change in momentum parallel to the plane.

In Figure 14.8 the impulse is:

$$mev - m(-v) = (1 + e)mv \text{ upwards}$$

In Figure 14.9 the impulse is:

$$meU \sin \alpha - m(-U \sin \alpha) = (1 + e)mU \sin \alpha \text{ upwards}$$

Whenever an impact takes place, energy is likely to be lost. In the cases illustrated in Figure 14.9, the *loss in kinetic energy* is:

> **Discussion point**
> What happens to the ball when $e = 0$ and $e = 1$?

$$\frac{1}{2}m(u^2+v^2)-\frac{1}{2}m(u^2+e^2v^2)=\frac{1}{2}m(1-e^2)v^2$$

or $$\frac{1}{2}m(1-e^2)U^2\sin^2\alpha$$

Example 14.4

A ball of mass 0.2 kg moving at $12\,\mathrm{m\,s^{-1}}$ hits a smooth horizontal plane at an angle of 75° to the horizontal. The coefficient of restitution is 0.5. Find:

(i) the impulse on the ball

(ii) the impulse on the plane

(iii) the kinetic energy lost by the ball.

Solution

(i) Figure 14.10 shows the velocities before and after impact.

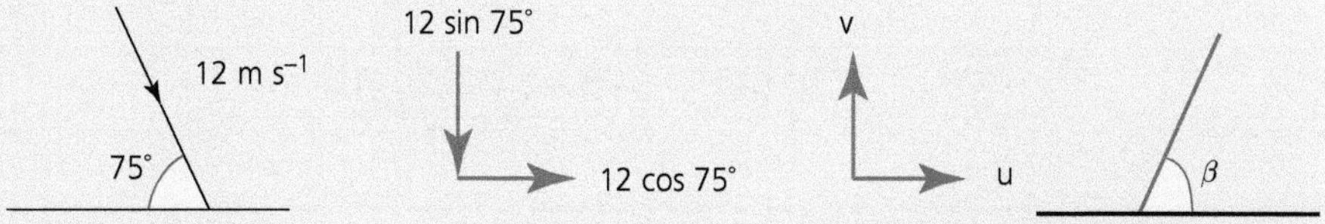

Figure 14.10

Parallel to the plane: $u = 12\cos 75°$ ← No change in velocity parallel to the plane

Perpendicular to the plane: $v = 0.5 \times 12\sin 75°$ ← Using Newton's law of impact with $e = 0.5$

$= 6\sin 75°$

The impulse on the ball = final momentum – initial momentum

$$\mathrm{I}=0.2\begin{pmatrix}12\cos75°\\6\sin75°\end{pmatrix}-0.2\begin{pmatrix}12\cos75°\\-12\sin75°\end{pmatrix}$$ ← Using directions **i** and **j** as shown

$$=\begin{pmatrix}0\\3.6\sin75°\end{pmatrix}$$

The impulse on the ball is 3.6 sin 75° **j**, that is, 3.48 N s perpendicular to the plane and upwards in the **j** direction.

(ii) By Newton's third law, the impulse on the plane is equal and opposite to the impulse on the ball. It is 3.48 N s perpendicular to the plane in the direction of $-$**j**.

(iii) The initial kinetic energy $=\frac{1}{2}\times0.2\times12^2=14.4\,\mathrm{J}$

Final kinetic energy $=\frac{1}{2}\times0.2\times\left[(12\cos75°)^2+(6\sin75°)^2\right]$

$= 4.32\,\mathrm{J}$

Loss in kinetic energy $= 13.4 - 4.32 = 10.1\,\mathrm{J}$ (3 s.f.)

Example 14.5

A ball moving with speed $10\,\mathrm{m\,s^{-1}}$ hits a smooth horizontal plane at an angle of 60° to the horizontal. The coefficient of restitution between the ball and the surface is $\frac{1}{3}$. The ball rebounds with speed v at an angle β with the surface.

(i) Find v.

(ii) Find β.

Solution

(i)

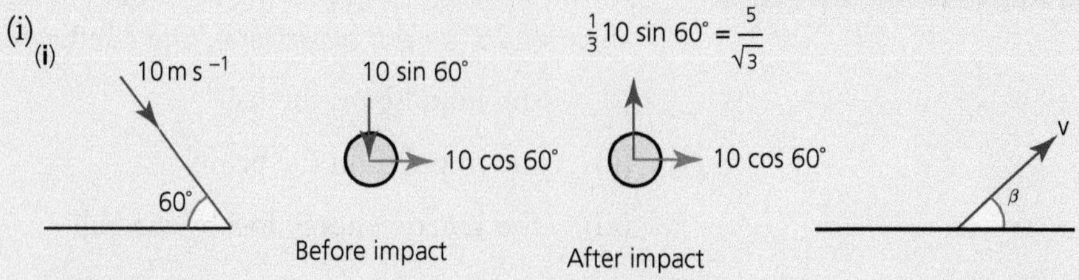

Figure 14.11

Using $\sin 60° = \frac{\sqrt{3}}{2}$ and $\cos 60° = \frac{1}{2}$

$$v = \sqrt{\left(\frac{5}{\sqrt{3}}\right)^2 + 5^2} = \sqrt{\frac{100}{3}} = 5.77\,\mathrm{m\,s^{-1}}$$

(ii) $\tan\beta = \dfrac{\frac{5}{\sqrt{3}}}{5} = \dfrac{1}{\sqrt{3}}$; $\beta = 30°$

Exercise 14.1

① A snooker ball of mass 0.08 kg is travelling with speed $3.5\,\mathrm{m\,s^{-1}}$ when it hits the cushion at an angle of 60°. After the impact the ball is travelling with speed $2\,\mathrm{m\,s^{-1}}$ at an angle of 30° to the cushion.

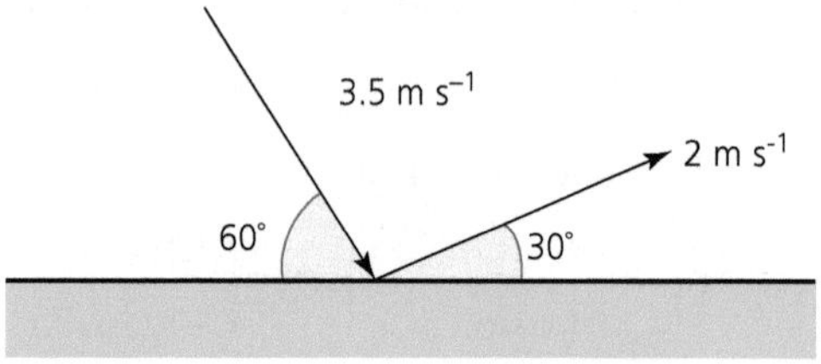

Figure 14.12

(i) Draw accurate scale diagrams to represent the following vectors:
the momentum of the ball before impact
the momentum of the ball after impact
the change in momentum of the ball during impact.

(ii) Use your answers to part (i) to **estimate** the magnitude and direction of the impulse acting on the ball.

(iii) Resolve the velocity of the ball before and after the impact into components parallel and perpendicular to the cushion.

(iv) Use your answers to part (iii) to **calculate** the impulse which acts on the ball during its impact with the cushion. Comment on your answers.

② A hockey ball of mass 0.15 kg is travelling with velocity $12\mathbf{i} - 8\mathbf{j}$ (in $\mathrm{m\,s^{-1}}$), where the unit vectors **i** and **j** are in horizontal directions parallel and perpendicular to the length of the pitch, and the vector **k** is vertically upwards. The ball is hit by Jane with an impulse $-4.8\mathbf{i} + 1.2\mathbf{j}$.

(i) What is the velocity of the ball immediately after Jane has hit it?

The ball goes straight, without losing any speed, to Fatima in the opposite team who hits it without stopping it. Its velocity is now 14**i** + 4**j** + 3**k**.

(ii) What impulse does Fatima give the ball?

(iii) Which player hits the ball harder?

③ Find the velocity of each of the following after one impact with a smooth plane.

(i) Initial velocity $4\,\mathrm{m\,s^{-1}}$ at 20° to the plane. Coefficient of restitution 0.5.

(ii) Initial velocity $10\,\mathrm{m\,s^{-1}}$ at 40° to the plane. Coefficient of restitution 0.1.

(iii) Initial velocity u $\mathrm{m\,s^{1}}$ at $\alpha°$ to the plane. Coefficient of restitution 0.8.

④ A ball of mass 0.1 kg moving at $10\,\mathrm{m\,s^{-1}}$ hits a smooth horizontal plane at an angle of 80° to the horizontal. The coefficient of restitution is 0.6. Find:

(i) the impulse on the ball

(ii) the impulse on the plane

(iii) the kinetic energy lost by the particle.

⑤ A particle of mass 0.05 kg moving at $8\,\mathrm{m\,s^{-1}}$ hits a smooth horizontal plane at an angle of 45° to the horizontal. The coefficient of restitution is 0.6. Find:

(i) the impulse on the particle

(ii) the impulse on the plane

(iii) the kinetic energy lost by the particle.

⑥ A ball of mass m kg moving at u $\mathrm{m\,s^{-1}}$ hits a smooth horizontal plane at an angle of $\alpha°$ to the horizontal. The coefficient of restitution is 0.

(i) Find the impulse on the ball.

(ii) Show that the kinetic energy lost is $\frac{1}{2}mu^2\sin^2\alpha$.

⑦ Two balls A and B, of masses 1.2 kg and 0.8 kg respectively, are rolling on a smooth horizontal floor when they collide. Initially their velocities are (4.2**i** + 2.6**j**) $\mathrm{m\,s^{-1}}$ and (1.2**i** – 0.4**j**) $\mathrm{m\,s^{-1}}$ respectively. After the collision the velocity of A is (1.4**i** +1.8**j**) $\mathrm{m\,s^{-1}}$. Find the velocity of B after the collision.

⑧ A firework of mass 0.16 kg is moving with velocity (1**i** + 2**j** + 35**k**) $\mathrm{m\,s^{-1}}$ when it explodes into two parts, of masses 0.06 kg and 0.1 kg respectively. Immediately after the explosion the velocity of the part of mass 0.06 kg is (2**i** + 3**j** + 50**k**) $\mathrm{m\,s^{-1}}$. Find the velocity of the part of mass 0.1 kg.

⑨ An alpha particle of mass 6.64×10^{-27} has initial velocity (0.23**i** + 0.11**j** + 5.40**k**) $\times 10^7\,\mathrm{m\,s^{-1}}$. It collides with a stationary gold nucleus of mass 1.32×10^{-25} kg. After the collision the velocity of the alpha particle is (–1.71**i** + 0.10**j** + 3.25**k**) $\times 10^7\,\mathrm{m\,s^{-1}}$. Find the velocity of the gold nucleus after the collision.

⑩ A ball is hit from level ground with initial components of velocity u_x $\mathrm{m\,s^{-1}}$ horizontally and u_y vertically. Assume the ball is a particle and ignore air resistance.

(i) Show that its horizontal range is $R = \frac{2u_xu_y}{g}$.

The ball bounces on the ground with coefficient of restitution 0.6.

(ii) How much further does it travel horizontally before the next bounce?

(iii) Find an expression for the horizontal range after the nth bounce.

(iv) By considering the sum of a geometric series, calculate the total horizontal distance travelled up to the sixth bounce.

⑪ A small marble is projected horizontally over the edge of a table 0.8 m high at a speed of $2.5\,\mathrm{m\,s^{-1}}$ and bounces on smooth horizontal ground with coefficient of restitution 0.7.

Calculate:

(i) the components of the velocity of the marble just before it hits the ground

(ii) its horizontal distance from the edge of the table when it first hits the ground

(iii) the horizontal distance travelled between the first and second bounces

(iv) the horizontal distance travelled between the nth and $(n + 1)$th bounces

(v) the number of bounces before the distance between bounces is less than 20 cm.

⑫ A smooth snooker ball moving at $2\,\mathrm{m\,s^{-1}}$ hits a cushion at an angle of 30° to the cushion.

The ball then rebounds and hits a second cushion which is perpendicular to the first. The coefficient of restitution for both impacts is 0.8.

(i) Find the direction of motion after each impact.

(ii) Find the magnitude of the velocity after the second impact.

(iii) Repeat parts (i) and (ii) for a ball moving at $u\,\mathrm{m\,s^{-1}}$ which hits the first cushion at an angle α. Assume the coefficient of restitution is e. Hence show that the direction of a ball is always reversed after hitting two perpendicular cushions and state the factor by which its speed is reduced.

⑬ A standard table tennis table is 1.52 m wide and 2.75 m long. It is divided across the middle by a net 15.25 cm high. A ball is served horizontally at $6\,\mathrm{m\,s^{-1}}$, without spin, from a point 0.3 m above the level of the smooth table. It hits the table at A and then rebounds and passes over the net to hit it again at B. The coefficient of restitution is 0.8.

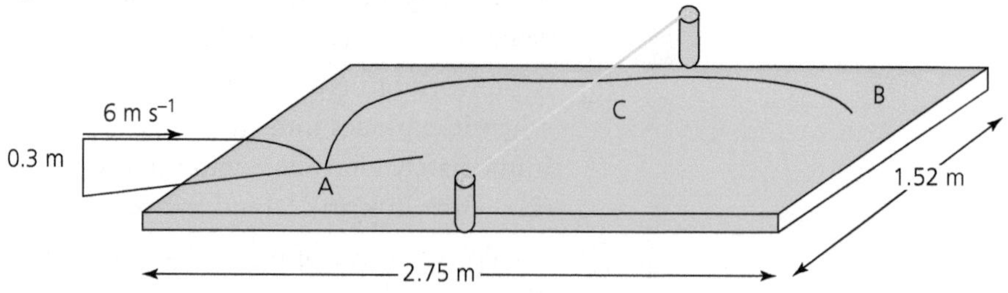

Figure 14.13

(i) Calculate the length AB.

The ball just passes over the net at a point C.

(ii) Calculate the two possible horizontal distances between B and C.

(iii) Given that B is in fact a point on the shorter edge of the table, find at what angle to the net the ball is served.

⑭ Two circular discs slide on a smooth horizontal surface. Disc A has mass 6 kg and disc B has mass 14 kg; both are initially at rest. A force of 12 N acts on disc A for 4 seconds and this disc then collides directly with disc B. The coefficient of restitution between the two discs is 0.25.

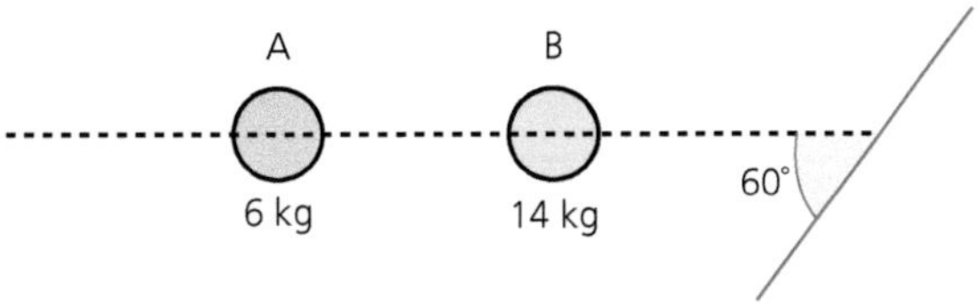

Figure 14.14

(i) Calculate the velocity of disc A before the collision.

(ii) Show that, after the collision, disc B has speed $3\,\mathrm{m\,s^{-1}}$ and find the new speed of disc A.

(iii) Calculate the impulse on disc A in this collision.

Disc B now collides with a smooth surface at 60° to the line of its motion, as shown in Figure 14.14. The speed of the disc after the collision is $1.6\,\mathrm{m\,s^{-1}}$.

(iv) Calculate the coefficient of restitution between the disc and the plane.

⑮ A ball is projected horizontally from a table top of height h with speed u. The coefficient of restitution between the ball and the ground is e.

(i) Find an expression for the time during which the ball is moving.

(ii) Find the total horizontal distance travelled.

⑯ The wind blowing against a sail can be modelled as a series of particles hitting the smooth sail at an angle of 30° and with zero coefficient of restitution. The wind blows at $20\,\mathrm{m\,s^{-1}}$ and the density of the air is $1.4\,\mathrm{kg\ m^{-3}}$. Calculate:

(i) the mass of air hitting one square metre of sail each second

(ii) the impulse of this air on the sail and hence the force acting on a $2\,\mathrm{m^2}$ sail.

2 Oblique impact of smooth elastic spheres

Two smooth spheres A of mass m_A and B of mass m_B collide. Immediately before impact the velocity of A is u at an angle α with the line of centres of the spheres, and the velocity of B is v at an angle β with the line of centres.

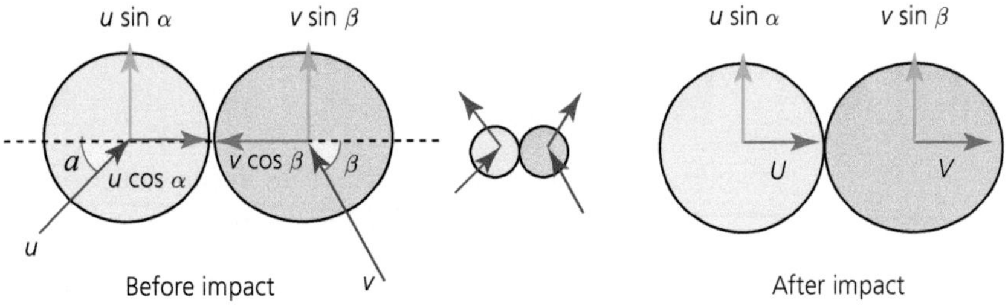

Figure 14.15

When analysing an impact like this you need to consider the components of the motion in two directions: perpendicular to the line of centres and along the line of centres.

Motion perpendicular to the line of centres

There is no impulse between the spheres in the direction of their common tangent at the point of contact and the momentum of each sphere in this direction is unchanged by the impact.

Hence the component velocities after the collision in this direction are $u \sin \alpha$ for A and $v \sin \beta$ for B.

Motion along the line of centres

Calling the components of the velocities in the direction of the line of centres U and V, conservation of momentum gives:

$$m_A u \cos \alpha - m_B v \cos \beta = m_A U + m_B V$$

The coefficient of restitution is e so that Newton's law of impact gives:

$$e(u \cos \alpha + v \cos \beta) = V - U$$

Speed of separation

Speed of approach

These two simultaneous equations are sufficient to determine U and V.

Once U and V are known, the velocities of A and B after the collision can be written in vector form as:

$$\mathbf{v}_A = U\mathbf{i} + u \sin\alpha\, \mathbf{j} \quad \text{and} \quad \mathbf{v}_B = V\mathbf{i} + v \sin\beta\, \mathbf{j}$$

where the directions along and perpendicular to the line of centres are denoted by **i** and **j**.

Example 14.6

In a game of snooker, the cue ball moving with speed $2\,\text{m s}^{-1}$ strikes a stationary red ball. The cue ball is moving at an angle of 60° to the line of centres of the two balls. Both balls are smooth and have the same mass m. The coefficient of restitution between the balls is $\frac{1}{2}$.

Find the velocities of the two balls after impact.

Solution

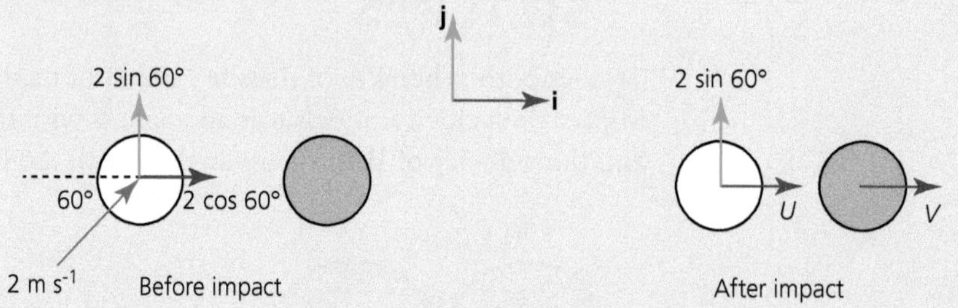

Figure 14.16

Let the component velocities in the direction of the line of centres be U for the cue ball and V for the red ball.

Conservation of momentum in the direction of the line of centres (**i**):

$$m \times 2 \cos 60° = mU + mV$$
$$1 = U + V \quad \text{(A)}$$

Divide by m and use $\cos 60° = 0.5$

Newton's law of impact:

$$e \times 2 \cos 60° = V - U$$

Speed of separation

Speed of approach

$$\frac{1}{2} = V - U \quad \text{(B)}$$

$$\text{(A)+(B)} \quad \frac{3}{2} = 2V \Rightarrow V = \frac{3}{4}$$

$$\text{(A)−(B)} \quad \frac{1}{2} = 2U \Rightarrow U = \frac{1}{4}$$

The velocity of the red ball is $\frac{3}{4}\mathbf{i}$; the velocity of the white ball is $\frac{1}{4}\mathbf{i} + 2\sin 60°\mathbf{j} = \frac{1}{4}\mathbf{i} + \sqrt{3}\mathbf{j}$.

The red ball moves with speed $0.75\,\mathrm{m\,s^{-1}}$ along the line of centres. The cue ball moves with speed $1.75\,\mathrm{m\,s^{-1}}$ at 82° to the line of centres.

$\sqrt{\left(\frac{1}{4}\right)^2 + 3} = \sqrt{\frac{49}{16}} = \frac{7}{4}$

$\theta = \arctan\left(\frac{\sqrt{3}}{0.25}\right) = 81.79°$

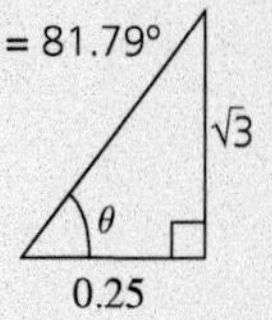

Example 14.7

A smooth sphere A of mass $2m$ moving with speed $4\,\mathrm{m\,s^{-1}}$ collides with a smooth sphere B of mass m moving with speed $2\,\mathrm{m\,s^{-1}}$. The velocity of A immediately before impact makes an angle of 45° to the line of centres. The velocity of B immediately before impact is at 90° to the line of centres. The coefficient of restitution between the two balls is 0.6.

(i) Draw a diagram showing the situation before and after the collision.

(ii) Calculate the velocities of the two spheres after impact.

(iii) Calculate the loss of kinetic energy sustained by the system during the impact.

Solution

(i) The velocities of the two spheres are shown as well as their components **along** and **perpendicular** to the line of centres.

The components perpendicular to the line of centres ($4\sin 45° = 2\sqrt{2}$ for A and 2 for B) are not affected by the collision.

The components along the line of centres are taken to be V_A and V_B.

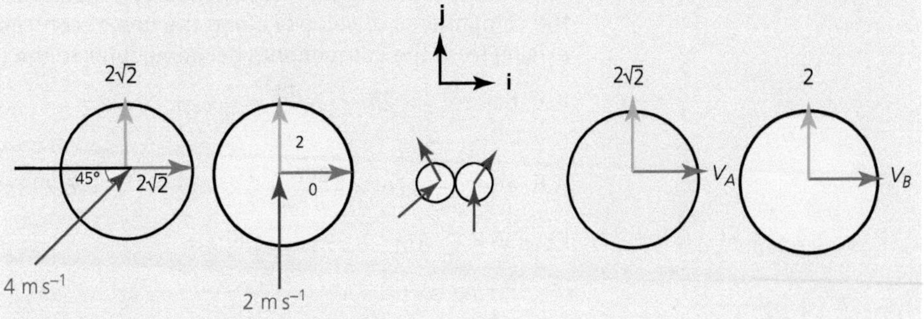

Figure 14.17

(ii) Conservation of momentum along line of centres:

$$2m \times 4\cos 45° = 2mV_A + mV_B$$

Using $\cos 45° = \frac{\sqrt{2}}{2}$ and dividing by m

$$4\sqrt{2} = 2V_A + V_B \qquad \text{(A)}$$

$\theta = \arctan\left(\frac{2\sqrt{2}}{1.32}\right) = 65°$

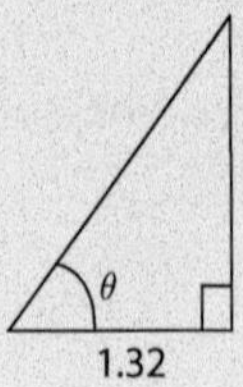

Newton's law of impact:

$e \times 4\cos 45° = V_B - V_A \qquad 2\sqrt{2}e = V_B - V_A \qquad \text{(B)}$

(A)–(B): $(4 - 2e)\sqrt{2} = 3V_A \qquad V_A = \frac{\sqrt{2}}{3}(4 - 2e)$

$4 - 2e = 4 - 2 \times 0.6$

$V_A = \frac{2.8\sqrt{2}}{3} = 1.319\ldots$

(A)+2(B): $4(1+e)\sqrt{2} = 3V_B$

$V_B = \frac{4\sqrt{2}}{3}(1+e)$ ← $4(1 + e) = 4(1 + 0.6)$

$V_B = \frac{6.4\sqrt{2}}{3} = 3.016\ldots$

$\sqrt{1.32^2 + (2\sqrt{2})^2} = \sqrt{1.32^2 + 8} = 3.12$

Velocity of A after impact: $1.32\mathbf{i} + 2\sqrt{2}\,\mathbf{j}$

A moves with speed $3.12\,\mathrm{m\,s^{-1}}$ at an angle of 65° to the line of centres.

Velocity of B after impact: $3.02\mathbf{i} + 2\mathbf{j}$

B moves with speed $3.62\,\mathrm{m\,s^{-1}}$ at an angle of 33.5° to the line of centres.

$\sqrt{3.016\ldots^2 + 2^2} = 3.62$

$\phi = \arctan\left(\frac{2}{3.016\ldots}\right) = 33.5°$

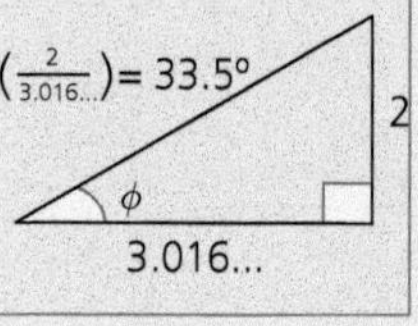

(iii) The kinetic energy of the system before the collision is equal to:

$$\frac{1}{2} \times 2m \times 4^2 + \frac{1}{2} \times m \times 2^2 = 18m$$

The kinetic energy of the system after the collision is equal to:

$$\frac{1}{2} \times 2m \times 3.12^2 + \frac{1}{2} \times m \times 3.62^2 = 16.29m$$

The loss in kinetic energy is:

$$18m - 16.29m = 1.71m$$

Note

This result could have been obtained by consideration of the contribution from the components of velocity along the line of centres only as there is no change arising from the components perpendicular to the line of centres.

K.E. before: $\frac{1}{2} \times 2m \times \left(2\sqrt{2}\right)^2 + \frac{1}{2} \times m \times 0 = 8m$

K.E. after: $\frac{1}{2} \times 2m \times \frac{2.8\sqrt{2}}{3}^2 + \frac{1}{2} \times m \times \frac{6.4\sqrt{2}}{3}^2 = 6.29\dot{3}m$

Loss in K.E. $8m - 6.29\dot{3}m = 1.70\dot{6}m$

Exercise 14.2

In questions 1–6, a smooth sphere A of mass m_A collides with a smooth sphere B of mass m_B, as shown in Figure 14.18.

The coefficient of restitution between the spheres is e.

Immediately before the collision, A is moving with speed u_A at an angle α with the line of centres and B is moving with speed u_B at an angle β with the line of centres.

Immediately after impact, A is moving with speed v_A at an angle α_A with the line of centres and B is moving with speed v_B at an angle β_B with the line of centres.

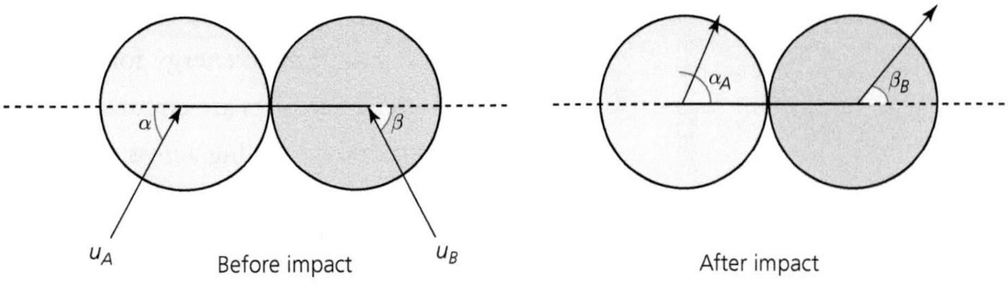

Figure 14.18

① $m_A = 4\,\text{kg}$, $m_B = 2\,\text{kg}$, $u_A = 2\,\text{m s}^{-1}$, $u_B = 4\,\text{m s}^{-1}$, $\alpha = \beta = 45°$, $e = 0.5$.
Calculate v_A, v_B, α_A and β_B.

② $m_A = m_B = m$, $\alpha = 60°$, $u_A = u$, $u_B = 0$, $e = 0.6$.
Calculate v_A, v_B, α_A and β_B.

③ $m_A = m_B = m$, $u_A = u_B = u$, $\alpha = 0°$, $\beta = 90°$, $e = 0.5$.
Calculate v_A, v_B, α_A and β_B.

④ $m_A = m_B = m$, $u_A = u_B = u$, $\alpha = 60°$, $\beta = 60°$, $e = 0.5$.
Calculate v_A, v_B, α_A and β_B.

⑤ $m_A = m$, $m_B = 5m$, $u_A = u$, $u_B = 0$, $\alpha = 60°$, $\alpha_A = 90°$.
Calculate e.

⑥ $m_A = m_B = m$, $u_B = 0$, $\alpha = 45°$, $e = \frac{2}{3}$.
Calculate α_A.

⑦ A white ball of mass 0.17 kg travelling with velocity $6\mathbf{i} + 4\mathbf{j}\,\text{m s}^{-1}$ hits a stationary red ball of mass 0.16 kg. After the impact the velocity of the white ball is $3\mathbf{i} + 3\mathbf{j}\,\text{m s}^{-1}$.

(i) Find the velocity of the red ball after the impact.

(ii) Find the magnitude of the impulse of the white ball on the red ball.

⑧ A small ball A of mass 0.03 kg travelling with velocity $5\mathbf{i} + 3\mathbf{j}\,\text{m s}^{-1}$ hits another small ball B of mass 0.02 kg travelling with velocity $-\mathbf{i} + \mathbf{j}\,\text{m s}^{-1}$. The impulse between the balls acts in the $\mathbf{i}$ direction, and the velocity of ball A after the collision is $\mathbf{i} + \alpha\mathbf{j}\,\text{m s}^{-1}$.

(i) Write down the value of α.

(ii) Find the velocity of B after the collision.

(iii) Find the value of the coefficient of restitution.

⑨ Two identical smooth balls of mass m are moving with equal speed u in opposite directions. The balls collide obliquely, so that the line of centres between the balls is at 30° to the direction of motion. Show that the loss in kinetic energy due to the impact is 75% of what it would be if the impact were direct.

⑩ A smooth sphere A of mass $2m$ moving with speed $2u$ collides with a smooth sphere B of mass m moving with speed u.

At the moment of impact, A is moving at 60° to the line of centres and B is moving at 90° to the line of centres.

The coefficient of restitution between the spheres is 0.5.

(i) Find the component of velocity along the line of centres after impact for each sphere.

(ii) Find the velocities of the spheres after impact.

(iii) Find the loss in kinetic energy for the system.

⑪ In this question all the discs are circular and have the same radius.

(i) A disc of mass m is sliding across a table when it collides with a stationary disc with the same mass. After the collision, the directions of motion of the two discs are at right angles.

Prove that the collision is perfectly elastic.

(ii) On another occasion the disc of mass m collides with a stationary disc of mass km, where $k > 1$, and the directions of their subsequent motion are at right angles. The coefficient of restitution is e.

Prove that $e = \frac{1}{k}$.

(iii) State a modelling assumption required for parts (i) and (ii).

⑫ Figure 14.19 illustrates a collision between two smooth spheres of equal mass m. Initially they are moving along parallel lines but in opposite directions. At impact the acute angle between their line of centres and the directions of their original movement is α. The coefficient of restitution in the collision is e. Before the impact both spheres have speed u.

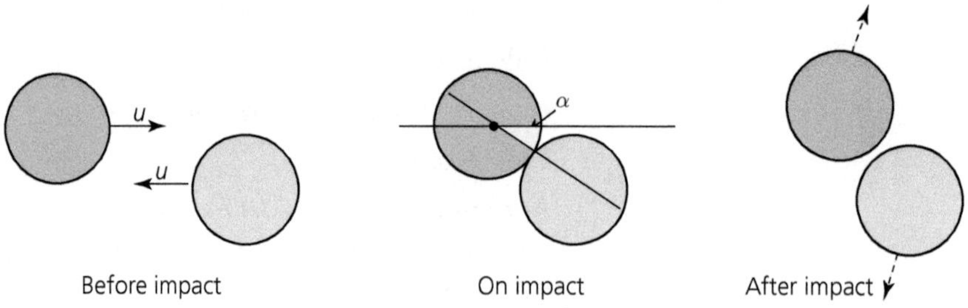

Figure 14.19

(i) Show that the loss of kinetic energy in the collision is $mu^2\cos^2\alpha(1-e^2)$.

(ii) Show that, in the case when $\alpha = 30°$ and $e = \frac{1}{3}$, the direction of motion of each of the spheres after impact is at right angles to its direction before impact.

⑬ Two uniform circular discs with the same radius, A of mass 1 kg and B of mass 5.25 kg, slide on a smooth horizontal surface and collide obliquely with smooth contact.

Figure 14.20 gives information about the velocities of the discs just before and just after the collision.

- The line XY passes through the centres of the discs at the moment of collision.
- The components parallel and perpendicular to XY of the velocities of A are shown.
- Before the collision, B is at rest, and after it is moving at $2\,\text{m s}^{-1}$ in the direction XY.

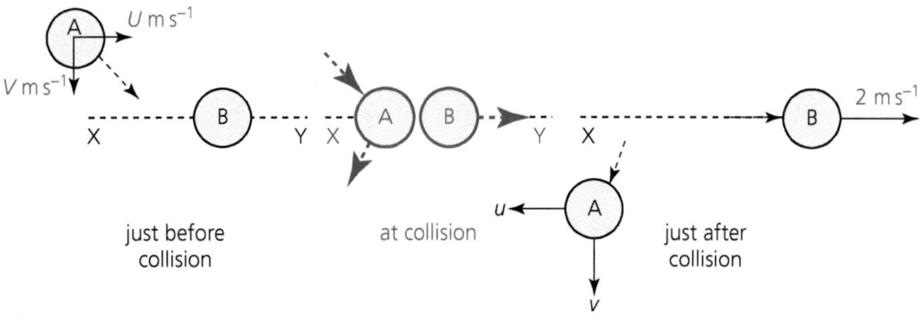

Figure 14.20

The coefficient of restitution between the two discs is $\frac{2}{3}$.

(i) Find the values of U and u.

(ii) What information in the question tells you that $v = V$?

The speed of disc A before the collision is $8.5\,\mathrm{m\,s^{-1}}$.

(iii) Find the speed of disc A after the collision.

⑭ Figure 14.21 shows a white snooker ball with centre W and a red one with centre R. The straight line through W and R passes through the centre, C, of one of the pockets. WR = 100 cm and RC = 40 cm.

Apart from their colour the balls are identical. Their diameter is 5.25 cm.

A model for this snooker table is that a ball will go into the pocket if the line of approach of its centre passes within 2.5 cm of the centre of the pocket

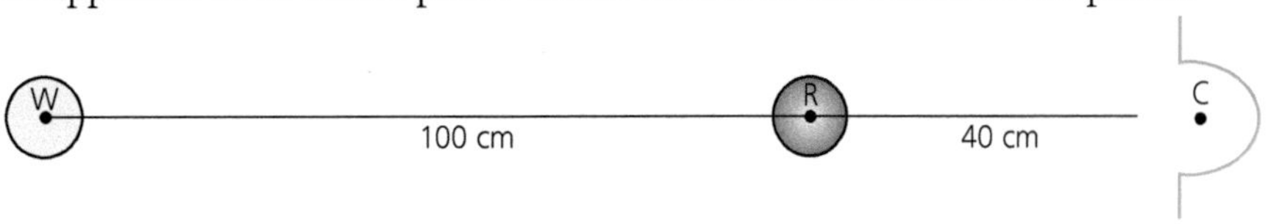

Figure 14.21

(i) A player tries to hit the white ball exactly along the straight line WRC so that the red ball will go into the pocket. Instead, however, he hits the ball at an angle α to the required line.

What happens to the red ball in the cases when (a) $\alpha = 0.5°$ (b) $\alpha = 0.15°$?

Figure 14.22 shows a different situation. There are two red balls with centres, R_1 and R_2, on the line WC. R_1R_2 = 20 cm and R_2C = 20 cm.

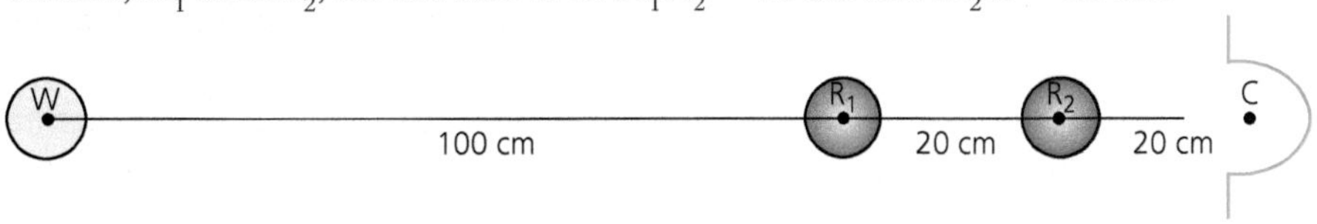

Figure 14.22

The player hits the white ball into the first red ball, which then hits the second red ball. If the shot is successful the second red ball goes into the pocket. A shot like this is called a 'plant'.

The player hits the white ball at an angle α to the line WC.

(ii) Show that, if $\alpha = 0.15°$, the shot is not successful.

(iii) Find, to 2 significant figures, the smallest value of α for which the shot is unsuccessful.

(iv) Explain why the plant is not a popular shot with serious snooker players.

KEY POINTS

1 Collision between a sphere and a fixed plane

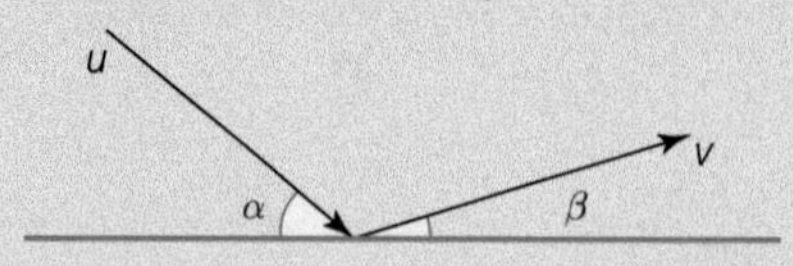

Figure 14.23

Component of velocity parallel to surface remains unchanged [$v \cos \beta = u \cos \alpha$]
Component of velocity perpendicular to surface: [$v \sin \beta = -eu \sin \alpha$]

Loss in kinetic energy: $\frac{1}{2}mu^2\sin^2\alpha(1-e^2)$

2 Oblique impact between smooth spheres

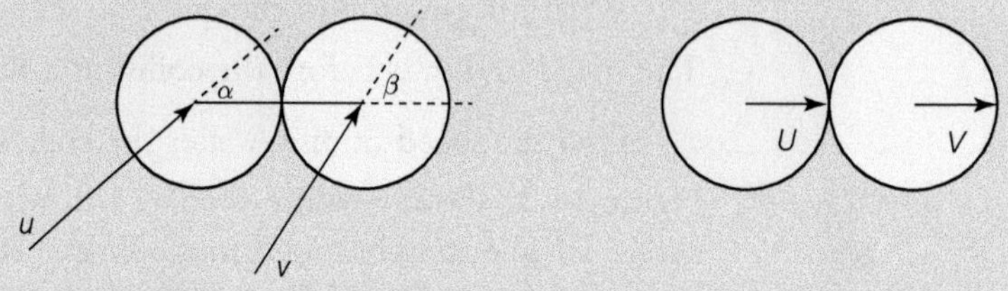

Figure 14.24

Perpendicular to line of centres

$u \sin \alpha$ and $v \sin \beta$ remain unchanged by the collision.

Along line of centres

Conservation of momentum:

$$m_A u\cos\alpha + m_B v\cos\beta = m_A U + m_B V \quad ①$$

Newton's law of impact:

$$V - U = e(u\cos\alpha - v\cos\beta) \quad ②$$

Equations ① and ② can be solved to find U and V.

LEARNING OUTCOMES

When you have completed this chapter, you should

- understand the term *oblique impact* and the assumptions made when modelling oblique impact
- know the meaning of Newton's experimental law and of the coefficient of restitution when applied to an oblique impact
- be able to solve problems involving impact between an object and a fixed smooth plane by considering components of motion parallel and perpendicular to the line of impulse
- be able to solve problems involving impact between two spheres by considering components of motion in directions parallel and perpendicular to the line of centres
- be able to calculate the loss of kinetic energy in an oblique impact
- solve problems involving impacts using vectors.

PS ① A small ring of mass 4 kg is threaded onto a smooth wire. The wire is bent into a circle of radius a m and fixed in a vertical plane. The ring slides round the wire. When it is at its highest point, the ring has speed of $3.5\,\mathrm{m\,s^{-1}}$ and the wire exerts a force of 9.8 N on it.

(i) Determine the possible values of a. [4 marks]

(ii) What is the largest possible speed of the ring? Give your answer correct to 3 significant figures. [3 marks]

P ② A snooker ball travelling with velocity **v** hits a smooth cushion at an angle of θ to the cushion. It rebounds and then hits a second smooth cushion at right angles to the first, as shown in Figure 1. At each impact the coefficient of restitution e between the ball and the cushion is the same. Show that after the second impact the velocity of the ball is $-e\mathbf{v}$. [5 marks]

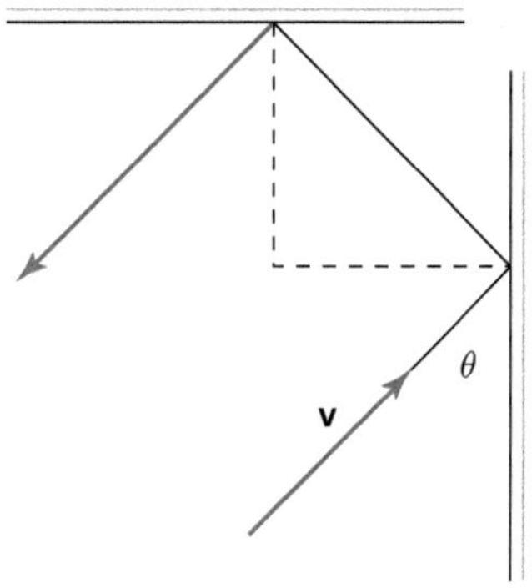

Figure 1

PS P M ③ A region of the plane between the line $x = \frac{a}{2}$ and the circle $x^2 + y^2 = a^2$ is shown shaded in Figure 2. The uniform solid S is formed by rotating this shaded region through 2π radians about the x-axis.

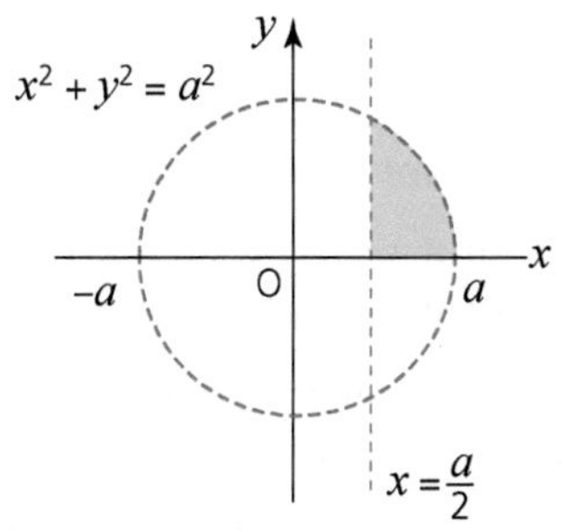

Figure 2

(i) Show that the centre of mass of S is at a distance $\frac{7a}{40}$ from the centre of its plane face. [6 marks]

S has mass M. A uniform thin rod of length l with density $\frac{27M}{40a}$ per unit length is attached to S at Q, the centre of its plane face; the rod is perpendicular to this face and lies on a z-axis with origin Q. S with the rod forms the object T shown in a side view in Figure 3 on the left.

Figure 3

(ii) Show that the centre of mass of T is at the point on the z-axis where

$$z = \frac{27l^2 - 14a^2}{2(40a + 27l)}.$$ [4 marks]

When $l = 2a$, the centre of mass of T is at the point G.

(iii) The object S is part of a sphere. Show that G is at the centre of that sphere. [1 mark]

(iv) When $l = 2a$, T is suspended from a point on the circumference of the circular face of S, so that T hangs in equilibrium with the rod below S. Find the angle the rod makes with the vertical. [4 marks]

Figure 3 on the right shows T placed on a horizontal plane with the rod not quite vertical. B is the point of contact of T with the plane.

(v) Why does the normal to the plane at B pass through G? [1 mark]

T is released from rest.

(vi) State with a reason what will happen if $l < 2a$. [1 mark]

PS M ④ A ball of mass 0.2 kg is thrown vertically upwards with speed $20\,\mathrm{m\,s^{-1}}$. Air resistance is modelled as $0.002v^2$ where v is the speed of the ball. Find the speed of the ball when it returns to the point from which it was thrown. [13 marks]

PS M ⑤ In this question take $g = 10$.

One end of a light elastic string with modulus 50 N is fixed to a point A. The other end is attached to a small object of weight 80 N.

The object is dropped from rest at A and falls vertically a distance of 10 m before coming instantaneously to rest.

(i) Find the maximum speed of the object as it falls. [10 marks]

(ii) State a modelling assumption you have made in addition to the information given in this question. [1 mark]

PS T ⑥ Figure 4 shows the path of a particle P moving in the Cartesian plane with origin O, drawn with graph-drawing software.

The position of P at time t s is $\mathbf{r} = (2t^3 - 3t^2 + 2)\mathbf{i} + (t-1)^2\mathbf{j}$, where $\mathbf{i}$ and $\mathbf{j}$ are unit vectors in the directions Ox and Oy and $-1 \le t \le 2$.

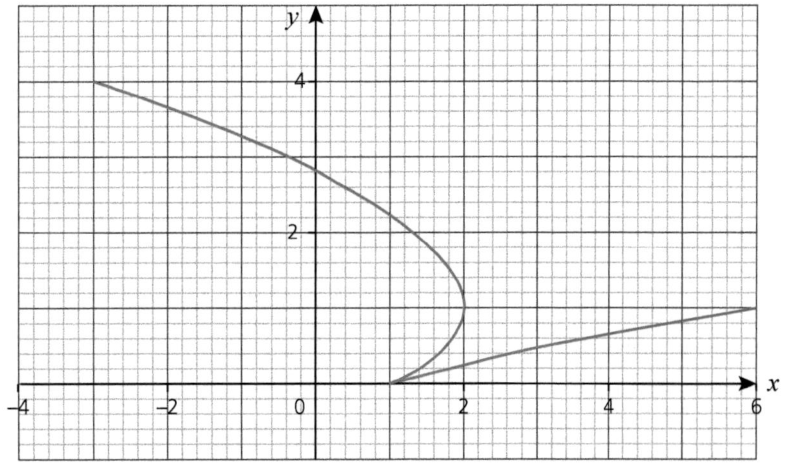

Figure 4

(i) Determine the time(s), if any, when P is instantaneously at rest. [3 marks]

(ii) Sketch a copy of the path of P and indicate the points where $t = -1, 0, 1$ and 2 and the direction of travel.

Describe briefly the motion of P about the time when $t = 0$.

Describe briefly the motion of P about the time when $t = 1$. [4 marks]

Chapter 1

Discussion point page 1

Mostly it will be vertically downwards and after some initial acceleration the velocity will be fairly constant. If there is a wind blowing the velocity will also have a horizontal component motion.

Exercise 1.1

1 (i) $-100, 900\,\text{m}$ (ii) $1, 9\,\text{m}$

2 (a) (i) 20,10m (ii) −10m
(iii) 50 m
(iv) $-6\text{ ms}^{-1}, 6\text{ ms}^{-1}$ for $0 \le t \le 5$; 0 ms^{-1}, 0 ms^{-1} for $5 \le t \le 7$; $6\frac{2}{3}, 6\frac{2}{3}\text{ ms}^{-1}$ for $7 \le t \le 10$
(v) -1 ms^{-1}
(vi) 5 ms^{-1}

(b) (i) 0, 20 m
(ii) 20m (iii) 60m
(iv) $5\text{ ms}^{-1}, 5\text{ ms}^{-1}$ for $0 \le t \le 2$; -5 ms^{-1}, 5 ms^{-1} for $2 \le t \le 6$; $5\text{ ms}^{-1}, 5\text{ ms}^{-1}$ for $6 \le t \le 12$
(v) $1\frac{2}{3}\text{ ms}^{-1}$
(vi) 5ms^{-1}

3 (i) 1 and $3\frac{2}{3}$, (ii) $t = 2\frac{1}{3}$,
(iii) $37\frac{2}{3}$

4 (i)

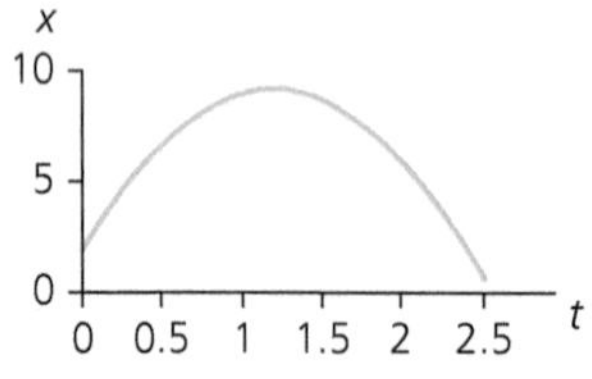

(ii) 2 m (iii) −1.25 m
(iv) 1.2 s; 9.2 m
(v) 15.65 m

5 (i) $1.958\dot{3}$ h
(ii) 51.06 km h^{-1}
(iii) 0 km h^{-1}

6 500 s

7 6.81 ms^{-1}

8 (i) 200 m (ii) 30 s
(iii) 150 m

9 (i) 7.5 mph
(ii) 10.91 mph

10 (i) $20\text{ ms}^{-1}, 0\text{ ms}^{-1}$
(ii)

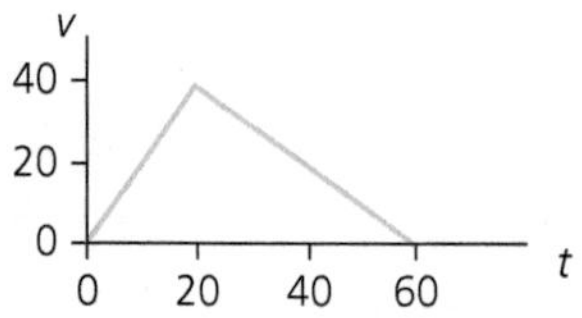

(iii) 1200 m

11 (i)

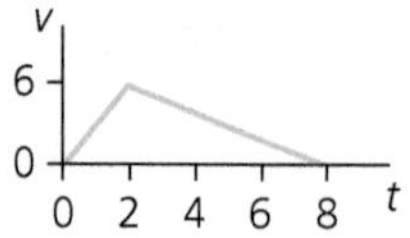

(ii) 24 m (iii) 1 ms^{-2}
(iv) 3 ms^{-1}

12 (i)

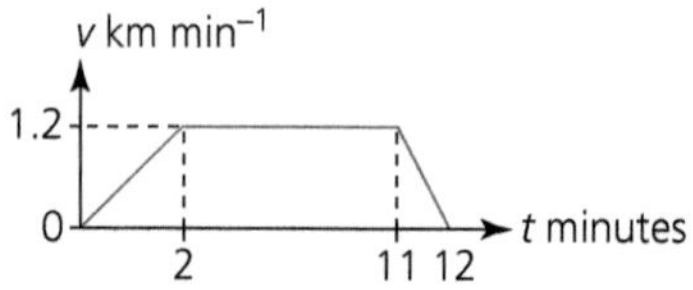

(ii) 12.6 km

13 (i) 500 m, 1500 m, 1500 m, −500 m (ii) 4000 m
(iii) 180 s

14 8.96 ms^{-1}

15 110 s

16 (i) $\frac{5}{54}\text{ ms}^{-2}$ (ii) $\frac{5}{18}\text{ ms}^{-2}$
(iii) $\frac{50}{3}\text{ ms}^{-1}$

Exercise 1.2

1 (i) 10 ms^{-1} (ii) −4 m
(iii) 5.66 ms^{-1} (iv) −24 m
(v) 15 ms^{-1}

2 2 ms^{-2}; 225 m

3 122.5 m

4 4.146 s after the first ball is thrown; -20.63 ms^{-1}; -15.83 ms^{-1}

5 (i) 5 ms^{-2} (ii) 10 ms^{-1}
(iii) 11 s (iv) $9.\dot{0}\dot{9}\text{ ms}^{-1}$

7 (i) 40 m (ii) 20.4 m

8 (i) Janet (ii) 5.62 m
(iii) 0.70 s

9 60 s; 1500 m

10 356.6 ms^{-1}

11 (i) $16\frac{2}{3}\text{ ms}^{-1}$ (ii) $\frac{5}{18}\text{ ms}^{-2}$
(iii) 50 ms^{-1}

12 19.6 ms^{-1}; 19.6 m

13 4.12 m

14 Sprinter

15 (i) 45 s (ii) $0.1234\ldots\text{ ms}^{-2}$
(iii) 31.24 m

16 (i)

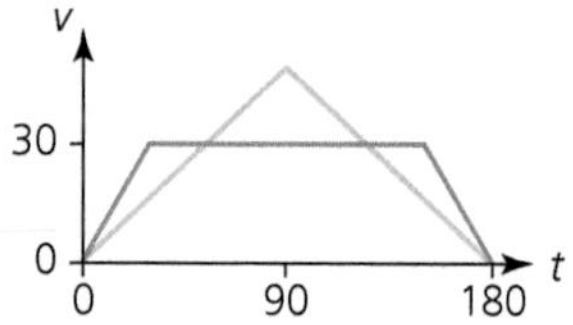

(ii) 4500 m (iii) $\frac{5}{9}\text{ms}^{-2}$
(iv) 360 m

17 (ii) 18 ms^{-1} (iii) 6.125 m

Exercise 1.3

1 (a) (i) $4 - 2t$ (ii) 2; 4
(iii) 2; 6

(b) (i) $10t - 3t^2$
(ii) 0; 0
(iii) 0 and $\frac{10}{3}$; $\frac{500}{27}$

(c) (i) $4t^3 - 2t$ (ii) 2; 0
(iii) 0 and $\pm\frac{1}{\sqrt{2}}$; $\frac{13}{8}$

2 $76\text{ ms}^{-1}, 42\text{ ms}^{-2}$

3 (i) $s = 2.5t^2 - 2t + 3$
(ii) $s = t^3 + 2t^2 - 1$

4 (i) $v = 6t^2 - 8t + 3$; $s = 2t^3 - 4t^2 + 3t + 5$
(ii) $v = \frac{1}{6}t^3 - \frac{1}{10}t^2 + t - \frac{1}{15}$
$s = \frac{1}{24}t^4 - \frac{1}{30}t^3 + \frac{1}{2}t^2 - \frac{1}{15}t + \frac{7}{120}$

5 38 m

6 (i) $t = 1$: $v = 0\text{ ms}^{-1}$, $a = -2\text{ ms}^{-2}$; $t = 2$: $v = 1\text{ ms}^{-1}$, $a = 4\text{ ms}^{-2}$
(ii) $t = 1$: 0 m; $t = \frac{5}{3}$: $\frac{4}{27}$ m
(iii) 10 ms^{-2}

7 16 m

8 (i) $0\text{ ms}^{-2}, 10\text{ ms}^{-1}$
(ii) $13.\dot{3}$ m (iii) $10.\dot{6}$ s

9 (i) 10 m (ii) $36 + 6t - 6t^2$
(iii) −2, 3; −34 m, + 91 m
(iv) 98 m (v) 3 times

10 (i) 0 s, 2 s (ii) 3 s
(iii) $\frac{27}{4}$ m (iv) 4 s

11 (i) 0 s, 6 s (ii) 32 m s^{-1}
(iii) 108 m

12 (i) $6t - 3t^2$; 0, 2
(ii) 0, 3 (iii) 24

13 (i) $v = 18\cos 3t - 24\sin 3t$
$a = -54\sin 3t - 72\cos 3t$

14 (i) 10 m s^{-1} for both
(ii) $13\frac{1}{3}$ m for A, 10 m for B
(iii) $10\frac{2}{3}$ s for A, 11 s for B
(iv) A wins by $\frac{1}{3}$ s and $3\frac{1}{3}$ m

15 John finishes in 2 h 54 m 45 s, Euan finishes in 2 h 55 m 9 s; John by 24 s or 34 m

Chapter 2

Exercise 2.1

1 (i) $6.\dot{6}\ \text{m s}^{-2}$ (ii) 10000 m s^{-2}
(iii) 0.1 m s^{-2}

2 16 000 N

3 (i) 2 m s^{-2}, 4 s (ii) 960 N

4 (i) 61.5 N (ii) 36.5 N
(iii) 49 N (iv) 36.5 N

5 (a) (i) 6.86 N (ii) 8.96 N
(iii) 4.76 N
(b) 9.8 m s^{-2}
(c) It will be left behind by the lift and will appear to fly into the air.

6 (i) $3\frac{4}{15}\ \text{m s}^{-2}$, $65\frac{1}{3}$ N
(ii) 1.4 m s^{-1} (iii) 0.1 m

7 (i)

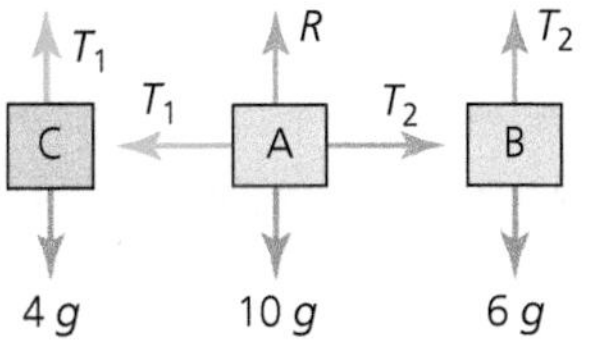

(ii) $T_2 - T_1 = 10a$
$6g - T_2 = 6a$
$T_1 - 4g = 4a$
(iii) 0.98 m s^{-2}, 43.1 N, 52.9 N

8 (i)

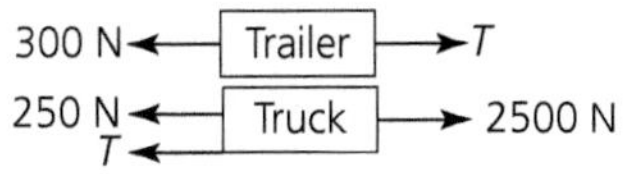

(ii) 1.22 m s^{-2} (iii) 726.6 N

9 (ii) 4100 N (iii) −0.1 m s^{-2}
(iv) 100 N

10 (i)

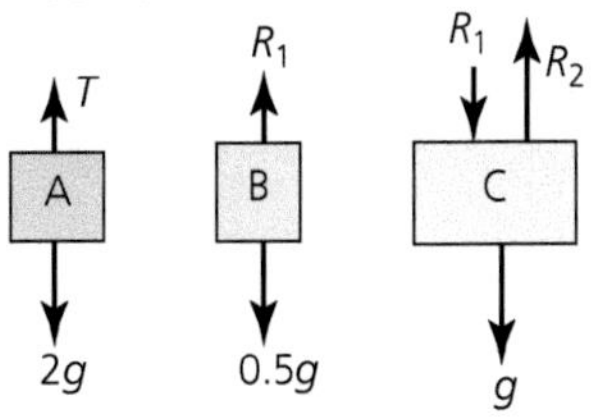

(ii) A: $2g - T = 2a$
B: $R_1 - 0.5g = 0.5a$
C: $R_2 - R_1 - g = a$
(iii) 1.4 m s^{-2}; 16.8 N; 5.6 N, 16.8 N

11 (i)

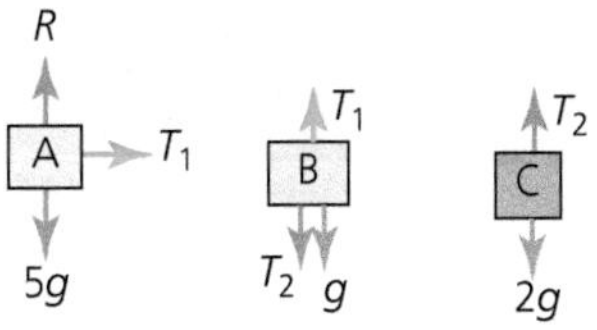

(ii) A: $5a = T_1$;
B: $a = g + T_2 - T_1$;
C: $2a = 2g - T_2$
(iii) 3.675 m s^{-2}, $T_1 = 18.375$ N, $T_2 = 12.25$ N

Exercise 2.2

1 (i) $9\mathbf{i} - 3\mathbf{j}$ (ii) $4\mathbf{i} - 2\mathbf{j}$
(iii) $-7\mathbf{i} + 2\mathbf{j}$ (iv) $4\mathbf{i} - 6\mathbf{j}$
(v) $-3\mathbf{i} + 11\mathbf{j}$ (vi) $-13\mathbf{i} + 9\mathbf{j}$

2 (i) $\mathbf{i} + 2\mathbf{j}$, $5\mathbf{i} + \mathbf{j}$, $7\mathbf{i} + 8\mathbf{j}$
(ii) $\overrightarrow{AB} = 4\mathbf{i} - \mathbf{j}$
$\overrightarrow{BC} = 2\mathbf{i} + 7\mathbf{j}$
$\overrightarrow{CA} = -6\mathbf{i} - 6\mathbf{j}$
(iii)

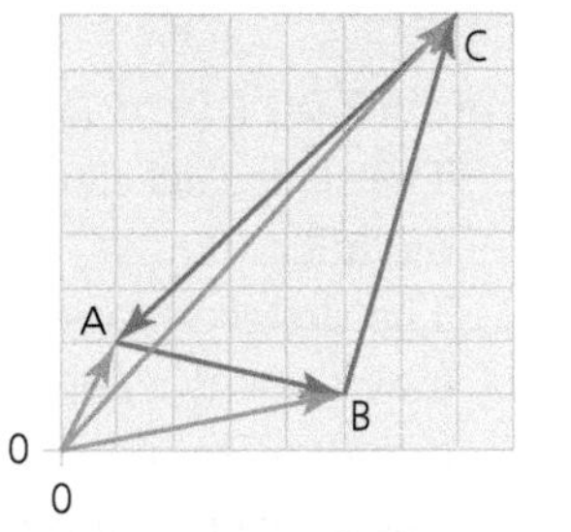

3 $9\mathbf{i} - 10\mathbf{j}$

4 (i) 13, −22.6° (ii) 25, 73.7°
(iii) 1.41, 135° (iv) 5, 53.1°
(v) 3.61, −56.3°
(vi) 2.24, −116.6°

5 (i) $5.64\mathbf{i} + 2.05\mathbf{j}$
(ii) $-5.36\mathbf{i} + 4.50\mathbf{j}$
(iii) $1.93\mathbf{i} - 2.30\mathbf{j}$
(iv) $-1.45\mathbf{i} - 2.51\mathbf{j}$

6 (i) $\frac{5}{13}\mathbf{i} + \frac{12}{13}\mathbf{j}$ (ii) $15\mathbf{i} + 36\mathbf{j}$

7 $8\mathbf{i} - 1.8\mathbf{j}$

8 (i) $2.30\mathbf{i} + 1.93\mathbf{j}$;
$-0.92\mathbf{i} + 2.54\mathbf{j}$;
$-2.42\mathbf{i} - 1.4\mathbf{j}$;
$1.7\mathbf{i} - 2.94\mathbf{j}$;
$\mathbf{R} = 0.66\mathbf{i} + 0.13\mathbf{j}$
(ii) $1.35\mathbf{i} + 2.34\mathbf{j}$; $-2\mathbf{i}$;
$-0.35\mathbf{i} - 1.97\mathbf{j}$;
$2.68\mathbf{i} - 1.55\mathbf{j}$;
$\mathbf{R} = 1.68\mathbf{i} - 1.18\mathbf{j}$

9

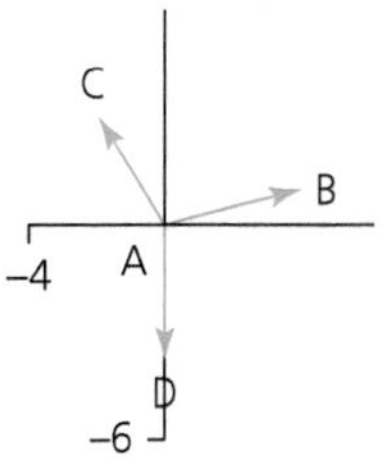

(i) $\begin{pmatrix} 4 \\ 5 \end{pmatrix}$ (ii) $\begin{pmatrix} -2 \\ 7 \end{pmatrix}$
(iii) $\begin{pmatrix} 6 \\ -2 \end{pmatrix}$ (iv) $\begin{pmatrix} -6 \\ 2 \end{pmatrix}$

10 (i) $\mathbf{a} = a\mathbf{i}$;
$\mathbf{b} = -b\cos\theta\,\mathbf{i} + b\sin\theta\,\mathbf{j}$
(ii) $\mathbf{a} + \mathbf{b} = (a - b\cos\theta)\mathbf{i} + b\sin\theta\mathbf{j}$; $|\mathbf{a} + \mathbf{b}|^2 = (a - b\cos\theta)^2 + (b\cos\theta)^2$
(iii) $c^2 = a^2 + b^2 - 2ab\cos\theta$

Discussion point page 44

Draw a vertical line to represent the weight, $10g = 98$ N. Then add the line of the force T_2 at 40° to the horizontal (note the length of the vector is unknown), and then the line of the force T_1 at 20° to the horizontal (70° to the vertical). C is the point at which these lines meet.

Discussion point page 45

The angles in the triangle are $180° - \alpha$, $180° - \beta$ and $180° - \gamma$. The sine rule holds. Using $\sin(180° - \alpha) = \sin\alpha$, $\sin(180° - \beta) = \sin\beta$ and $\sin(180° - \gamma) = \sin\gamma$ results in Lami's theorem.

Exercise 2.3

1 (i) −49 N, −78 N
(ii) 1 N, 2 N
(iii) −1 N, −2 N

2 (i)

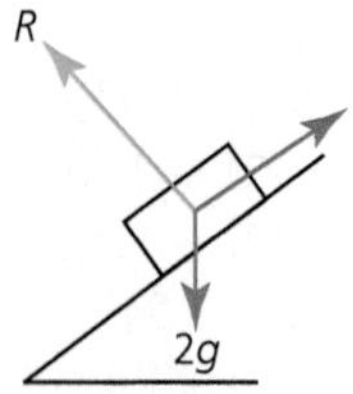

(ii) 15.0 N (iii) 12.6 N

3 5.83 N, 31°

4 (i) 98 N

(ii)

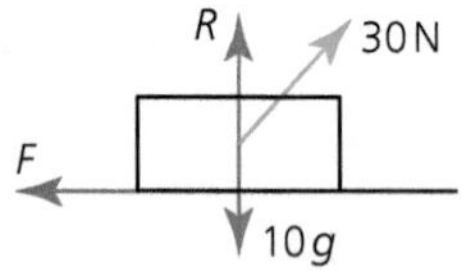

(iii) 70.8 N; 12.7 N

5 15 N

6 (i)

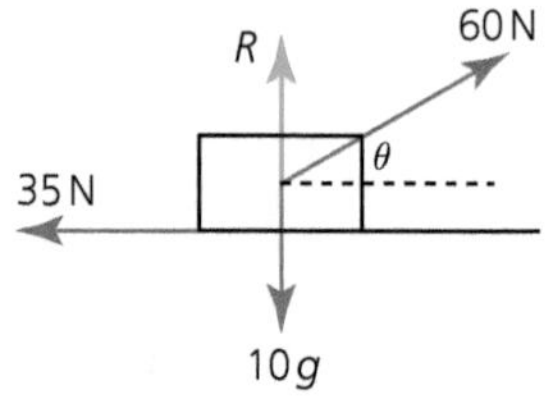

(ii) 54.3° (iii) 49.3 N

7 20 N, 16.9 N

8 (i)

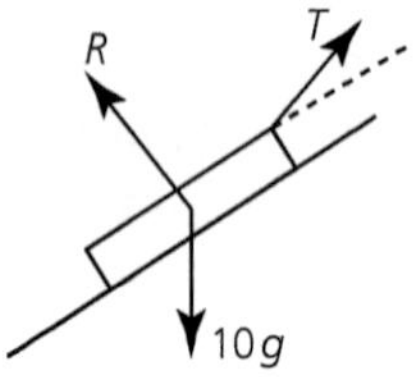

(ii) 50.7 N, 71.7 N

9 (i)

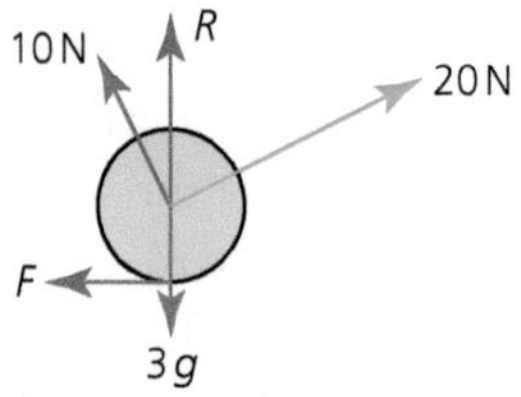

(ii) 7.15 N

(iii) 11.90 N left

10 (ii) $42.6\mathbf{i} + 82.5\mathbf{j}$; 92.8 N at 62.7° to the horizontal

(iii) 32.6 N, –94.4°

11 (i) $5000 \cos 15° + T \cos 25°$ along l;
$5000 \sin 15° - T \sin 25°$ perpendicular to l

(ii) 3062 N (iii) 7605 N

12 (i)

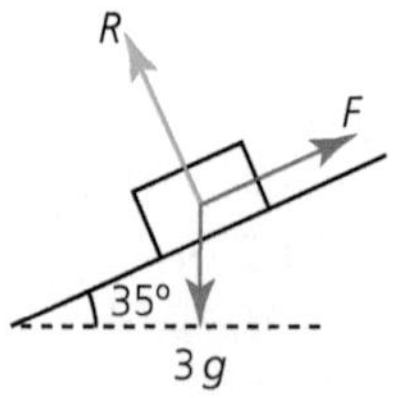

(ii) $(-3g \sin 35° + F)$ and $(-3g \cos 35° + R)$

(iii) 16.9 N, 24.1 N

(iv) 33.7 N

13 (i)

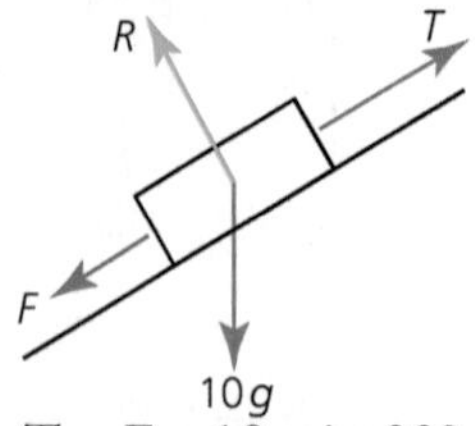

(ii) $T - F - 10g \sin 30°$ and $R - 10g \cos 30°$

(iii) 19.6 N (iv) 3 kg

14 $T_{AB} = 196$ N in tension,
$T_{AC} = 261.\dot{3}$ N in tension,
$T_{AD} = 326.\dot{6}$ N in compression

15 (i) $T \sin 65° = 735 - R$

(ii) 810.98 N, 82.75 kg

(iii) 342.7 N

16 (i) 525 N (ii) 13.1°, 517.5 N

Discussion point page 51 (top)

It is much easier to choose to resolve in directions which ensure that one component of at least one unknown force is zero.

Discussion point page 51 (bottom)

Start with AB and BC. Then draw a line in the right direction for CD and another perpendicular line through A. These lines meet at D.

Discussion point page 52

(i) The sledge accelerates up the hill.

(ii) The sledge is stationary or moving with constant speed (forces in equilibrium).

(iii) The acceleration is downhill.

Exercise 2.4

1

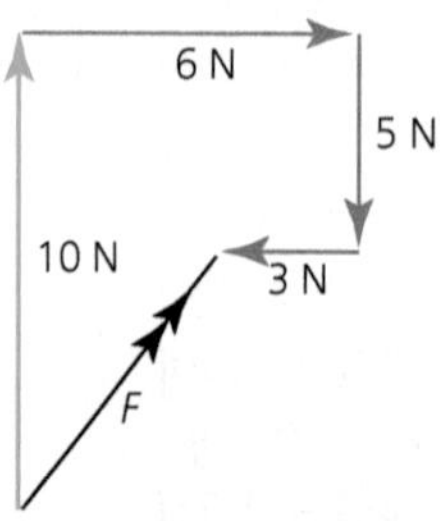

(iii) $\mathbf{F} = 3\mathbf{i} + 5\mathbf{j}$, $F = 5.83$ N at 59° to the horizontal.

2

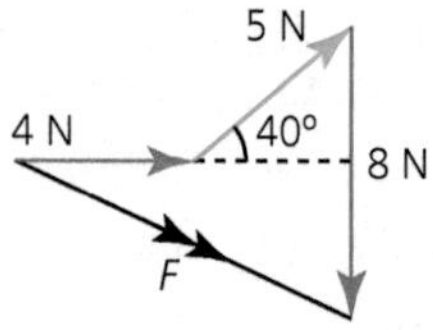

(iii) $\mathbf{F} = 7.83\mathbf{i} - 4.79\mathbf{j}$,
$F = 9.18$ N, 31.4° below horizontal.

3

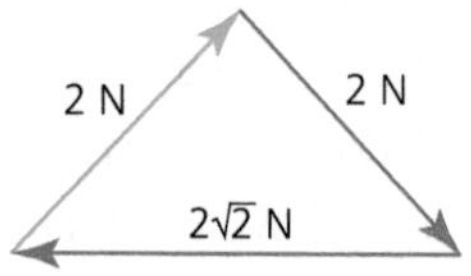

(iii) $\mathbf{F} = \mathbf{0}$

4

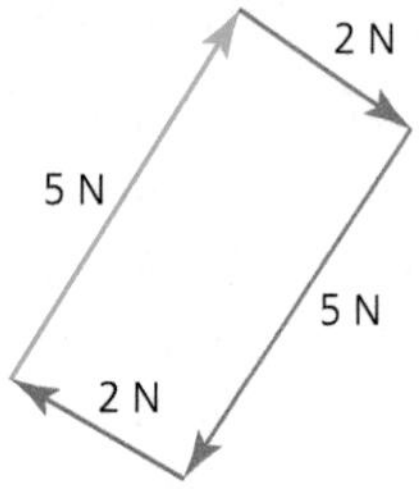

(iii) $\mathbf{F} = \mathbf{0}$

5

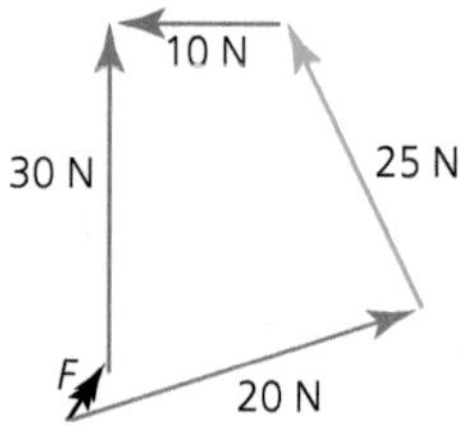

(iii) $\mathbf{F} = 0.34\,\mathbf{i} + 0.23\,\mathbf{j}$,
$F = 0.41$ N at 34° to the slope.

6

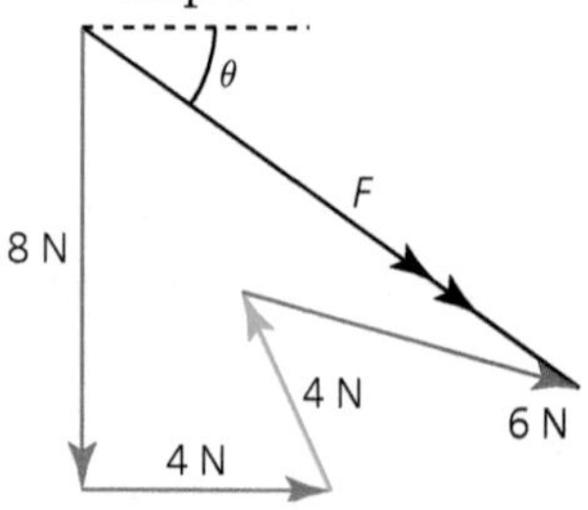

(iii) $\mathbf{F} = 7.14\,\mathbf{i} - 7.26\,\mathbf{j}$,
$F = 10.2$ N, $\theta = -45.5°$.

7 42.9 N, bearing of 300°

8 (i) $7.73\mathbf{i} + 20.67\mathbf{j}$

(ii) 22.1 N at 69.5° to the horizontal

(iii) $\mathbf{a} = 5.15\mathbf{i} + 13.78\mathbf{j}$

9 (i) 6 N at 30° to the horizontal

(ii) 3.6 m s^{-1}; 5.4 m from O

10 7.81 N, 26.3°

11 $P = 10$ N, $Q = 17.3$ N

12 $Q = P\sqrt{\frac{5}{2}}$, 142°

Chapter 3

Discussion point page 58 (top)

No, they would quickly become lowland goats. Although they are very good at balancing (and so using moments), this is used in conjunction with friction to stop them sliding down steep mountain slopes.

Discussion point page 58 (bottom)

Assumptions: Cars are treated as particles, frictional force with the road is uniform, road is horizontal, use linear motion with constant deceleration.

Discussion point page 59

A downward slope would extend the skid so u is an overestimate; opposite for upward slope. A smaller final speed would indicate a lower u while a higher final speed would indicate a higher u for the same length of skid. Treating the car and driver as a particle means discounting the effects of air resistance. In reality this would reduce the skid making u an underestimate.

Discussion point page 60 (top)

The brakes don't lock. Friction acts between the brake pads and the wheels.

Discussion point page 60 (bottom)

Forwards when pedalling, backwards when freewheeling.

Exercise 3.1

1 (i) 0.082 (ii) 0.020

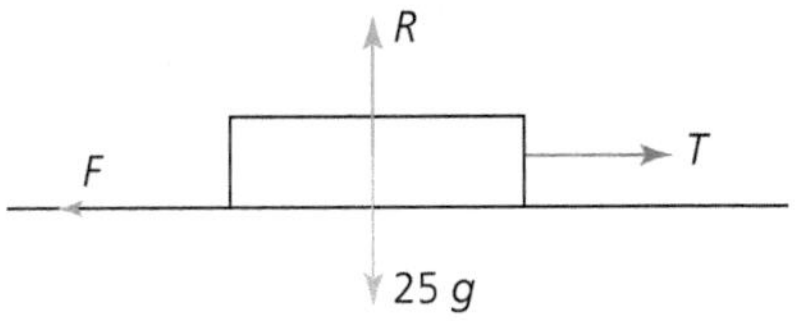

2 0.245

3 0.068

4 0.68

5 (a) $a = 2.156\ \text{m s}^{-2}$; $T = 61.15$ N; $F = 35.3$ N

(b) $a = 0.22\ \text{m s}^{-2}$; $T = 4.79$ N; $F = 3.92$ N

(c) $a = 0\ \text{m s}^{-2}$; $T_1 = 58.8$ N; $T_2 = 39.2$ N; $F = 19.6$ N

(d) $a = 0.065\dot{3}\ \text{m s}^{-2}$; $T_1 = 78.9$ N; $T_2 = 97.3$ N; $F = 17.6$ N

6 0.60

7 (i) $0.8\ \text{m s}^{-2}$ (ii) 0.04 N (iii) 0.082 (iv) 40 m

8 (i) $7.35\ \text{m s}^{-2}$ (ii) $17.66\ \text{m s}^{-1}$ (iii) 59.9 m

9 (i) 34.3 N (ii) 35.2 N

10 (i) $5\ \text{m s}^{-2}$ (ii) 4.29 N; 44.4 N; 0.097 (iii) $3.28\ \text{m s}^{-2}$; $8.10\ \text{m s}^{-1}$

11 11.6 m

12 (i) $0.408\ \text{m s}^{-2}$ (ii) 2.21 s (iii) $0.48\ \text{m s}^{-1}$

13 151 N < T < 1341 N

14 (i) $T = \dfrac{100}{\cos\alpha + 0.5\sin\alpha}$ (ii) 26.6°, 89.4 N

15 (i) 148.4 N (ii) 5.88 N

Chapter 4

Discussion point page 73

The pliers consist of two first class levers: the forces applied tighten the grip on the nut. An extra force at right angles to the previous forces is then applied to tighten the nut.

The adjustable wrench consists of one first class lever. This fits the nut head exactly so that all the force produced is used to tighten the nut.

Discussion point page 79

The sails produce forces at right angles to the mast and so produce a moment on the mast about its base. The tensions in the stays have components perpendicular to the mast acting at its top. The moment of these components helps to balance that of the force from the sails and so makes it less likely that the mast will break.

Exercise 4.1

1 (i) −10 N m (ii) +25.2 N m (iii) −0.945 N m (iv) −11.73 N m

2 (i) +0.48 N m (ii) +2.88 N m (iii) +6.2 N m (iv) 0 N m

3 (i) $33\frac{1}{3}$ N; $16\frac{2}{3}$ N (ii) 35 N; 55 N (iii) 35 N; 75 N

4 5.36 m

5 $\frac{1}{6}$ m from fulcrum on the lighter child's side

6 $0.37 < x < 1.63$

7 (i)

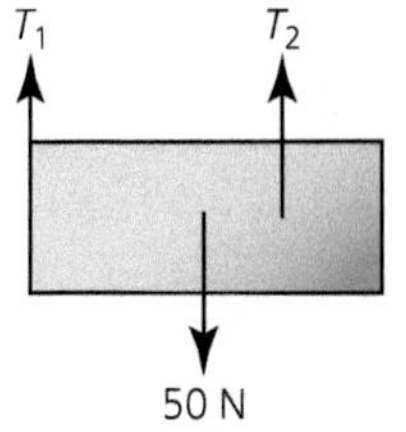

(ii) $T_1 = 16\frac{2}{3}$ N; $T_2 = 33\frac{1}{3}$ N

8 12.5 N and 7.5 N

9 (i) $R_X = 61.2\dot{4}$ N; $R_Y = 66.7\dot{5}$ N (ii) 14.06 kg

10 (i) 280 kg (ii) 28 kg

11 $X = 8$ N; $Y = 12$ N

12 (i) 220.5 N (ii) 294 N

13 The resultant has magnitude 2 N, is pointing downwards, and its line of action is 7.5 m to the right of A.

14 (i) $\frac{1}{4}g(25 + 5m_1 - m_2)$ (ii) $m_1 = 4\frac{1}{6}$ kg; $m_2 = 5\frac{5}{6}$ kg

Discussion point page 86 (top)

There are two answers. Either it doesn't matter because if the force is downwards it will be negative upwards, or, and better, taking moments about A at the right-hand end shows it must be upwards to counteract the moment of the weight.

Discussion point page 86 (bottom)

No, the rod is symmetrical about its centre so the forces must cancel each other out exactly.

Exercise 4.2

1 (i) 6 N m (ii) −10.72 N m (iii) 22.98 N m (iv) 0

(v) -4.24 N m
(vi) 4.24 N m

2 David and Hannah (by radius × 0.027 N m)

3 (i) 5915.5 kg
(ii) $4531.5 \sec\theta$ kg

4 (i) 42.4 N (ii) 27.7 N
(iii) 30.1 N

5 (i) $T\cos 30° = 0.866T$; $T\sin 30° = 0.5T$
(iii) 30 N m
(v) $R_H = 8.04$ N, $R_V = 15.36$ N
(vi) (a) 33.69° (b) 3.23 m
(vii) $T = \frac{30}{3.23} = 9.28$ N

6 (i) 1405.26 N
(ii) 638 N, 1611 N
(iii) 1611 × 3 = 1405 sin 55° × 4.2
(iv) (a) The jib stays put.
(b) The jib will rotate in an anticlockwise direction.

7 (i)

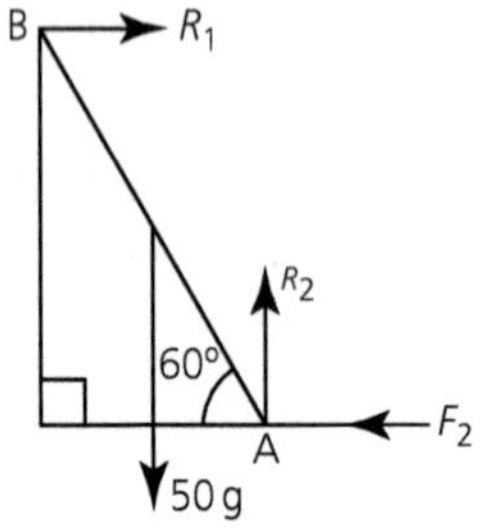

(ii) 0 N m (iii) 141.5 N
(iv) 141.5 N; $\mu \geq 0.29$
(v) 141.5 × 6 sin 60° + 490 × 3 cos 60° − 490 × 6 cos 60° = 0

8 (i)

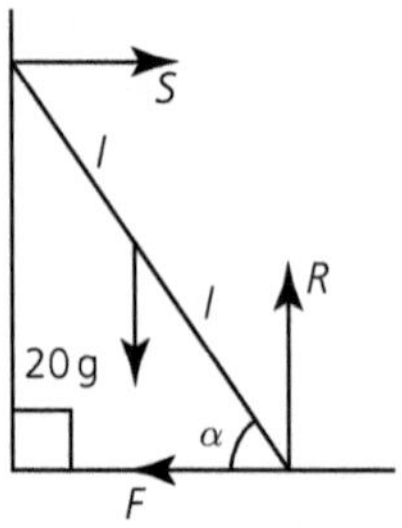

(ii) (a) 56.6 N, 56.6 N, 196 N
(b) 98 N, 98 N, 196 N
(iii) (a) 0.29 (b) 0.5

9 (i)

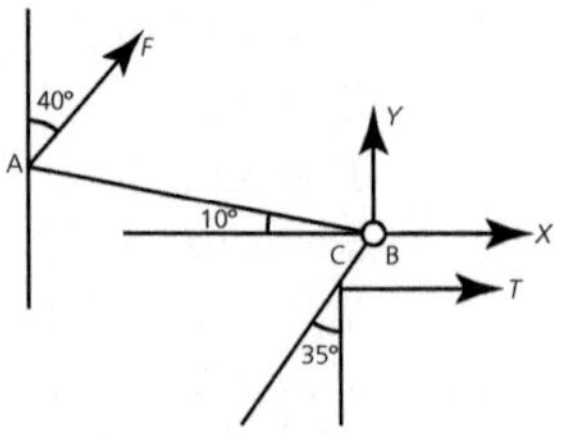

(ii) 162 N (iii) 61.7 N

10 (i) 8000 + 10000 sin 45° − 3000 − 14000 sin 60° = −53.3 N
10 000 cos 45° − 14 000 cos 60° = 71.1 N
$\sqrt{(53.3)^2 + 71.1^2}$ = 88.8 N < 100 N
(ii) 1 600 000 N m
(iii) 529 N, 529 N

11 (i)

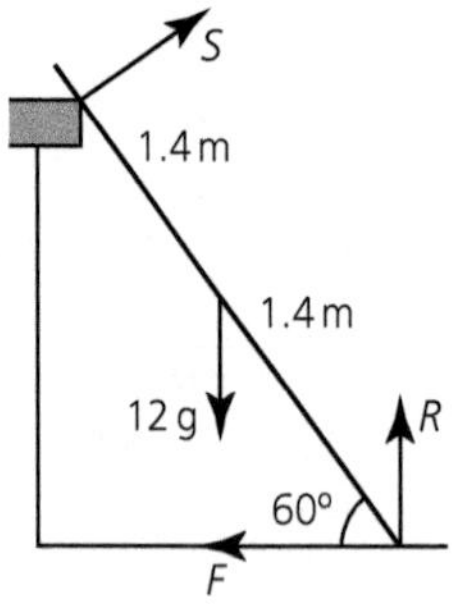

(ii) 25.5 N, 102.9 N
(iii) 0.514 (iv) 2.25 m

12 (i)

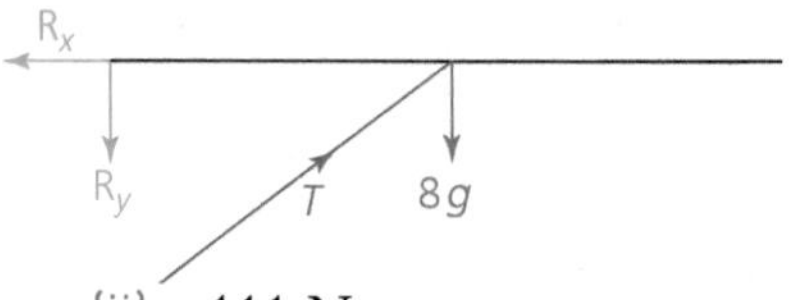

(ii) 111 N
(iii) 1500 N
(iv) 1170 N at 65.2° to the left of the downward vertical

13 (i) 15 N
(ii) $\mu \geq 0.962$ (3 s.f.)

14 (i) MX = 0.2 m, XC = 0.8 m
(ii) arctan(0.05) = 2.86°
(iii) 1456.5 N, 1664.6 N

15 $\tan\theta = \frac{1}{2}\tan\phi$

16 (ii) $\mu \geq 0.328$

Chapter 5

Discussion point page 95

Water is captured when the tide is high and allowed to flow away when the tide is low. The flowing water turns turbines, which generate electricity. So the gravitational potential energy of the water is converted into electrical energy. Thus the tidal wave is the source of the energy. The tidal wave is caused by the gravitational pull of the Moon on the Earth's surface and so the energy originates from the Earth–Moon system, resulting in the Moon getting very slightly further away from the Earth with every tide.

Exercise 5.1

1 (i) 2500 J (ii) 40 000 J
(iii) 5.6×10^9 J
(iv) 3.7×10^{28} J (v) 10^{-25} J

2 (i) 1000 J (ii) 1070 J
(iii) 930 J (iv) None

3 (i) 4320 J (ii) 4320 J
(iii) 144 N
(iv) $a = 144 \div 60 = 2.4$
$v = \sqrt{2 \times 2.4 \times 30} = 12$

4 (i) 540 000 J, no
(ii) 3600 N (iii) No

5 (i) 500 000 J (ii) 6667 N

6 (i) (a) 5250 J
(b) −13 750 J
(ii) (a) 495 250 J
(b) 476 250 J

7 (i) 64 J (ii) Dissipated
(iii) 64 J (iv) 400 N
(v) 89.4 m s^{-1}

8 (i) 314 600 J (ii) 8279 N
(iii) Dissipated as heat and sound
(iv) Some of the work is dissipated as heat

9 18.6 m s^{-1}

10 (i) 240 N (ii) 5.5 m
(iii) 1320 J
(iv) 0.5 m s^{-2}, 270 N, 270 J
(v) 960 J, 90 J

Discussion point page 110

More work cycling into the wind, less if at an angle, minimum if the wind is behind.

Exercise 5.2

1 (i) 9.8 J (ii) 94.5 J
(iii) −58.8 J (iv) −58.9 J

2 (i) −27.44 J (ii) 54.88 J
(iii) −11.76 J

3 17.64 J

4 23 284.8 J

5 (i) (a) 1504 J (b) 280 J
(ii) (a) 15.65 ms^{-1}
(b) 16.15 ms^{-1}

6 (i) 2122 J (ii) The same

7 (i) 2.8 ms^{-1}

8 4.2 ms^{-1}

9 (i) 0.512 ms^{-1} (ii) 35.3°

10 (i) 7.67 ms^{-1} (ii) 3.43 m

11 (i) $\theta_0 = \cos^{-1}\left(1 - \frac{u^2}{2gl}\right)$ (ii) $139T$

Exercise 5.3

1 (i) 271 N (ii) 13.4 ms^{-1}

2 (i) 45 N (ii) 6.75 cm

3 4570 N

4 (i) (a) 1701 J
(b) 8.69 ms^{-1}
(ii) (a) Unaltered
(b) Decreased

5 (i) 1750 J
(ii) 1750 J, 8.37 ms^{-1}
(iii) 50°
(iv) It is always perpendicular to the motion.

6 (i) 153 743 J (ii) 20 000 J
(iii) The car is not raised by 200 m but by 200 sin 5°.
(iv) 137 743 J

7 (i) 156.8 J
(ii) $1.96(80 - x)$
$= 156.8 - 9.6t^2$
(iii) $0 \le t \le 4.04$
(iv) 10 ms^{-1} (v) 90 J

8 (i) 34 300 J, 21 875 J
(ii) 248.5 N (iii) 5061 N

9 (i) 9.8 ms^{-2}
(ii) $1.47(10t - 4.9t^2)$,
$0 \le t \le 2.04$
(iii) 5.10 m, 10**i**
(iv) 10**i** + 10**j**, 14.14 ms^{-1}, 15J
(v) No air resistance; no

10 (i) 109.16 ms^{-1}
(ii) 114.6 N
(iii) The heavier (relatively less affected by resistance)

11 (i) 12 J, 8.7612 J
(ii) 3.24 J (iii) 0.217 N
(iv) 14.05 ms^{-1}

12 (i) 591.6 J (ii) 758 700 J

13 (i) 960 J (ii) 2352 J
(iii) 2392 J (iv) 16.9°

Exercise 5.4

1 (i) 308.7 J (ii) 37 044 J
(iii) 10.29 W

2 (i) 2352 J (ii) 1176 W
(iii) 1881.6 W; 0 W; 2822.4 W

3 (i) 31 752 J (ii) 16 200 J
(iii) 15 98.4 J (iv) 1332 N
(v) Power of the winch = 1598.4 J

4 (i) 703 N
(ii) The mass of the car

5 576 N

6 245 kW

7 (i) 560 W (ii) 168 000 J

8 (i) $2 \neq \frac{1}{2}(0+3)\times 1.5$
(ii) 0.241 W

9 (i) 20 ms^{-1}
(ii) 0.0125 ms^{-2}
(iii) 25 ms^{-1}

10 (i) 1.6×10^7 W
(ii) 0.0025 ms^{-2}
(iii) 5.7 ms^{-1}

11 (i) 16 (ii) 320 N
(iii) 6400 W
(iv) (a) 1.98 ms^{-2}
(b) 1.12 ms^{-2}

12 (i) $DF = \frac{15000}{15}$
$DF - k \times 15^{\frac{1}{2}} = 1500 \times 0.4$
$k = 103$
(ii) $\frac{P}{30} = k\,30^{\frac{1}{2}}$
$P = 17000W$

13 (i) Driving force $= \frac{10000}{20}$
$= 500$
$\left(\frac{10000}{20}\right) - 1300$
$+ 800g \sin\alpha = 0$
$\sin\alpha = \frac{5}{49}$
(ii) $800(22.1)g \sin\alpha + 1300(22.1) + \frac{1}{2}(800)(8^2)$
$= 72010J$
$\left(\frac{720101}{t}\right) = 202000$ so
$t = 3.6(0)$ s

14 (i) 2000 N (ii) 2609 N
(iii) 32 s; 15 584 W

15 (i) 33.3 $\mathrm{m\,s^{-1}}$
(ii) 18.35 $\mathrm{m\,s^{-1}}$
(iii) 0.78 $\mathrm{m\,s^{-2}}$

16 (i) 1.1 $\mathrm{m\,s^{-2}}$ (ii) 750 m

Practice Questions: Set 1 (page 122)

1 36 $\mathrm{km\,h^{-1}}$ = 10 $\mathrm{m\,s^{-1}}$
4 minutes = 240 s, 5 minutes = 300 s and 2 minutes = 120 s

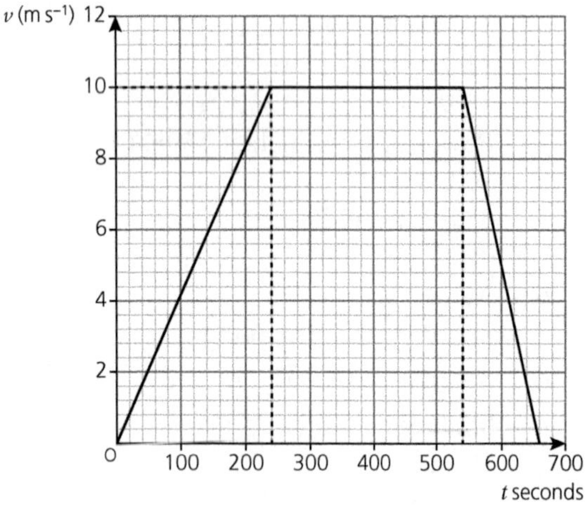

(i) Total distance travelled
= area under graph
$= \frac{1}{2}(660 + 300) \times 10$
= 4800 m
= 4.8 km

2 (i) $s = 18 - 24t + 9t^2 - t^3, 0 \le t \le 5,$

$\frac{ds}{dt} = -24 + 18t - 3t^2$
$= -3(t-4)(t-2)$
$= 0$

$v = 0$ when $-24 + 18t - 3t^2 = 0$
So $t = 2s$ or $t = 4s$

(i) $s(2) = -2, s(4) = 2$

(ii) When $t = 0, s = 18$ mm
From $t = 0$ to $t = 2$
distance travelled: 18 + 2 = 20 m
From $t = 2$ to $t = 4$
distance travelled: 2 + 2 = 4 m
From $t = 4$ to $t = 5$
distance travelled: 2 + 2 = 4 mm
Total distance is 28 m.

3 (i)

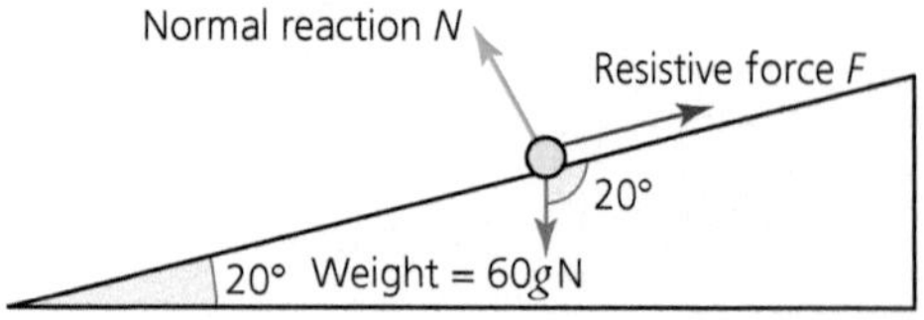

(ii) Parallel to the slope: Weight $60g \cos 20°$ down the slope
Perpendicular to the slope: Weight $60g \cos 20°$ into the slope

(iii) At constant speed ⇒ no acceleration
⇒ no net force on skier

$\Rightarrow R = 60g \cos 20° = 552.539..$
$= 553$ N (to 3 s.f.)

$\Rightarrow F = 60g \sin 20° = 201.107....$
$= 201$ N (to 3 s.f.)

(iv)

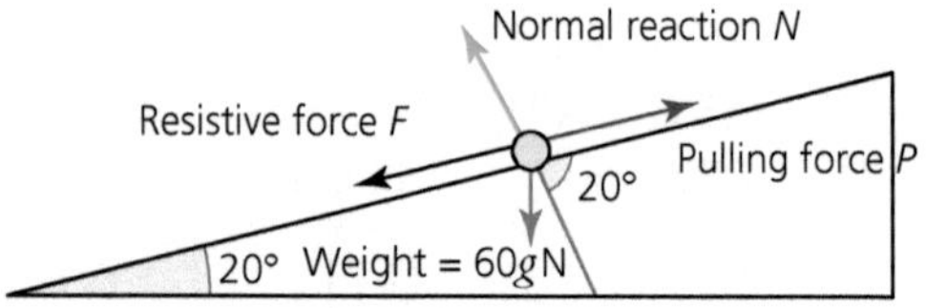

Resolve parallel to the slope
$P - F - 60g \sin 20 = 0$
$P = F + 60g \sin 20 = 2 \times 60g \sin 20$
= 402.215... = 402 N (to 3 s.f.)

(v)

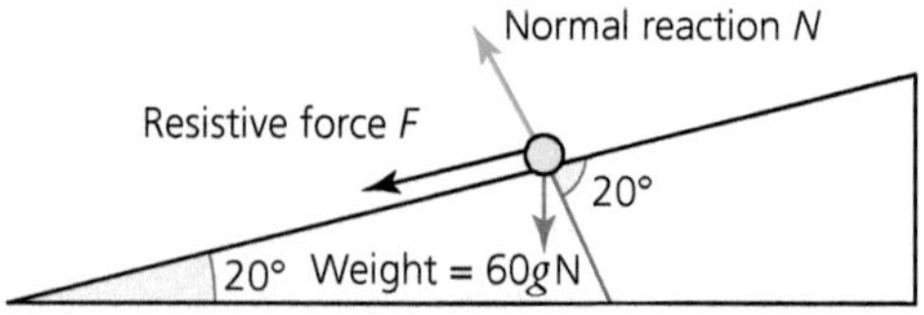

Resolve along the slope
$-F - 60g \sin 20 = 60a$
$-2 \times 60g \sin 20 = 60a$
$a = g \sin 20$
Acceleration is constant
$s = ?\ u = 8, v = 0, a = -g \sin 20°,$
$v^2 = u^2 + 2as$
$\Rightarrow 0 = 64 - 2g \sin 20s$
$\Rightarrow s = 9.547... = 9.5$ m (2 s.f.)

4 (i)

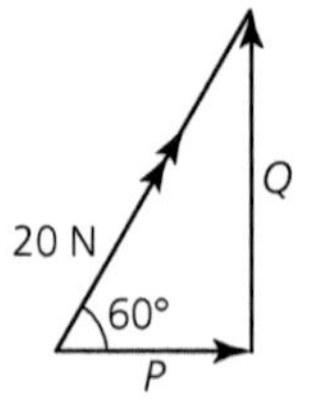

$|\mathbf{P}| = 20 \cos 60 = 10$
$|\mathbf{Q}| = 20 \sin 60 = 10\sqrt{3}$
So the magnitude of P is 10 N, and the magnitude of Q is $10\sqrt{3} = 17.3$ N

(ii) $-3\mathbf{P} + \sqrt{3}\mathbf{Q} = -30\mathbf{i} + \sqrt{3} \times 10\sqrt{3}\mathbf{j}$
$= -30\mathbf{i} + 30\mathbf{j}$

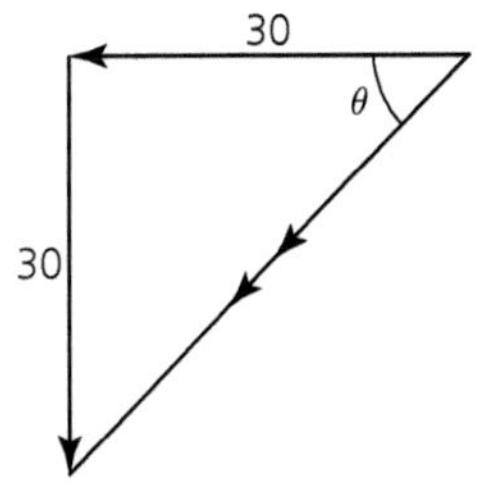

Magnitude $= \sqrt{30^2 + 30^2} = 30\sqrt{2}$

Direction $\tan\theta = \dfrac{30}{30}$ so $\theta = 45°$ with the negative i direction as shown in the diagram

5 (i) (a) Taking moments about B: $1000 \times 1 + 1500 \times 2.5 = N_A \times 5$

$\Rightarrow \quad N_A = 1650$ N

(b) Resolving vertically:

$N_A + N_B = 3500$

so $N_B = 1850$ N

(ii) Let the tension in BC be T N.

Taking moments about A:

$1000 \times 1.5 + 1500 \times 2.5 + 1000 \times 4$

$= T \times 5 \sin 30°$

$\Rightarrow \quad T = 3700$ N

6 (i) $F = mg\sin 11°$

$\Rightarrow \mu = \tan 11°$

$= 0.194$ (3 s.f.)

(ii) $F' = (\tan 11)R', R' = mg\cos 40°$,

$mg\sin 40° - F' = ma$

$\Rightarrow mg\sin 40° -$

$\tan 11°(mg\cos 40°)$

$= ma$

$\Rightarrow a = 4.84\text{ m s}^{-1}$

(iii) $s = 10,\ u = 0,\ v = ?\ a = 4.84,$

$v^2 = u^2 + 2as \Rightarrow v = 9.84\text{ m s}^{-1}$

(iv)

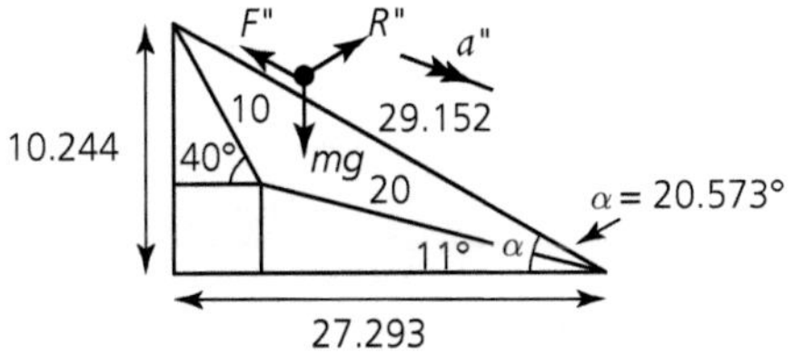

$F'' = \mu R'', R'' = mg\cos\alpha,$

$mg\sin\alpha - F'' = ma''$

$\Rightarrow g\sin(24.68) - \tan 11(g\cos 24.68)$

$= a'' = 2.361$

$s = \sqrt{10.244^2 + 22.293^2} = 24.534,$

$a = 2.361, u = 0, v = ?$

$v^2 = u^2 + 2as \Rightarrow v = 10.8\text{ m s}^{-1}$ (3 s.f.)

Chapter 6

Discussion point page 125 (top)

$t = 0.1 \Rightarrow 20 = -10 + 0.1a$

$\Rightarrow a = 300 \Rightarrow F = 0.06 \times 300 = 18\text{ N}$

$t = 0.015 \Rightarrow a = 30 \div 0.015$

$= 2000 \Rightarrow F = 0.06 \times 2000 = 120\text{ N}.$

'Average' means it stays the same over the time period.

Discussion point page 125 (bottom)

Cricket ball: momentum is 6 N s; kinetic energy is 120 J

Train: momentum is 200 N s;
kinetic energy is 1 J

Exercise 6.1

1 (i) 500 N s
(ii) 20 000 N s
(iii) 2.8×10^8 N s
(iv) 2×10^{-22} N s

2 (i) 18 200 N s
(ii) 0.002 25 N s
(iii) 3 N s
(iv) 10 N s

3 (i) 15 N
(ii) 20 m
(iii) 20 m s^{-1}
(iv) 300 J, work = K.E. gain
(v) 30 N s, impulse = gain in momentum

4 (i) $0.2v - 0.2 \times 5$

$= 20 \times 0.1 \Rightarrow v = 15\text{ m s}^{-1}$

(ii) $v = 5 + \left(\dfrac{20}{0.2}\right) \times 0.1$

$= 15$ m s^{-1}

(iii) They give the same answer.

5 (i) 1.2 N s upwards
(ii) 2 s

(iii) 0
(iv) 1.2 Ns

6 (i) 2.125 Ns
(ii) (a) 21.25 N
(b) 42.5 N
(iii) smaller impulse on hands as it increases the time taken for the ball to stop

7 (i) 11 800 Ns
(ii) 99 000 N
(iii) $11g\,\mathrm{m\,s^{-2}}$
(iv) lower deceleration

8 (i) 5.42 $\mathrm{m\,s^{-1}}$
(ii) 108.4 Ns
(iii) 108.4 Ns
(iv) 542 N

9 (i) +30 000 Ns
(ii) −15 000 Ns
(iii) −45 000 Ns
(iv) the impulse
(v) 450 000 N

10 (i) 12 800 Ns
(ii) 5.12 $\mathrm{m\,s^{-1}}$

Discussion point page 131

Between impact and separation the car travels 0.625 m, and the van travels 0.125 m.

Exercise 6.2

1 195.45 $\mathrm{m\,s^{-1}}$

2 (i) 2 $\mathrm{m\,s^{-1}}$
(ii) 1.5 $\mathrm{m\,s^{-1}}$

3 (i) 25.6 $\mathrm{m\,s^{-1}}$
(ii) 4444 Ns forward
(iii) 4444 Ns backwards

4 (i) $1\frac{2}{3}\,\mathrm{m\,s^{-1}}$
(ii) 1670 Ns forward on car, backwards on lorry

5 (i) 0.623 $\mathrm{m\,s^{-1}}$
(ii) 9.97 Ns
(iii) 997 N

6 (i) 4990 $\mathrm{m\,s^{-1}}$
(ii) 5000.001 $\mathrm{m\,s^{-1}}$

7 (i) 3 $\mathrm{m\,s^{-1}}$
(ii) Impulse 1500 Ns is too great

8 (i) 0
(ii) M: −0.75 $\mathrm{m\,s^{-1}}$, A: 1.05 $\mathrm{m\,s^{-1}}$
(iii) M: −52.5 Ns, A: +52.5 Ns
(iv) 0

9 (i) 49 000 J
(ii) 7 $\mathrm{m\,s^{-1}}$
(iii) 4 $\mathrm{m\,s^{-1}}$
(iv) 42.9%

10 (i) 10 $\mathrm{m\,s^{-1}}$
(ii) 24 000 Ns
(iii) 24 000 Ns
(iv) 966 000 N
(v) 0.5 m

11 (i) 1 $\mathrm{m\,s^{-1}}$
(ii) 9 $\mathrm{m\,s^{-1}}$
(iii) 21 $\mathrm{m\,s^{-1}}$
(iv) 33 $\mathrm{m\,s^{-1}}$

12 (i) 0.196 $\mathrm{m\,s^{-1}}$
(ii) 0.385 $\mathrm{m\,s^{-1}}$
(iv)

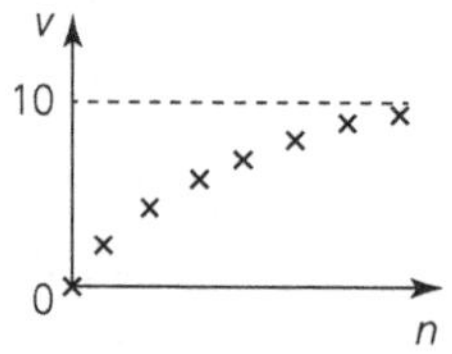

(v) faster; ball has negative momentum

13 (i) $\frac{2}{3}\,\mathrm{m\,s^{-1}}$
(iii) true

Discussion point page 136

The tennis ball will rebound higher than the cricket ball. Heights of second bounces will be lower than those of first bounces.

Exercise 6.3

1 (i) $\frac{2}{3}$
(ii) 1.44 $\mathrm{m\,s^{-1}}$
(iii) $\frac{3}{4}$
(iv) 3.2 $\mathrm{m\,s^{-1}}$

2 (i) 0.3
(ii) 0
(iii) 0.95
(iv) 1

3 (i) 0.8
(ii) 1.62 Ns
(iii) 2.43 J

4 (i) 4.43 $\mathrm{m\,s^{-1}}$
(ii) 3.98 $\mathrm{m\,s^{-1}}$
(iii) 0.9
(iv) 0.149 J
(v) 0.149 J
(vi) 0.656 m

5 (a) (ii) 2.5 $\mathrm{m\,s^{-1}}$, 3.5 $\mathrm{m\,s^{-1}}$
(iii) 3.75 J
(b) (ii) −0.5 $\mathrm{m\,s^{-1}}$; 2.5 $\mathrm{m\,s^{-1}}$
(iii) 33.75 J
(c) (ii) 1.2 $\mathrm{m\,s^{-1}}$; 1.2 $\mathrm{m\,s^{-1}}$
(iii) 4.8 J
(d) (ii) −1 $\mathrm{m\,s^{-1}}$; 2 $\mathrm{m\,s^{-1}}$
(iii) 0 J
(e) (ii) −0.5 $\mathrm{m\,s^{-1}}$; 1 $\mathrm{m\,s^{-1}}$
(iii) 2.25 J
(f) (ii) 2 $\mathrm{m\,s^{-1}}$; 4 $\mathrm{m\,s^{-1}}$
(iii) 96 J

6 (i) 1 $\mathrm{m\,s^{-1}}$
(ii) 0.2
(iii) 450 Ns
(iv) 900 J

7 (i) 19.8 $\mathrm{m\,s^{-1}}$
(ii) 0.76
(iii) 1740 Ns
(iv) 4175 J
(v) a low one

8 (i)

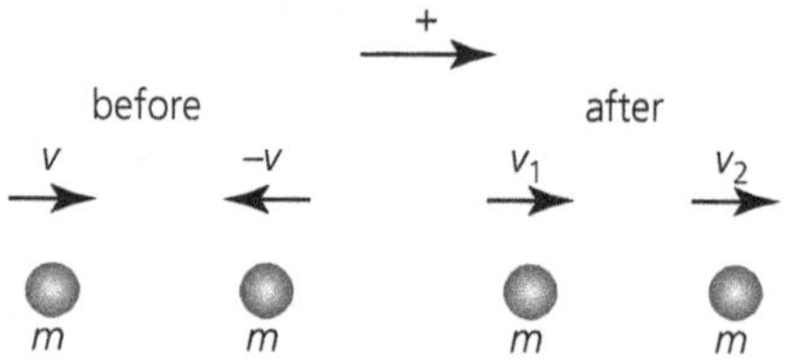

(ii) $-ev$, ev
(iv) Kinetic energy cannot be gained during a collision.

9 $\frac{13}{32}, \frac{15}{32}, \frac{9}{8}\,\mathrm{m\,s^{-1}}$

10 $-\frac{47}{16}, \frac{7}{16}\,\mathrm{m\,s^{-1}}$

11 (ii) $-2 \le v \le 2$

12 (i) 1.5 $\mathrm{m\,s^{-1}}$
(ii) 3 $\mathrm{m\,s^{-1}}$

13 (i)

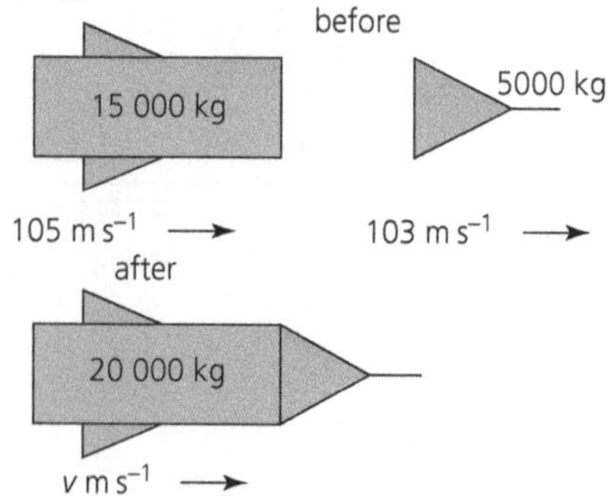

(ii) 104.5 $\mathrm{m\,s^{-1}}$
(iii) 2 $\mathrm{m\,s^{-1}}$ forwards
(iv) 18.73 kg

14 (i) 180 N s

(ii) The only forces acting are due to the impact. These are *internal* to the pair of particles but *external* to each separate particle.

(iii) $\frac{2}{9}$

(iv) $m = 24$; 120 N s in opposite direction to A's original motion

(v) 8 kg; it would go backwards

15 (i)

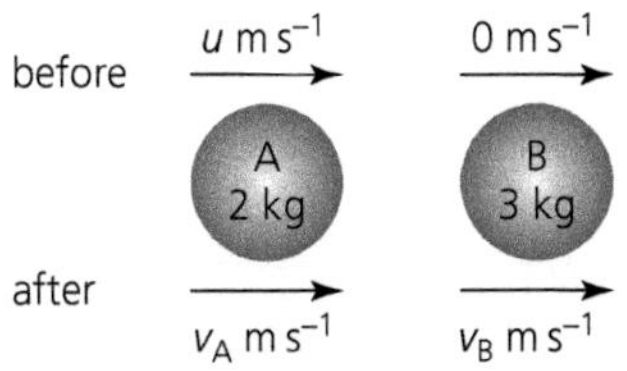

(ii) $2u = 2v_A + 3v_B$;

$eu = v_B - v_A; v_B = \frac{2}{5}u(1+e)$

(iii) $e > \frac{2}{3}$

(iv) $e = \frac{5}{6}; \frac{11}{60}u^2$ J

16 (i) $\sqrt{\frac{2h}{g}}, \sqrt{2hg}$

(ii) e^2h

(iii) he^{2n}

(iv) $\sqrt{\left(\frac{2h}{g}\right)}(1+2e)$,

$\left(\sqrt{\frac{2h}{g}}\right)(1 + 2e + \ldots + 2e^{n-1})$

(vi) $\frac{h(1+e^2)}{(1-e^2)}$

18 $v_A = \frac{1}{2}(1-e)u;\ v_B = \frac{1}{4}(1-e^2)u;\ v_C = \frac{1}{4}(1+e)^2 u$

Chapter 7

Discussion point page 148

e.g. Cube: $V = x^3$, $[V] = L^3$

Cone: $V = \frac{1}{3}\pi r^2 h$, $[V] = L^3$

Sphere: $V = \frac{4}{3}\pi r^3$, $[V] = L^3$

Activity 7.1 page 150

Quantity	Formula	Dimensions	S.I. unit
Area	$l \times w$	L^2	m^2
Volume	$l \times w \times h$	L^3	m^3
Speed	$\frac{d}{t}$	LT^{-1}	$m s^{-1}$
Acceleration	$\frac{v}{t}$	LT^{-2}	$m s^{-2}$
g	acceleration	LT^{-2}	$m s^{-2}$
Force (= mass × acceleration)	$F = ma$	MLT^{-2}	N, newton
Weight	mg	MLT^{-2}	N, newton
Kinetic energy	$\frac{1}{2}mv^2$	ML^2T^{-2}	J, joule
Gravitational potential energy	mgh	ML^2T^{-2}	J, joule
Work	Fs	ML^2T^{-2}	J, joule
Power	Fv	ML^2T^{-3}	W, watt
Impulse	Ft	MLT^{-1}	N s

Quantity	Formula	Dimensions	S.I. unit
Momentum	mv	MLT^{-1}	N s
Pressure (= force/area)	force/area	$ML^{-1}T^{-2}$	$N m^{-2}$
Density	mass/volume	ML^{-3}	$kg m^{-3}$
Moment	Fd	ML^2T^{-2}	N m
Angle	$\theta = s/r$	dimensionless	radian
Gravitational constant (G)	$F = \frac{Gm_1m_2}{d^2}$	$M^{-1}L^3T^{-2}$	$N m^2 kg^{-2}$
Coefficient of friction	$F = \mu R$	dimensionless	–
Coefficient of restitution	v separation/v approach	dimensionless	–

Exercise 7.1

1 (i) All L^2T^{-2}; consistent
(ii) All L; consistent
(iii) All MLT^{-2}; consistent
(iv) L.H.S. MLT^{-2}, R.H.S. ML^2T^{-2}; inconsistent
(v) L.H.S. ML^2T^{-2}, R.H.S. MLT^{-1}; inconsistent
(vi) All MLT^{-2}; consistent
(vii) L.H.S. ML^2T^{-2}, R.H.S. MLT^{-2}; inconsistent
(viii) All ML^2T^{-2}; consistent
(ix) L.H.S. ML^2T^{-3}, R.H.S. L^2T^{-3}; inconsistent

2 (i) MLT^{-2} (ii) ML^2T^{-3}
(iii) ML^2

3 (i) $[v] = LT^{-1}$, $[h] = L$, $[\rho] = ML^{-3}$, $[g] = LT^{-2}$
(ii) $\alpha = \frac{1}{2}, \beta = 0, \gamma = \frac{1}{2}, v = k\sqrt{hg}$
(iii) Deep water
(iv) No difference

4 (i) $t = kd^{\alpha} g^{\beta}$
(ii) $\alpha = \frac{1}{2}, \beta = -\frac{1}{2}, t = k\sqrt{\frac{d}{g}}$
(iii) $k = 150$
(iv) 36.7 s

5 (ii) $T = k\sqrt{\frac{a}{g}}$
(iii) $k = 7.70$

6 (i) $e = \frac{\text{velocity}}{\text{velocity}}$
(ii) $\alpha = 2, \beta = 0, \gamma = -1$, $h = \frac{kv^2}{g}$
(iii) h is independent of m so both bounce to the same height
(iv) because e is dimensionless and is included in k
(v) $h = \frac{e^2v^2}{2g}$
(vi) $k = \frac{e^2}{2}$ is dimensionless

7 (ii) $x + y = 3$
(iii) $R = 6.72 \times 10^6 \times \frac{r^4}{a}$
(iv) $0.213\ m^3\ s^{-1}$

8 (i) $V = \frac{kmg}{r\eta}$
(ii) $m = \frac{4}{3}\pi r^3 \rho$
(iii) $V = \frac{k_1 r^2 \rho g}{\eta}$
(iv) 0.113 cm

9 (i) π is the circumference of a circle divided by its diameter; dimensionless
(ii) $M^{-1} L^3T^{-2}$
(iii) 1.54×10^9
(iv) π (dimensionless) is independent of units, G (not dimensionless) is dependent on its units

10 (i) $M^{-1}L^3T^{-2}$
(ii) 1.002
(iii) $0.0123M_E$, $0.273R_E$, $0.165g_E$
(iv) $0.379g_E$

11 (ii) $ML^{-1}T^{-2}$, ML^{-3}
(iii) $\alpha = -1, \beta = \frac{1}{2}, \gamma = -\frac{1}{2}$; by experiment or analysis
(iv) 1.2
(v) much greater; $A \propto \rho c^2$ and $c_{water} \gg c_{air}$, $\rho_{water} \gg \rho_{air}$

12 (i) $M^{-1}L^3T^{-2}$
(ii) $t = k\sqrt{\frac{r_0^3}{Gm}}$
(iii) Yes
(iv) $t = \frac{k_1}{\sqrt{G\rho_0}}$

13 (i) $f = \frac{k}{l}\sqrt{\frac{T}{m}}$
(ii) $f = \frac{1}{2l}\sqrt{\frac{T}{m}}$
(iii) 316.2 cycles s^{-1}

14 (iii) MT^{-1}
(iv) Dimensionless
(v) $\varepsilon = \frac{kcu}{mg}$, $R = R_M\left(1 - \frac{kcu}{mg}\right)$

15 (i) T^2L^{-3}

(ii) 2.98×10^{-19}

(iii)

Mercury	0.241
Venus	0.615
Earth	1
Mars	1.874
Jupiter	11.9
Saturn	29.5
Uranus	84.1
Neptune	165

Chapter 8

Discussion point page 161

Forces which pull them towards the centre of the circle.
Gravity pulls it in.
It moves off at a tangent.
No.

Exercise 8.1

1 (i) 8.2 rad s^{-1}
(ii) 4.7 rad s^{-1}
(iii) 3.5 rad s^{-1}

2 2865 rpm

3 (i) (a) 0.033 rpm
(b) 0.0035 rad s^{-1}
(ii) 0.24 $m s^{-1}$

4 32.5 rad s^{-1}

5 (i) 50 rad s^{-1}
(ii) 150 rad s^{-1}

6 (i) 3820 rpm
(ii) 2080 rpm

7 (i) 1.99×10^{-7} rad s^{-1}
(ii) 7.27×10^{-5} rad s^{-1}
(iii) 465 $m s^{-1}$
(iv) about 290 $m s^{-1}$ at latitude 51.5°

8 2.29:1

9 (i) 61.7 J
(ii) Points on a large object would travel with different speeds

10 (i) big: 0.126 $m s^{-1}$, small: 0.00140 $m s^{-1}$
(ii) 90:1; the radius is also involved

11 (i) 4.91 m
(ii) 12.3 $m s^{-1}$

12 (i) $v = 2\cos t\mathbf{i} - 2\sin t\mathbf{j} - \frac{1}{2}\mathbf{k}$
(ii) $|v| = \sqrt{4.25} = 2.06$ $m s^{-1}$
(iii) $\mathbf{a} = -2\sin t\mathbf{i} - 2\cos t\mathbf{j}$; magnitude 2 $m s^{-2}$ horizontally towards the vertical axis

Activity 8.1 page 171

When you turn fast enough, the coin flies off the card. When the card is tilted it stays put at higher angular speeds.

Discussion point page 172

The answer is described in the text that follows.

Discussion point page 174

1 Resolve perpendicular to the slope:

$$R - mg\cos\alpha = m\frac{v^2}{r}\sin\alpha$$

Then parallel to the slope.

No slipping down if

$$mg\sin\alpha - F = m\frac{v^2}{r}\cos\alpha,$$

and $F < \mu R$. No slipping up if

$$mg\sin\alpha + F = m\frac{v^2}{r}\cos\alpha, \text{ and}$$

$F < \mu R$.

Substitute for F and R and rearrange.

2 The bend is safe at 30 mph. In general, bends are safer for large r. As long as $\mu > \tan\alpha$, there is no lower limit for v and then α can be increased in order to increase the upper limit.

Exercise 8.2

1 (i) Neither, both have $\omega = 0.75$ rad s^{-1}.
(ii) No, because they have the same angular speed.
(iii) 13.5 $m s^{-2}$, 11.25 $m s^{-2}$
(iv) towards the centre for circular motion

2 (i) 7.2 $m s^{-2}$
(ii) 16 $m s^{-2}$
(iii) 4.8 $m s^{-2}$

3 (i) (a) neither slips
(b) B slips, A doesn't
(c) both slip
(ii) A slips first, radius matters, mass doesn't matter

4 (i) accelerates because direction changes
(ii) 11.25 $m s^{-2}$
(iii) 2250 N
(iv) No, outside wheels go faster so force is greater

5 (i) T for fixed seats
(ii) F, as $v = r\omega$ so speed depends on r.
(iii) F, as $a = r\omega^2$ so acceleration depends on r.

6 (i) (a) 0.5 rad s^{-1}
(b) 1 $m s^{-2}$
(c) 60 N towards centre
(ii) skater is a particle

7 B has greater force because greater acceleration

8 (i) (a) $\frac{(2\times10^7)}{\sqrt{r}}$ (3 s.f.)
(b) $\pi r^{\frac{3}{2}}\times10^{-7}$ s
(ii) $T^2 = \pi^2\times10^{-14}r^3$
(iii) 4.23×10^7 m

9 (i) 263 N
(ii) The weight of the sphere is very small compared with the tension of the cord.
(iii) 23 $m s^{-1}$

10 (i) 5.71×10^{-3} $m s^{-2}$
(ii) 1.77×10^{30} kg
(iii) Any planet in this orbit would have the same period whatever its mass

11 (i) Vertical force required to balance weight
(ii) 12.57 rad s^{-1}
(iii)

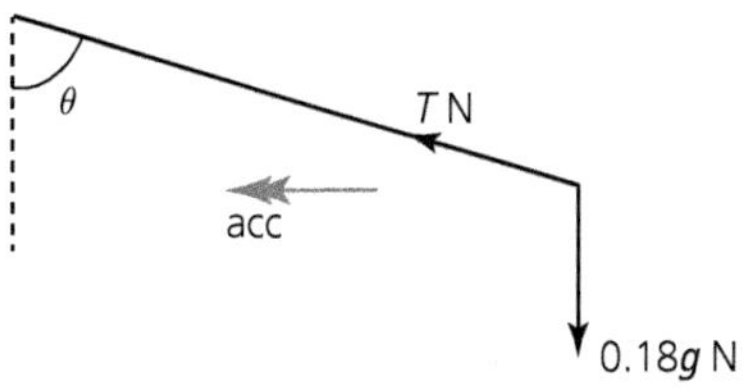

(iv) $T\sin\theta = mr\omega^2 = 0.18 \times 0.8\sin\theta \times 12.57^2$;
$T\cos\theta = mg = 1.764$

(v) $\arccos\left(\frac{1.764}{0.18 \times 0.8 \times 12.57^2}\right) = 85.55...°$

(vi) 22.8 N

12 (i) 44 mph (19.8 m s^{-1})

(ii) 4 mph (1.98 m s^{-1}) faster

13 (i) 6272 N

(a) The car is about to skid on a bend.

(b) The car is accelerating or braking and is about to skid.

(ii) 69 mph (30.7 m s^{-1})

(iii)

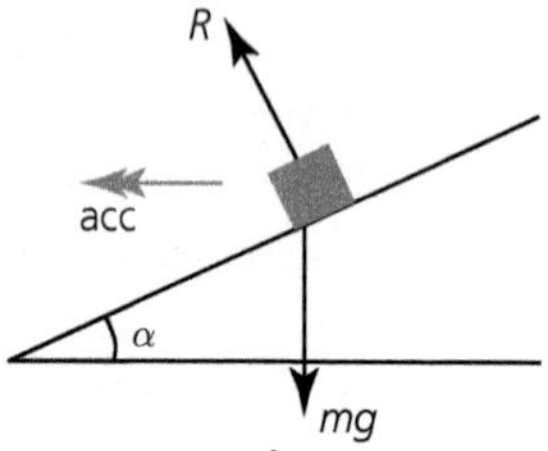

(iv) $R\sin\alpha = \frac{mv^2}{r}$, $R\cos\alpha = mg$

(vi) 10.8° or 0.189 rad

14 (i) $\frac{\pi}{30}\text{rad s}^{-1}$

(ii) $\frac{\pi}{3}\text{ m s}^{-1}$

(iii) No tangential acceleration

(iv) $40g\cos\theta - R\cos\phi = \frac{4}{9}\pi^2$

(v) 388.1, 30.3°

15 (i) $M = 0.6m$

(ii) 5.72 rad s^{-1}

16 (ii) 2.8 m s^{-1}

(iii) 1.35 s

17 (ii) $6T_1 + 8T_2 = 30$; $T_1 = 0.57\text{ N}$, $T_2 = 3.32\text{ N}$

Practice Questions: Set 2 (page 181)

1 [Fuel consumption in litres per 100 km] = $L^3 \div L = L^2$
Need to express in m^2
1 litre per 100 km is $10^{-8} m^2$.

2 $32\cos 30° - 5g\sin 10° - F = 5a$
$N + 32\sin 30° - 5g\cos 10° = 0$
$F = 0.4N$
$a = 1.26\text{ m s}^{-2}$

3 (i) $v_A = \frac{U}{3}(2-e)$,

$v_B = \frac{2U}{3}(1+e)$

(ii) PCLM with coalescence giving
$v_D = \frac{U}{6}(2+2e-3k)$

(iii) Need $\frac{U}{3}(2-e) > \frac{U}{6}(2+2e-3k)$ so ...
$k > \frac{2}{3}(2e-1)$.

(iv) Either: linear momentum is conserved through the whole of the process of obtaining E. Or: Equate initial and final momentum so $2mU - mkU = 4mv_E$ so v_E is independent of e.

Put $k = \frac{4}{9}$ to give
$v_E = \frac{7U}{18}$

That the final answer is independent of e comes neatly from considering initial and final momenta but the other method gets full marks.

4 (i) Use of $P = Fv$
$F - 1200 \times 9.8 \times 0.1 - 250$
$= 1200 \times 0.7$
(so $F = 2266$)
$P = 33\,990$ so about 34 kW.

(ii) $0 - \frac{1}{2} \times 1200 \times 12^2$

$$= -\begin{pmatrix} 1200 \times 9.8 \times 0.1 \\ +1200 \times 9.8 \times 0.4 \\ \times\cos(\sin^{-1}(0.1)) \end{pmatrix}$$

$d - 1500$

86 400 – 1500
$= d \times 5856.42...$ so
$d = 14.496...$ so 14.5 m (3 s. f.)

(iii) Coulomb's law applies; slope is uniformly steep; slope is uniformly rough; slides in a straight line; ...

5 (i) Moment A $5\sin\alpha \times T - 2.5W\cos\alpha = 0$
so $T = \frac{\cos\alpha}{2\sin\alpha}W$
$T = F$; $R = W$; $F = \mu R$
so $\mu = \frac{\cos\alpha}{2\sin\alpha} = \frac{1}{2\tan\alpha}$.

(ii) Doesn't say on the point of slipping so $F \le \mu R$

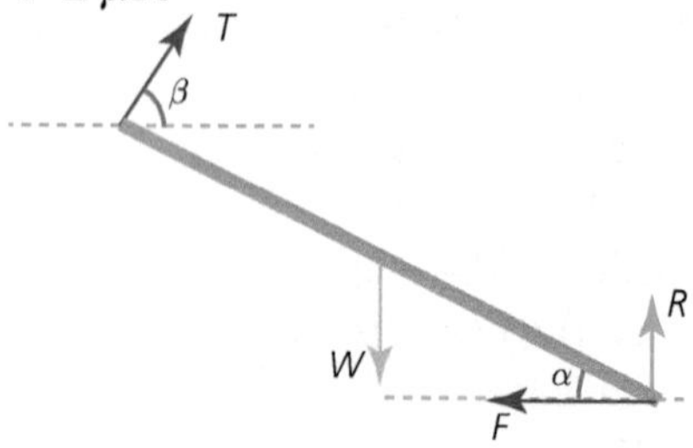

Values of $\sin\beta$, $\cos\alpha$ etc

$T \sin\beta + R - W = 0;$

$F = T \sin\alpha;$

$5T - 2.5W \cos\alpha = 0$

$\mu \geq \frac{12}{41}$ (0.2926…)

6 (i) $T \cos BAC = 0.01g$
$T + T \sin BAC = 0.01 \times 0.3\omega^2$
$T = 0.1225$ N
(ii) $\omega^2 = 65.3$
Time $= 2\pi/\omega$
$= 0.777$ seconds

7 (i) Tension in the string is mg when system in equilibrium.
c.w. moment is $0.25g \times 1.6\sin(\theta)$; a.c moment is $mg \times 2\sin(\phi)$
(ii) 1.35 rad
(iii) The a.c. moment is greater than the c.w. moment so the system will move a.c.
(iv) One or more assumptions are not correct. Most likely there is friction at the hinge or on the string passing over the pulley.

Chapter 9

Discussion point page 185

Yes; the centre of mass is vertically below P.

Discussion point page 187

$$4 \times 1\frac{2}{15} + 5 \times \frac{2}{15} = 6 \times \frac{13}{15}$$

Exercise 9.1

1 (i) 0.2 m
(ii) 0
(iii) −0.72 m
(iv) 1.19 m
(v) +0.275 m
(vi) 0.36 m
(vii) −0.92 m
(viii) 0.47 m

2 2.18 m from 20 kg child
3 4.2 cm
4 4680 km
5 0.92 m
6 3.33 mm from centre
7 2.95 cm
8 1.99 kg
9 42 kg
10 $\frac{m_2 l}{(m_1 + m_2)}$ from m_1 end
11 (i) 3.35 m, tips over
(ii) 4.55 tonnes
(iii) $L(l-d) < Md + C(a+d)$, $C(a-d) < Md$
(iv) $\frac{2Mad}{(l-d)(a-d)}$

Exercise 9.2

1 (i) (2.3, −0.3)
(ii) (0, 1.75)
(iii) $\left(\frac{1}{24}, \frac{1}{6}\right)$
(iv) (−2.7, −1.5)
2 $(5, 6\frac{1}{3})$
3 (i) (20, 60)
(ii) (30, 65)
(iii) (30, 60)
4 23 cm
5 (i) (3, 2)
(ii) $\left(1\frac{1}{6}, 1\frac{1}{6}\right)$
(iii) (1.6, 1.6)
6 (i) (1.5, −1.5)
(ii) (1.5, −2.05)
7 (i) 0.2 cm below O
(ii) 9.1°
8 24.4°
9 (i) Using $\mathbf{v} = \mathbf{u} + \mathbf{a}t$ gives $t = 1$ for the x-coordinate, −1 for the y-coordinate and −3 for the z-coordinate. So there is no single time at which all three coordinates are correct.
(ii) You cannot in general apply this vector equation to find individual components.

10 (i) (0.5a, 1.2a)
(ii) 3.9°
(iii) 2m
11 8.78 cm from the base on the axis of symmetry
12 (i) (28, 60)
(ii) (52, 60)
(iv) 40 cm
13 (i) (a) (10, 2.5)
(b) (12.5, 5)
(c) (15, 7.5)
(d) (17.5, 10)
(e) (20, 12.5)
(ii) 5
(iii) (9 + n, 2.5n), 11
(iv) 102.5 cm
14 (i) 2.25
(ii) 0.56 m; not feasible as it would not stay within the shape
(iii) 0.40, $\left(\frac{1}{2}, 1\frac{1}{2}\right)$
16 $\left(-1, \frac{4}{\pi}\right)$
17 (i) (a) $\left(\frac{4m+M}{8m+4M}\right)h$
(b) $\frac{h}{2}\left(\frac{M\alpha^2 + m}{M\alpha + m}\right)$

Chapter 10

Exercise 10.1

1 12.65 m s^{-1}
2 6.32 m s^{-1}; bearing 072°
3 $\begin{pmatrix} 12t \\ 0 \\ 10 \end{pmatrix}$; $\begin{pmatrix} 12mt \\ 0 \\ 10m \end{pmatrix}$
4 $\begin{pmatrix} \frac{5}{4}t^3 + 2t \\ \frac{1}{2}t^3 + 1 \\ \frac{3}{4}t^2 + 5t + 3 \end{pmatrix}$
5 (i) $-0.1\mathbf{i} + 0.2\mathbf{j}$, $5\mathbf{i} + 3\mathbf{j}$;
(ii) $6\frac{2}{3}$ s, 6.13 m s^{-1};
(iii) 39.6 m, 51.8°
6 (i) 1.97 s
(ii) 4.74 m

7 45.1 m

8 (ii) 884 m

9 39.8° or 82.2°

10 15.26°

11 (i) $\begin{pmatrix} 8 \\ -6 \\ 4 \end{pmatrix}, \begin{pmatrix} 4 \\ -3 \\ 2 \end{pmatrix}$;

(ii) $\begin{pmatrix} -30 \\ 15 \\ 10 \end{pmatrix}$;

(iii) 5 s

12 13 $\mathrm{m\,s^{-2}}$; bearing = 247°

13 (i) $\mathbf{v} = 2t^2\mathbf{i} + (6t - t^2)\mathbf{j}$;

$\mathbf{r} = \frac{2}{3}t^3\mathbf{i} + \left(3t^2 - \frac{1}{3}t^3\right)\mathbf{j}$

(ii) 2 s, 11.31 $\mathrm{m\,s^{-1}}$

(iii) 10.75 m, 29.7°

14 (i) $4.33\mathbf{i} - 2.5\mathbf{j}$

(ii) $\mathbf{v} = 14.33\mathbf{i} + 2.5\mathbf{j}$;

$\mathbf{r} = 76.67\mathbf{i} - 8.33\mathbf{j}$

15 (i) 73.5 m, 045°

(ii) $\begin{pmatrix} 20 \\ 30t - 3t^2 \end{pmatrix}$ cannot be 0 as $v_x = 20$ for all t.

(iii) 5 s

(iv) 77.6 $\mathrm{m\,s^{-1}}$

16 (ii) $3\mathbf{i} + 6\mathbf{k}$

(iii) 6.71 m

(iv) 63.4°

17 (i) 3 $\mathrm{m\,s^{-2}}$

(iii) $(1.2t + 0.9t^2)\mathbf{i} + (1.6t + 1.2t^2)\mathbf{j}$

(iv) $58.5\mathbf{i} + 63\mathbf{j}$

18 (i) $\mathbf{v} = -2\lambda t \sin \lambda t^2 \mathbf{i} + 2\lambda t \cos \lambda t^2 \mathbf{j} + 2\lambda t \mathbf{k}$;

$\mathbf{a} = (-2\lambda \sin \lambda t^2 - (2\lambda t)^2 \cos \lambda t^2)\mathbf{i} + (2\lambda \cos \lambda t^2 - (2\lambda t)^2 \sin \lambda t^2)\mathbf{j} + 2\lambda\mathbf{k}$

(iii) $4m\lambda^2 t^2$

(iv) $4m\lambda$

Exercise 10.2

1 (i) $\frac{dv}{dt} = 5t + 1$; 12 $\mathrm{m\,s^{-1}}$

(ii) $v\frac{dv}{dx} = \frac{2}{5+x}$; $2\sqrt{\ln 2}$ $\mathrm{m\,s^{-1}}$

(iii) $v\frac{dv}{dx} = \frac{2}{(1+x)^2}$; $\sqrt{2}$ $\mathrm{m\,s^{-1}}$

(iv) $\frac{dv}{dt} = 9 - v^2$; $\frac{1}{6}\ln(2)$ s

(v) $v\frac{dv}{dx} = v^2 + 1$; $\frac{1}{2}\ln 2$ m

(vi) $\frac{dv}{dt} = v^2 + 1$; $\frac{\pi}{4}$

(vii) $v\frac{dv}{dx} = \frac{2}{(2+x)^3}$; 0.53 $\mathrm{m\,s^{-1}}$

(viii) $\frac{dv}{dt} = 2\sin 3t$; $\frac{2}{3}$ $\mathrm{m\,s^{-1}}$

2 (i) $\begin{pmatrix} 10 - 2t \\ 20 - 10t \end{pmatrix}$; $\begin{pmatrix} 10t - t^2 \\ 20t - 5t^2 \end{pmatrix}$

(ii)

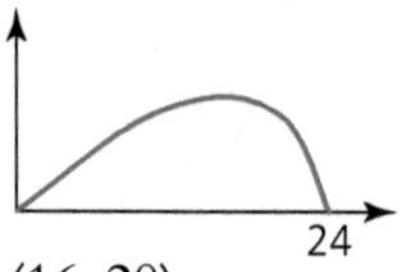

(iii) (16, 20)

3 (i) (a) $v = At$

(b) $v = ct - te^{-t^2}$

(ii) (a) $v = \sqrt{As - 1}$

(b) $v = ce^{-s^2} + e^{-s^2 - 2s}$

4 (ii) $69e^{-0.2t} - 49$

(iii) $345(1 - e^{-0.2t}) - 49t$

(iv) 16.1 m

5 (ii) 3.93 m

6 (ii) $v = 10e^{-0.2t} + 0.5e^{-1.2t}$

7 (ii) $2040(1 - e^{-0.005t})$

(iii) 126.4 m

8 (ii) $v = 16\left(1 - e^{-\frac{1}{8}t}\right)$

(iii) 47.1 m

9 (i) $v = (2t + 3)\cos t$

(ii) $0 \le t < \frac{\pi}{2}$

10 (ii) $\frac{2U^{1.5}}{3k}$

11 (i) 1.002 s

(ii) 7.98 m

(iii) $v = 8(1 - e^{-1.25t})$

(iv) $x = 8t - 6.4(1 - e^{-1.25t})$

12 (i) $a = 2x(x^2 - 4)$; 2.625 N

(ii) $2\left(\frac{1 - e^{-4t}}{1 + e^{-4t}}\right)$

(iii) 2 m

13 (A) (i) $k = \frac{3mu^2}{8s}$

(ii) $[k] = \mathrm{MLT^{-2}}$

(iii) The probe never leaves the gas cloud.

(iv) $\frac{4s}{3}$

(B) (i) $k = \frac{mu}{2s}$

(ii) $[k] = \mathrm{MT^{-1}}$

(iii) The probe never leaves the gas cloud.

(iv) $2s$

(C) (i) $k = \frac{m \ln 2}{s}$

(ii) $[k] = \mathrm{ML^{-1}}$

(iii) $\frac{u}{8}$

(iv) $3s$

Discussion point page 222 (top)

The equation becomes $v^2 = u^2 + 2\mathbf{a} \bullet \mathbf{s}$, which is the vector version of $v^2 = u^2 + 2as$.

Discussion point page 222 (bottom)

(i) The magnitude of the final velocity is $\sqrt{56}$.

(ii) It is impossible to deal with the components of the equation separately. The direction of the final velocity cannot be found, only its magnitude.

Exercise 10.3

1 9 J

2 1.22 kW

3 6.8 J

4 (i) $9 \times 10^4\,\mathrm{m\,s^{-1}}$

(ii) $5.39 \times 10^4\,\mathrm{m\,s^{-1}}$ (unchanged)

5 25.2 J

6 $z = 0.3$

7 $x = 15$

8 (i) 25 $\mathrm{m\,s^{-1}}$

(ii) 20 $\mathrm{m\,s^{-1}}$

9 24 $\mathrm{m\,s^{-1}}$

10 (i) $\frac{35}{12}$ J

Chapter 11

Discussion point page 228

At both the bottom and the top the contact force is in the vertically upwards direction. It is about 4×10^{-6}% smaller at the top.

Half way up or down the value of the vertical component of the contact force is the mean of those at the top and bottom and is equal to your weight. However the contact force also has a component acting horizontally, towards the axis of the Eye, with magnitude about 2×10^{-6}% of your weight.

Exercise 11.1

1 (i) 0.02 rad s^{-2}
(ii) 900 rad

2 (i) 6.28 rad s^{-2}
(ii) 4 revs

3 (i) $4\,\text{rad}\,s^{-1}$
(ii) $0.0005\,\text{rad}\,s^{-2}$
(iii) 16 000 rad
(iv) 32 000 m

4 $9.42\ \text{m}\,\text{s}^{-1}$

5 (i) area = total angle turned through

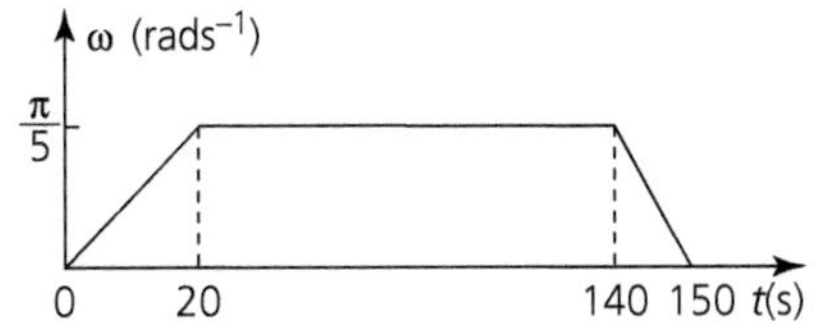

(ii) 84.82 rad, 254 m
(iii) $1.18\ \text{m}\,\text{s}^{-2}$

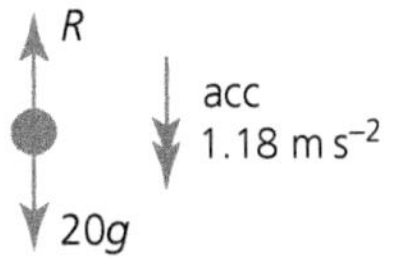

(iv) $0.03\,\pi\ \text{m}\,\text{s}^{-2}$ vertically upwards and $0.03\,\pi^2\ \text{m}\,\text{s}^{-2}$ horizontally towards the centre.

Discussion point page 237

No, see text that follows.

Activity 11.1 page 237

If the string breaks the object will fly off at a tangent to the circle. If a rod were used rather than a string, the motion would be the same for 1 and 2. For 3, when a string is used, the object leaves the circle and falls in a parabola. On a rod, it swings back as a pendulum.

Discussion point page 239

$T = mr\omega^2 - mg\cos\alpha$, but $R = mg\cos\beta - mr\omega^2$ so $T > 0$ if ω is sufficiently large and $R > 0$ if ω is sufficiently small.

Discussion point page 241

(i) and (iv)

Exercise 11.2

1 (i) A: $4\ \text{m}\,\text{s}^{-2}$ B: $40\ \text{m}\,\text{s}^{-2}$
(ii) (a) A yes, B No
(b) A no, B yes
(c) A no, B yes
(d) A yes, B yes

2 (A) (i) $22.2m$ J
(ii) complete revolutions; $4.98\ \text{m}\,\text{s}^{-1}$
(iii) (a) $73.8m$ N towards O
(b) $15m$ N towards O
(B) (i) $18m$ J
(ii) stops; 1.84 m
(iii) (a) $18m$ N towards O
(b) $9m$ N away from O
(C) (i) $4.74m$ J
(ii) stops, 0.48 m
(iii) (a) $6.49m$ N away from O
(b) $9.49m$ N away from O

3 (ii) $2mg$

4 (ii) $R = \dfrac{mv^2}{a} + mg\cos\theta$

$v^2 = u^2 - 2ga(1 - \cos\theta) = ga(1 + 2\cos\theta)$

$\Rightarrow R = mg(1 + 3\cos\theta)$

5 (i) $0.186mg$ J
(iv) 0.598 m
(v) No, it leaves the track

6 (ii) $3mg$

7 (i) $0.8g$ J, $6.35\ \text{m}\,\text{s}^{-1}$
(ii) $\sqrt{9 + 1.6g(1 - \cos\theta)}$
(iii) (a) 0.725 N
(b) 30.125 N
(iv)

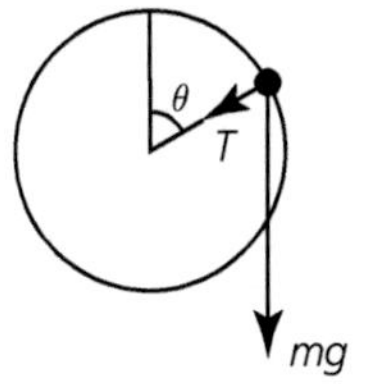

$T = 15.43 - 14.7\cos\theta$, $g\sin\theta$

8 (i) $82\ \text{m}\,\text{s}^{-1}$, $53\ \text{m}\,\text{s}^{-1}$
(ii) $67.2\ \text{m}\,\text{s}^{-2}$, $28.6\ \text{m}\,\text{s}^{-2}$
(iii)

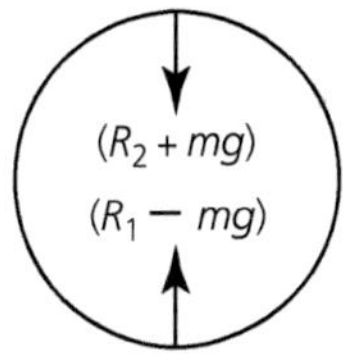

$R_1 = 5393$ N,
$R_2 = 1316$ N
(iv) He would fail to complete the loop

(v) 138 m

9 (i) 15 cm
(ii) 3.45 rad s^{-1}
(iii) 1.9 rad s^{-2}
(iv) Girl lets go before reaching the vertical

10 (i) Almost zero speed at the top of the loop not sufficient
(ii) 20 m
(iii) It stops below the centre and returns to C; 8 m

11 (i) 12 ms^{-1}, 27 mph
(ii) Traffic used to travel more slowly.
(iii) Increase the radius by making the approaches less steep.

12 (i) K.E. = $\frac{1}{2} \times 200 \times 21^2$
= 44 100
The energy equation including K.E. and P.E. gives
$200g \times 20 + \frac{1}{2} \times 200v^2$
= 44 100
$v = 7$ ms^{-1}
(ii) radial acceleration =
4.9 ms^{-2};
$R = -980$ N
Force from track is up so could not operate.
(iii) 14.7ms^{-2}; 8.49ms^{-2}
$\arctan\left(\dfrac{\frac{\sqrt{3}}{2}g}{14.7}\right) = 30°$

13 (i) $v^2 = gl(2\cos\theta - 1)$
(iii) $2mg$ when $\theta = 0$
(iv) Perpendicular to AB
(v) 0.32rad

Chapter 12

Discussion point page 251

Use energy considerations. See the investigation at the end of this chapter.

Exercise 12.1

1 (i) 49N, 245N
(ii) 98N, 32.$\dot{6}$N
(iii) 0.98N, 4.9N

2 (i) 20 N
(ii) 20 N
(iii) Tensions required to double the length is the same. There is a 20 N force at the fixed end in part (i).

3 (i)

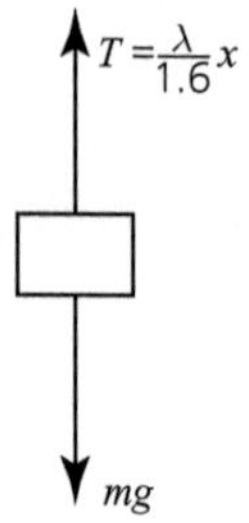

9.8 Nm^{-1}

4 (i) 4.9 N
(ii) 0.625 kg
(iii) 1.2 m

5 (i) 30 N
(ii) 3
(iii) Spring becomes fully compressed with fewer than seven blocks.

6 $-40\text{N} < \text{force} < 80\text{N}$

7 (i) 0.03N
(ii) 42cm
(iii) 0.135N

8 (i) $\lambda = 0.3375$, $l = 0.45$
(ii) 0.1125

Exercise 12.2

1 (i) 60 N
(ii) 0.04 m
(iii) 2400 N; could be two strings together (side by side)

2 (i) 12 000 N
(ii) 80 000 Nm^{-1}
(iii) 0.05 m
(iv) 0.02 m

3 (i) 7000 N
(ii) 7000 N, 10 000 Nm^{-1}
(iii) 4000 N

4 (i) 198 N
(ii) 654 N
(iii) 118%
(iv) 51.6 m

5 (i) $T = F$ for each spring,
$\frac{Fl_0}{\lambda_1}, \frac{Fl_0}{\lambda_2}$

6 (i) $(0.3 - x)$ m
(ii) $16x$ N, $25(0.3 - x)$ N
(iii) 0.183

7 (i) $2.2 - h$ m, $h - 1.2$ m
(ii) $44 - 20h$ N, $30h - 36$ N
(iii) 1.2 m
(iv) 20 N, 0 N

8 (i) $\frac{l_0}{\lambda}mg\sin\alpha$
(ii) (a) $\frac{l_0}{\lambda}mg(\mu\cos\alpha + \sin\alpha)$
(b) $\frac{l_0}{\lambda}mg(\sin\alpha - \mu\cos\alpha)$

9 (i) 1000 N
(ii) 0.024 m
(iii) $R = 5000h - 730$

10 (ii) 0.306 m
(iii) An elastic band is unlikely to pass smoothly over a peg.

11 (i) 5.1 kg
(ii) 0.8784 m
(iii) 59.8 N
(iv) 3.52 kg

12 (i) (b) $\frac{g}{80n}$ m
(iii) 4
(iv) 0.098 m

13 $\frac{\lambda d}{l_0} = mg \Rightarrow \lambda = \frac{mgl_0}{d}$
x_1 = extension of top half;
x_2 = extension of bottom half
$\Rightarrow$ displacement $= \frac{1}{2}(x_1 - x_2)$
Equilibrium: $\frac{2\lambda}{l_0}x_1 = \frac{2\lambda}{l_0}x_2 + mg$
$\Rightarrow x_1 = x_2 + \frac{1}{2}d$
$\Rightarrow$ displacement $= \frac{1}{4}d$

14 1.3m

Exercise 12.3

1 (i) 4 J
(ii) 0.25 J
(iii) 1 J
(iv) 0.0625 J

2 (i) 0.75 J

(ii) 5.48 $\mathrm{m\,s^{-1}}$

3 (i) 0.006 67 J

(ii) 0.577 $\mathrm{m\,s^{-1}}$

4 (i) 5×10^4 J

(ii) 7.07 $\mathrm{m\,s^{-1}}$

(iii) 1.29 m

(iv) 7.07×10^4 N, 35.4 $\mathrm{m\,s^{-2}}$

(v) Truck moves back along the rail at 5 $\mathrm{m\,s^{-1}}$ if other forces ignored.

5 0.433 m, 0.067 m

6 (i) B is in equilibrium

(ii) 0.8 m, 6 N

(iii) 2.7 J

(iv) 10 $\mathrm{m\,s^{-1}}$

7 (i) 562.5 J

(ii) 0.15

(iii) 0.8 $\mathrm{m\,s^{-1}}$

(iv) $1440 = 25\,000x_1^2 + 20\,000x_2^2$, $5x_1 = 4x_2$; $x_1 = 0.16$, $x_2 = 0.2$

8 (i) EE gain = $44.1x^2 \div (2 \times 0.75)$

PE loss = $1.8g(0.75 + x)$

$[x^2 - 0.6x - 0.45 = 0]$

Extension is 1.03 m

(ii) $\dfrac{44.1 \times 1.03}{0.75} - 1.8 \times 9.8 = -1.8\ddot{x}$

Acceleration is $-24.0\,\mathrm{m\,s^{-2}}$

9 (i) 0.4, 1

(ii) It does not go slack.

(iii) 1.125 m

Activity 12.1 page 274

For a 90 kg person, the maximum extension is 33.2 m for a rope 12 m long giving rise to a deceleration of 19.7 m $\mathrm{s^{-2}}$.

For a 60 kg person the maximum extension is 27.1 m for a rope 18 m long giving rise to a deceleration of 26.3 m $\mathrm{s^{-2}}$.

Exercise 12.4

1 (i) $5h^2$ J

(ii) $0.2gh$ J

(iii) 0.392

2 $2l_0$

3 $l_0\left(1 + \dfrac{mg}{\lambda}\right)$

4 (ii) 0.1294

5 0.463 m

6 (i) 1 J

(iii) 0.2 m

7 (i) 0.1098 m

(ii) 0.149 m

8 Conservation of energy:

$$\frac{1}{2}\left(\frac{\lambda}{l_0}\right)(3l_0)^2 = mg \times 4l_0$$

$$\Rightarrow \lambda = \frac{8}{9}mg$$

Maximum tension:

$$T = \frac{\lambda}{l_0} \times 3l_0 = \frac{8}{3}mg$$

9 (i) $\arccos\left(\dfrac{g}{\omega^2 l}\right)$

(ii) $\arccos\left(\dfrac{g(\lambda - ml_0\omega^2)}{\omega^2 l_0 \lambda}\right)$

10 (i) 0.8 m

(ii) $98(x - 0.5)$ N, $98(2 - x)$ N

(iii) 57.3 J

(iv) 0.81 $\mathrm{m\,s^{-1}}$

11 (i) $\dfrac{mgl_0}{\lambda}$

(ii) $mg\left(l_0 + \dfrac{mg}{2\lambda}\right)$

(iii) $\dfrac{m^2g^2l_0}{\lambda}$

(iv) (ii) > (iii), external work done to move block

(v) $\dfrac{mg}{M}$

12 (iii) $-122\ \mathrm{m\,s^{-2}}$

13 $\sqrt{\dfrac{8}{3}gl}$

14 (ii) 14.06 $\mathrm{m\,s^{-1}}$

Chapter 13

Exercise 13.1

1 (i) (a)

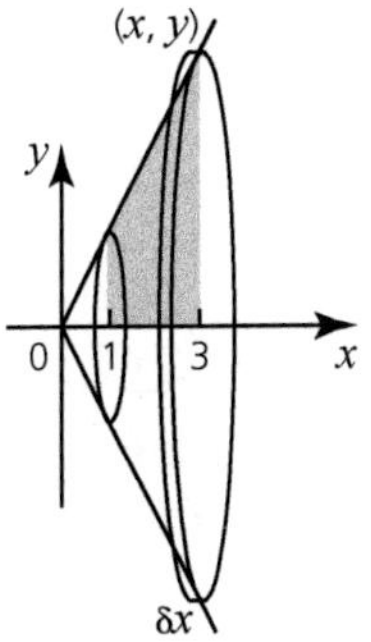

(b) $\dfrac{104}{3}\pi$

(ii) (a)

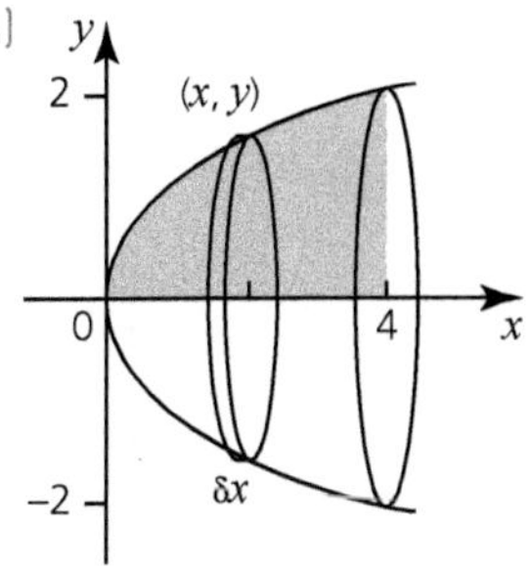

(b) 8π

(iii) (a)

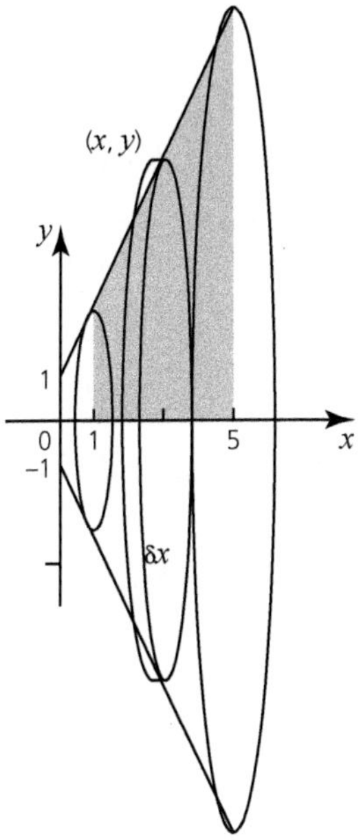

(b) $\dfrac{652}{3}\pi$

(iv) (a)

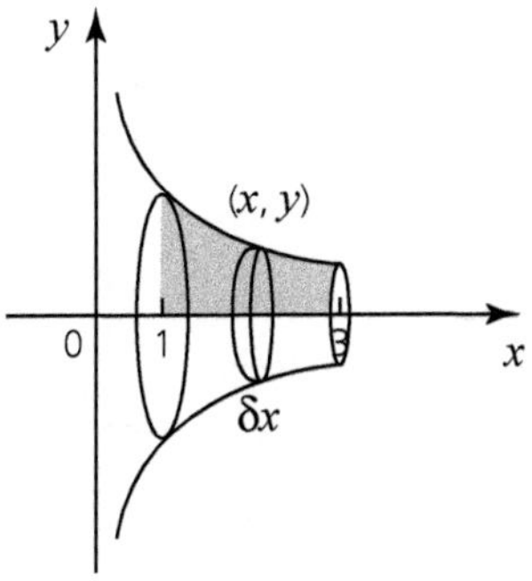

(b) $\dfrac{2}{3}\pi$

(v) (a)

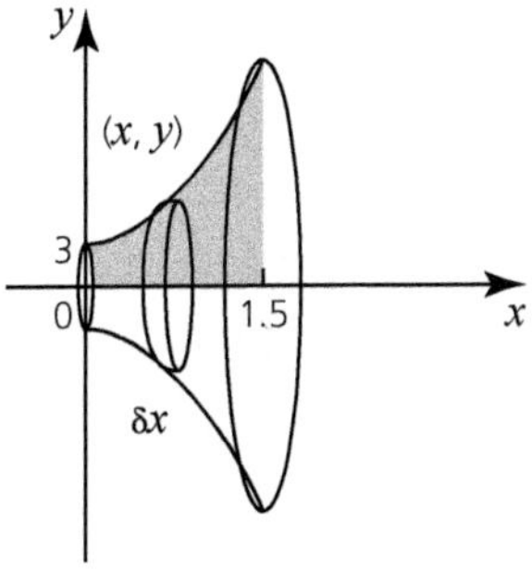

(b) $\frac{9}{2}\pi(e^3 - 1)$

(vi) (a)

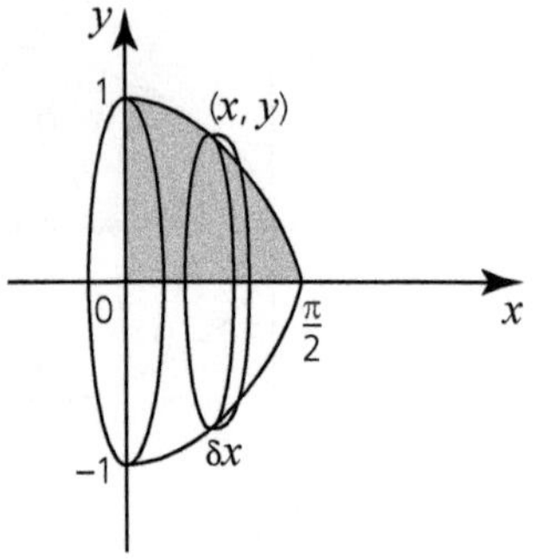

(b) $\frac{1}{4}\pi^2$

2 (i) (a)

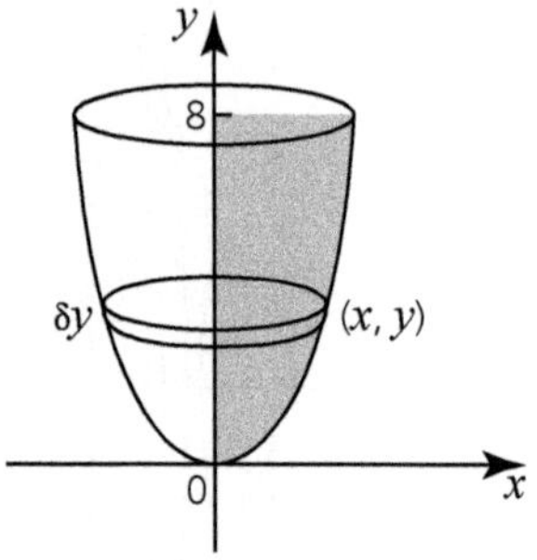

(b) $\frac{96}{5}\pi$

(ii) (a)

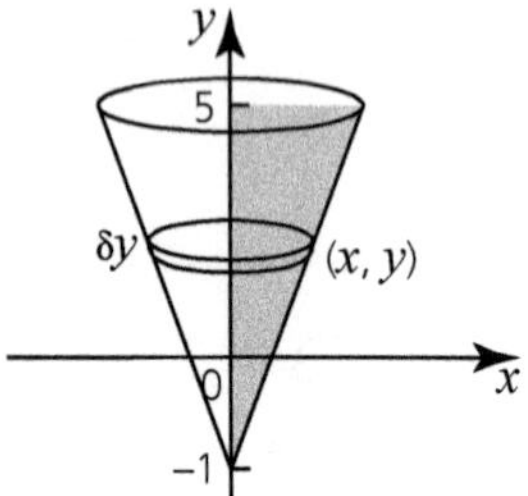

(b) 18π

(iii) (a)

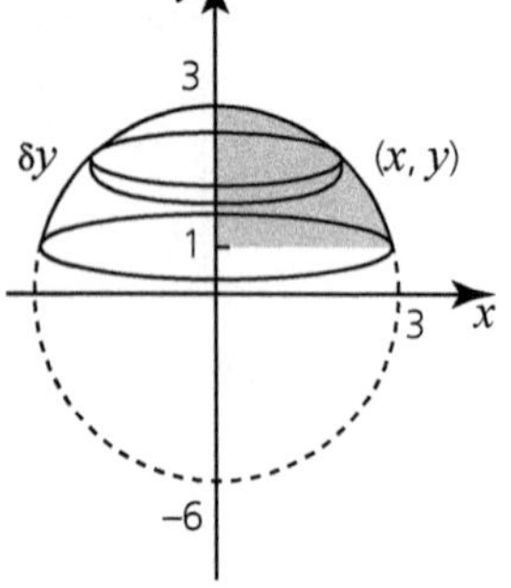

(b) $\frac{28}{3}\pi$

3 (i) $y = \frac{rx}{h}$

(ii) 0.235 l

4 $34\frac{1}{3}\pi$

5 (i)

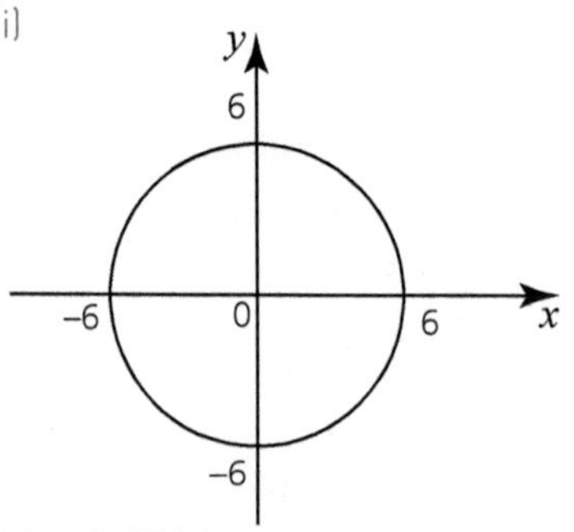

(ii) 0.235 l

6 (i)

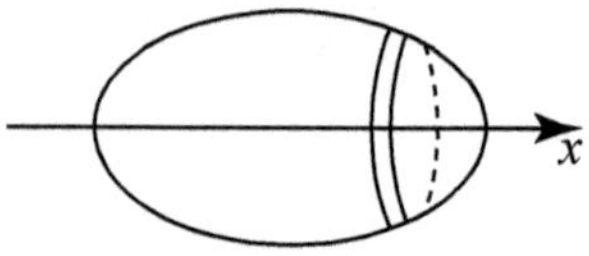

(iii) $\frac{2}{3}\pi b^2(a+b)$

7 (i)

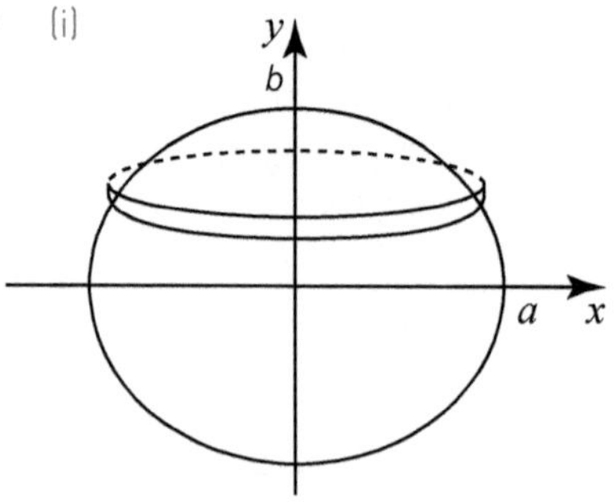

(ii) $a \approx 4.73 \times 10^{19}$ m;

$b \approx 4.26 \times 10^{19}$ m;

$V \approx 4 \times 10^{59}$ m^3

8 16π

9 $34\frac{1}{3}$

10 (iii) 101.775π

11 (iii) 3.2×10^5 m^3

12 (i)

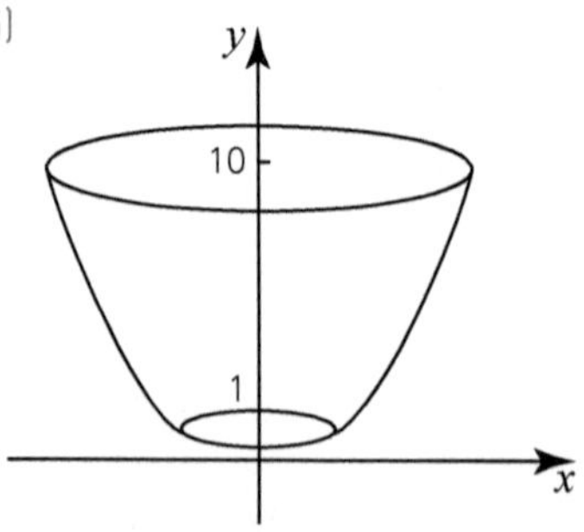

(ii) (a) 2.36 (b) 5.83

(c) 9.03

13 (i) A (−2, 0), B (2, 0)

(ii) 11.29

(iii) 4765 cm^3 = 4.765 litres

Exercise 13.2

1 (a) For sketches see Exercise 13.1 question 1.

(b) (i) (2.31, 0)

(ii) (2.67, 0)

(iii) (3.70, 0)

(iv) (1.65, 0)

(v) (1.08, 0)

(vi) (0.47, 0)

2 (a) For sketches see Exercise 13.1 question 2.

(b) (i) (0, 5)

(ii) (0, 3.5)

(iii) (0, 1.71)

3 (i)

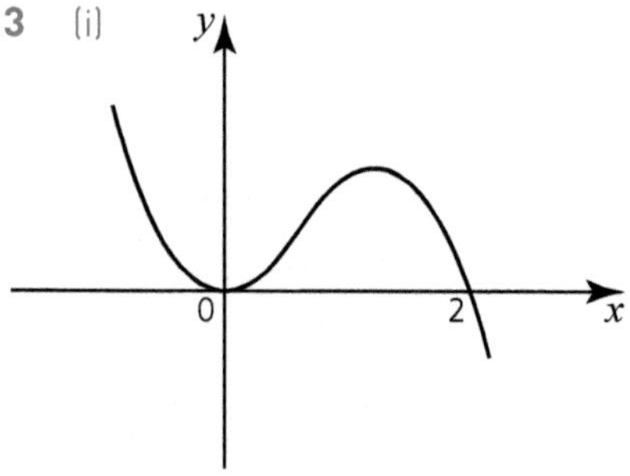

(ii) $\frac{128}{105}\pi$

(iii) (1.25, 0)

4 16.7°

5 (i)

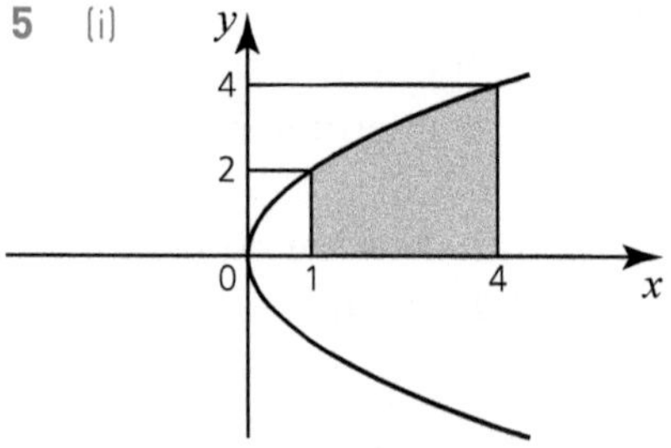

(ii) $V = 30\pi$; (2.8, 0)

(iii) (a) 2 , 4

(b) $\frac{62}{5}\pi$

(c) (0, 3.39)

6 3.9 cm

7 (i)

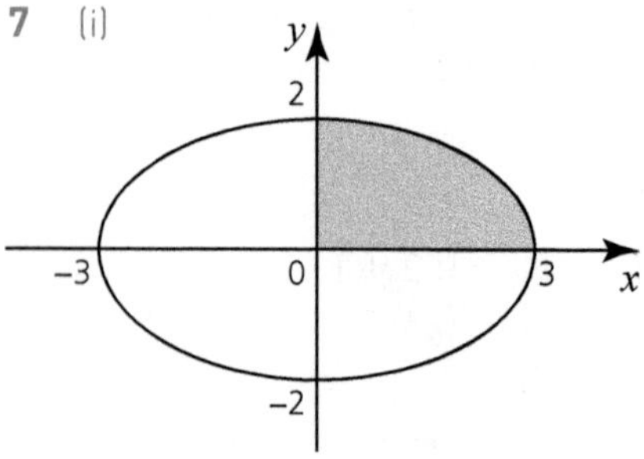

(ii) $V = 8\pi$; (1.125, 0)

8 4.76°

9 (i)

	Clown	Cone	Hemisphere
Mass	$\frac{1}{3}\pi r^2\rho(2r+h)$	$\frac{1}{3}\pi r^2 h\rho$	$\frac{2}{3}\pi r^3\rho$
Distance of c.o.m. above O	$\bar{y}$	$\frac{1}{4}h$	$-\frac{3}{8}r$

(ii) $\left(\frac{2}{3}r+\frac{1}{3}h\right)\bar{y}=\frac{1}{3}h\times\frac{1}{4}h-\frac{2}{3}r\times\frac{3}{8}r$

(iii) $\sqrt{3}:1$

(iv) upright

10 (i) Using σ as mass per unit area

	Whole container	Cylinder base	Cylinder walls	Cone
Mass	$132\pi\sigma$	$9\pi\sigma$	$108\pi\sigma$	$15\pi\sigma$
Distance of c.o.m. above O	$\bar{y}$	0	9	$19\frac{1}{3}$

(ii) 9.56 cm

(iii) 17.42°

(iv) The centre of mass will be lower so it is less likely to topple.

11 (i) $\frac{64}{3}\pi$

(ii) (1.6, 0)

(iii) 74.6°

12 (i)

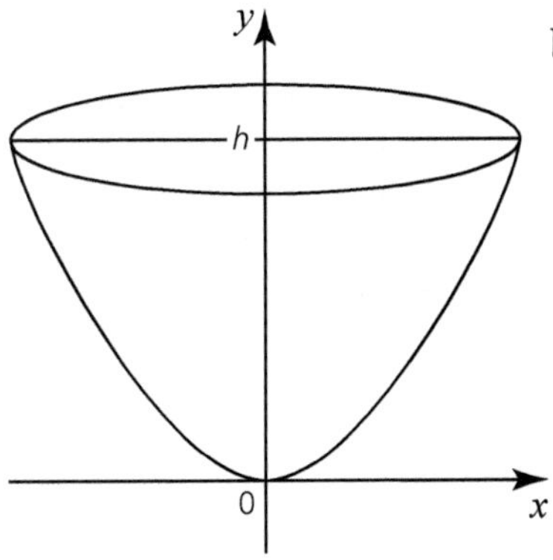

$V=\frac{\pi h^2}{2k}$

(ii) $\frac{1}{3}h$

(iii)

	Solid block	Glass	Part removed
Mass	$\frac{9^2\pi}{2k}\rho$	$\frac{\pi}{2k}\left(9^2-8.8^2\right)\rho$	$\frac{8.8^2\pi}{2k}\rho$
Distance of c.o.m. below rim	$\frac{1}{3}\times 9$	d	$\frac{1}{3}\times 8.8$

(iv) 7.3 cm

(v) 22.4°

13 (iii) $1-4\varepsilon$

Activity 13.1 page 300

About 8 : 11; see Example 13.8

Exercise 13.3

1 (a) (i) $\bar{x}=0$

(ii)

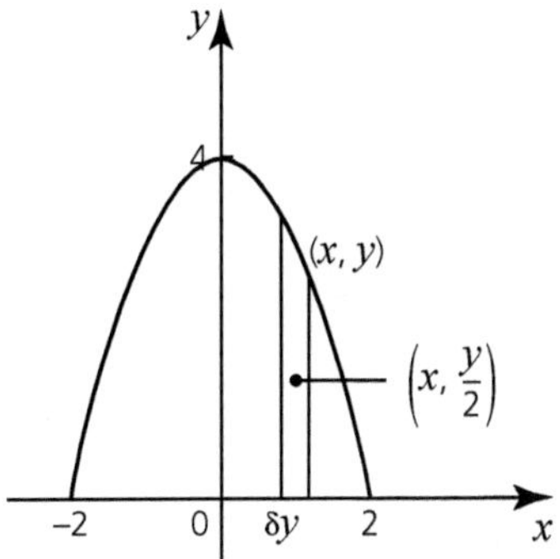

(iii) $\left(4-x^2\right)\delta x$

(iv) (0, 1.6)

(b) (i) $\bar{y}=0$

(ii)

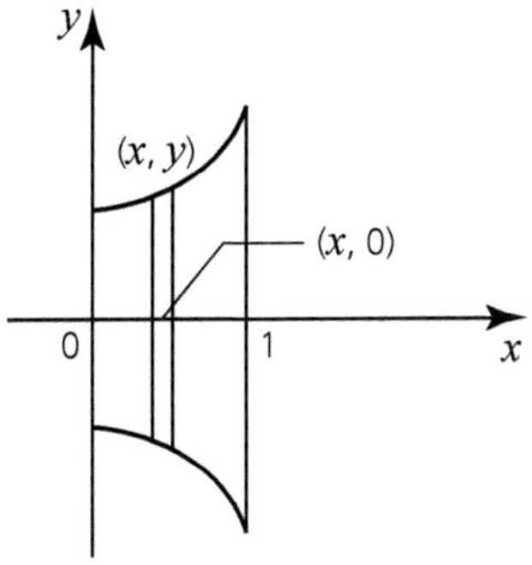

(iii) $2e^x\delta x$

(iv) (0.58, 0)

(c) (i) $\bar{y}=0$

(ii)

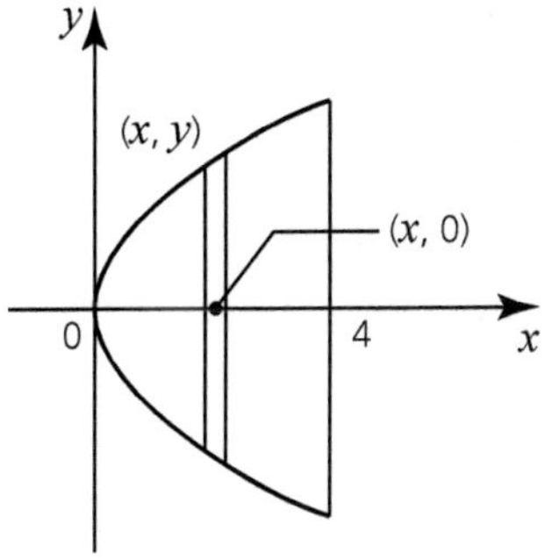

(iii) $4\sqrt{x}\delta x$

(iv) (2.4, 0)

(d) (i) $\bar{x} = \frac{\pi}{2}$

(ii) 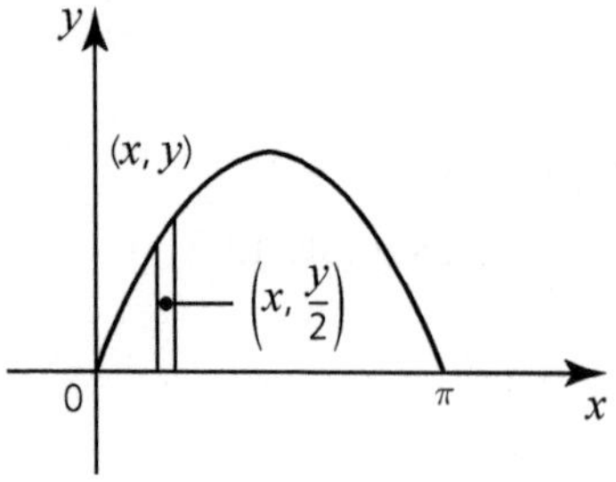

(iii) $\sin x \; \delta x$

(iv) $\left(\frac{\pi}{2}, \frac{\pi}{8}\right)$

2 (i) 36 cm^2

(ii) $y = -2x + 12$

(iii) $(2, 4)$

3 33.7°

4 36.9°

5 $\left(\frac{3}{4}\ln 2, \frac{3}{8}\ln 2\right)$

6 (i) 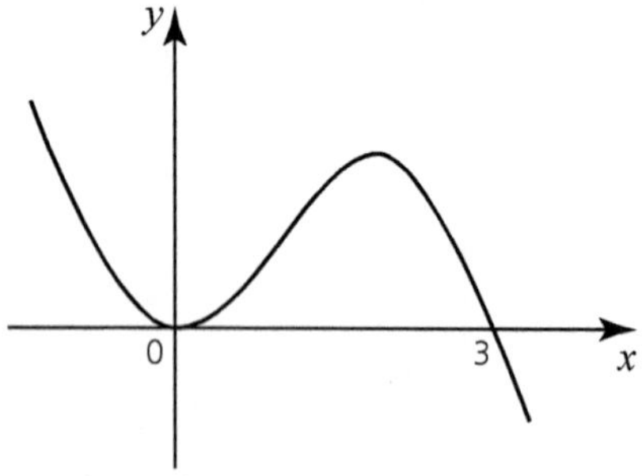

(ii) $(1.8, 1.54)$

7 (i) 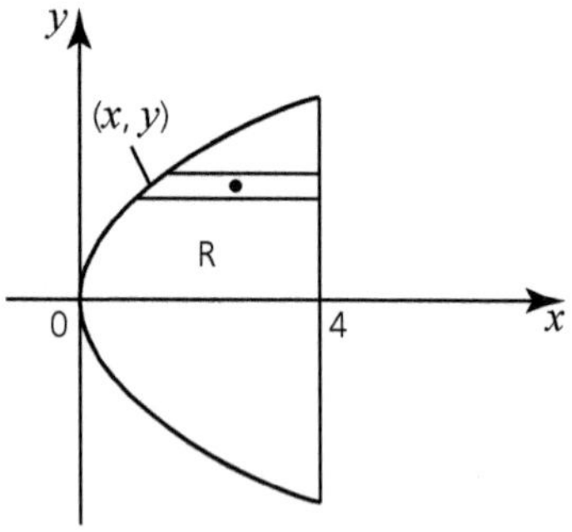

(ii) $(4 - x)\delta y, \frac{4 + x}{2}$

(iii) $(2.4, 0)$

8 (i) $\left(2, 2\frac{5}{12}\right)$

(ii) $\left(3, 2\frac{2}{3}\right)$

(iii) $\left(2, 2\frac{7}{24}\right)$

(iv) $\left(3, 2\frac{5}{8}\right)$

9 (i) $(1.08, 0.95)$

(ii) The centre of each strip is on PP′

(iii) G_1 and G_2 are both $\frac{1}{3}$ PD from QR so G_1G_2 is parallel to QR. G lies on G_1G_2 and PH:HD = 2:1 so GP:GP′ = 2:1.

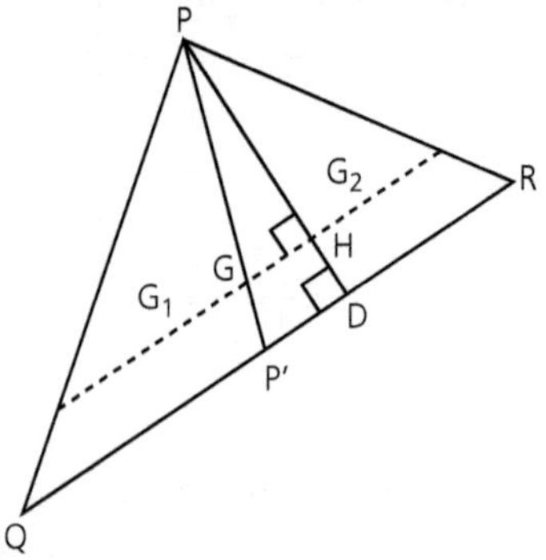

10 (ii) $(0.75, 0.3)$

(iii) $(0.447, 0.516)$

11 (i) outer semicircle: $2\pi, \left(1 + \frac{8}{3\pi}, 4\right)$

inner semicircle: $\frac{\pi}{2}, \left(1 + \frac{4}{3\pi}, 4\right)$

rectangle: 6, (0.5, 3)

(ii) $(1.16, 3.44)$

(iii) 18.63°

12 (i) 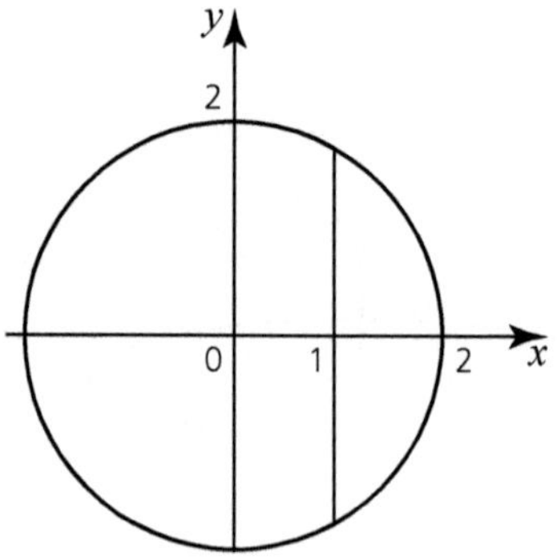

(iii) 1.41

(iv) 1.09 from centre

(v) 32.2°

13 (i) $\left(\frac{3}{8}, 0\right)$

(ii) $\left(\frac{3}{4}, 0\right)$

(iii) $\left(\frac{9}{8}, 0\right)$

(iv) 48.4°

14 $\left(\frac{3}{8}\sqrt{2}, 2\right)$

15 $(0, 2)$

16 (ii) $\left(0, \frac{4r}{\pi}\right)$

Discussion point page 308 (top)

The bus is likely to topple. Toppling depends on the relative mass of upstairs and downstairs passengers.

Discussion point page 308 (bottom)

In the first case it slides, in the second case it topples. The bus is similar to the second case.

Discussion point page 309

There is a resultant moment about the edge E.

Discussion point page 311

Yes when $\mu = 0.5$ and $\alpha = 26.6°$.

Exercise 13.4

1 (i) 27.44 N (ii) 34.3 N
(iii) slide

2 (i) 19.6μ (ii) 5.88 N
(iii) $\mu < 0.3$ (iv) $\mu > 0.3$

3 (i) 14.0° (ii) 18.4°
(iii) sliding

4 It slides

5 (a) (i) 22.51 N
(ii) 21.96 N
(iii) topples
(b) (i) 22.76 N
(ii) 25.90 N (iii) slides
63.4°, 22.36 N

6 (i) (a) 50 by 20
(b) 20 by 10
(ii) The shortest side is perpendicular to the plane of the slope for maximum likelihood of sliding.
(iii) (a) $\mu < 0.2$ (b) $\mu > 5$

7 (i) $\frac{1}{3}a(25+2.5a)x_G$

$$= 25\times 2.5 + 2.5a\times\left(5+\frac{1}{3}a\right)$$

$$x_G = \frac{a^2+15a+75}{3(a+10)} \qquad \text{AG}$$

(ii) $\frac{a^2+15a+75}{3(a+10)} = 5$

$a = 5\sqrt{3}$

(iii) $(25+2.5a)y_G$

$$= 25\times 2.5 + 2.5a\times\left(\frac{2}{3}\times 5\right)$$

$$y_G = \frac{10a+75}{3(a+10)} \text{ or } 2.89$$

$$\tan\theta = \frac{x_G}{y_G} = \frac{5}{y_G}$$

$$\theta = 60$$

Solving for a $a = 8.66$ or $5\sqrt{3}$

8 (i) It stays put.
(ii) It topples.

9 $T\times\frac{4}{5}l = T\times\frac{3}{5}l + W\times\frac{l}{2}$

$\Rightarrow T = 2.5W$

Chapter 14

Discussion point page 316

The cue ball should be struck in such a direction that when it reaches the blue ball, the line joining the centres of the balls is in the direction of the hole. The red ball cannot be potted from this position as the black ball is in the way. It would be possible for the cue ball to hit the black ball so that it then sends the red ball into the hole, but this is not allowed in snooker.

Discussion point page 318

The red ball was initially stationary so its final momentum is equal to the impulse it has received. This is equal in magnitude but opposite in direction to the impulse **J** acting on the white ball. So its direction is 47° from the **i** direction.

Discussion point page 321

When $e = 0$, the ball does not rebound and moves only along the plane. All the kinetic energy from the motion perpendicular to the plane is lost. When $e = 1$, the collision is perfectly elastic and there is no loss in kinetic energy.

Exercise 14.1

1 (i)

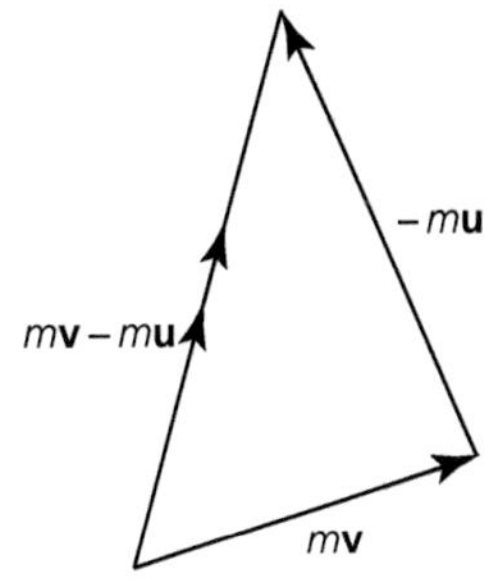

(ii) 0.32 Ns at 85° to the horizontal

(iii) $\begin{pmatrix}1.75\\-3.03\end{pmatrix}$ $\begin{pmatrix}1.73\\1\end{pmatrix}$

Answers

(iv) $\mathbf{J} = 0.08\begin{pmatrix}-0.02\\4.03\end{pmatrix}$

2 (i) $-20\mathbf{i}$
(ii) $5.1\mathbf{i} + 0.6\mathbf{j} + 0.45\mathbf{k}$
(iii) Fatima

3 (i) $\begin{pmatrix}3.76\\0.68\end{pmatrix}$ (ii) $\begin{pmatrix}7.66\\0.64\end{pmatrix}$ (iii) $\begin{pmatrix}u\cos\alpha\\0.8u\sin\alpha\end{pmatrix}$

4 (i) 1.58 Ns in $\mathbf{j}$ direction;
(ii) 1.58 Ns in $-\mathbf{j}$ direction;
(iii) 3.10 J

5 (i) 0.45 Ns in $\mathbf{j}$ direction
(ii) 0.45 Ns in $-\mathbf{j}$ direction
(iii) 0.512 J

6 (i) $mu\sin\alpha$ Ns
(ii) $\frac{1}{2}mu^2 - \frac{1}{2}mu^2\cos^2\alpha = \frac{1}{2}mu^2\sin^2\alpha$

7 $(5.4\mathbf{i} + 0.8\mathbf{j})$ m s^{-1}.

8 $(0.4\mathrm{i} + 1.4\mathrm{j} + 26\mathrm{k})$ m s^{-1}

9 $(0.976\mathrm{i} + 0.005\mathrm{j} + 1.08\mathrm{k})\times10^6$ m s^{-1}.

10 (i) time of flight $= \frac{2u_y}{g}$; range $= \frac{2u_xu_y}{g}$
(ii) 0.6 R
(iii) $0.6^n \times R$ (iv) $2.38R$

11 (i) $\begin{pmatrix}2.5\\-0.4\end{pmatrix}$
(ii) 1.01 m (iii) 1.41 m
(iv) 2.02×0.7^n (v) 7

12 (i) at 24.8° to cushion after first impact; at 60° to cushion after second impact
(ii) 1.6 m s^{-1}
(iii) at β to cushion with $\tan\beta = e\tan\alpha$; at $90° - \alpha$ to second cushion, speed is reduced by e^2

13 (i) 2.38 m
(ii) 0.65 m; 1.73 m
(iii) 53°

14 (i) 8 m s^{-1} (ii) 1 m s^{-1}
(iii) -42 Ns (iv) 0.214

15 (i) $\sqrt{\frac{2h}{g}}\left(\frac{1+e}{1-e}\right)$ (ii) $\sqrt{\frac{2h}{g}}\left(\frac{1+e}{1-e}\right)u$

16 (i) 14 kg (ii) 280 N

Exercise 14.2

1 1.58 m s^{-1}, 3.16 m s^{-1}; 116.6°, 63.4°

2 $1.23u$, $0.4u$, 85°, 0°

3 $\frac{1}{4}u$, $\frac{5}{4}u$, 0°, 53°

4 $0.90u$, $0.90u$, 106.1°, 73.9°

5 0.2

6 80.5°

7 (i) $3.1875\mathbf{i} + 1.0625\mathbf{j}$
(ii) 0.538 Ns (3 s.f.)

8 (i) 3
(ii) $5\mathbf{i} + \mathbf{j}$
(iii) $\frac{2}{3}$

9 Loss in K.E. for direct impact $= mu^2(1 - e^2)$
Loss in K.E. in oblique impact $= \frac{3}{4}mu^2(1-e^2)$

10 (i) $\frac{1}{2}u$; u
(ii) A: 1.80 u at 74°; B: $u\sqrt{2}$ at 45°
(iii) $\frac{1}{4}mu^2$

11 (i)

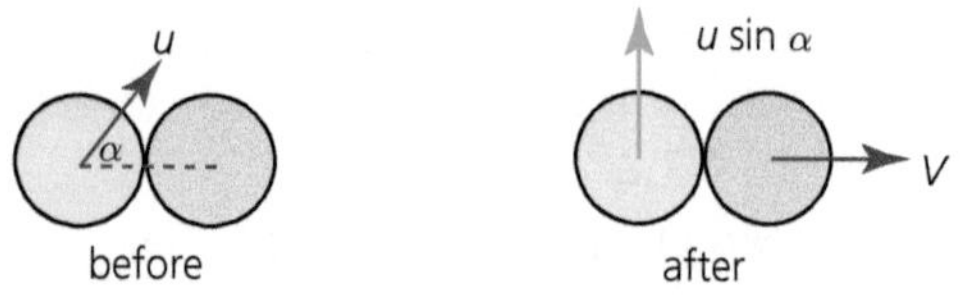

Conservation of momentum $mu\cos\alpha = mV$
Newton's law of impact:
$V = eu\cos\alpha \Rightarrow e = 1$

(ii) Conservation of momentum:
$mu\cos\alpha = kmV$
Newton's law of impact:
$V = eu\cos\alpha \Rightarrow ke = 1$

(iii) The contact between the two discs is smooth.

12 (i) $2 \times [\frac{1}{2}mu^2(1-e^2)\cos^2\alpha]$
(ii)

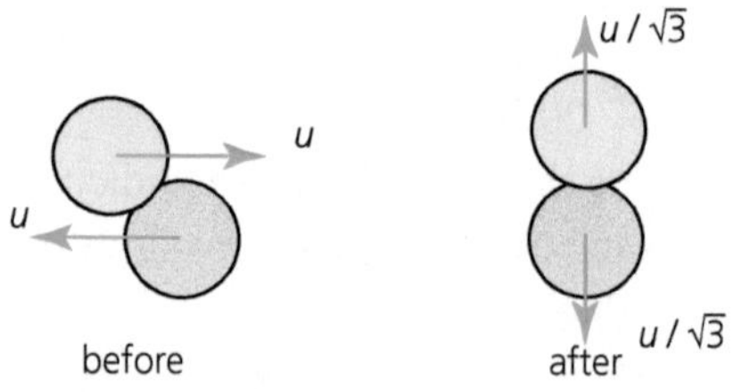

13 (i) $U = 7.5$, $u = 3$
(ii) The contact is smooth
(iii) 5 m s^{-1}

14 (i) (a) It is 6.38 cm off line and so does not go into the pocket.
(b) It is 1.89 cm off line and so goes into the pocket.
(ii) It is 2.69 cm off line and so does not go into the pocket.
(iii) 0.14° (to 2 s.f.)
(iv) A higher level of accuracy is required than is the case for a shot with a single impact. Any error in the original direction is increased in the second impact.

Practice Questions: Set 3 (page 333)

1 (i) Two cases: $4g \pm 9.8 = \frac{4 \times 3.5^2}{a}$ giving $a = 1$ or $\frac{5}{3}$.

(ii) Must be at the bottom with the larger a.
Using conservation of energy, $v^2 = \frac{931}{12}$ so $v = 8.81 \text{ m s}^{-1}$ (3 s.f.)

2 Velocity before first impact $= \mathbf{v} = v\begin{pmatrix} \sin\theta \\ \cos\theta \end{pmatrix}$

Velocity after first impact $= v\begin{pmatrix} -e\sin\theta \\ \cos\theta \end{pmatrix}$

Velocity after second impact $= v\begin{pmatrix} -e\sin\theta \\ -e\cos\theta \end{pmatrix}$

$= -e\mathbf{v}$ as required.

3 (i) $V = \int_{\frac{a}{2}}^{a} (\pi y^2)\,dx = \pi\int_{\frac{a}{2}}^{a} (a^2 - x^2)\,dx = \frac{5a^3\pi}{24}$

$\rho V\bar{x} = \rho\int_{\frac{a}{2}}^{a} (\pi x y^2)\,dx = \rho\pi\int_{\frac{a}{2}}^{a} (a^2x - x^3)\,dx$

$= \frac{9a^4\pi\rho}{64}$

so $\bar{x} = \frac{27a}{40}$. This is $\frac{27a}{40} - \frac{a}{2} = \frac{7a}{40}$ from the plane face.

(ii) $\left(M + \frac{27M}{40a}l\right)\bar{z} = -M \times \frac{7a}{40} + \frac{27M}{40a} \times \frac{l^2}{2}$ so

$\bar{z} = \frac{27l^2 - 14a^2}{2(40a + 27l)}$.

(iii) $l = 2a$ gives $\bar{y} = \frac{a}{2}$

(iv) G is vertically below point of suspension.
Angle required = angle between radius and rod $= \cos^{-1}(\frac{1}{2}) = 60°$

(v) When $l = 2\alpha$ the shape will balance as the weight and normal contact force both go through G.

(vi) If $l > 2a$, the c.o.m. will be nearer the top of the rod and so will have a moment about the point of contact and the shape will fall over.

4 For upwards motion, $0.2v\frac{dv}{ds} = -0.2g - 0.002v^2$

$\Rightarrow \quad v\frac{dv}{ds} = -(9.8 + 0.01v^2)$

$\Rightarrow \quad \int \frac{v\,dv}{(9.8 + 0.01v^2)} = -\int ds$

$\Rightarrow \quad 50\ln(9.8 + 0.01v^2) = -s + c$

$s = 0, v = 20$ so $c = 50 \ln (13.8)$

$\Rightarrow \quad s = 50\ln\left(\frac{13.8}{9.8 + 0.01v^2}\right)$

Maximum height is when $v = 0$

$\Rightarrow \quad s = 50\ln\left(\frac{13.8}{9.8}\right)$

For downwards motion, $0.2v\frac{dv}{ds} = 0.2g - 0.002v^2$

$\Rightarrow \quad v\frac{dv}{ds} = 9.8 - 0.01v^2$

$\Rightarrow \quad \int \frac{v\,dv}{(9.8 - 0.01v^2)} = \int ds$

$\Rightarrow \quad -50\ln(9.8 - 0.01v^2) = s + c$

$s = 0, v = 0$ so $c = -50 \ln (9.8)$

$\Rightarrow \quad s = 50\ln\left(\frac{9.8}{9.8 - 0.01v^2}\right)$

When the ball returns to its original point, the two values of s are equal. Hence

$50\ln\left(\frac{13.8}{9.8}\right) = 50\ln\left(\frac{9.8}{9.8 - 0.01v^2}\right)$

$\Rightarrow \quad \frac{13.8}{9.8} = \frac{9.8}{9.8 - 0.01v^2}$

$\Rightarrow \quad 135.24 - 0.138\text{v2} = 96.04$

$\Rightarrow \quad v = \sqrt{284.05...} = 16.85 = 16.85...$

The speed of the ball when it returns to the point from which it was thrown is 16.9 m s^{-1} (3 s.f.).

5 (i) Maximum speed is when the object has zero acceleration.
Need first to find natural length, a.
Conservation of energy from top to bottom gives

$80 \times 10 = \frac{1}{2a} \times 50 \times (10 - a)^2$ so

$32a = (10 - a)^2$ and $a^2 - 52a + 100 = 0$.

This gives $a = 2$ or $a = 50$. Hence $a = 2$ in this scenario.
For zero acceleration tension in string equals weight of object so if this happens when extension is e, $80 = \frac{50}{2}e$ so $e = \frac{16}{5}$.
Conservation of energy from top to this extension gives

$80 \times \left(2 + \frac{16}{5}\right) = \frac{1}{2} \times \frac{80}{10} \times v^2 + \frac{1}{2} \times \frac{50}{2} \times \left(\frac{16}{5}\right)^2$

This gives $v^2 = 72$ and $v = 6\sqrt{2}$.

(ii) Elastic string obeys Hooke's law; negligible air resistance; other answers possible

6 (i) $\mathbf{v} = (6t^2 - 6t)\mathbf{i} + 2(t - 1)\mathbf{j}$; $\mathbf{v} = \mathbf{0}$ only when $t = 1$ as both components must be zero.

(ii) (–3, 4), (2, 1), (1, 0), (6, 1); arrows
Travelling in negative y direction but goes from positive x to negative x directions through instantaneous zero speed in x-direction at $t = 0$ [the point (2, 1)]
Comes instantaneously to rest at a cusp or equivalent.

Index